16

THE PMP® CERTIFICATION EXAM STUDY GUIDE

ROSALDO DE JESUS NOCÊRA
PMP, PMI-SP, PMI-RMP, MCTS

THE PMP® CERTIFICATION EXAM STUDY GUIDE

CRC Press
Taylor & Francis Group
Boca Raton London New York

CRC Press is an imprint of the
Taylor & Francis Group, an **informa** business

CRC Press
Taylor & Francis Group
6000 Broken Sound Parkway NW, Suite 300
Boca Raton, FL 33487-2742

Printed in the United States of America on acid-free paper
Version Date: 20120612

International Standard Book Number: 978-1-4665-0383-0 (Paperback)

Visit the Taylor & Francis Web site at
http://www.taylorandfrancis.com

and the CRC Press Web site at
http://www.crcpress.com

Loving thanks to my children, Marcela,
Murilo, and Maurício Nocêra.

The Author

Rosaldo de Jesus Nocêra, PMP, PMI-SP, PMI-RMP, MCTS

As the author of 12 books addressing variations of the work planning and control subject, some of which have been adopted in academic teaching, Rosaldo de Jesus Nocêra has always worked in the project management field. His professional experience has been developed mainly in managing projects, working for more than 20 years with implementing large projects.

The author has worked as a civil engineer and holds a bachelor's degree in business administration, with postgraduate studies in industrial buildings, he is certified as a PMP® (Project Management Professional) by the Project Management Institute (PMI®) as well as a MCTS (Microsoft Certified Technology Specialist - Project Management with Project 2007) by Microsoft. He was the first civil engineer in Brazil to achieve the PMI-SP (Scheduling Professional) certification. Also, he is certified as a PMI-RMP (Risks Management Professional).

As a businessman and consultant, he has provided project management consulting services for large companies, including multinational companies, in addition to leading courses along with his team of instructors in São Paulo across company and institutions in different Brazilian cities. His books and courses on work planning and control with MS-Project did much to refine the technique of civil construction professionals and to professionalize jobsite work.

Nowadays, taking a step further in fulfilling the purpose of sharing his experience, he is publishing this book, the first one of its kind to be published by a Brazilian author.

The author hopes this book will be a guide for all professionals interested in achieving the PMP® certification.

After reaching that goal, the author is at readers' disposal by e-mail at nocera@rjn.com.br.

For information on other books and training, visit www.rjn.com.br.

Foreword

Chaos, criticality, speed, competition, riot. These are perhaps the key words that occur to any professional when viewing the current business reality. Globalization has played an extremely modifying role in the behavior of society and of all organizations.

Challenges are overcome every day, such as when Chilean miners were rescued and during the pre-salt exploration projects in Brazil. On the other hand, we know that after every challenge is overcome countless challenges arise, most of which are a result of an innovation and competition of massive movement.

When thinking about the concepts of projects and project management, we are not dealing with something new. Project management had its origins in the industrial environment nearly a century ago. Even PMI® has existed for 42 years. It is a middle-aged entity. Therefore, the natural question is: "Why is there a growing interest in project management?" The basis to answer that question is not the concept of projects but the applicability of such a concept.

A society that in the past was clearly based on routine, is now faced with the challenge of the new. Every day we are faced with less routine and more innovation. And innovation puts organizations at a zone of low comfort, limitations, and critical by definition. To manage tasks performed under such limitations, companies need to adopt new work processes and patterns, at which point project management is introduced.

Managing projects is nothing more than applying the right and adequate tools to manage tasks, aiming for better results. That is: RESULT. If we look at the evaluation of results obtained in projects such as the Standish Group Chaos Report in 1994, we will find that more than 84% of projects either failed or achieved only partial results. In 2006, that figure was reduced to 65%.

Improvement may seem small. However, if we imagine that the world has a GDP (Gross Domestic Product) of 100 trillion dollars and that, according to studies conducted by the PMI® and the Economist Intelligence Unit, approximately 25% of the world economy is in projects, we will realize that this amounts to 25 billion dollars, nearly twice the U.S. economy and 20 times the Brazilian economy. That means that improving from 84% to 65% within 12 years represents a major breakthrough.

And in order to prove that not everything is flowers, we virtually stagnated in enhancing project results in the period ranging between 2006 and 2010. It is speculated that this is due to the global crisis that erupted in 2008.

Others say that challenges have become steadily larger; a third strand upholds that low qualification and the huge gap of talents are the major responsible issues for difficulties found.

While searching best results, several initiatives have been consolidated over the years. Just as an example, in Brazil there are about 10,000 certified PMP®s, 13 PMI® regional offices, one IPMA (International Project Management Association) regional office and more than 20,000 graduate and executive MBA students. Can you image this scenario replicated around the whole world?

Training and qualifying people are the core of Rosaldo Nocêra' work. A work that follows the impeccable care of his other publications, now focused on the PMP® certification by the PMI®, a leading certification in the market, with more than 300,000 certified professionals in 180 countries.

All of these initiatives increasingly contribute to developing Brazil, causing us to have a deserved prominent place in the global society and to seize the long years of prosperity ahead of us. After all, promoting progress and success is much more than just taking an opportunity. It is the duty of all of us toward our successors.

Best wishes and enjoy constant success.

Ricardo Viana Vargas, MSc, CSM, PMP

Ricardo Viana Vargas is a specialist in project management, portfolio, and risk. Having authored 10 books in this area over the past 15 years, he has been responsible for more than 80 large projects in several countries, in oil, energy, infrastructure, telecommunications, IT and finance, with a portfolio of managed investments exceeding 18 billion dollars. He was the first Latin American volunteer to be elected to serve as chairman of the board of the Project Management Institute (PMI®), the world's largest organization focused on project management, with about 500,000 members and certified professionals in 175 countries.

Acknowledgements

Thanks to Taylor & Francis publishing house, represented by Mr. John Wyzalek, for having believed in this book.

Thanks to all of those who took part in and contributed to preparing this book, especially to

- Paula Corrêa and Rayane Carreiro, layout professionals in charge of the entire book, including its cover;
- Tania Zanquini, of Job Technical Translations, for general translation and spelling;
- Ricardo Viana Vargas, for having given me the honor of writing the book's foreword.

Rosaldo de Jesus Nocêra
May 2012

Introduction

Welcome!

That's it. Welcome to the wonderful world of the project management. Or more specifically: **Welcome to the wonderful world of the PMI® project management.**

If you have purchased this book, I assume that, being either a beginner or an experienced professional in project management, your desire is obtaining the PMP® certification and being professionally recognized by the largest and most important project management institution in the world! You are taking a big step in your career. The benefits of certification and the application of project management techniques and best practices are many and will hardly be exhausted throughout your professional life. You will identify such benefits as soon as you obtain the certification. And, of course, they will reflect positively on other areas of your life. Just like it was and has been to me. It is as the PMI® states:

"Good things happen when you get involved with the PMI®"

Let's take this journey together!

Rosaldo de Jesus Nocêra, PMP, PMI-SP, PMI-RMP, MCTS
May 2012

Summary

Chapter 3 Project management processes

Chapter 4 Project Integration Management

Chapter 5 Project Scope Management

Chapter 1

INTRODUCTION TO PMP® PREPARATORY

1. Introduction
2. The Project Management Institute - PMI®
3. Eligibility for PMP® Certification
4. Information about PMP® exam
5. Didactic material presentation
6. Study plan
7. Study recommendations

- Initial test
- Answer key

1.1 INTRODUCTION

The purpose of this chapter is to present information necessary for eligibility, recommendations, study plan, and an initial valuation test for those aiming to obtain the certified Project Management Professional (PMP®) of the Project Management Institute (PMI®).

1.2 THE PROJECT MANAGEMENT INSTITUTE - PMI*

Founded in 1969 in the United States and currently with members in more than 170 countries, the PMI® adds more than 300,000 certified professionals in project management (PMP®), making this the most important worldwide certification related to this profession.

PMI® aims to expand knowledge in project management through a framework that includes the following:

- Certification of Professionals — testing and certifying the knowledge of the professionals in project management through certification programs
- Education training in project management
- Researching and analyzing of current practices of project management
- Publications - journal and magazines specialized in project management
- Standards - developing methodologies and standards for project management, such as the *PMBOK® Guide* (Guide to the Project Management Body of Knowledge)
- Congresses and seminars on project management

1.2.1 THE *PMBOK® GUIDE*

The *PMBOK® Guide*, now in its fourth edition (2009), aims at disseminating knowledge and best practices in project management involving, for projects in general, 42 processes of project management, divided into 9 areas of knowledge, namely:

- ***Project Integration Management***
- ***Project Scope Management***
- ***Project Time Management***
- ***Project Cost Management***
- ***Project Quality Management***
- ***Project Human Resources Management***
- ***Project Communication Management***
- ***Project Risk Management***
- ***Project Procurement Management***

* Website: www.pmi.org;

1.3 ELIGIBILITY FOR PMP® CERTIFICATION

To obtain the PMP® Certification, the professional should meet certain education and experience requirements, agree and adhere to the Code of Professional Conduct, participate in classroom training, and pass the PMP® Certification Exam.

The classroom training shall have a minimum workload of 35 hours of lessons.

As proof of experience, there are two categories:

- Class I (graduated professionals) - 4,500 hours and 36 months of experience in the last six years;
- Class II (professionals who completed high school) - 7,500 hours and 60 months of experience in the last eight year.

Applicant must demonstrate their experience by completing the form directly at PMI® website (www.pmi.org) in English. After filling, the PMI® will review your eligibility and, within a maximum of 10 days, inform you about the acceptance of your order or request proof of your experience.

Note: Proof of experience is made randomly by the PMI® computer, covering approximately 10% of the applicants. In this case, your immediate boss or client(s) must attest to your experience. Documentation should be mailed to the PMI® (USA), which will return within 10 days after receipt of it.

After approval, the applicant must pay the exam fee. The fees (at the time of this writing) were

- PMI® Members - US$405
- Non members - US$555

After that, the applicant must schedule to take the exam in one of the locations indicated by PMI®.

1.4 INFORMATION ABOUT PMP® EXAM

The exam lasts four hours and consists of 200 multiple choice questions (average 72 seconds per question). There is one correct alternative only. You must hit a minimum of 65% (130 questions) to be approved. The result comes out soon after where the exam took place.

The following table shows the percentage of the exam questions in relation to the project management processes groups.

PROJECT MANAGEMENT PROCESS GROUPS		QUESTIONS
1.	Project Initiating	13%
2.	Project Planning	24%
3.	Project Executing	30%
4.	Project Monitoring and controlling	25%
5.	Project Closing	8%

1.5 DIDACTIC MATERIAL PRESENTATION

The book is divided into the following chapters and appendices:

- **Chapter 1:** Introduction to PMP® Preparatory
- **Chapter 2:** Project Management Fundamentals (corresponding to *PMBOK® Guide*, Chapters 1 and 2)
- **Chapters 3 to 12:** Referring to the areas of knowledge in project management (corresponding to *PMBOK® Guide*, Chapters 3 to 12)
- **Chapter 13:** Ethics and Professional Responsibility
- **Appendix 1:** Preparatory for the Exam Day
- **Appendix 2:** Glossary

Each chapter has two parts. One part applies to theory and the other provides some exercises.

1.6 STUDY PLAN

The preparatory exam will require that you are familiar with the *PMBOK® Guide* and all project management processes, including inputs, tools and techniques, and outputs of each process. In addition, it will require other knowledges on project management, which are not constant in the *PMBOK® Guide*. The latter requirement is based on your information that you have already worked at least 4,500 hours in project management. However, we know that even with experience, it may be that one or another area or project management tool was rarely used by you and therefore is less known. Thus, in preparing this book, I tried to do so in such a way to be very complete, avoiding leaving gaps in your knowledge.

In order to ensure your learning is efficient, I suggest you follow, in the specified sequence, the following study plan:

1st Do the initial test in the end of this chapter, and note your score in the follow-up sheet located in the last page of this book. The initial test has 50 questions and should be answered within one hour.

2nd Read the *PMBOK® Guide* carefully. Using a pen mark, highlight the points that you do not know or understand.

3rd Study Chapter 2 - Introduction to Project Management, trying to familiarize yourself with the basic terms of project management, the influence of organizational structures as well as other important topics. Study the constant reminders to the exam described in this chapter. At the end of the chapter, do the corresponding exercises. In multiple choice questions, "study" the answers. Most of them are detailed so that you may also learn from them. If you have not achieved a minimum score of 85% of correct answers, you should re-examine the points with gaps in your knowledge.

4th Review Chapter 3 - Project Management Processes, using the posters attached to the book, to overview the processes and their location in the project management process groups (Initiating, Planning, Executing, Monitoring and controlling, and Closing) as well as the inputs, tools and techniques, and outputs of the processes. Follow the same study guidelines described in Chapter 2. I recommend answering the multiple choice questions on a separate sheet, as you are going to answer them once more when completing the study of the 9 areas of knowledge.

5th Review Chapters 4 to 12 - related to the 9 areas of knowledge in project management, to try to understand:

- What should be developed in each area of knowledge, and what is the right sequence to be followed? In addition, you should also know in which process group each process of all areas of knowledge is located.
- The reasons of each process input. That is, which information do you need to develop the process?
- The reasons of each process tool and technique. That is, how will you develop the product of the process?
- The reasons of each process output. In other words, what you should produce for each process?
- When reviewing each area and process, try to understand the impact of the product of every process on other processes and also the global context of your project by viewing the project documents that may be implied or should be updated because of the respective product process.
- Study the reminders to the exam described in each chapter. At the end of the chapter, do the corresponding exercises. In multiple choice questions, "study" the answers. Most of them are detailed so that you may also learn from them. If you have not achieved a minimum score of 85% of correct answers, you should re-examine those gaps in your knowledge.

6th Review Chapter 3 once more - Project Management Process, and redo the multiple choice exercises therein provided. Probably, you will find those exercises less difficult. If you have not achieved the minimum score of 85%, review the chapter again.

7th Review Chapter 13 - Ethics and Professional Responsibility. At the end of the chapter, do the corresponding exercises. In multiple choice questions, "study" the answers. Most of them are detailed so that you may also learn from them. If you have not achieved a minimum score of 85%, you should re-examine the gaps in your knowledge.

8th Review Appendix 2 - Glossary. There you will find definition of the term used in project management, which are important for the exam.

9th Select 50 questions from chapters and answer them within 1 hour. Study all the answers. Repeat the process until your minimum score remains above 85%. Record the scores in the Follow-up Sheet available on the last page of the book.

10th Read Appendix 1 - Preparatory for the Exam Day. The information therein is relevant for your success in the real exam!

1.7 STUDY RECOMMENDATIONS

1st You should have a good knowledge of the *PMBOK® Guide* - 4th Edition (2009). Do not use previous versions!

2nd You should have the "eyes of PMI®"! Practical experience in project management will help a lot, but it will not grant you the right to disagree or not to accept the principles and techniques defined by the PMI®. These issues should be discussed when you become a PMP®.

3rd It is important to consider that you are working on large projects, where all project management processes should be developed and applied to tools and techniques provided by PMI®.

4th Always choose the best option from those alternatives you think may be the correct ones.

5th Several multiple choice questions contain traps! They also occur in the exam!

6th The exercises in the book, as well as in the exam, provide a number of long questions with lots of information. Always try to identify what really matters in the question.

7th You should memorize a couple of formulas for the exam. First of all, try to understand them.

8th Study all answers, even those that you have already set. Some answers provide tips to be memorized for the exam. First, try to understand them, and next, memorize them.

9th Use the mock test as many times as you can! This practice will give you confidence and peace of mind for the exam day!

10th It is important to keep a minimum score of 85% in mock test - and afterward, decide when are you going to do the exam. If you do not get that score or rarely get it, do not delude yourself. All you have to do is to study more. Enjoy your studies and good luck!

Initial Test

1. A project is
   a. Ongoing effort undertaken to create a product, service, or result
   b. Ongoing effort undertaken to manufacture a given product or service
   c. Temporary effort undertaken to create a product, service, or exclusive result
   d. Set of activities developed in a process or system

2. What is project management?
   a. Application of knowledge and skills to the project activities in order to meet their requirements
   b. Application of knowledge, skills, tools and techniques to the project activities in order to meet their requirements
   c. Application of tools and techniques to the project activities in order to meet their requirements
   d. Application of the best practices to achieve the project objectives

3. The Project management process groups are
   a. Initiating, Planning, Executing, Monitoring and controlling, and Closing
   b. Definition, Initiating, Planning, Executing, Monitoring and controlling, and Closing
   c. Evaluation, Decision, Planning, Executing, Monitoring and controlling, and Closing
   d. Decision, Planning, Executing, Monitoring and controlling, and Closing

4. Portfolio management refers to
   a. Management of the project financing levels, aiming at the decision making regarding the choice of the projects
   b. Integrated management of the organization-related project portfolio
   c. Set of related projects managed in a coordinated manner to obtain benefits and control that would not be available if they were individually managed
   d. Set of projects or programs and other works, gathered to facilitate the effective management in order to achieve the strategic business objectives

5. Program management refers to

a. Management of the project financing levels, aiming at the decision making regarding the choice of projects

b. Integrated management of the organization non related projects

c. Set of related projects, managed in a coordinated manner to obtain benefits and control that would not be available if they were individually managed

d. Set of projects or programs and other works, gathered to facilitate the effective management in order to achieve the strategic business objectives

6. A training company authorizes a project to create a new course to increase its revenue. Which is the strategic consideration of project authorization related to this example?

a. Market demand

b. Opportunity or business strategic need

c. Technological progress

d. Legal requirement

7. The effective project management requires the manager has the features from the listed options, except

a. Knowledge in project management

b. Performance, ability to perform

c. Technical knowledge in project product

d. Personal, referring to the behavior in project execution

8. All projects, whether large or small, simple or complex, can be mapped by the cycle of life of the option:

a. Initiating, Planning, Executing, Monitoring and controlling, and Closing

b. Initiating, Organization and preparation, Executing and Closing

c. Definition, Planning, Executing and Closing

d. Definition, Initiating, Planning, Executing, Monitoring and controlling, and Closing

9. Regarding the cycle of life, the following information are true, except

a. Cost and personnel levels are low at the beginning, reaching a maximum value in execution and fall quickly as the project is concluded

b. The influence of stakeholders is greatest early in the project, and falls over the project

c. The ability to influence the final characteristics of the project product, with no significant impact on costs, is lower at the beginning and becomes increasingly greater as the project progresses

d. The risks and uncertainties are greater at the beginning of the project and decrease as the project runs

10. In a functional organizational structure, the project manager's authority is

a. Limited

b. Low or inexistent

c. Low to moderate

d. Moderate to high

11. Who does control the budget of the project in a projectized organizational structure?

a. Operation manager

b. Functional manager

c. Project manager

d. Functional manager and project manager

12. The project management process group, where the processes are performed in order to define the project scope, refine the objectives, and develop the actions required to reach the purposes for which the project was created is called

a. Monitoring and controlling

b. Planning

c. Initiating

d. Executing

13. The project management process group whose project management processes are developed to follow up, review, and regulate the project progress and performance is called

a. Planning

b. Monitoring and controlling

c. Executing

d. Closing

14. All items listed are non compliance costs related, except

a. Rework

b. Disposal

c. Loss of destructive testing

d. Responsibilities

15. A structured and independent review to determine whether the project activities comply with the policies, processes, and procedures of the organization and the project is called

a. Inspection

b. Quality audit

c. Periodic evaluation

d. Analysis of the processes

16. The difference between inspection and prevention is

a. The inspection is intended to keep errors within the limits of control and the prevention aims to keep errors within the upper and lower limits

b. The prevention aims to keep errors out of the reach of the client and the inspection is intended to keep errors out of the process

c. The prevention aims to keep errors out of the process and the inspection is intended to keep errors out of the reach of the client

d. The inspection is intended to keep errors within the limits of tolerance and the prevention aims to keep errors within the upper and lower limits

17. One theory asserts that the project teams can go through stages of development, which usually occur in sequence. But it is not rare for a team to become blocked in a specific stage or regress to an earlier stage, or even skip a step. These steps, in sequence, are

a. Formation, conflict, agreement, and performance

b. Formation, conflict, agreement, performance, and dispersion

c. Formation, development, agreement, performance, and dispersion

d. Formation, development, conflict, agreement, and performance

18. The work required to deliver a product, a service, or a result with the specified features and functions is called

a. Project scope

b. Product scope

c. Statement of work

d. Product of the project

19. The technique of collecting information that examines the project from the point of view of its strengths, weaknesses, opportunities, and threats to increase the extent of the risks considered in project management is called

a. Root cause analysis

b. SWOT analysis

c. Decision tree analysis

d. Monte Carlo analysis

20. A schedule activity having low total gap is called

a. Critical activity

b. Near-critical activity

c. Critical path activity

d. Predecessor activity

21. The calculation of early start date and early finish date for incomplete parts of all network diagram activities is called

a. Backward pass

b. Critical path

c. Forward pass

d. Pass from right to the left

22. The type of cost reimbursable contract where the buyer reimburses the supplier for allowable costs (defined by the contract) and the supplier is entitled to a bonus if the set performance criteria are met is called

a. Cost plus fixed fee

b. Cost plus incentive fee

c. Reimbursable costs

d. Fixed price plus incentive fee

23. The type of contract in which the supply unit values are defined before execution and the performed quantities are measured, thus generating the value to be invoiced by the supplier, is called

a. Time and material

b. Guaranteed fixed price

c. Fixed price plus incentive fee

d. Cost plus fixed fee

24. The technique used by the schedule network analysis that modifies the project schedule so that it takes into account the resource limit is called

a. Critical path method

b. Critical chain method

c. Precedence Diagramming Method (PDM)

d. Schedule compression

25. Those factors that, for planning purposes, are considered true, real, or right, requiring no evidence or proof, are called

a. Restrictions

b. Project information

c. Assumptions

d. Historical records

26. You have been hired as an expert for a construction company, to be responsible for the demolition of part of an industry that will be expanded. You will report directly to the construction manager. The company previously announced you will be released when you complete the demolition phase. In this case, which kind of organizational structure are you in?

a. Functional

b. Projectized

c. Strong matrix

d. Balanced matrix

27. Your company has been called by an organization to implement an electronic invoice issuing system. This project should be ready within three months and will require the installation of appropriate computers in the company and the training the accounts receivable staff. What is the origin of this project?

a. Technological progress

b. Legal requirement

c. Client request

d. Organizational need

28. The company you work for is willing to open a new branch in another state to meet market demand. There are four possibilities of capital to be studied, but the company is able to open only branch at the moment. Studies have shown: Capital A Project, with a return period of 18 months and NPV (Net Present Value) of $50,000; Capital B Project, with a payback of 24 months and NPV of $52,000 Capital C Project, with a return period of 24 months and NPV of $51,000, and Capital D Project, with a return period of 30 months and NPV of $60,000. Which option should your company choose?

a. Capital B Project

b. Capital D Project

c. Capital C Project

d. Capital A Project

29. W&W Co. is ready to open a new branch of its store network in another city, and it has two options: Washington Project with a payback period of 32 months and IRR (Internal Rate of Return) of 6.25%; New York Project, with a return period of 36 months and IRR of 6.7%. Which project would you recommend for your company?

a. Washington Project, because it has a lower return period

b. Washington Project, because IRR is smaller

c. New York Project, because IRR is greater

d. New York Project, because return period is greater

30. You have contracted for your project an equipment supplier that has already worked on several other projects of yours and it has always met the delivery deadlines. In this new project, you expect you can rely on this supplier´s equipment on June 20. This is an example of

a. Restriction

b. Requirement

c. Term

d. Assumption

31. Let´s suppose you are managing a project to install a large computer network in a given company. You have already developed several very similar projects and know that 14 hours are required to install each server. As there are 5 servers, you have estimated this activity to conclude in 70 hours. Which kind of estimating techniques have you employed?

a. Analogous estimate

b. Three-point estimate

c. Parametric estimate

d. Bottom-up estimate

32. You are starting the preparation of the project network diagram and using the Precedence Diagramming Method (PDM). What kind of logical relationship is used more often by PDM?

a. End-to-end

b. Start-to-start

c. Start-to-end

d. End-to-start

33. While developing the network diagram of your project, you have set the graph of the following figure. What is the critical path?

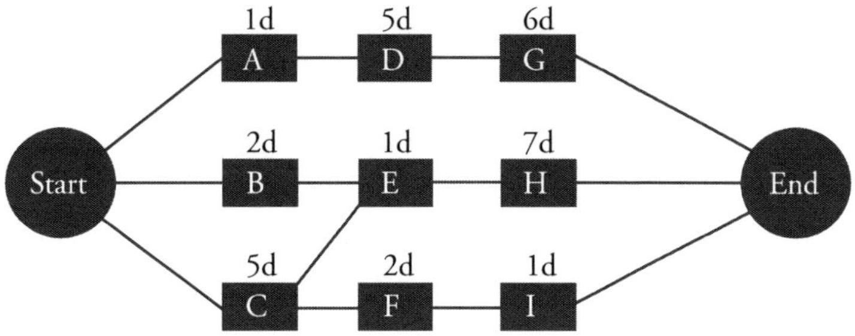

a. Start-A-D-G-End

b. Start-B-E-H-End

c. Start-C-F-I-End

d. Start-C-E-H-End

34. The preliminary schedule developed by your project team is exceeding the stipulated contract period. You thought about solutions and additional resources from the department in charge obtained of releasing resources. These resources shall be used in several project activities to reduce the duration, as well as to adjust the schedule to the term. Which technique are you using?

a. Fast tracking

b. Crashing

c. Resource leveling

d. Resource compensation

35. You are developing the human resources plan, and one of the tools and techniques you are using is a RACI-format matrix graph. What does the acronym RACI mean?

a. Responsible for execution - responsible for approval - consulted - informed

b. Report to - updated - consulted - informed

c. Resource - assignment - to consult - to inform

d. Responsible - to assign - to consult - to inform

36. You are the manager of a project that has a tight schedule and for which delays are not allowed. One action you are taking to comply with the deadline is promising three days of paid time off as well as a closing party. This is an example of

a. Theory of termination warranty

b. Maslow's theory

c. Theory of expectations

d. Juran's theory

37. A manager that follows Y theory believes that

a. People will work hard if they have proper motivation and expectations

b. People will endeavor for money and power only

c. People will endeavor to achieve a high level of knowledge

d. People will endeavor for good result expectations

38. A key skill inherent to a project manager should be

a. Ability to negotiate

b. Ability to communicate

c. Ability to influence

d. Ability to troubleshoot

39. You are the team member in charge of updating the project schedule. The project manager asks you to reduce the project time limit. After analyzing the situation, you tell the manager that this is likely to increase the likelihood of risks. What kind of reduction technique are you planning to use?

a. Compression

b. Fast tracking

c. Anticipation

d. Resource leveling

40. The technique that says that all team members and managers must constantly observe opportunities for quality improvements is called:

a. 5S

b. Kaizen

c. Total quality management

d. Zero defect

41. Joseph Juran enunciated a theory in which stakeholders and clients expectations are met or exceeded. What is the name of this theory?

a. Zero defect

b. Customer service

c. Theory of expectations

d. Adequacy to the use

42. The technique that simulates the schedule and cost variables several times in order to calculate a distribution of duration results or probable cost is called

a. Monte Carlo analysis

b. Probabilities analysis

c. Sensitivity analysis

d. Statistical sampling

43. You have been assigned to participate in a project in a country very different from yours. Furthermore, professionals from other countries are working on this project too. This issue is causing some confusion on project execution because of

a. Cultural differences

b. Language differences

c. Non acceptance of subordination by some members living in the country of execution.

d. Short project life cycle

44. The dependence directly linked to the nature of ongoing work is called

a. Required dependency

b. Arbitrated dependency

c. Dependency between activities

d. Dependency restricted to the work

45. The sensitivity analysis data diagram, whose variables with major effect are shown in horizontal bars at the top of the chart and go down according to the effect reduction is called

a. Cause-and-effect diagram

b. Control diagram

c. Fishbone diagram

d. Tornado diagram

46. When a scheduled activity can be delayed without delaying the early start of the successor activity, we say that the activity is

a. Sale float

b. Successor float

c. Total float

d. Free float

47. The motivational theory, according to which we have five basic needs, is called

a. Theory of expectations

b. McGregor's theory

c. Deming's theory

d. Maslow's theory

48. The amount of damage or opportunities that a risk event offers to the project is called

a. Probability

b. Impact of risk

c. Set of positive and negative risks

d. Set of risks

49. You have been assigned to make a presentation of the ongoing project to the client within three days. Although the project was going well, yesterday you heard of a problem in the manufacture of imported equipment, which will cause a three-week delay on the project. You and your team have already studied all the possibilities of reducing the delay, but you were not able to reach a conclusion about the matter. This risk of delay in supply has not been included in the risk management processes by the team. What should you do during the presentation to your client?

a. You would tell the customer that this was an unforeseen risk in the project and that once the supplier was considered as reliable

b. You should present the actual situation of the problem that occurred and the delay of the project, informing the customer that the risk was not predicted by you

c. You would tell the customer that you will take strong measures regarding the supplier

d. You would tell the client that this issue usually happens in projects

50. Your company has been invited to participate in a project in a foreign country. You are preparing the proposal, when you are informed that, to participate in the project, your company must pay a high value to the foreign country's government minister. What should be the attitude of the company?

a. Do not pay the amount and take part of the bidding

b. Consider the value as a participation fee

c. Pay the amount and take part of the bidding

d. Do not pay the amount because this is a bribe

Answer key

1. C. Project is temporary effort undertaken to create a product, service, or exclusive result.

2. B. Project management is the application of knowledge, skills, tool, and techniques to the project activities in order to meet their requirements.

3. A. The Project management process groups are Initiating, Planning, Executing, Monitoring and controlling, and Closing.

4. D. Portfolio management refers to a set of projects or programs and other works, gathered to facilitate the effective management in order to achieve the strategic business objectives. Note that questions B and C refer to related projects (feature of programs).

5. C. Set of related projects, managed in a coordinated manner to obtain benefits and control that would not be available if they were individually managed.

6. B. An example of market demand: a car company authorizing a project to produce more economic cars because of the shortage of gasoline. An example of technological progress: an electronics manufacturer authorizes a project to develop a laptop faster and cheaper, because of progress in technology. An example of legal requirement: the company authorizes a project to implement the electronic invoice issuing to satisfy a governmental law. The example of business strategic opportunity or need is described in the question.

7. C. The technical knowledge of the project product is not defined as a characteristic of the effective project management. Other mentioned features are the characteristics defined by the *PMBOK® Guide*.

8. B. The project life cycle includes initiating, organization and preparation, executing and closing.

9. C. The ability to influence the final characteristics of the project product, with no significant impact on costs, is higher at the beginning and becomes increasingly greater as the project progresses to its closing.

10. B. In a functional organizational structure, the project manager's authority is low or inexistent.

11. C. In this type of organization, the project manager has high authority and controls the budget.

12. B. Planning includes the project management process group, where the processes are performed in order to define the project scope, refine the objectives, and develop the actions required to reach the purposes for which the project was created.

13. B. During Monitoring and controlling, the processes are developed to follow up, review, and regulate the project progress and performance.

14. C. Loss of destructive testing is considered a non compliance cost. The non compliance costs, e.g. the money spent during and after the project due to failures, can arise from:

- Internal failure costs (failures find by the project): rework, disposal.
- Costs of external failures (failures found by the customer): responsibilities, guarantee work, loss of business.

15. B. Quality audit is a structured and independent review to determine whether the project activities comply with the policies, processes, and procedures of the organization and the project.

16. C. Keep it in mind for the test: The prevention aims to keep errors out of the process, and the inspection is intended to keep errors out of the reach of the client.

17. B. The team development stages are: Formation, conflict, agreement, performance, and dispersion.

18. A. The project scope is the work that needs to be done to deliver a product, service, or result with the specified features and functions.

19. B. The SWOT analysis considers the strengths, weaknesses, opportunities, and threats.

20. B. A schedule activity having low total gap is called near-critical activity. When delayed, it can entering the critical path and become critical (with no gap).

21. C. Forward pass is the calculation of early start date and early finish date for incomplete parts of all network diagram activities.

22. B. The type of cost reimbursable contract where the buyer reimburses the supplier for allowable costs (defined by the contract) and the supplier is entitled to a bonus if the set performance criteria are met, is called cost plus incentive fee contract.

23. A. The type of contract in which the supply unit values are defined before execution and the performed quantities are measured, thus generating the value to be invoiced by the supplier, is called time and material (or unit prices):

24. B. The technique used by the schedule network analysis that modifies the project schedule so that it takes into account the resource limit is called critical chain method.

25. C. Those factors that for planning purposes, are considered true, real, or right, requiring no evidence or proof, are called assumptions.

26. B. Normally, in projectized organizations, it is used to release the team components when the respective members conclude the works, and usually they do not have a place to return. These organizations are focused on the projects.

27. B. The project was born from the requirement to issue electronic invoices, coming up with a law or decree. So, it is a legal requirement.

28. B. The choice should be done by the project presenting the largest NPV, regardless of the payback period.

29. C. The New York Project because the IRR is greater.

30. D. You expect to receive the equipment on the due date since you can rely on the supplier. This is an example of an assumption.

31. C. The parametric estimate uses a statistical relation and other variables (e.g., square feet under construction) to calculate a cost estimate for duration or activity cost. In this issue, the estimate is 14 hours per server.

32. D. End-to-Start relationship is the most used in PDM.

33. D. If the forward passes are calculated, you are going to get option A = 12 days; option B = 10 days; option C = 8 days; option D = 13 days. Option D is the critical path.

34. B. The schedule compression (crashing) is the application of additional resources to the activities in order to reduce their duration. The compression preference should be the critical path activities to anticipate the end of the project.

35. A. The acronym RACI means: responsible for execution - responsible for approval - consulted - informed.

36. C. The theory of expectations says that people are motivated by the prospect of good, feasible, and reasonable results.

37. A. Y theory says that people will give their best if they're given proper motivation and expectations.

38. B. The project manager spends about 90% of his or her time communicating.

39. B. Fast tracking, the technique of overlapping the schedule activities that were previously planned to be held consecutively, is a technique that increases the probability of risks and often causes rework.

40. B. Kaizen means continuous improvement in Japanese. It is a technique of quality.

41. D. For the test, keep in mind: Juran = Adequacy to the use

42. A. Monte Carlo analysis is a technique that simulates the schedule and cost variables several times in order to calculate a distribution of the duration results or probable cost: This technique is developed in the processes Perform quantitative risk analysis and Develop schedule.

43. A. The main cause of relationship difficulties among team members on a project with professionals from several countries is culture differences.

44. A. Dependence directly linked to the nature of the work is a required dependency, also called hard logic.

45. D. The Tornado diagram shows the variables with the greatest effect at the top of the chart, and from top to bottom, shows the effect decreasing. The diagram has the shape of a tornado, or an inverted cone.

46. D. Free float is the time that an activity can be delayed without delaying the early start of the successor activity.

47. D. Maslow's theory states that we have five basic needs that follow a hierarchy:

- basic physical needs
- safety and security needs
- social needs
- esteem needs and
- self-realization needs.

48. B. The amount of damage (losses) or opportunities (earnings) that a risk event offers to the project is called impact of risk.

49. B. The project manager should present the reality of the problem and take responsibility for any error he or his project team commits.

50. D. The company should refuse to make payment because this is a bribe.

Chapter 2

PROJECT MANAGEMENT FUNDAMENTALS

1. Introduction
2. What is a project?
3. Project life cycle
4. What is project management?
5. Relationship between project management process groups
6. Project management benefits
7. Project Management Body of Knowledge (*PMBOK® Guide*)
8. Areas of expertise
9. Project management context
10. The project manager
11. Stakeholders
12. Organizational influences on the project
13. Environmental factors applied to project management

- Additional information and reminders for the exam
- Supplementary exercises
- Questions
- Answer key

2.1 INTRODUCTION

This chapter presents the definitions of the project and project management as well as the fundamentals that are the basis for managing a project.

2.2 WHAT IS A PROJECT?

The term *project* comes from Latin *projectu* and means to cast forth, i.e., an idea created to execute or perform something into the future; a plan; an intent; a purpose.

In its purest form, we can define *project* as a project to be carried out within a certain scheme, sketch, or risk of a work to be performed. However, using the term *project* includes a set of actions, activities, material, and human resources and all items necessary to implement what was imagined or desired.

According to the Project Management Institute (PMI®)

> *A project is a temporary effort undertaken to create a product, a service or an exclusive result.*

This definition takes the characteristics of a project into account:

- **Temporary**

  All projects have a well-defined start and finish. The end is reached when the project objectives are achieved, when it is defined that it is no longer possible to achieve such goals, or when the project need no longer exists and is closed.

- **Exclusive products, services, or results**

  A project creates unique deliverables as a product, a capability of producing something, or a result, such as final drawings or documents.

- **Progressive elaboration**

  Progressive elaboration means developing in steps and continuing by increments. For example, when implementing an industry, the process characteristics will be the basis for the basic engineering project, which, in turn, will be the basis for manufacturing and construction drawings.

Project versus operational work

An important issue is the distinction between project and operational work. The project purpose is defining, achieving and then completing goals. Operational work is meant to keep the organization running and does not always have a defined start or end. Operational work generally uses the same process to produce a given result.

Table 2.1 shows the main differences between project and operational work.

TABLE 2.1 PROJECT VERSUS OPERATIONAL WORK

PROJECT	OPERATIONAL WORK
Defined start and finish	Non defined and non definitive start and finish
Temporary	Continuous - the process is continuously repeated
Produces a single product or service (exclusive)	Produces the same product or service repeatedly
Resources devoted to the project	Resources dedicated to the operation

How projects are originated

Projects often stem from the following considerations:

- **Market demand**

  When, for example, an industry decides to expand its manufacturing area due to increased sales of a product.

- **Organizational need**

  When, for example, a company decides to implement a computerized sales system to better serve customers.

- **Client request**

  When, for example, a company applies for paving the streets of its industrial park.

- **Legal requirement**

  When, for example, the government sets forth the obligation to issue electronic invoices from a certain date onward.

- **Technological progress**

  When, for example, a cell phone company authorizes a project to develop a new generation of such devices.

- **Social need**

  When, for example, a public body authorizes the construction of a school to attend to a neighborhood lacking that feature.

Project examples

Project examples can be

- development of a new product
- implementation of a new software application
- implementation of a new production line
- expansion of industrial units
- construction of new plants
- construction of buildings and
- construction of roads

2.3 PROJECT LIFE CYCLE

By definition, a project has a defined start and end, and it comprises by intermediate phases defining its life cycle. In general, any project can have a life cycle with the following stages:

- Project start
- Organization and preparation
- Project work execution
- Project closing

The following figure illustrates the project life cycle and the level of use of the resources (financial, equipment, and personnel) over the cycle.

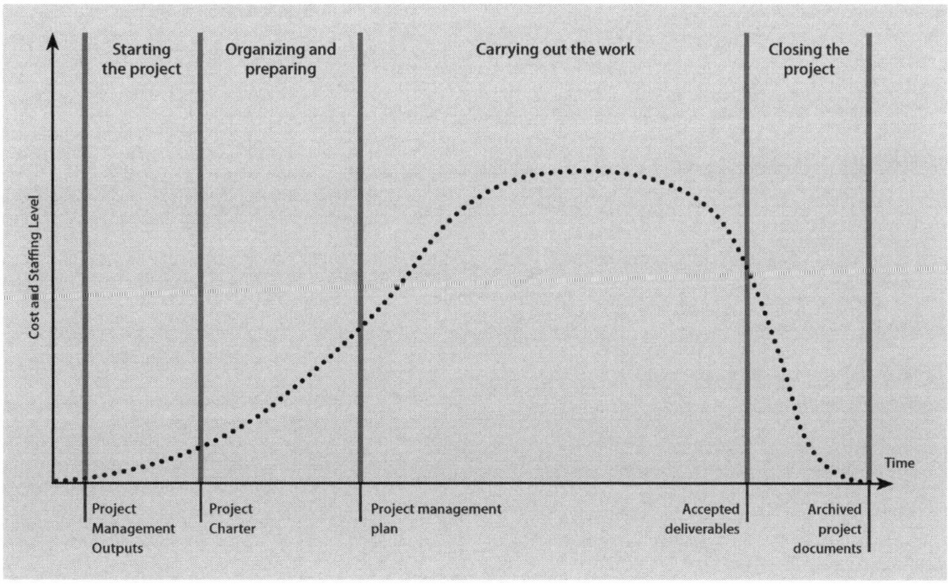

SOURCE: ***PMBOK® Guide***

The project start is generally defined when the organization identifies a business opportunity that it wishes to seize and authorizes feasibility studies or the project begins. In the previous figure (dashed line), one can observe that the resource application (money, equipment, and personnel) are low at first, reach a maximum value in the work execution, and is quickly reduced at closure. Phases of a project life cycle are sequential and, according to *PMBOK® Guide*, their closure is related to the following project management activities (addressed throughout the book):

END OF PHASE	PROJECT MANAGEMENT ACTIVITY
Starting	Charter Issuance
Organizing and preparing	Project Management Plan Issuance
Carrying out the work	Accepted deliverables
Closing	Archived project documents

Other features of most project life cycles, illustrated in the figure below, are as follows:

- The influence of stakeholders, the risks, and the uncertainties are larger at the project start and tend to decrease during the project execution;
- The costs are minor changes at the project start and tend to increase during the project execution.

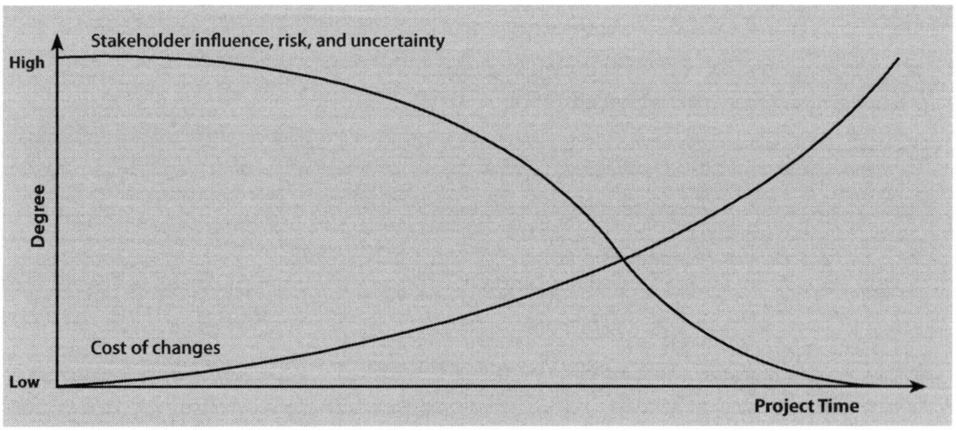

SOURCE: *PMBOK® Guide*

2.4 WHAT IS PROJECT MANAGEMENT?

Project management, although always present in the life of man, started to be structured and defined as a discipline since 1940, when important programs requiring specific structuring were developed. Among such programs, are the Manhattan Project (construction of the first atomic bomb) and the Polaris submarine. This project management structuring started by recognizing the need to establish concepts, techniques, and processes driving those in charge for compliance with goals related to technical performance, time, cost, and quality.

According to PMI®, project management is the application of knowledge, skills, tools, and techniques to project activities in order to meet their requirements. Project management is performed by applying and integrating project management processes. Such processes are gathered together into five groups, called project management process groups:

- Initiating process group
- Planning process group
- Executing process group
- Monitoring and controlling process group
- Closing process group

Managing a project includes

- Identifying requirements;
- Adapting to different needs, concerns, and expectations of the stakeholders as the project is planned and performed and
- Balancing conflicting constraints of the project, including, but not limited to
    - Scope
    - Quality
    - Schedule
    - Budget
    - Resources an
    - Risks.

2.5 RELATIONSHIP BETWEEN PROJECT MANAGEMENT PROCESS GROUPS

The relationship between process groups is more complex than the basic PDCA (Plan-Do-Check-Act) cycle[1], in view of the interactions between the groups. In the PDCA cycle, the result of a part of the cycle becomes the input of the other part. In interactions among project management process groups, the monitoring and controlling process group interacts with all other groups.

1 The PDCA cycle: defined by Shewhart and modified by Deming

Figure 2.1 shows the basic PDCA cycle, and Figure 2.2 shows the relationship between project management process groups.

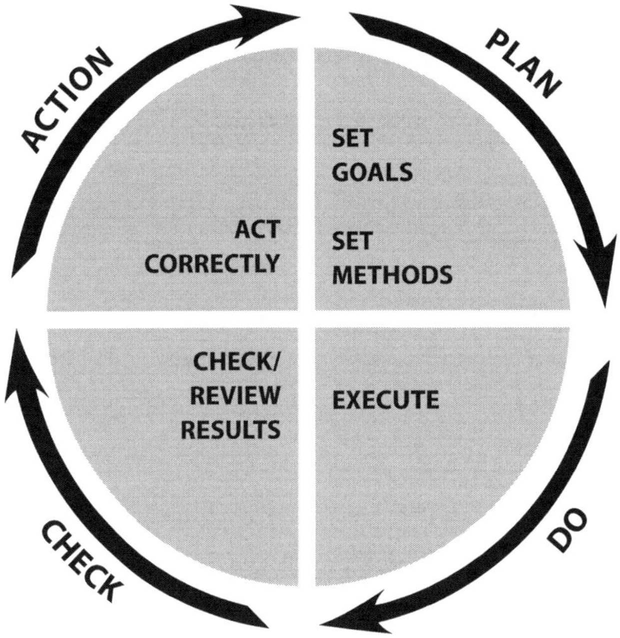

Fig. 2.1 - PDCA cycle.

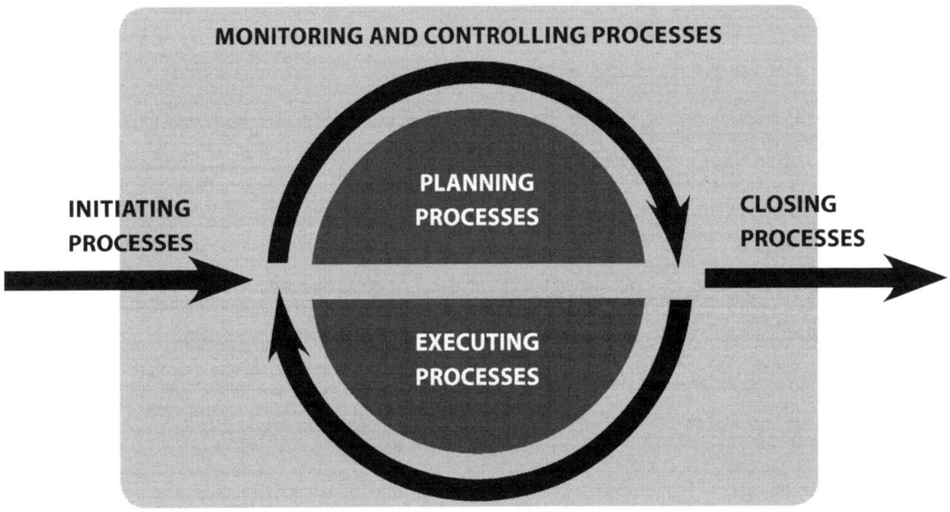

Fig. 2.2 - Mapping between project management process groups and the PDCA cycle.

2.6 PROJECT MANAGEMENT BENEFITS

The benefits of project management in an organization are usually related to the following aspects of the project product delivery:

1 Technical – the result of the project product, as required

2 Delivery deadline – obtaining the product on the project requested date

3 Cost – the final cost according to the plan

4 Customer satisfaction – with the final product, deadline and cost

5 Satisfaction of project stakeholders and team members

The amount and degree of benefits obtained with the project management implementation are factors resulting directly from effective implementation of project management processes and monitoring of such processes. For example, the planning processes implementation requires adequate effort and monitoring to provide the execution team with a clear view on how and when work should be performed, under which conditions, and at which cost. Otherwise, inadequate and unrealistic planning causes the project to divert from goals, often causing injury or even rendering the project itself inappropriate or unacceptable.

2.7 PROJECT MANAGEMENT BODY OF KNOWLEDGE (*PMBOK® GUIDE*)

The *PMBOK® Guide* aims to promote knowledge and the best practices when managing projects involving

- Five (5) groups of project management processes (Initiating, Planning, Executing, Monitoring and controlling, and Closing – presented throughout the book)
- Nine (9) areas of expertise for projects in general
    - ***Project Integration Management***
    - ***Project Scope Management***
    - ***Project Time Management***
    - ***Project Cost Management***
    - ***Project Quality Management***
    - ***Project Human Resource Management***
    - ***Project Communications Management***
    - ***Project Risk Management***
    - ***Project Procurement Management***
- Forty-two (42) project management processes (presented throughout the book)

2.8 AREAS OF EXPERTISE

According to PMI®, toward an effective project management, the project team must have knowledge and skills in at least five areas of expertise:

- Project management body of knowledge
- Knowledge, rules and regulations of the application area
- Understanding the project environment
- General management knowledge and skills
- Interpersonal skills

Figure 2.3 shows the relationship between these five areas of expertise, showing that they overlap and cannot exist alone.

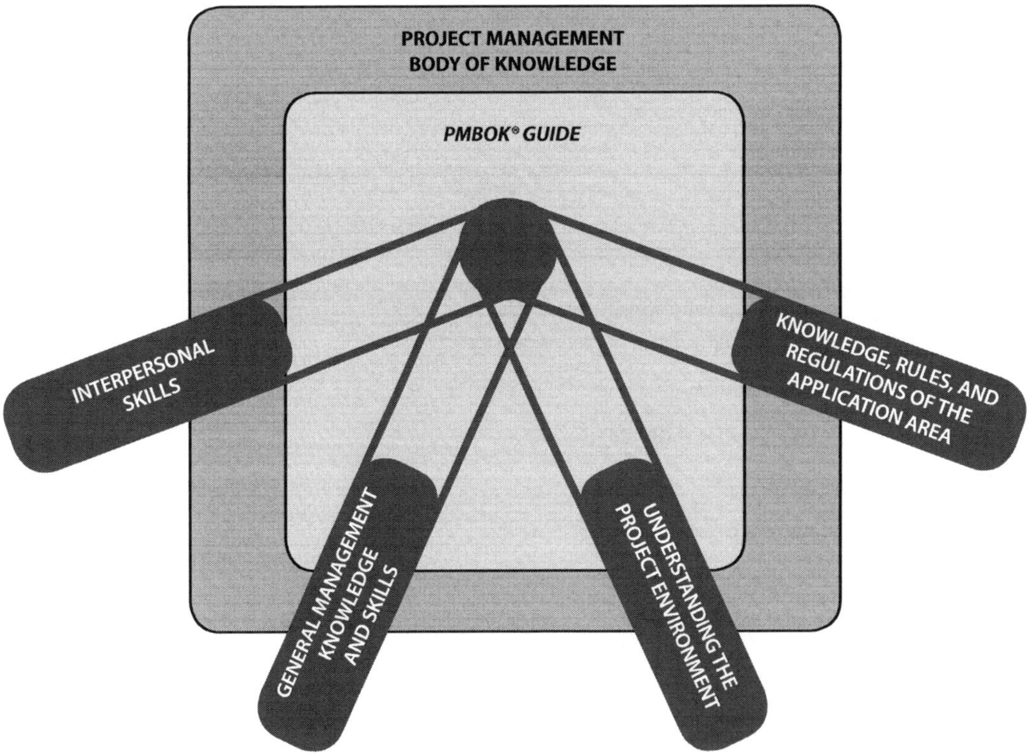

Fig. 2.3 - Areas of expertise required for the project management team.

2.8.1 KNOWLEDGE, RULES, AND REGULATIONS OF THE APPLICATION AREA

Application areas are categories of projects that generally have a set of standards and practices, often codified in regulations. These areas may be the organization functional departments, such as marketing department, legal department, etc. Examples can also be technical elements, e.g., software engineering or management expertise such as new product development.

2.8.2 PROJECT ENVIRONMENT UNDERSTANDING

The project team must acquire a project environment understanding and understand how cultural, social, economic, physical, and political factors influence the project execution.

2.8.3 GENERAL MANAGEMENT KNOWLEDGE AND SKILLS

The project team must have knowledge of the project support disciplines, such as accounting, purchasing, manufacturing, logistics, information technology, safety practices, among other, that influence the project development.

2.8.4 INTERPERSONAL SKILLS

The project team and especially the project manager must have or develop interpersonal skills, such as effective communication, leadership, influence on the organization, motivation, negotiation and conflict management, troubleshooting, among others.

2.9 PROJECT MANAGEMENT CONTEXT

In some organizations, a project can be inserted into a broader project management context, including program management, portfolio management, and project office.

2.9.1 PROGRAM MANAGEMENT

Program management is the centralized and coordinated management of a group of projects in order to achieve the program strategic goals and benefits. Therefore, hierarchically, a program has control over its projects and subprojects. For example, construction companies that have their annual construction program with several projects.

2.9.2 PORTFOLIO MANAGEMENT

Portfolio is a collection of projects or programs grouped together in order to make management easier and meet strategic business objectives. The portfolio management has the goal of including projects and programs that meet the strategic objectives and excluding projects not meeting such goals. Hierarchically, the portfolio has control over its programs, projects, and subprojects.

2.9.3 SUBPROJECTS

Subprojects are divisions of the project into more manageable components, usually executed by an organization external to the project or the organization functional unit. As an example, we may have subprojects related to the process or phase of the project life cycle (procurements for a project), related to human resources skills (service execution by electricians), or related to specialized technology (transformer testing program for a substation).

2.9.4 PROJECT MANAGEMENT SCHEMATIC VIEW, PROGRAMS, AND PORTFOLIOS

In a simple view, managing projects, programs, and portfolios may have the following schematic view:

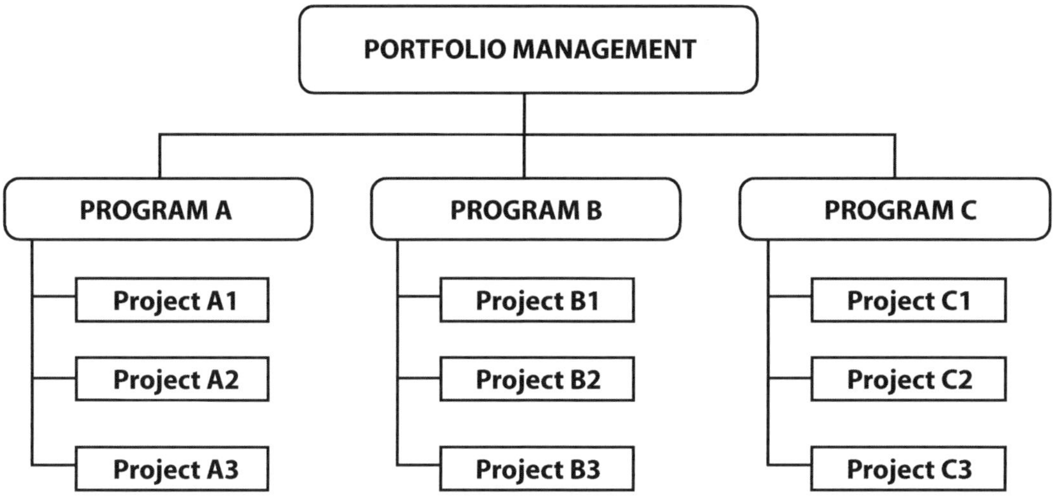

In the previous view, all projects belong to the same level as well as programs ultimately managed by portfolio management. However, according to the importance of each project, the organization may choose to consider a project in the same program level.

Programs can be grouped and managed by the portfolio management, which can be in turn managed by the integrated portfolio management.

The following figure shows a variance example of the above presented view.

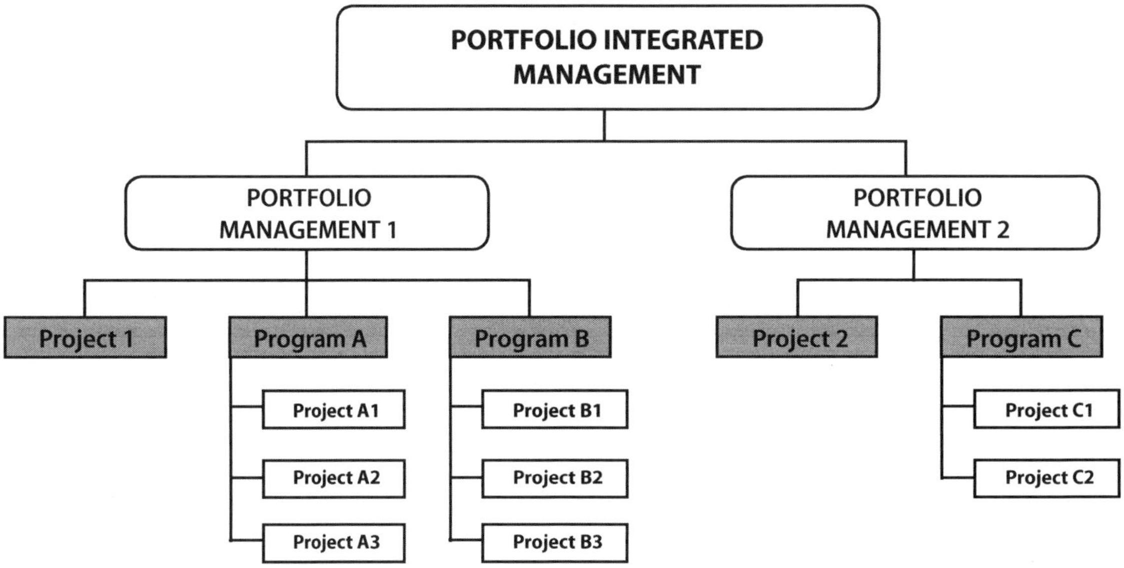

2.9.5 PROJECT OFFICE

Project or Program Management Office (PMO) is a department of the organization that centralizes the program management. Generally, PMO has, alone or grouped, the following attributions:

- Identifying, developing, and providing methodology, best practices, and rules for the organization project management;
- Coordinating project management within the organization, providing training on project management, tools, and software applications to be used;
- Coordinating, in a centralized way, communications management among projects, configuration management, and management of the global quality standards of projects.

2.10 THE PROJECT MANAGER

The project manager is the individual assigned by the execution organization to achieve the project objectives.

The project manager must have, in addition to the skills of the specific area, the following characteristics:

- **Knowledge:** It is what the project manager knows about project management.
- **Performance:** It is what the project manager is capable of performing while applying his knowledge of project management.
- **Personnel:** It is the project manager's behavior during the project execution. The project manager must seek personal effectiveness by means of right actions in order to direct the team to achieve the project objectives and balance its constraints.

2.11 STAKEHOLDERS

Stakeholders are individuals or organizations (such as customers, sponsors, the execution organization, or the audience) actively involved in the project or whose interests can be positively or negatively affected by the project execution or completion. They can also influence the project, its deliverables, and the project team members.

Stakeholders have different responsibility and authority levels when participating in a project, and they can change over the project's life cycle. Stakeholders' responsibility and authority range from occasional contributions in studies and group dynamics to the project sponsorship, which includes providing financial and political support.

Identifying stakeholders and understanding their relative degree of influence on a project are critical issues. The failure to identify a stakeholder may extend the schedule and substantially increase costs.

Project stakeholders include

- **Customers/users:** Individuals or organizations that will use the product, the service, or the project result. Customers/users may be internal and/or external in relation to the execution organization. In some areas of application, the terms customers and users are those who will use it directly.

- **Sponsor:** The individual or group providing financial resources, in cash or in-kind, to the project. The sponsor leads the project through the commitment or selection process until formal authorization and plays a significant role in developing the initial scope and the charter.

- **Portfolio managers/portfolio analysis committee:** Portfolio managers are those in charge of high-level governance of a number of projects or programs that may or may not be interdependent. They analyze each project according to its return on investment, its amount, risks associated with the project adoption, and other attributes.

- **Program managers:** They are responsible for managing related projects in a coordinated manner to obtain benefits and control not available when they are individually managed.

- **Project Management Office:** A Project Management Office (PMO) is an organizational body or entity assigned with several responsibilities related to the centralized and coordinated management of projects under its domain. The responsibilities of a PMO can range from providing support to project management functions to the actual responsibility for direct management of a project.

- **Project managers:** Project managers are assigned by the execution organization to achieve project objectives. The project manager is the leader responsible for communication with all stakeholders, especially with the sponsor, the project team, and other key stakeholders. The project manager is at the center of interactions between stakeholders and the project.

- **Project teams:** A project team comprises by the project manager, the project management team, and other team members who perform the work but are not necessarily involved with project management.

- **Functional managers:** Functional managers are key people who play a managerial function within an administrative or functional area of business, such as human resources, finance, accounting, or procurements. The functional manager can provide advice on a particular project subject or service.

- **Operation managers:** Operations managers have a managerial function in a key business area, such as research and development, design, manufacture, supply, testing, or maintenance. Depending on the project type, a formal delivery occurs after it is completed, in order to transfer its technical documentation and other permanent records to the hands of the appropriate operations management group.

- **Business suppliers/partners:** Vendors, suppliers, or contractors are external companies that have entered into a supply contract of components or services required to do the project. Business partners are also external companies, but they have a special relationship with the company, sometimes obtained through a certification process.

2.12 ORGANIZATIONAL INFLUENCES ON THE PROJECT

A project is subject to the influences of the organization that it belongs to or that is being developed. Such influences can be generated by the organization culture and policies, procedures, rules, beliefs, expectations, and, more directly, by the company's organizational structure.

2.12.1 ORGANIZATIONAL STRUCTURE

Recognizing the company's organizational structure in which the project will be developed is critically important for project management, since it will generate the answers regarding where resources will be obtained, how all communications must be planned and conducted, what the project manager's decision power is, among others.

2.12.1.1 FUNCTIONAL ORGANIZATION

In such an organization, employees are grouped by expertise, such as production, marketing, and accounting, and each employee has a well-defined superior.

Figure 2.4 shows the typical organization chart of a functional organization.

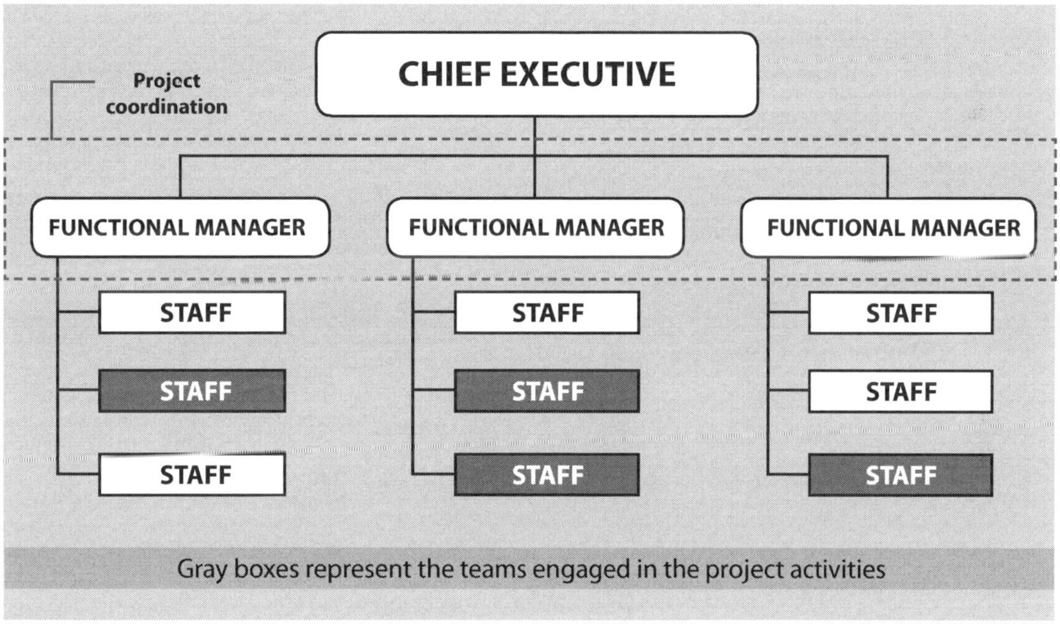

SOURCE: *PMBOK® Guide*

Fig. 2.4 - Functional organization.

The main characteristic of this type of organization is that projects are usually developed within a department, and, if information from other departments is necessary, communication occurs through functional managers. Professionals in this organization prioritize their technical careers over the project, and project managers have little or no authority, depending almost entirely on the functional manager.

2.12.1.2 PROJECTIZED ORGANIZATION

The projectized organization is at the opposite end of the functional organization. In this case, team members are allocated close to one another, allowing a more efficient project organization.

Figure 2.5 shows the typical organization chart by projects.

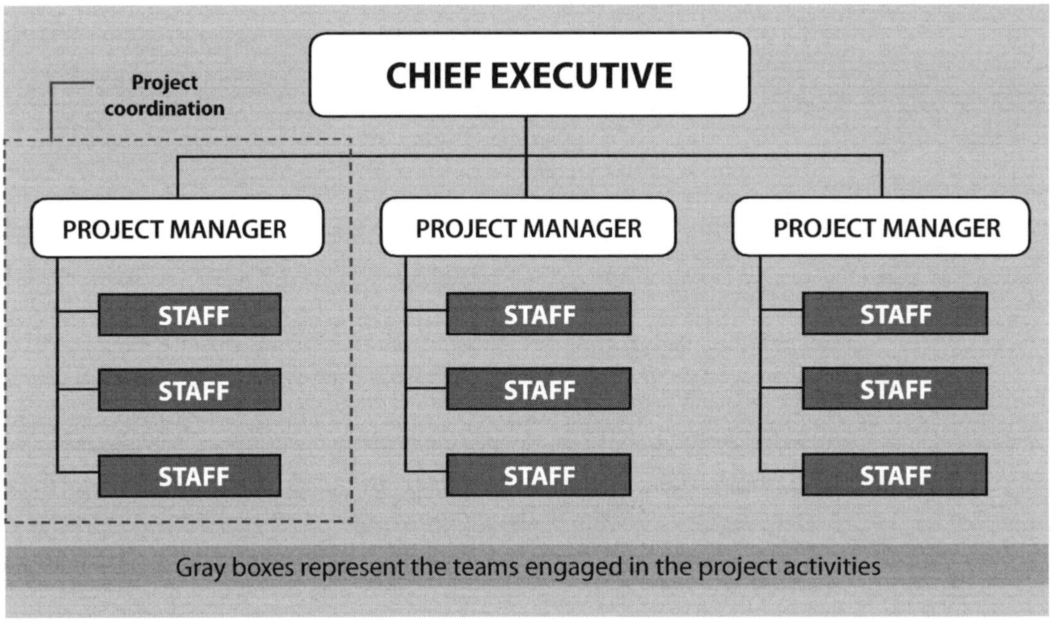

SOURCE: ***PMBOK® Guide***

Fig. 2.5 - Projectized organization.

The main characteristic of this type of organization is that the project team members, although multidisciplinary, report directly to the project manager. In addition to promoting more effective communication than a functional organization, this promotes the loyalty of employees to the project.

2.12.1.3 MATRIX ORGANIZATION

The matrix organization is a combination of the characteristics of functional organizations and by projects. From the project management perspective, this type of organization can be of three types, according to the decision-making power exercised by the project manager.

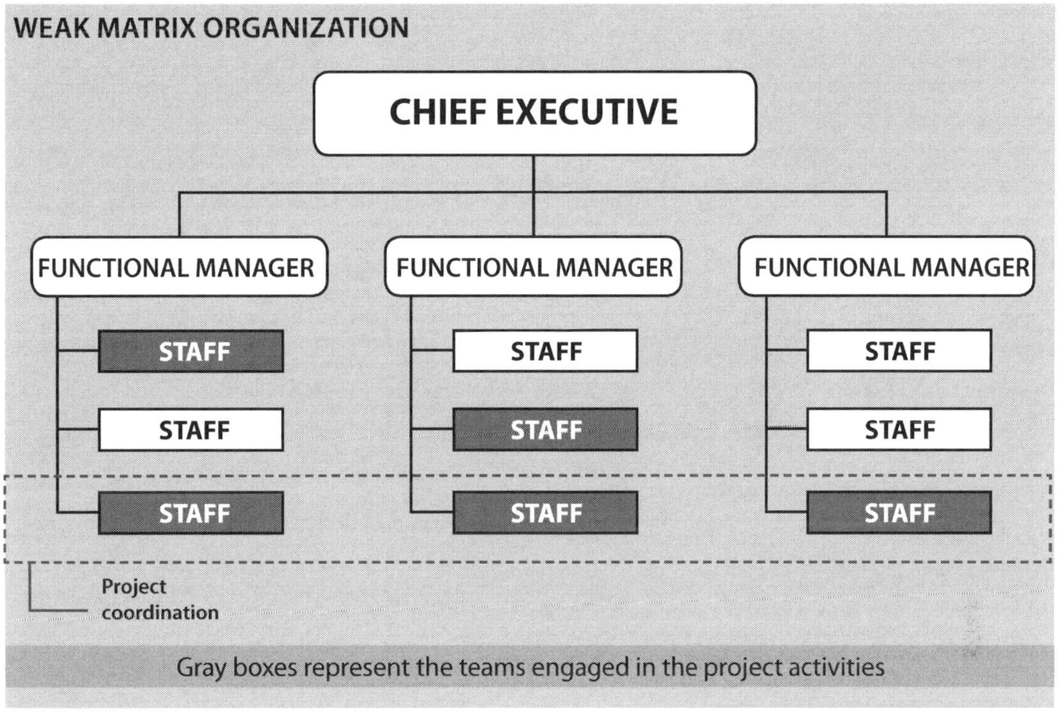

SOURCE: *PMBOK® Guide*

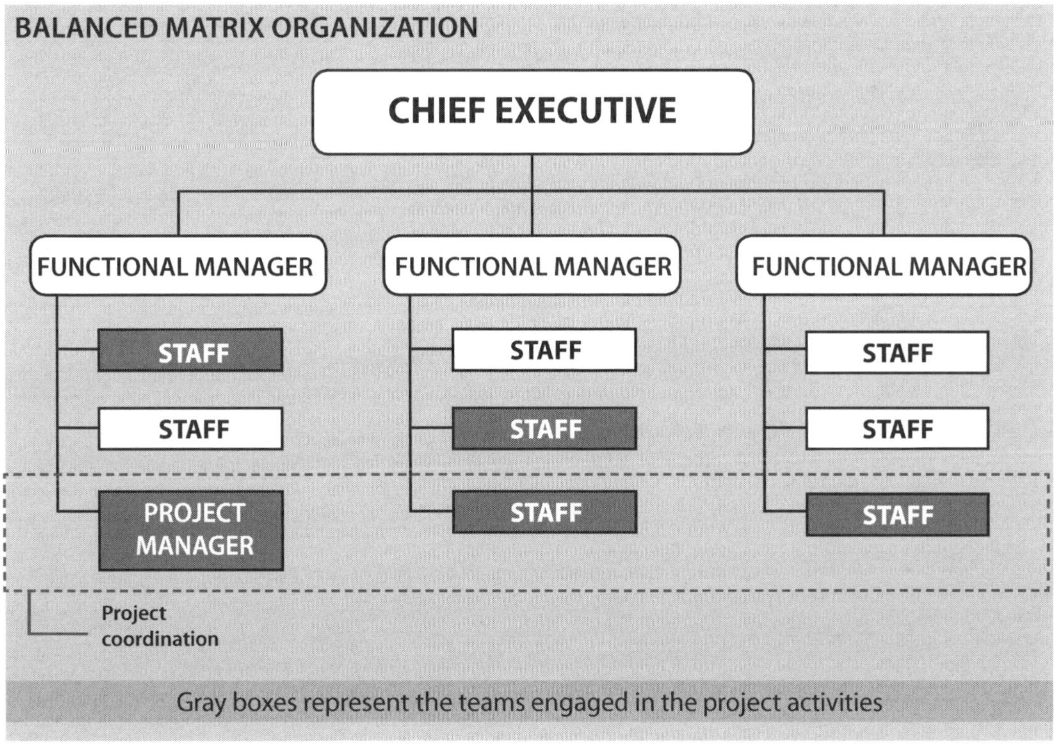

SOURCE: *PMBOK® Guide*

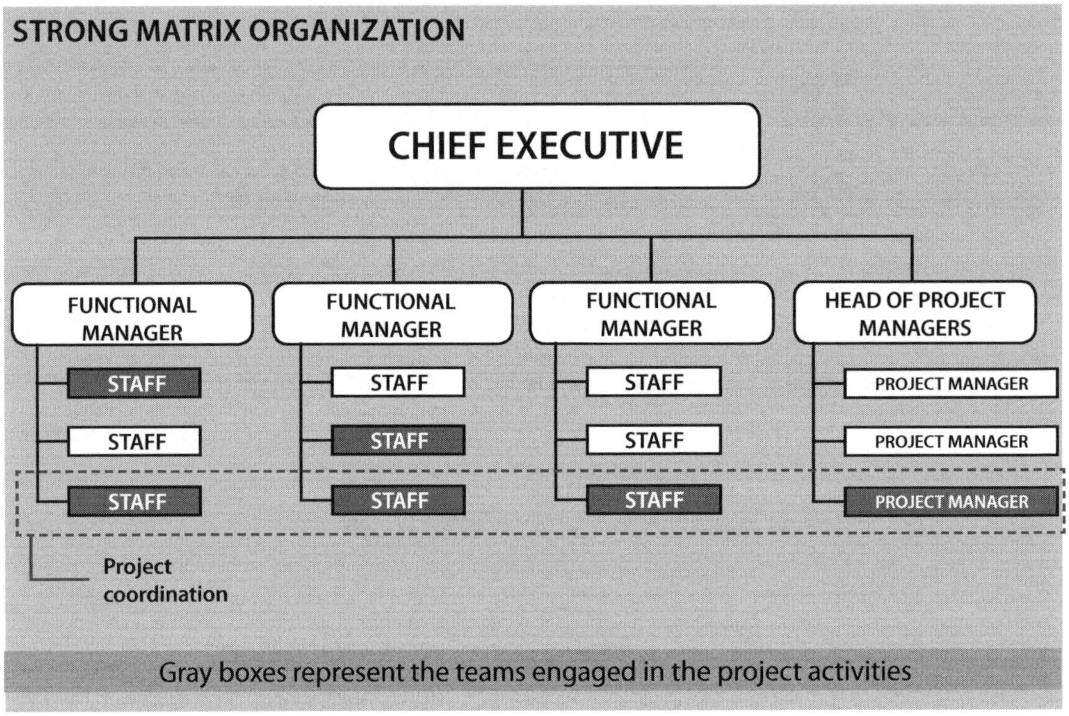

SOURCE: ***PMBOK® Guide***

Matrix organizations are combinations of the characteristics of the functional organization and the organization by project, intended to maximize their strengths.

While in the weak matrix, power is with the functional manager, in the strong matrix, power is with the project manager, and the balanced matrix attempts to share this power between the functional manager and the project manager. In a weak matrix, the project manager position is equivalent to that of a project facilitator (without any decision power) or a project coordinator (with some decision power) subject to a higher-level manager.

2.12.1.4 COMPOSITE ORGANIZATION

Some organizations may use an organizational structure involving, at several levels, the structures addressed above. For example, a typical functional organization can, at any given time, create a special team to manage a critical or important project.

The following figure shows an example of such a structure.

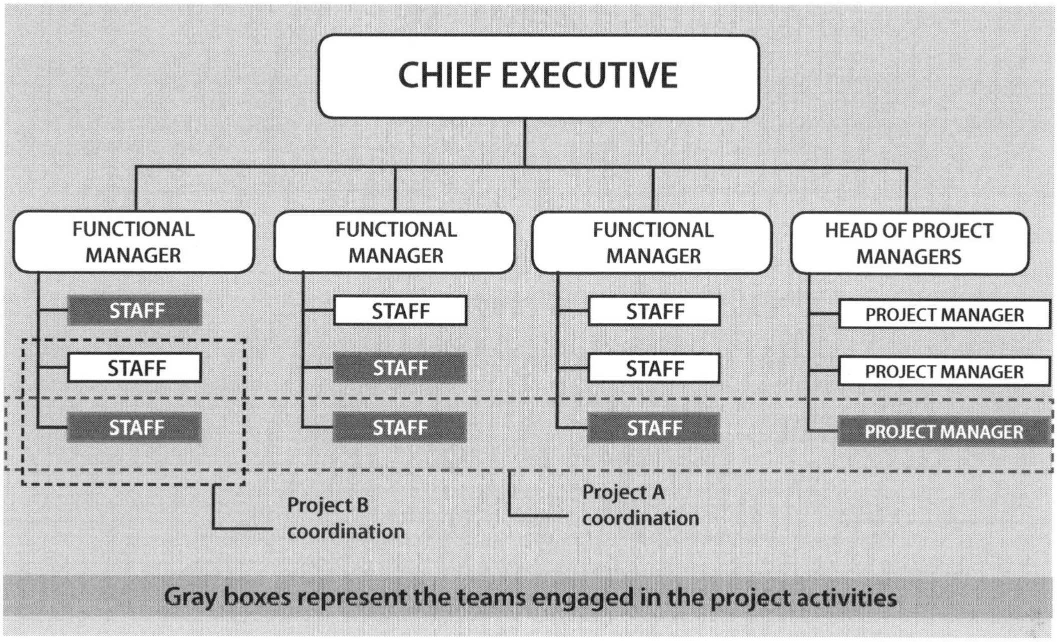

SOURCE: *PMBOK® Guide*

The table below shows a comparison among organizational structures.

TABLE 2.2 ORGANIZATIONAL STRUCTURE INFLUENCES ON PROJECTS

Project characteristics / Organization structure	Functional	Weak Matrix	Balanced	Strong	By project
Project manager authority	Little or none	Limited	Low to moderate	Moderate to high	High to almost total
Resource availability	Little or none	Limited	Low to moderate	Moderate to high	High to almost total
Who controls the project budget	Functional manager	Functional manager	Mixed	Project manager	Project manager
Project manager position	Part time	Part time	Full time	Full time	Full time
Project management administrative team	Part time	Part time	Part time	Full time	Full time

SOURCE: *PMBOK® Guide*

2.13 ENVIRONMENTAL FACTORS APPLIED TO THE PROJECT MANAGEMENT

Project management must take into account enterprise factors influencing the project. Such factors can be considered as input information or tools when developing project management processes. Ultimately, as part of the lessons learned from the project, such factors can be revised, making it outputs of the project management processes in question and therefore inputs and tools for the company's future projects.

2.13.1 ENTERPRISE ENVIRONMENTAL FACTORS

Recognizing and considering the influences of the enterprise environmental factors in project management is essential to develop the project management processes. Such factors are considered as inputs and can be

- Organizational culture and organizational structure;
- Organizational culture related to project management;
- General infrastructure for project management;
- Functions and departments interlinked to project management;
- The company human resources and applicable policies;
- The company information system;
- The company procurement and contracting policies;
- External factors influencing the company, such as governmental standards, quality standards, market conditions, the project social and economic local environment, and others;
- Any other factors influencing or that may directly or indirectly influence project management.

2.13.2 ORGANIZATIONAL PROCESS ASSETS

Organizational process assets can be any and all processes, policies, and procedures of the company as well as the knowledge base acquired by the company on previous projects. Therefore, such assets can be grouped into two categories and can include, for example

Processes, policies, and procedures of the company

- Project management policy
- Project management specific procedures
- Project management procedures
- Quality policy
- Quality procedures
- Safety policy and health at work
- Work instructions
- Templates and standard forms
- The organization communication requirements

The company knowledge base

- Historical information of previous project management such as time, scope, cost, work breakdown structure, and others
- Information regarding problems and troubleshooting in previous projects
- Information on labor productivity, equipment, and services for use in estimates
- Activity cost information from previous projects for use in estimates
- Lessons learned by the company throughout its existence

2.13.3 PROJECT SELECTION

Project selection is the process of assessing a project or a group of projects in order to select one or a few projects that match the company-defined objectives and criteria.

Project selection methods are

- Scoring templates and
- Economic templates.

Economic templates cover the following methods:

- Return on investment period,
- Net present value, and
- Internal rate of return.

Attachment I to this chapter presents further reading on project selection

2.13.4 CONTRACT

Reviewing the contract is essentially important for project management, because at the project start, the contract and the documents belonging to it present the highest level of detail of the project scope.

In the contract, in addition to the project characteristics and peculiarities, the following items must be reviewed:

- Scope of services
- Location where services will be performed, facilities, or local difficulties
- Deadlines for mobilization, service execution, and demobilization
- Documents contained in the contract (drawings, specifications, quantity spreadsheets, etc.)
- Contractor obligations and responsibilities — related to labor, material and equipment supply, and service performance
- Contractor obligations and responsibilities
- Contracting and payment method
- The guarantee bank letter requirement

- Price adjustment
- Services performed measurement criteria
- Services performed acceptance criteria

2.13.5 PROJECT MANAGEMENT METHODOLOGY

The existence of a project management methodology, which often comes down to a standard or procedure, must be checked and analyzed in terms of adapting the management of the project in question. Changes to methodology, aiming at adapting the project in question, must be previously authorized by senior management and, therefore, become part of the company historical records.

2.13.6 PROJECT MANAGEMENT INFORMATION SYSTEM (PMIS)

The project management information system is the set of programs available within the company in order to help manage projects. This system must have the capability of helping manage the project from the beginning to the end and must include features to make the integration of stakeholders easier as well as to make communications and records easier, and enable monitoring changes related to scope, time and cost, among others.

2.13.7 EXPERT JUDGMENT

Expert judgment is a way of obtaining more knowledge about a technical or project management detail. It is used as an input or tool in several project management processes and can be obtained from several sources, including

- Consultants
- Other units of the organization
- Project stakeholders
- Manufacturers and suppliers of equipment and services, and
- Technical and professional associations.

2.13.8 ASSUMPTIONS AND CONSTRAINTS

- **Assumptions**

  Factors considered, for planning purposes, as true, real, or certain, even without proof or documentation:

  - Financial resource availability
  - Availability of qualified personnel
  - Deadlines for suppliers' deliverables

- **Constraints**

  Internal or external factors limiting the project options, which may affect the project or process performance:

  - Scope
  - Costs
  - Deadlines
  - Quality
  - Resources
  - Technology
  - Legal obligations

Attachment I

PROJECT SELECTION

PROJECT SELECTION

Project selection is the process of assessing a project or a group of projects in order to select one or a few projects that match the company-defined objectives and criteria.

1 PROJECT SELECTION CRITERIA

Project selection criteria involve factors that contribute, either positively or negatively, to a project selection decision. Such factors are directly related to the organizational goals. They are usually related to the project product and the benefits brought about by this product to the company. Project selection criteria are associated with areas of the organization such as production, marketing, finance, human resources, and information technology.

Project selection criteria may differ from organization to organization. For example, for a construction company entering market in a region where it is not operating yet, this criterion may be the most important at this point, while for another construction company already operating in the same region, the criterion related to obtaining certain profit might be more important now.

Therefore, a list of criteria should be developed and each criterion must have, for every project, its relative contribution importance set in order to achieve the organization objectives. The following list shows some of the criteria that must be considered in selecting a project associated with areas of the organization.

MARKETING AND SALES CRITERIA

- Increased market potential
- Increased market share
- Time for increasing market share
- Customer acceptance and satisfaction
- Project life cycle
- Product quality
- Consumer safety
- Increased company reputation
- Possibility of competitive prices
- Probability of creating products from their original

PRODUCTION CRITERIA

- Technology requirements
- Installation time and production start
- Production requirements: raw materials, equipment, energy, etc
- Production learning time
- Production unit time

- Production unit cost
- Production losses and waste
- End product quality
- Quality control procedures

FINANCIAL CRITERIA

- Profitability
- Investment present value
- Need for cash flow and its impact on the company
- Time of return on investment
- Time until the break-even point (when total expenditure equals the cost and part of the invested amount is returned)
- Magnitude of the required investment
- Investment risk degree

ORGANIZATIONAL CRITERIA

- Increased productivity
- Impact on the enterprise image among consumers and suppliers
- Compliance with environmental protection requirements
- Compliance with governmental requirements
- Impact on the company information system
- Suppliers' vulnerability

PERSONAL CRITERIA

- Changes to working conditions
- Training needs
- Required professional skills
- Employees increased morale
- Changes to the length of the working day
- Changes to work team type and characteristics
- Employees reaction
- Additional needs of communication means and methods

2 PROJECT SELECTION METHODS

Project selection methods are used to assess the project benefits or compare measurable benefits among projects, enabling selection of one or more projects among those possible.

Project selection methods are

- Scoring templates and
- Economic templates.

Economic templates cover the following methods:

- Return on investment period
- Net present value
- Internal rate of return

2.1 SCORING TEMPLATES

A scoring model is a method that basically uses the sum of scores for each relevant project selection criterion in order to obtain the project score.

Criterion selection

Selecting appropriate criteria is essentially important to create the scoring template. This selection must result in a list of relevant criteria, unlike the detailed list provided in item 1 above. However, for more effective use, such criteria can be decomposed.

Scoring template construction

In order to construct a scoring template, the following items must be defined:

- Selection criteria, separated by group or type
- Relative weights of each set of criteria, according to their degree of importance in the project selection
- Relative weights of each criterion according to the degree of importance in the set of criteria

Project scoring

- Each project analyzed will obtain a scoring value in each criterion that, when multiplied by its relative weight within the set of criteria, will result in the score related to the set of criteria.
- The sum of scores of criteria within a set of criteria will result in the score of this group related to the project selection.
- The sum of scores of all sets of criteria will result in the project scoring.
- Projects with the highest score must be listed in priority in relation to those with lower scores.

The following spreadsheet shows an example of the project scoring template for projects A, B, and C. In this example, project C has been assigned the highest score and must be selected.

LOGO

PROJECT SCORING

ESTIMATE CRITERIA	WEIGHT OF THE GROUP	WEIGHT OF THE CRITERIA	SCORING		
			PROJECT A	PROJECT B	PROJECT C
1. MARKETING/SALES	**30%**				
1.1. Market participation		10%	7	8	9
1.2. Customer satisfaction		40%	6	7	8
1.3. Product life cycle		30%	8	8	7
1.4. Company's reputation		20%	6	6	9
2. PRODUCTION	**20%**				
2.1. Unit production cost		60%	9	8	6
2.2. Installation/production time		25%	5	6	8
2.3. Losses and rejections		15%	9	7	8
3. FINANCE	**40%**				
3.1. Profitability		20%	7	8	9
3.2. Return on investment period		25%	8	6	7
3.3. Investment current value		25%	8	6	7
3.4. Investment risk level		30%	7	8	7
4. ORGANIZATIONAL	**10%**				
4.1. Productive increase		70%	6	8	7
4.2. Organizational image improvement		30%	5	5	6
PROJECT FINAL SCORING			**7.18**	**7.14**	**7.39**

2.2 ECONOMIC METHODS

Project selection economic methods ignore the technical criteria and consider the investment cost and the return of the amount invested in the project. The most common economic methods are return on investment period, net present value, and internal rate of return.

Return on investment period

The return on investment period is the time required for the company to recover the money invested in the project. It compares the initial investment to the cash inflows expected during the product or service lifetime.

Assuming an initial investment of $200,000 on a project whose output provides a monthly cash inflow of $20,000, we would have a Return on Investment Period by dividing the initial investment provided by the expected inflows:

Return on investment period = $200,000 / $20,000 = 10 months

The return on investment period is conservative and the least accurate among economic methods, mainly for the reasons below:

- The method outcome — in units of time — does not express the difference among projects based on the orders of magnitude of investment and cash inflows.
- The method does not consider the possibility of a project having a slower, but more durable, return, which can be a considerable advantage for the company.
- The method does not consider a product life cycle. A project may have a short return on investment period, but at the end of that period, the project product may enter into obsolescence, which could render the initial investment unfeasible.
- Difficulty to determine the cash inflow amount, in view of currency depreciation over the period of return and the possibilities of increasing the product sales value in that period.

Net present value

The *net present value* method, also named *discounted cash flow* considers the value of money over time, the inflows (return) and outflows (expenses) of cash flow (net amount).

The formula to calculate the *net present value* is

$$\text{NPV} = \frac{FV}{(1+i)^n}$$

Where

FV = *future value*

i = *interest rate*

n = *period*

As an example, let's compare the three following projects:

Chapter 2 - Project Management Fundamentals

Project A

- expected future value (less expenses) = $250,000
- annual interest rate = 5%
- period = 3 years

$$NPV = (\$250{,}000) / (1 + 0.05)^3 = \$215{,}959$$

Project B

- expected future value (less expenses) = $280,000
- annual interest rate = 7%
- time = 3 years

$$NPV = (\$280{,}000) / (1 + 0.07)^3 = \$228{,}563$$

Project C

- expected future value (less expenses) = $280,000
- annual interest rate = 10%
- time = 2 years

$$NPV = (\$280{,}000) / (1+0.10)^2 = \$228{,}563$$

It is observed that Project C, with a higher annual interest rate, resulted in the best choice among the three projects.

Internal rate of return

The Internal Rate of Return (IRR) is the discount rate when the present value of cash flow is zero, i.e., when the net present value of inflows equals the initial investment.

The Internal Rate of Return calculation is the most complex of all cash flow techniques and must be prepared using a computer. In general, projects with a higher IRR are considered as better than those with a lower IRR.

2.2.1 CONSIDERATIONS ON ECONOMIC METHODS

Economic methods require that data on future return and the resulting costs expected for the project are expected. Even though these data may not have great difficulty, there will always be a degree of uncertainty, which is the main drawback of applying economic methods. In contrast, after obtaining these data, economic methods are easily viewed and enable easy comparison of projects and other capital investment opportunities.

Additional information and reminders for the exam

- In order to be considered successful, a project must meet or exceed stakeholders' expectations.
- OPM3: an organizational maturity template for project management of PMI®. It was developed to assist organizations determine their level of maturity in project management.
- Management by Objectives (MBO): definition of enterprise objectives, periodic assessment, and implementation of corrective actions. The MBO will only work if fully supported by the senior management.

- **Organizational influences on the project**

1 Functional structure

- Team members have a single head.
- Professionals are grouped by expertise.
- Professionals specialize in their specific areas and not in project management.
- Professionals are "faithful" to the department, not so much to the project.
- The functional manager has full authority over team members.
- The project manager has little or no authority, and he acts more like an communications assistant or coordinator and cannot make decisions on a personal level. The project manager can be referred to simply as coordinator, facilitator, or consignor of projects.

2 Structure by project

- Professionals are grouped by project.
- Professionals are dedicated to the project.
- Professionals, at the end of each project, proceed to another project or are dismissed — usually there is not an assignment location for the professional at the organization structure.
- The functional manager has no authority over team members.
- The project manager has full authority over the project and the team members and is responsible for all decisions and project results.
- There may be double functions and facilities when there are simultaneous projects.
- There is no project coordinator or facilitator role.

3 Matrix structure

- Professionals usually report to more than one boss.
- The functional manager and the project manager share responsibilities and authority, which requires well-defined policies and procedures.
- The control of resource use is more complex when using the mixed management system.
- At the end of each project, professionals usually proceed to another project or return to their place of origin.
- Communications are more complex than in other organizations.

- **Project Selection**

1 Present value

$PV = FV/(1 + i)^n$, where

FV = future value
i = interest rate
n = periods

2 Net present value

If NPV is greater than zero, it is a good investment.
The one with the highest NPV must be selected.

3 Internal rate of return (IRR)

The project with the highest IRR must be selected.

4 Return period

The project with the lower return period must be selected.

5 Benefit-cost ratio

The project with the highest index must be selected.

6 Opportunity cost

Opportunity cost is the amount that the company fails to obtain with a project by choosing another one and is represented by the project net present value not selected. Example: the company chooses project A with a NPV of $500,000 over project B with an NPV of $100,000. The opportunity cost of project A is $100,000.

Supplementary exercises

1. Are the examples below related to projects or processes?

1	A baby room renovation	☐ project	☐ process
2	Wash the car every Friday	☐ project	☐ process
3	Dog walking every day	☐ project	☐ process
4	Preparing a Valentine's Day dinner	☐ project	☐ process
5	Making a vacation trip	☐ project	☐ process
6	Organizing a lecture	☐ project	☐ process
7	Organizing a trade show	☐ project	☐ process
8	Fueling the car every 3 days	☐ project	☐ process
9	Developing a control spreadsheet of the personal budget	☐ project	☐ process
10	Renovating the beach house	☐ project	☐ process

2. Link the project sources in the left column with the corresponding projects in the right column:

Market demand •	• Emergency unit construction
Organizational need •	• Development of a new generation of computer processors
Customer request •	• Implementation of an industry wastewater treatment plant
Legal requirement •	• Expansion of a manufacturing area to meet sales growth
Technological advancement •	• Renovation of the industry administration building
Social need •	• Implementation of a sales computerized system to better serve customers

3. Name three characteristics of each type of organizational structure.

1 Functional

____
____
____
____
____

2 By project

____
____
____
____
____

3 Matrix

____
____
____
____
____

4. Complete each sentence below with one of the options listed, taking into account that you are the project manager in a company organized by projects.

1. I am the ____________________ of the project.
2. The project team reports ____________________.
3. The project team is grouped ____________________.
4. Team members know that, at the end of the project, they can ____________________.
5. I have ____________________ to use resources.
6. I ____________________ to the functional manager.
7. The functional manager ____________________ authority over team members.
8. Communications in my project are ____________________ complex than in matrix organizations.

Full authority – no – more – facilitator – directly to me – by expertise – be dismissed – report to – do not report to the functional manager – responsible for the success – in the project room – return to the place of origin – little authority – has no – less.

Questions

1. The project conflicting constraints include but are not limited to
   a. Scope, cost, schedule, and customer satisfaction
   b. Scope, quality, schedule, budget, resources, and risks
   c. Scope, cost, schedule, customer satisfaction, and budget
   d. Scope, cost, quality, and customer satisfaction

2. In terms of scope, all alternatives are correct, except the following:
   a. In projects, the scope is progressively developed during the project life cycle
   b. Programs have a broader scope and provide more significant benefits
   c. Portfolios have a business scope that changes according to the organization strategic goals
   d. Programs have projects with non related scopes

3. In terms of change, all alternatives are correct, except the following:
   a. Project managers expect changes and implement processes in order to maintain managed and controlled changes
   b. Changes that occur in projects do not influence the program to which it is related
   c. Program managers must expect changes both inside and outside the program and be prepared to manage them
   d. Portfolio managers continually monitor changes in the wider organization environment

4. A training company authorizes a project to create a new course in order to increase its revenue. This is an example of which project authorization strategic consideration?
   a. Market demand
   b. Business opportunity or strategic need
   c. Technological progress
   d. Legal requirement

5. All questions refer to the Project Management Office (PMO), except the following:
   a. An organizational entity to which several responsibilities related to the centralized and coordinated project management are assigned
   b. It can provide support functions to project management

c. It does not provide members to project teams

d. May be responsible for the direct management of a project

6. The following options address the differences between the role of a project managers and a PMO, except

a. The project manager manages constraints (scope, schedule, cost, quality, etc.) of individual projects, while the PMO manages methodologies, standards, global risk/opportunity, and interdependencies among projects at the company level

b. The project manager focuses on the project specified objectives, while the PMO manages major program scope changes that can be seen as potential opportunities to better achieve business objectives

c. The project manager manages resources allocated to the project, except for resources allocated by the PMO, while the PMO manages the resources allocated by it

d. The project manager controls the resources assigned to the project in order to best meet the project objectives, while the PMO uses shared organizational resources among all projects

7. The following options are enterprise environmental factors, except

a. Culture, structure, and organizational processes

b. Government or industry standards

c. Lessons learned from other projects

d. Infrastructure (equipment and existing installations)

8. The following options are enterprise environmental factors, except

a. Information on labor productivity, equipment, and services

b. Market conditions

c. Stakeholders' risk tolerance

d. Political climate

9. The following options are the enterprise organizational process assets, except

a. Historical information of previous project management

b. Information related to the occurrence, and troubleshooting in previous projects

c. The company culture and structure

d. Lessons learned by the company throughout its existence

10. The following options are the enterprise organizational process assets, except

a. Information on time, scope, and cost in previous projects

b. Channels of communication defined by the company

c. Information on labor productivity from previous projects

d. Previous work breakdown structures

11. All options are basic types of relationships between project phases, except

a. Non linear

b. Sequential

c. Overlapping

d. Interactive

12. All options are related to a project with a sequential relationship between phases, except

a. A phase that can begin only after the previous phase is completed

b. The allowance at overlapping between phases

c. The step-by-step approach that reduces uncertainties

d. Limiting the schedule reduction options

13. All of them are characteristics of functional managers, except the following:

a. Functional managers directly address production and maintenance of the company's salable products

b. Functional managers can provide advice on a particular subject or project services

c. Functional managers have their own permanent staff to perform continuous work

d. Functional managers play a role within an administrative or functional area of business, such as finance, human resources, accounting, or procurements

14. In a balanced matrix structure, the project manager's authority is

a. Limited

b. Little or none

c. Low to moderate

d. Moderate to high

15. In an organizational projectized structure, the project manager's authority is

a. Limited

b. Little or none

c. Low to moderate

d. High to almost total

16. In a balanced matrix structure, resource availability is

a. Moderate to high

b. Limited

c. Low to moderate

d. Little or none

17. The difference between organizational process assets and enterprise environmental factors is

a. Organizational process assets restrict and limit the options of project management; environmental factors limit the use of organizational resources in the project

b. Organizational process assets provide guidelines and criteria for adapting the organization's processes to specific needs of the project; environmental factors may restrict the options for project management

c. Environmental factors provide project management templates and standards, and organizational process assets provide project management standards and procedures

d. Environmental factors are related to standards, and organizational process assets are related to the organization infrastructure

18. To be considered as successful, a project

a. Must be accepted by the sponsor

b. Must meet or exceed stakeholders' expectations

c. Has its product transferred to the production line

d. Must obtain formal acceptance of deliverables

19. Which of the following options is directly related to the degree of authority of the project manager?

a. The project manager's head authority

b. The project manager's communication skills

c. Organizational structure

d. The project manager's technical level

20. Which of the following best describes the advantage of the functional structure for employees?

a. The organization is focused on projects

b. Teams are grouped and defined for each project

c. The chain of command is explicit, and employees report to one manager

d. The project manager has full authority in the project

21. You have been assigned to be part of a project team, with a well-defined function. You will report to both the manager in charge and the infrastructure director. They both share the responsibility for the project and there is a balance of power between them. In this case, which kind of organizational structure are you in?

a. Balanced matrix

b. Weak matrix

c. Projectized

d. Functional

22. You are the manager of an ongoing project, more specifically in the planning process group. You have had difficulties with stakeholders, but you know that you will still find difficulties ahead. What is the project management process group where stakeholders' influence is larger?

a. Initiating

b. Planning

c. Executing

d. Monitoring and controlling

23. Your company won the bid to build a school in a certain area of the city the company headquarters. You have been appointed as the project manager, and during your first visit to the work site, you find that this would be the first school in that area, which makes you very proud to collaborate with the education of residents in that area. What is the origin of this project?

a. Social progress

b. Technological progress

c. Social need

d. Market demand

24. In a functional organization, who has power to give orders to team members?

a. The project manager

b. The functional manager

c. The team

d. The integrated matrix

25. All of them are characteristics of a project, except

a. Temporary

b. Defined start and finish

c. Interrelated activities

d. Continuously repeated work

26. A team is continuously working on manufacturing a new product and, even after a month, it cannot clearly define the project scope statement, making it difficult to fully understand the situation. What is really happening?

a. The team has managed to identify the product scope

b. The team is working on a process, not a project

c. The project charter has not clearly defined the project objectives

d. The team has not yet identified the project product

27. There is a great discussion between project managers in an organization in which project is more important. One manager says yours has a higher cost and brings a higher return to the company. The other states that your project adds more value to the business and requests priority for resources to be available for the project. Who should decide on priorities among the company projects?

a. The project manager

b. Project management teams

c. The project management office

d. The financial management

28. Legal requirements to be implemented in the organization, market demand and customer request, are all examples of

a. Reasons to develop the project charter

b. Reasons for initiating projects

c. Reasons to define project stakeholders

d. Reasons to define the project sponsor

29. Lessons learned are BETTER completed by the

a. Project manager

b. Project team

c. Sponsor

d. Stakeholders

30. A company is interested in creating historical records of current projects and using that information for future projects. Which is the BEST way to accomplish it?

a. Record the project management plans

b. Create lessons learned

c. Record schedule and network diagrams

d. Create status reports

31. Project A has an IRR (Internal Rate of Return) of 27.5%. Project B has an IRR of 26%. Project C has an IRR of 28%. Project D has an IRR of 28.3%. Which would be the best project?

a. Project A

b. Project B

c. Project C

d. Project D

32. When comparing the following projects by means of the internal rate of return, which one would be the best option?

a. IRR = 16.4%

b. IRR = 18.4%

c. IRR = 18.6%

d. IRR = 18.92%

Answer key

Supplementary exercises

1. 1 - project; 2 - process; 3 - process; 4 - project; 5 - project; 6 - project; 7 - project; 8 - process; 9 - project; 10 - project.

2. Link the project sources in the left column with the corresponding projects in the right column:

Market demand	Emergency unit construction
Organizational need	Development of a new generation of computer processors
Customer request	Implementation of an industry wastewater treatment plant
Legal requirement	Expansion of a manufacturing area to meet sales growth
Technological advancement	Renovation of the industry administration building
Social need	Implementation of a sales computerized system to better serve customers

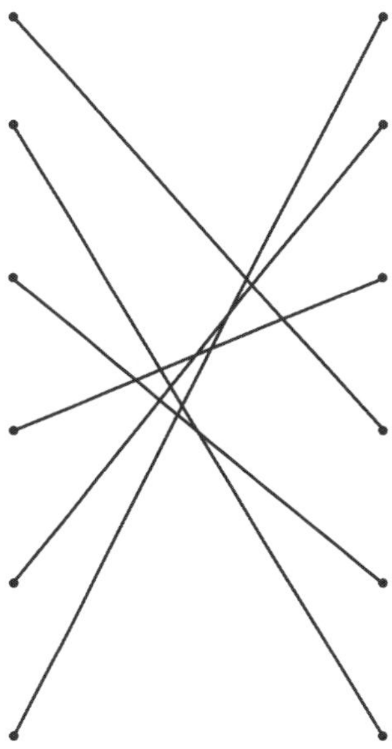

3. 1
- Team members have one boss
- The project manager has little authority
- Professionals are grouped by expertise

2
- Professionals, at the end of the project, proceed to another project or are dismissed
- The project manager has full authority
- Professionals are grouped by project

3
- Communications are more complex
- Professionals usually report to more than one boss
- The functional manager and the project manager share the responsibility and authority

4. 1 - responsible for the success; 2 - directly to me; 3 - in the project room; 4 - be dismissed; 5 - full authority; 6 - do not report; 7 - has no; 8 - less.

Questions

1. B. The project conflicting constraints include, but are not limited to scope, quality, schedule, budget, resources, and risks.

2. D. A program is a set of related projects. It is important to understand the different scope considerations for projects, programs, and portfolios, described in options A, B, and C.

3. B. A project change can influence the program to which it is connected. It is important to understand the different change considerations for projects, programs, and portfolios, described in options A, C, and D.

4. B. An example of market demand: a car company authorizing a project to produce more economic cars because of the shortage of gasoline. An example of technological progress: an electronics manufacturer authorizes a project to develop a laptop faster and cheaper because of the progress in technology. An example of legal requirement: the company authorizes a project to implement the electronic invoice issuing to satisfy a governmental law. An example of business strategic opportunity or need is described in the question.

5. C. PMO can provide members to be part of project teams. It is important to learn the characteristics of a PMO, addressed in options A, B, and D.

6. C. Regardless of who allocated resources in the project, in a projectized company, as is the case now, they are controlled in the project environment by the project manager. It is important to learn the differences between the role of project managers and of a PMO, addressed in A, B, and D.

7. C. Lessons learned are organizational process assets. The other options are enterprise environmental factors.

8. A. Information on labor productivity, equipment, and services are organizational process assets of the company. The other options are enterprise environmental factors.

9. C. The company culture and structure are enterprise environmental factors. The other options are organizational process assets.

10. B. Channels of communication are environmental factors of the company. The other options are organizational process assets.

11. A. The basic types of relationships between phases of a project are sequential, overlapping, and interactive.

12. B. The type of relationship enabling overlay is the overlapping relationship, not the sequential one. The other options are characteristics of the phase sequential relationship.

13. A. Functional managers are usually related to the organization's administrative areas. Professionals who deal with the production and maintenance of sales products in the company are operations managers.

14. C. In a balanced matrix structure, the project manager's authority is low to moderate.

15. D. In a projectized organizational structure, a project manager's authority is from high to almost total.

16. C. In a balanced matrix structure, resource availability is low to moderate.

17. B. This question is to differentiate:

- Organizational process assets are related to providing guidelines and criteria to adapt the organization processes to specific needs of the project.
- Enterprise environmental factors are factors that may restrict the options for managing the project, such as the company's culture and infrastructure, project management information systems, market conditions, political climate, stakeholders' risk tolerance, and so forth.

18. B. A project is considered successful when it meets or exceeds stakeholders' expectations. The other options characterize of the project closing but do not measure whether the project was successful.

19. C. The project manager's degree of authority is directly related to the company's organizational structure. In a projectized company, the manager has full authority of the project. On the other hand, in a functional organization, the project manager has little or no authority, working more as a facilitator.

20. C. The advantage to employees in a functional structure is the ability to view a clear chain of command and to report to one manager. The other options refer to organization by projects.

21. A. In the balanced matrix organizational structure, employees usually report to two or more managers who share the authority and responsibility for the project.

22. A. In the initiating phase, the influence of stakeholders is higher than in other phases of the project. It defines stakeholders' requirements and expectations, and, at the planning, on the other hand, such requirements are considered in the project so that the influence is reduced by meeting requirements.

23. C. Note that the city hall in the nearby city has decided to build a school to meet a social needs, residents still did not have a school in the area.

24. B. In a functional organization, the functional manager gives orders to team members.

25. D. If the work is repeated on a daily basis, it is probably related to an operation such as manufacturing.

26. B. If the work has now started the continuous manufacture of a product, then this is not a project but a process. The project charter is not applicable in this case.

27. C. The project management office is, among other things, designed to define priorities among projects, always complying with the organization's policies. The manager and teams cannot decide on other projects as the financial management cannot decide single-handedly on the course of the organization's ongoing projects.

28. B. All of them are reasons for initiating projects.

29. D. Given that stakeholders involve the team, the manager, and the sponsor, the best option is "stakeholders".

30. B. Lessons learned may comprise several documents, including those discussed in other options.

31. D. The higher the rate of return, the better the expected return for the project.

32. D. The best option is the project with the highest rate of return.

Chapter 3

PROJECT MANAGEMENT PROCESSES

1. Introduction
2. Project management process groups
3. Interaction among process groups
4. Project management knowledge areas
5. Knowledge areas overview
6. Project management process mapping

- Additional information and reminders for the exam
- Supplementary exercises
- Questions
- Answer key

3.1 INTRODUCTION

This chapter presents the project management process groups, their interactions, project knowledge areas, and process mapping within such areas.

3.2 PROJECT MANAGEMENT PROCESS GROUPS

The five management processes groups presented in the poster attached to the book have the following key features and actions:

Initiating

The Initiating process group must begin when there is a consensus that the project must be started. Although it does not take much time or many resources, this group is very important for the project to be successful. Here the project manager is selected and defined, stakeholders are identified, the enterprise need or the project reason is recorded, project objectives are determined, and assumptions and constraints are recorded. This information is documented in the project charter. In summary, Initiating involves

- Determining the project objectives
- Appointing the project manager
- Identifying stakeholders and
- Documenting and publishing the project charter.

Planning

The Planning process group involves determining the project scope (what must be done), defining the team and their roles and responsibilities (who must do it), schedule development (when it must be done), and budget (at what cost), determining standards and quality metrics, risk identification, establishing what must be purchased or acquired, the project management plan (how it must be done) and its approval, and the project initial meeting. In summary, Planning involves

- Documenting and publishing the project scope statement
- Developing the Work Breakdown Structure (WBS)
- Project schedule development
- Resource needs determination
- Definition of purchases and procurements
- Project budget development and
- Developing and publishing the project management plan.

Executing

The Executing process group is where the project work is performed. It involves mobilizing the work Executing team, the actual work execution according to the plan, following specifications and standards, implementing approved changes and defect repair, developing the team, and selecting and hiring suppliers.

Executing is the phase where more resources are spent, whether human, material, or financial. In summary, Executing involves

- Allocation and development of the work execution team;
- Allocation of resources required to perform the job;
- Project management plan execution; and
- Project work execution.

Monitoring and controlling

The Monitoring and controlling process group is also where project work is being executed, but the focus is on the work verification and measurement to confirm compliance with the plan. In the event of discrepancies between Planning and Executing, corrective or preventive measures are taken to realign the project as planned. This verification and measurement consider the scope, time, cost, quality baselines, identified risks, and any other parameters defined in the project management plan as well as the occurrence of new risks to achieve the project objectives. In summary, Monitoring and controlling involves

- Measuring project performance as compared to baselines;
- Variance determination and consequent recommendations for corrective or preventive actions;
- Assessment of the corrective action taken;
- Risk audit;
- Performance reports execution; and
- Contract administration.

Closing

The Closing process group includes confirmation that the work complies with requirements, formal product acceptance by the customer, issuing final performance reports, record indexing and archiving, updating the lessons learned knowledge base, project closing, and project resource release. In summary, Closing involves

- Obtaining formal acceptance of deliverables;
- Archiving project records;
- Documentation of lessons learned; and
- Project closing formalizing.

3.3 INTERACTION AMONG PROCESS GROUPS

The processes of the project management process groups are connected, and they interact with one another throughout the project execution. Many of the process outputs are subsequent processes inputs, which become inputs from other subsequent processes and so on, until the project ends.

An input generally defines "what do I need before doing?" while an output generally defines "what will I have when it ends?" Generally, after obtaining process inputs, we use project management tools and techniques to get the desired or required outputs.

Figure 3.1 shows interaction among process groups.

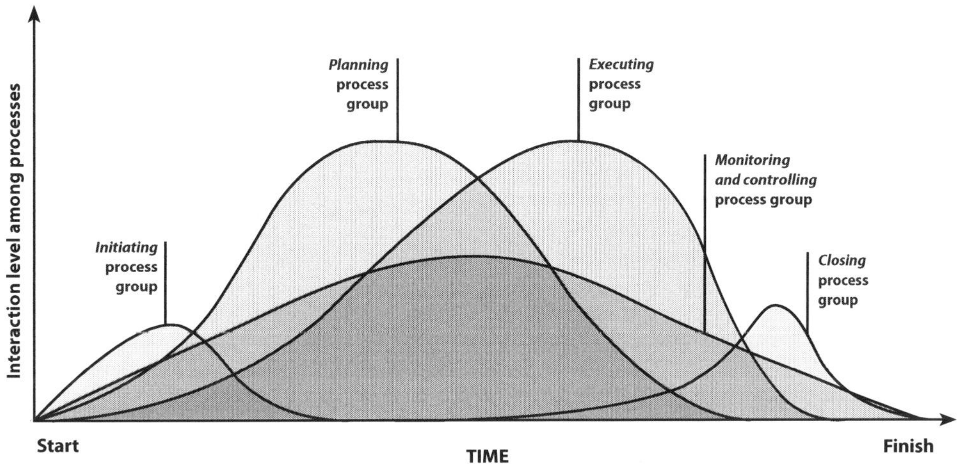

Fig. 3.1 - Interaction among process groups in a project.

It is important to note that the project management process groups are not project phases. When a large project is divided into distinct phases, all process groups can be considered in each project phase.

3.4 PROJECT MANAGEMENT KNOWLEDGE AREAS

PMI® establishes the following 9 knowledge areas that include 42 project management processes.

3.4.1 PROJECT INTEGRATION MANAGEMENT

The Project Integration Management knowledge area includes the processes required for the effective integration of all processes necessary to accomplish the project objective within the organization-defined procedures.

Integration management processes include:

1 ***Develop Project Charter***

2 ***Develop Project Management Plan***

3 ***Direct and Manage Project Execution***

4 ***Monitor and Control Project Work***

5 ***Perform Integrated Change Control***

6 ***Close Project or Phase***

3.4.2 PROJECT SCOPE MANAGEMENT

The Project Scope Management knowledge area is mainly what is or not included in the project, and it includes the processes required to ensure that the project covers all required work, and only that work, to complete the project successfully.

Scope management processes include:

1 ***Collect Requirements***

2 ***Define Scope***

3 ***Create WBS***

4 ***Verify Scope***

5 ***Control Scope***

3.4.3 PROJECT TIME MANAGEMENT

The Project Time Management knowledge area includes the processes required to complete the project within the defined deadline.

Time management processes include:

1 ***Define Activities***

2 ***Sequence Activities***

3 ***Estimate Activity Resources***

4 ***Estimate Activity Durations***

5 ***Develop Schedule***

6 ***Control Schedule***

3.4.4 PROJECT COST MANAGEMENT

The Project Cost Management knowledge area includes the processes required to complete the project within the approved budget.

Cost management processes include:

1 ***Estimate Costs***

2 ***Determine Budget***

3 ***Control Costs***

3.4.5 PROJECT QUALITY MANAGEMENT

The Project Quality Management knowledge area includes the processes required for quality policies to be implemented to meet the project needs.

Quality management processes include:

1 ***Plan Quality***

2 ***Perform Quality Assurance***

3 ***Perform Quality Control***

3.4.6 PROJECT HUMAN RESOURCE MANAGEMENT

The Project Human Resource Management knowledge area includes the processes organizing and managing the project team.

Human Resource management processes include:

1 ***Develop Human Resource Plan***

2 ***Acquire Project Team***

3 ***Develop Project Team***

4 ***Manage Project Team***

3.4.7 PROJECT COMMUNICATIONS MANAGEMENT

The Project Communications Management knowledge area includes the processes required to ensure generation, collection, distribution, storage, retrieval, and destination of project information in a timely and appropriate manner.

Communication management processes include:

1 ***Identify Stakeholders***

2 ***Plan Communications***

3 ***Distribute Information***

4 ***Manage Stakeholder Expectations***

5 ***Report Performance***

3.4.8 PROJECT RISK MANAGEMENT

The Project Risk Management knowledge area includes the project risk identification, analysis, response, and Monitoring and controlling processes.

Risk management processes include:

1 ***Plan Risk Management***

2 ***Identify Risks***

3. ***Perform Qualitative Risk Analysis***

4 ***Perform Quantitative Risk Analysis***

5 ***Plan Risk Responses***

6 ***Monitor and Control Risks***

3.4.9 PROJECT PROCUREMENT MANAGEMENT

The Project Procurement Management knowledge area includes the processes of purchasing or acquiring products, services, or results required outside the project team to perform the work.

Procurement management processes include:

1 ***Plan Procurements***

2 ***Conduct Procurements***

3 ***Administer Procurements***

4 ***Close Procurements***

3.5 KNOWLEDGE AREAS OVERVIEW

The following figure shows the knowledge areas overview, indicating the PMI®-related chapters.

KNOWLEDGE AREAS OVERVIEW

CHAPTER 4 - *PMBOK® GUIDE*
PROJECT INTEGRATION MANAGEMENT

1. Develop Project Charter
2. Develop Project Management Plan
3. Direct and Manage Project Execution
4. Monitor and Control Project Work
5. Perform Integrated Change Control
6. Close project or phase

CHAPTER 5 - *PMBOK® GUIDE*
PROJECT SCOPE MANAGEMENT

1. Collect Requirements
2. Define Scope
3. Create WBS
4. Verify Scope
5. Control Scope

CHAPTER 6 - *PMBOK® GUIDE*
PROJECT TIME MANAGEMENT

1. Define Activities
2. Sequence Activities
3. Estimate Activity Resources
4. Estimate Activity Durations
5. Develop Schedule
6. Control Schedule

CHAPTER 7 - *PMBOK® GUIDE*
PROJECT COST MANAGEMENT

1. Estimate Costs
2. Determine Budget
3. Control Costs

CHAPTER 8 - *PMBOK® GUIDE*
PROJECT QUALITY MANAGEMENT

1. Plan Quality
2. Perform Quality Assurance
3. Perform Quality Control

CHAPTER 9 - *PMBOK® GUIDE*
PROJECT HUMAN RESOURCE MANAGEMENT

1. Develop Human Resource Plan
2. Acquire Project Team
3. Develop Project Team
4. Manage Project Team

CHAPTER 10 - *PMBOK® GUIDE*
PROJECT COMMUNICATIONS MANAGEMENT

1. Identify Stakeholders
2. Plan Communications
3. Distribute Information
4. Manage Stakeholder Expectations
5. Report Performance

CHAPTER 11 - *PMBOK® GUIDE*
PROJECT RISK MANAGEMENT

1. Plan Risk Management
2. Identify Risks
3. Perform Qualitative Risk Analysis
4. Perform Quantitative Risk Analysis
5. Plan Risk Responses
6. Monitor and Control Risks

CHAPTER 12 - *PMBOK® GUIDE*
PROJECT PROCUREMENT MANAGEMENT

1. Plan Procurements
2. Conduct Procurements
3. Administer Procurements
4. Close Procurements

3.6 PROJECT MANAGEMENT PROCESS MAPPING

KNOWLEDGE AREAS PROCESSES	PROJECT MANAGEMENT PROCESS GROUPS (PROCESSES NUMBERED ACCORDING TO *PMBOK® GUIDE*)				
	INITIATING PROCESS GROUP	PLANNING PROCESS GROUP	EXECUTING PROCESS GROUP	MONITORING AND CONTROLLING PROCESS GROUP	CLOSING PROCESS GROUP
CHAPTER 4 - *PMBOK® GUIDE* PROJECT INTEGRATION MANAGEMENT	*4.1 Develop Project Charter*	*4.2 Develop Project Management Plan*	*4.3 Direct and Manage Project Execution*	*4.4 Monitor and control project work* *4.5 Perform Integrated Change Control*	*4.6 Close project or phase*
CHAPTER 5 - *PMBOK® GUIDE* PROJECT SCOPE MANAGEMENT		*5.1 Collect Requirements* *5.2 Define Scope* *5.3 Create WBS*		*5.4 Verify Scope* *5.5 Control Scope*	
CHAPTER 6 - *PMBOK® GUIDE* PROJECT TIME MANAGEMENT		*6.1 Define Activities* *6.2 Sequence Activities* *6.3 Estimate Activity Resources* *6.4 Estimate Activity Durations* *6.5 Develop Schedule*		*6.6 Control Schedule*	
CHAPTER 7 - *PMBOK® GUIDE* PROJECT COST MANAGEMENT		*7.1 Estimate Costs* *7.2 Determine Budget*		*7.3 Control Costs*	
CHAPTER 8 - *PMBOK® GUIDE* PROJECT QUALITY MANAGEMENT		*8.1 Plan Quality*	*8.2 Perform Quality Assurance*	*8.3 Perform Quality Control*	
CHAPTER 9 - *PMBOK® GUIDE* PROJECT HUMAN RESOURCE MANAGEMENT		*9.1 Develop Human Resource Plan*	*9.2 Acquire Project Team* *9.3 Develop Project Team* *9.4 Manage Project Team*		
CHAPTER 10 - *PMBOK® GUIDE* PROJECT COMMUNICATIONS MANAGEMENT	*10.1 Identify Stakeholders*	*10.2 Plan Communications*	*10.3 Distribute Information* *10.4 Manage Stakeholder Expectations*	*10.5 Report Performance*	
CHAPTER 11 - *PMBOK® GUIDE* PROJECT RISK MANAGEMENT		*11.1 Plan Risk Management* *11.2 Identify Risks* *11.3 Perform Qualitative Risk Analysis* *11.4 Perform Quantitative Risk Analysis* *11.5 Plan Risk Responses*		*11.6 Monitor and Control Risks*	
CHAPTER 12 - *PMBOK® GUIDE* PROJECT PROCUREMENT MANAGEMENT		*12.1 Plan Procurements*	*12.2 Conduct Procurements*	*12.3 Administer Procurements*	*12.4 Close Procurements*

3.6.1 PROJECT INTEGRATION MANAGEMENT

PROJECT INTEGRATION MANAGEMENT OVERVIEW

PMBOK® GUIDE, CHAPTER 4

4.1 DEVELOP PROJECT CHARTER

1. Inputs
    - Project statement of work
    - Business case
    - Contract
    - Enterprise environmental factors
    - Organizational process assets
2. Tools and techniques
    - Expert judgment
3. Outputs
    - Project charter

4.2 DEVELOP PROJECT MANAGEMENT PLAN

1. Inputs
    - Project charter
    - Outputs from planning processes
    - Enterprise environmental factors
    - Organizational process assets
2. Tools and techniques
    - Expert judgment
3. Outputs
    - Project management plan

4.3 DIRECT AND MANAGE PROJECT EXECUTION

1. Inputs
    - Project management plan
    - Approved change requests
    - Enterprise environmental factors
    - Organizational process assets
2. Tools and techniques
    - Expert judgment
    - Project management information system
3. Outputs
    - Deliverables
    - Work performance information
    - Change requests
    - Project management plan updates
    - Project document updates

4.4 MONITOR AND CONTROL PROJECT WORK

1. Inputs
    - Project management plan
    - Performance reports
    - Enterprise environmental factors
    - Organizational process assets
2. Tools and techniques
    - Expert judgment
3. Outputs
    - Change request
    - Project management plan updates
    - Project document updates

4.5 PERFORM INTEGRATED CHANGE CONTROL

1. Inputs
    - Project management plan
    - Work performance information
    - Change requests
    - Enterprise environmental factors
    - Organizational process assets
2. Tools and techniques
    - Expert judgment
    - Change control meetings
3. Outputs
    - Change request status updates
    - Project management plan updates
    - Project document updates

4.6 CLOSE PROJECT OR PHASE

1. Inputs
    - Project management plan
    - Accepted deliverables
    - Organizational process assets
2. Tools and techniques
    - Expert judgment
3. Outputs
    - Final product, service, or result transition
    - Organizational process assets updates

3.6.2 PROJECT SCOPE MANAGEMENT

PROJECT SCOPE MANAGEMENT OVERVIEW

PMBOK® GUIDE, CHAPTER 5

5.1 COLLECT REQUIREMENTS

1. Inputs
   - Project charter
   - Stakeholder register
2. Tools and techniques
   - Interviews
   - Focus groups
   - Facilitated workshops
   - Group creativity techniques
   - Group decision making techniques
   - Questionnaires and surveys
   - Observations
   - Prototypes
3. Outputs
   - Requirements documentation
   - Requirement management plan
   - Requirements traceability matrix

5.2 DEFINE SCOPE

1. Inputs
   - Project charter
   - Requirements documentation
   - Organizational process assets
2. Tools and techniques
   - Expert judgment
   - Product analysis
   - Alternatives identification
   - Facilitated workshops
3. Outputs
   - Project scope statement
   - Project document updates

5.3 CREATE WBS

1. Inputs
   - Project scope statement
   - Requirements documentation
   - Organizational process assets
2. Tools and techniques
   - Decomposition
3. Outputs
   - Work breakdown structure (WBS)
   - WBS dictionary
   - Scope baseline
   - Project document updates

5.4 VERIFY SCOPE

1. Inputs
   - Project management plan
   - Requirements documentation
   - Requirements traceability matrix
   - Validated deliverables
2. Tools and techniques
   - Inspection
3. Outputs
   - Accepted deliverables
   - Change requests
   - Project document updates

5.5 CONTROL SCOPE

1. Inputs
   - Project management plan
   - Work performance information
   - Requirements documentation
   - Requirements traceability matrix
   - Organizational process assets
2. Tools and techniques
   - Variance analysis
3. Outputs
   - Work performance measurements
   - Organizational process assets updates
   - Change requests
   - Project management plan updates
   - Project document updates

3.6.3 PROJECT TIME MANAGEMENT

PROJECT TIME MANAGEMENT OVERVIEW

PMBOK® GUIDE, CHAPTER 6

6.1 DEFINE ACTIVITIES

1. Inputs
   - Scope baseline
   - Enterprise environmental factors
   - Organizational process assets
2. Tools and techniques
   - Decomposition
   - Rolling wave Planning
   - Templates
   - Expert judgment
3. Outputs
   - Activity list
   - Activity attributes
   - Milestone list

6.2 SEQUENCE ACTIVITIES

1. Inputs
   - Activity list
   - Activity attributes
   - Milestone list
   - Project scope statement
   - Organizational process assets
2. Tools and techniques
   - Precedence diagramming method (PDM)
   - Dependency determination
   - Applying leads and lags
   - Schedule network templates
3. Outputs
   - Project schedule network diagrams
   - Project document updates

6.3 ESTIMATE ACTIVITY RESOURCES

1. Inputs
   - Activity list
   - Activity attributes
   - Resource calendar
   - Enterprise environmental factors
   - Organizational process assets
2. Tools and techniques
   - Expert judgment
   - Alternatives analysis
   - Published estimating data
   - Bottom-up estimating
   - Project management software
3. Outputs
   - Activity resource requirements
   - Resource breakdown structure
   - Project document updates

6.4 ESTIMATE ACTIVITY DURATIONS

1. Inputs
   - Activity list
   - Activity attributes
   - Activity resource requirements
   - Resource calendars
   - Project scope statement
   - Enterprise environmental factors
   - Organizational process assets
2. Tools and techniques
   - Expert judgment
   - Analogous estimating
   - Parametric estimating
   - Three-point estimates
   - Reserve analysis
3. Outputs
   - Activity duration estimates
   - Project document updates

6.5 DEVELOP SCHEDULE

1. Inputs
   - Activity list
   - Activity attributes
   - Project schedule network diagrams
   - Activity resource requirements
   - Resource calendars
   - Activity duration estimates
   - Project scope statement
   - Enterprise environmental factors
   - Organizational process assets
2. Tools and techniques
   - Schedule network analysis
   - Critical path method
   - Critical chain method
   - Resource leveling
   - "What if?" scenario analysis
   - Applying leads and lags
   - Schedule compression
   - Scheduling tool
3. Outputs
   - Project schedule
   - Schedule baseline
   - Schedule data
   - Project document updates

6.6 CONTROL SCHEDULE

1. Inputs
   - Project management plan
   - Project schedule
   - Work performance information
   - Organizational process assets
2. Tools and techniques
   - Performance reviews
   - Variance analysis
   - Project management software
   - Resource leveling
   - "What if?" scenario analysis
   - Adjusting leads and lags
   - Schedule compression
   - Scheduling tool
3. Outputs
   - Work performance measurements
   - Organizational process assets updates
   - Change requests
   - Project management plan updates
   - Project document updates

3.6.4 PROJECT COST MANAGEMENT

PROJECT COST MANAGEMENT OVERVIEW

PMBOK® GUIDE, CHAPTER 7

7.1 ESTIMATE COSTS

1. Inputs
    - Scope baseline
    - Project schedule
    - Human resource plan
    - Risk register
    - Enterprise environmental factors
    - Organizational process assets
2. Tools and techniques
    - Expert judgment
    - Analogous estimating
    - Parametric estimating
    - Bottom-up estimating
    - Three-point estimates
    - Reserve analysis
    - Cost of quality (COQ)
    - Project management estimating software
    - Vendor bid analysis
3. Outputs
    - Activity cost estimates
    - Basis of estimates
    - Project document updates

7.2 DETERMINE BUDGET

1. Inputs
    - Activity cost estimates
    - Basis of estimates
    - Scope baseline
    - Project schedule
    - Resource calendars
    - Contracts
    - Organizational process assets
2. Tools and techniques
    - Cost aggregation
    - Reserve analysis
    - Expert judgment
    - Historical relationships
    - Funding limit reconciliation
3. Outputs
    - Cost performance baseline
    - Project funding requirements
    - Project document updates

7.3 CONTROL COSTS

1. Inputs
    - Project management plan
    - Project funding requirements
    - Work performance information
    - Organizational process assets
2. Tools and techniques
    - Earned value management
    - Forecasting
    - To-complete performance index (TCPI)
    - Performance reviews
    - Variance analysis
    - Project management software
3. Outputs
    - Work performance measurements
    - Budget forecasts
    - Organizational process assets updates
    - Change requests
    - Project management plan updates
    - Project document updates

3.6.5 PROJECT QUALITY MANAGEMENT

PROJECT QUALITY MANAGEMENT OVERVIEW

PMBOK® GUIDE, CHAPTER 8

8.1 PLAN QUALITY

1. Inputs
   - Scope baseline
   - Stakeholder register
   - Cost performance baseline
   - Schedule baseline
   - Risk register
   - Enterprise environmental factors
   - Organizational process assets
2. Tools and techniques
   - Cost-benefit analysis
   - Cost of quality (COQ)
   - Control charts
   - Benchmarking
   - Design of experiments
   - Statistical sampling
   - Flowcharting
   - Proprietary quality management methodologies
   - Additional quality Planning tools
3. Outputs
   - Quality management plan
   - Quality metrics
   - Quality checklists
   - Process improvement plan
   - Project document updates

8.2 PERFORM QUALITY ASSURANCE

1. Inputs
   - Project management plan
   - Quality metrics
   - Work performance information
   - Quality control measurements
2. Tools and techniques
   - Plan Quality and Perform Quality Control tools and techniques
   - Quality audits
   - Process analysis
3. Outputs
   - Organizational process assets updates
   - Change requests
   - Project management plan updates
   - Project document updates

8.3 PERFORM QUALITY CONTROL

1. Inputs
   - Project management plan
   - Quality metrics
   - Quality checklists
   - Work performance measurements
   - Approved change requests
   - Deliverables
   - Organizational process assets
2. Tools and techniques
   - Cause-and-effect diagram
   - Control charts
   - Flowcharting
   - Histogram
   - Pareto chart
   - Run chart
   - Scatter diagram
   - Statistical sampling
   - Inspection
   - Approved change requests review
3. Outputs
   - Quality control measurements
   - Validated changes
   - Validated deliverables
   - Organizational process assets updates
   - Change requests
   - Project management plan updates
   - Project document updates

3.6.6 PROJECT HUMAN RESOURCE MANAGEMENT

PROJECT HUMAN RESOURCE MANAGEMENT OVERVIEW

PMBOK® GUIDE, CHAPTER 9

9.1 DEVELOP HUMAN RESOURCE PLAN

1. Inputs
    - Activity resource requirements
    - Enterprise environmental factors
    - Organizational process assets
2. Tools and techniques
    - Organization charts and position descriptions
    - Networking
    - Organizational theory
3. Outputs
    - Human resource plan

9.2 ACQUIRE PROJECT TEAM

1. Inputs
    - Project management plan
    - Enterprise environmental factors
    - Organizational process assets
2. Tools and techniques
    - Pre-assignment
    - Negotiation
    - Acquisition
    - Virtual teams
3. Outputs
    - Project staff assignments
    - Resource calendars
    - Project management plan updates

9.3 DEVELOP PROJECT TEAM

1. Inputs
    - Project staff assignments
    - Project management plan
    - Resource calendars
2. Tools and techniques
    - Interpersonal skills
    - Training
    - Team-building activities
    - Ground rules
    - Co-location
    - Recognition and rewards
3. Outputs
    - Team performance assessments
    - Enterprise environmental factors updates

9.4 MANAGE PROJECT TEAM

1. Inputs
    - Project staff assignments
    - Project management plan
    - Team performance assessments
    - Performance reports
    - Organizational process assets
2. Tools and techniques
    - Observation and conversation
    - Project performance appraisals
    - Conflict management
    - Issue log
    - Interpersonal skills
3. Outputs
    - Enterprise environmental factors updates
    - Organizational process assets updates
    - Change requests
    - Project management plan updates

3.6.7 PROJECT COMMUNICATIONS MANAGEMENT

PROJECT COMMUNICATIONS MANAGEMENT OVERVIEW

PMBOK® GUIDE, CHAPTER 10

10.1 IDENTIFY STAKEHOLDERS

1. Inputs
   - Project charter
   - Procurement documents
   - Enterprise environmental factors
   - Organizational process assets
2. Tools and techniques
   - Stakeholder analysis
   - Expert judgment
3. Outputs
   - Stakeholder register
   - Stakeholder management strategy

10.2 PLAN COMMUNICATIONS

1. Inputs
   - Stakeholder register
   - Stakeholder management strategy
   - Enterprise environmental factors
   - Organizational process assets
2. Tools and techniques
   - Communication requirements analysis
   - Communications technology
   - Communication models
   - Communication methods
3. Outputs
   - Communications management plan;
   - Project document updates

10.3 DISTRIBUTE INFORMATION

1. Inputs
   - Project management plan
   - Performance reports
   - Organizational process assets
2. Tools and techniques
   - Communication methods
   - Information distribution tools
3. Outputs
   - Organizational process assets updates

10.4 MANAGE STAKEHOLDER EXPECTATIONS

1. Inputs
   - Stakeholder register
   - Stakeholder management strategy
   - Project management plan
   - Issue log
   - Change log
   - Organizational process assets
2. Tools and techniques
   - Communication methods
   - interpersonal skills
   - Management skills
3. Outputs
   - Organizational process assets updates
   - Change requests
   - Project management plan updates
   - Project document updates

10.5 REPORT PERFORMANCE

1. Inputs
   - Project management plan
   - Work performance information
   - Work performance measurements
   - Budget forecasts
   - Organizational process assets
2. Tools and techniques
   - Variance analysis
   - Forecasting methods
   - Communication methods
   - Reporting systems
3. Outputs
   - Performance reports
   - Organizational process assets updates
   - Change requests

3.6.8 PROJECT RISK MANAGEMENT

PROJECT RISK MANAGEMENT OVERVIEW

PMBOK® GUIDE, CHAPTER 11

11.1 PLAN RISK MANAGEMENT

1. Inputs
   - Project scope statement
   - Cost management plan
   - Schedule management plan
   - Communications management plan
   - Enterprise environmental factors
   - Organizational process assets
2. Tools and techniques
   - Planning meetings and analysis
3. Outputs
   - Risk management plan

11.2 IDENTIFY RISKS

1. Inputs
   - Risk management plan
   - Activity cost estimates
   - Activity duration estimates
   - Scope baseline
   - Stakeholder register
   - Cost management plan
   - Schedule management plan
   - Quality management plan
   - Project documents
   - Enterprise environmental factors
   - Organizational process assets
2. Tools and techniques
   - Documentation reviews
   - Information gathering techniques
   - Checklist analysis
   - Assumptions analysis
   - Diagramming techniques
   - SWOT analysis
   - Expert judgment
3. Outputs
   - Risk register

11.3 PERFORM QUALITATIVE RISK ANALYSIS

1. Inputs
   - Risk register
   - Risk management plan
   - Project scope statement
   - Organizational process assets
2. Tools and techniques
   - Risk probability and impact assessment
   - Probability and impact matrix
   - Risk data quality assessment
   - Risk categorization
   - Risk urgency assessment
   - Expert judgment
3. Outputs
   - Risk register updates

11.4 PERFORM QUANTITATIVE RISK ANALYSIS

1. Inputs
   - Risk register
   - Risk management plan
   - Cost management plan
   - Schedule management plan
   - Organizational process assets
2. Tools and techniques
   - Data gathering and representation techniques
   - Quantitative risk analysis and modeling techniques
   - Expert judgment
3. Outputs
   - Risk register updates

11.5 PLAN RISK RESPONSES

1. Inputs
   - Risk register
   - Risk management plan
2. Tools and techniques
   - Strategies for negative risks or threats
   - Strategies for positive risks or opportunities
   - Contingent response strategies
   - Expert judgment
3. Outputs
   - Risk register updates
   - Risk-related contract decisions
   - Project management plan updates
   - Project document updates

11.6 MONITOR AND CONTROL RISKS

1. Inputs
   - Risk register
   - Project management plan
   - Work performance information
   - Performance reports
2. Tools and techniques
   - Risk reassessment
   - Risk audits
   - Variance and trend analysis
   - Technical performance measurement
   - Reserve analysis
   - Status meetings
3. Outputs
   - Risk register updates
   - Organizational process assets updates
   - Change requests
   - Project management plan updates
   - Project document updates

3.6.9 PROJECT PROCUREMENT MANAGEMENT

PROJECT PROCUREMENT MANAGEMENT OVERVIEW

***PMBOK® GUIDE*, CHAPTER 12**

12.1 PLAN PROCUREMENTS

1. Inputs
    - Scope baseline
    - Requirements documentation
    - Teaming agreements
    - Risk register
    - Risk-related contractual decisions
    - Activity resource requirements
    - Project schedule
    - Activity cost estimates
    - Cost performance baseline
    - Enterprise environmental factors
    - Organizational process assets
2. Tools and techniques
    - Make-or-buy analysis
    - Expert judgment
    - Contract types
3. Outputs
    - Procurement management plan
    - Procurement work statements
    - Make-or-buy decisions
    - Procurement documents
    - Source selection criteria
    - Change requests

12.2 CONDUCT PROCUREMENTS

1. Inputs
    - Project management plan
    - Procurement documents
    - Source selection criteria
    - Qualified seller list
    - Seller proposals
    - Project documents
    - Make-or-buy decisions
    - Teaming agreements
    - Organizational process assets
2. Tools and techniques
    - Bidder conferences
    - Proposal evaluation techniques
    - Independent estimates
    - Expert judgment
    - Advertising
    - Internet search
    - Procurement negotiations
3. Outputs
    - Selected sellers
    - Procurement contract award
    - Resource calendars
    - Change requests
    - Project management plan updates
    - Project document updates

12.3 ADMINISTER PROCUREMENTS

1. Inputs
    - Procurement documents
    - Project management plan
    - Contract
    - Performance reports
    - Approved change requests
    - Work performance information
2. Tools and techniques
    - Contract change control system
    - Procurement performance reviews
    - Inspections and audits
    - Performance reporting
    - Payment system
    - Claims administration
    - Records management system
3. Outputs
    - Procurement documentation
    - Organizational process assets updates
    - Change requests
    - Project management plan updates

12.4 CLOSE PROCUREMENTS

1. Inputs
    - Project management plan
    - Procurement documentation
2. Tools and techniques
    - Procurement audits
    - Negotiated settlements
    - Record management system
3. Outputs
    - Closed procurements
    - Organizational process assets updates

Additional information and reminders for the exam

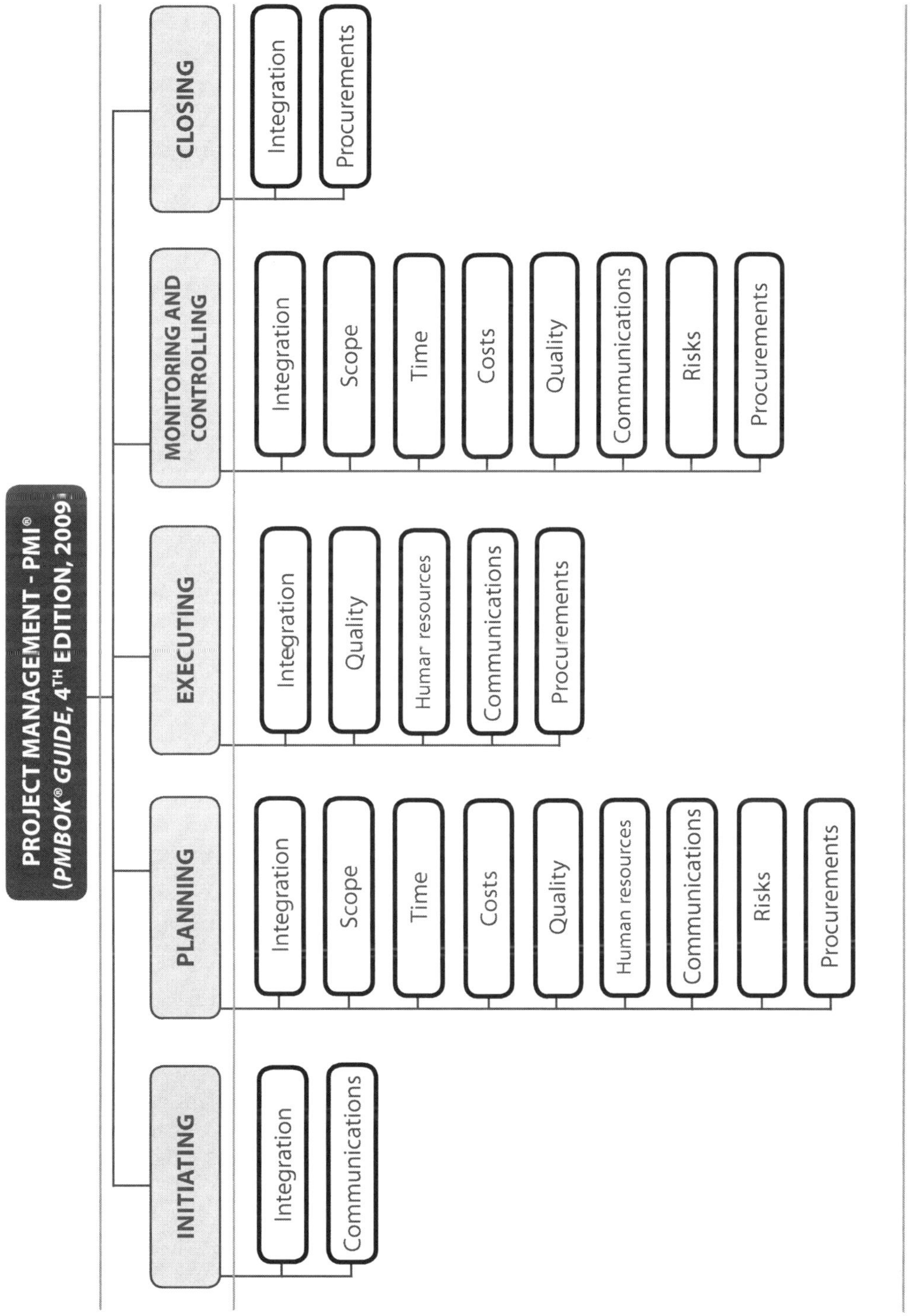

Supplementary exercises

1. Indicate the integration knowledge area processes and in which project management process groups they are found.

Initiating	Planning	Executing	Monitoring and controlling	Closing

2. Indicate the scope knowledge area processes and in which project management process groups they are found.

Initiating	Planning	Executing	Monitoring and controlling	Closing

3. Indicate the time knowledge area processes and in which project management process groups they are found.

Initiating	Planning	Executing	Monitoring and controlling	Closing

4. Indicate the cost knowledge area processes and in which project management process groups they are found.

Initiating	Planning	Executing	Monitoring and controlling	Closing

5. Indicate the quality knowledge area processes and in which project management process groups they are found.

Initiating	Planning	Executing	Monitoring and controlling	Closing

6. Indicate the human resource knowledge area processes and in which project management process groups they are found.

Initiating	Planning	Executing	Monitoring and controlling	Closing

7. Indicate the communications knowledge area processes and in which project management process groups they are found.

Initiating	Planning	Executing	Monitoring and controlling	Closing

8. Indicate the risks knowledge area processes and in which project management process groups they are found.

Initiating	Planning	Executing	Monitoring and controlling	Closing

9. Indicate the procurement knowledge area processes and in which project management process groups they are found.

Initiating	Planning	Executing	Monitoring and controlling	Closing

Check your answers using the process flowchart of each knowledge area.

Questions

1. Project management is the application of knowledge, skills, tools, and techniques to project activities in order to meet their requirements. This knowledge application requires effective management of appropriate processes. The following options are about the project management process, except for:

   a. A set of interrelated actions and activities performed to achieve a predefined product, result, or service

   b. It is characterized by its applicable inputs, tools, and techniques and the resulting outputs

   c. It must consider organizational process assets and enterprise environmental factors

   d. Some people do not consider organizational process assets and/or enterprise environmental factors

2. The project management process group where processes are performed to define the new project or a new phase of an existing project by obtaining permission to start the project or phase is named

   a. Monitoring and controlling

   b. Planning

   c. Initiating

   d. Executing

3. The project management process group where processes are performed to define the project scope, refine objectives, and develop a course of action necessary to achieve the objectives for which the project was created is named

   a. Monitoring and controlling

   b. Planning

   c. Initiating

   d. Executing

4. The project management process group whose processes are performed to execute the work defined in the project management plan in order to meet its specifications is named

   a. Planning

   b. Monitoring and controlling

   c. Executing

   d. Initiating

5. The project management process group whose processes are developed to track, revise, and regulate the project progress and performance is named

a. Planning

b. Monitoring and controlling

c. Executing

d. Closing

6. The project management process group whose processes are developed to identify all areas where changes to the plan are required and to start such changes is named

a. Planning

b. Closing

c. Executing

d. Monitoring and controlling

7. The project management process group whose processes are performed to, among other things, identify areas where changes to the plan are required is named

a. Integration

b. Scope

c. Monitoring and controlling

d. Perform Integrated Change Control

8. All of the following processes are part of Monitoring and controlling, except

a. Perform Integrated Change Control

b. Control Scope

c. Verify Scope

d. Perform Quality Assurance

9. All of the following processes are part of Executing, except

a. Direct and Manage Project Execution

b. Perform Quality Assurance

c. Verify Scope

d. Distribute Information

10. All of the following processes are part of Planning, except

a. Identify Stakeholders

b. Collect Requirements

c. Define Activities

d. Identify Risks

11. The development sequence of project human resource processes is

a. Develop Human Resource Plan, Acquire Project Team, Manage Project Team, and Report Team Performance

b. Develop Human Resource Plan, Acquire Project Team, Manage Project Team, and Develop Project Team

c. Develop Human Resource Plan, Acquire Project Team, Develop Project Team, and Manage Project Team

d. Acquire Project Team, Develop Human Resource Plan, Develop Project Team, and Manage Project Team

12. The Control Scope process is developed in the Monitoring and controlling processes group. The Verify Scope process is developed in the following process group:

a. Monitoring and controlling

b. Closing

c. Executing

d. Planning

13. In Closing process group, in terms of scope, which process is developed?

a. Close Project or Phase

b. Close Procurements

c. Verify Scope

d. None of the above

14. The Define Scope process is developed in Planning while the Control Scope process is developed in Monitoring and controlling. In which knowledge area is the Verify Scope process developed?

a. Planning

b. Executing

c. Scope

d. Closing

15. In which process groups are Integration knowledge area processes developed?

a. Initiating, Planning, Monitoring and controlling, and Closing

b. Initiating, Planning, Executing, Monitoring and controlling, and Closing

c. Initiating, Planning, Executing, Monitoring and controlling

d. Planning, Executing, Monitoring and controlling, and Closing

16. In which process groups are Scope knowledge area processes developed?

a. Planning, Monitoring and controlling

b. Initiating, Planning, Executing, Monitoring and controlling, and Closing

c. Initiating, Planning, Executing, Monitoring and controlling

d. Planning, Executing, Monitoring and controlling, and Closing

17. In which process groups are Time knowledge area processes developed?

a. Initiating, Planning, Monitoring and controlling, and Closing

b. Planning, Executing, Monitoring and controlling

c. Initiating, Planning, Executing, Monitoring and controlling

d. Planning and Monitoring and controlling

18. In which process groups are Costs knowledge area processes developed?

a. Initiating, Planning, Monitoring and controlling, and Closing

b. Planning, Monitoring and controlling

c. Initiating, Planning, Executing, Monitoring and controlling

d. Planning, Monitoring and controlling, and Closing.

19. In which process groups are Quality knowledge area processes developed?

a. Initiating, Planning, Monitoring and controlling, and Closing

b. Planning, Executing, Monitoring and controlling, and Closing

c. Planning, Executing and Monitoring and controlling

d. Planning, Monitoring and controlling

20. In which process groups are Human Resource knowledge area processes developed?

a. Initiating, Planning, Executing, Monitoring and controlling

b. Planning, Executing, Monitoring and controlling, and Closing

c. Planning, Executing, Monitoring and controlling

d. Planning and Executing

21. In which process groups are Communications knowledge area processes developed?

a. Initiating, Planning, Monitoring and controlling, and Closing

b. Planning, Executing, Monitoring and controlling, and Closing

c. Initiating, Planning, Executing, and Monitoring and controlling

d. Planning, Executing, and Monitoring and controlling

22. In which process groups are Risks knowledge area processes developed?

a. Planning and Monitoring and controlling

b. Planning, Executing, Monitoring and controlling, and Closing

c. Planning, Executing, and Monitoring and controlling

d. Planning and Executing

23. In which process groups are Procurements knowledge area processes developed?

a. Initiating, Planning, Monitoring and controlling, and Closing

b. Planning, Executing, Monitoring and controlling, and Closing

c. Initiating, Planning, Executing and Monitoring, and controlling

d. Planning, Executing, and Monitoring and controlling

24. How many project management processes in the project Integration knowledge area are there?

a. 4

b. 7

c. 6

d. 5

25. How many project management processes in the project Scope knowledge area are there?

a. 4

b. 3

c. 6

d. 5

26. How many project management processes in the project Time knowledge area are there?

a. 4

b. 3

c. 6

d. 5

27. How many project management processes in the project Costs knowledge area are there?

a. 3

b. 4

c. 6

d. 5

28. How many project management processes in the project Quality knowledge area are there?

a. 4

b. 6

c. 3

d. 5

29. How many project management processes in the project Human resource knowledge area are there?

a. 4

b. 3

c. 6

d. 5

30. How many project management processes in the project Communications knowledge area are there?

a. 4

b. 3

c. 6

d. 5

31. How many project management processes in the project Risks knowledge area are there?

a. 4

b. 7

c. 6

d. 5

32. How many project management processes in the project Procurements knowledge area are there?

a. 4

b. 3

c. 6

d. 5

33. The process of developing a document to formally authorize a project or a phase and the initial requirements documentation that meet stakeholder needs and expectations is called

a. Identify Stakeholder Requirements

b. Collect Requirements

c. Develop Project Charter

d. Develop Project Management Plan

34. The process of identifying all people or organizations that may be affected by the project and documenting information relevant to their interests, engagement, and impact on the project success is called

a. Identify Stakeholder Requirements

b. Collect Requirements

c. Develop Project Charter

d. Identify Stakeholders

35. The process of documenting the actions required to define, prepare, integrate, and coordinate all auxiliary plans is called

a. Identify Stakeholder Requirements

b. Develop Project Management Plan

c. Develop Project Charter

d. Collect Requirements

36. The process of defining and documenting stakeholder needs in order to achieve the project objectives is called

a. Define Scope

b. Collect Requirements

c. Develop Project Charter

d. Develop Project Management Plan

37. The process of developing a project and product detailed description is called

a. Define Scope

b. Collect Requirements

c. Develop Project Charter

d. Develop Project Management Plan

38. The process of estimating types and quantities of materials, people, equipment, or supplies required to complete each activity is called

a. Estimate Activity Resources

b. Estimate Schedule Resources

c. Estimate Project Resources

d. Estimate Costs

39. The process of analyzing activity sequences, their durations, required resources, and constraints in order to create the project schedule is called

a. Develop Network Diagram

b. Develop WBS

c. Develop Schedule

d. Develop Schedule Template

40. The process of identifying the project and product quality requirements and/or standards in addition to the documentation of how the project will achieve compliance is called

a. Estimate Quality

b. Plan Quality

c. Define Quality Metrics

d. Define Quality Requirements

41. The process of identifying and documenting roles, responsibilities, required skills, and hierarchical relationships in the project is called

a. Develop Human Resource Plan

b. Staffing Management Plan

c. Human Resource Plan

d. Plan Human Resources

42. The process of determining the stakeholders' information needs and defining a communication approach is called

a. Identify Requirements

b. Plan Communications

c. Report Performance

d. Direct Communications

43. The process of determining which risks can affect the project and documenting their characteristics is called

a. Plan Risk Responses

b. Risk Management Plan

c. Plan Risk Management

d. Identify Risks

44. The process of prioritizing risks for further analysis or action by assessing and combining their occurrence and impact probability is called

a. Perform Quantitative Risk Analysis

b. Perform Qualitative Risk Analysis

c. Plan Risk Responses

d. Identify Risks

45. The process of numerically analyzing the identified risk effect on the project overall objectives is called

a. Perform Quantitative Risk Analysis

b. Perform Qualitative Risk Analysis

c. Plan Risk Responses

d. Identify Risks

46. The process of developing options and actions to increase opportunities and reduce threats to project objectives is called

c. Plan Risk Management

b. Identify Risks

c. Risk Response Planning

d. Manage Risks

47. The process of documenting the project purchasing decisions, specifying the approach and identifying potential suppliers is called

a. Procurement Management Plan

b. Conduct Procurements

c. Administer Procurements

d. Plan Procurements

48. The process of performing the work defined in the project management plan in order to achieve its objectives is called

a. Monitor and Control Project Work

b. Verify Scope

c. Direct and Manage Project Execution

d. Control Scope

49. The process of auditing quality requirements of the results of quality control measurement to ensure that quality standards and appropriate operational definitions are used is called

a. Quality Inspection

b. Perform Quality Assurance

c. Perform Quality Control

d. Plan Quality

50. The process of confirming the availability of human resources and obtaining the team required to complete the project assignments is called

a. Develop Project Team

b. Mobilize Human Resources

c. Acquire Project Team

d. Manage Project Team

51. The process of improving competences, team interaction, and the team global environment in order to improve the project performance is called

a. Develop Project Team

b. Train Project Team

c. Acquire Project Team

d. Manage Project Team

52. The process of monitoring the performance of team members, providing feedback, resolving issues, and managing changes in order to optimize the project performance is called

a. Perform Integrated Change Control

b. Develop Project Team

c. Direct and Manage Work Execution

d. Manage Project Team

53. The process of making relevant information available to stakeholders interested in the project as planned is called

a. Report Performance

b. Manage Stakeholder Expectations

c. Manage Project Information

d. Distribute Information

54. The process of obtaining suppliers' responses, selecting a supplier, and awarding a contract is called

a. Conduct Procurements

b. Administer Procurements

c. Suppliers Proposal Analysis

d. Implement Procurements

55. The process of monitoring, assessing, and adjusting progress in order to meet the performance objectives defined in the project management plan is called

a. Monitor and Control Project Work

b. Report Performance

c. Direct and Manage Project Execution

d. Manage Project Team

56. The process of assessing all change requests, approving and managing changes in their deliverables, organizational process assets, documents and project management plan is called

a. Lessons learned from the project

b. Monitor and Control Project Work

c. Perform Integrated Change Control

d. Control Scope

57. The process of formalizing the acceptance of the project finished deliverables is called

a. Verify Scope

b. Control Scope

c. Check Deliverables

d. Monitor and Control Project Work

58. The process of monitoring the project scope and product scope progress as well as managing changes to the scope baseline is called

a. Verify Scope

b. Control Scope

c. Check Deliverables

d. Monitor and Control Project Work

59. The process of monitoring the project toward its progress update as well as managing changes to the schedule baseline is called

a. Verify Scope

b. Update Schedule

c. Control Schedule

d. Develop Schedule

60. The process of monitoring and recording results of the quality activity execution to assess performance and recommend required changes is called

a. Perform Quality Control

b. Verify Quality

c. Quality Inspection

d. Audit Quality

61. The process of collecting and distributing performance information, including progress reports, progress measurements, and forecasts is called

a. Report Information

b. Distribute Information

c. Report Performance

d. Inform Stakeholders

62. The process of implementing risk response plans, tracking identified risks, monitoring residual risks, identifying new risks, and assessing the risk process throughout the project is called

a. Plan Risk Management

b. Plan Risk Responses

c. Monitor and Control Risks

d. Risk Assessment

63. The process of managing procurement relationships and monitoring contract performance, making changes and corrections as required, is called

a. Administer Procurements

b. Conduct Procurements

c. Evaluate Procurements

d. Monitor and Control Procurements

64. When managing the project integration after developing the Develop Project Charter and the Develop Project Management Plan processes, the next process is

a. Monitor and Control Project Work

b. Direct and Manage Project Execution

c. Perform Integrated Change Control

d. Check Project Work

65. When managing the project integration after developing the Develop Project Charter and the Direct and Manage Project Execution processes, the next process is

a. Perform Integrated Change Control

b. Check Project Work

c. Monitor and Control Project Work

d. Close Project or Phase

66. When managing the project integration after developing the Direct and Manage Project Execution and the Monitor and Control Project Work processes, the next process is

a. Perform Integrated Change Control

b. Check Project Work

c. Monitor and Control Project Work

d. Close Project or Phase

67. When managing the project integration, after the Monitor and Control Project Work and the Perform Integrated Change Control processes, the next process is

a. Perform Integrated Change Control

b. Check project work

c. Monitor and Control Project Work

d. Close Project or Phase

68. During the Project Scope Management after the Collect Requirements process, the next process is

a. Define Activities

b. Identify Stakeholders

c. Define Scope

d. Create WBS

69. During the Project Scope Management after the Define Scope process, the next process is

a. Define Activities

b. Create WBS

c. Verify Scope

d. Control Scope

70. During the Project Scope Management after the Create WBS process, the next process is

a. Define Activities

b. Develop Schedule

c. Define Scope

d. Control Scope

71. During the Project Scope Management after the Verify Scope process, the next process is

a. Define Activities

b. No process

c. Verify Scope

d. Control Scope

Answer key

1. D. Organizational process assets and/or the enterprise environmental factors must be considered in all project management processes, even if they are not explicitly listed as inputs in the process specification.

2. C. Initiating includes the project management process group where processes are performed to define the new project or a new phase of an existing project by obtaining permission to start the project or phase.

3. B. Planning includes the project management process group where processes are performed to define the project scope, refine objectives, and develop a course of action necessary to achieve the objectives for which the project was created.

4. C. In Executing, processes are accomplished to perform the work defined in the project management plan in order to meet its specifications.

5. B. In Monitoring and controlling, processes are developed to track, revise, and regulate the project progress and performance.

6. D. Monitoring and controlling also aims to identify all areas where changes to plan are required and such corresponding changes start.

7. C. Options A and B are project management knowledge areas, not process groups. Option D is a process of the Integration knowledge area. The only process group is Monitoring and controlling.

8. D. The Perform Quality Assurance process is part of the Executing processes group.

9. C. The Verify Scope process is part of the Monitoring and controlling processes group.

10. A. Identify Stakeholders is a process of the Initiating group.

11. C. The development sequence of project human resource processes is Develop Human Resource Plan, Acquire Project Team, Develop Project Team, and Manage Project Team.

12. A. The Verify Scope process is developed in the Monitoring and controlling processes group.

13. D. In terms of scope, no process is developed in the Closing process group.

14. C. That's easy, isn't it? There is only one knowledge area among those options: Scope! The other options are process groups.

15. B. Integration processes are developed in all project management process groups.

16. A. Processes of the Scope knowledge area are developed in the Planning and Monitoring and controlling process groups.

17. D. Time knowledge area processes are developed in the Planning and Monitoring and controlling processes groups.

18. B. Costs knowledge area processes are developed in the Planning and Monitoring and controlling processes groups.

19. C. Quality knowledge area processes are developed in the Planning, Executing, and Monitoring and controlling processes groups.

20. D. Human Resource knowledge area processes are developed in the Planning and Executing processes groups. Note that it is the only knowledge area with processes only in these two process groups.

21. C. Communications knowledge area processes are developed in the Initiating, Planning, Executing, and Monitoring and controlling processes groups.

22. A. Risks knowledge area processes are developed in the Planning and Monitoring and controlling processes groups.

23. B. Procurements knowledge area processes are developed in the Planning, Executing, Monitoring and controlling, and Closing processes groups.

24. C. There are six processes in the project Integration knowledge area: Develop Project Charter, Develop Project Management Plan, Direct and Manage Project Execution, Monitor and Control Project Work, Perform Integrated Change Control, and Close Project or Phase.

25. D. There are five processes in the project Scope knowledge area: Collect Requirements, Define Scope, Create WBS, Verify Scope and Control Scope.

26. C. There are six processes in the project Time knowledge area: Define Activities, Sequence Activities, Estimate Activity Resources, Estimate Activity Durations, Develop Schedule, and Control Schedule.

27. A. There are three processes in the project Costs knowledge area: Estimate Costs, Determine Budget, and Control Costs.

28. C. There are three project management processes in the project Quality knowledge area: Plan Quality, Perform Quality Assurance, and Perform Quality Control.

29. A. There are four project management processes in the project Human resource knowledge area: Develop Human Resource Plan, Acquire Project Team, Develop Project Team, and Manage Project Team.

30. D. There are five project management processes in the project Communications knowledge area: Identify Stakeholders, Plan Communications, Distribute Information, Manage Stakeholder Expectations, and Performance Report.

31. C. There are six project management processes in the project Risks knowledge area: Plan Risk Management, Identify Risks, Perform Risk Qualitative Analysis, Perform Quantitative Risk Analysis, Plan Risk Responses, and Monitor and Control Risks.

32. A. There are four project management processes in the project Procurements knowledge area: Plan Communications, Conduct Procurements, Administer Procurements, and Close Procurements.

33. C. Develop Project Charter is the process of developing a document to formally authorize a project or a phase and the initial requirements documentation that meet stakeholder needs and expectations.

34. D. Identify Stakeholders is the process of identifying all people or organizations that may be affected by the project and documenting information relevant to their interests, engagement, and impact on the project success. Option A is part of that process.

35. B. Develop Project Management Plan is the process of documenting actions required to define, prepare, integrate, and coordinate all auxiliary plans.

36. B. Collect Requirements is the process of defining and documenting stakeholder needs in order to achieve the project objectives.

37. A. Define Scope is the process of developing a project and product detailed description.

38. A. Estimate Activity Resources is the process of estimating types and quantities of materials, people, equipment, or supplies required to complete each activity.

39. C. Develop Schedule is the process of analyzing activity sequences, their durations, required resources, and constraints in order to create the project schedule.

40. B. Plan Quality is the process of identifying the project and product quality requirements and/or standards as well as the documentation of how the project will achieve compliance.

41. A. Develop Human Resource Plan is the process of identifying and documenting roles, responsibilities, skills required, and hierarchical relationships in the project.

42. B. Plan Communications is the process of determining the stakeholders' information needs and defining a communication approach.

43. D. Identify Risks is the process of determining which risks may affect the project and documenting their characteristics.

44. B. Qualitative Risk Analysis is the process of prioritizing risks for further analysis or action by assessing and combining their occurrence and impact probability.

45. A. Quantitative Risk Analysis is the process of numerically analyzing the effect of risks identified in the project overall objectives.

46. C. Plan Risk Responses is the process of developing options and actions to increase opportunities and reducing threats to the project objectives.

47. D. Plan Procurements is the process of documenting the project purchasing decisions, specifying the approach, and identifying potential suppliers.

48. C. Direct and Manage Project Execution is the process of performing the work defined in the project management plan to achieve its goals.

49. B. Perform Quality Assurance is the process of auditing quality requirements of the results of quality control measurement to ensure that quality standards and appropriate operational definitions are used.

50. C. Acquire Project Team is the process of confirming the availability of human resources and obtaining the team required to complete the project assignments.

51. A. Develop Project Team is the competence improvement, team interaction, and the team global environment process to enhance the project performance.

52. D. Manage Project Team is the process of monitoring the performance of team members, provide feedback, resolve issues, and manage changes in order to optimize the project performance.

53. D. Distribute Information is the process of making relevant information available to stakeholders in the project as planned.

54. B. Conduct Procurements is the process of obtaining supplier's responses, selecting a supplier, and awarding a contract.

55. A. Monitor and Control Project Work is the process of monitoring, assessing, and regulating progress in order to meet performance objectives defined in the project management plan.

56. C. Perform Integrated Change Control is the process of assessing all change requests, approving and managing changes in their deliverables, organizational process assets, documents and project management plan.

57. A. Verify Scope is the process of formalizing acceptance of completed deliverables of the project.

58. B. The process of monitoring the project scope and product scope progress as well as managing changes to the scope baseline.

59. C. Control Schedule is the process of monitoring the project toward its progress update as well as managing changes to the schedule baseline.

60. A. Perform Quality Control is the process of monitoring and recording results of the quality activity execution to assess performance and recommend required changes.

61. C. Report Performance is the process of collecting and distributing performance information, including progress reports, progress measurements, and forecasts.

62. C. Monitor and Control Risks is the process of implementing risk response plans, tracking identified risks, monitoring residual risks, identifying new risks, and evaluating the risk process throughout the project.

63. A. Administer Procurements is the process of managing procurement relationships and monitoring contract performance, making changes and corrections as required.

64. B. The Develop Project Management Plan process follows the Develop Project Management Plan process. Please note: after preparing the plan, the team will start the project work – under its guidance and management. During the work development by the team, it is necessary to Monitoring and controlling the work and, where appropriate, performs the project required change control. After all changes are implemented and controlled and deliverables are accepted, the last management integration process occurs – Close Project or Phase.

65. C. The Monitor and Control Project Work process follows the Direct and Manage Project Execution process.

66. A. The Perform Integrated Change Control process follows the Monitoring and controlling project work process.

67. D. The Close Project or Phase process follows the Perform Integrated Change Control process.

68. C. The Define Scope process follows the Collect Requirements process. Note the following: requirements are first collected before defining the project scope. Afterward, the WBS is developed. Other processes will be developed for the project work execution. After that, in terms of scope, there are only Verify Scope and Control Scope processes left.

69. B. The Create WBS process follows the Define the scope process.

70. C. The Define Scope process follows the Create WBS process. Note the following: requirements are first collected before defining the project scope. Afterward, the WBS is developed. Other processes will be developed for the project work execution. In terms of scope, the next process is Verify Scope (formalizing deliverables acceptance and revision) and Control Scope (monitoring the project and product scope progress and managing scope baseline changes).

71. D. The Control Scope process follows the Verify Scope process.

Chapter 4

PROJECT INTEGRATION MANAGEMENT

1. Introduction
2. Project Integration Management processes
3. Integration management in project initiating
4. Integration management in project planning
5. Integration management in project executing
6. Integration management in project monitoring and controlling
7. Integration management in project closing

- Additional information and reminders for the exam
- Supplementary exercises
- Questions
- Answer key

4.1 INTRODUCTION

This chapter will introduce the project management processes in the Integration knowledge area, their relevant inputs, tools, techniques, and outputs.

4.2 PROJECT INTEGRATION MANAGEMENT PROCESSES

According to *PMBOK® Guide*, the Project Integration Management includes processes and activities required to identify, define, combine, unify, and coordinate the several processes and activities of the management process groups.

The Project Integration Management processes are the following:

- **Develop Project Charter**

  The process of developing a document that formally authorizes a project or a phase and documents the initial requirements that satisfy the stakeholder's needs and expectations.

- **Develop Project Management Plan**

  The process of documenting the actions required to define, prepare, integrate, and coordinate all subsidiary plans.

- **Direct and Manage Project Execution**

  The process of performing the work defined in the project management plan to achieve the project's objectives.

- **Monitor and Control Project Work**

  The process of tracking, reviewing, and regulating the progress in order to meet the performance objectives defined in the project management plan.

- **Perform Integrated Change Control**

  The process of reviewing all change requests, approving changes, and managing changes to the deliverables, organizational process assets, project documents, and the project management plan.

- **Close Project or Phase**

  The process of finalizing all activities of all project management process groups in order to formally finish the project or phase.

The following flowchart shows the relationship among the Project Integration Management processes and their locations across the project management process groups.

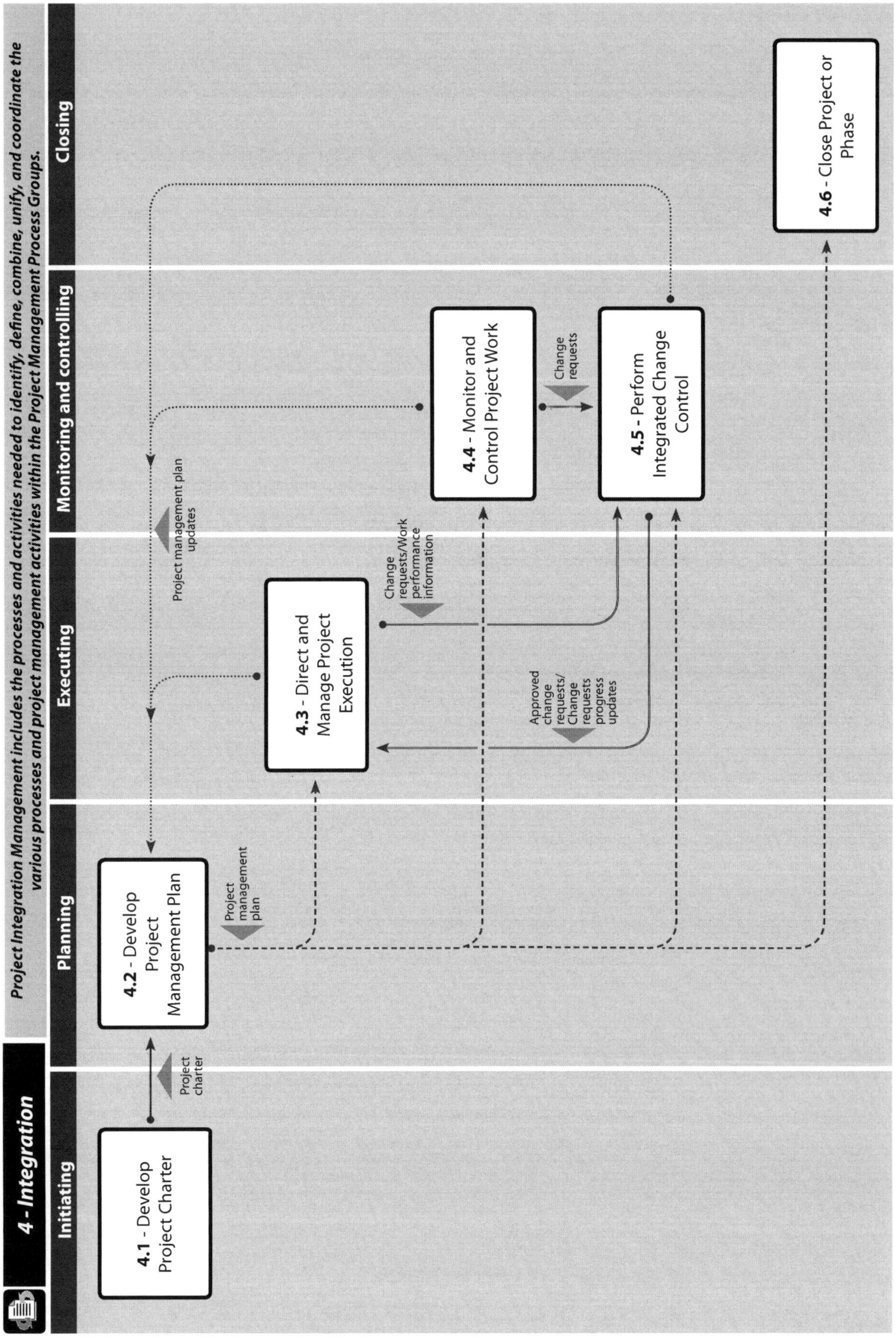
4 - Integration
Project Integration Management includes the processes and activities needed to identify, define, combine, unify, and coordinate the various processes and project management activities within the Project Management Process Groups.
Initiating
Planning
Executing
Monitoring and controlling
Closing
4.1 - Develop Project Charter
Project charter
4.2 - Develop Project Management Plan
Project management plan
4.3 - Direct and Manage Project Execution
Project management plan updates
Change requests/Work performance information
Approved change requests/Change requests progress updates
4.4 - Monitor and Control Project Work
Change requests
4.5 - Perform Integrated Change Control
4.6 - Close Project or Phase

4.3 INTEGRATION MANAGEMENT IN PROJECT INITIATING

According to PMI®, the integration management in project initiating is composed of a process, namely:

- ***Develop Project Charter***

However, for the mentioned process development, we need the preliminary implementation of several actions related to the project initiating.

4.3.1 ACTIONS RELATED TO THE INTEGRATION MANAGEMENT IN PROJECT INITIATING

4.3.1.1 SELECT AND DESIGNATE THE PROJECT MANAGER

The project manager selection and assignment must be one of the first actions taken by the top management or the project sponsor. From the designation, the project has a person in charge for its success or failure. Gradually, especially after the issuance of the Project charter, actions and interferences by the top management and the sponsor decrease, while actions and responsibilities of the project manager grow until project closing.

Selecting the project manager must take into account following criteria:

- Leadership
- Technical credibility
- Administrative credibility
- Interpersonal and communication skills
- Knowledge of tools and techniques for project management and proven experience in their implementation
- Ability to promote motivation in the project team
- Ability to solve problems
- Ability to solve conflicts

4.3.1.2 RECOGNIZE THE COMPANY CULTURE AND EXISTING SYSTEMS

The recognition of the company culture and management systems of existing projects must be one of the early activities of the project manager. This activity, in addition to the business environment recognition, shall provide the project manager with the foundation to propose alternatives for some processes and project management procedures of the organization, or adaptations thereof, as well as the analysis of the project management systems used and required for the project.

4.3.1.3 COLLECT HISTORICAL INFORMATION

The collection of historical information related to projects performed by the company will provide the project manager and the project team with the possibility of improving and refining estimates of time, cost, human resource needs, and project materials as well as to predict possible variations and anticipate possible risks.

Among the historical information to be collected are the following:

- Resource estimates for the activities
- Compositions of unit costs of services
- Work breakdown structure models
- Network diagrams and schedules
- Progress follow-up reports
- Risk follow-up reports
- Lessons learned reports

4.3.1.4 IDENTIFY THE BUSINESS NEED

Identifying the business need recognizes the reasons that led the company to start the project. These reasons are considered throughout the project life cycle and shall direct the planning, executing and controlling, approval of changes, and the project scope management.

4.3.1.5 DEFINE THE PROJECT MISSION

The project mission definition for the project chart must be as succinct and clear as possible to leave no doubt concerning the mission. For example, to build a company's new plant, the project mission would be "To construct a new plant of company X in New York, USA."

4.3.1.6 DETERMINE THE PROJECT GOALS

The project goals definition consists of establishing guidelines for project development. These guidelines can be related to time, cost, quality, level of consumer acceptance, and any other factors determining the project. For the project charter, these guidelines must be short and direct. For example, for the new plant of company X quoted above, we can set the following goals: Plant start of operation: September 2012. Total cost of implantation: $25 million.

4.3.1.7 IDENTIFY THE PROJECT CONSTRAINTS

Usually a project is subject to the occurrence of constraints related to time, cost, quality, and other issues intrinsic to the project. The need of a given resource for a certain period can be a constraint. The top management guidelines, as well as the contractual clauses of a contracted service, can be considered as restrictions. We may have a project with a time constraint to complete, limited costs, a quality-specific requirement, or a combination of two constraints. The project manager must work to distinguish the main constraint of the project once it directs the project goals and planning. All constraints must be accordingly documented and recorded in the project charter. With the progress of the project, these constraints may be revised or even discarded.

4.3.1.8 IDENTIFY THE PROJECT ASSUMPTIONS

Assumptions are statements regarded as true but which can be wrong. They can be defined by all stakeholders in the project. The project manager must work to list and validate all assumptions. As an example of assumptions, we can have the contract execution date, the project start date, the start date of a particular project phase, suppliers' delivery times, availability of certain resources when necessary, among others. Validation consists in the assumption of formal documentation. This documentation can contain a contingency plan in case the assumption does not occur. For example, for a generator supply contract, we can establish that, in the event of equipment delivery delay, the supplier will bear the costs of renting an alternative generator until the equipment delivery is accomplished.

4.3.1.9 DETERMINE THE BASIC PROJECT TEAM

The determination of the basic project team consists of identifying the project manager and, if possible, indicating the basic project team. That is, it is not necessary that the entire project team is defined, but one must know the key persons or those that are already defined to compose the team.

4.3.1.10 DETERMINE THE RESOURCES ORIGIN

The resources origin determination consists of recognizing from where the resources will be provided, which departments or sectors of the company will contribute to the project required resources, or whether individuals will be hired from outside the organization.

4.3.2 DEVELOP PROJECT CHARTER (*PMBOK® GUIDE*, PROCESS 4.1)

The project charter is the document that formally authorizes a project or a project phase. It is usually issued by the project sponsor outside the organization, with power to finance the project. The sponsor may be, for example, a company or government agency issuing the project charter in response to a need for the project.

The project charter associates the project to the operational work of the company and provides the high-level requirements of the project.

The project charter informs everyone involved who project manager is and what his authority level is, inclusively regarding the application of resources necessary to the project execution.

4.3.2.1 DEVELOP PROJECT CHARTER: INPUTS, TOOLS AND TECHNIQUES, AND OUTPUTS

INPUTS

1 **Project statement of work**

The project statement of work is the document that records the description of products or services to be provided by the project. Generally, for external projects, the project statement of work is part of the bid document or the contract issued by the customer. For internal projects, this statement is usually issued by the project sponsor or initiator. The project statement of work makes reference to the following:

- The business need of doing business, usually based on market demand, technological advance, legal requirements, or government regulation
- The product scope description to be supplied by the product
- The strategic business plan and goals to be considered by the project

2 **Business case**

The description of the business case provides the necessary information from a business point of view in order to determine whether the project has (or not) investment feasibility. Overall, the business case will include a description of business need and cost-benefit analysis to justify the project. The business case can be caused by one of the following considerations:

- Market demand
- Organizational need
- Customer request
- Technological advancement
- Social need

In the case of multiphase projects, the business case description must be periodically reviewed to ensure that the project is on track to meet the business objectives.

3 **Contract**

The contract contains the whole information on the scope, deadlines, quality criteria, and other requirements, and it must be considered in this process.

4 **Enterprise environmental factors**

The enterprise environmental factors as the organization's quality standards, government regulations, market conditions, and others must be considered in this process.

5 **Organizational process assets**

The organizational process assets, such as the company's project management policy, quality policy and procedures, work instructions, templates, standard forms, historical information, lessons learned, and others, must be considered in this process.

TOOLS AND TECHNIQUES

1 **Expert judgment**

The use of expert judgment to establish the project charter may arise from several sources, such as

- Other units of the organization;
- Consultants;
- Stakeholders, including users, sponsors, and others;
- Technical and professional associations;
- Industrial groups;

- Suppliers and manufacturers and;
- Project Management Office (PMO).

OUTPUTS

1 Project charter

The project charter documents the main features of the project, such as

- Purpose of the project, product description and scope, and time and resources required to perform it;
- Designated project manager;
- Business need and those users who will receive the project product;
- Description of the project deliverables;
- Identified assumptions, constraints, and risks; and
- Other relevant information of the project.

The form on page 145 exemplifies a project charter.

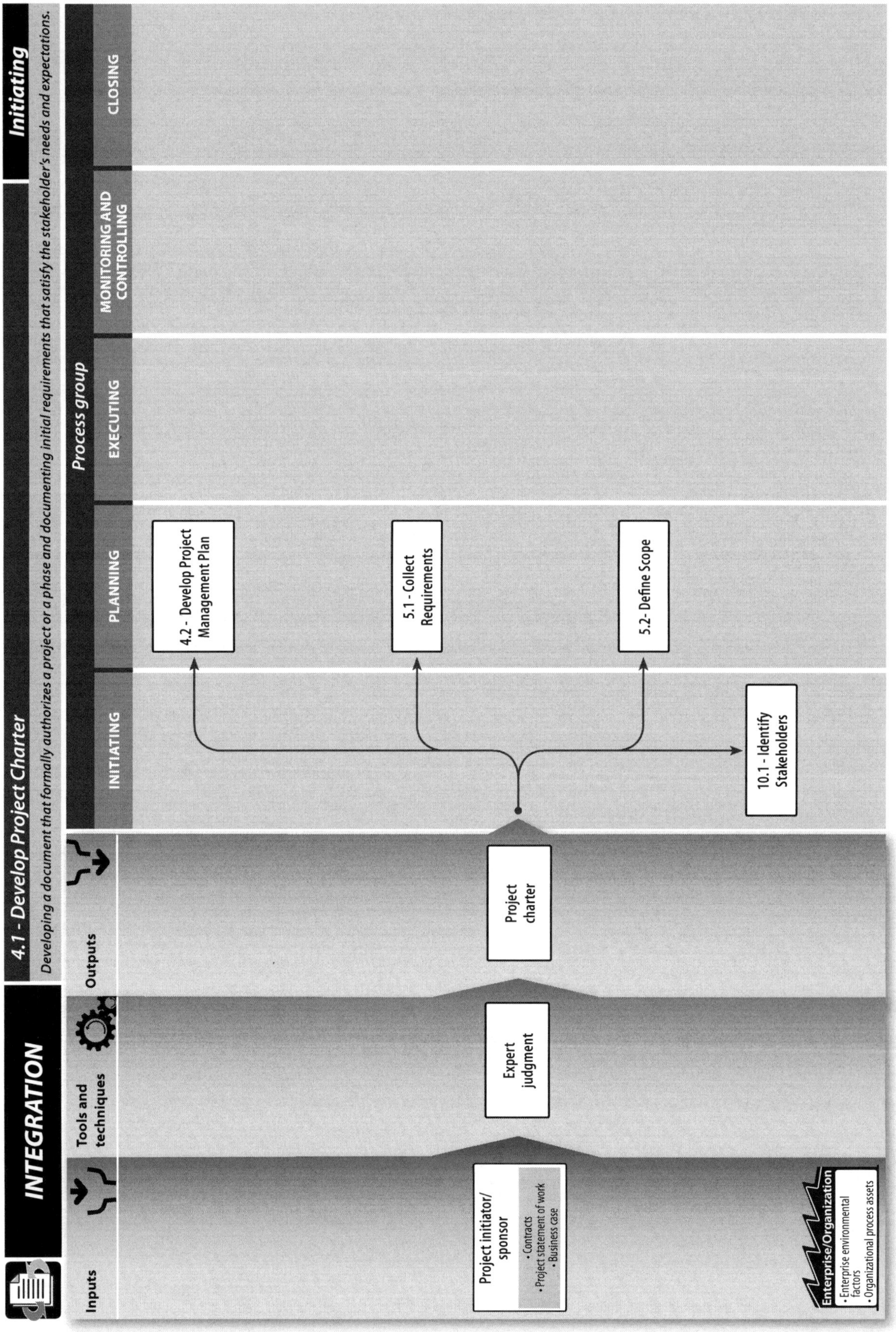
INTEGRATION
4.1 - Develop Project Charter
Initiating
Developing a document that formally authorizes a project or a phase and documenting initial requirements that satisfy the stakeholder's needs and expectations.
Inputs
Tools and techniques
Outputs
Process group
INITIATING
PLANNING
EXECUTING
MONITORING AND CONTROLLING
CLOSING
Project initiator/ sponsor
• Contracts
• Project statement of work
• Business case
Enterprise/Organization
• Enterprise environmental factors
• Organizational process assets
Expert judgment
Project charter
4.2 - Develop Project Management Plan
5.1 - Collect Requirements
5.2- Define Scope
10.1 - Identify Stakeholders

LOGO	PROJECT	PROJECT CHARTER	Rev.: Date: Sheet ___ of ___

AUTHOR:	
INITIATING	Include the project name and the assigned project manager.
SYNOPSIS	Summary of relevant aspects of the project. **Why** (purpose), **what** (product description/scope), **when** (time), and **how much** (resources).
ENTERPRISE NEED	Identify the enterprise need and users who will receive and benefit from the project product.
PRODUCT AND DELIVERY DESCRIPTION	Identify what will be delivered at the project completion. Sufficiently describe the product in order to make it possible for the project team to develop it.
PROJECT MANAGEMENT	Indicate project management standards and procedures to be used.
ASSUMPTIONS, CONSTRAINTS, AND RISKS	Indicate known assumptions, constraints, and risks.
RESOURCES	Indicate the resources necessary or available for the project. Indicate financial, personnel, and materials resources.
COMMUNICATION	Indicate the required communication between the sponsor and the project team.
ACCEPTANCE	Indicate the method and the sponsor's criteria to accept deliverables.
CHANGE MANAGEMENT	Indicate procedures to be used in order to make and document changes in the project charter
OTHER	Identify any other factor relevant to the project.
APPROVED BY: ____________________	**PROJECT MANAGER:** ____________________

4.4 INTEGRATION MANAGEMENT IN PROJECT PLANNING

According to PMI®, the management integration in project planning is composed of a process, namely:

- ***Develop Project Management Plan***

4.4.1 DEVELOP PROJECT MANAGEMENT PLAN (*PMBOK® GUIDE,* PROCESS 4.2)

The project management plan is the documentation of those actions required to define, prepare, integrate, and coordinate all auxiliary plans into a project management plan. The project management plan defines how the project is performed, monitored, controlled and closed.

The development of the project management plan is the activity to create a well-accepted, approved, realistic, and formal.

According to PMI®, the project management plan includes

- The project management processes applicable to the project, selected by the project management team
- The implementation level of each selected process
- Description of tools and techniques to be used for this process
- How the selected processes shall be used to manage the specific project
- How the work shall be performed to accomplish the project objectives
- How changes shall be monitored and controlled
- How the configuration management shall be performed
- How the performance measurement baseline shall be maintained and updated
- The need and the communication techniques between stakeholders
- The project life cycle and, in the case of multiphase projects, the project-associated phases

The project management plan may be summarized or detailed, and it may consist of auxiliary plans, which are detailed up to the required project level. These auxiliary plans include, but are not limited to

- Project scope management plan
- Schedule management plan
- Cost management plan
- Quality management plan
- Human resources management plan
- Communications management plan
- Risk management plan and
- Procurement management plan

Other documents may also be part of the project management plan, including

- Milestone list
- Schedule baseline
- Cost baseline
- Quality baseline and
- Risk register.

4.4.1.1 DEVELOP PROJECT MANAGEMENT: INPUTS, TOOLS AND TECHNIQUES, AND OUTPUTS

INPUTS

1 **Project charter**

The project charter herein described documents the main features of the project and must be considered in this process.

2 **Outputs from planning processes**

The outputs from planning processes described in Chapters 5 to 12 are integrated to create the project management plan. All the management auxiliary plans and their baselines must be considered as inputs in this process. On the other side, any updating on the auxiliary plans shall generate an updating in the project management plan as well.

3 **Enterprise environmental factors**

Enterprise environmental factors, such as project management infrastructure, project management systems, organizational structure, industrial standards, governmental rules, and others must be considered in this process.

4 **Organizational process assets**

The organizational process assets such as the policy of the company's project management, quality policy and procedures, work instructions, templates and standard forms, performance measurement criteria, procedures for change implementation, historical information, lessons learned, and others must be considered in this process.

TOOLS AND TECHNIQUES

1 **Expert judgment**

The use of expert judgment to establish the project management plan may contribute to

- Directing the process to meet the project needs
- Developing technical and management details to be included in the plan
- Determining resources and skill levels to perform the project work
- Setting the configuration management level to be applied to the project and
- Determining which documents of the project should be part of the change integrated control process.

OUTPUTS

1 **Project management plan**

Described in this chapter, item 4.4.

INTEGRATION

4.2 - Develop Project Management Plan

Planning

The process of documenting the actions necessary to define, prepare, integrate, and coordinate all subsidiary plans.

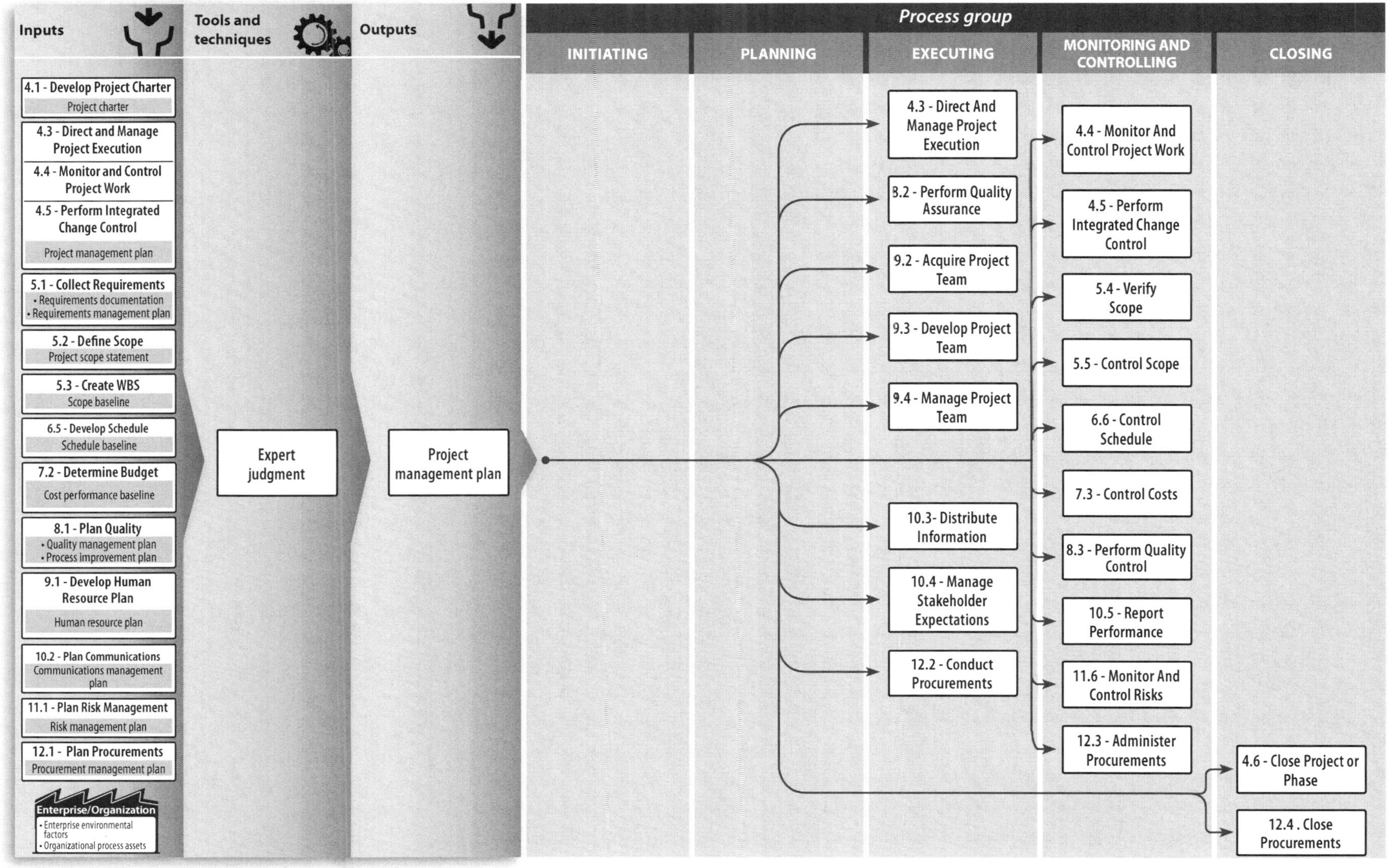

4.5 INTEGRATION MANAGEMENT IN PROJECT EXECUTING

According to PMI®, the integration management in project executing is composed of a process, namely:

- ***Direct and Manage Project Execution***

4.5.1 DIRECT AND MANAGE PROJECT EXECUTION (*PMBOK® GUIDE*, PROCESS 4.3)

The process of Direct and Manage Project Execution is the execution of activities by the manager and the project team in order to fulfill the project management plan and perform the work defined in the project scope description. In this process, the functions of the project manager are to obtain and apply resources required to the project management, to integrate the project team among its members and the suppliers and contractors, guiding the execution of activities, and to manage the approved preventive and corrective measures implementation, as well as the approved defect corrections.

Direct and Manage Project Execution also requires the approved changes in implementation, including:

- **Corrective action.** Documented guidance so that the project work is performed in such a way its expected future performance conforms to the management plan.
- **Preventive action.** Documented guidance to perform a given activity that may reduce the likelihood of the project risk-associated negative consequences.
- **Defect repair.** The formal documented identification of a given defect in a project component with the recommendation to repair or completely replace the defective component.

4.5.1.1 DIRECT AND MANAGE PROJECT EXECUTION: INPUTS, TOOLS AND TECHNIQUES, AND OUTPUTS

INPUTS

1 **Project management plan**

The project management plan and its auxiliary plans depict the main input for this process.

2 **Approved change requests**

Changes found by the project team or other stakeholders, considered as necessary for the project and that change the project scope, must be analyzed in the Monitoring and controlling processes, and, if approved, they must be considered as input for this process.

3 **Enterprise environmental factors**

The environmental issues recognition is relevant in the Direct and Manage Project Execution. The organization type of the company, the relationship between internal departments and the organization, between the organization and other companies participating in the project, between the organization and government agencies, as well as logistics and politics-related issues, should be checked for their impact on this process.

4 **Organizational process assets**

Policies, procedures, and guidelines related to direction and management of the company's project execution must be considered, including historical information from previous projects, management processes and procedures, previous project defect register, lessons learned, and any other information relevant to the process.

TOOLS AND TECHNIQUES

1 **Expert judgment**

The use of expert judgment to direct and manage the project execution may arise from several sources, such as

- Other units of the organization;
- Consultants;
- Stakeholders, including users, sponsors, and others; and
- Project Management Office (PMO).

2 **Project management information system**

The project management information system is the system used by the project team to manage the project activities.

OUTPUTS

1 **Deliverables**

Deliverables are products, services, or results, subject matter of the project, as defined in the Work Breakdown Structure (WBS), the WBS dictionary, and the project scope statement.

2 **Work performance information**

In the process, the work performance information should be distributed by routine collecting of data, including schedule progress, eventual delays and their causes, critical path activities, activities presenting delays, and actions for recovery and other important data for managing the work. Costs incurred and the status of deliverables are also information from the work performance.

3 **Change requests**

If changes occur during this process, they shall be forwarded for review and approval, and, if approved, they should be implemented.

4 **Project management plan updates**

The project management plan and its auxiliary plans should be updated according to this process information.

5 Project document updates

Project documents that can be updated include, but are not limited to

- Requirements documentation
- Project registers (issues, assumptions, etc.)
- Risk register, and
- Stakeholder register.

INTEGRATION

4.3 - Direct and Manage Project Execution

Executing

The process of performing the work defined in the project management plan to achieve the project's objectives.

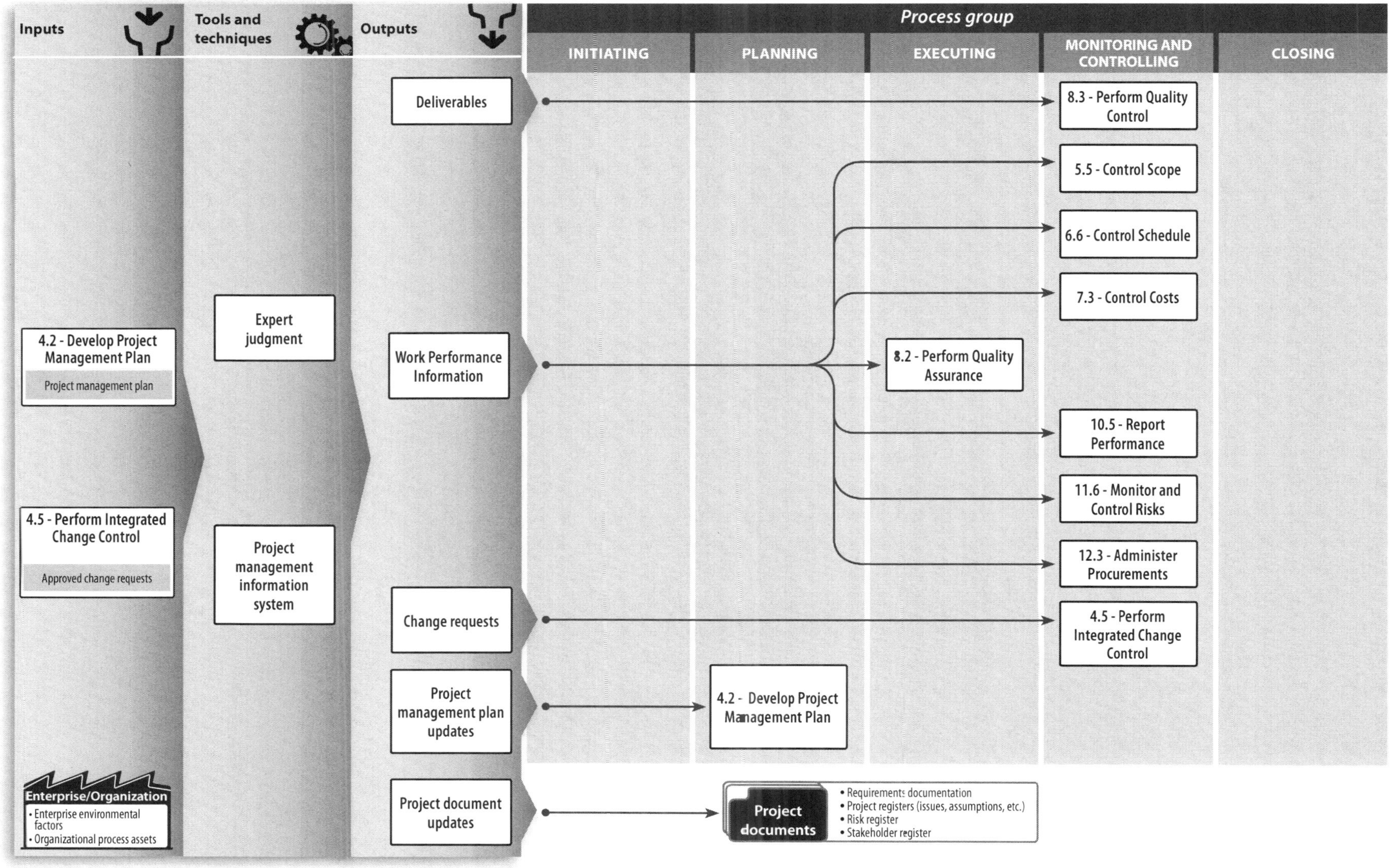

4.6 INTEGRATION MANAGEMENT IN PROJECT MONITORING AND CONTROLLING

According to PMI®, the management integration in project monitoring and controlling is composed of two processes, namely:

- ***Monitor and Control Project Work***
- ***Perform Integrated Change Control***

4.6.1 MONITOR AND CONTROL PROJECT WORK (*PMBOK® GUIDE*, PROCESS 4.4)

Process to track, review, and adjust the progress toward achieving the performance objectives defined in the project management plan. According to PMI®, this process is related to

- Comparison of actual performance to the project management plan;
- Performance evaluation in order to determine whether preventive or corrective actions are indicated and recommend such actions as necessary;
- Analyzing, following-up, and monitoring of project risks to ensure risks are identified, the progress is reported, and feedback plans for proper risks are being performed;
- Maintenance of a correct and accurate information database concerning the project product(s) and associated documentation until the end of the project;
- Supply of information to support the progress reports, progress measurements, and forecasts;
- Providing forecasts to update current cost and information about the current schedule;
- Monitoring the implementation of approved changes when and as they occur.

4.6.1.1 CONTROL AND MANAGE PROJECT EXECUTION: INPUTS, TOOLS AND TECHNIQUES, AND OUTPUTS

INPUTS

1 **Project management plan**

The project management plan and its auxiliary plans depict the main input for this process.

2 **Performance reports**

Work performance information contained in performance reports must be considered in this process. They should contain the information and test results related to cost and time, compared with the baseline of the performance measurement. As examples, these reports may contain schedules, milestone, schedules, resource utilization histograms, and earned value management.

3 **Enterprise environmental factors**

The environmental factors of the organization, which can influence the process Monitor and Control Project Work, including, but not limited to, the following:

- Industry standards related to the product, quality and others
- Industry standards by associations, related to the product, quality and others
- System of work authorization of the organization
- Risk tolerance of stakeholders and
- Project management information system of the company as implementation schedules software, configuration management system and information collecting and distributing system.

4 **Organizational process assets**

Organizational process assets may influence the Monitor and Control Project Work process by means of policies and procedures of project management, report templates, historical information, and lessons learned from previous projects.

TOOLS AND TECHNIQUES

1 **Expert judgment**

Expert opinion to monitor and control the project work can originate from several sources, such as

- Other units of the organization,
- Consultants and contractors hired specifically for this assignment,
- Stakeholders as members of the project team, and
- Project Management Office (PMO).

OUTPUTS

1 **Change requests**

As a result of comparing between expected and current results, change requests can cause expansion, adjustment, or reduction of the project scope or the product scope. Such changes can impact the project management plan, project documents, and deliverables. Changes may include

- Corrective action,
- Preventive action, and
- Defect repair.

2 **Project management plan updates**

The project management plan and its auxiliary plans must be updated, including, but not limited to

- Schedule management plan,
- Cost management plan,
- Quality management plan,
- Scope baseline,

- Schedule baseline, and
- Cost baseline.

3 **Project document updates**

Project documents that can be updated include, but are not limited to

- Forecasts,
- Performance reports, and
- Issue log.

4.4 - Monitor and Control Project Work

Monitoring and controlling

The process of tracking, reviewing, and regulating the progress to meet the performance objectives defined in the project management plan.

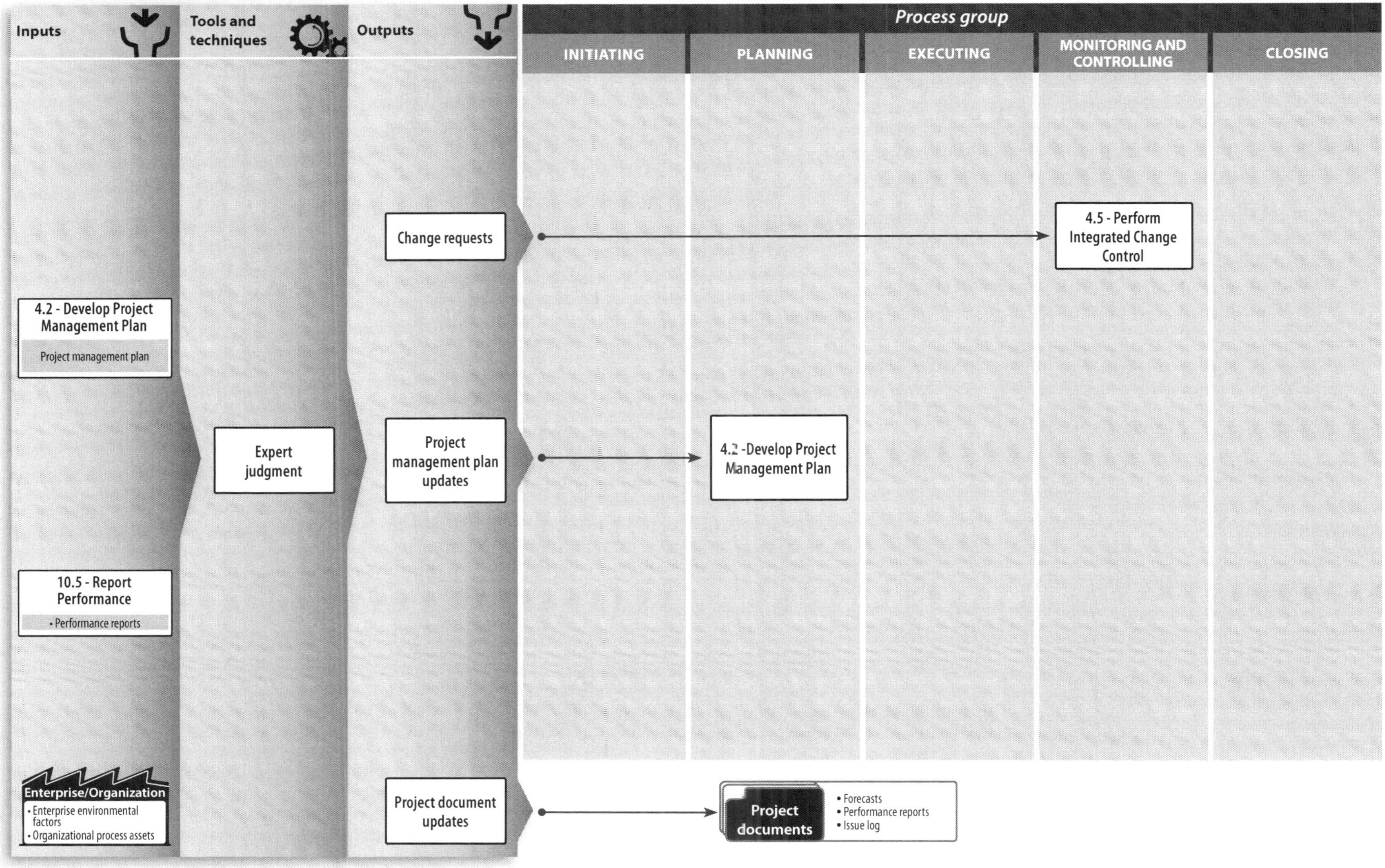

4.6.2 PERFORM INTEGRATED CHANGE CONTROL (*PMBOK® GUIDE*, PROCESS 4.5)

The process of reviewing all change requests, approving changes and controlling changes in deliverables in the organizational process assets, project documents, and the project management plan. Such activities, according to the PMI®, include

- Identifying that a change needs to occur or has occurred;
- Controlling factors that might hamper the integrated change control so that only approved changes are implemented;
- Reviewing and approving requested changes;
- Managing approved changes when and as they occur, regulating the flow of requested changes;
- Maintaining the integrity of baselines by releasing only approved changes to be incorporated into products or services and maintaining the related project configuration and the Planning documentation;
- Reviewing and approving all recommended corrective and preventive actions;
- Controlling and updating the scope, cost, budget, schedule, and quality requirements, based on changes approved by means of the coordination of changes throughout the project. For example, a proposed schedule change will often impact cost, risk, quality, and personnel;
- Assessing total impact documentation on requested changes, and
- Determining defect repair validation.

4.6.2.1 PERFORM INTEGRATED CHANGE CONTROL: INPUTS, TOOLS AND TECHNIQUES, AND OUTPUTS

INPUTS

1 **Project management plan**

The project management plan and its auxiliary plans depict the main input for this process.

2 **Work performance information**

Work performance information is the major cause of recommended corrective and preventive actions and must be considered in this process.

3 **Change requests**

Change requests generated in the Monitor and Control Project Work process must be considered in this process. These changes may be related to corrective or preventive actions and defect repair.

4 **Enterprise environmental factors**

Enterprise environmental factors as well as the project management information system, schedule execution software applications, configuration management system and the information collection and distribution system must be considered in this process.

5 **Organizational process assets**

The organizational process assets may influence the process Perform Integrated Change Control through policies and procedures for project management, change control procedures, historical information, and lessons learned from previous projects.

TOOLS AND TECHNIQUES

1 **Expert judgment**

The use of expert judgment to carry out the integrated change control can be obtained from several sources, including

- Other units of the organization;
- Consultants;
- Stakeholders, such as members of the project team and project product users; and
- Project Management Office (PMO).

2 **Change control meetings**

The change control meetings are held by the change control board, and they are intended to review, approve, or reject the change requests. All decisions of the changes control board are documented and communicated to stakeholders.

OUTPUTS

1 **Change request status updates**

The current status of change requests, approved or not, must be documented in the requested change register.

2 **Project management plan updates**

The project management plan and its auxiliary plans should be updated according to these approved and implemented changes.

3 **Project document updates**

All and any project document that has been influenced by the process Perform Integrated Change Control should be updated as

- Change request log and
- Change request analysis.

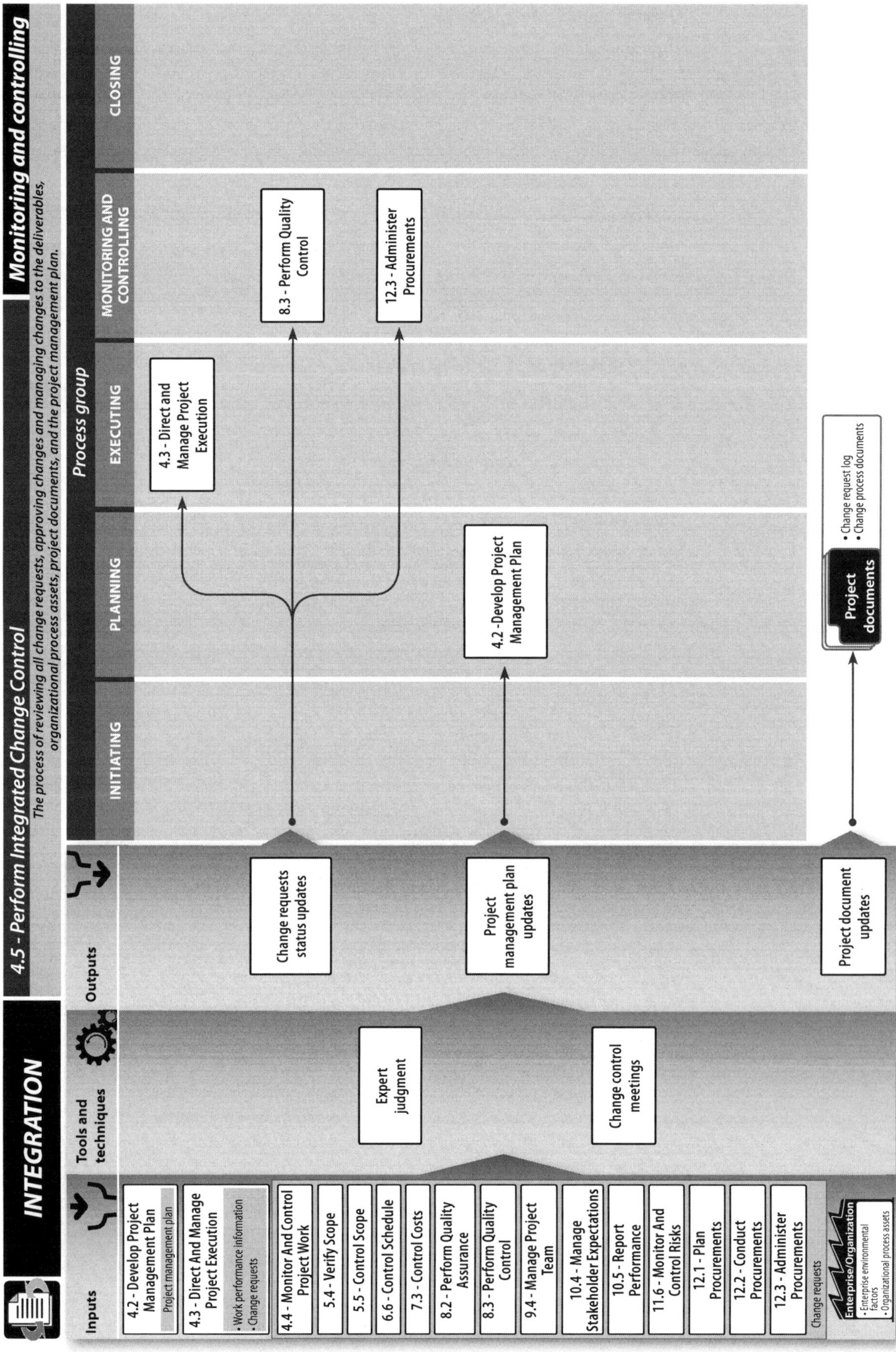
INTEGRATION
4.5 - Perform Integrated Change Control
Monitoring and controlling
The process of reviewing all change requests, approving changes and managing changes to the deliverables, organizational process assets, project documents, and the project management plan.
Inputs
Tools and techniques
Outputs
Process group
INITIATING
PLANNING
EXECUTING
MONITORING AND CONTROLLING
CLOSING
4.2 - Develop Project Management Plan
Project management plan
4.3 - Direct And Manage Project Execution
• Work performance information
• Change requests
4.4 - Monitor And Control Project Work
5.4 - Verify Scope
5.5 - Control Scope
6.6 - Control Schedule
7.3 - Control Costs
8.2 - Perform Quality Assurance
8.3 - Perform Quality Control
9.4 - Manage Project Team
10.4 - Manage Stakeholder Expectations
10.5 - Report Performance
11.6 - Monitor And Control Risks
12.1 - Plan Procurements
12.2 - Conduct Procurements
12.3 - Administer Procurements
Change requests
Enterprise/Organization
• Enterprise environmental factors
• Organizational process assets
Expert judgment
Change control meetings
Change requests status updates
Project management plan updates
Project document updates
4.3 - Direct and Manage Project Execution
8.3 - Perform Quality Control
12.3 - Administer Procurements
4.2 - Develop Project Management Plan
Project documents
• Change request log
• Change process documents

4.7 INTEGRATION MANAGEMENT IN PROJECT CLOSING

According to PMI®, the management integration in project closing is composed of a sole process, namely:

- ***Close Project or Phase***

4.7.1 CLOSE PROJECT OR PHASE (*PMBOK® GUIDE*, PROCESS 4.6)

The Close Project or Phase process involves all the activities of project completion or a given phase of the project. This process establishes procedures for coordinating activities necessary to verify and document project deliverables, verifying and documenting the reasons for the project cancellation before completion (aborted), if any.

The projects are closed for a range of reasons, including

- Those successfully concluded,
- Those canceled before completion (aborted), and
- Those transformed in continuous operation.

There are four formal types of project Closing:

- **Absorption:** when projects become continuous operation, that is, the project is absorbed by the operation.
- **Integration:** when the project ends because of lack of resources, that were transferred to another project elsewhere in the organization.
- **Exhaustion:** when project funds are no longer provided and the project will fade to extinction. Examples of Closing by exhaustion may be the order cancellation by the customer and the appearance of higher priority projects.
- **Extinction:** when the project achieves its goals, and the project is naturally closed as a process that was already expected to occur.

4.7.1.1 CLOSE PROJECT OR PHASE: INPUTS, TOOLS AND TECHNIQUES, AND OUTPUTS

INPUTS

1 **Project management plan**

The project management plan and its auxiliary plans depict the main input for this process.

2 **Accepted deliverables**

Deliverables represent the project purpose and must be taken into account in this process.

3 **Organizational process assets**

Organizational process assets, such as policies and procedures related to project Closing, must be taken into account in this process.

TOOLS AND TECHNIQUES

1 **Expert judgment**

Expert opinion may be used as an aid in the process execution to close the contract, by means of consultants, users of the project product(s), and other stakeholders.

OUTPUTS

1 **Final product, service, or result transition**

Contract closure must only occur upon formal acceptance and delivery of the product, service, or result in the contract.

2 **Organizational process assets updates**

The Close Project or Phase process can identify new processes or opportunities for improvements in the organization project Closing procedures and policies. All documentation related to the contract closure must be taken into account and filed as lessons learned from the project.

INTEGRATION

4.6 - Close Project or Phase

Closing

The process of finalizing all activities across all of the Project Management Process Groups to formally complete the project or phase.

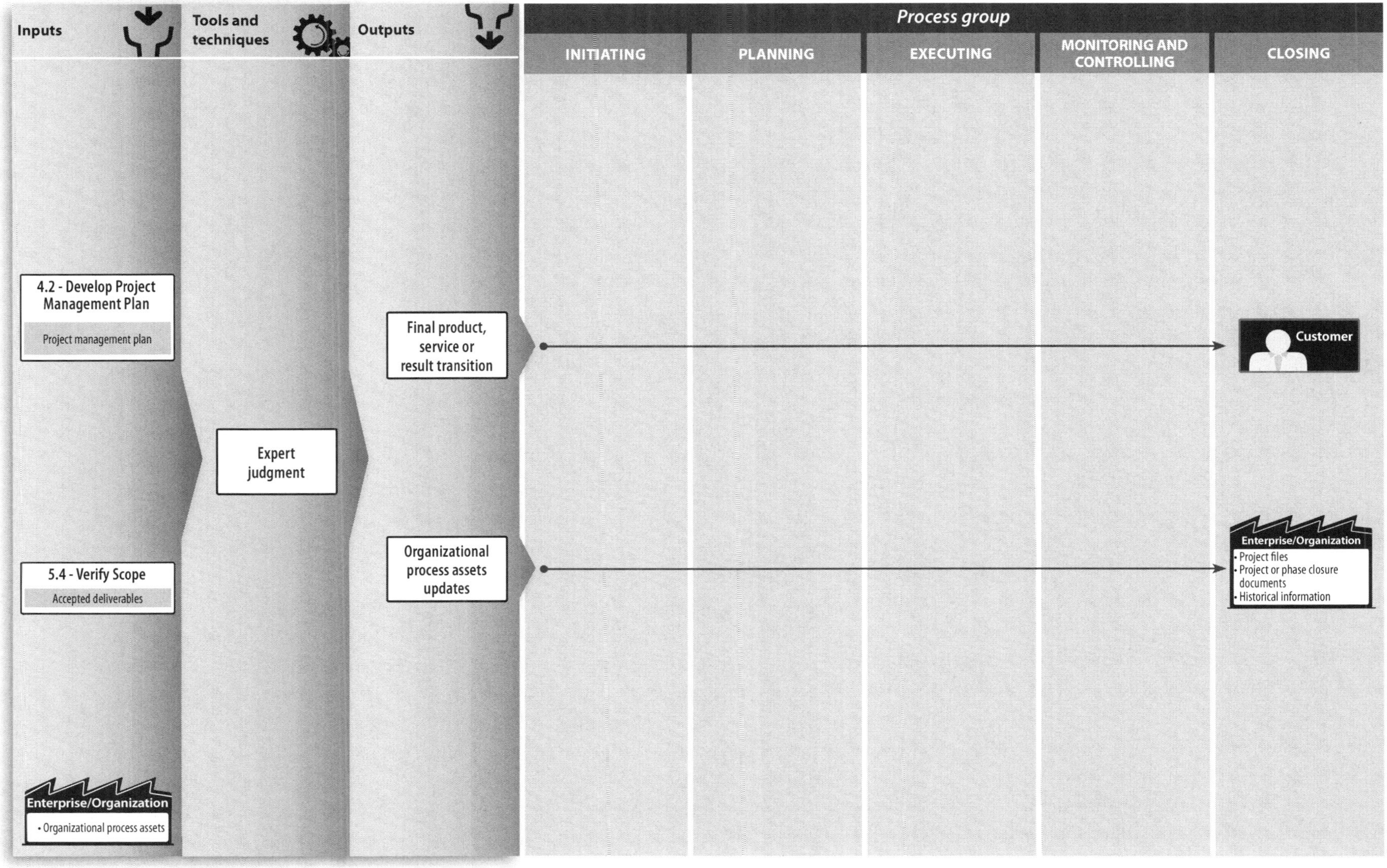

Additional information and reminders for the exam

- The project manager's major role is performing the project integration, with the effective management of stakeholders and the project team.
- The project requires integration that communications are effective throughout the project stages.
- The sponsor is the individual in charge of financing the project, and he plays an important role in all important decisions of the project.
- Developing the project charter is the first process developed in the project. In all projects!
- The project charter formally authorizes the project. Without a charter, the project cannot be started.
- The project charter authorizes the project manager to perform the project work, assign and track resources, spend money, and use other features of the company.
- The project charter documents the project assumptions and constraints.
- The project charter does not include details on what will be produced and how it will be produced. Two inputs of the project charter are the contract and the project statement of work. The contract is what was agreed upon to be executed. The statement of work lists all project deliverables that the project manager and his team must produce.
- An important factor on which the manager must focus is the prevention of unnecessary changes.
- Preventive action involves taking action before potential deviations from the project performance baseline in order to reduce the nonoccurrence or impact of such deviations.
- Corrective action involves taking action to realign the project performance damaged by deviations in relation to their baseline.
- Defect repair represents the rework required when a delivery or project component does not meet requirements.
- Changes are approved in the change integrated control.

Supplementary exercises

1. In regards to the Project Integration area of knowledge, indicate to which management processes group(s) each element is related and explain why. Follow the project charter example.

1. Project charter

   [X] Initiating [X] Planning [ ] Executing [ ] Monitoring/controlling [ ] Closing

   The project charter is the output of the Develop Project Charter (Initiating) process and the input of the Develop Project Management Plan (Planning) process.

2. Project statement of work

   [ ] Initiating [ ] Planning [ ] Executing [ ] Monitoring/controlling [ ] Closing

3. Project management plan

   [ ] Initiating [ ] Planning [ ] Executing [ ] Monitoring/controlling [ ] Closing

4. Expert judgment

   [ ] Initiating [ ] Planning [ ] Executing [ ] Monitoring/controlling [ ] Closing

5. Business case

   [ ] Initiating [ ] Planning [ ] Executing [ ] Monitoring/controlling [ ] Closing

6. Change control meetings

☐ Initiating ☐ Planning ☐ Executing ☐ Monitoring/controlling ☐ Closing

7. Work performance information

☐ Initiating ☐ Planning ☐ Executing ☐ Monitoring/controlling ☐ Closing

8. Result transition

☐ Initiating ☐ Planning ☐ Executing ☐ Monitoring/controlling ☐ Closing

9. Contract

☐ Initiating ☐ Planning ☐ Executing ☐ Monitoring/controlling ☐ Closing

10. Change requests

☐ Initiating ☐ Planning ☐ Executing ☐ Monitoring/controlling ☐ Closing

11. Change requests status updates

☐ Initiating ☐ Planning ☐ Executing ☐ Monitoring/controlling ☐ Closing

12. Approved change requests

☐ Initiating ☐ Planning ☐ Executing ☐ Monitoring/controlling ☐ Closing

13. Accepted deliverables

☐ Initiating ☐ Planning ☐ Executing ☐ Monitoring/controlling ☐ Closing

14. Project management information system

☐ Initiating ☐ Planning ☐ Executing ☐ Monitoring/controlling ☐ Closing

15. Deliverables

☐ Initiating ☐ Planning ☐ Executing ☐ Monitoring/controlling ☐ Closing

Check your answers by referring to the inputs, tools and techniques, and outputs of processes in Chapter 3.

2. Complete the sentences below, stating whether the option refers to input, tool/technique, or output, and identifying the corresponding project management process.

1. Business case is ____________ of the process ____________________ ____________.
2. Accepted deliverables are ____________ of the ____________________ process.
3. Management information system is a ____________________ of the ____________ ____________________ process.
4. Change control meetings are ____________________ of the ____________________ process.
5. Contract is a ____________ of the ____________________ ____________ process.
6. Change requests are ____________________ of the ____________ ____________ process.
7. Change requests are ____________________ of the ____________ ____________ process.
8. Product, service, or result transition is a ____________________ of the ____________________ process.
9. Performance reports are ____________________ of the ____________ ____________ process.
10. Work performance information is ____________________ of the ____________________ process.
11. Work performance information is ____________________ of the ____________________ process.
12. Outputs of Planning processes are ____________________ of the ____________________ process.

Questions

1. In the Integration area of knowledge, approved change requests are inputs of which process?

a. Direct and Manage Project Execution

b. Monitor and Control Project Work

c. Perform Integrated Change Control

d. Develop Project Management Plan

2. The document providing the required information from a business viewpoint in order to determine whether or not the project justifies the investment is named:

a. Project charter

b. Statement of work

c. Business case

d. Business need

3. All of the following options are part of an effective change management plan, except

a. Procedures

b. Report standards

c. Meetings

d. Lessons learned

4. The document detailing the business needs, the current understanding of customers' needs, and the new product, service, or result that intend to satisfy, as project justification, the high-level requirements, the high-level project description, the high-level risks, the assigned project manager, and others is named:

a. Project charter

b. Project scope statement

c. Statement of work

d. Requirements register

5. Who must Integration be the primary role of?

a. Project manager

b. Project team

c. Sponsorship

d. Stakeholders

6. All the following are inputs of the Develop Project Charter, except

a. Contract

b. Stakeholder register

c. Project statement of work

d. Enterprise environmental factors

7. All of the following are inputs of the Direct and Manage Project Execution process, except

a. Project management plan

b. Enterprise environmental factors

c. Organizational process assets

d. Work performance information

8. You are the project manager and have received a change request from a customer, which is easy to implement and does not change the schedule. What are you supposed to do first?

a. Implement the change to meet the customer's need

b. Obtain permission from the sponsor for the implementation

c. Refer to the change control board

d. Assess the impact on other project constraints

9. All of the following are inputs of the Monitor and Control Project Work process, except

a. Project management plan

b. Performance reports

c. Organizational process assets

d. Change requests

10. All of the following are inputs of the Monitor and Control Project Work process, except

a. Enterprise environmental factors

b. Performance reports

c Project document updates

d. Organizational process assets

11. A project is undergoing many changes in its charter. Who is responsible for deciding whether such changes are necessary?

a. Project manager

b. Project team

c. Sponsorship

d. Stakeholders

12. All of the following are outputs of the Monitor and Control Project Work process, except

a. Performance reports

b. Change requests

c Project management plan updates

d. Project document updates

13. All of the following options are inputs of the Perform Integrated Change Control process, except

a. Project management plan

b. Change requests status updates

c. Work performance information

d. Organizational process assets

14. In regards to changes, the project manager must focus his attention on:

a. Analyzing changes

b. Monitoring and recording changes

c. Notifying the sponsor about changes

d. Avoiding unnecessary changes

15. All of the following options are inputs of the Perform Integrated Change Control process, except

a. Change request status updates

b. Project management plan updates

c. Change control meetings

d. Project document updates

16. An approved corrective action is an input of

a. Verify Scope

b. Direct and Manage Project Execution

c. Develop Project Charter

d. Develop Schedule

17. The project manager is developing the project management plan. In which knowledge area is he working on?

a. Planning

b. Executing

c. Initiating

d. Integration

18. The project team is using the project management information system to properly direct and manage the project execution within the standards defined by the organization. He is also using the help of experts in this process. The team is at which project management process group?

a. Integration

b. Direct and Manage Project Execution

c. Executing

d. Monitoring and controlling

19. An expert was hired to analyze the project performance reports and assist the project team to monitor and control the project work. The project involves several thousand dollars and is experiencing cost and time problems. Which project management process group is the expert and the project team working on?

a. Integration

b. Executing

c. Monitoring and controlling

d. Monitor and Control Project Work

20. The constant deadline and cost problems occurring in the project caused the company to hire an expert to analyze the project performance reports and to assist the project team to monitor and control the project work. The report analysis tends to show that one of the leading suppliers may be one of the major schedule delays leading to increased costs. Which project management knowledge area is the expert and the project team working on?

a. Integration

b. Executing

c. Monitoring and controlling

d. Monitor and Control Project Work

21. The project manager started a change control weekly meeting so that several stakeholders are Change requests in the project scope. Such requests have caused schedule delays and increased the project costs. The work breakdown structure has undergone the addition of several work packages. These meetings are attended by the project manager, the team, and some stakeholders. Which project management process group is the project manager and the team working on?

a. Perform Integrated Change Control

b. Integration

c. Monitoring and controlling

d. Monitor and control work

22. The project manager is concerned with the several scope changes that the project has been undergoing due to requests from stakeholders. He gathered together change requests already performed and scheduled a meeting with the project team, of which some experts in this project type, to review such changes. Which project management knowledge area are the project manager and the team working on?

a. Perform Integrated Change Control

b. Integration

c. Monitoring and controlling

d. Monitor and control work

23. The project team is performing inspections in validated deliverables to check the scope. The project has undergone several scope changes, leaving the sponsor concerned about costs and deadlines. The project has a CPI of 0.87 and a SPI of 0.89. In which project management process groups is the team working on?

a. Verify Scope

b. Monitoring and controlling

c. Control Scope

d. Scope

24. Which of the following is true regarding the project charter?

a. The project charter must be published by the senior management

b. The project charter must be published by the project manager

c. The project charter must be published by the sponsor

d. The project charter must be published by the stakeholder

25. The configuration management system involves developing the following activities, except

a. Configuration identification

b. Configuration progress record

c. Audit

d. Variance analysis

26. The project manager and his team are analyzing the project's actual performance to verify whether a corrective action is necessary. Which process is he working on?

a. Report Performance

b. Perform Integrated Change Control

c. Monitor and Control Project Work

d. Manage Project Team

27. Formal types of project closing are the following, except

a. Exhaustion

b. Absorption

c. Integration and extinction

d. Operation

28. All the options are grounds for project closing, except

a. Those canceled or eliminated before the closure

b. Those successfully concluded

c. Those transferred to other organizations

d. Those transformed into continuous operation

29. All the following are examples of a project closing by exhaustion, except

a. Other higher-priority projects for the organization

b. The project budget is reduced

c. The customer stops the request

d. The project has become a continued operation

30. When the project ends because resources (people, equipment, etc.) are shared in other areas or allocated to other projects, we say that the project was completed by

a. Integration

b. Exhaustion

c. Extinction

d. Absorption

Answer key

Supplementary exercises

2. 1 - Input - Develop Project Charter

2 - Input - Close Project or Phase

3 - Tool - Direct and Manage Project Execution

4 - Tool/technique - Perform Integrated Change Control

5 - Input - Develop Project Charter

6 - Outputs - Monitor and Control Project Work

7 - Inputs - Perform Integrated Change Control

8 - Input - Close Project or Phase

9 - Outputs - Monitor and Control Project Work

10 - Outputs - Direct and Manage Project Execution

11 - Inputs - Perform Integrated Change Control

12 - Inputs - Develop Project Management Plan

Questions

1. A. Approved change requests are inputs of the Direct and Manage Project Execution process.

2. C. Business case is the document providing the required information from a business viewpoint in order to determine whether or not the project justifies the investment. Typically, the business need and cost-benefit analysis are contained in the business case to justify the project.

3. D. Lessons learned are records related to the project to serve as examples for other projects. Such records are not part of the change management plan.

4. A. The project charter is the document detailing the business needs, current understanding of customers' needs, and the new product, service, or result that you intend to meet, as the project justification, high-level requirements, high-level project description, high-level risks, the milestone schedule summary, the budget summary, and other information.

5. A. Integration is an essential responsibility of the project manager.

6. B. The stakeholder record is drawn up after the project charter. It is an output of the Identify Stakeholders process.

7. D. During the exam, remember in Executing, Monitoring and controlling, and Closing, the project management plan is an input of all processes. Options B and C are inputs of the process. The information on the work performance is an input of the process.

8. D. Even if it is a customer's request, the first action to be taken is assessing the impacts of such request on the project scope, cost, quality, risks, and resources and sending it to the change control board for approval or rejection.

9. D. Note that "change requests" are outputs of processes; if they were "approved change requests", they could be inputs of processes (except for the Perform Integrated Change Control process). Options B and C are inputs of the process.

10. C. Please note: the term "update" is not an input of the process but a process output. Options B and C are inputs of the process.

11. C. The responsibility for deciding whether changes are necessary is the sponsor's, since he is issuer of the Project charter.

12. A. Performance reports are an input of this process. Something worthwhile to be remembered: Change requests are always outputs of processes, except for the Perform Integrated Change Control process. Also, realize the following: the term "upgrade" always refers to outputs of processes.

13. B. Please note: the term "update" always refers to the outputs of processes. If all of them are inputs and only one of them is not, it is not necessary to analyze the other options.

14. D. Project managers must be proactive, so avoiding unnecessary changes is the best answer.

15. C. Please note: the term "update" always refers to the outputs of processes. The only option left is C, change control meetings, which is a tool of the process.

16. B. Approved corrective action is an input of Direct and Manage Project Execution process.

17. D. The project manager is working on the Integration knowledge area and on the Planning process group.

18. C. The project management information system and expert opinion are tools and techniques of the Direct and Manage Project Execution process, in the Executing process group and the Integration knowledge area.

19. C. The expert (expert judgment) is a tool of the Monitor and Control Project Work process, while performance reports are inputs of this process. They are working on the Monitoring and controlling process group and the Integration knowledge area.

20. A. The expert (expert judgment) is a tool of the Monitor and Control Project Work process, while performance reports are inputs of this process. They are working on Monitoring and controlling process group and the Integration knowledge area.

21. C. If you have paid close attention to the question and the answer options, you must have realized that there is only one project management process group from the options: Monitoring and controlling.

22. B. If you have paid close attention to the question and the answer options, you must have realized that there is only one project management knowledge area: integration. The process in question is the Perform Integrated Change Control, and the Perform Integrated Change Control group is Monitoring and controlling.

23. B. In the answer options, there is only one project management process group: Monitoring and controlling. The process in question is Verify Scope (inspections are tools of this process), and the knowledge area is scope. The rates presented are irrelevant information in the question.

24. C. The project charter must be published by the sponsor of the project. Note that he or she is also a stakeholder and can also be from senior management, however, not any party or any management individual must publish the project charter.

25. D. The variance analysis is not an activity associated with the configuration management. Other options are activities associated with the configuration management.

26. C. The project actual performance analysis as compared to the expected performance and the verification of the corrective measure need is an integral part of the Monitor and Control Project Work process.

27. D. The term "transaction" is related to the period after completing the project by absorption – projects become continued operations of a business unit. The important aspect in this question is knowing formal types of project closing.

28. C. Even if a project is transferred to another organization, it remains as a project. Other options are reasons for project terminations.

29. D. When the project has become a continued operation, we say that it was finished by absorption. Other options are examples of closure by exhaustion.

30. A. The end of a project due to the transfer of its resources to other projects is named Closing by integration.

Chapter 5

PROJECT SCOPE MANAGEMENT

1. Introduction
2. Project Scope Management processes
3. Product scope versus project scope
4. Scope management in project planning
5. Scope management in project monitoring and controlling

- Additional information and reminders for the exam
- Supplementary exercises
- Questions
- Answer key

5.1 INTRODUCTION

This chapter will introduce the project management processes in the Scope knowledge area, their relevant inputs, tools, techniques, and outputs.

5.2 PROJECT SCOPE MANAGEMENT PROCESSES

According to *PMBOK® Guide*, the Project Scope Management includes the processes required to ensure that the project contains all necessary work, and only what is necessary, to successfully complete the project.

Project Scope Management processes are

- **Collect Requirements**

  This process defines and documents the stakeholder needs in order to achieve the project objectives.

- **Define Scope**

  This process develops a project and product detailed description.

- **Create WBS**

  This process breaks down the project deliverables and works into smaller more easily manageable components.

- **Verify Scope**

  This process formalizes the acceptance of the finished project deliverables.

- **Control Scope**

  This process monitors the project scope and product scope progress as well as manages the scope baseline changes.

The following flowchart displays the relationship among the Project Scope Management processes and their locations across the Project management process groups.

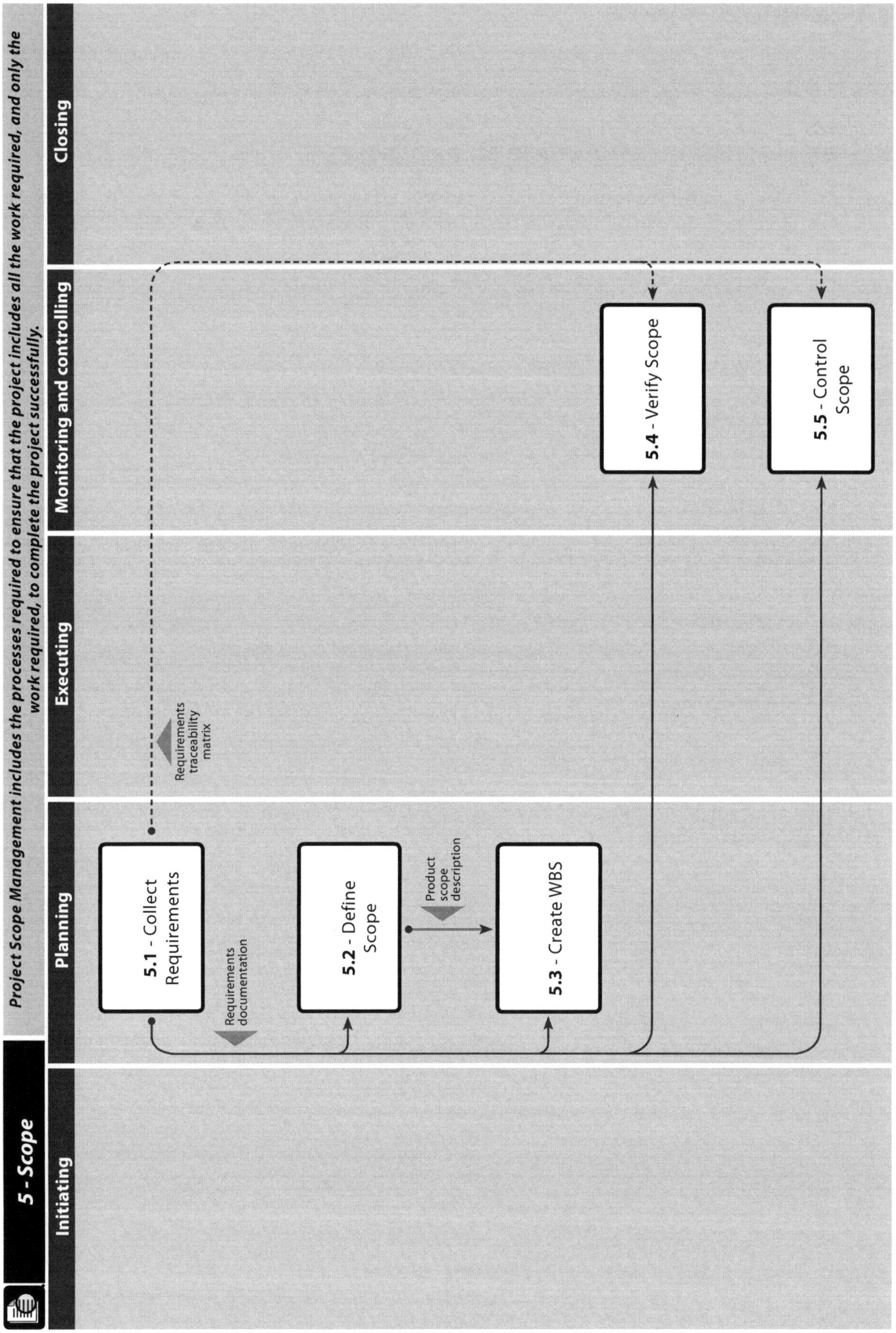
5 - Scope
Project Scope Management includes the processes required to ensure that the project includes all the work required, and only the work required, to complete the project successfully.
Initiating
Planning
Executing
Monitoring and controlling
Closing
5.1 - Collect Requirements
5.2 - Define Scope
5.3 - Create WBS
5.4 - Verify Scope
5.5 - Control Scope
Requirements documentation
Product scope description
Requirements traceability matrix

5.3 PRODUCT SCOPE X PROJECT SCOPE

Within the project, the term scope can refer to

- **Product scope**

  Features and functions describing a product, service, or result.

- **Project scope**

  The work that needs to be performed to deliver a product, service, or result according to the specified features and functions.

Project Scope Management must be integrated to other processes of the knowledge areas, so that the project work result is delivering the specified product scope. The project scope completion is measured against the project management plan, the project scope statement, the Work Breakdown Structure (WBS) and the related WBS dictionary; however, the product scope completion is measured against the product requirements.

5.4 SCOPE MANAGEMENT IN PROJECT PLANNING

Project Scope Management includes the processes required to ensure that the project contains all the necessary work, and only that work, to successfully complete the project. Scope management is primarily concerned with defining and controlling what is or not included in the project. In addition, in practice, it is a constant verification whether the entire work is being completed, not enabling people to randomly include unexpected work without the authorized change and preventing additional or superfluous work from being included.

The scope management in project management comprises three processes, namely

- ***Collect Requirements***
- ***Define Scope***
- ***Create WBS***

5.4.1 COLLECT REQUIREMENTS (*PMBOK® GUIDE*, PROCESS 5.1)

Collect Requirements is the process of defining and documenting stakeholder needs in order to achieve the project objectives. Requirements include quantification and documentation of the needs and expectations of customers, sponsors, users, and other stakeholders. Such requirements need to be adequately clarified, reviewed, and detailed to enable evaluation once the project is started. Requirements are the foundation of the WBS. The development of the Collect Requirements process is started with information from the project charter (Chapter 4) and stakeholder register (Chapter 5).

5.4.1.1 COLLECT REQUIREMENTS: INPUTS, TOOLS AND TECHNIQUES, AND OUTPUTS

INPUTS

1 **Project charter**

The charter provides the project high-level requirements as well as the project product high-level description and must be taken into account in this process.

2 **Stakeholder register**

The Stakeholder register records the stakeholder requirements and expectations and must be taken into account in this process.

TOOLS AND TECHNIQUES

1 **Interviews**

Interviews are formal or informal approaches directly performed with stakeholders in order to obtain information aimed at helping identifying and defining features and functions of the desired project deliverables.

2 **Focus groups**

Focus groups are meetings gathering prequalified experts and interested stakeholders together to reach consensus about the product, service, or result. Such meetings are developed through interactive discussions among participants, as guided by a coordinator.

3 **Facilitated workshops**

Facilitated workshops are sessions are developed with the presence of stakeholders to jointly define the requirements of the product, service, or result. In addition to dealing with differences among stakeholders, the workshops strengthen relationships, better communication among participants and troubleshooting.

4 **Group creativity techniques**

Some group techniques can be used to identify project and product requirements, including

- **Brainstorming**

  A group work technique designed to release participants' imagination and creativity toward ideas and solutions about a particular subject.

- **Nominal group technique**

  A technique based on brainstorming and a voting process to define ideas and solution for a future brainstorming or discussion prioritization.

- **Delphi technique**

  A technique consisting of drafting a questionnaire to be sent to experts who can be in different locations in order to obtain ideas on the subject concerned. Answers are summarized and redistributed to experts for further comment. One of the advantages of this technique is participants' anonymity, which rules out the possibility of judging ideas and helps them to be more genuine.

- **Mind maps**

  A technique consisting of consolidating individual ideas on a mind map.

- **Affinity diagram**

  A technique designed to share a large number of ideas with groups for revision and analysis.

5 **Group decision-making techniques**

Some group decision making techniques can be used to create, classify, and prioritize requirements, among which are

- **Unanimous decision**

  All group members agree on the same choice.

- **Decision by majority**

  More than 51% of participants in the group define a choice.

- **Plurality**

  The largest subgroup of the group defines a choice when there is no decision by majority.

- **Dictatorial decision (dictatorship)**

  A component makes the decision on behalf of the group.

6 **Questionnaires and surveys**

Questionnaires and surveys are sets of questions made to a large number of people, when a fast response return is needed. In this technique, it may be appropriate using the statistical analysis of responses.

7 **Observations**

Observations consist of visual verification of how services and processes are performed, particularly when individuals have a hard time defining or are reluctant to submit their requirements.

8 **Prototypes**

Prototypes mean obtaining information on requirements using a model performed before the project.

OUTPUTS

1 **Requirements documentation**

Requirements documentation is recording the individual requirements of each stakeholder that can be performed at a high level at first and be detailed in depth, as the requirement becomes known. The registration form can be a simple list of requirements and priorities, or more elaborate, containing information, such as, among others, the following:

- Requirement description and its importance to achieve the project objectives;
- Requirement-related assumptions and constraints;

- Impact on the project cost and schedule;
- Requirement quality metrics and acceptance criteria;
- Requirement impact on other organizational departments or areas such as technology, sales, production, maintenance, and others;
- Requirement-related training; and
- Other relevant information on requirements.

2 Requirements management plan

Requirements management plan documents how they will be reviewed, documented, and managed throughout the project life cycle. Components of the plan include, but are not limited to, the following:

- How requirements activities will be planned, tracked, and reported
- How configuration management activities, such as change control, impact analysis, and others, will be developed
- Information on requirements prioritization
- Metrics to be used for subsequent requirements verification

3 Requirements traceability matrix

Requirements traceability matrix consists of a table displaying the origin of each requirement and where it is located in the project life cycle, ensuring that each requirement will add value to the business and is related to the project and business objectives. The matrix final intention is ensuring that requirements approved in the requirements documentation are delivered at the end of the project. The matrix must encompass all types of requirements, among which may be listed

- Requirements related to business needs, opportunities, goals, and objectives;
- Requirements related to project objectives;
- Requirements related to the WBS scope and deliverables;
- Requirements related to product design;
- Requirements related to product development;
- Requirements related to tests; and
- Other relevant requirements for the project and the business.

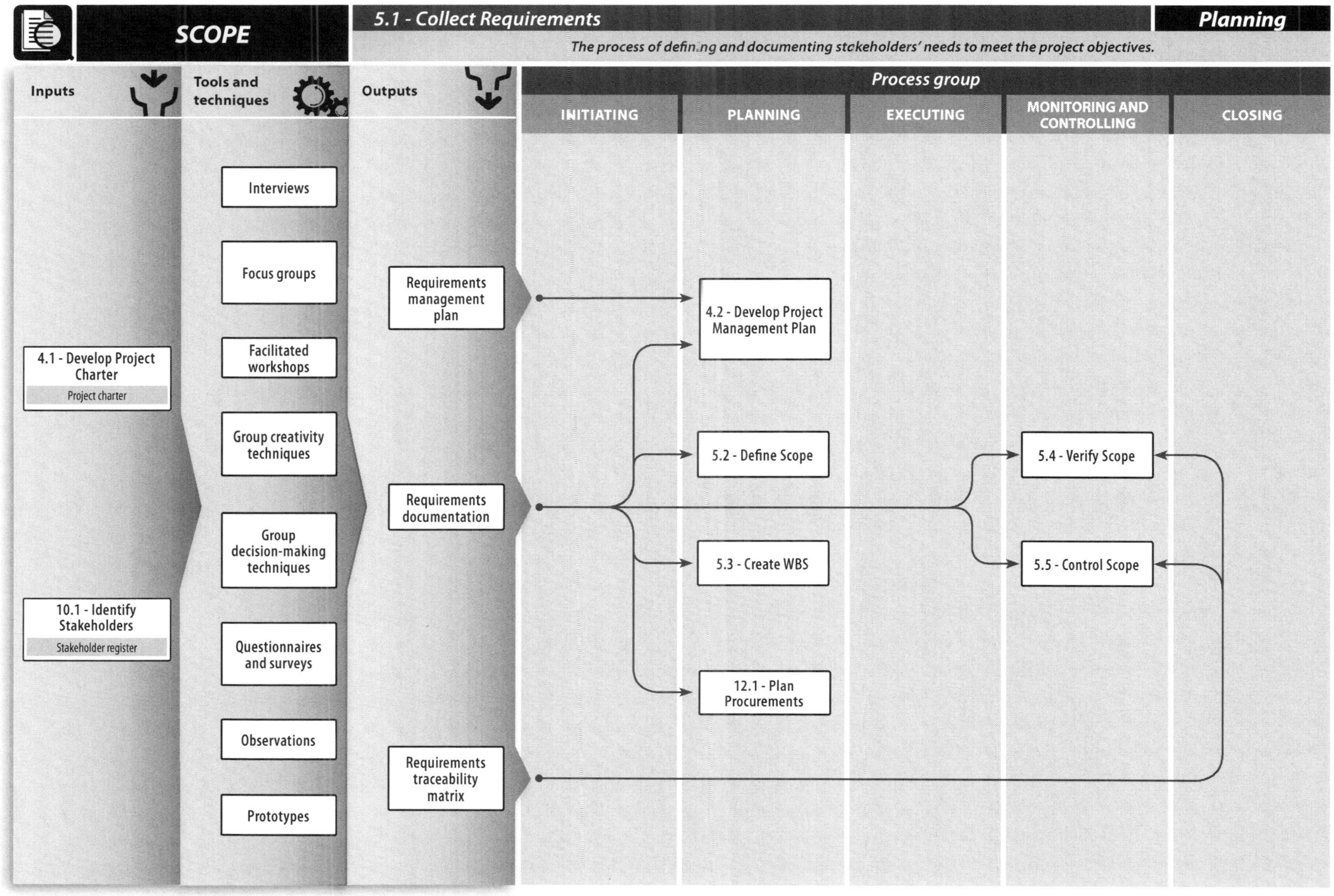
SCOPE
5.1 - Collect Requirements
Planning
The process of defining and documenting stakeholders' needs to meet the project objectives.
Inputs
Tools and techniques
Outputs
Process group
INITIATING
PLANNING
EXECUTING
MONITORING AND CONTROLLING
CLOSING
4.1 - Develop Project Charter
Project charter
10.1 - Identify Stakeholders
Stakeholder register
Interviews
Focus groups
Facilitated workshops
Group creativity techniques
Group decision-making techniques
Questionnaires and surveys
Observations
Prototypes
Requirements management plan
Requirements documentation
Requirements traceability matrix
4.2 - Develop Project Management Plan
5.2 - Define Scope
5.3 - Create WBS
12.1 - Plan Procurements
5.4 - Verify Scope
5.5 - Control Scope

5.4.2 DEFINE SCOPE (*PMBOK® GUIDE*, PROCESS 5.2)

Define Scope is developing a project and product description as the basis for future project decisions. The project scope statement must consider major deliverables, assumptions and constraints documented at the project initiating. In the Planning phase, the project scope is defined in more detail as more information on the project becomes known. The project scope statement provides a common understanding of the project scope among stakeholders as well as the exclusions scope. It enables the project team to develop a more detailed planning, serves as a guide during project execution, and defines the baseline to evaluate scope change requests or add new services to the project.

5.4.2.1 DEFINE SCOPE: INPUTS, TOOLS AND TECHNIQUES, AND OUTPUTS

INPUTS

1 **Project charter**

The project charter provides the project high-level requirements as well as the project product high-level description and must be taken into account in this process.

2 **Requirements documentation**

Requirements documentation must be taken into account in this process.

3 **Organizational process assets**

The organizational process assets such as the policy of the company's project management, quality policy and procedures, work instructions, templates and standard forms, performance measurement criteria, change implementation procedures, historical information, lessons learned, and others should be considered in this process.

TOOLS AND TECHNIQUES

1 **Expert judgment**

Expert judgment to define the project scope can be obtained from several sources, including

- Other units within the organization;
- Consultants;
- Stakeholders, including users, sponsors, and others;
- Team members;
- Suppliers and manufacturers; and
- Project Management Office (PMO).

2 **Product analysis**

The objective of the product analysis is verifying the project objectives and turning them into tangible requirements and deliverables. The product analysis may include techniques such as product breakdown, systems analysis, and value engineering, among others.

3 **Alternatives identification**

The alternatives identification is performed through techniques used to generate different approaches to execute and perform the work, the most common being brainstorming, which is a meeting where participants talk about their ideas on a given subject, the best ones being selected and analyzed.

4 **Facilitated workshops**

Facilitated workshops must be used in this process.

OUTPUTS

1 **Project scope statement**

The project scope statement describes, in detail, the project's deliverables and the work required to create those deliverables. In short, it must include, but not be limited to, the following information:

- Product scope description,
- Project requirements,
- Scope exclusions,
- Project deliverables,
- Deliverables acceptance criteria, and
- Constraints and assumptions.

2 **Project document updates**

Project documents that may be updated include but are not limited to

- Stakeholder register,
- Requirements documentation, and
- Requirements traceability matrix.

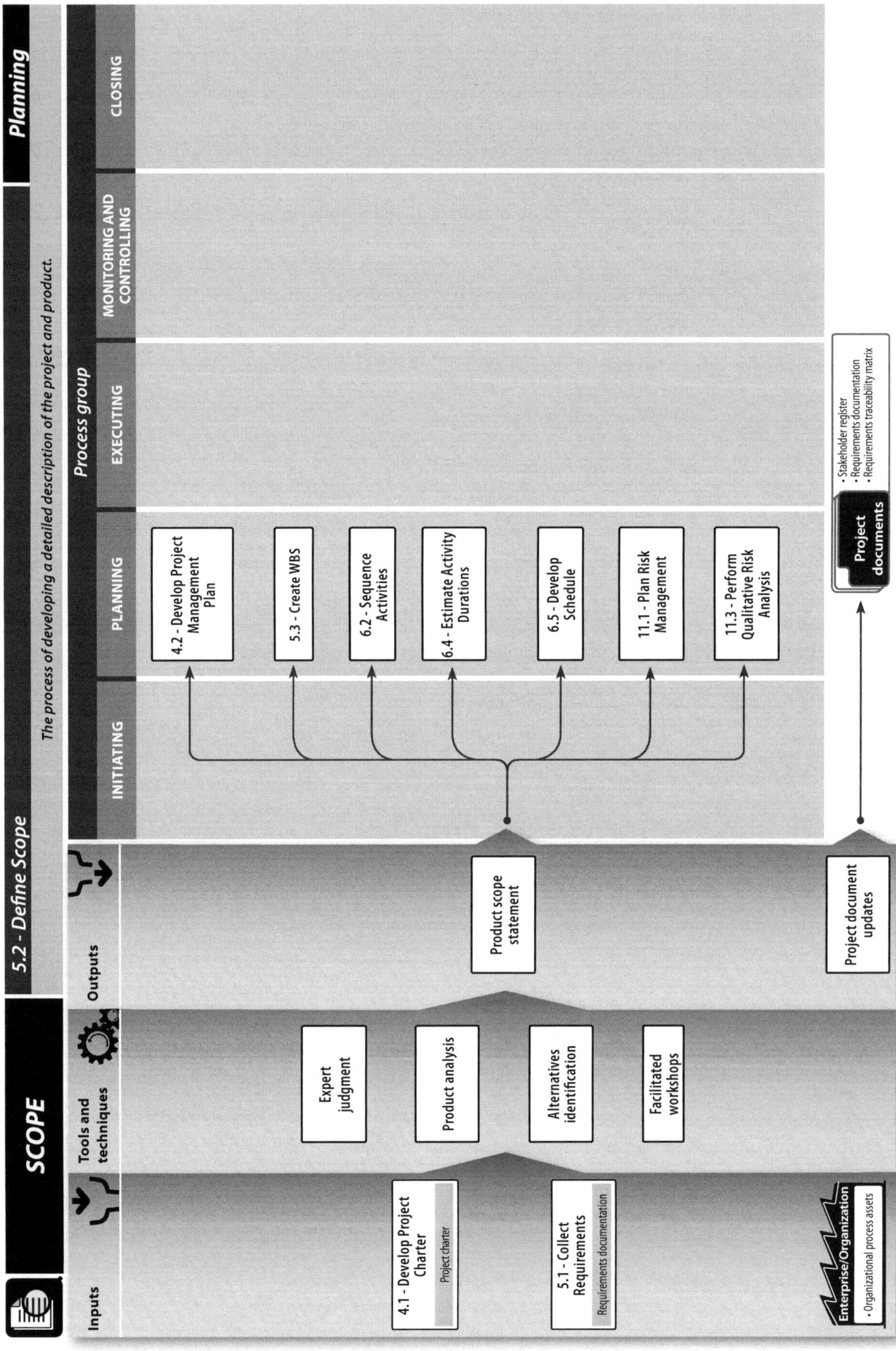
SCOPE
5.2 - Define Scope
Planning
The process of developing a detailed description of the project and product.
Inputs
Tools and techniques
Outputs
Process group
INITIATING
PLANNING
EXECUTING
MONITORING AND CONTROLLING
CLOSING
4.1 - Develop Project Charter
Project charter
5.1 - Collect Requirements
Requirements documentation
Enterprise/Organization
• Organizational process assets
Expert judgment
Product analysis
Alternatives identification
Facilitated workshops
Product scope statement
Project document updates
4.2 - Develop Project Management Plan
5.3 - Create WBS
6.2 - Sequence Activities
6.4 - Estimate Activity Durations
6.5 - Develop Schedule
11.1 - Plan Risk Management
11.3 - Perform Qualitative Risk Analysis
Project documents
• Stakeholder register
• Requirements documentation
• Requirements traceability matrix

LOGO	PROJECT	PROJECT SCOPE STATEMENT	Rev.: Data: Sheet ___ of ___

1 **PROJECT OBJECTIVE(S)**

Describes the project objective(s) - what the project intends to achieve.

2 **PRODUCT SCOPE**

Describes the features of the product, service, or work to be delivered by the project.

3 **PROJECT REQUIREMENTS**

Describe the condition or capability that must be met or exist in the project deliverables to comply with a contract, standard, specification, or other formal documents.

4 **SCOPE EXCLUSIONS**

Describe what is not included in the project scope.

5 **PROJECT DELIVERABLES**

Describe the project deliverables, including ancillary results, such as documents, reports, etc.

6 **ACCEPTANCE CRITERIA**

Describe the process and the acceptance criteria of finished products.

7 **PROJECT SPECIFICATION**

Identify the specification documents that the project must comply with.

8 **LINKS WITH OTHER PROJECTS**

Indicate, if any, interdependencies with other organization projects.

9 **CONSTRAINTS**

Describe project constraints especially related to cost, schedule, scope, and quality.

Include, if any, dates identified in item 11 - Schedule milestone.

10 **ASSUMPTIONS**

Indicate assumptions made by the Planning team to date.

ELABORATED BY:	APPROVED BY:

5.4.3 CREATE WBS (*PMBOK® GUIDE*, PROCESS 5.3)

The WBS is a hierarchical decomposition oriented toward delivering the work to be performed by the project team in order to achieve the project objectives and create the required deliverables. WBS is the major Planning tool and must be developed in all projects, regardless their size or complexity. Without WBS, the project tends to have a larger amount of change requests, the project schedule tends to be compromised and budget tends to be constantly exceeded and may even render the project unfeasible.

WBS can be represented as a list of activities or in graphic form, which is the best view.

5.4.3.1 CREATE WBS: INPUTS, TOOLS AND TECHNIQUES, AND OUTPUTS

INPUTS

1 **Project scope statement**

The project scope statement, described earlier in this chapter, is the major input of this process.

2 **Requirements documentation**

The requirements documentation, described earlier in this chapter, must be taken into account in this process.

3 **Organizational process assets**

The organizational process assets such as the policy of the company's project management, quality policy and procedures, work instructions, templates and standard forms, performance measurement criteria, change implementation procedures, historical information, lessons learned and others should be considered in this process.

TOOLS AND TECHNIQUES

1 **Decomposition**

Decomposition is the subdivision of project deliverables into smaller more manageable components and usually involves the following activities:

- Identifying the deliverables and related work
- Structuring and organizing the WBS
- Decomposing the WBS highest levels in lower level detailed components (top-down technique)
- Developing and assignment identification codes to the WBS components
- Verifying that the degree of decomposition level - whether it is necessary and sufficient

The decomposition of the WBS higher-level components requires the work subdivision for each one of the deliverables into products, services, or verifiable results. Each component must be clearly and completely defined and assigned to an execution organizational unit.

The WBS must not be confused with other types of analytical structures, such as an organization chart, which refers to the project organization, a Resource Breakdown Structure (RBS), or even a Risk Breakdown Structure.

OUTPUTS

1 **Work Breakdown Structure (WBS)**

The WBS is the major output of this process (see example in the end of the chapter).

2 **WBS dictionary**

The WBS dictionary provides more detailed descriptions of the work packages, and its contents must include component identification code, component title, component description, activities to generate the product, product acceptance criteria, and others (see example in the end of the chapter).

3 **Scope baseline**

Scope baseline is a component of the project management plan and includes

- Product scope statement,
- WBS, and
- WBS dictionary.

4 **Project document updates**

Project document that may be updated include but are not limited to

- Requirements documentation

SCOPE

5.3 - Create WBS

Planning

The process of subdividing project deliverables and project work into smaller, more manageable components.

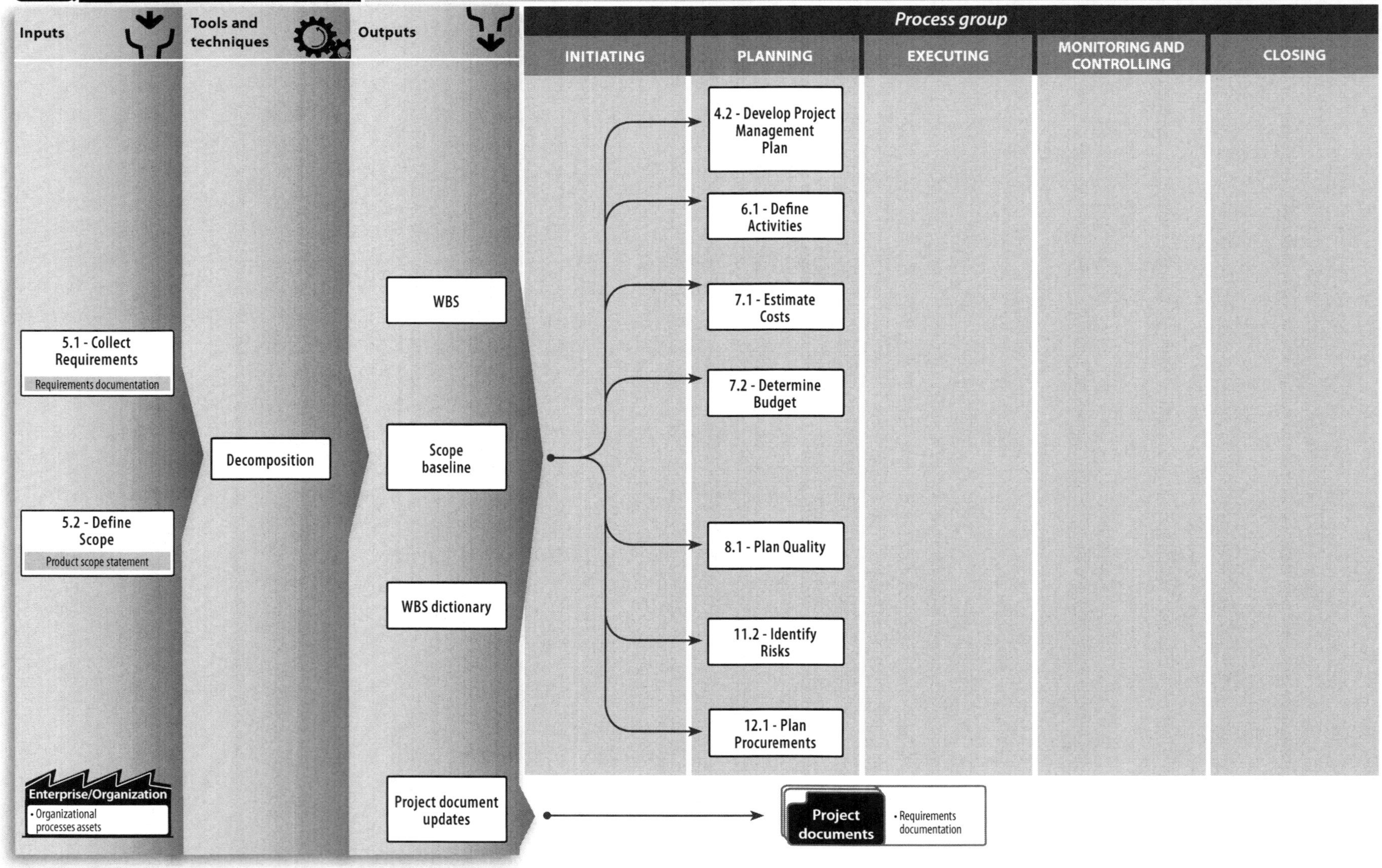

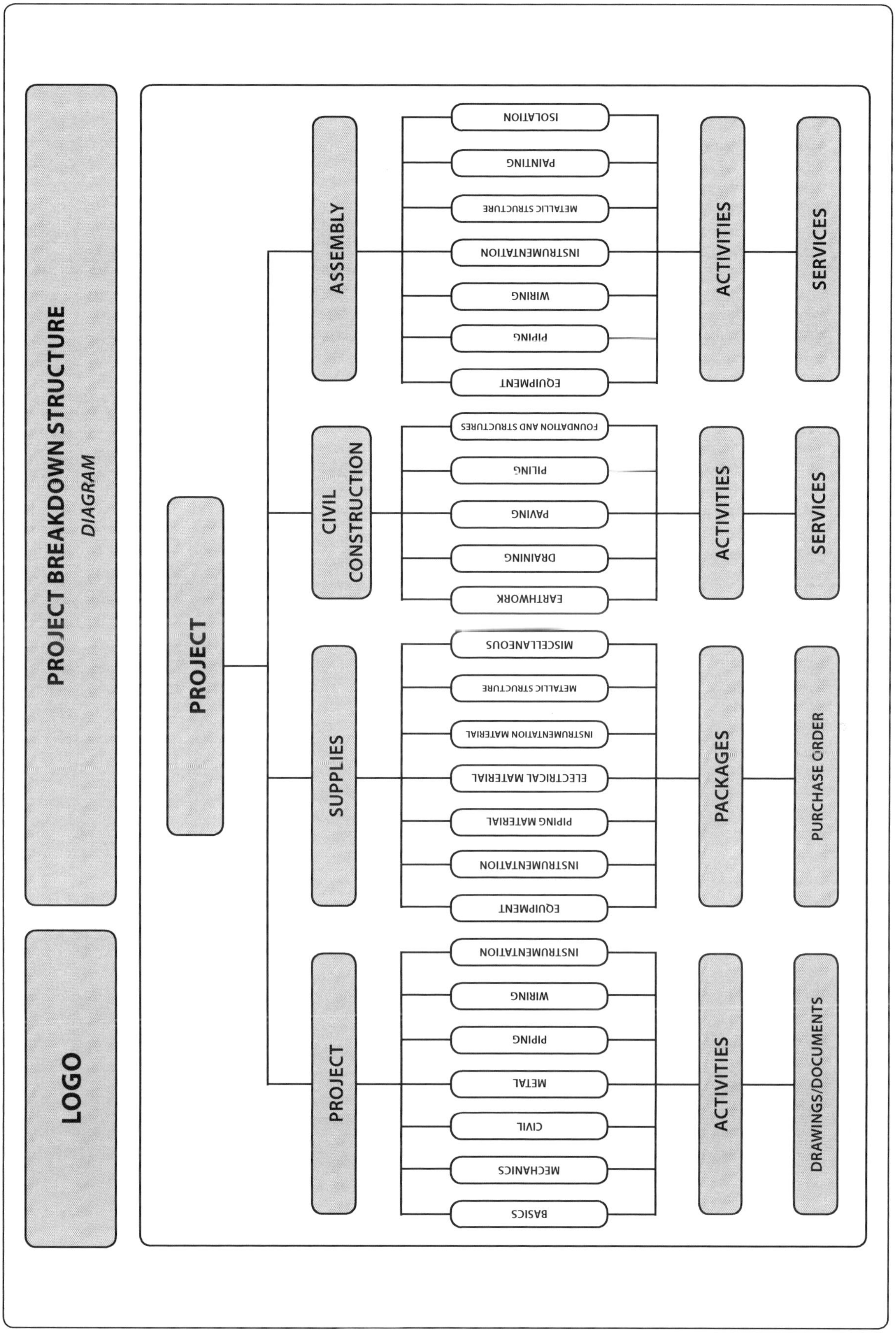
LOGO
PROJECT BREAKDOWN STRUCTURE
DIAGRAM
PROJECT
PROJECT
BASICS
MECHANICS
CIVIL
METAL
PIPING
WIRING
INSTRUMENTATION
ACTIVITIES
DRAWINGS/DOCUMENTS
SUPPLIES
EQUIPMENT
INSTRUMENTATION
PIPING MATERIAL
ELECTRICAL MATERIAL
INSTRUMENTATION MATERIAL
METALLIC STRUCTURE
MISCELLANEOUS
PACKAGES
PURCHASE ORDER
CIVIL CONSTRUCTION
EARTHWORK
DRAINING
PAVING
PILING
FOUNDATION AND STRUCTURES
ACTIVITIES
SERVICES
ASSEMBLY
EQUIPMENT
PIPING
WIRING
INSTRUMENTATION
METALLIC STRUCTURE
PAINTING
ISOLATION
ACTIVITIES
SERVICES

LOGO	PROJECT	WBS DICTIONARY	Rev.: Data: Sheet ___ of ___

WBS IDENTIFICATION	WORK PACKAGE	DESCRIPTION	ACCEPTANCE CRITERIA
WBS element number	WBS work package name	Description of work package, containing specification, functionality, quality, etc.	What will be (or not) taken into account to accept the work package delivery

ELABORATED BY: **APPROVED BY:**

5.5 SCOPE MANAGEMENT IN PROJECT MONITORING AND CONTROLLING

Scope management in project monitoring and controlling consists of the following processes:

- *Verify Scope*
- *Control Scope*

5.5.1 VERIFY SCOPE (*PMBOK® GUIDE*, PROCESS 5.4)

Verify Scope consists of verifying whether the work was performed according to the project management plan, the scope management plan, the WBS, and the WBS dictionary and obtaining formal acceptance of deliverables by stakeholders. If the project has been stopped or canceled, this process must document the extent to which the project was completed. This documentation will serve as historical information if the project is resumed. While quality control is related to evaluating the work results for compliance with quality requirements, scope verification is related to acceptance of work results.

5.5.1.1 VERIFY SCOPE: INPUTS, TOOLS AND TECHNIQUES, AND OUTPUTS

INPUTS

1 **Project management plan**

The project management plan and especially the scope management plan must be taken into account in this process.

2 **Requirements documentation**

The Requirements documentation, which is one of the outputs of the Collect Requirements process, must be taken into account in this process.

3 **Requirements traceability matrix**

The Requirements traceability matrix, which is one of the outputs of the Collect Requirements process, must be taken into account in this process.

4 **Validated deliverables**

Validated deliverables are deliverables that have been completed and verified as to accuracy, through the Perform Quality Control process.

TOOLS AND TECHNIQUES

1 **Inspection**

Inspections are verification, exam, and measurement activities to verify whether the work performed is according to the acceptance requirements and criteria defined for the project. Inspections can be

- **Partial**

  A partial inspection is the one performed in a product execution intermediate stage aiming to check the proper use of components, which are not always verifiable after the product execution. An example of that is a manufacture partial inspection of large-sized equipment, intended to anticipate potential problems with the use of inadequate or nonspecified components.

- **Final**

  A final inspection is the one performed after product execution through visual, dimensional inspection, tests, and other exams.

Results of such inspections can be:

- **Approved**

  The product is considered approved when meeting the requirements and acceptance criteria defined in the project.

- **Corrected**

  Correction occurs when the product is found noncompliant with the requirements and acceptance criteria defined in the project and must be corrected. Correction often makes a new verification inspection necessary.

- **Rejected**

  The product is rejected when it is found noncompliant with requirements and acceptance criteria and cannot be repaired.

OUTPUTS

1 **Accepted deliverables**

The Verify Scope process documents deliverables which have complied with requirements and acceptance criteria and were accepted.

2 **Change requests**

Completed deliverables not accepted are formally documented with the nonacceptance reasons. Such deliverables require a change request to repair the defect. Change requests are processed for revision and availability during the Perform Integrated Change Control process.

3 **Project document updates**

Any and all project documents that have been influenced by the Verify Scope process must be updated.

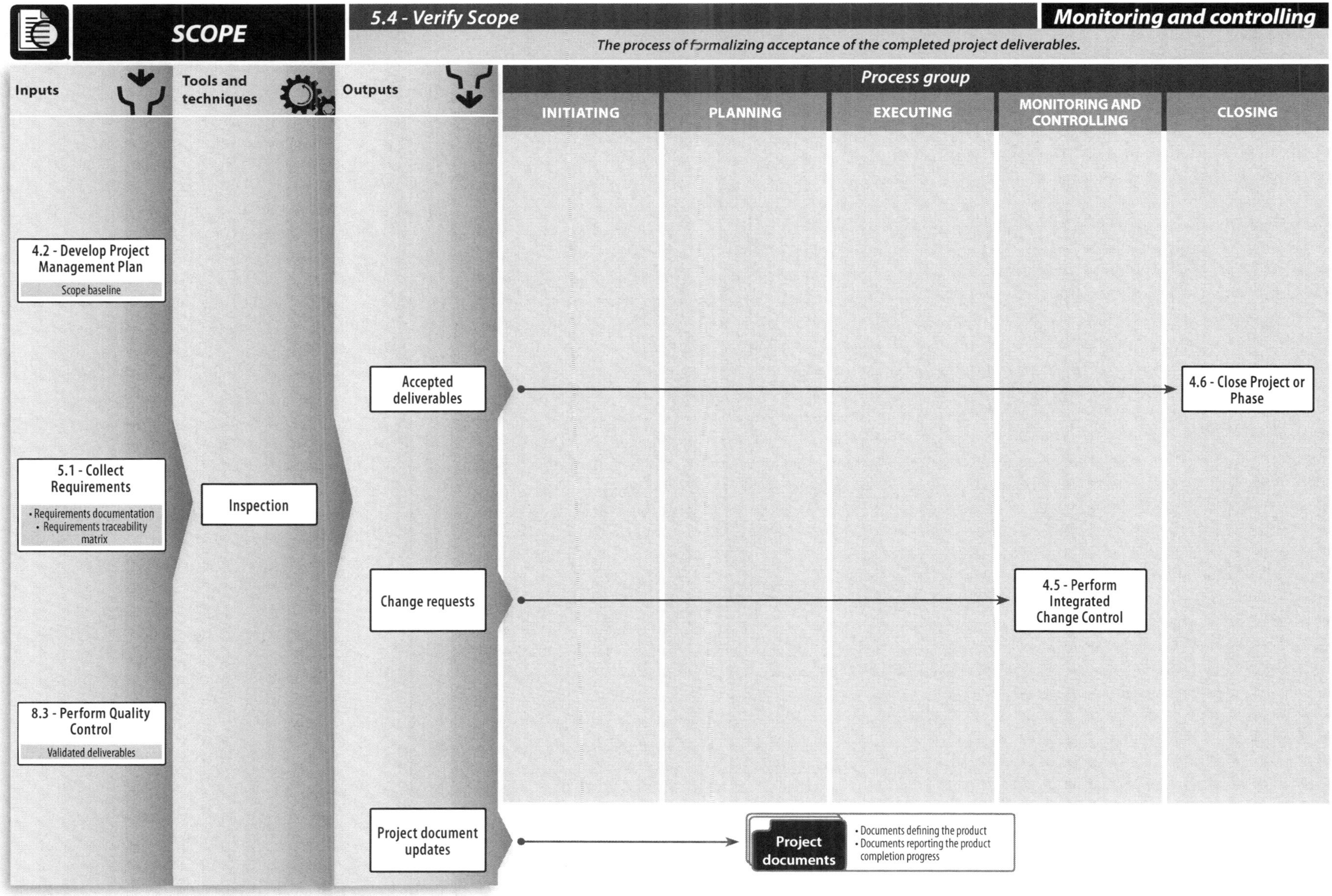
SCOPE
5.4 - Verify Scope
Monitoring and controlling
The process of formalizing acceptance of the completed project deliverables.
Inputs
Tools and techniques
Outputs
Process group
INITIATING
PLANNING
EXECUTING
MONITORING AND CONTROLLING
CLOSING
4.2 - Develop Project Management Plan
Scope baseline
5.1 - Collect Requirements
• Requirements documentation
• Requirements traceability matrix
8.3 - Perform Quality Control
Validated deliverables
Inspection
Accepted deliverables
Change requests
Project document updates
4.6 - Close Project or Phase
4.5 - Perform Integrated Change Control
Project documents
• Documents defining the product
• Documents reporting the product completion progress

5.5.2 CONTROL SCOPE (*PMBOK® GUIDE*, PROCESS 5.5)

It is the process of monitoring the product scope and project scope and managing changes in the scope baseline. Every change request or recommendation that might change the WBS is considered as a scope change and must be analyzed under all aspects influencing the project, such as cost, schedule, quality, risk, and others. Such changes, which may be related to the project scope or the product scope, must be processed and controlled by an integrated control system based on the scope baseline.

5.5.2.1 CONTROL SCOPE: INPUTS, TOOLS AND TECHNIQUES, AND OUTPUTS

INPUTS

1 **Project management plan**

The project management plan and especially the scope management plan must be taken into account in this process.

2 **Work Performance Information**

Information on the work performance information contained in performance reports must be taken into account in this process. Such information can be related to the project progress, initiated deliverables and their progress, and completed deliverables.

3 **Requirements documentation**

The requirements documentation, which is one of the outputs of the Collect Requirements process, must be taken into account in this process.

4 **Requirements traceability matrix**

The requirements traceability matrix, which is one of the outputs of the Collect Requirements process, must be taken into account in this process.

5 **Organizational process assets**

The organizational process assets that may influence the Control Scope process, such as project management policies and procedures, scope control procedures, reporting templates, historical information, and lessons learned from previous projects must be taken into account in this process.

TOOLS AND TECHNIQUES

1 **Variance analysis**

Variance in the project actual performance in relation to performance expected in the scope baseline must be analyzed in order to verify the need for corrective or preventive actions.

OUTPUTS

1 **Work performance measurements**

Measurements may include a comparison between the current and the planned technical performance or other scope performance measurements. Such information must be documented and notified to stakeholders.

2 **Organizational process assets updates**

The Scope control process may identify new processes or opportunities for improvements in the organization standards, quality procedures, and policies. Such updates may relate to the causes of variances, chosen corrective actions, and the reasons and lessons learned from this process.

3 **Change requests**

The Control Scope process may result in change requests in the scope baseline or other components of the project management plan. Such change requests can be corrective actions, preventive actions and defect repair. Change requests are processed for revision and availability during the Perform Integrated Change Control process.

4 **Project management plan updates**

The Project management plan and, in particular, the Scope management plan must be updated after changes are approved as a result of the Control Scope process.

5 **Project document updates**

Project documents that may be updated include, but are not limited to

- Requirements documentation, and
- Requirements traceability matrix.

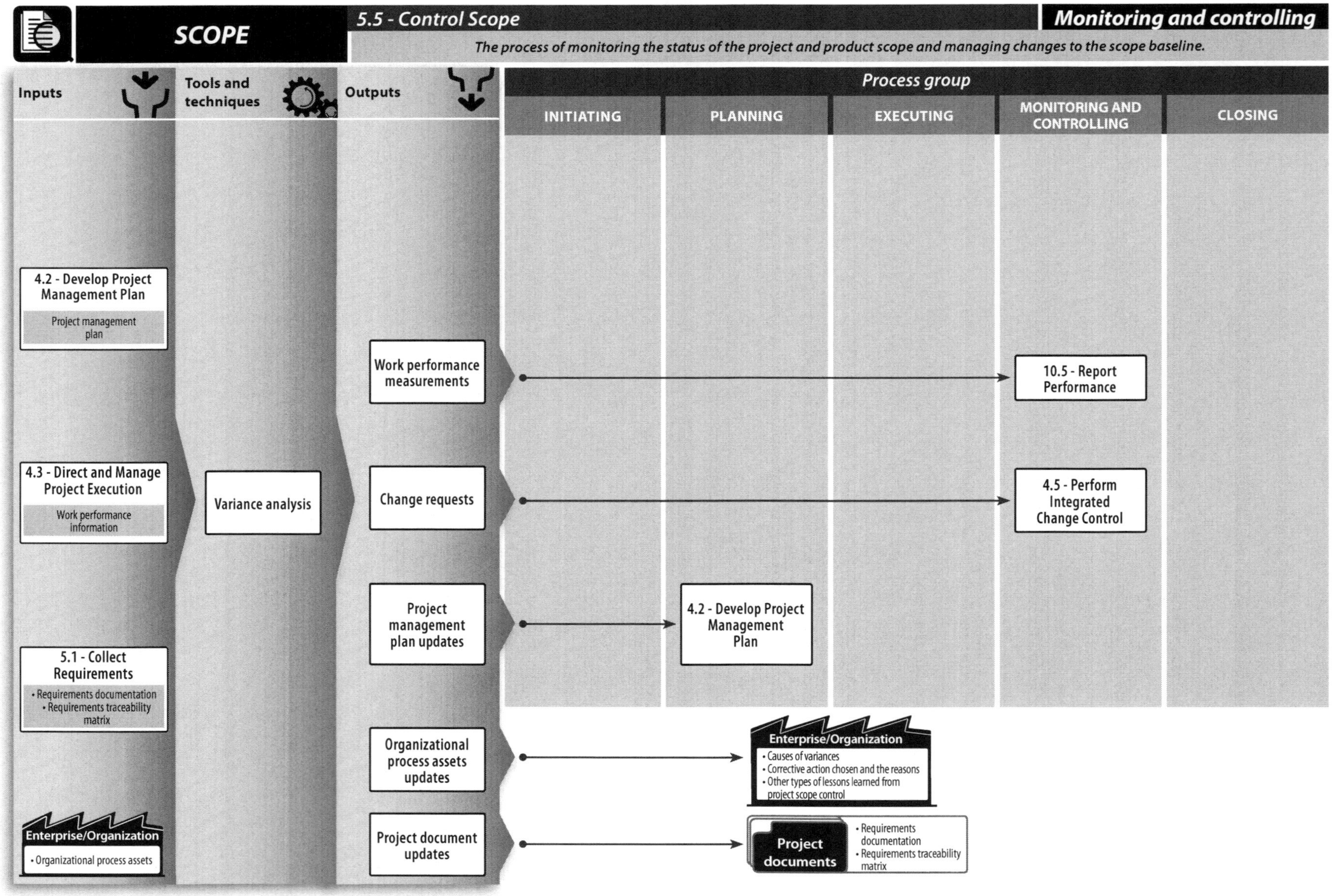

SCOPE
5.5 - Control Scope
Monitoring and controlling
The process of monitoring the status of the project and product scope and managing changes to the scope baseline.
Inputs
Tools and techniques
Outputs
Process group
INITIATING
PLANNING
EXECUTING
MONITORING AND CONTROLLING
CLOSING
4.2 - Develop Project Management Plan
Project management plan
4.3 - Direct and Manage Project Execution
Work performance information
5.1 - Collect Requirements
• Requirements documentation
• Requirements traceability matrix
Enterprise/Organization
• Organizational process assets
Variance analysis
Work performance measurements
Change requests
Project management plan updates
Organizational process assets updates
Project document updates
10.5 - Report Performance
4.5 - Perform Integrated Change Control
4.2 - Develop Project Management Plan
Enterprise/Organization
• Causes of variances
• Corrective action chosen and the reasons
• Other types of lessons learned from project scope control
Project documents
• Requirements documentation
• Requirements traceability matrix

Additional information and reminders for the exam

- Product scope: represents the project product requirements. What is the intended product or end result?

- Project scope: it is the project work to deliver the product scope. What must be done to deliver the product or achieve the end result?

- The PMP® exam is focused only on the project scope, not on the product scope.

- Scope management is aimed to develop all the required project work — and nothing more than the required work!

- The Scope management plan shows how to develop the Project scope statement, such as creating the WBS and verifying that all work is being developed and how to Control Scope changes. It is part of the project management plan.

- The WBS is a decomposition of the work into more easily manageable levels. The last WBS level must comprise the work packages. When the work is broken down, new information is found, which must be added to the Scope management plan and the Project scope statement, if changes are approved (such information is considered as changes and they must be submitted to the Change Control Board for analysis and approval or rejection).

- The WBS numbering system identifies the level of each WBS element.

- The WBS dictionary is a document containing detailed descriptions of the WBS work packages.

- The scope baseline comprises the Project scope statement, the WBS, and the WBS dictionary.

- In all projects, the WBS must be used.

- The WBS must include only the required project deliverables. Deliverables not included in the WBS are not part of the project. Making additional changes or superfluous work on the project is not allowed.

- The WBS does not have any dependencies.

- The Control Scope process includes monitoring the project scope and product scope as well as managing changes to the scope baseline.

- The Verify Scope process does NOT mean verifying the scope as defined in the Planning! The Verify Scope process means *formal acceptance of deliverables* by the customer or sponsor! In other words, in this process, meetings are held with the customer or sponsor towards formal acceptance of deliverables.

- The Quality Function Deployment (QFD) used in the manufacturing industry is an example of Collect Requirements workshop. This workshop begins by identifying the customer's needs. Such needs are also referred to as Voice of the Customer (VOC).

Supplementary exercises

1. Regarding the project scope knowledge area, indicate to which management processes group(s) each element is related and explain why. Follow the project scope statement example.

1. Product scope description

☐ Initiating ☒ Planning ☐ Executing ☐ Monitoring/controlling ☐ Closing

The Project Scope Statement is an output of the Define Scope process and an input of the Create WBS process, both of which are Planning processes.

2. Project charter

☐ Initiating ☐ Planning ☐ Executing ☐ Monitoring/controlling ☐ Closing

3. WBS

☐ Initiating ☐ Planning ☐ Executing ☐ Monitoring/controlling ☐ Closing

4. Inspection

☐ Initiating ☐ Planning ☐ Executing ☐ Monitoring/controlling ☐ Closing

5. Stakeholder register

☐ Initiating ☐ Planning ☐ Executing ☐ Monitoring/controlling ☐ Closing

6. Prototypes

☐ Initiating ☐ Planning ☐ Executing ☐ Monitoring/controlling ☐ Closing

7. Variance analysis

☐ Initiating ☐ Planning ☐ Executing ☐ Monitoring/controlling ☐ Closing

8. Accepted deliverables

☐ Initiating ☐ Planning ☐ Executing ☐ Monitoring/controlling ☐ Closing

9. Product analysis and alternatives identification

☐ Initiating ☐ Planning ☐ Executing ☐ Monitoring/controlling ☐ Closing

10. Work performance measurements

☐ Initiating ☐ Planning ☐ Executing ☐ Monitoring/controlling ☐ Closing

11. Interviews and group dynamics

☐ Initiating ☐ Planning ☐ Executing ☐ Monitoring/controlling ☐ Closing

12. Change requests

☐ Initiating ☐ Planning ☐ Executing ☐ Monitoring/controlling ☐ Closing

13. Requirements traceability matrix

☐ Initiating ☐ Planning ☐ Executing ☐ Monitoring/controlling ☐ Closing

14. Decomposition

☐ Initiating ☐ Planning ☐ Executing ☐ Monitoring/controlling ☐ Closing

15. Scope baseline

☐ Initiating ☐ Planning ☐ Executing ☐ Monitoring/controlling ☐ Closing

2. Complete the sentences below, stating whether the option refers to input, tool/technique, or output, and identify the corresponding project management process.

1. Decomposition is a ____________________ of the ________________________________ process.
2. Variance analysis is a ________________________ of the ____________________________ ______________ process.
3. Accepted deliverables are ____________________ of the ______________________________ ______________ process.
4. Requirements documentation is a __________________________ of the ________________ ______________________________ process.
5. Project Scope Statement is a ____________________________ of the ________________ ______________________________ process.
6. Project Scope Statement is a ____________________________ of the ________________ ______________________________ process.
7. Alternatives identification is a ___________________________ of the ________________ ______________________________ process.
8. WBS dictionary is a ______________________________ of the ______________________ ______________________ process.
9. Requirements documentation is a __________________ of the ______________________ ______________________________ process.
10. Requirements traceability matrix is a ____________________________ of the __________ ____________________________________ process.
11. Requirements traceability matrix is a __________________________________ of __________ ____ processes.
12. Group creativity techniques are ____________________________ of the ________________ ____________________________________ process.
13. Validated deliverables are ______________________ of the ____________________________ process.
14. Facilitated workshops are ____ of the ____________________________________ process.
15. Inspection is a ________________________ of the ____________________________________ process.

Questions

1. In Project Scope Management, the process immediately preceding the Verify Scope process is
   a. Define Activities
   b. Define Scope
   c. Control Scope
   d. Create WBS

2. Which are the two processes that generate inputs to the Create WBS process?
   a. Develop Project Management Plan and Collect Requirements
   b. Collect Requirements and Define Scope
   c. Develop Project Management Plan and Define Scope
   d. Identify Stakeholders and Define Scope

3. Regarding the Project Breakdown Structure, all options are true, except
   a. The project is created with the help of the project team
   b. The project is broken down to the activity level
   c. Each WBS level is a smaller part of the upper level
   d. The project includes only the work required to create deliverables

4. Which are the processes that generate inputs to the Define Scope process?
   a. Develop Project Charter and Collect Requirements
   b. Identify Stakeholders and Develop Project Charter
   c. Develop Project Management Plan and Collect Requirements
   d. Identify Stakeholders and Develop Project Management Plan

5. Which are the processes that generate inputs to the Verify Scope process?
   a. Develop Project Management Plan and Collect Requirements
   b. Develop Project Management Plan, Collect Requirements, and Perform Quality Control
   c. Collect Requirements, Create WBS, and Define Scope
   d. Collect Requirements, Perform Quality Control, and Develop Project Management Plan

6. A scope change was requested by a project stakeholder. The Change Control Board has carefully analyzed the request and decided to reject it. The project manager was upset with that decision. What is he supposed to do?

a. Support the stakeholder and ask the board for explanations

b. Record the change request and its corresponding result

c. Advise the board to create more flexible rules for approving changes

d. Tell the stakeholder that he will ensure approval of the next request

7. The document containing the scope baseline is

a. Project scope

b. Product scope statement

c. Project management plan

d. Requirements documentation

8. Processes that generate inputs to the Control Scope process are

a. Develop Project Management Plan, Direct and Manage Project Execution, and Verify Scope

b. Develop Project Management Plan, Collect Requirements, and Verify Scope

c. Direct and Manage Project Execution, Verify Scope, and Collect Requirements

d. Develop Project Management Plan, Direct and Manage Project Execution and Collect Requirements

9. The Define Scope process generates outputs that become inputs of all processes listed, except

a. Develop Project Management Plan

b. Sequence Activities

c. Estimate Activity Durations

d. Estimate Costs

10. The Define Scope process generates outputs that become inputs of all processes listed, except

a. Perform Quantitative Risk Analysis

b. Develop Schedule

c. Plan Risk Management

d. Perform Quantitative Risk Analysis

11. The major output of the Verify Scope process is

a. Change requests

b. Project scope statement update

c. Formal acceptance of deliverables by the customer

d. Change requests documents

12. The Create WBS process generates outputs that become inputs of all processes listed, except

a. Determine Budget

b. Plan Quality

c. Control Scope

d. Identify Risks

13. The Create WBS process generates outputs that become inputs of all processes listed, except

a. Develop Project Management Plan

b. Verify Scope

c. Define Activities

d. Estimate Costs

14. The project manager fails to obtain from team members adequate information on their percent of work completed. Team members claim they do not know exactly what to do and therefore cannot measure their percent of work completed. This is an example of

a. Lack of the project scope statement

b. Lack of cooperation and commitment among team members

c. Lack of the work breakdown structure

d. Lack of clarification meetings on the work

15. Only one of the processes listed receives an output from the Create WBS process. Which process is that?

a. Plan Procurements

b. Control Scope

c. Verify Scope

d. Plan Risk Management

16. The Verify Scope process provides outputs to all items listed, except

a. Project documents

b. Control Scope process

c. Close Project or Phase process

d. Perform Integrated Change Control process

17. After working with projects for several years, you have been hired as the projects general manager of a new company. Project managers in that company do not use the work breakdown structure in their projects and they think you are forcing it and causing them to perform unnecessary work. One of the convincing ways you can resort to is

a. Saying that it is not necessary in some projects

b. Saying that they can develop summarized WBSs

c. Saying that it helps them to prevent some work from being forgotten

d. Saying that it is the only way of identifying risks

18. All listed processes generate outputs that become inputs of the Verify Scope process, except

a. Develop Project Management Plan

b. Perform Quality Control

c. Create WBS

d. Collect Requirements

19. All listed processes generate outputs that become inputs of the Control Scope process, except

a. Verify Scope

b. Collect Requirements

c. Develop Project Management Plan

d. Direct and Manage Project Execution

20. In Project Scope Management, requirements documentation is an input of all the processes listed, except

a. Define Scope

b. Create WBS

c. Control Scope

d. Collect Requirements

21. All options are part of the scope baseline, except

a. Work breakdown structure

b. Product scope description

c. WBS dictionary

d. Scope management plan

22. In the Collect Requirements process, focused sessions that gather multifunctional stakeholders together to define product requirements are named:

a. Brainstorming

b. Focus groups

c. Facilitated workshops

d. Interviews

23. At what stage of the project, must the Verify Scope process be performed?

a. At the beginning of each phase of the project

b. Throughout the project

c. At the end of each phase of the project

d. During the Executing processes

24. The QFD used in the manufacturing industry, is an example of

a. Collect Requirements workshop

b. Collect Requirements brainstorming

c. Collect Requirements interview

d. Collect Requirements focus groups

25. The project manager is breaking the work down so that the scope is clearer and more manageable. He intends to present the result as a hierarchy tree structure. To what extent must he break it down?

a. Physical areas

b. Activity list

c. Schedule activities

d. Work packages

26. The Quality Function Deployment (QFD), a kind of workshop used to Collect Requirements, starts by collecting customer needs. Such customers' needs are also known as

a. Consumer Expectations (CE)

b. Customer Requirements (CR)

c. Customer Opinion (CO)

d. Voice of the Customer (VOC)

27. All of the following project management processes are related to the project scope, except

a. Define Scope

b. Define Activities

c. Create WBS

d. Collect Requirements

28. A new team member has asked the project manager which document contained detailed descriptions of work packages. What must the manager have shown that member?

a. Project scope statement

b. WBS dictionary

c. Scope management plan

d. Activity list

29. All of the following options are inputs of the Define Scope process, except

a. Project charter

b. Requirements documentation

c. Stakeholder register

d. Organizational process assets

30. All of the following options are outputs of the Collect Requirements process, except

a. Requirements management plan

b. Requirements documentation

c. Project document updates

d. Requirements traceability matrix

31. The project manager is sought by a team member who suggests an improvement to the scope that, despite being beyond the scope defined in the project charter, will be welcomed by the customer. The manager responds to the member that the team must focus on developing the entire project work and only on the required work. This answer from the manager is an example of

a. Effective change management

b. Change analysis

c. Scope decomposition

d. Scope management

32. All of the following options are outputs of the Create WBS process, except

a. Work Breakdown Structure

b. WBS dictionary

c. Project scope statement

d. Scope baseline

33. A PMP® professional is trying to convince the new project manager of the company to develop the Work Breakdown Structure, as the latter is struggling to view the project scope. In his attempt, one of the arguments upheld by the PMP® professional is saying that the WBS can be used to

a. Show the individuals responsible for each work package

b. Communicate with the customer

c. Show details of work packages

d. Show the project business need

34. All of the following options are not tools or techniques of the Collect Requirements process, except

a. Interviews

b. Requirements documentation

c. Project scope statement

d. Stakeholder register

35. All of the following options are not tools or techniques of the Define Scope process, except

a. Decomposition

b. Product analysis

c. Scope statement

d. Stakeholder register

36. All of the following options are not tools or techniques of the Create WBS process, except

a. Expert judgment

b. Alternatives identification

c. Product analysis

d. Decomposition

37. All of the following options are not outputs of the Define Scope process, except

a. Requirements documentation

b. Past projects scope

c. Procedure to define project scopes

d. Product scope description

38. All of the following options are outputs of the Create WBS process, except

a. Scope baseline

b. Product scope description

c. Decomposition

d. Activity list

39. All of the following options are inputs of the Verify Scope process, except

a. Project management plan

b. Requirements documentation

c. Requirements traceability matrix

d. Accepted deliverables

40. All of the following options are not tools or techniques of the Verify Scope process, except

a. Requirements analysis

b. Inspection

c. WBS analysis

d. Baseline analysis

41. All of the following options are outputs of the Verify Scope process, except

a. Accepted deliverables

b. Project document updates

c. Validated deliverables

d. Change requests

42. The WBS can be better expressed as an effective aid to communication among the

a. Project team

b. Project stakeholders

c. Project customer and manager

d. Project manager and team

43. All of the following options are not tools or techniques of the Control Scope process, except

a. Work performance measurements

b. Variance analysis

c. Requirements documentation

d. Change requests

Answer key

Supplementary exercises

2. 1 - Technique - Create WBS

2 - Technique - Control Scope

3 - Outputs - Verify Scope

4 - Output - Collect Requirements

5 - Output -Define Scope

6 - Input - Create WBS

7 - Tool/Technique - Define Scope

8 - Output - Create WBS

9 - Input - Define Scope

10 - Output - Collect Requirements

11 - Input - Verify Scope and Control Scope

12 - Techniques - Collect Requirements

13 - Inputs - Verify Scope

14 - Techniques - Define Scope

15 - Tool - Verify Scope

Questions

1. D. Create WBS is the process immediately preceding the Verify Scope process, taking into account the Project Scope Management. Note the following: requirements are first collected before defining the project scope. Afterward, the WBS is developed. Other processes will be developed for the project work execution. In terms of scope, the next process is Verify Scope (formalizing deliverables acceptance and revision) and Control Scope (monitoring the project and product scope progress and managing scope baseline changes).

2. B. Collect Requirements process generates the requirements documentation input, and Define Scope process generates the Project scope statement.

3. B. WBS is deployed only to the work packages level and provides the basis for the schedule activities list.

4. A. Develop Project Charter process generates project charter input, and Collect Requirements process generates the requirements documentation input.

5. B. Processes generating inputs to the Verify Scope process are Plan project management (scope baseline), Perform Quality Control (validated deliverables), and Collect Requirements (requirements documentation and requirements traceability matrix).

6. B. With regards to option A: The board, when approving or rejecting a request, usually defines the criteria for approving or rejecting the requested change. Supporting the stakeholder is valid, provided it shows no disrespect to the board decision. With regards to option C: "flexible" rules to approve the changes will inevitably increase the project scope and costs. Regarding option D: the project manager cannot promise approval of any change! This is the role of the Change Control Board. What the project manager must do is accept the board decision.

7. C. The project management plan contains the scope baseline, comprising Project scope statement, WBS, and WBS dictionary.

8. D. Processes generating inputs to the Control Scope process are Develop Project Management Plan (project management plan), Direct and Manage Project Execution (work performance information), Collect Requirements (requirements documentation, requirements traceability matrix).

9. D. The Define Scope process does not generate outputs to the Estimate Costs process. It provides the Project scope statement output to the following processes: Create WBS, Develop Project Management Plan, Sequence Activities, Estimate Activity Durations, Develop Schedule, Plan Risk Management, and Perform Qualitative Risk Analysis.

10. A. The Define Scope process does not generate outputs to the Perform Quantitative Risk Analysis process. It provides the Project scope statement output to the following processes: Create WBS, Develop Project Management Plan, Sequence Activities, Estimate Activity Durations, Develop Schedule, Plan Risk Management and Perform Qualitative Risk Analysis.

11. C. In the exam, remember: the major output of the Verify Scope process is "to obtain formal acceptance of deliverables by the customer."

12. C. The Create WBS process does not generate a direct output to the Control Scope process. It provides the Scope baseline output to the following processes: Develop Project Management Plan, Define Activities, Estimate Costs, Determine Budget, Plan Quality, Identify Risks, and Plan Procurements.

13. B. The Create WBS process does not generate a direct output to the Verify Scope process. It provides the Scope baseline output to the following processes: Develop Project Management Plan, Define Activities, Estimate Costs, Determine Budget, Plan Quality, Identify Risks, and Plan Procurements.

14. C. The Project scope statement process defines the high-level work, not being the best option. Lack of cooperation and commitment may occur, but dealing only with that will not "show" work packages. Lack of meetings can also jeopardize the project progress, but meetings alone will not show work packages. What team members are actually lacking to "view" the work is the Work Breakdown Structure, which defines work packages.

15. A. Out of the processes listed, the only one receiving the Scope baseline output of the Create WBS process is Plan Procurements. In addition to that process, the other ones receiving the same output are Develop Project Management Plan, Define Activities, Estimate Costs, Determine Budget, Plan Quality, and Identify Risks.

16. B. The Verify Scope process does not provide outputs to the Control Scope process. It provides the Change requests output to the Perform Integrated Change Control process, the Accepted deliverables output to the Close Project or Phase process, and the Project document updates output to the project documents.

17. C. Option A is not valid: the WBS is required for all projects. Option B is not valid: there is no summarized WBS. It must show work packages, nothing less than that. Option D states that the WBS is the only way to Identify Risks. The WBS helps identifying risks by work package, but there are other ways to Identify Risks. One of the reasons to use the WBS is prevent any work from being forgotten.

18. C. The Create WBS process does not directly provide an output to the Verify Scope process. It receives the Scope baseline output (which contains the WBS) of the Develop Project Management Plan process, the Validated deliverables output of the Perform Quality Control process, and the Requirements documentation and requirements traceability matrix outputs of the Collect Requirements process.

19. A. The Verify Scope process provides an output to the Control Scope process. The Scope control process receives the Project management plan output from the Develop Project Management Plan process, the Work performance information output from the Direct and Manage Project Execution process, and the Requirements documentation and requirements traceability matrix outputs from the Collect Requirements process.

20. D. Requirements documentation is an output of the Collect Requirements process and an input to all other Project Scope Management processes.

21. D. Scope management plan is not part of the scope baseline.

22. C. Focused sessions that gather multifunctional stakeholders together to define product requirements are named facilitated workshops.

23. C. One of the outputs of the Verify Scope process is the formalization of deliverables, which occur at the end of each project phase – e.g., at the end of design, at the end of execution, at the end of tests, C is the best answer.

24. A. The QFD, used in the manufacturing industry, is an example of a Collect Requirements workshop.

25. D. What the manager is elaborating is the Work Breakdown Structure! The WBS last level of decomposition includes work packages.

26. D. Customer needs are also known as Voice of the Customer (VOC).

27. B. The Define Activities process is part of the Time area of knowledge.

28. B. The WBS dictionary shows descriptions of each element (work package) of the WBS. The other options do not have descriptive details of work packages.

29. C. Stakeholder register was dealt with in the previous process (Collect Requirements), which generated an output named Requirements documentation. Therefore, there is no need to review it once again.

30. C. Remember: from all five Project Scope Management processes, the one with outputs not containing project document updates is Collect Requirements. When requirements are collected, it is necessary to define how they will be documented, tracked and managed.

31. D. Scope management involves focusing on getting the work done in order to achieve the objectives defined in the project charter and no additional work - this is scope management.

32. C. The Project scope statement is defined in the Define Scope process and is an input of the Create WBS process.

33. B. The WBS does not show title names (that is developed in human resource plan). Details of work packages are shown at the WBS dictionary. The project business need is shown in the project charter. The WBS is aimed to facilitate communication among all stakeholders, including the customer.

34. A. The question, asked more clearly, is "Which of the following options IS a tool or technique of the Collect Requirements process?" In the exam, remember: requirements documentation, scope statement and stakeholder register are NOT tools or techniques of any project management process! They are either inputs or outputs! Interviews are techniques of the Collect requirements process.

35. B. The question, asked more clearly, is "Which of the following options IS a tool or technique of the Define Scope process?" Note that the scope statement and the stakeholder register are "documents", not tools and techniques! Decomposition is a technique of the Create WBS process. Product analysis is one of the tools and techniques of the Define Scope process.

36. D. The question, asked more clearly, is "Which of the following options IS a tool or technique of the Create WBS process?" Remember this for the exam: the only technique used in the Create WBS process is decomposition! The other options are tools or techniques of other processes.

37. D. The question, asked more clearly, is "Which of the following options IS an output of the Define Scope process?" The major product (output) of the Define Scope process is the Project scope statement. Requirements documentation is performed in the Collect Requirements process and is an input of the Define Scope process. Questions B and C refer to organizational process assets, which are inputs of Project Management processes.

38. A. The question, asked more clearly, is "Which of the following options IS an output of the Create WBS process?" The statement of work scope is defined in the Define Scope process. Decomposition is a technique of the Create WBS process, not an output. The activity list is only elaborated afterward, in the Define Activities process. The scope baseline (Project scope statement, WBS, and WBS dictionary) is a process output.

39. D. Verify Scope is the process of formalizing acceptance of completed deliverables of the project. Therefore, option D is a process output.

40. B. Remember for the exam: the only tool of Verify Scope process is the inspection!

41. A. Let us understand the process:

    1. The project team developed a delivery.

2. The delivery was validated by the quality control team (sometimes by a project external team) in the Perform Quality Control process. This resulted in a validated deliverable – process input.
3. The project team conducted inspection of the delivery with regards to acceptance requirements and acceptance of the product – a process tool.
4. The team delivered it to the sponsor or customer and received the receipt formal documentation (if accepted by the sponsor or customer) – this resulted in an accepted deliverable – a process output.

42. B. "Stakeholders" includes all of the other options. All stakeholders can benefit from communications through the WBS.

43. B. The question, asked more clearly, is "Which option is tool of the Control Scope process?" Remember during the exam: the term "analysis" always refers to the tool and the technique. Variance analysis is the only tool in the process.

Chapter 6

PROJECT TIME MANAGEMENT

1. Introduction
2. Project Time Management processes
3. Time management in project planning
4. Time management in project monitoring and controlling

Attachment I	Project Planning concepts and techniques
Attachment II	Supplementary reading on activity resource estimates
Attachment III	Supplementary reading on activity duration estimates
Attachment IV	Supplementary reading on network diagrams
Attachment V	Supplementary reading on bar schedule
Attachment VI	Supplementary reading on critical chain method

- Additional information and reminders for the exam
- Supplementary exercises
- Questions
- Answer key

6.1 INTRODUCTION

This chapter will introduce the project management processes in the Time knowledge area, their relevant inputs, tools, techniques, and outputs.

6.2 PROJECT TIME MANAGEMENT PROCESSES

According to *PMBOK® Guide*, the Project Time Management includes the processes required to manage the project timely completion.

Project Time Management processes are

- **Define Activities**

  The process of identifying particular actions to be performed to produce the project deliverables.

- **Sequence Activities**

  The process of identifying and recording relationships among project activities.

- **Estimate Activity Resources**

  The process of estimating types and quantities of materials, people, equipment, or supplies to be required to complete particular activities with the estimated resources.

- **Estimate Activity Durations**

  The process of estimating, as closely as possible, the number of work periods to be required to complete particular activities with the estimated resources.

- **Develop Schedule**

  The process of analyzing activity sequences, their durations, required resources, and schedule constraints in order to create the project schedule.

- **Control Schedule**

  It is the process of monitoring the project toward its progress as well as managing changes to the schedule baseline.

The following flowchart displays the relationship among the Project Time Management processes and their locations across the project management process groups.

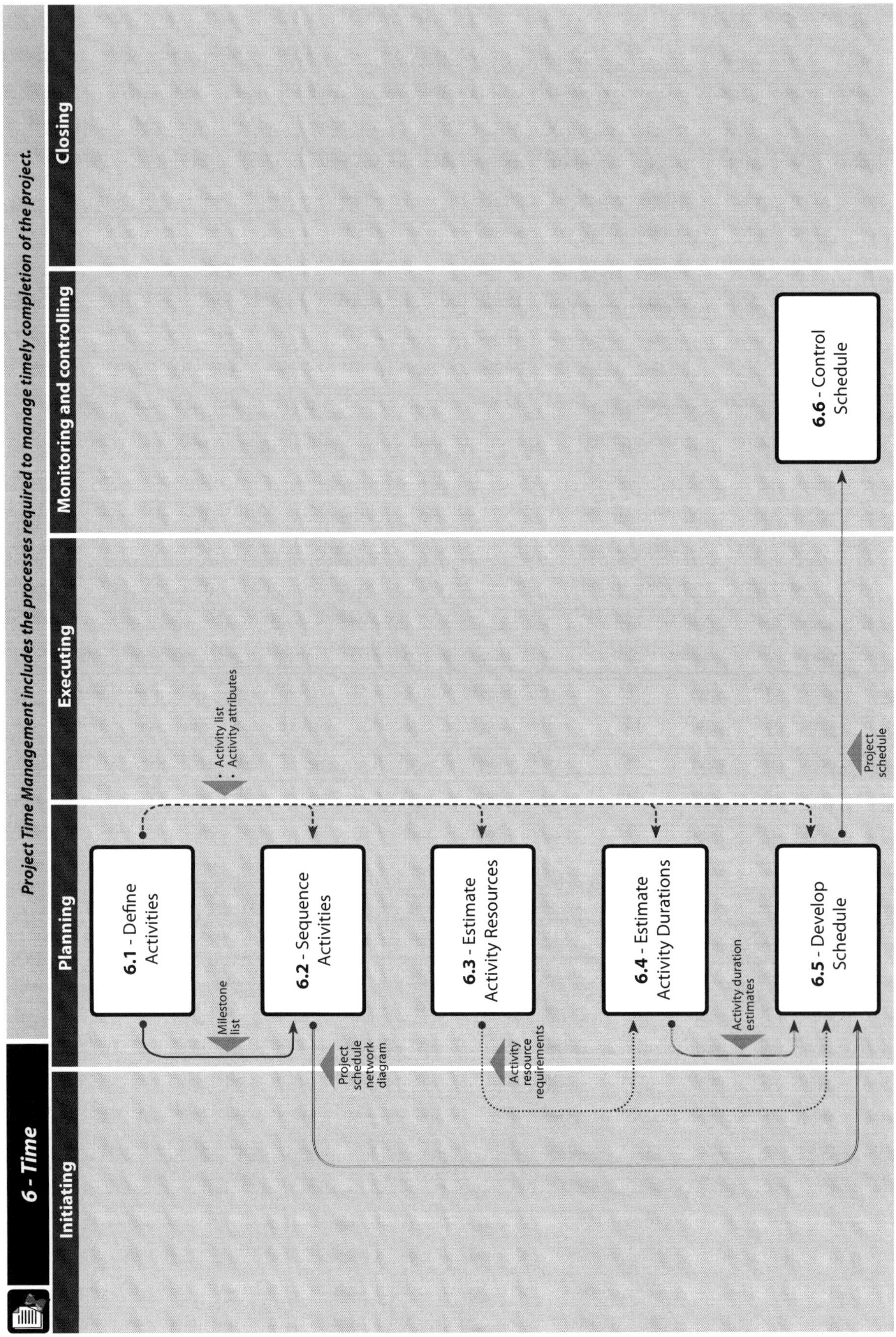

6 - Time
Project Time Management includes the processes required to manage timely completion of the project.
Initiating
Planning
Executing
Monitoring and controlling
Closing
6.1 - Define Activities
6.2 - Sequence Activities
6.3 - Estimate Activity Resources
6.4 - Estimate Activity Durations
6.5 - Develop Schedule
6.6 - Control Schedule
• Activity list
• Activity attributes
Milestone list
Project schedule network diagram
Activity resource requirements
Activity duration estimates
Project schedule

6.3 TIME MANAGEMENT IN PROJECT PLANNING

According to PMI®, the time integration in project Planning comprising five processes, namely

- ***Define Activities***
- ***Sequence Activities***
- ***Estimate Activity Resources***
- ***Estimate Activity Durations***
- ***Develop Schedule***

6.3.1 DEFINE ACTIVITIES (*PMBOK® GUIDE*, PROCESS 6.1)

Activity definition is developing the work packages defined in the Work Breakdown Structure in more easily manageable schedule activities representing the project deliverables. Activities must reach a level at which it is possible to estimate the activity duration and resources that can be monitored and controlled in the schedule.

6.3.1.1 DEFINE ACTIVITIES: INPUTS, TOOLS AND TECHNIQUES, AND OUTPUTS

INPUTS

1 **Scope baseline**

The scope baseline, comprised by the project scope statement, the WBS, and the WBS dictionary must be considered as an input in this process.

2 **Enterprise environmental factors**

Enterprise environmental factors, including the management information systems of projects and software applications, must be considered when defining activities.

3 **Organizational process assets**

Organizational process assets, including policies and procedures as well as lessons learned when defining activities of other projects, must be considered when defining such activities.

TOOLS AND TECHNIQUES

1 **Decomposition**

Decomposition is subdividing work packages into smaller more easily manageable components to comprise the schedule activities. In general, decomposition is performed by performers or individuals responsible for work packages.

2 **Rolling wave planning**

Rolling wave planning is planning progressive elaboration as information on activities becomes more detailed. Therefore, activities to be performed in the short term may be detailed in the schedule, while little known activities to be developed in the long term can be maintained at the milestone level until detailed information is made available.

3 **Templates**

Activity lists from previous projects or activity list templates developed by the company can be used in order to make the project activity list development easier. What is important when using activity list templates from previous projects is verifying the previous project peculiarities and characteristics not to cause erroneous interpretations when defining activities of the current project.

4 **Expert judgment**

Team members who participated in other projects and consultants can help define the project activities.

OUTPUTS

1 **Activity list**

Activity list is a list of all planned activities to be performed in the project. Schedule activities, obtained from the decomposition of work packages, are not part of the WBS. According to the rolling wave Planning concept, it may be necessary to revise the activity list as the project progresses, by including new activities or deleting activities removed from the project scope.

2 **Activity attributes**

Attributes are descriptive and explanatory supplements of the activity. Activity attributes may include the following:

- **Activity identifier**

  Usually this attribute is derived from the classification system generally used by the company in all projects. For example, a construction company may have a group of masonry services, and, within such group, each type of masonry has an identification code used in all company projects.

- **Activity code**

  This attribute is used to identify which WBS work package contains the schedule activity. The activity code generally supplements the WBS work package code. For example, the equipment assembly work package of Area 02 of an industry being implemented is coded EA.02 (with EA meaning **e**quipment **a**ssembly and 02 indicating the area); assembling a centrifugal pump (an schedule activity) in this area could be coded EA.02.BB-001 (with BB-001 being the pump tag or identifier).

- **Other attributes**

  Other attributes of the activity are also indicated, such as activity description, predecessor and successor activities, logical relationships with other activities, required resources, imposed dates, constraints, and assumptions defined for the activity.

3 **Milestone list**

The milestone list displays all milestones set on a contractual basis and those defined in the project requirements by historical information or expert judgment. Therefore, it may enlist project phases, a phase start or end, area release dates for work start-up, among others.

TIME

6.1 - Define Activities

Planning

The process of identifying the specific actions to be performed to produce the project deliverables.

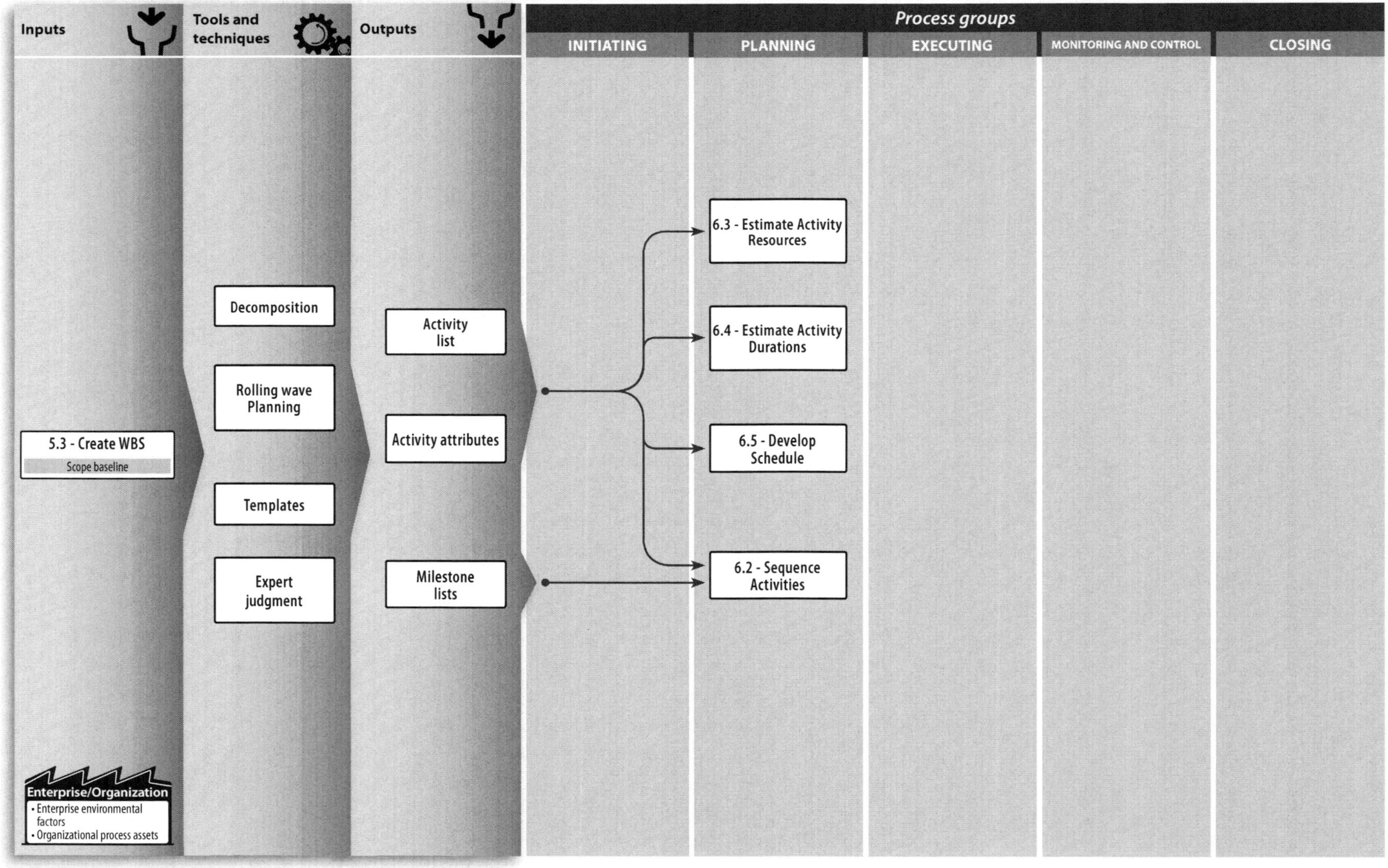

6.3.2 SEQUENCE ACTIVITIES (*PMBOK® GUIDE*, PROCESS 6.2)

Sequence Activities involves identifying and recording logical relationships among schedule activities. The ultimate goal of sequencing activities is having a network diagram with all project activities and their relationships to be used as a support to obtain a realistic and achievable schedule. When sequencing activities, the application of activity leads or delays must also be considered, according to the execution possibilities and constraints of each activity. Therefore, sequencing must be performed by individuals with technical skill to perform particular services of activities.

Sequence Activities can be performed manually or through particular software applications generally available on the market. Manual diagram elaboration requires much work and must be only applied to small projects.

6.3.2.1 SEQUENCE ACTIVITIES: INPUTS, TOOLS AND TECHNIQUES, AND OUTPUTS

INPUTS

1 **Activity list**

The activity list is one of the major inputs of sequencing activities.

2 **Activity attributes**

Activity attributes are also the major inputs of the sequencing activities.

3 **Milestone list**

The milestone list is also one of the major inputs of sequencing activities.

4 **Project scope statement**

The project scope statement, including deliverables, assumptions, and constraints, must be considered when sequencing activities.

5 **Organizational process assets**

The organizational process assets, including procedures and policies as well as lessons learned when sequencing activities of other projects, must be considered in this process.

TOOLS AND TECHNIQUES

1 **Precedence Diagramming Method (PDM)**

The PDM is a tool for implementing a network diagram that uses nodes (or boxes) to represent activities whose interdependencies are connected by arrows.

Attachment IV contains supplementary reading on precedence diagrams

2 **Dependency determination**

Three types of dependencies are used to define the sequence of activities: mandatory dependencies, arbitrated dependencies, and external dependencies.

Attachment I contains supplementary reading on dependencies

3 **Applying leads and lags**

Applying a lead (also referred to as lead time) to an activity enables anticipating that activity in time. Applying a lag (also referred to as lead time) to an activity enables anticipating that activity in time.

Attachment I contains supplementary reading on leads and lags

4 **Schedule network templates**

Network diagrams from previous projects or network diagram templates developed by the company can be used in order to make the project network diagram development easier. What is important when using network diagram templates from previous project is verifying the previous project peculiarities and characteristics not to cause erroneous interpretations when defining activities of the current project.

OUTPUTS

1 **Project schedule network diagrams**

(see Attachment IV of this chapter).

2 **Project document updates**

Some project documents can be updated, such as

- Activity list,
- Activity attributes, and
- Risk register.

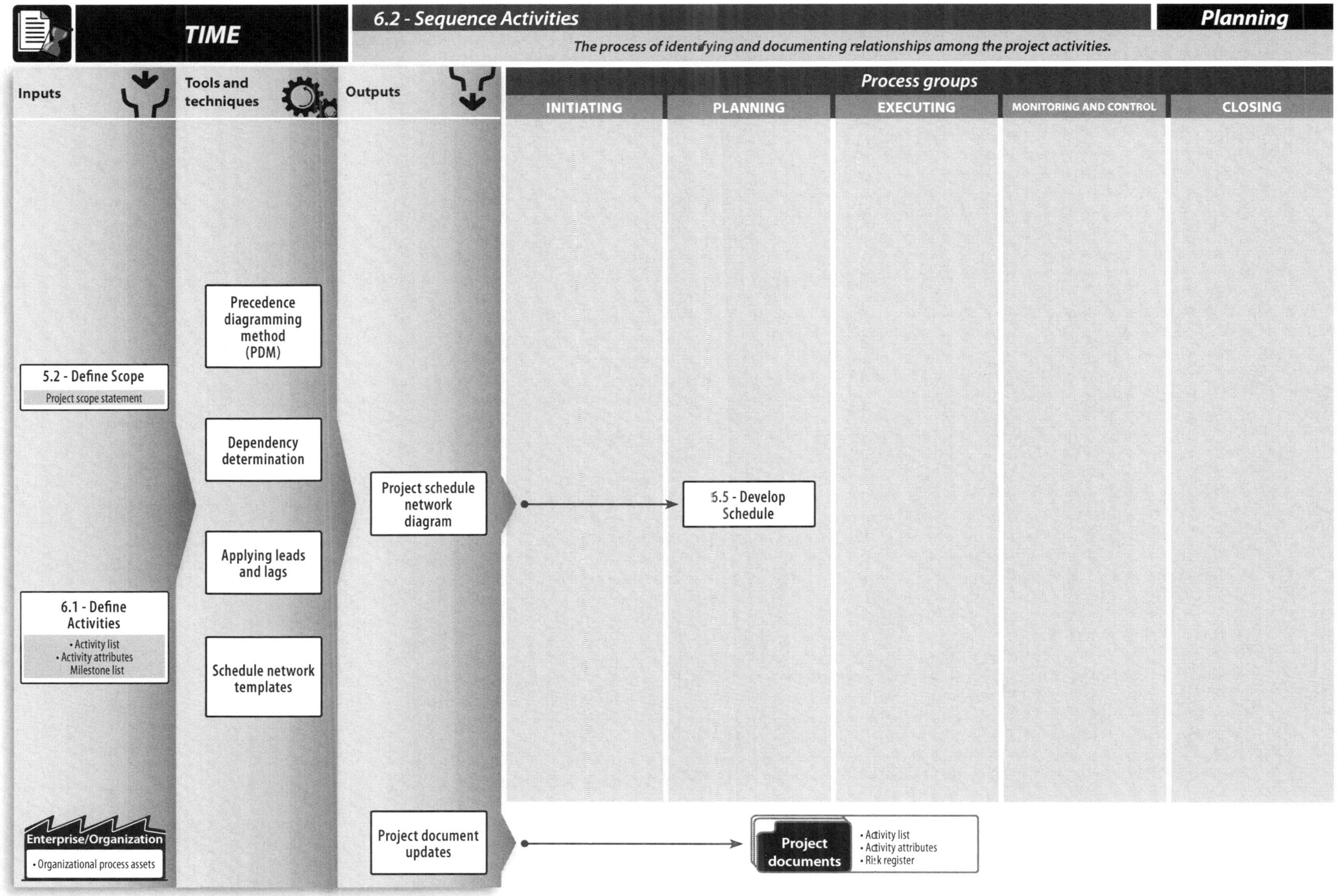
TIME
6.2 - Sequence Activities
Planning
The process of identifying and documenting relationships among the project activities.
Inputs
Tools and techniques
Outputs
Process groups
INITIATING
PLANNING
EXECUTING
MONITORING AND CONTROL
CLOSING
5.2 - Define Scope
Project scope statement
6.1 - Define Activities
• Activity list
• Activity attributes
Milestone list
Enterprise/Organization
• Organizational process assets
Precedence diagramming method (PDM)
Dependency determination
Applying leads and lags
Schedule network templates
Project schedule network diagram
Project document updates
6.5 - Develop Schedule
Project documents
• Activity list
• Activity attributes
• Risk register

6.3.3 ESTIMATE ACTIVITY RESOURCES (*PMBOK® GUIDE*, PROCESS 6.3)

Resources are any facilitators contributing to the activity execution and can be divided into three types: human resources, equipment resources, and material resources.

Estimate resource activities involve determining which resources and how many and when they must be available for the activity execution.

> ***Attachment II contains supplementary reading on resource estimating***

6.3.3.1 ESTIMATE ACTIVITY RESOURCES: INPUTS, TOOLS AND TECHNIQUES, AND OUTPUTS

INPUTS

1 **Activity list**

The activity list presented earlier in this chapter identifies activities that will require resources.

2 **Activity attributes**

Activity attributes presented earlier in this chapter provide information on activities and the resources they will require.

3 **Resource calendars**

The resource calendar informs the existence and availability of the resources required to perform the activity, either within the company or by external agents. For resources from the company itself, the quantity and time of use must be set, and the internal acceptance from resource providers must be obtained. For resources from external sources, at the time of purchase or contract, the quantity and period of use of each resource must be recorded.

4 **Enterprise environmental factors**

Enterprise environmental factors can provide information on resource availability, skills of available resources, among others.

5 **Organizational process assets**

Organizational process assets can contribute information on labor productivity as well as equipment and information about the equipment purchase or lease.

TOOLS AND TECHNIQUES

1 **Expert judgment**

Team members, individuals who participated in other projects and consultants can help estimate the project activity resources.

2 **Alternative analysis**

The alternative analysis is the technique of raising alternative possibilities for the activity execution, which may change the type and quantity of resources to be used. The abovementioned expert judgment may submit and analyze such alternatives.

3 **Published estimating data**

Some technical books and journals publish data on the composition of services that can be used in activity resource estimating.

4 **Bottom-up estimating**

Bottom-up estimating is a resource estimating technique that considers recognizing the need for more detailed resources at each activity. At each level, resources are accrued to comprise the estimating at the next higher level until the activity estimating level is reached.

5 **Project management software**

Project management softwares can help classifying, planning, and managing resources.

OUTPUTS

1 **Activity resource requirements**

The recognition of the resources required for the activity is the goal of this process. Such recognition determines the types and quantities of resources required for each schedule activity. Determination of when resources to be required will be obtained with the Develop Schedule process.

2 **Resource Breakdown Structure (RBS)**

RBS is a hierarchical representation of resources required to develop activities, separated by resource category and type. Similar to an organization chart, RBSs are used to enable easy viewing of resources to be used. The most widely used is the human resources RBS, but equipment and material resources RBSs can be employed too.

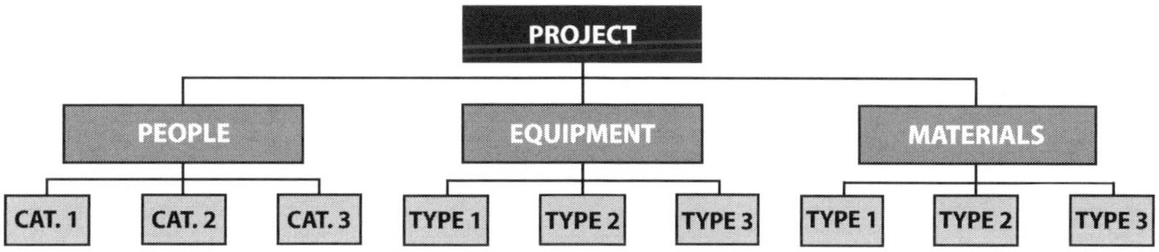

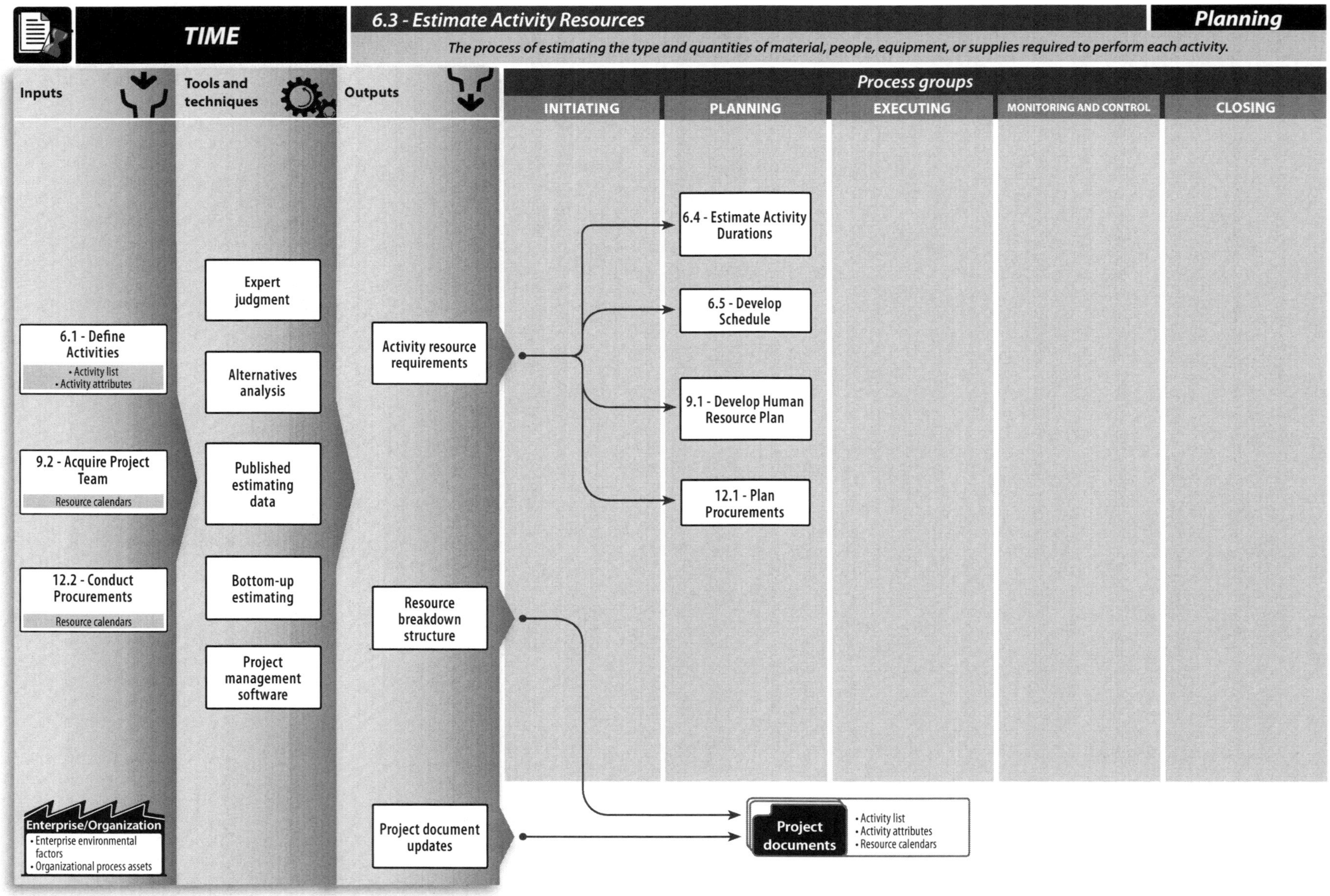
TIME
6.3 - Estimate Activity Resources
Planning
The process of estimating the type and quantities of material, people, equipment, or supplies required to perform each activity.
Inputs
Tools and techniques
Outputs
Process groups
INITIATING
PLANNING
EXECUTING
MONITORING AND CONTROL
CLOSING
6.1 - Define Activities
• Activity list
• Activity attributes
9.2 - Acquire Project Team
Resource calendars
12.2 - Conduct Procurements
Resource calendars
Enterprise/Organization
• Enterprise environmental factors
• Organizational process assets
Expert judgment
Alternatives analysis
Published estimating data
Bottom-up estimating
Project management software
Activity resource requirements
Resource breakdown structure
Project document updates
6.4 - Estimate Activity Durations
6.5 - Develop Schedule
9.1 - Develop Human Resource Plan
12.1 - Plan Procurements
Project documents
• Activity list
• Activity attributes
• Resource calendars

3 **Project document updates**

Some project documents must be updated, such as

- Activity list,
- Activity attributes, and
- Resource calendar.

6.3.4 ESTIMATE ACTIVITY DURATIONS (*PMBOK® GUIDE*, PROCESS 6.4)

Estimate Activity Durations consists in determining the number of time periods required to perform the activity, based on the activity quantity of work and the quantity of required and available resources.

6.3.4.1 ESTIMATE ACTIVITY DURATIONS: INPUTS, OUTPUTS AND TOOLS AND TECHNIQUES

INPUTS

1 **Activity list**

The activity list, described earlier in this chapter, must be taken into account in this process.

2 **Activity attributes**

Activity attributes must be considered in this process.

3 **Activity resource requirements**

The estimated activity duration must consider the resources required to perform the activity.

4 **Resource calendars**

The estimated duration must consider the availability calendar of resources required to perform the activity.

5 **Project scope statement**

In addition to other pieces of information contained in the project scope statement, constraints on delivery dates must be considered when estimating the activity duration.

6 **Enterprise environmental factors**

Enterprise environmental factors can provide information that can influence the estimated activity duration.

7 **Organizational process assets**

Organizational process assets can contribute information on durations of similar activities in previous projects, information on labor productivity as well as equipment, and information related to the periods of time required to allocate resources to activities.

TOOLS AND TECHNIQUES

1 **Expert judgment**

Team members, individuals who participated in other projects, and consultants can help estimate the project activity resources.

2 **Analogous estimating**

Analogous estimating, also referred to as top-down estimating, is a technique commonly used in the project initial phase, when there is no detailed information on the activities. In this technique, the identification, in previous projects, of activities similar to those of the project in question, is used to assume the activity duration.

Attachment III contains supplementary reading on analogous estimating

3 **Parametric estimating**

Activity duration parametric estimating applies productivity rates in the work formula, with such indices being defined through product mass studies.

Attachment III contains supplementary reading on parametric estimating

4 **Three-point estimates**

Consideration of risks in activity duration estimates can be performed using the so-called three-point estimating technique, applied to values obtained both from analogous estimating and parametric estimating.

Attachment III contains supplementary reading on three-point estimating

5 **Reserves analysis**

Reserves are duration lungs estimated for the project in order to anticipate unknown risk events that might delay the duration of some activities. Such reserves are estimated for the project as a whole and are not estimated individually for each activity. As the project progresses, such reserves are reviewed and changed to longer or shorter time, when more accurate information on the project is known.

OUTPUTS

1 **Activity duration estimates**

Activity duration estimates are quantitative assessments of the likely number of work periods to be required to complete an activity. Duration estimates do not include any lag. They may include a few indications of the range of potential results. For instance,

- 2 weeks ± 2 days to indicate that the activity will take at least 8 days and no more than 12 (assuming a 5 day workweek);
- 15% probability of exceeding 3 weeks to indicate a high probability - 85% - that the activity will take 3 weeks or less.

2 **Project document updates**

Some project documents must be updated, such as

- Activity attributes. Activity attributes changed by change requests approved in the Estimate Activity Durations process must be updated. Such changes to attributes can occur by applying estimating techniques, by expert judgment or by the estimating itself, which may change the resource type.
- Assumptions learned from developing the estimated activity duration as skill levels and resource availability.

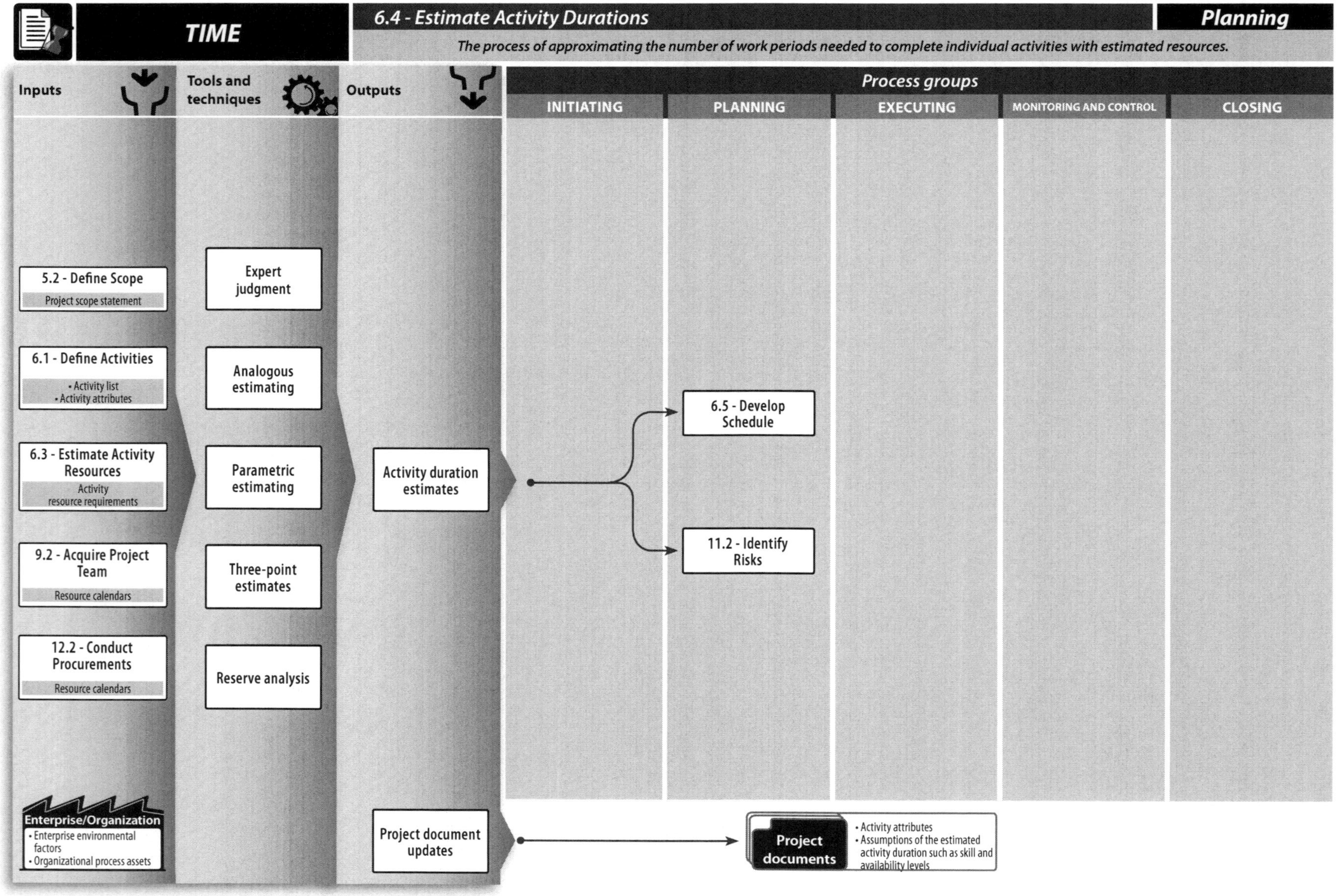
TIME
6.4 - Estimate Activity Durations
Planning
The process of approximating the number of work periods needed to complete individual activities with estimated resources.
Inputs
Tools and techniques
Outputs
Process groups
INITIATING
PLANNING
EXECUTING
MONITORING AND CONTROL
CLOSING
5.2 - Define Scope
Project scope statement
6.1 - Define Activities
• Activity list
• Activity attributes
6.3 - Estimate Activity Resources
Activity resource requirements
9.2 - Acquire Project Team
Resource calendars
12.2 - Conduct Procurements
Resource calendars
Enterprise/Organization
• Enterprise environmental factors
• Organizational process assets
Expert judgment
Analogous estimating
Parametric estimating
Three-point estimates
Reserve analysis
Activity duration estimates
Project document updates
6.5 - Develop Schedule
11.2 - Identify Risks
Project documents
• Activity attributes
• Assumptions of the estimated activity duration such as skill and availability levels

6.3.5 DEVELOP SCHEDULE (*PMBOK® GUIDE*, PROCESS 6.5)

Develop Schedule means setting start and end dates to project activities. Although the schedule development continues throughout the project, the objective in this process is obtaining a schedule that is well accepted, approved, realistic, and formal.

Refer to attachments to this chapter

6.3.5.1 DEVELOP SCHEDULE: INPUTS, TOOLS AND TECHNIQUES, AND OUTPUTS

INPUTS

1 **Activity list**

Earlier described in this chapter.

2 **Activity attributes**

Earlier described in this chapter.

3 **Project schedule network diagrams**

Earlier described in this chapter.

4 **Activity resource requirements**

Earlier described in this chapter.

5 **Resource calendars**

Earlier described in this chapter.

6 **Activity duration estimates**

Earlier described in this chapter.

7 **Project scope statement**

In addition to other pieces of information contained in the project scope statement, constraints on delivery dates must be considered in this process.

8 **Enterprise environmental factors**

Enterprise environmental factors can provide information, such as which schedule execution tool must to be used, among others.

9 **Organizational process assets**

Organizational process assets can provide information on the project calendar, such as workdays and days when activities are not developed as well as a shift calendar.

TOOLS AND TECHNIQUES

All tools and techniques have been listed in this section and presented in detail in the attachments to this chapter.

1 **Schedule network analysis**

2 **Critical path method**

3 **Critical chain method**

4 **Resource leveling**

5 **What-if scenario analysis**

6 **Applying leads and lags**

7 **Schedule compression**

8 **Scheduling tool**

OUTPUTS

1 **Project schedule**

The project schedule must set a project start date and an end date. In general, it is graphically represented and in one of the following formats:

Network diagram

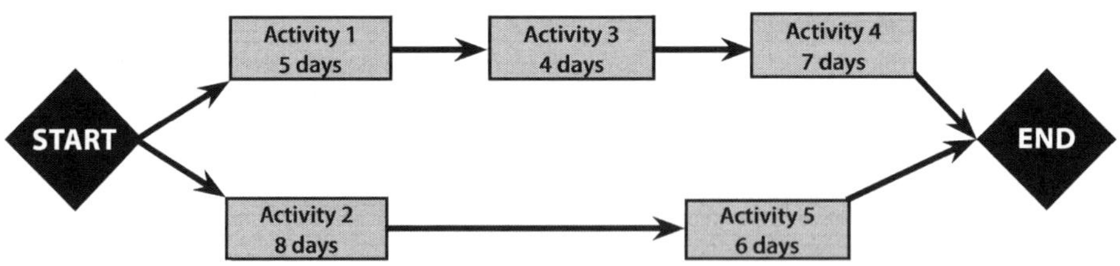

Bar chart

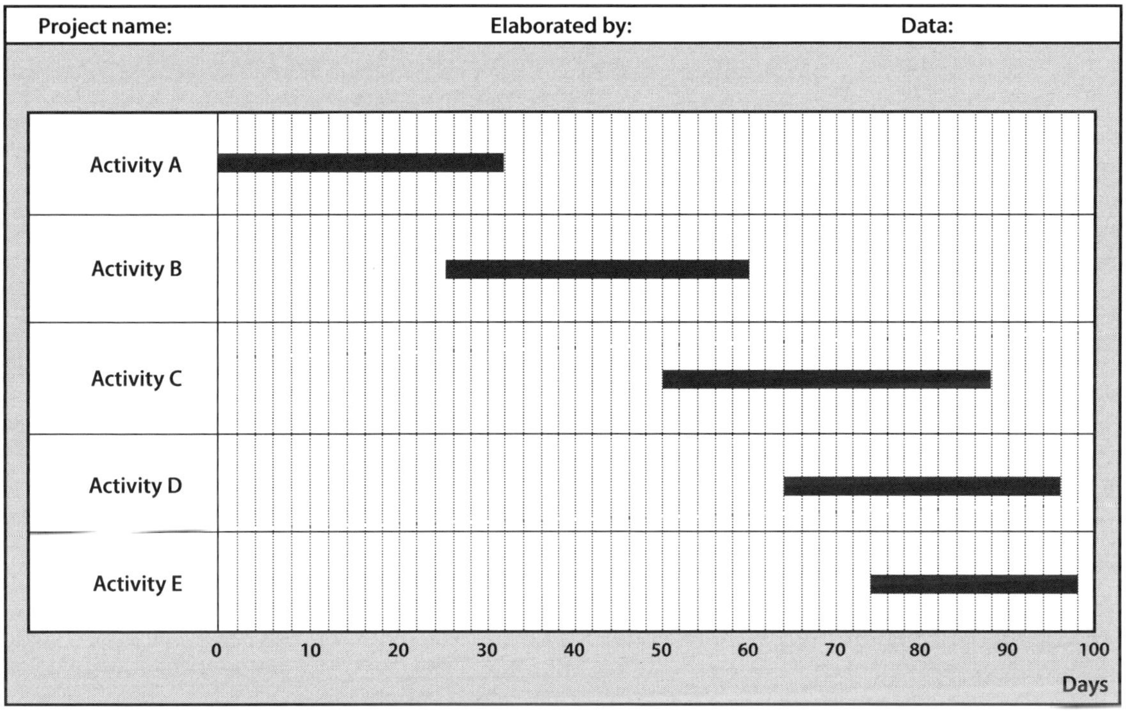

Milestone charts

Project name: Elaborated by: Data:

Event	Jan	Feb	Mar	Apr	May	Jun	Jul	Aug
Sign the contract			△▼					
Complete the specifications				△				
Revise the drawing					△			
Teste the subsystem						△		
Production - 1st delivery							△	
Complete the production plan								△

Planned = △
Current = ▼

2 **Schedule baseline**

The schedule baseline is a schedule version accepted and approved by the project team and will be the basis for comparing the project progress.

3 **Schedule data**

The schedule data includes all information influencing the schedule development, such as assumptions and constraints, attributes, activity attributes, calendars, resources, reserves and others.

4 **Project document updates**

During the project schedule execution, changes to resources initially scheduled may occur, mainly due to the resource leveling process. Such changes can be related to the resource type, the quantity scheduled, or even the addition of new features. Therefore, some project documents must be updated as

- Activity resource requirements,
- Activity attributes,
- Project calendar, and
- Risk register.

TIME

6.5 - Develop Schedule

Planning

The process of analyzing activity sequences, durations, resource requirements, and schedule constraints to create the project schedule.

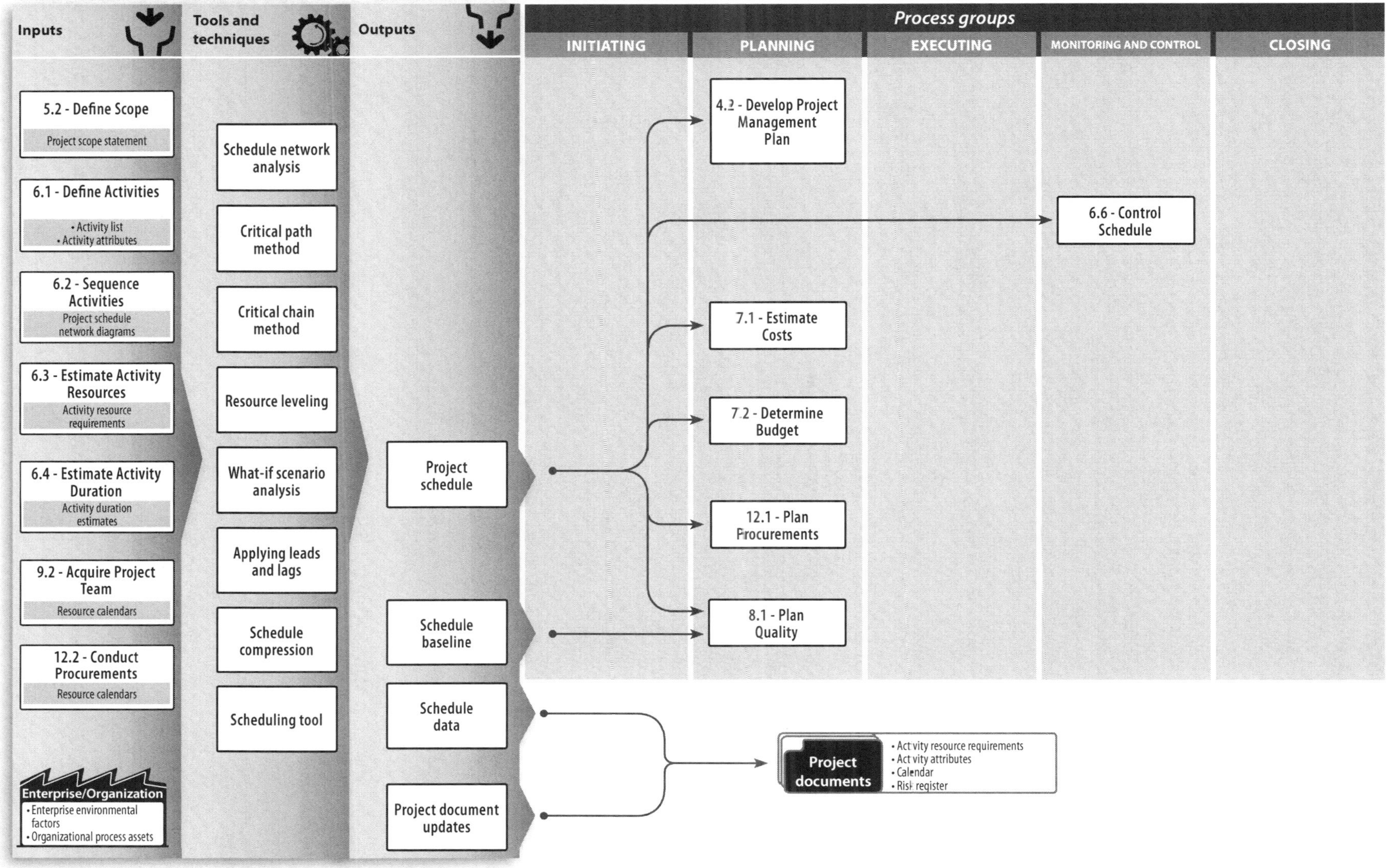

6.4 TIME MANAGEMENT IN PROJECT MONITORING AND CONTROLLING

According to PMI®, the time management in project monitoring and controlling is composed of the following process:

- ***Control Schedule***

6.4.1 CONTROL SCHEDULE (*PMBOK® GUIDE*, PROCESS 6.6)

Control Schedule is the process of monitoring the project progress and managing changes to the schedule baseline. Schedule control uses particular tools, such as comparison bar charts, progress lines, deviation charts, and the network diagram. When recovering from lags is desired, the schedule compression technique is used to redesign lagged activities or future activities.

6.4.1.1 CONTROL SCHEDULE: INPUTS, TOOLS AND TECHNIQUES, AND OUTPUTS

INPUTS

1 **Project management plan**

The project management plan and especially the schedule management plan must be taken into account as an input in this process.

2 **Project schedule**

The latest version of the project schedule set and approved is the major input of this process.

3 **Work performance information**

Performance reports provide current information on the project performance such as activities started, their progress, and which activities have already been completed.

4 **Organizational process assets**

Organizational process assets may influence the Control Schedule process by means of project management policies and procedures, schedules control methods, reporting templates, historical information, and lessons learned from previous projects.

TOOLS AND TECHNIQUES

1 **Performance reviews**

Performance reviews, obtained by reviewing the earned value, are used to evaluate the current deadline performance and the project future performance estimate.

Progress reports provide information such as actual dates or the activity new start and end dates scheduled, the project physical progress percentage, and information used to define preventive or corrective actions related to schedule changes.

2 **Variance analysis**

The current schedule variance with the schedule baseline provides important information for taking corrective and preventive actions regarding schedule deviations.

3 **Project management software**

The project management software is the automated tool for managing the project schedule. In the Control Schedule, it can be used to simulate future deadline situations.

4 **Resource leveling**

Resource leveling is used to optimize resource distribution throughout the project timing.

5 **What-if scenario analysis**

The what-if scenario analysis is used to analyze alternative scenarios to realign the schedule as planned.

6 **Adjusting leads and lags**

Adjustments to the schedule leads and lags are used to realign the schedule as planned.

7 **Schedule compression**

Schedule compression, just like fast tracking, is a technique used to realign the schedule as planned.

8 **Scheduling tool**

The tool used in the schedule execution can be a particular software application for schedule execution and network diagrams.

OUTPUTS

1 **Work performance measurements**

Information obtained from the earned value management must be recorded and reported to stakeholders.

2 **Organizational process assets updates**

The Control Schedule process can identify new processes or opportunities for improvements in the organization standards, procedures, and quality policies. Such updates may relate to the causes of variances, corrective actions chosen, and the reasons and lessons learned from this process.

3 **Change requests**

The Control Schedule process can result in change requests in the schedule baseline or another component of the project management plan. Change requests are processed for revision and availability during the Perform Integrated Change Control process.

4 **Project management plan updates**

The project management plan and, in particular, the schedule management plan must be updated after changes are approved as a result of the Control Schedule process.

5 **Project document updates**

Any and all project documents that have been influenced by the Control Schedule process must be updated, such as

- Project schedule network diagram, and
- Project schedule.

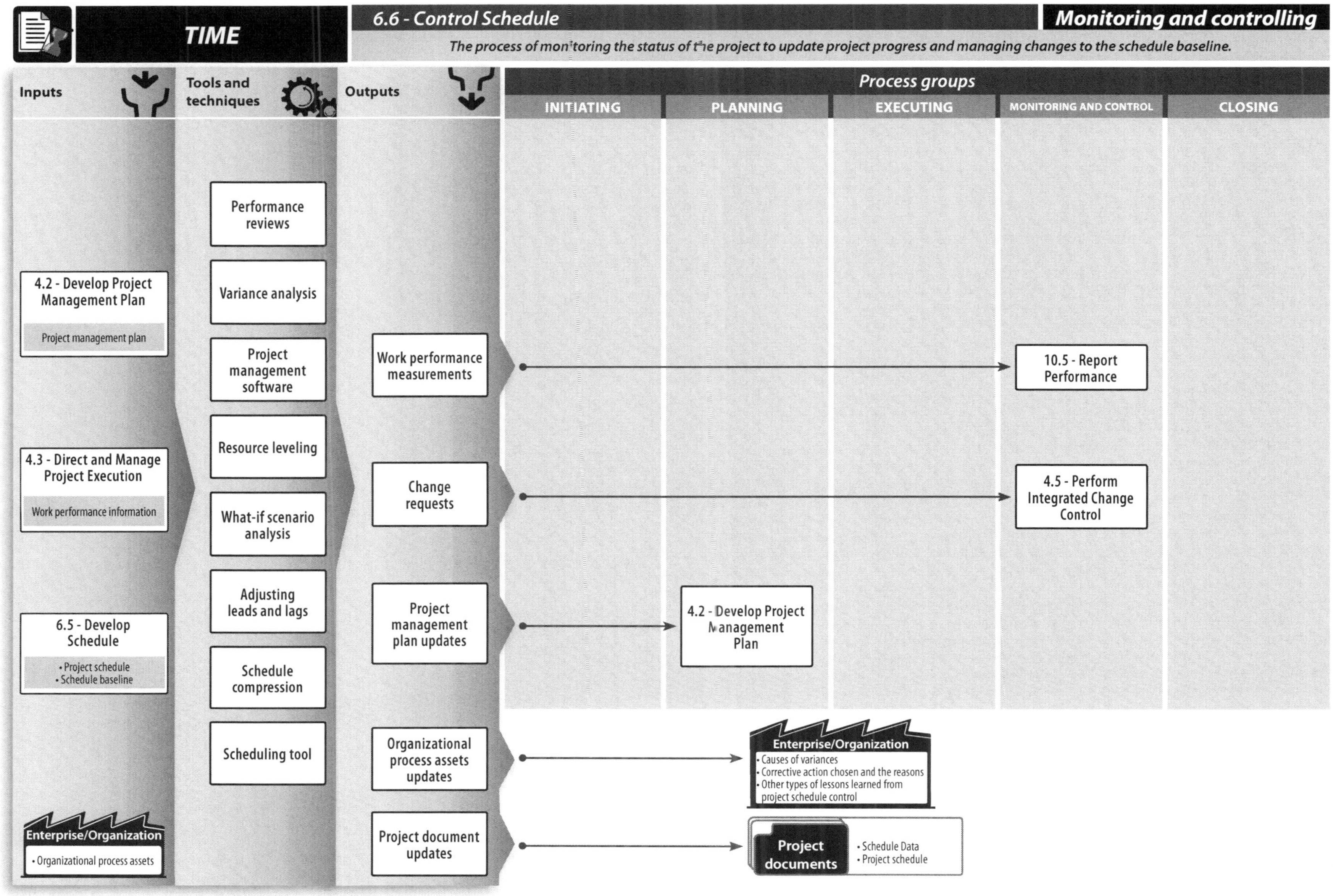
TIME
6.6 - Control Schedule
Monitoring and controlling
The process of monitoring the status of the project to update project progress and managing changes to the schedule baseline.
Inputs
Tools and techniques
Outputs
Process groups
INITIATING
PLANNING
EXECUTING
MONITORING AND CONTROL
CLOSING
4.2 - Develop Project Management Plan
Project management plan
4.3 - Direct and Manage Project Execution
Work performance information
6.5 - Develop Schedule
• Project schedule
• Schedule baseline
Enterprise/Organization
• Organizational process assets
Performance reviews
Variance analysis
Project management software
Resource leveling
What-if scenario analysis
Adjusting leads and lags
Schedule compression
Scheduling tool
Work performance measurements
Change requests
Project management plan updates
Organizational process assets updates
Project document updates
10.5 - Report Performance
4.5 - Perform Integrated Change Control
4.2 - Develop Project Management Plan
Enterprise/Organization
• Causes of variances
• Corrective action chosen and the reasons
• Other types of lessons learned from project schedule control
Project documents
• Schedule Data
• Project schedule

Attachment I

PROJECT PLANNING CONCEPTS AND TECHNIQUES

PROJECT PLANNING CONCEPTS AND TECHNIQUES

1 ROLLING WAVE PLANNING

According to PMI®, rolling wave planning is a form of progressive elaboration Planning where the work to be performed in the near term is planned in detail at a low WBS level, while in the long term, it is planned for components in a relatively high WBS level. Therefore, schedule activities can exist in multiple detail levels throughout the project life cycle.

When starting some projects, we only have information about the project's *earlier* phase, while details on other phases appear according to the project progress. Therefore, at the project start, for example, there can be activities only at the milestone or detail level of few activities.

Rolling wave planning can also occur on a large project comprising several subprojects. It is possible to detail activities of one or a few subprojects at an *earlier* phase while other subprojects will only have their activity breakdown as the project progresses or after a few previous subprojects are completed.

As good practice, *PMBOK® Guide* indicates that the work to be performed within one or two reporting periods in the future must be planned in detail, as the work is completed during the current period.

2 ACTIVITIES AND MILESTONE

An activity is the component of a work performed during the project progress. The exception is a ghost activity to be described later on.

Schedule activity

A schedule activity is a different component of the work scheduled during the project progress. It usually has an estimation of the required duration, cost, and resources.

Summary activity

A group of schedule activities gathered together and related at any summary level and displayed/ reported as a single activity at the summary level.

Ghost activity

An activity with zero duration used to display a logical relationship in the arrow diagramming method. Ghost activities are used when representing logical relationships either thoroughly or completely with diagram activity arrows is not possible. They are usually represented by a dotted line with an arrowhead.

Predecessor activity

The schedule activity that determines when the logical successor activity can be started or ended.

Successor activity

The schedule activity that follows a predecessor activity, as determined by the logical relationship between them.

Critical activity

Any schedule activity on a critical path of the project schedule.

Near-critical activity

Any schedule activity with a low total float. Any lag occurring in this activity may turn it into critical.

Milestone

A significant schedule point or event, usually representing the project phase start or end. A milestone is not an activity — while an activity is associated with the duration and work, a milestone is only one point and has no work or duration.

3 ACTIVITY SEQUENCING

The creation of a project Planning involves, in addition to listing activities and estimating durations, determining the relationship among such activities. In practicality, there are no projects without relationships among activities. Applying activity relationships enables viewing how activities are related to each other and to project milestones and how the project must be developed. This process is referred to as Sequence Activities. Sequence Activities must follow a logical order and the planner is supposed to have working knowledge of the execution process and the project priorities.

3.1 DEPENDENCIES

There are three types of dependencies among activities:

- **Mandatory dependency.** It is the dependence that underlies the nature of the work to be performed. It is also referred to as strict logic. An example is the logic behind building a wall and then perform the coating on it.
- **Arbitrated dependency.** Dependence is determined or chosen by the planner or performer based on experience and suggestions and can be changed. Therefore, it is also referred to as preferred, preferential, or flexible logic.
- **External dependency.** Dependence is based on needs, wishes, and impositions external to the project, for example, procuring a license from government environmental agencies. Another example is the deadline imposition of equipment supply on suppliers who have the technology of such equipment.

3.2 RELATIONSHIP TYPES AMONG ACTIVITIES

There are four types of relationships among activities:

Finish-to-Start (FS)

Activity B can only be started after activity A is completed

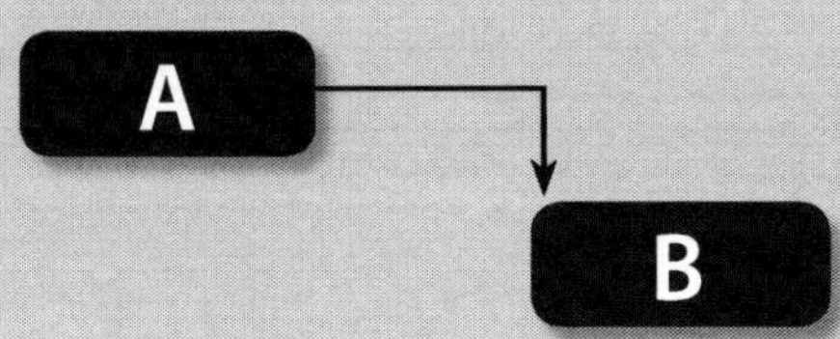

Examples

- Foundation block (activity B) can only be started after piling (activity A) that block.
- Concrete work (activity B) can only be started after the truck mixer arrives (activity A).

Notes

- The FS link is the most common among link types.

Start-to-Start (SS)

Activities A and B must be started at the same time

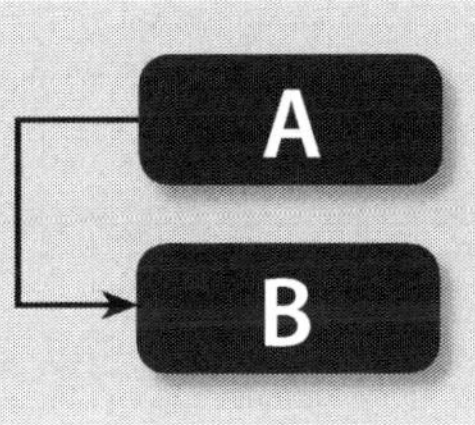

Examples

- The bending hardware activity (activity B) must be started as soon as hardware is received (activity A).
- The concrete mixing activity (activity B) must be started as soon as concrete launching is started (activity A).

Note

- The SS link can be used both by technical necessity and as a result of the objective of overlapping two activities and reducing the project deadline.

Finish-to-Finish (FF)

Activities A and B must be completed at the same time

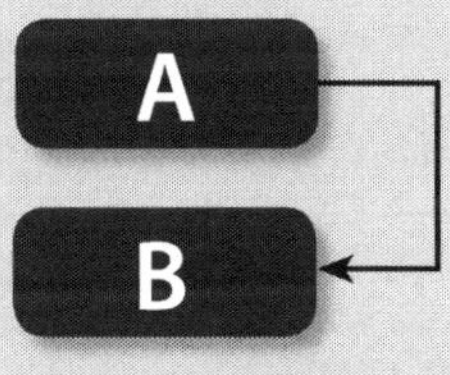

Example

- At the end of the work, worksite (activity A) and labor (activity B) demobilization work must be completed at the same time.

Note

- The FF link can be used both by technical necessity and as a result of the objective of overlapping two activities and reducing the project deadline.

Start-to-Finish (SF)

Activity B can only be completed when activity A is started.

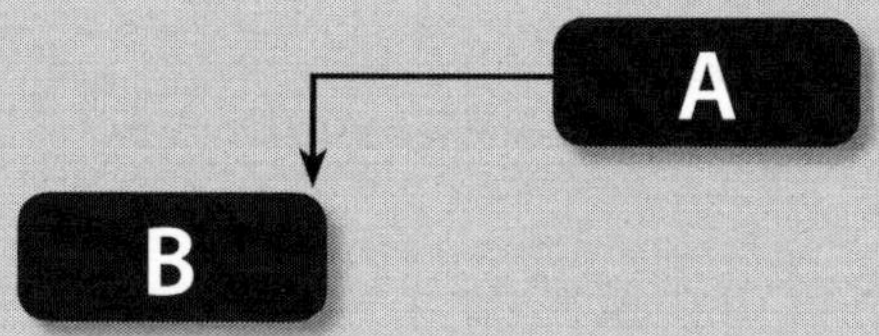

Example

- The company's current printed matter (activity B) must be used until the new ones arrive from the print shop (activity A).

Note

- The SF link occurs less frequently than other links.

3.3 LEAD AND LAG (LEAD TIME AND LAG TIME)

LEAD
(LEAD TIME)

Lead is overlapping dependent activities in order to reduce the project deadline.

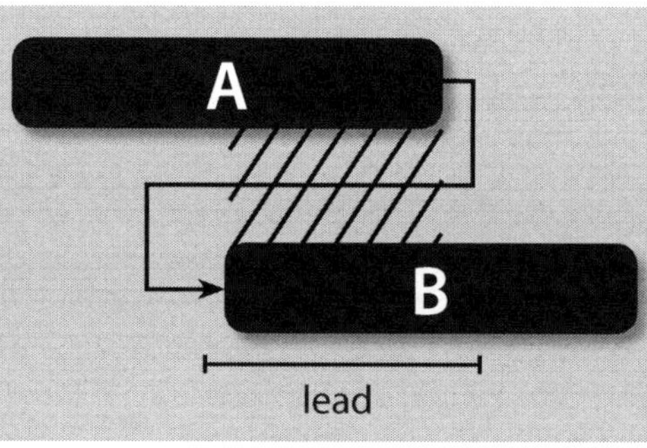

Examples

- Excavation (activity B) to perform foundation blocks can be started five days before completing piling (activity A) of the entire construction area.
- Concrete structure services (activity B) can be started when 50% of foundations (activity A) are completed.

LAG
(LAG TIME)

A lag is a waiting time among dependent activities usually applied as a result of a technical necessity.

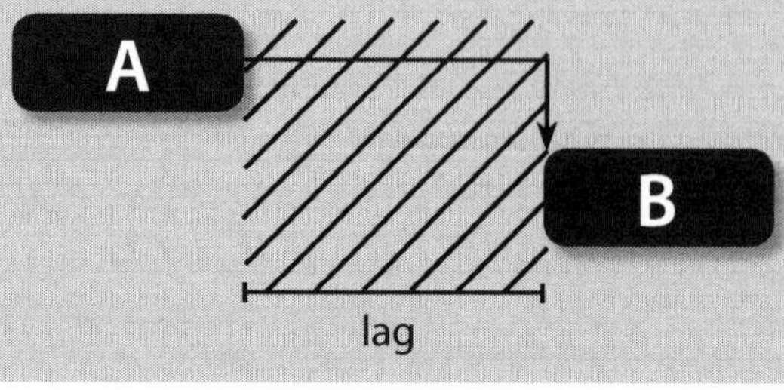

Example

- After concreting a beam (activity A), it is necessary to wait a few days before starting to de-form it (activity B) as a result of concrete curing.

4 CONSTRAINTS

It is possible to specify that an activity must start on a certain date or that it must not end after a certain date. When doing that, we apply a constraint (a set of limitations on an activity start date or end date) to an activity.

For example, if the earthwork company completes its services and releases the area to start construction on a given date X, it is possible to consider that the first construction activity will have the following constraints applied:

- not start before date X or
- start on date X.

Constraints may be flexible, semiflexible, or inflexible, according to their association with dates.

Flexible — not associated with a particular date
Semiflexible — associated with a particular date but not limited by it
Inflexible — associated with a particular date for start or end

In the previous example, we may:

• not start before date X	a semiflexible constraint associated with date X, but not limited by it, that is, the activity can start on any date after date X
• start on date X	inflexible constraint, since the activity must be started on date X

5 RESOURCES

Any individual, equipment, material, or item that contributes to a project activity completion is considered a resource.

Examples:

- a foreman, bricklayer, carpenter, construction worker, concrete mixer truck, crane, cement, sand, gravel, tiles.

5.1 RESOURCE TYPES

WORK RESOURCES

Labor resources are individuals and equipment that, in order to perform activities, spend time or work (a foreman, carpenter, concrete mixer, truck, etc.).

MATERIAL RESOURCES

Material resources are supplies, stocks, or other consumable items used to complete project activities (cement, sand, gravel, etc.).

When distributing material resources, the unit of measure (kilograms, meters, cubic meters) is considered and the quantity to be consumed in the activity is specified. In order to deal with the resource overallocation issue, it is possible to use the allocation of more resources, overtime, and resource leveling.

RESOURCE LEVELING

Resource leveling is a distribution technique of resources allocated to an activity or project in order to eliminate overallocation or to obtain a uniform distribution of such resources. This leveling can be performed manually in network diagrams or using project management softwares that perform leveling. Automatic leveling considers parallel activities that share the same resource and the displacement of such activities in a sequence, which can lead to lags in the project.

6 WORK FORMULA

The work formula to be used in Planning is

Work = duration × quantity of resources

Where

- **Working** is the total quantity of hours scheduled or provided of one or more resources (labor or equipment) to perform an activity. Example: 120 hours for a bricklayer to perform the masonry activity.
- **Duration** is the time period scheduled or required to complete an activity. Example: a 15-day duration is scheduled to perform the masonry activity.
- **Quantity of resources** is the quantity scheduled or required resources (labor or equipment) to complete an activity. Example: you will need to allocate a bricklayer (8 hours a day) for 15 days to perform the masonry activity — 8 hours/day * 15 days = 120 hours for the bricklayer.

Attachment II

SUPPLEMENTARY READING ON ACTIVITY RESOURCE ESTIMATES

ACTIVITY RESOURCE ESTIMATES

1 INTRODUCTION

Any and all projects, simple or complex, large or small, short or long, require the use of human resources, materials, or equipment. The very definition of activity is associated with work, and work requires human resources and/or equipment resources.

2 BASIC ESTIMATING RULES

When performing estimates, some basic rules can be followed:

- Consider that labor resources will have a productivity of no more than 80% of their productive time.
- Use the experience of other people in the company knowledgeable on previous projects.
- Consult, whenever possible, the judgment of experts internal or external to the company.
- Consider that people working on several projects have lower productivity because of transition between projects.
- Seek tolerance agreement in estimates with the sponsor in order to provide unscheduled services.
- Adjust estimates according to the approved scope changes.
- Keep all stakeholders informed about estimates and their changes.

3 RESOURCE ESTIMATE TYPES

The three most common resource estimate methods required to perform the activity are

- single estimating,
- analogous estimating, and
- parametric estimating.

Self-explanatory single estimating is used alone when applying another estimate is not possible. Other estimates can be used together to supplement one an other and to tune the process.

3.1 SINGLE ESTIMATING

Single estimating is used when there is only one judgment about the quantity of resources required to perform the activity. This judgment may come from a specialist's historical record or by the planner's plain guess.

Single estimating is a method that must not be used only when we have better information but in cases where deliverables are totally innovative products; their use may be unavoidable in some activities.

Using single estimating too frequently can cause the following effects on the project:

- The created schedule does not have the credibility on the quantity of resources and the execution deadline.
- Estimators tend to increase their estimates so that they will not be regarded as responsible for lags.
- The project tends to use more resources as a result of the above effect.
- The project tends to be more expensive because of the increased use of resources.

Single estimating must only be used rarely when we do not want to know activity details, and this information will only be known after the activity is developed.

3.2 ANALOGOUS ESTIMATING

Analogous estimating is a technique commonly used in the project's initial phase when there is no detailed information on the activities. In this technique, the identification in previous projects of activities similar to those of the project in question are used to assume the required resources. We can imagine the application of a ceramic floor in an area of a given size that consumed a certain quantity of resources in the previous project. In the current project, the consideration would be the quantity of resources required for the current area when applying the same type of ceramic tile.

One caution to be exerted when using this technique is obtaining records about the reliability of the previous project: how they were collected, what problems occurred during execution, if there was lag in material delivery, if human resources were quickly allocated and actually used, and if there were leftover materials and others.

3.3 PARAMETRIC ESTIMATING

Parametric estimating is a technique using values related to resource consumption per unit of measure defined by product mass studies. Such values represent the resource productivity rate per unit of measure. For example, after performing studies, the conclusion was reached that a bricklayer consumes X hours to run a square meter of masonry in a given specification. Similarly, the conclusion was reached that Y bricks are spent to build a square meter of masonry. In order to define resources in a new project, it is possible to use the historical consumption rates per unit of measure multiplied by the particular quantities of each service of this new project.

Such data can be obtained in the following ways:

- **External sources**

  External sources for data collection toward estimating parameters are publications, data from other companies, or public archives. The great advantage of using such sources is the availability of such data. However, for a company wishing to use such data, there is always the uncertainty of how data were collected, what the procedures used in studies were, and the reliability of results. Either way, the company may, while using parameters, evaluate and obtain their compliance with the service execution process.

- **Estimate creation**

  Creating your own estimates, in contrast, which are able to provide reliability, demand time, labor, and financial resources from the company, which may, depending on the quantity and diversity of products, become impractical or unfeasible. The great difficulty in creating estimates is related to this repetitive collection, using the same technological process and determining variables that influence results. Creating your own estimates must also consider mathematical analyses such as variable regression (scatter diagram) and the learning curve, which considers growing productivity according to the quantity performed. Therefore, the creation of your own estimates must be used in particular products, which can be repeated in the short term and that may reflect economies of scale for the company.

4 WHAT-IF SCENARIO ANALYSIS

The what-if scenario analysis is the technique to create estimate alternative scenarios. In order to estimate resources, such scenarios can be answered by other questions, as explained below:

- What if lower than expected productivity takes place?
- What if we find some difficulty in allocating certain scheduled resources?
- What if the company starts a new project?
- What if a strike bursts during the project execution?

5 RESOURCE REQUIREMENTS

Estimating resource activities requires, in addition to setting the quantity of resources, defining resource requirements such as type, origin, and other information necessary to properly identify the resource.

Attachment III

SUPPLEMENTARY READING ON ACTIVITY DURATION ESTIMATES

ACTIVITY DURATION ESTIMATE

1 INTRODUCTION

An activity duration is closely linked to the quantity of resources allocated as well as the productivity of each resource and the activity features. When the quantity of work required to perform the activity as well as the quantity of resources available for that activity is known, it is possible to determine its duration by dividing the work by the quantity of resources, as seen in Attachment I to this chapter (see work formula). However, we cannot indefinitely increase the quantity of resources and wait the duration to decrease proportionally, since the excess of resources in an activity ultimately reduces productivity or hinders execution. In addition, there are other variables that must be considered when estimating activity durations, such as preparing the environment for the activity execution, material resource allocation at the appropriate time, equipment and material preparation time, and even external factors such as rain events, which may affect the activity duration.

2 DURATION ESTIMATE TYPES

Usual methods for estimating activity durations are

- single estimating,
- analogous estimating, and
- parametric estimating.

2.1 SINGLE ESTIMATING

Single estimating of an activity duration is used when there is only one judgment about the activity duration.

Considerations on resource single estimating available in Attachment II to this chapter must be used for the duration single estimating.

2.2 ANALOGOUS ESTIMATING

Analogous estimating is a technique commonly used in the project initial phase when there is no detailed information on the activities. In this technique, the identification, in previous projects, of activities similar to those of the project in question is used to assume the activity duration. We can imagine working on a brick area that required a certain quantity of days to be completed. In the current project, consideration would be the time required to perform the current masonry area of the same type.

Issues raised about caution when using analogous estimating on resources, available in Attachment II, are also valid to estimate analogous duration.

2.3 PARAMETRIC ESTIMATING

Activity duration parametric estimating applies productivity rates in the work formula, with such indices being defined through product mass studies.

Considerations for resource parametric estimating presented in Attachment II to this chapter must be made for duration parametric estimating.

3 RISK CONSIDERATION IN DURATION ESTIMATES

As with resource and activity cost estimates, risk consideration must be used when estimating activity durations. Such risks may be related to work features, interference arising from allocating resources that impact duration, risks associated with parallel activities, risks related to "path convergence"* and even external factors such as weather. But not only threat-posing risks must be considered; opportunity-posing risks must also be remembered and taken into account. Both risk mitigation of threats and opportunity leverage related to an opportunity risk can mean the difference between success and failure of a project.

3.1 THREE-POINT ESTIMATES

Consideration of risks in activity duration estimates can be performed using the so-called three-point estimating technique, applied to values obtained both from analogous estimating and parametric estimates. Such estimates do not generally consider variance, providing a unique estimating value, which is the first of the three points required by the three-point estimating. The other two points are usually defined by individuals who know the work, namely, by expert judgment. This technique uses value beta distribution, as shown in the following chart.

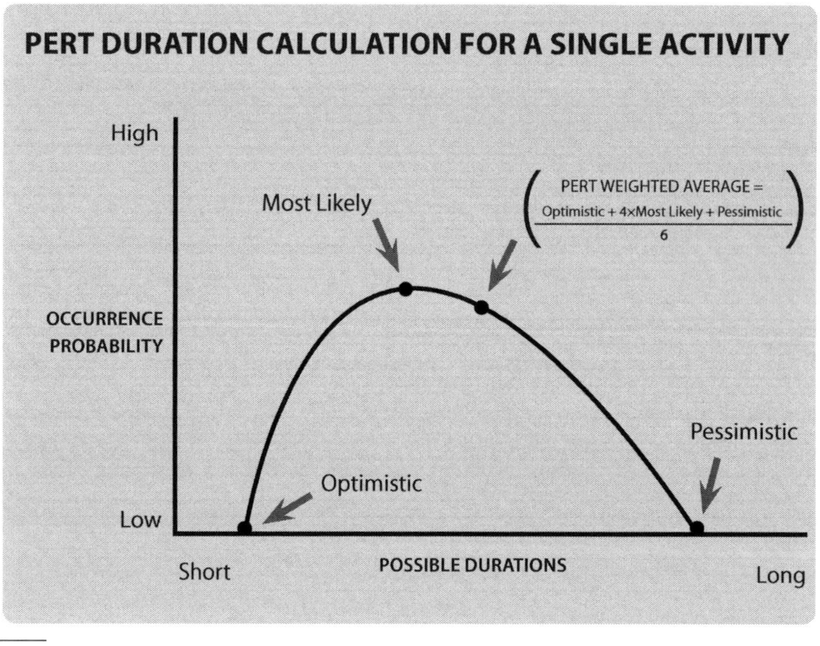

* **Patch convergence** network diagram sites where multiple activities are predecessors of a successor one, increasing the execution risk of that successor activity.

In order to consider risks in the activity duration, the following steps can be used:

- **Step 1**
  Define the activity with the best likely duration estimating (the most likely duration).
- **Step 2**
  Define the duration estimate if all goes well and without any problems (optimistic duration).
- **Step 3**
  Define some problems that may occur and impact duration.
- **Step 4**
  Define duration estimate if all such problems occurred (pessimistic duration).

With this information at hand, using the PERT (Program Evaluation and Review Technique) formula, it is possible to obtain the activity estimated duration.

$$D = (O + 4ML + P)/6$$

Where

D = Estimated duration

O = Optimistic duration

ML = Most likely duration

P = Pessimistic duration

Estimate duration define as such must be the goal to be achieved to complete the activity.

The activity standard deviation is given by the formula

$$SD = (P - O)/6$$

The activity variance is given by:

$$V = [(P - O)/6]^2$$

CONSIDERATIONS ON THE THREE-POINT ESTIMATES

The three-point estimates uses the weighted average between the optimistic (O), the pessimistic (P), and the most likely estimate, providing an expected duration (D) estimate based on the risk consideration.

The **activity** expected duration and the **activity** standard deviation are used to consider the **activity** variance interval.

Variance is only used in calculating the **project** total deviation.

See the example below:

Activity	Most likely duration	Pessimistic duration	Optimistic duration	Expected duration	Standard deviation	Variance	Activity interval (for standard deviation 1)
Activity 1	30	40	26	31	2.33	5.42	31 days ± 2.33 days
Activity 2	20	36	16	22	3.33	11.08	22 days ± 3.33 days
Activity 3	25	35	21	26	2.33	5.42	26 days ± 2.33 days
Activity 4	45	62	40	47	3.66	13.39	47 days ± 3.66 days
Activity 5	60	82	50	62	5.33	28.44	62 days ± 5.33 days
Sum				188		63.75	

Each estimate interval is defined by the activity expected duration minus or plus the standard deviation.

The project duration interval is given by the sum of the expected durations of each activity and the sum or reduction of the **project standard deviation** (and not the sum of the standard deviations of activities). The project standard deviation is given by the square root of the sum of activity variances ($\sqrt{61.75} = 7.98$)

Therefore, for this project we have

Project duration estimate = 188 days ± 7.98 days

Rounding up = 188 days ± 8 days

The activity duration intervals calculated in a particular year takes into account a standard deviation, that is, considering the 68.26% probability of occurrence in that interval. An example of activity 1:

- Activity 1 has a 68.26% probability of having its duration between 31 days ± 2.33 days (28.67 to 33.33 days).

If two standard deviations are considered, the occurrence probability is 95.46%. An example of activity 1:

- Activity 1 would have a 95.46% probability of having its duration between 31 days ± 4.66 days (26.34 to 35.66 days)

If three standard deviations are considered, the occurrence probability is 99.73%. For activity 1, we would have

- Activity 1 would have a 99.73% probability of having its duration between 31 days ± 6.99 days (24.01 to 37.99 days)

The same considerations apply to other activities and to the project itself.

The same information herein contained is valid for cost estimates of activities.

4 WHAT-IF SCENARIO ANALYSIS

The what-if scenario analysis is the technique used to create estimate alternative scenarios. In order to estimate the activity duration, such scenarios can be answered by other questions, as explained below:

- What if we used another way to complete the activity?
- What if weather conditions are worse than expected?
- What if lower than expected productivity takes place?
- What if we find some difficulty in allocating certain scheduled resources?
- What if the company starts a new project?
- What if there is a strike during the project execution?

Attachment IV

SUPPLEMENTARY READING ON NETWORK DIAGRAMS

NETWORK DIAGRAMS

1 INTRODUCTION

Network diagram techniques were first used in the 50s in order to show a work flowchart presenting activity relationships in addition to bar charts used in Planning. Among the several network diagram techniques, two were more developed and used the Arrow Diagramming Method (ADM) and the Precedence Diagramming Method (PDM). In addition to these two, another method to consider is the Conditional diagramming method, which allows loops among activities.

2 INFORMATION REQUIRED TO DEVELOP NETWORK DIAGRAMS

In order to develop network diagrams, several information must be available to the planner, among which the following are key:

- **Project scope**

  Defined by the project scope statement and any and all documents that may help to define project activities.

- **Defining the Planning detail level**

  The detail level must be based on the WBS work packages and defined in order to enable activity identification, relationships among them, and progress monitoring.

- **Resource availability**

  For each activity or group of activities, the availability of necessary resources in terms of availability quantity and period must be verified.

- **Setting the project calendars**

  The project standard calendar must be set and, if any, special calendars for particular activities or resources.

3 GOOD PRACTICES FOR NETWORK DIAGRAM EXECUTION

Some practices apply to network diagram execution:

- Each element of the project scope, as defined in the WBS, must be supported by an activity or activities in the network diagram, which supplement the scope of this element.
- Activities must be described on an individual basis, including a verb, at least an object and common and clarifying adjectives.
- After creating the activity list, the activity performance order must be defined.
- In order to prevent incorrect or artificial relationships, initial activity sequencing must be determined independently of resource availability. After initial activity sequencing is completed, discretionary dependencies may be inserted.
- A network diagram must have only one start and one end.

- Each activity must have at least one predecessor activity, except for the start activity.
- Each activity must have at least one successor activity, except for the end activity.
- Constraints must not be used to change the network diagram logic.
- Resources required to complete each activity must be considered when determining the activity duration, whether the resources are currently available for that activity or not.
- After determining the network diagram logic, productivity and availability of each resource required to perform the activity must be considered.

4 NETWORK DIAGRAM ADVANTAGES AND DISADVANTAGES

The major advantage of network diagrams is providing the project manager and those involved in the work execution with a graphical view of the overall project, activity sequencing, and the project critical path, enabling Monitoring and controlling of critical activities.

In contrast, network diagrams can become confusing to less experienced professionals in Planning, particularly when the project has many interrelated activities. Furthermore, for very dynamic projects or with frequent changes, network diagrams tend to become cumbersome and unproductive.

5 PRECEDENCE DIAGRAMMING METHOD (PDM)

The PDM, also referred to as Node Activity Method (NAM), enters the activity information in boxes representing diagram nodes and uses arrows only to indicate the relationship among activities, thus, rendering it possible to show the four types of relationships among activities. This method determines the *earlier* date and the *later* date that each activity can start and determines the *earlier* date and the *later* date when each activity can be completed.

5.1 GRAPHICAL REPRESENTATION OF PRECEDENCE DIAGRAM NODES

The most usual manner to represent precedence diagram nodes is presented in the figure below:

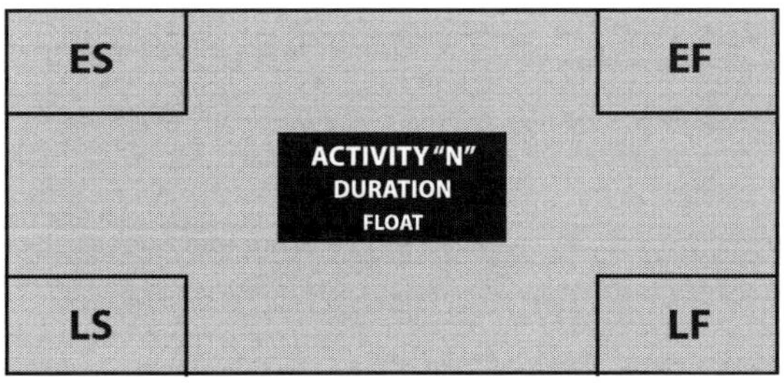

Where

ES = Early start

LS = Later start

EF = Early finish

LF = Later finish

5.2 FLOAT TYPES

There are three types of floats to be considered in the project: total float (fluctuation), free float (fluctuation), and project float (fluctuation).

- **Total float**

  The lag time allowed for an activity without delaying the project finish date or a project milestone.

- **Free float**

  The lag time allowed for an activity without delaying the *early* start date of any of its successors.

- **Project float**

  The lag time allowed for a project without delaying the finish date imposed by the client or externally determined.

Total float can be calculated by the following formulas:

Float = *Later* Start Date (LS) – *Early* Start Date (ES)

or

Float = *Later* Finish Date (LF) – *Early* Finish Date (EF)

5.3 FLOAT CALCULATION

An activity float calculation enables identifying the *early* or *later* date when it can be started or the *early* or *later* date when it can be completed without the project.

Diagram *early* and *later* dates are obtained from the forward pass and the backward pass, respectively.

- **Forward pass.** Calculation of the diagram *early* dates, beginning at the project start through its finish, considering activity dependencies. It is the to left-to-right pass.

- **Backward pass.** Calculation of the diagram *later* dates, returning from the project finish through its start, considering activity dependencies. It is the right-to-left pass.

5.4 BUILDING A PRECEDENCE DIAGRAM (PDM) WITH FINISH-START RELATIONSHIP

In order to develop the precedence diagram example with finish-start relationships among activities, let us consider the following activity list and their relationships:

Activity	Predecessors	Duration
Activity 1	Start	5 days
Activity 2	Start	8 days
Activity 3	1	4 days
Activity 4	3	7 days
Activity 5	2	6 days
END	4, 5	0 days

The figure below represents the precedence diagram.

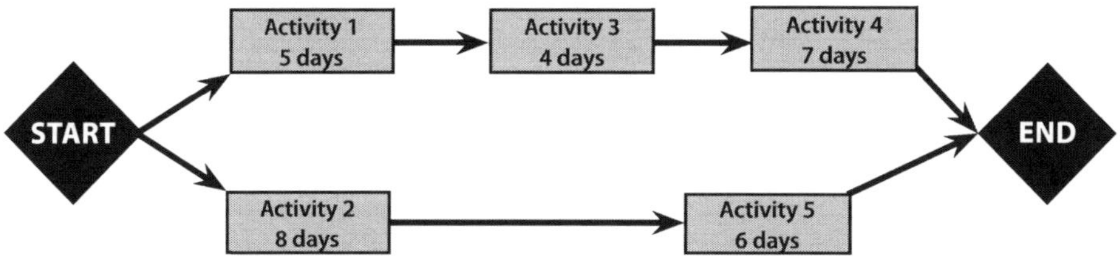

5.4.1 CRITICAL PATH DETERMINATION

Critical path is the longest path of the network diagram and represents the shortest time to complete the project. In order to determine it, it is necessary to know the duration of all possible paths of the project.

In the precedence diagram above, we have the following paths and durations:

- **1st path**

  Start - Activity 1 - Activ. 3 - Activ. 4 - End

  Duration = 5 + 4 + 7+ 2 = 18 days

- **2nd path**

  Start - Activity 2 - Activ. 5 - End

  Duration = 8 + 6 + 2 = 16 days

By definition, the project critical path is the path number 1, which has the longest duration (18 days).

5.4.2 DETERMINATION OF EARLY, LATER, AND FLOAT DATES

5.4.2.1 *Early* dates – diagram forward pass

In order to determine the *early* dates of activities, the diagram forward pass (left to right) is used, following the steps below:

1. Start with zero for the activity ES.
2. Add the activity duration to obtain the activity *early* finish.
3. Recognizing that the successor activity *early* start is the predecessor activity *early* finish, repeat the value from step 2 for activity 3.
4. Repeat steps 2 and 3 for activities 3 and 4.
5. Start with zero for activity 2.
6. Repeat steps 2 and 3 for activities 2 and 5.

The figure below shows these steps and the result obtained for the forward pass.

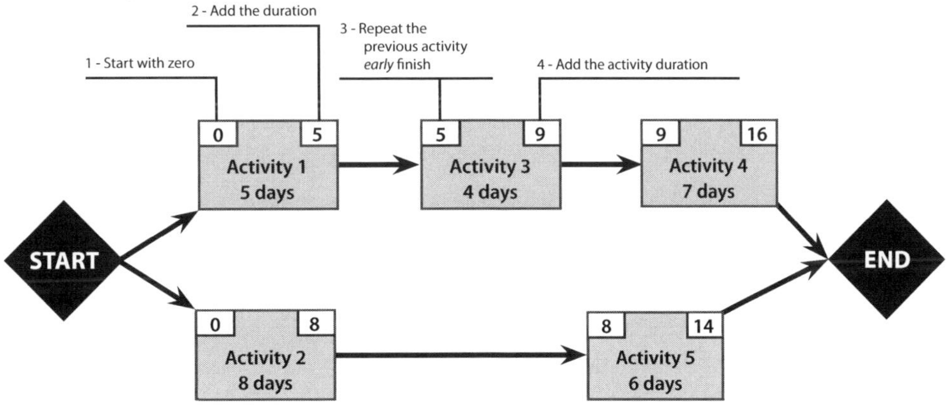

5.4.2.2 Later dates – diagram backward pass

In order to determine the *later* dates of activities, the diagram backward pass (right to left) is used, following the steps below:

1. Consider the *early* finish *later* date found on the forward pass as the *later* finish date of each activity. In the example, date 16 is the finish of activity 4 and date 14 is the finish of activity 5. Consider 16 as the finish date of each activity.
2. Subtract activity duration 4 to obtain the *later* start of this activity (16 – 7 = 9).
3. Repeat this LS value for successor activity LF.
4. Repeat steps 2 and 3 for activities 3 and 1.
5. Start with 16 for the LF of activity 5.
6. Repeat steps 2 and 3 for activities 2 and 5.

The figure below shows such steps and the result obtained for the backward pass.

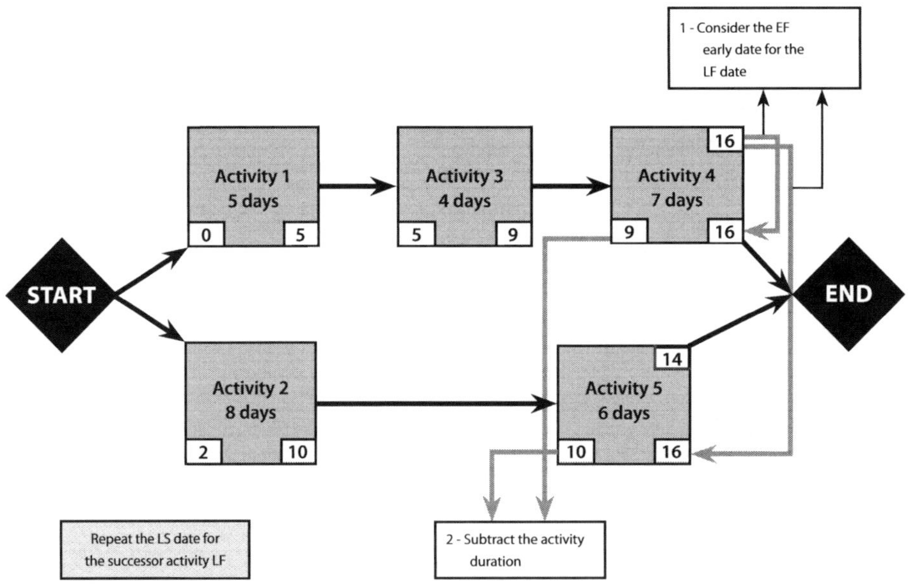

The following figure shows the result of applying the forward and backward passes to the Network diagram.

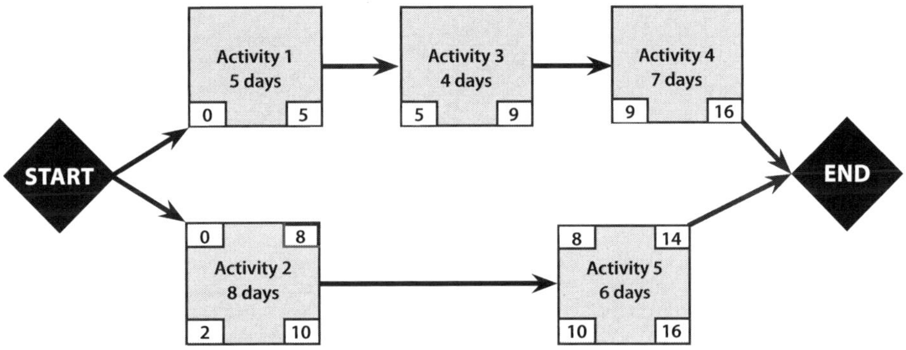

5.4.2.3 Total float calculation

In order to determine the *later* dates of activities, the diagram backward pass (right to left) is used, following the steps below:

- **Activity float 1** = LS – ES = 0 – 0 = 0 days
  or = LF – EF = 5 – 5 = 0 days
- **Activity float 3** = 0 days
- **Activity float 4** = 0 days
- **Activity float 2** = LS – ES = 2 – 0 = 2 days **or**
  LF – EF = 10 – 8 = 2 days
- **Activity float 5** = 2 days

5.4.2.4 Critical path identification

Observing the example, it is possible to see that there are some activities (1, 3, and 4) with total float equal to zero, therefore identifying the project critical path.

To recap, the critical path is

- the network longest path,
- the *earliest* time to complete the project, and
- the path through which activities have zero total float.

The following figure shows the example critical path.

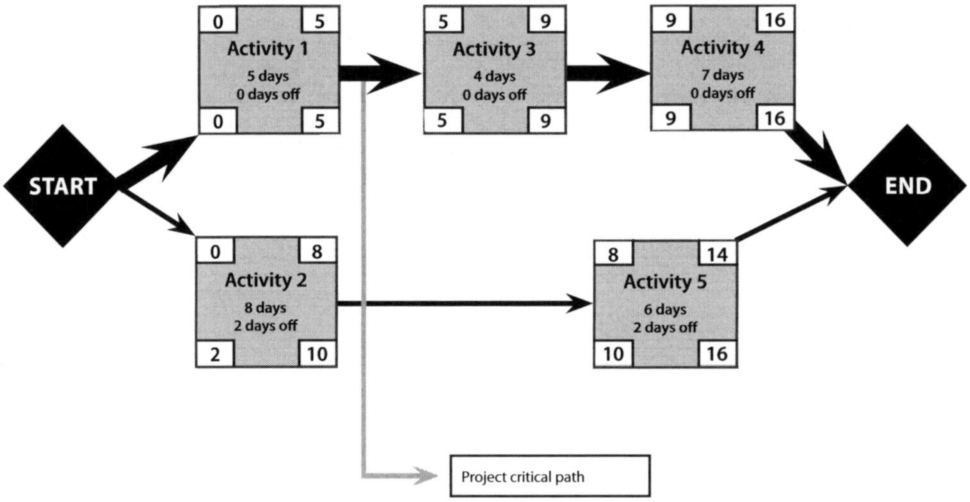

5.4.2.5 Free float calculation

The free float of an activity can be determined by the difference between the successor activity *early* finish and the activity *early* finish analyzed.

Free float = Successor ES – Activity EF

In the example, the only free float activity is activity 5, which can delay its *early* finish by 2 days without damaging the following activity, which coincidentally in this case, is the project end.

5.5 PROJECT SCHEDULE DURATION REDUCTION

There are two techniques to reduce the schedule duration without reducing its scope:

- *Schedule compression (crashing)*. The project schedule compression consists of reducing durations of activities or some of them that are part of the project critical path. This duration reduction can be applied as a result of
    - better assessment of the initially estimated duration,
    - allocation of more resources (labor and/or equipment) to activities, and
    - allocation of more effective resources (labor and/or equipment) to activities.
- *Fast tracking*. Applying fast track consists of changing the relationship type among activities, modifying serial execution simultaneously with such activities. The best way to achieve fast tracking is breaking down work packages into smaller packages to enable fast tracking.

6 CONDITIONAL DIAGRAM METHOD

The Conditional Diagramming Method (CDM) involves diagramming techniques enabling the use of activities among loops and conditional variances among activities. Techniques involve the GERT (Graphical Evaluation and Review Technique) diagram and Dynamic Systems templates. Loop and conditional deviations are the result of decisions (Yes/No) about a fact or choice among alternatives.

The figures below show examples of such diagrams.

CDM 1

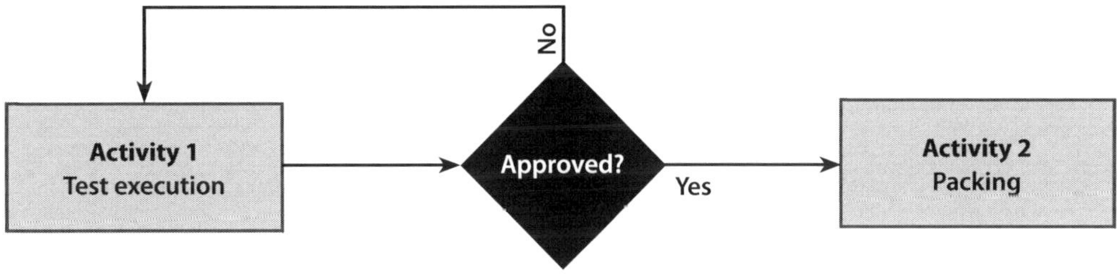

CDM 2

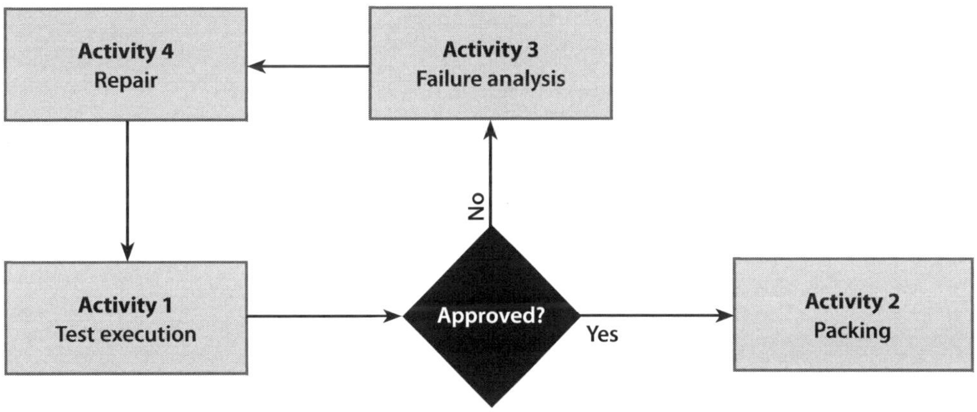

Chapter 6 - Project Time Management

CDM 3

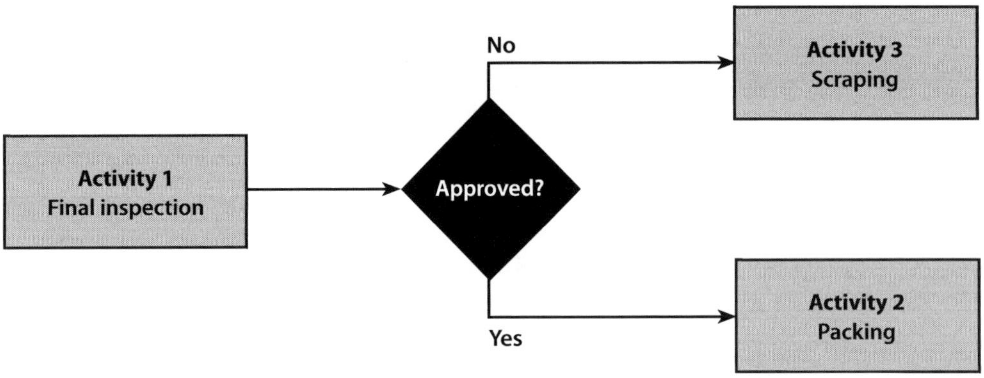
Activity 1
Final inspection
Approved?
No
Yes
Activity 3
Scraping
Activity 2
Packing

Attachment V

SUPPLEMENTARY READING ON BAR SCHEDULE

BAR SCHEDULES

1 INTRODUCTION

The bar schedule, also referred to as Gantt chart, was created by the engineer and scientist Henry L. Gantt in 1917, with the objective of being a production control tool. Since it is easy to use, it is one of the most used tools in project management. It basically consists of a list of project activities on the left and their respective durations represented by bars on a time scale on the right.

The figure below is a bar schedule example.

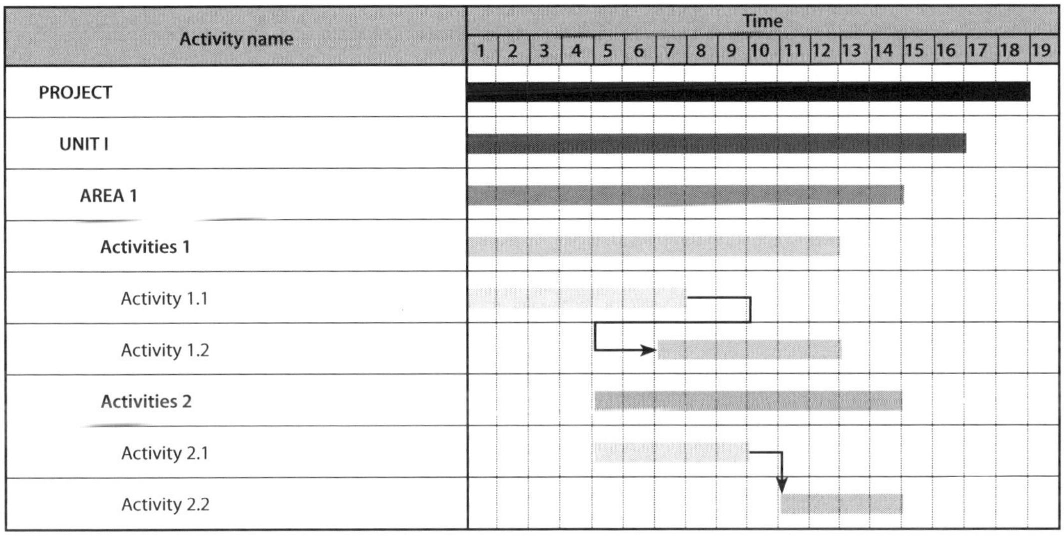

2 INFORMATION REQUIRED TO DEVELOP A BAR SCHEDULE

In order to develop a bar schedule, several pieces of information must be available to the planner. If the bar schedule is elaborated after the network diagram execution, such information will have been previously released, thus making the Gantt chart execution easier. However, if the bar schedule is performed without the precedence of a network diagram, the following information is fundamental for its execution:

- **Project scope**

  Defined by the project scope statement and any and all documents that may help define project activities.

- **Defining the planning detail level**

  The detail level must be based on the WBS work packages and defined in order to enable activity identification, relationships among them, and progress monitoring.

- **Resource availability**

  For each activity or group of activities, the availability of necessary resources in terms of availability quantity and period must be verified.

- **Setting the project calendars**

  The project standard calendar must be set and, if any, special calendars for particular activities or resources.

3 GOOD PRACTICES FOR BAR SCHEDULE EXECUTION

Some practices apply to bar schedule execution:

- Each element of the project scope, as defined in the WBS, must be supported by an activity or activities in the bar schedule, which supplement the scope of this element.
- The bar schedule must have at least two milestones: the project start and project end.
- Activities must be described on an individual basis, including a verb, at least an object, and common and clarifying adjectives.
- After creating the activity list, the activity performance order must be defined.
- In order to prevent incorrect or artificial relationships, initial activity sequencing must be determined independently of resource availability. After initial activity sequencing is completed, discretionary dependencies may be inserted.
- Each activity must have at least one predecessor activity, except for the early activity.
- Each activity must have at least one predecessor activity, except for the early activity.
- Constraints must not be used to change the bar schedule logic.
- The work represented by a bar schedule activity, once started, must be completed without interruption (except for calendar nonbusiness days). If an activity work needs to be stopped to be restarted at a *later* date, it is recommended that the activity is divided into two or more activities, considering such stop points.
- The work represented by a bar schedule activity must be set so that the activity duration is less than twice the refresh cycle. This enables a start and end report of an activity within one or two update cycles, allowing management to focus on performance and corrective actions.
- Resources required to complete each activity must be considered when determining the activity duration, whether the resources are currently available for that activity or not.
- After determining the network bar schedule, productivity and availability of each resource required to perform the activity must be considered.
- When the bar schedule is completed, a baseline must be defined to allow comparing progress with the original plan.

4 BAR SCHEDULE LEVELS

According to PMI®, the schedule can be divided into five detail levels:

- **Level 1 - Executive summary**

  A one-page schedule summary with the major contractual milestones and activities summarized.

- **Level 2 - Management summary**

  A four- or five-page schedule, including Level 1 plus activities summarized by area or main equipment.

- **Level 3 - Publication schedule**

  A schedule with major milestones, key engineering, procurement, construction, electromechanical assembly, commissioning, and start-up elements. This schedule is the monthly report feed basis.

- **Level 4 - Execution planning**

  Schedule with activities lasting longer than one week. Used to support construction, electromechanical assembly and commissioning staff in their global planning.

- **Level 5 - Detailed planning (programming)**

  Work schedule to be used in the field, usually with activities lasting less than one week.

5 BAR SCHEDULE ADVANTAGES AND DISADVANTAGES

The bar schedule has the advantage of being easily assimilated by all participants of the project. It also allows comparing between the project current status to planning and the resource allocation to resources distributed throughout the project lifetime.

In contrast, the bar schedule, when used for large projects, does not easily recognize dependencies among activities.

Attachment VI

SUPPLEMENTARY READING ON CRITICAL CHAIN METHOD

CRITICAL CHAIN METHOD

1 INTRODUCTION

The critical chain method, also known as critical current method, was developed by Israeli physicist Eliyahu Goldratt and is an application of the Theory of Constraints (TOC) to project management.

According to PMI®, critical chain is a schedule network analysis technique that modifies the project schedule so that it can take limited resources into account. Critical chain combines deterministic approaches with probabilistic approaches.

The critical chain method is a technique aimed at obtaining a schedule with highly reduced deadlines by means of reduced time estimates of activities and creating resource lungs.

The major focus of critical chain method is the use of resources and how estimates can be influenced by human behavior. Therefore, unlike other methods, the critical chain method has the following characteristics:

- Critical chain, which is the network longest path, considers the dependency of activities and resources.
- Duration estimates are assumed at 50% probability, while other tools use 95% probability. This dramatically reduces estimated durations.
- When estimating resources and durations any contingencies that may increase such estimates are neglected.
- The method requires the use of resources dedicated to the project, since resource productivity must be as large as possible without interruption during the activity execution, except for days not worked.

2 FACTORS INFLUENCING ESTIMATES

There are two human behavior-related factors that must be considered as far as estimates are concerned:

- **Student syndrome**

  Imagine a student who is assigned by the teacher to deliver a task within 5 days. The student initially imagines the task, asks the teacher for another 2 days to deliver it, and the teacher accepts it. The student, now with 7 days to finish the task, re-evaluates and verifies that it can be completed in 5 days. The student starts the task only after the first 2 days, at the risk of not delivering or getting more tired than usual. For projects, that means saying that negotiated breaks do not prevent lags and the use of a larger quantity of resources.

- **Parkinson's law**

  If an activity can be developed within 3 days, but, at the performer's request, two additional days are granted, even if the activity is started at time zero, the tendency is it is extended throughout the 5 days. The tendency of human behavior is performing it slower or even fine-tuning or beautifying the activity, until reaching, in this example, the 5-day deadline.

There is an enterprise factor that must be considered about estimates:

- **Multi activity environment**

  For organizations performing multiple projects simultaneously, it is common to use the same resource for two or more projects, so that resource productivity can be diminished, given the required setup between one project and another. In the critical chain method, there is no resource exchange in an activity that is not completed for another activity. That means that when an activity is started, it will be performed until it is finished, without interruption.

3 CRITICAL CHAIN METHOD BRIEF DESCRIPTION

Since the critical chain proposal is to reduce the effects caused by the factors above, the following actions are generally adopted:

- **Obtaining realistic estimates**

  That means obtaining the answer the question: "Which resources are actually required to perform this activity?" In such estimates, extensions related to any kind of contingency must not be considered.

- **Inserting precedences of activity and resource constraints**

  Defining precedences related to performing activities and to using activities such as productivity and resource availability.

- **Identifying the project critical chain**

  This is the critical path related to the use of project resources, that is, the project critical chain.

- **Setting resource objectives**

  Resources must clearly define how many hours estimated as realistic can be spent on activity development.

- **Creating a resource hours lung**

  The creation of a resource hour lung for the project and the critical chain activities protect the project against estimate variances, which may occur since they were obtained without any fat or addition. Lung hours must be defined to be used *as late as possible* when activities will be developed and, therefore, become known.

- **Protecting critical resources**

  People key to the project and who usually perform it receive a reserve hour lung for potential estimate overruns.

- **Defining activities as *as early as possible***

  This definition causes the activity to start at the *as early as possible* date, avoiding the student syndrome.

- **Monitoring resources**

  The project manager must, throughout the critical chain period, monitor hours spent by the resource and hours required to complete the activity.

The figure below shows a critical chain example.

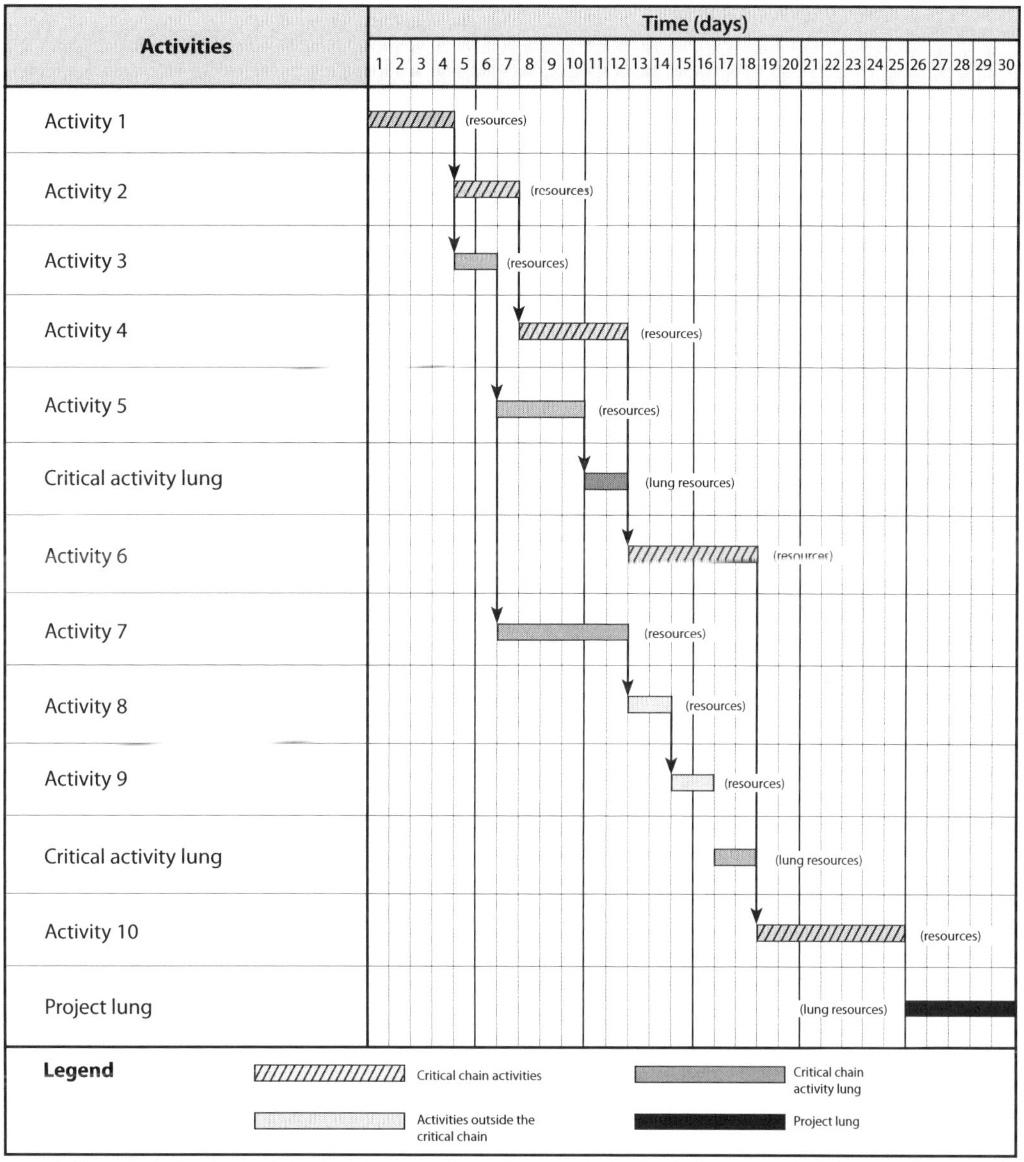

By applying critical chain in project management, it is possible to achieve a 20% to 25% reduction in the completion schedule deadline. Results like that render the project team as reliable and generate positive reviews from customers.

4 CRITICAL CHAIN METHOD ADVANTAGES AND DISADVANTAGES

The advantages of the critical chain method, in addition to reducing schedule time, are related to human behavior. Defining the *as early as possible* start, reducing estimates, and defining the "project-assigned resource" leads participants to pursue project objectives, to have greater commitment and productivity as well as achieving a level of excellence in activity execution.

A disadvantage of the critical chain method is related to its own application, namely, in environments where several projects are performed simultaneously and use the same resources, the method is not applicable, due to the loss of resource productivity.

One cause of failure during the application is the need for the company cultural change in order to define the goal of achieving the level of excellence in service execution and obtaining the team's commitment.

Additional information and reminders for the exam

- Milestones are significant project events, such as area release date by the customer, a phase end, among others. Milestones have zero duration.

- The creation of parametric estimating can be given by

    - Regression analysis (scatter diagram) and
    - Learning curve.

- Three-point estimating, also referred to as PERT (Technical Evaluation and Review Technique) analysis, uses the following formulas:

    Expected activity duration = $\frac{(P + 4ML + O)}{6}$

    Activity duration standard deviation = $(P - O)$

    Activity duration variance (standard deviation squared) = $(P - O)^2$

- The Monte Carlo analysis can show, in terms of time, the probability that the project be completed at any particular date or any activity likely to be on the critical path as well as the project overall risk.

- Critical path is the longest path schedule and determines the shortest time to complete the project. Critical path has zero float.

- In a project, more than one critical path may exist. You must be able to identify critical paths of projects and their durations.

- The most critical path is the path whose activities have low total float and, should any delay occur, can become a critical path. It can also become critical if the original critical path is shortened.

- **Floats**

    - **Total float:** how long an activity can be delayed without delaying the project finish date or the intermediate milestone
    - **Free float:** how long an activity can be delayed without delaying the early start date of its successor activity(ies).
    - **Project float:** how long a project can be delayed without delaying the finish date set by the client, the sponsor, or senior management.

- A negative float indicates the project is delayed.
- Fast tracking can result in rework, requires more attention from the project team, and usually increases risk.
- Compression always results in increased project costs.
- Resource leveling is used when dealing with resource constraints, such as limited quantity or resource availability.
- A milestone chart shows only major events. They are generally part of senior management reports.
- The project schedule can be a network diagram, a milestone chart, or a bar chart.
- Rules to consider physical progress percentage:
    - **50/50 Rule:** an activity is considered as 50% complete when it is started and 100% when it is completed.
    - **20/80 Rule:** an activity is considered as 20% complete when it is started and 100% when it is completed.
    - **0/100 Rule:** an activity is considered as 100% complete when it is completed.
- Heuristics is defined as a general rule.
    - A deadline-related heuristic example: foundations take 15% of the construction deadline.
    - A cost-related heuristic example: engineering services represent 5% of the total project.

Supplementary exercises

1. In regards to the Project time area of knowledge, indicate to which management processes group(s) each element is related and explain why. Follow the Activity list example.

1. Activity list

   ☐ Initiating ☒ Planning ☐ Executing ☐ Monitoring/controlling ☐ Closing

   The Activity list is an output of the Define Activities process and an input of the Sequence Activities, Estimate Activity Resources, Estimate Activity Durations, and Develop Schedule processes, which are all the Planning process.

2. Project schedule network diagram

   ☐ Initiating ☐ Planning ☐ Executing ☐ Monitoring/controlling ☐ Closing

3. Critical path method

   ☐ Initiating ☐ Planning ☐ Executing ☐ Monitoring/controlling ☐ Closing

4. Resource leveling

   ☐ Initiating ☐ Planning ☐ Executing ☐ Monitoring/controlling ☐ Closing

5. Activity attributes

   ☐ Initiating ☐ Planning ☐ Executing ☐ Monitoring/controlling ☐ Closing

6. Analogous estimating and parametric estimating

☐ Initiating ☐ Planning ☐ Executing ☐ Monitoring/controlling ☐ Closing

7. Applying leads and lags

☐ Initiating ☐ Planning ☐ Executing ☐ Monitoring/controlling ☐ Closing

8. What-if scenario analysis

☐ Initiating ☐ Planning ☐ Executing ☐ Monitoring/controlling ☐ Closing

9. Milestone list

☐ Initiating ☐ Planning ☐ Executing ☐ Monitoring/controlling ☐ Closing

10. Scheduling tool

☐ Initiating ☐ Planning ☐ Executing ☐ Monitoring/controlling ☐ Closing

11. Adjusting leads and lags

☐ Initiating ☐ Planning ☐ Executing ☐ Monitoring/controlling ☐ Closing

12. Project schedule

☐ Initiating ☐ Planning ☐ Executing ☐ Monitoring/controlling ☐ Closing

13. Schedule compression

☐ Initiating ☐ Planning ☐ Executing ☐ Monitoring/controlling ☐ Closing

14. Bottom-up estimating

☐ Initiating ☐ Planning ☐ Executing ☐ Monitoring/controlling ☐ Closing

15. Decomposition

☐ Initiating ☐ Planning ☐ Executing ☐ Monitoring/controlling ☐ Closing

2. Complete the sentences below, stating whether the option refers to input, tool/technique, or output, and identify the corresponding project management process.

1. Three-point estimates is a ______ of the ______ process.
2. Bottom-up estimating is a ______ of the ______ process.
3. Decomposition is a ______ of the ______ process.
4. Schedule network analysis is a ______ of the ______ process.
5. Resource leveling is a ______ of the ______ process.
6. Schedule baseline is a ______ of the ______ process.
7. Schedule compression is ______ of ______ processes.
8. Variance analysis is a ______ of the ______ process.
9. Applying leads and lags are ______ of ______ processes.
10. Project schedule network diagram is a ______ of the ______ process.
11. Parametric estimating is ______ of ______ processes.
12. Adjusting leads and lags are ______ of the ______ process.
13. Schedule data are ______ of the ______ process.
14. Activity attributes are ______ of the ______ process.
15. Milestone list is a ______ of the ______ process.

Questions

1. All of the following options are inputs of Define Activities process, except
   a. Activity attributes
   b. Organizational process assets
   c. Enterprise environmental factors
   d. Scope baseline

2. All of the following options are inputs of Sequence Activities process, except
   a. Activity list
   b. Activity attributes
   c. Milestone list
   d. Project document updates

3. All of the following options are inputs of Estimate Activity Resources, except
   a. Activity list
   b. Alternatives analysis
   c. Resource availability
   d. Activity attributes

4. All of the following options are inputs of Estimate Activity Durations process, except
   a. Parametric estimating
   b. Activity list
   c. Activity attributes
   d. Resources required for activities

5. All of the following options are inputs of Develop Schedule process, except
   a. Activity list
   b. Activity duration estimates
   c. Network diagram
   d. Cost estimating

6. All of the following options are tools or techniques of Define Activities process, except

a. Activity attributes

b. Rolling wave Planning

c. Expert judgment

d. Decomposition

7. All of the following options are tools or techniques of Sequence Activities process, except

a. Precedence diagramming method

b. Project network diagram

c. Applying leads and lags

d. Dependency determination

8. All of the following options are tools or techniques of Estimate Activity Resources, except

a. Resource breakdown structure

b. Expert judgment

c. Published estimating data

d. Bottom-up estimating

9. All of the following options are not tools or techniques of Estimate Activity Durations process, except

a. Expert judgment

b. Analogous estimating

c. Three-point estimates

d. Resource estimating

10. All of the following options are tools or techniques of Develop Schedule process, except

a. Network diagram analysis

b. Critical path method

c. Expert judgment

d. Schedule compression

11. All of the following options are tools or techniques of Develop Schedule process, except

a. Network diagram

b. Critical path method

c. Critical chain method

d. Resource leveling

12. All of the following options are outputs of Define Activities process, except

a. Activity list

b. Templates

c. Activity attributes

d. Milestone list

13. All of the following options are outputs of Estimate Activity Resources, except

a. Resources required for activities

b. Resource breakdown structure

c. Resource availability

d. Project document updates

14. All of the following options are outputs of Develop Schedule process, except

a. Project schedule

b. Resource leveling

c. Schedule baseline

d. Project document updates

15. All of the following options are not inputs of Define Activities process, except

a. Activity list

b. Scope baseline

c. Activity attributes

d. Expert judgment

16. All of the following options are not inputs of Sequence Activities process, except

a. Leads and lags

b. Dependency determination

c. Activity attributes

d. Precedence diagramming method

17. All of the following options are not tools or techniques of Define Activities process, except

a. Decomposition

b. Product analysis

c. Alternatives identification

d. Scope baseline

18. All of the following options are not tools or techniques of Sequence Activities process, except

a. Activity list

b. Expert judgment

c. Applying leads and lags

d. Decomposition

19. All of the following options are not tools or techniques of Estimate Activity Resources, except

a. Activity list

b. Bottom-up estimating

c. Organizational process assets

d. Enterprise environmental factors

20. All of the following options are not tools or techniques of Estimate Activity Durations process, except

a. Data published to help estimates

b. Bottom-up estimating

c. Parametric estimating

d. Activity duration estimates

21. All of the following options are not tools or techniques of Develop Schedule process, except

a. Resource leveling

b. Duration estimating

c. Activity list

d. Network diagram

22. All of the following options are not outputs of Define Activities process, except

a. Expert judgment

b. Decomposition

c. Activity list

d. Rolling wave Planning

23. All of the following options are not outputs of Sequence Activities process, except

a. Dependency determination

b. Project network diagram

c. Applying leads and delays

d. Precedence diagramming method

24. All of the following options are not outputs of Estimate Activity Resources, except

a. Bottom-up estimating

b. Resource breakdown structure

c. Expert judgment

d. Alternatives analysis

25. All of the following options are inputs of Control Schedule process, except

a. Project schedule

b. Project management plan

c. Schedule variance analysis

d. Work performance information

26. All of the following options are tools or techniques of Control Schedule process, except

a. Performance reviews

b. Variance analysis

c. Project management software

d. Project schedule

27. All of the following options are tools or techniques of Control Schedule process, except

a. Adjusting leads and lags

b. What-if scenario analysis

c. Work performance information

d. Schedule compression

28. All of the following options are not outputs of Control Schedule, except

a. Work performance measurement

b. Performance reviews

c. Variance analysis

d. What-if scenario analysis

29. The project manager is concerned with the physical progress of your project and is reviewing the sequence of activities with the least flexible schedule. Which technique is he using?

a. Precedence diagramming method

b. Critical chain method

c. Schedule compression

d. Critical path method

30. A dependency determining that an activity is completed before another one is started is an example of

a. External dependency

b. Arbitrated dependency

c. Mandatory dependency

d. Decisive dependency

31. When estimating an activity duration, an optimistic 15-day forecast and another pessimistic 21-day forecast were collected. Which is the activity standard deviation?

a. 6

b. 1

c. 3

d. 2

32. Heuristics is best well defined as a

a. Control technique

b. Planning tool

c. Scope definition tool

d. General rule

33. Applying lags in the start-to-start dependency relationship among activities causes

a. The predecessor activity to be completed later

b. Activities to be started at the same time

c. The successor activity to be started later than its predecessor

d. Activities to be always completed at the same time

34. Which of the following is correct?

a. In a schedule, there can be only positive floats

b. In a schedule, there can only be one critical path

c. The network diagram always changes according to the schedule date

d. Critical path shows the minimum time that the project will take

35. The duration of a schedule milestone:

a. Equals the phase duration it represents

b. Equals zero

c. Equals one

d. Equals the activity duration that defines it

36. An activity free float is determined:

a. By its lag time allowed without delaying the next activity start

b. By its allowed lag time without delaying the project end

c. By its allowed lag time without delaying the early start date of the next activity

d. By its lag time allowed without delaying the successor activity start

37. An activity free total is determined:

a. By its lag time allowed without delaying the next activity start

b. By its allowed lag time without delaying the project end

c. By its allowed lag time without delaying the early start date of the next activity

d. By its lag time allowed without delaying the successor activity start

38. You are reviewing the project schedule and find that an activity can be delayed by 3 days without delaying the successor activity early start and 8 days without delaying the project end. You conclude that this activity:

a. Has an 8-day free float and a 3-day total float

b. Has a 3-day free float and an 8-day total float

c. Has an 11-day total float

d. Has a 5-day free float

39. A schedule activity is the predecessor of another one, which is the last activity of the schedule critical path. The float between them is 3 days. That means:

a. The predecessor activity is on the critical path

b. The successor activity can be delayed by 3 days without compromising the project end

c. The predecessor activity has a 3-day total free float

d. The predecessor activity has no float since its successor is on the critical path

40. The project manager is concerned with a schedule activity, because its estimated duration was determined using the estimating technique. However, one team member convinces the manager that this activity has a 2-day total float, hence there is no reason to worry. Even so, the manager does not feel satisfied because:

a. The team member above elaborated the estimated activity duration

b. This activity has a 2-day free float as well

c. If the activity is delayed, it may delay the project end

d. He believes this activity will be delayed

41. A company is having trouble assigning resources to its projects due to the resource availability and the number of ongoing projects. In a given project, if the project schedule and cost are not as important as the quantity of resources allocated to each month, which is the best technique to be applied in the schedule?

a. Schedule compression

b. Fast tracking to schedule activities

c. The Monte Carlo analysis

d. Resource leveling

42. During Planning, the project team estimated durations and then created the schedule, which resulted in a very long-term project. What is wrong with this scenario?

a. The team did not apply schedule compression

b. The team did not elaborate the project network diagram before creating the schedule

c. The team did not apply the Monte Carlo analysis estimates

d. The team did not apply resource leveling

43. The project team is using weighted average term estimates to analyze the project network diagram. In this case, what type of analysis is being used?

a. Duration analysis method

b. Critical path method

c. CPM

d. PERT analysis

44. You are working on a project and it is necessary to cut off 2 days from deadline. Based on the data below, which activity would you like to cut off?

Activity	Predecessor	Duration
Start	None	0
A	Start	1
B	Start	2
C	Start	8
D	A	8
E	B, C	1
F	C	2
G	D	4
H	E	7
I	F	1
End	G, H, I	0

a. Activity D

b. Activity B

c. Activity C

d. Activity G

45. You are working on a project and it is necessary to cut off 2 days from the deadline. Based on the data below, which activity would you like to cut off?

Activity	Predecessor	Duration
Start	None	0
A	Start	2
B	Start	3
C	Start	4
D	A	8
E	B, C	4
F	C	7
G	D	6
H	E	5
I	F	2
End	G, H, I	0

a. Activity D

b. Activity B

c. Activity C

d. Activity H

46. You are working on a project and it is necessary to cut off 3 days from the deadline. Based on the data below, which activity would you try to reduce and what would happen to the project?

Activity	Predecessor	Duration
Start	None	0
A	Start	2
B	Start	3
C	Start	4
D	A	8
E	B, C	4
F	C	7
G	D	6
H	E	5
I	F	2
End	G, H, I	0

a. Activity D and the project will have 3 critical paths

b. Activity B and the project will have a ghost activity

c. Activity C and the project will have 2 critical paths

d. Activity H and the project will have 2 critical paths

47. You are working on a project and it is necessary to cut off 2 days from the deadline. Based on the data below, which activity would you try to reduce and how many critical paths would the project have?

Activity	Predecessor	Duration
Start	None	0
A	Start	5
B	Start	2
C	A, B	3
D	B	4
E	C	3
F	D	3
End	E,F	0

a. Activity A and the project will have 2 critical paths

b. Activity D and the project will have 2 critical paths

c. Activity C and the project would have a critical path

d. Activity F and the project would have a critical path

48. You are working on a project and it is necessary to cut off 2 days from the deadline. Based on the data below, the duration of which activities would you try to reduce, considering the minimum activities to be changed?

Activity	Predecessor	Duration
Start	None	0
A	Start	2
B	Start	1
C	Start	4
D	A	6
E	B, C	4
F	C	7
G	D	5
H	E	5
I	F	2
End	G, H, I	0

a. Activity D

b. Activity B

c. Activity C

d. Activity H

Answer key

Supplementary exercises

2. 1 - Tool/technique - Estimate Activity Durations

2 - Tool technique - Estimate Activity Resources

3 - Technique - Define Activities

4 - Tool/technique - Develop Schedule

5 - Tool/technique - Control Schedule

6 - Output - Develop Schedule

7 - Tool/technique - Develop Schedule and Control Schedule

8 - Tool/technique - Control Schedule

9 - Techniques - Sequence Activities and Develop Schedule

10 - Output - Sequence Activities

11 - Tool/technique - Estimate Activity Durations

12 - Techniques - Control Schedule

13 - Output - Develop Schedule

14 - Outputs -Define Activities

15 - Outputs -Define Activities

Questions

1. A. Activity attributes will be defined as the activity list is executed or after it. Therefore, they are outputs of the Define Activities process.

2. D. Remember: Project document updates are never considered as process inputs — they are always outputs!

3. B. Alternatives analysis is a technique of Estimate resources process, which is raising alternative possibilities for the activity execution, which may change the type and quantity of resources to be used.

4. A. Parametric estimating (using productivity indexes based on product mass studies) is a technique for estimating the activity duration, not an input of the process.

5. D. During the exam, when the schedule is mentioned, it means a physical schedule (not a physical-financial one). In order to develop the physical schedule, you do not need cost estimating.

6. A. Decomposition (of WBS work packages during activities), expert judgment and rolling wave Planning (a development Planning characteristic) are tools or techniques of Define Activities process. Activity attributes is a process output.

7. B. The project network diagram is the major process of Sequence Activities process.

8. A. The resource breakdown structure can only be performed after resource estimating. It is a process output.

9. D. Resource estimating is a process input. The other options are process tools or techniques.

10. C. Expert judgment is not a tool or technique of the Develop Schedule process.

11. A. Pay attention: option A is labeled as network diagram, which is a process input. If you had written network diagram analysis, it would be a technique. The other options are process tools or techniques.

12. B. Templates are tools used to define in the Define Activities process.

13. C. Resource availability information are inputs of Estimate Activity Resources process.

14. B. Resource leveling is one of the techniques of Schedule development, not a process output.

15. B. Note that the question is "Which of the following IS an input of the Define Activities process?". The major input of this process is the Scope baseline (project scope statement, WBS, and WBS dictionary). The activity list and the activity attributes are process outputs. Expert judgment is a tool, not a process input.

16. C. Note that the question is "Which of the following IS an input of the Sequence activities process?" In this question, only option C is an input of this process. Activity attributes were defined in the previous process, named "Define Activities." All other options are process tools and techniques.

17. A. The question, asked more clearly, is "Which of the following options IS a tool or technique of the Define Activities process?" Option D is a process output. Product analysis and identification of alternatives are performed in the Define Scope process, which occurs before Create WBS and Define Activities processes. The decomposition of work packages in WBS is one of the techniques and tools of this process.

18. C. The question, asked more clearly, is "Which of the following options IS a tool or technique of the Sequence Activities process?" The activity list is a process input. Expert judgment and decomposition are not tools and techniques of the process.

19. B. The question, asked more clearly, is "Which of the following options IS a tool or technique of the Estimate Activity Resources process?" The activity list is a process input. Organizational process assets and enterprise environmental processes are always inputs of any project management process. Bottom-up estimating is one of the tools of the Estimate Activity Resources process.

20. C. The question, asked more clearly, is "Which of the following options IS a tool or technique of the Estimate Activity Durations process?" Data published to help estimate and bottom-up estimating do not

apply to duration (only resource estimating does). Activity duration estimates is the process output itself. Parametric estimating is one of the techniques applicable to Duration estimating.

21. A. The question, asked more clearly, is "Which of the following options IS a tool or technique of the Develop Schedule process?" Activity list, Network diagram, and Duration estimating are not tools or techniques. They are inputs or outputs of processes. Resource leveling is a technique of the Develop Schedule process.

22. C. The question, asked more clearly, is "Which of the following options IS an output of the Define Activities process?" The only output, among options presented by the question, of Define Activities is the activity list. The other options are process tools and techniques.

23. B. The question, asked more clearly, is "Which of the following options IS an output of the Sequence Activities process?" The major product (output) of the Sequence Activities process is the project network diagram. The other options are process tools and techniques.

24. B. The question, asked more clearly, is "Which of the following options IS an output of the Estimate Activity Resources process?" In the exam, remember: the terms bottom-up estimating, expert judgment, and analysis always refers to tools and techniques. The resource breakdown structure is one of the outputs of the Estimate Activity Resources process.

25. C. What do you need to control the schedule? The schedule itself, the project management plan (which includes the schedule management plan, and the work (performance) progress information. Therefore, options A, B, and D are process inputs. The schedule variance analysis is a process technique.

26. D. The project schedule is not a tool or technique. It is a product (an output) of the Develop Schedule process and an input of the Control Schedule process.

27. C. In order to control the schedule (through tools and techniques), you first need to have (input) information on the work performance – option C. The other options are tools and techniques.

28. A. In the exam, remember: whenever the term analysis comes up, it refers to a tool or technique. It will never be an input or output. Option A is a process output.

29. D. Critical path method shows the sequence of activities with the least flexibility.

30. C. If dependency determines that the activity be completed before another one starts, it is mandatory, not arbitrary. There is not any suggestion that it is external. The term decisive dependency is not used.

31. B. Standard deviation is calculated by the formula $d = (P - O)/6 = (21 - 15)/6 = 1$

32. D. Heuristics is best defined as a general rule. Examples might be cost per square foot, cost per code line, and others.

33. C. Applying lags causes the successor activity to start later than its predecessor, in case of a start-to-start dependency. Option D can only be possible where the predecessor activity has a duration equal to the sum of the duration of the successor activity and the waiting time, but that's not necessarily true, as stated in this option.

34. D. In a schedule, if an activity is delayed, it has a negative float. In a schedule, it may exist more than one critical path. The network diagram may or may not change when a schedule date is changed, depending on dependencies, floats, and the reason to change the schedule. Critical path confirms the minimum time to complete the project.

35. B. A milestone only shows the start or end of a project phase or a series of activities without duration.

36. C. By definition, an activity free float is determined by the lag time allowed without delaying the next activity early start date.

37. B. By definition, total float is determined by the lag time allowed for that activity without delaying the project end.

38. B. By definition, we have: 1) An activity free float is determined by the lag time allowed for that activity without delaying the next activity early start date – therefore, free float is 3 days. 2) Total float is determined by the total lag time allowed for that activity without delaying the project end – therefore, 8 days.

39. C. Option A is not correct – if it has a float, it does not belong to the critical path. Option B: the activity is the last one on the critical path; therefore, if it is delayed, the project end may likewise be delayed. Option D is not correct either, since it has been stated that it has a 3-day float between it and its successor. Option C is correct: it can be delayed by 3 days without delaying the successor and without delaying the project end.

40. C. Pay attention: what matters now is the possible lag to the project end. If the activity is delayed by 2 days, the total float is zero it, and it will be on the critical path or create another schedule critical path. If it is delayed by more than 2 days, it will delay the project end.

41. D. Applying compression and fast tracking can result in project time and cost as well as applying larger quantities of resources. Monte Carlo analysis does not apply directly to resources. Resource leveling is the best option.

42. B. Question C might be correct, but it does not necessarily apply the Monte Carlo analysis estimates. Compression (option A) and resource leveling (option D) are techniques that can be applied to the schedule, but they are not mandatory. The project network diagram preparation is mandatory before creating the schedule.

43. D. Note that option A is a made-up term and options B and C are the same thing. The PERT analysis is a weighted average to calculate activity durations.

44. C. If you create the network diagram, the result will be

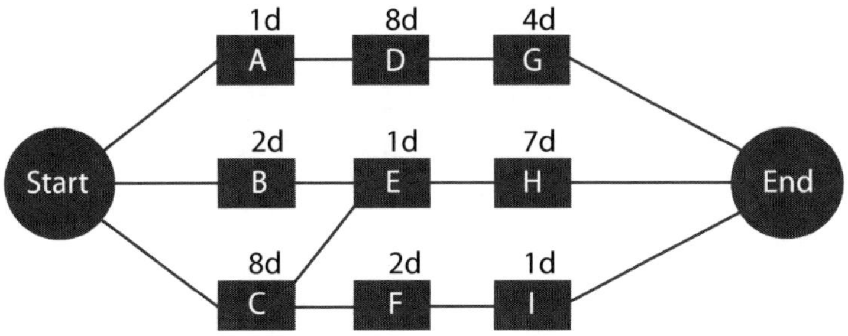

If you elaborate a network diagram, the following forward passes will be obtained:

- Start-A-D-G-End duration = 13d
- Start-B-E-H-End duration = 10d
- Start-C-F-I-End duration = 11d
- Start-C-E-H-End duration = 16d – critical path

If anticipating the project end by 2 days is desired, it would be necessary to reduce the Activity C duration by 2 days. It would be also possible to reduce Activity H duration by 2 days, but it is always preferable to reduce the duration of the first activities. In addition, activity H is not an answer option.

45. A. If you create the network diagram, the result will be:

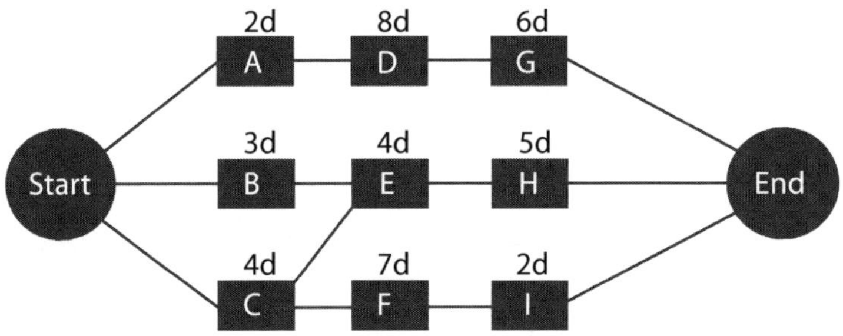

There are 4 forward passes:

- Start-A-D-G-End duration = 16d – critical path
- Start-B-E-H-End duration = 12d
- Start-C-F-I-End duration = 13d
- Start-C-E-H-End duration = 13d

If we would like to cut off 2 days from the project end, it would be necessary to eliminate 2 days from activity D. It would also be possible to eliminate 2 days from activity G, but it is always preferable to reduce the duration of the first activities. In addition, activity H is not an answer option.

46. A. If you create the network diagram, the result will be

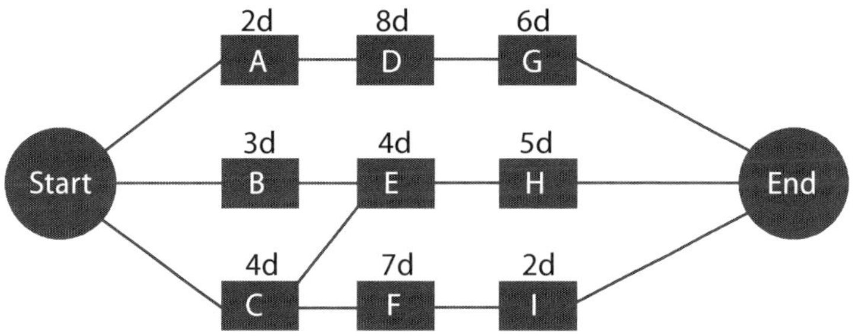

There are 4 forward passes:

- Start-A-D-G-End duration = 16d – critical path
- Start-B-E-H-End duration = 12d
- Start-C-F-I-End duration = 13d
- Start-C-E-H-End duration = 13d

If we would like to cut off 3 days from the project end, it would be necessary to eliminate 3 days from activity D. It would also be possible to eliminate 2 days from activity G, but it is always preferable to reduce the duration of the first activities. In addition, activity G is not an answer option. Reducing activity D by 3 days, the project would have 3 critical paths

47. A. If you create the network diagram, the result will be:

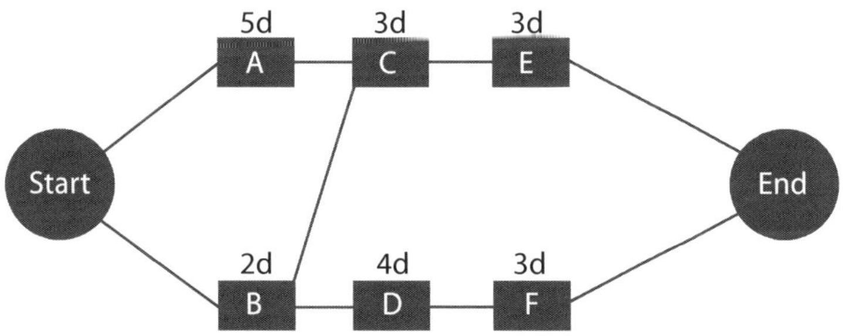

There are 3 forward passes:

- Start-A-C-E-End duration = 11d – critical path
- Start-B-C-E-End duration = 8d
- Start-B-D-F-End duration = 9d

If we would like to cut off 2 days from the project end, it would be necessary to eliminate 2 days from activity A. It would be also possible to reduce activity C or E by 2 days, but it is always preferable to reduce the duration of the first activities. Note that the project now has 2 two critical paths lasting 9 days each.

48. A. If you create the network diagram, the result will be

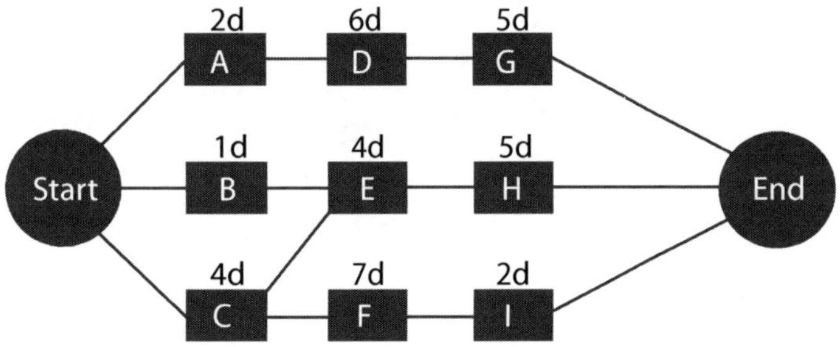

There are 4 forward passes:

- Start-A-D-G-End duration = 13d – critical path
- Start-B-E-H-End duration = 11d
- Start-C-F-I-End duration = 13d – critical path
- Start-C-E-H-End duration = 13d – critical path

For the first critical path (Start-A-D-G-End), the ideal would be reducing activity D by 2 days, which is the longest on that path. For other critical paths, considering it is necessary to change the minimum number of activities, the ideal would be reducing activity C duration by 2 days. Note, however, that such changes cause the project to have 4 critical paths, which, in terms of project management, increase risks.

Chapter 7

PROJECT COST MANAGEMENT

1. Introduction
2. Project Cost Management processes
3. Costs in projects
4. Project account plan
5. Cost management plan
6. Cost management in project planning
7. Cost management in project monitoring and controlling

Attachment I	Cost of quality
Attachment II	Earned value management

- Additional information and reminders for the exam
- Supplementary exercises
- Questions
- Answer key

7.1 INTRODUCTION

This chapter will introduce the project management processes related to the Cost knowledge area, their respective inputs, tools, techniques, and outputs.

7.2 PROJECT COST MANAGEMENT PROCESSES

According to *PMBOK® Guide*, the Project Cost Management includes the processes involved in estimates, budgets, and cost control, so that the project can be completed within the approved budget.

The Project Cost Management processes are

- **Estimate Costs**

  The development process of a monetary resources cost estimate required to complete the project activities.

- **Determine Budget**

  The process of aggregating individual activity estimated work packages in order to establish a cost authorized baseline.

- **Control Costs**

  It is the process of monitoring the project progress in order to update budget and managing changes made to the cost performance baseline.

The following flowchart displays the relationship among the Project Cost Management processes and their locations across the project management process groups.

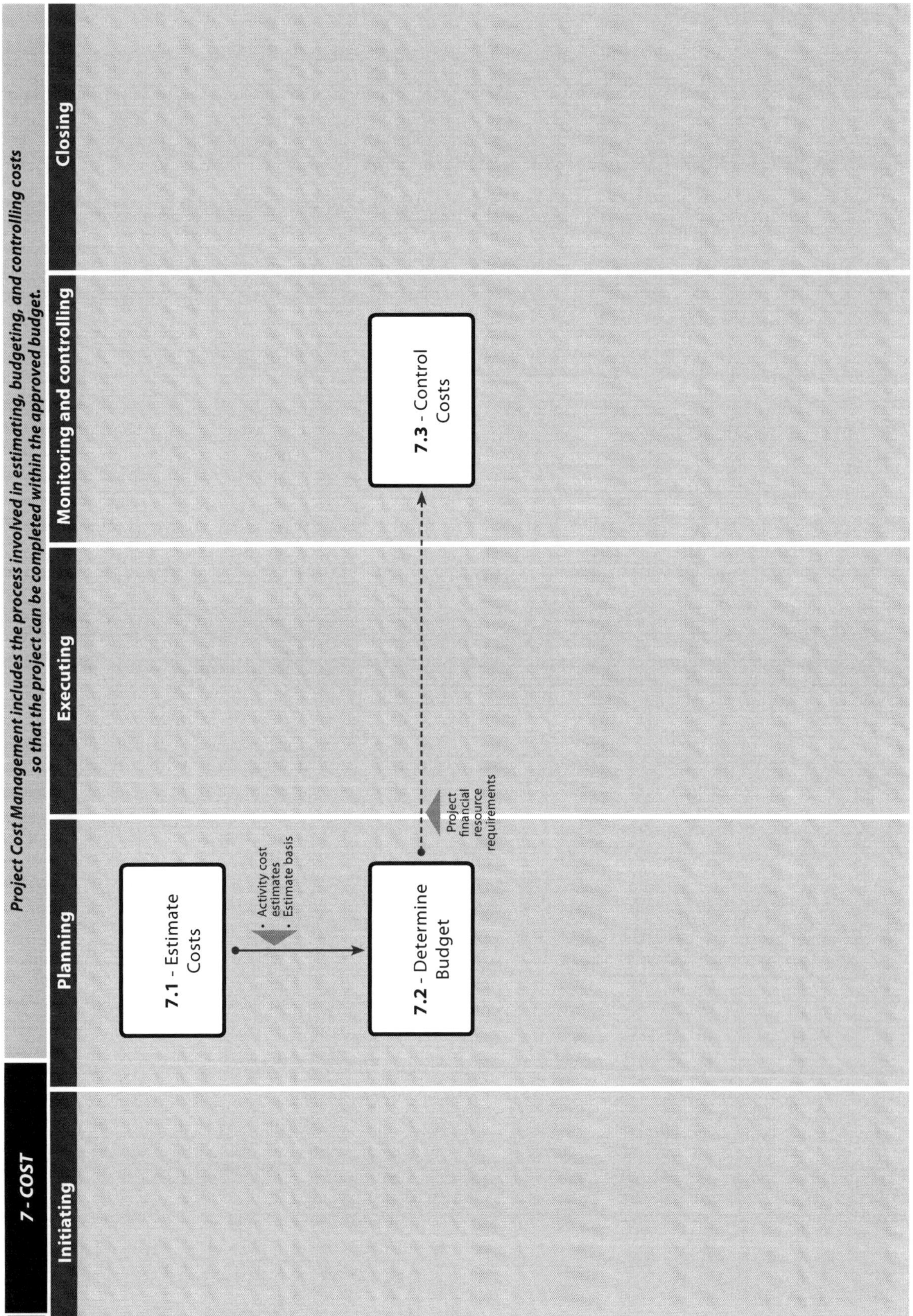
7 - COST
Project Cost Management includes the process involved in estimating, budgeting, and controlling costs so that the project can be completed within the approved budget.
Initiating
Planning
Executing
Monitoring and controlling
Closing
7.1 - Estimate Costs
• Activity cost estimates
• Estimate basis
7.2 - Determine Budget
Project financial resource requirements
7.3 - Control Costs

7.3 COSTS IN PROJECTS

For all projects, irrespective of their type and size, there is no need to use resources to perform activities. These features, which can be human, equipment, or materials, cost money to the company or to the project owner. Apart from this type of cost, named direct cost, there are other costs that must be considered in the project, such as the management salaries, office maintenance expenses, and office supplies.

- **Cost**

  Cost is the monetary value or price of a project activity or component. This value comprises the sum of all costs involved in the project activity or component performance.

- **Direct cost**

  Direct cost is the cost directly associated with a work activity performance, that is the monetary value to be disbursed due to the use of resources specific to that activity. As an example, we can have cost related to the project team working hours, cost of materials used in the activity, cost related to equipment lease used exclusively for the activity, among others.

- **Indirect cost**

  Indirect cost is the cost incurred by the company for several projects and their operation. This cost is not directly associated with the performance of an activity work and usually comes from sharing the company expenses among several projects. As an example, we can have: the company's maintenance expenses, senior management salaries, accounting staff salaries, company's communication expenses, among others.

- **Fixed cost**

  Fixed cost does not vary according to the amount of work related to a particular activity and complies with various thresholds. As an example, the cost of renting a room for the project will not change and will comply with the maximum room occupancy.

- **Variable cost**

  Variable cost varies proportionately according to production and the amount of work. As an example, we have material costs of an activity, which vary according to the amount of work of that activity.

7.3.1 OTHER DEFINITIONS AND CONSIDERATIONS RELATED TO PROJECT COSTS

- **Activity unit cost**

  The activity unit cost is the sum of all costs incurred when Executing an activity service unit. For example, the company has a database record stating that the unit cost to run a square meter of masonry is $45.

- **Activity total cost**

  The activity total cost is the sum of all costs incurred when Executing an activity. For example, the company needs to run 100 m^2 of masonry at the unit cost of $45. The masonry activity total cost will be $4,500.

- **Sunk cost**

  Sunk cost is the value that has been spent on the project without any control, which must not be used in the project continuity decision analysis.

- **Cost of opportunity**

  Opportunity cost is the cost associated with the benefit of one or more business rejected opportunities based on choosing an opportunity. As an example, a company decides to reduce production of component A to enable production of a new component in the same manufacturing line. The opportunity cost of manufacturing the new component is the amount that the company will fail to sell because of lower production of component A.

- **Cost of quality**

  Cost of quality is the cost incurred to obtain quality or it is the cost attributed to poor quality in the product or service. This cost may be due to assessment and prevention, internal or external failures, or injury caused to users or customers.

- **Cost of taxes**

  Cost of taxes is the cost related to the payment of taxes on the project product or service. The cost of taxes can be related to (municipal, state, or federal) jurisdiction or a triggering event (services, circulation of products, and others).

- **Contingency reserve**

  Contingency reserve is a monetary value added to the project budget to be used to deal with "known unknown" (known and not forecast) risk events occurring in the project. The sum of the project budget and the contingency reserve will be the project cost performance baseline.

- **Management reserve**

  Management reserve is a monetary value added to the project to be used when dealing with risks or changes not forecast in the project. This reserve is usually managed by the project owner or sponsor. The sum of cost performance baselines and the management reserve will be the project's final budget.

7.4 PROJECT ACCOUNT PLAN

The project account plan is an accounting system or coding used to monitor project costs, usually based on the company's chart of accounts. Similar to WBS, the chart of accounts is a split of the project budget into smaller shares (accounts), so they are easier to control.

In order to be usual, the Project account plan must have the following features:

- Comply with the accounting system principles used
- Comply with the company's accounting standards
- Enable correlation with the company's chart of accounts
- Develop adequately according to the company and the project size
- Enable adaptations and a larger development, if necessary

- Be clear and enable analysis of its components
- Enable effective communication of required management information

7.5 COST MANAGEMENT PLAN

Cost management plan is a document formalizing activities related to execution and updates of the project cost estimates and budget. In addition to information on how to perform such activities, the plan must specify individuals authorized to make changes to the project estimates and budget.

7.6 COST MANAGEMENT IN PROJECT PLANNING

According to PMI®, cost management on Project Planning comprises two processes:

- ***Estimate Costs***;
- ***Determine Budget***.

7.6.1 ESTIMATE COSTS (*PMBOK® GUIDE*, PROCESS 7.1)

The main question asked throughout the project life cycle is: "How much will the project cost?" Or, better yet, "After all, how much will the project cost?". This is only possible to know when the project is completed. You can run an estimate based on information currently available. Cost estimate is the process of forecasting a future result in terms of costs based on information currently available. As the project progresses and the resulting knowledge about its details increases, a new, more accurate estimate must be performed. In an initial stage of the project, estimates can be of the "gross magnitude order" type. In a second stage, estimates may be either analog or top-down, with greater precision than the first estimate. After defining activities, estimates may be of the bottom-up type, using the sum of costs of all resources to be used in all project activities with all indirect costs to define the project cost.

7.6.1.1 ESTIMATE COSTS: INPUTS, TOOLS AND TECHNIQUES, AND OUTPUTS

INPUTS

1 **Scope baseline**

- **Project scope statement**

  The project scope statement contains information related to the project cost, such as assumptions and constraints, and must be considered when estimating costs.

- **Work Breakdown Structure (WBS)**

  The WBS, containing information on work packages and project deliverables, must be considered when estimating costs.

- **WBS dictionary**

  The WBS dictionary, containing detailed information on WBS components, must be considered when estimating costs.

2 **Project schedule**

The project schedule defines types and quantities of resources required to perform each activity and must be considered when estimating costs.

3 **Human resource plan**

The human resource plan provides information on the company's human resource policy, such as salaries and rewards of the project team and must be considered when estimating costs.

4 **Risk register**

The risk register provides information on identified risks, root causes, and uncertain project assumptions and must be considered when estimating costs.

5 **Enterprise environmental factors**

Environmental factors must be considered when estimating costs related to:

- **Market conditions**

  Lack or scarcity of resources in the market that may negatively impact the project cost must be verified. Likewise, special offers and conditions of supply of certain resources that can positively impact the project cost must be verified.

- **Commercial databases**

  It must be verified whether there are information on costs, such as price list of materials and equipment, manpower assignment, and performance of special services.

6 **Organizational process assets**

Policies, procedures, and guidelines related to the company's cost estimates must be considered, including historical cost information from previous projects, cost estimate templates, lessons learned, and any other information on the company's cost estimate.

TOOLS AND TECHNIQUES

1 **Expert judgment**

The use of expert judgment to define the project scope estimate can be obtained from several sources, including

- Other units of the organization;
- Consultants;
- Stakeholders, including users, sponsors, and others;
- Technical and professional associations;
- Industrial groups;
- Suppliers and manufacturers; and
- Project Management Office (PMO).

2 **Analogous estimating**

Analogous estimating, also called *top-down*, uses expert opinion to estimate project costs based on costs of previous projects. It is usually used in the project's early stages, when details about project activities are not known yet.

3 **Parametric estimating**

Parametric estimating is a technique that uses values related to resource consumption by unit of measure defined by means of product mass studies and may be used when estimating costs of project activities.

4 **Bottom-up estimating**

Bottom-up estimating is a cost estimating technique that considers the cost of each item of work in its most detailed level possible. The sum of costs at this level is added to compose the cost of the next higher level and so on, until it reaches the desired level of cost estimates.

5 **Three-point estimates**

Risk consideration when estimating activity costs may be performed using the so-called three-point estimates technique, which is applied to values obtained both from analogous estimating and parametric estimating. Three-point estimates consider activity costs based on

- **Most likely cost (ML)**

  Activity cost based on defining realistic efforts and forecast expenses to perform an activity.

- **Optimistic cost (O)**

  Activity cost based on analyzing the most optimistic scenario possible to perform the activity.

- **Pessimistic cost (P)**

  Activity cost based on analyzing the most pessimistic scenario possible to perform the activity.

Having this information at hand, using the PERT (*Program Evaluation and Review Technique*) formula, it is possible to obtain the activity Expected Cost (EC).

Expected Cost = (P + 4ML + O)/6

The expected cost must be the goal to be achieved in order to complete the activity.

6 **Reserve analysis**

In the cost estimating process, activity contingency reserves must be analyzed and gathered together in a single contingency reserve. This analysis must be carefully performed to avoid the tendency to exaggerate reserve applications to activities.

7 **Cost of quality (COQ)**

Cost of quality must be considered when preparing activity cost estimates.

8 **Project management estimating software**

Software applications for project management and estimate executions are used to support the elaboration of estimate spreadsheets.

9 **Vendor bid analysis**

One way to obtain cost estimates is to consult with suppliers accredited by the company that have a high level of knowledge at the activity as well as proven reliability when showing and presenting these costs.

OUTPUTS

1 **Activity cost estimates**

Activity cost estimates are quantitative assessments of likely costs required to execute the project work. They can be presented in a summary form or in detail. Costs are estimated for all resources applied when estimating activity costs. This includes, but is not limited to, direct labor, materials, equipment, services, facilities, information technology, and special categories, such as inflation allowance or contingency costs. Indirect costs, if included in the project estimate, may be included at the activity level or higher levels.

2 **Basis of estimates**

Information leading to the activity cost estimates must be listed in detail to provide tracking, verification, and comparison with the activity actual cost.

3 **Project document updates**

Project documents that must be updated include risk register and any other document related to this process.

7.1 - Estimate Costs

The process of developing an approximation of the monetary resources needed to complete project activities.

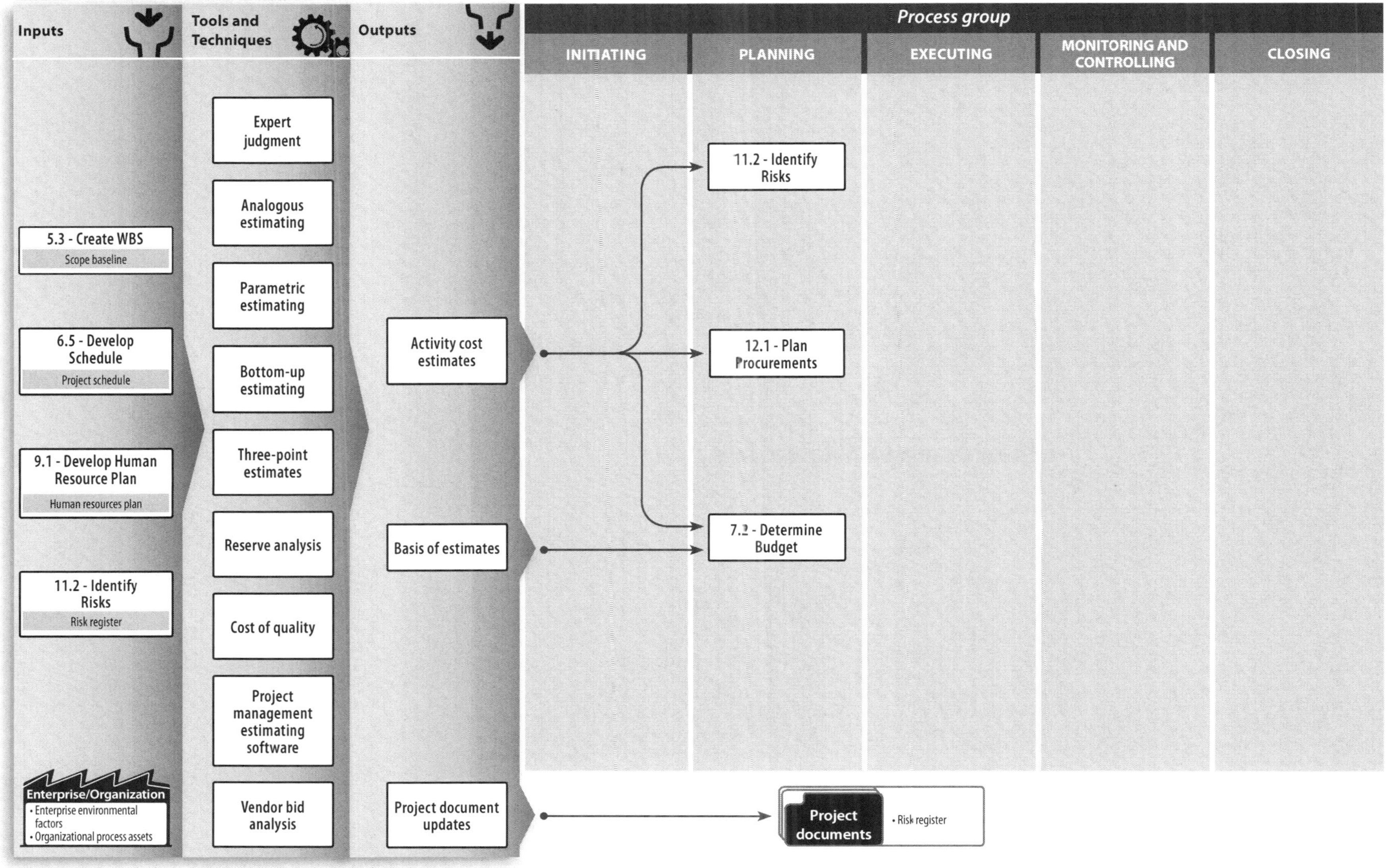

7.6.2 DEVELOP BUDGET (*PMBOK® GUIDE*, PROCESS 7.2)

The Determine Budget process is the bottom-up aggregation of the project cost estimates. This process starts by gathering together the estimated costs of activities that compose the cost of work packages. The cost aggregation of work packages will make up the control account cost. Aggregation of control accounts will compose the project cost. The sum of the project cost and the contingency reserve will make up the project cost performance baseline. The cost performance baseline added to the management reserve will compose the project final budget.

The figure below shows a sample budget diagram.

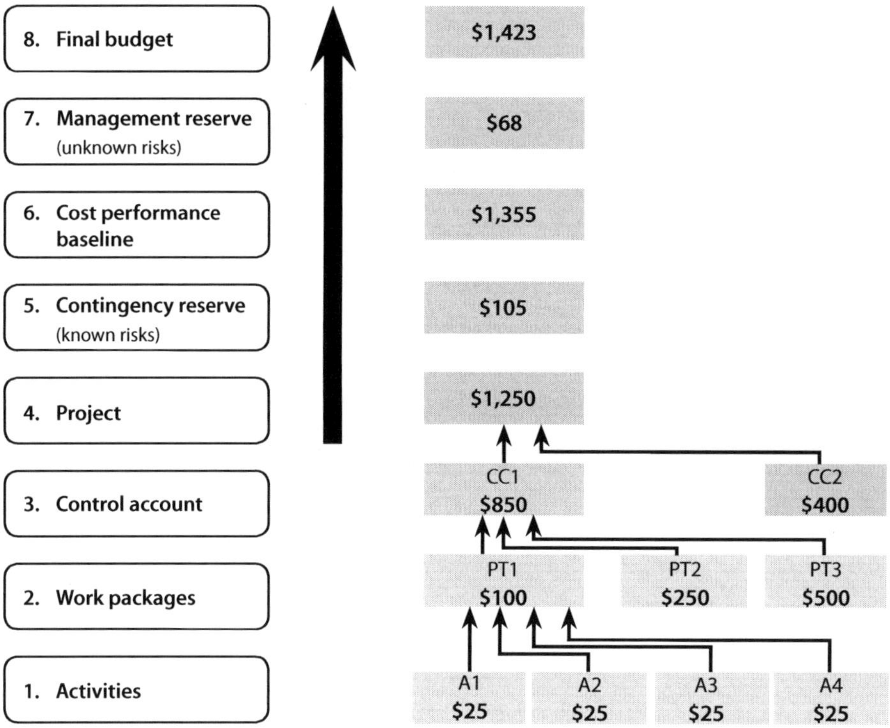

7.6.2.1 DETERMINE BUDGET: INPUTS, TOOLS AND TECHNIQUES, AND OUTPUTS

INPUTS

1 **Activity cost estimates**

Cost estimates of activities are the major inputs of the Determine Budget process.

2 **Basis of estimates**

Information leading to the activity estimated costs must be considered in the Determine Budget process.

3 **Scope baseline**

- **Project scope statement**

  The project scope statement, covering information related to project costs, such as assumptions and constraints, must be considered in this process.

- **Work Breakdown Structure (WBS)**

  The Work Breakdown Structure (WBS), containing information on work packages and project deliverables, must be considered in this process.

- **WBS dictionary**

  The WBS dictionary, containing detailed information on the WBS components, must be considered in this process.

4 **Project schedule**

Information related to start and finish of schedule activities will be used to define the financial resource needs across the project.

5 **Resource calendars**

Resource calendars must be verified whether there is work on special days or times requiring the payment of additional amounts to resources.

6 **Contracts**

Procurement and contracting costs, information related to payments and any other information related to costs in contracts, must be considered in this process.

7 **Organizational process assets**

Policies, procedures, and guidelines related to determining the company's budgets must be considered, including historical cost information from previous projects, budget templates, lessons learned, and any other information on this process.

TOOLS AND TECHNIQUES

1 **Cost aggregation**

Described in item 7.6 above.

2 **Reserve analysis**

Contingency and management reserves must have their values set to cover expenses with known risks and unknown risks; both are not forecast in the project budget.

3 **Expert judgment**

Using expert judgment to define the project budget can be obtained from several sources, such as

- Other organization units;
- Consultants;
- Stakeholders, including users, sponsors, and others;

- Technical and professional associations;
- Industrial groups;
- Suppliers and manufacturers; and
- Project Management Office (PMO).

4 **Historical relationships**

Any historical relationship, such as supplies and previous contracting, that can provide information on parametric or analogous estimating must be used in this process.

5 **Funding limit reconciliation**

Reconciliation consists in comparing and adapting budget values with the financing values defined by the customer or organization.

OUTPUTS

1 **Cost performance baseline**

Cost performance baseline is the sum of the project budget and the contingency reserve.

Since project expenses start slowly and increase gradually until a certain point of the project and then eventually decrease until reaching the project end, cost performance baseline can be represented by an S curve, as shown by the figure below.

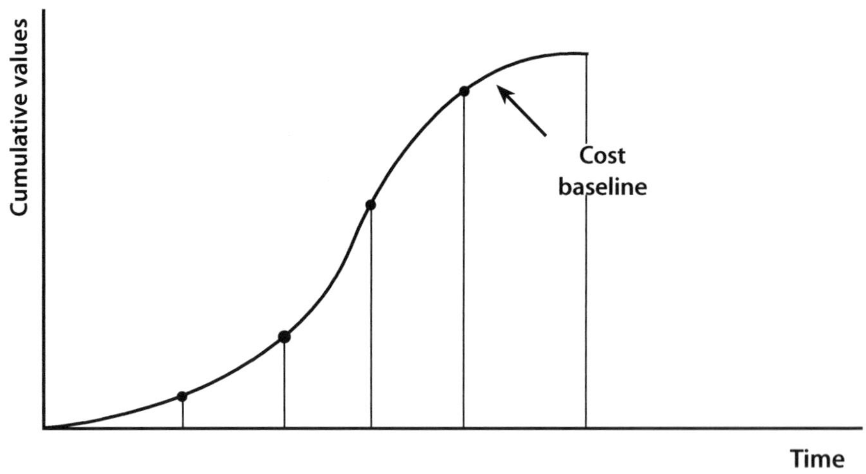

2 **Project funding requirements**

The project financing need, either in whole or by periods of time, derives from the cost performance baseline by adding a margin to forecast a faster start or cost overrun. Initial financing generally starts at the organization, and, subsequently, there are financing inputs from the customer or financial agency. The following chart shows the project financing need.

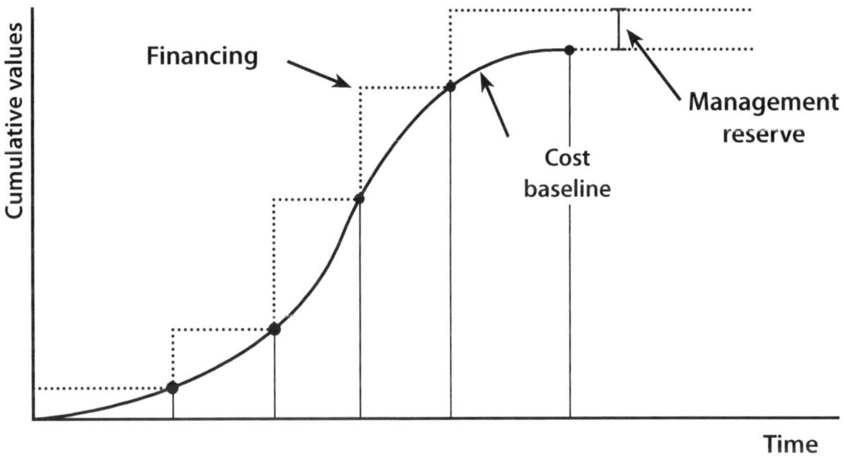

3 **Project document updates**

Project documents that must be updated include, but are not limited to

- Risk register,
- Cost estimate, and
- Project schedule.

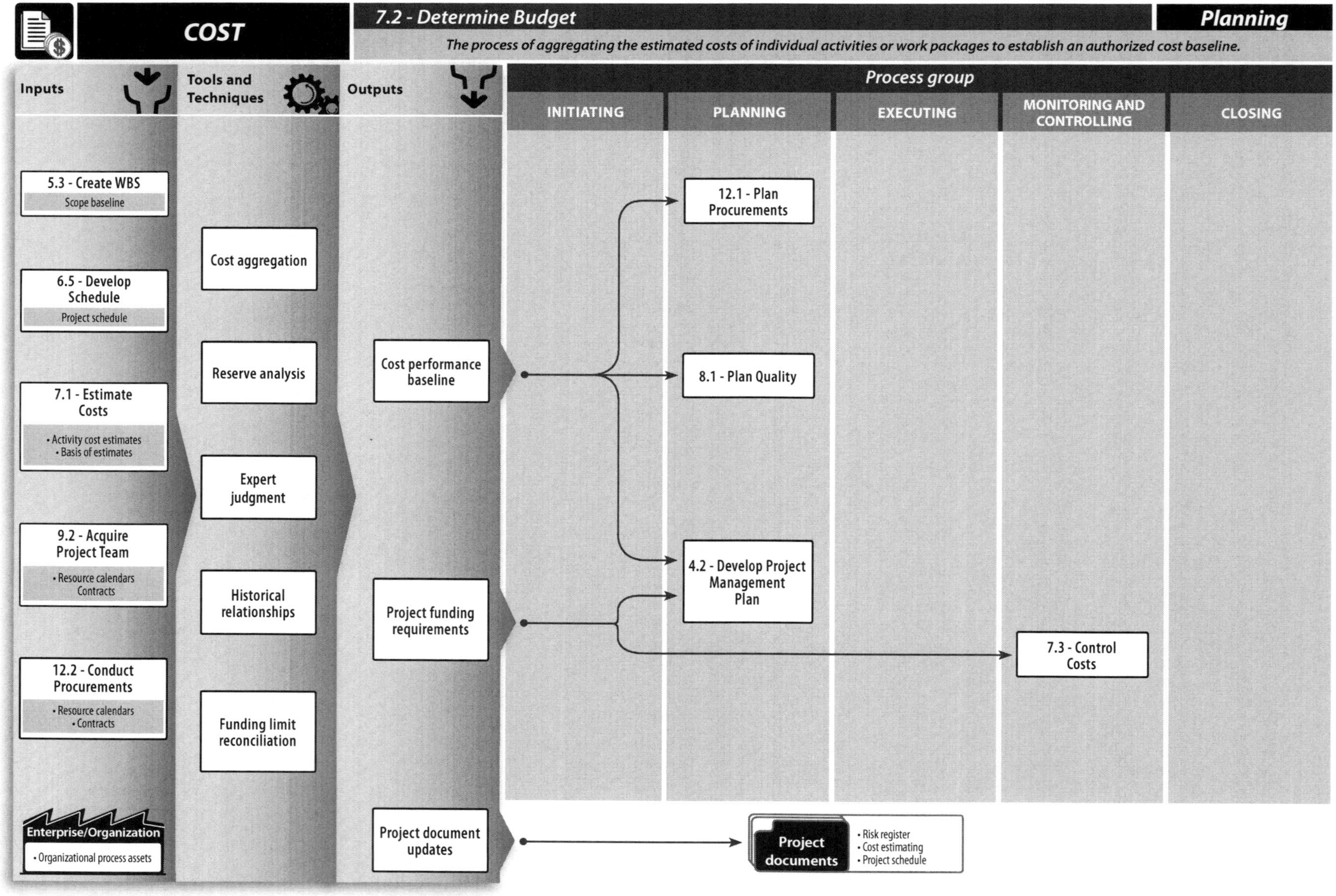

COST
7.2 - Determine Budget
Planning
The process of aggregating the estimated costs of individual activities or work packages to establish an authorized cost baseline.
Inputs
Tools and Techniques
Outputs
Process group
INITIATING
PLANNING
EXECUTING
MONITORING AND CONTROLLING
CLOSING
5.3 - Create WBS
Scope baseline
6.5 - Develop Schedule
Project schedule
7.1 - Estimate Costs
• Activity cost estimates
• Basis of estimates
9.2 - Acquire Project Team
• Resource calendars
Contracts
12.2 - Conduct Procurements
• Resource calendars
• Contracts
Enterprise/Organization
• Organizational process assets
Cost aggregation
Reserve analysis
Expert judgment
Historical relationships
Funding limit reconciliation
Cost performance baseline
Project funding requirements
Project document updates
12.1 - Plan Procurements
8.1 - Plan Quality
4.2 - Develop Project Management Plan
7.3 - Control Costs
Project documents
• Risk register
• Cost estimating
• Project schedule

7.7 COST MANAGEMENT IN PROJECT MONITORING AND CONTROLLING

According to PMI®, cost management in project monitoring and controlling is composed of the following process:

- *Control Costs.*

7.7.1 CONTROL COSTS (*PMBOK® GUIDE*, PROCESS 7.3)

This process monitors the project progress in order to update and manage its budget and manage changes made to cost performance baselines. The purpose of this control is to prevent unauthorized costs to be included in the project and to ensure that any change to influence the cost performance baseline are agreed upon and authorized according to the project financing thresholds.

7.7.1.1 CONTROL COSTS: INPUTS, TOOLS AND TECHNIQUES, AND OUTPUTS

INPUTS

1 **Project management plan**

The project management plan, its auxiliary plans, and the cost management plan as well as cost performance baselines must be considered in this process.

2 **Project funding requirements**

The project financing need, establishing the management contingency reserve thresholds, must be considered in this process.

3 **Work performance information**

Performance reports provide information on the project costs and must be considered in this process.

4 **Organizational process assets**

Organizational process assets, such as cost control policies and procedures, cost control tools, cost control templates, and other types, must be considered in this process.

TOOLS AND TECHNIQUES

1 **Earned value management**

The project performance measurement analysis is performed by means of the Earned Value Management (EVM), indicating the comparison between the planned and aggregate values and the actual costs incurred when performing work in a given point of the project.

2 **Forecasting**

Forecasting of future conditions in the project are performed according to information on the project performance, such as estimate at completion, estimate to complete, and other information available at the time of forecast.

3 **To-complete performance index**

The To-Complete-Performance-Index (TCPI), presented in this chapter Attachment II, is the ratio between the work remaining to be completed and the funds remaining to be spent on a certain date of the project.

4 **Performance reviews**

Performance reviews is performed by examining the earned value.

5 **Variance analysis**

Variance analysis is performed by examining the earned value.

6 **Project management software**

The project management software can help to apply the earned value management and monitoring results.

OUTPUTS

1 **Work performance measurements**

Performance measurements, obtained by analyzing the earned value, are documented in this process and reported to stakeholders.

2 **Budget forecasts**

Budget forecasts to complete the project, obtained from analyzing the earned value, are documented in this process and reported to stakeholders.

3 **Organizational process assets updates**

The Control Costs process can identify new processes or opportunities for improvements in the organization standards, cost control procedures, and policies.

4 **Change requests**

The Control Scope process can result in change requests in the cost performance baseline or another component of the project management plan. Change requests are processed for revision and availability during the Perform Integrated Change Control process.

5 **Project management plan updates**

The project management plan and in particular the cost management plan as well as the cost performance baseline must be updated as to approved changes occurring as a function of the Control Costs process.

6 **Project document updates**

The project documents that can be updated include, among others

- Cost estimates and
- Basis of estimates.

COST

7.3 - Estimate Costs

Monitoring and controlling

The process of monitoring the status of the project to update the project budget and managing changes to the cost baseline.

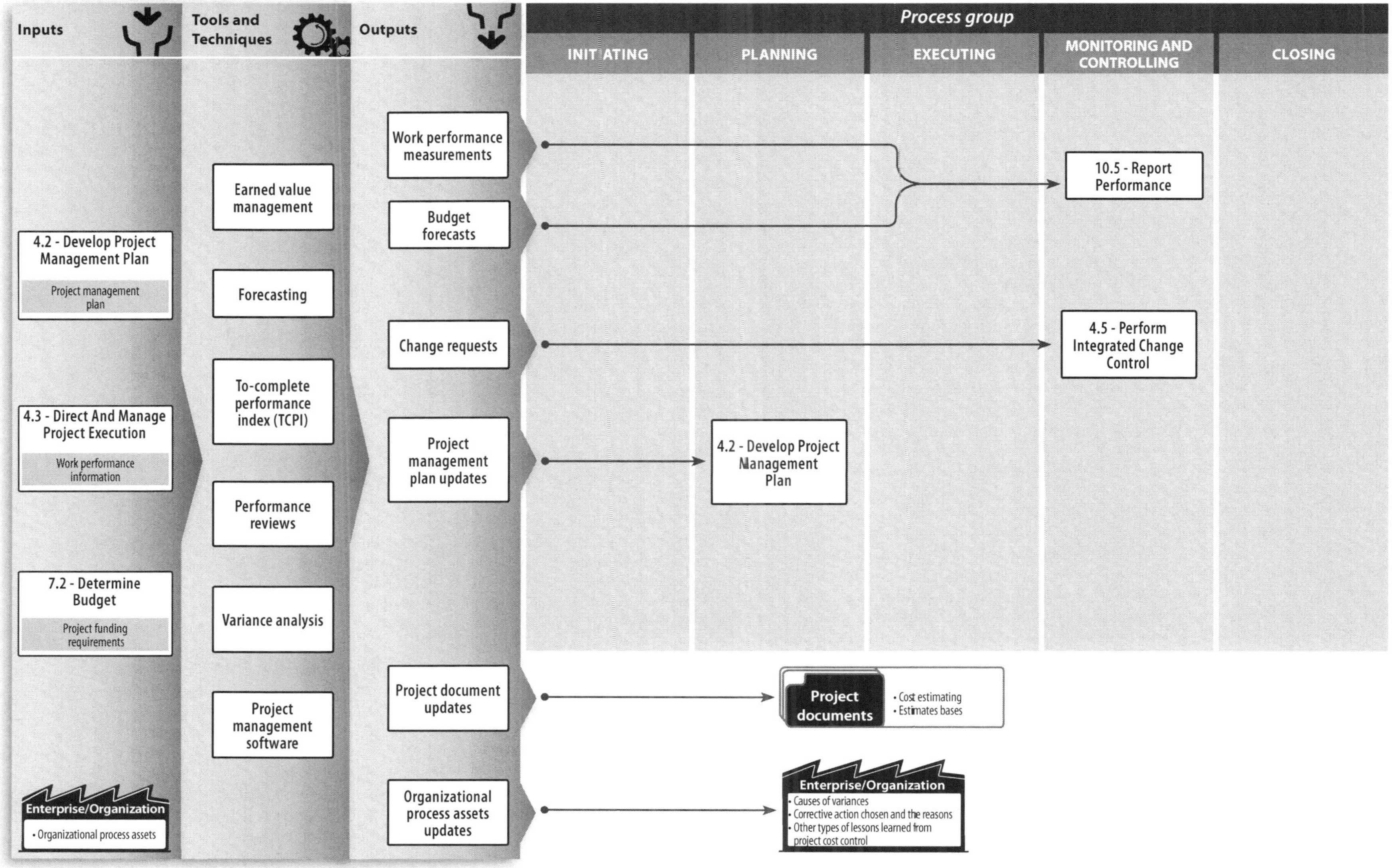

Attachment I

COST OF QUALITY

COST OF QUALITY

1 DEFINITION

Cost of quality is the cost incurred to obtain quality or to attribute it to poor quality in the project product or service. This cost may be due to assessment and prevention, internal or external failures, or injury caused to users or customers.

2 COST OF QUALITY TYPES

Cost of quality can be classified into two groups: actual costs of quality and costs of nonquality.

2.1. COSTS OF QUALITY

Costs of quality are costs related to the efforts required to achieve quality and can be classified into three groups.

2.1.1 COSTS OF THE QUALITY SYSTEM

Costs of the quality system are preventive costs incurred during the quality system implementation and management. As an example, we have

- implementation costs of the quality department;
- costs of salaries, administrative expenses, and other expenses of the quality department;
- courses and training of the quality department staff; and
- execution cost of quality reports.

2.1.2 ASSESSMENT COSTS

Assessment costs are preventive costs incurred to reach and maintain the product or service quality requirements.

Such costs generally derive from inspections, quality audits, and tests, such as

- suppliers assessment,
- inspection of suppliers' product or service,
- receipt inspection,
- product storage audit,
- quality audit in the production process, and
- finished product test.

2.1.3 MARKETING COSTS

Marketing costs are preventive ad incurred in researches to define customers' or users' acceptance criteria and satisfaction level. As examples, we have

- research to define the characteristics and requirements of the product to be developed and
- postsales research to identify customers' or users' acceptance and satisfaction level.

2.2 COST OF NONQUALITY

Costs of nonquality are costs related to poor quality of the product or service. Such costs can be classified into three groups.

2.2.1 INTERNAL FAILURE COSTS

Internal failure costs are incurred to correct failures in the company's environment, from design and project to manufacturing and shipping stages. As examples, we have

- hourly cost of design staff to redesign the product,
- cost of replacing damaged parts in production,
- cost of machine hours spent in non-compliant manufacturing parts,
- cost of tests conducted to determine defect causes, and
- cost of production scrap and waste.

2.2.2 EXTERNAL FAILURE COSTS

External failure costs are incurred to correct failures in the company's external environment after delivering a product or service to a customer or user. As an example, we have

- external failure inspection cost;
- complaint treatment cost;
- product return cost (transport, repair, product new shipment, etc.);
- discontinued product cost;
- quality assurance cost (replacement parts, free service execution, etc.);
- fines imposed by the customer or user;
- cost related to damage reimbursement to customers or users; and
- cost related to losing the customer.

Attachment II

EARNED VALUE MANAGEMENT

EARNED VALUE MANAGEMENT

1 INTRODUCTION

Earned Value Management (EVM) is a method used to analyze the project performance by comparison of planned and added values and actual costs incurred when performing work in a given point of the project. This method uses the original cost estimate and saves it with a baseline and the actual current work to show whether actual costs incurred are within the budget. The function of this technique, also called cumulative value, is making it possible, any time after the project start, verifying whether spent amounts correspond to the expected amounts, and whether the remaining money and time are sufficient to complete the project.

The figure below shows values considered in the earned value management.

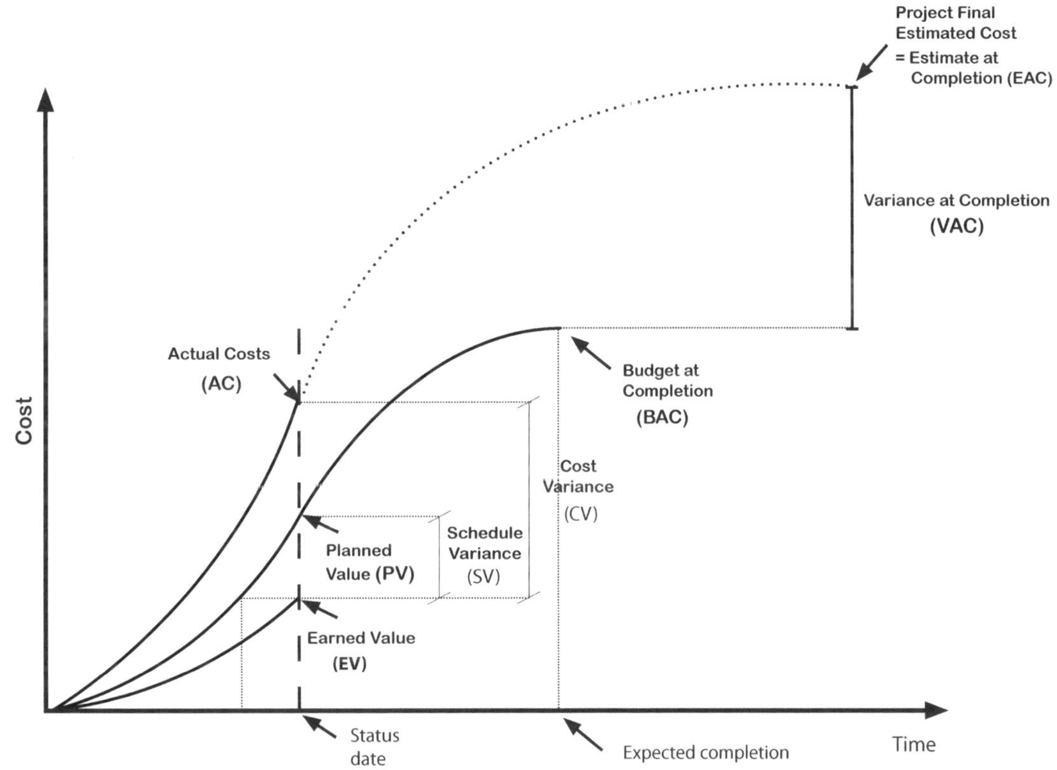

2 ANALYSIS KEY VALUES

The EVM considers three key values to analyze the project performance:

- **Planned value**

  Planned Value (PV) is the baseline cost of a WBS activity or element until the status date selected, based on costs of allocated resources over any fixed costs associated with the activity (or the WBS element). For example, an activity with a baseline cost of $1,000, distributed evenly throughout two months; at the end of the last day of the first month, PV must be $500, since half of this activity must have been performed.

- **Actual Cost**

  Actual Cost (AC) is the cost actually required to complete the activity (or the WBS element) until the status date. For example: an activity had a Planned Value (PV) of $1,000 to be completed, but $1,200 were spent. This amount is the activity AC.

3 PERFORMANCE REVIEWS INDEXES

Based on key elements – PV, AC, and EV – and the forecast cost amount at the activity final date (Budget at Completion – BAC), we can obtain several activity or project levels of current performance and future performance trends. The following table shows these indices and what they indicate:

ABBREVIATION	DESCRIPTION	INDICATION
PV	Planned Value	Which is the planned value at the activity status date?
AC	Actual Cost	Which is the actual cost at the activity status date?
EV	Earned Value	Which is the earned value at the activity status date?
BAC	Budget at Completion	Which is the total budgeted cost for the activity?

ANALYSIS AND FORECASTS RELATED TO TIME			FORMULA
SV	Schedule Variance	How ahead or behind schedule is the project?	SV = EV – PV
SV%	Schedule Variance Percentage	How ahead or behind schedule are we in percentage terms?	$SV\% = \frac{SV}{PV} 100$
SPI	Schedule Performance Index	How effectively are we using the time in the project?	SPI = EV/PV

ANALYSIS AND FORECASTS RELATED TO COST			FORMULA
CV	Cost Variance	How below or above budget is the project?	**CV = EV – AC**
CV%	Cost Variance Percentage	How above or below budget are we in percentage terms?	**CV% = (CV / EV)*100**
CPI	Cost Performance Index	How effectively have we been using resources?	**CPI = EV / AC**
TCPI	To-Complete Performance Index	How effectively should we use the remaining resources?	**TCPI = (BAC – EV) / (BAC – AC)** **OR** **TCPI = (BAC – EV) / (EAC – AC)** **(If BAC is no longer valid)**
EAC	Estimate at Completion (EAC)	How much is the project likely to cost?	**EAC = AC + (BAC – EV)** **OR** **EAC = AC + [(BAC – EV)/CPI] = BAC / CPI**
VAC	Variance at Completion	Which is the cost variance at the end of the project?	**VAC = BAC – EAC**
ETC	Estimate to Complete (ETC)	What is the forecast cost to complete the remaining work?	**ETC = EAC - AC**

3.1 SCHEDULE VARIANCE - SV

(Are we behind or ahead of schedule?)

Schedule Variance (SV) determines how ahead of or behind schedule the activity or project is. SV is calculated by subtracting the PV from the Earned Value (EV). SV is shown in terms of value (money) when the cost used is in terms of hours when effort is used.

SV = EV – PV

- A SV positive value is favorable — it indicates that the activity or project is ahead of schedule;
- A SV negative value is unfavorable — it indicates that the activity or project is behind schedule;
- A SV zero value indicates that the activity or project is on schedule.

3.2 SCHEDULE VARIANCE PERCENTAGE - SV%

(How behind or ahead of schedule are we in percentage terms?)

Schedule Variance Percentage (SV%) indicates how ahead of or behind schedule the project is in terms of percentages of completed work on a given day.

Schedule Variance Percentage (SV%) can be expressed as a percentage of the SV divided by the PV.

SV% = (SV / PV)*100

- A positive SV% indicates the progress percentage of a work performed in relation to schedule.
- A negative SV% indicates the delay percentage of a work performed in relation to schedule.

3.3 SCHEDULE PERFORMANCE INDEX - SPI

(How effectively are we using time in the project?)

Schedule Performance Index (SPI) is an index showing efficiency of the time used by the project team in relation to schedule. SPI can be expressed by dividing the EV by the PV:

SPI = EV / PV

An SPI higher than 1 indicates that the project team's actual performance is higher than planned.

An SPI lower than 1 indicates that the project team's actual performance is lower than planned. This can be represented.

An SPI equal to 1 indicates that the project team's actual performance is the same as planned. This can be represented.

4 ANALYSIS AND FORECASTS RELATED TO COST

4.1 COST VARIANCE - CV

(Are we below or above the budget?)

Cost Variance (CV) indicates whether the activity or project is below or above budget and is determined by subtracting the AC from EV.

CV = EV – AC

- A CV positive value is favorable — it indicates that the project is spending less than the budget.
- A CV negative value is unfavorable — it indicates that the project is spending more than the budget.

4.2 COST VARIANCE PERCENTAGE - CV%

(How above or below budget are we in percentage terms?)

Cost Variance Percentage (CV%) indicates how above or below budget a project is in percentage terms.

An CV% positive value indicates the percentage below budget; an CV% negative value indicates the percentage above budget. An CV% can be expressed as a percentage by dividing the CV by the EV.

CV% = (CV / EV)*100

4.3 COST PERFORMANCE INDEX (CPI)

(How effectively have we been using our resources?)

Earned Value (EV) and Actual Cost (AC) can also be used to calculate the Cost Performance Index (CPI), which is one of the clearest indicators of effective resource use in the project. CPI is obtained by dividing the EV by the AC.

CPI = EV / AC

A CPI value higher than 1 is favorable – it indicates that the effective resource use is higher than expected.

A CPI value of 1 is favorable – it indicates that the effective resource use is the same as expected. This can represent:

A CPI value lower than 1 is unfavorable – it indicates that the effective resource use is lower than expected.

4.4 TO-COMPLETE-PERFORMANCE-INDEX

(How effectively should we use the remaining resources?)

The To-Complete-Performance-Index (TCPI) shows which efficiency must be applied to the remaining work so that the project can reach the BAC. TCPI is calculated by dividing the remaining work by the remaining budget.

TCPI = (BAC – EV) / (BAC – AC)

or

TCPI = (BAC – EV) / (EAC – AC) or (if BAC is no longer valid)

- A TCPI higher than 1 indicates that a larger performance is required in the remaining work to remain on budget.
- A TCPI lower than 1 indicates that the current performance is above expectations and that it can be reduced and still remain on budget.

4.5 ESTIMATE AT COMPLETION (EAC)

(How is the project likely to cost?)

EAC indicates the project's likely final cost if the current performance trend continues for the remaining project work. At the beginning of the project, EAC usually tends to equal the project BAC, but as the project progresses, the trend is that EAC changes.

When analyzing variances that occur in a project to determine EAC, we must consider three hypotheses.

HYPOTHESIS 1

Variances will continue in the project

It is considered that variances that occurred in the past will continue in the project with the same intensity. EAC, in this case, can be calculated by the formula:

EAC = AC + [(BAC – EV)/CPI] = BAC / CPI

That is, EAC is the sum of the AC so far with the earned value remaining to complete the project (BAC – EV), considering the current performance (CPI). The missing value is the subtraction of the earned value to the project (this value is already incorporated into the project) at the BAC date (which at the project start represents the earned value expected for the project). The division of the remaining aggregated work by the CPI applies the current performance index to the project's remaining earned value.

HYPOTHESIS 2

Variances occurred are not expected for the remaining project section

It is considered that variances occurred, but they will not continue occurring in the remaining project section. EAC, in this case, can be calculated by the formula:

$$EAC = AC + (BAC - EV)$$

EAC is the sum of the AC so far and the earned value remaining to complete the project (BAC – EV), not considering the current performance (CPI). The missing value is the subtraction of the earned value to the project (this value is already incorporated into the project) at the BAC date (which at the project start represents the earned value expected for the project).

4.6 VARIANCE AT COMPLETION (VAC)

(Which cost variance is likely to be at the end of the project?)

VAC indicates how much the project will be below or above budget, based on accrued performance until the analysis date and can be defined by subtracting the EAC from the BAC.

$$VAC = BAC - EAC$$

- A VAC negative value indicates the amount to be overspent in the project.
- A VAC positive value indicates the amount to be saved in the project.

4.7 ESTIMATE TO COMPLETE (ETC)

ETC is the cost expected to be spent from the status date in order to complete the activity. The ETC formula is

$$ETC = EAC - AC$$

Additional information and reminders for the exam

- The value analysis, also called value engineering, is performed in order to find a cheaper way of performing the same job.

- The estimated magnitude order is performed at the project start, and the variance range is high and can reach up to ± 50%. The budget estimate is performed in Planning and variance can range from –10 to +25%. The final estimate is performed during the project execution and can range from –5% to +10%.

- The cost performance baseline comprises the sum of the project budget and the contingency reserve.

- The contingency reserve is expected to be used in case of known and unexpected risks.

- **Cost types**

  1 **Variable or fixed cost**

    - **Variable costs:** change according to the amount or quantity of work produced. Examples: cost of materials and raw materials used in manufacturing, cost of production staff salaries.
    - **Fixed costs:** do not change when the amount or quantity of work produced is modified. Examples: rent, property taxes.

  2 **Direct or indirect cost**

    - **Direct costs:** directly associated with the project work. Examples: cost of the team working hours, costs of team training, travel and accommodation of team members.
    - **Indirect costs:** costs incurred by the company toward several projects and their operation. Examples: senior management salaries, plant maintenance expenses, the company's communication expenses.

- The product life cycle cost includes the operation and maintenance analysis throughout the product lifetime to check whether such costs are lower than the project cost savings.

- There are two types of depreciation: linear depreciation (the same yearly amount) and accelerated depreciation. Accelerated depreciation can be calculated in two ways, by adding up the year digits and by double reducing balance.

- The law of diminishing returns means that from a certain point, the more someone invests in something, the lower the return will be.

- The three-point estimates, also called PERT analysis, uses the following formulas:

Expected activity cost = **(P + 4ML + O) / 6**

Activity cost standard deviation = **(P – O) / 6**

Activity cost variance (standard deviation squared) = $[(P - O) / 6]^2$

Supplementary exercises

1. In regards to the Project Costs area of knowledge, indicate to which management processes group(s) each element is related and explain why. Follow the example of the project financial requirements.

1. Project financial resource requirements

   ☐ Initiating ☒ Planning ☐ Executing ☒ Monitoring/controlling ☐ Closing

   These requirements are outputs of the Determine Budget (Planning) process and inputs of the Control Costs (Monitoring and controlling) process.

2. Risk register

   ☐ Initiating ☐ Planning ☐ Executing ☐ Monitoring/controlling ☐ Closing

3. Forecasting

   ☐ Initiating ☐ Planning ☐ Executing ☐ Monitoring/controlling ☐ Closing

4. Reserve analysis

   ☐ Initiating ☐ Planning ☐ Executing ☐ Monitoring/controlling ☐ Closing

5. Performance reviews

   ☐ Initiating ☐ Planning ☐ Executing ☐ Monitoring/controlling ☐ Closing

6. Three-point estimates

☐ Initiating ☐ Planning ☐ Executing ☐ Monitoring/controlling ☐ Closing

7. Estimates bases

☐ Initiating ☐ Planning ☐ Executing ☐ Monitoring/controlling ☐ Closing

8. To-complete-performance-index (TCPI)

☐ Initiating ☐ Planning ☐ Executing ☐ Monitoring/controlling ☐ Closing

9. Change requests

☐ Initiating ☐ Planning ☐ Executing ☐ Monitoring/controlling ☐ Closing

10. Scope baseline

☐ Initiating ☐ Planning ☐ Executing ☐ Monitoring/controlling ☐ Closing

11. Contracts

☐ Initiating ☐ Planning ☐ Executing ☐ Monitoring/controlling ☐ Closing

12. Supplier's proposal analysis

☐ Initiating ☐ Planning ☐ Executing ☐ Monitoring/controlling ☐ Closing

13. Work Performance Information

☐ Initiating ☐ Planning ☐ Executing ☐ Monitoring/controlling ☐ Closing

14. Budget forecasts

☐ Initiating ☐ Planning ☐ Executing ☐ Monitoring/controlling ☐ Closing

15. Work performance measurements

☐ Initiating ☐ Planning ☐ Executing ☐ Monitoring/controlling ☐ Closing

2. Complete the sentences below, stating whether the option refers to input, tool/technique, or output, and identify the corresponding project management process.

1. Three-point estimates is a ______ of the ______ process.
2. Cost aggregation is a ______ of the ______ process.
3. Earned value management is a ______ of the ______ process.
4. The project financial resources requirements are ______ of the ______ process.
5. The project financial resources requirements are ______ of the ______ process.
6. Basis of estimates are ______ of the ______ process.
7. Basis of estimates are ______ of the ______ process.
8. Contracts are ______ of the ______ process.
9. Reserve analysis is a ______ of ______ processes.
10. Cost performance baseline is a ______ of the ______ process.
11. Budget forecasts are ______ of the ______ process.
12. Supplier's proposal analysis is a ______ of the ______ process.

Questions

1. The Estimate Costs process receives inputs of the following processes:
    a. Create WBS, Develop Schedule, Develop Human Resource Plan, Define Scope, and Identify Risks
    b. Create WBS, Develop Schedule, Develop Human Resource Plan, and Identify Risks
    c. Define Scope, Create WBS, Develop Schedule, and Develop Project Management Plan
    d. Define Scope, Define Activities, Develop Schedule, and Develop Project Management Plan

2. The Estimate Costs process generates outputs that become inputs of the following processes:
    a. Determine Budget, Plan Procurements, and Plan Risk Management
    b. Plan Procurements, Develop Project Management Plan, and Determine Budget
    c. Plan Procurements, Identify Risks, and Determine Budget
    d. Develop Project Management Plan, Determine Budget, Plan Procurements, and Plan Risk Management.

3. The Estimate Costs process generates outputs to all processes listed, except
    a. Develop Project Management Plan
    b. Plan Procurements
    c. Identify Risks
    d. Determine Budget

4. All listed processes generate outputs that become inputs of the Estimate Costs process, except
    a. Create WBS
    b. Define Scope
    c. Develop Schedule
    d. Identify Risks

5. All listed processes generate outputs that become inputs of the Determine Budget process, except
    a. Plan Procurements
    b. Develop Schedule
    c. Create WBS
    d. Estimate Costs

6. All listed processes generate outputs that become inputs of the Determine Budget process, except

a. Conduct Procurements

b. Define Scope

c. Acquire Project Team

d. Estimate Costs

7. The Define budget process generates outputs that become inputs of all processes listed, except

a. Plan Procurements

b. Plan Quality

c. Verify costs

d. Control Costs

8. The Define budget process generates outputs that become inputs of all processes listed, except

a. Develop Project Management Plan

b. Plan Quality

c. Control Costs

d. Control budget

9. The Control Costs process receives inputs generated by all processes listed, except

a. Develop Project Management Plan

b. Determine Budget

c. Direct and Manage Project Execution

d. Estimate Costs

10. The Control Costs process generates outputs that become inputs to all projects listed, except

a. Report Performance

b. Perform Integrated Change Control

c. Determine Budget

d. Develop Project Management Plan

11. The three dimensions of earned value management are

a. Planned value, earned value, and current value

b. Planned value, earned value, and actual cost

c. Time, cost, and budget

d. Time, cost, and earned value

12. All of the following options are inputs of the Estimate Costs process, except

a. Estimate details

b. Human resource plan

c. Scope baseline

d. Project schedule

13. All of the following options are inputs of the Determine Budget process, except

a. Activity cost estimates

b. Cost performance baseline

c. Contracts

d. Estimate details

14. All of the following options are tools or techniques of the Estimate Costs process, except

a. Expert judgment

b. Analogous estimating

c. Parametric estimating

d. Activity cost estimates

15. All of the following options are tools or techniques of the Estimate Costs process, except

a. Estimate details

b. Supplier's proposal analysis

c. Cost of quality

d. Reserve analysis

16. All of the following options are tools or techniques of the Estimate Costs process, except

a. Expert judgment

b. Resource estimating

c. Parametric estimating

d. Reserve analysis

17. All of the following options are tools or techniques of the Determine Budget process, except

a. Cost aggregation

b. Reserve analysis

c. Cost performance baseline

d. Expert judgment

18. All of the following options are outputs of the Estimate Costs process, except

a. Cost performance baseline

b. Activity cost estimates

c. Estimate details

d. Project document updates

19. All of the following options are outputs of the Determine Budget process, except

a. Cost performance baseline

b. Cost performance measurements

c. Financial resource requirements

d. Project document updates

20. All of the following options are not tools or techniques of the Estimate Costs process, except

a. Cost of quality

b. Cost performance baseline

c. Scope baseline

d. Cost aggregation

21. All of the following options are not tools or techniques of the Determine Budget process, except

a. Parametric estimating

b. Activity cost estimating

c. Bottom-up estimating

d. Cost aggregation

22. All of the following options are not outputs of the Estimate Costs process, except

a. Analogous estimating

b. Reserve analysis

c. Activity cost estimating

d. Parametric estimating

23. All of the following options are not outputs of the Determine Budget process, except

a. Historical relationships

b. Reserve analysis

c. Cost aggregation

d. Cost performance baseline

24. All of the following options are inputs of the Control Costs process, except

a. Project management plan

b. Forecasting

c. Work performance information

d. Financial resource requirements

25. All of the following options are outputs of the Control Costs process, except

a. Work performance measurement

b. To-Complete Performance Index

c. Budget forecasts

d. Change requests

26. All of the following options are outputs of the Control Costs process, except

a. Organizational process assets updates

b. Project management plan updates

c. Forecasting

d. Change requests

27. In order to obtain the EAC (Estimate at Completion), we use the BAC (Budget at Completion) value and:

a. Divide it by the SPI

b. Divide it by the CPI

c. Multiply it by the CPI

d. Multiply it by the SPI

28. In an ongoing project, we have EV = 300, AC = 350, and PV = 330. What is the project CV?

a. –30

b. 50

c. –20

d. –50

29. In an ongoing project, we have EV = 500, AC = 650, and PV = 600. What is the project CV?

a. –150

b. 50

c. –100

d. –50

30. In a project in progress, we have CV = –50, AC = 350, and PV = 330. What is the project EV?

a. 400

b. 300

c. 280

d. 380

31. In a project in progress, we have CV = –20, AC = 120, and PV = 110. What is the project EV?

a. 130

b. 90

c. 100

d. 140

32. The project is in progress with a CPI (Cost Performance Index) of 0.91. This means that

a. Currently, the project has spent 91% of the planned amount

b. The forecasting shows that the project finishes spending 91% of the budget

c. For every $1 invested, the project receives only $0.91

d. The project is progressing at 91% of the planned rate

33. The project is in progress and has an SPI (Schedule Performance Index) of 0.92. This means that

a. The project is progressing at 92% of the planned rate

b. The project is ahead of schedule

c. The project has spent 92% of the expected time so far

d. The forecasting is finishing the project with a deadline 8% shorter

34. In which project management process group a magnitude order estimate is performed?

a. Initiating

b. Planning

c. Executing

d. Monitoring and controlling

35. Cost performance baseline is an output of which project management process?

a. Plan cost management

b. Estimate Costs

c. Determine Budget

d. Control Costs

36. The project team is under training to work with a software application used at the project management. This training cost is:

a. Indirect cost

b. Direct cost

c. Fixed cost

d. Opportunity cost

37. The project team is trying to reduce the project cost without reducing the project scope. The team is performing a

a. Cost estimate

b. Benchmark analysis

c. Value analysis

d. Cost versus scope analysis

38. The budgeted amount of the work actually performed is the

a. Planned Value (PV)

b. Earned Value (EV)

c. Cost Variance (CV)

d. Actual Cost (AC)

39. In the Determine Budget process, the project team defined a contingency reserve amount. This amount must be

a. Out of the budget

b. Absent from the cost performance baseline

c. Added to the project basic project in order to offset risks

d. Added to the project control accounts

40. Cost performance baseline comprises

a. The project basic costs and the contingency reserve

b. The project basic costs and the management reserve

c. The project basic costs plus control accounts costs

d. The final budget less contingency reserve

41. The PV can be interpreted, when performing the earned value management, as

a Which is the estimated value of the work actually performed?

b. What is the estimated value of the planned work?

c. What is the actual cost incurred for the performed work?

d. How much have we budgeted for the project total effort?

42. The EAC can be interpreted when performing the earned value management, such as

a. How much have we budgeted for the project total effort?

b. From this moment onward, how much do we expect to spend to complete the project?

c. At this point, which is our forecasting for the project total cost?

d. How much below or above the budget do we expect to have at the end of the project?

43. In order to obtain a present value of $250,000 within three years with an expected interest rate of 12% per year, what is the investment amount today?

a. $177,945

b. $201,341

c. $201,947

d. $183,823

44. If we invest today an amount of $210,000 at an interest rate of 12% per year, what will the present value be within three years?

a. $263,424

b. $285,200

c. $285,600

d. $295,034

45. Project A will last 36 months and has a Net Present Value (NPV) of $2,000,000. Project B will last 48 months and has a NPV of $2,350,000. Project C will last 60 months and has an NPV of $2,500,000. Which project would you choose to be performed by your company?

a. Project A

b. Project B

c. Project C

d. Either project B or C, as both have the same return rate

46. Your company is performing an analysis of potential projects, based on the Internal Rate of Return (IRR). Project A has an IRR of 18% and a 24-month term; project B has an IRR of 17% and a 22-month term; project C has an IRR of 20% and a 24-month term. Which project would you indicate to your company?

a. Either project A or C, as both have the same return rate

b. Project C

c. Project B

d. Project A

47. Costs already spent on the project must be considered when analyzing the project continuation?

a. Yes, they may impact on financing

b. Yes, as they determine the project assessment

c. No, as they are sunk costs — not considered in this analysis

d. No, as they are recurring costs

48. Depreciation types include the following options, except

a. Sum of digits of the year

b. Straight-line depreciation

c. Double reducing balance

d. Slowed depreciation

49. Your company has asked you to prepare a budget to reach a decision whether a project that was started and discontinued last year should be resumed. In the budget, you would include all the following options, except

a. Variable costs

b. Direct costs

c. Sunk costs

d. Fixed costs

50. Which of the following sequences represents linear depreciation?

a. $160, $140, $120

b. $100, $120, $140

c. $100, $120, $160

d. $100, $100, $100

Answer key

Supplementary exercises

2. 1 - Tool/technique - Estimate Costs

2 - Technique - Determine Budget

3 - Technique - Control Costs

4 - Outputs - Determine Budget

5 - Inputs - Control Costs

6 - Inputs - Determine Budget

7 - Outputs - Estimate Costs

8 - Inputs - Determine Budget

9 - Tool/technique - Estimate Costs and Determine Budget

10 - Output - Determine Budget

11 - Outputs - Control Costs

12 - Tool/technique - Estimate Costs

Questions

1. B. The Estimate Costs process receives as inputs: the baseline of the Create WBS process; the project schedule of the Develop Schedule process; the human resources plan of the Develop Human Resource Plan process; the risk register of the Identify Risks process.

2. C. The Estimate Costs process generates estimated outputs of activity costs and estimated bases to the Determine Budget process, and the Activity cost estimates output to the Plan Procurements and Identify Risks processes.

3. A. The Estimate Costs process generates estimated outputs of activity costs and estimated bases to the Determine Budget process, and the Activity cost estimates output to the Plan Procurements and Identify Risks processes.

4. B. The Estimate Costs process receives as inputs: the baseline of the Create WBS process; the project schedule of the Develop Schedule process; the human resources plan of the Develop Human Resource Plan process; the risk register of the Identify Risks process.

5. A. The Determine Budget process receives as inputs: activity and basis cost estimates of the Estimate Costs process; scope baseline of the Create WBS process (this time we disagree with the *PMBOK® Guide*, as WBS does not contain the scope baseline as the project management plan does); project schedule of the Develop Schedule process; resource calendar of the Acquire Project Team process; resource calendar and contracts of the Perform procurements process.

6. A. The Determine Budget process receives as inputs: activity and basis cost estimates of the Estimate Costs process; scope baseline of the Create WBS process (this time we disagree with the *PMBOK® Guide*, as WBS does not contain the scope baseline as the project management plan does); project schedule of the Develop Schedule process; resource calendar of the Acquire Project Team process; resource calendar and contracts of the Perform procurements process.

7. C. Verify costs process does not exist. The Determine scope process generates the following outputs to other processes: cost performance baseline for Plan Procurements, Plan Quality, and Develop Project Management Plan processes and the project financial resources requirements to the Control Costs process. In addition, it provides updates to the project documents.

8. D. The Control budget process does not exist. The Determine scope process generates the following outputs to other processes: cost performance baseline for Plan Procurements, Plan Quality, and Develop Project Management Plan processes and the project financial resources requirements to the Control Costs process. In addition, it provides updates to the project documents.

9. D. The Control Costs process do not receive inputs directly from the Estimate Costs process. It receives the following inputs: project management plan of the Develop Project Management Plan process; work performance information of the Direct and Manage Project Execution process; financial resource requirements of the Determine Budget process.

10. C. The Control Costs process does not generate outputs to the Determine Budget process. The outputs of the Control Costs process are Work performance measurements and budget forecasts to the Report Performance process; change request to the Perform Integrated Change Control process; project management plan updates of the Develop Project Management Plan process.

11. B. The three dimensions of earned value management are planned value, earned value, and actual cost.

12. A. In order to Estimate Costs, you need the schedule, the human resource plan, and the scope baseline (scope statement, WBS, and WBS dictionary). Estimate details is one of the results (outputs) of the process.

13. B. In order to prepare the budget, you need, among other inputs, the estimate, estimate details, and the amounts contained in contracts already entered into. The cost performance baseline is the budget final value; therefore, it is a process output.

14. D. The Estimate Costs process name means estimating activity costs. Therefore, option D is a process (output) product.

15. A. Cost estimate details are products (outputs) of the Estimate Costs process.

16. B. The activity resource estimate was performed in the Estimate Activity Resources process, in the Time knowledge area.

17. C. The cost performance baseline is the budget final amount (a process output), adequate, and reconciled to the appropriate financing thresholds, which will be a comparison actual cost amounts.

18. A. The cost performance baseline will only be obtained by implementing the budget, in the Determine budget process.

19. B. The term measurement is related to control. Cost performance measurements are developed in Monitoring and controlling, in the Control Costs process.

20. A. The question, asked more clearly, is "Which of the following options IS a tool or technique of the Estimate Costs process?" Remember that (cost, scope) baseline is never a tool: it is an input or output of processes. Cost aggregation is a tool of the Determine Budget process. Cost of quality (even if you believe it would be clearer as an input) is a tool of the Estimate Costs process.

21. D. The question, asked more clearly, is "Which of the following options IS a tool or technique of the Determine Budget process?" Parametric estimating, bottom-up estimating and activity costs are tools of the Estimate Costs process. Cost aggregation is a bottom-up technique to add up costs until reaching the budget amount. Note that aggregation is a bottom-up technique, not a bottom-up estimate.

22. C. The question, asked more clearly, is "Which of the following options IS an output of the Estimate Costs process?" The process name already implies that we should obtain cost estimates. The other options are related to tools and techniques.

23. D. The question, asked more clearly, is "Which of the following options IS an output of the Determine Budget process?" The first three options are process tools and techniques. The cost performance baseline (budget at completion) is the major output of the Determine Budget process.

24. B. Forecasting (option B) referred to here is the EAC, obtained by analyzing the earned value. Both the earned value management and forecasting are Cost control techniques.

25. B. The To-Complete-Performance-Index (TCPI) is obtained by analyzing the earned value. Remember that the term "analysis" always refers to process tools and techniques. The other options are process outputs.

26. C. Forecasting (option C) referred to here is the EAC, obtained by analyzing the earned value. Remember that the term "analysis" always refers to process tools and techniques. The other options are process outputs.

27. B. EAC formula is BAC/CUMULATIVE CPI

28. D. CV = EV–AC.

29. A. CV = EV–AC.

30. B. CV = EV–AC, where EV = CV + AC. Note that CV is negative.

31. C. CV = EV–AC, where EV = CV + AC. Note that CV is negative.

32. C. A CPI value lower than 1.0 indicates an excess cost to the work performed (CPI = EV/AC). Option C is correct.

33. A. An SPI value lower than 1.0 indicates that less work was performed, as compared to the original plan (SPI = EV/PV). Option A is correct.

34. A. The magnitude order estimate is performed during the Project initiating, when little is known about the project. This estimate has a wide range.

35. C. The cost performance baseline is an output of the Determine Budget process.

36. B. If the team is being trained toward a project need, cost is directly related to the project. This cost is the direct cost.

37. C. Value analysis (or value engineering) seeks more cost-effective ways of performing the same work. Terms used in options B and D have been made up.

38. B. The budgeted amount of the work actually performed is the earned value, obtained from the project earned value management.

39. C. The contingency reserve must be added to the project basic costs, which compose the cost performance baseline.

40. A. The cost performance baseline comprises the project basic costs plus the contingency reserve. Management reserve (option B) is any additional amount of separate funds assigned to cover unforeseen risks or project changes and is not included in the cost performance baseline. Basic costs already include the costs of control accounts (option C). Option D is incorrect.

41. B. Option A is the interpretation of EV; option C is the AC; option D is the BAC.

42. C. Option A is the interpretation of the BAC; option B is the ETC (Estimate to Complete); option D is Variance at Completion (VAC).

43. A. The present value is calculated by the formula $PV = FV/(1 + i)^n$, where FV is the Future Value, i is the interest rate, and n the number of periods.

44. D. The present value is calculated by the formula $PV = FV/(1 + i)^n$, where FV is the Future Value, i is the interest rate, and n the number of periods. The Future Value is, therefore, $FV = PV (1 + i)^n$.

45. C. The project deadline is not relevant in this case, as it was already considered when calculating the NPV. The best project is the one with the highest NPV!

46. B. The term is not relevant in this case, as it was already considered when calculating the IRR. The best project is the one with the highest IRR, i.e., project C.

47. C. Remember for the exam: sunk costs (costs already spent) must not be considered when deciding whether a project must continue with problems or not.

48. D. Option D is a made-up name. There are two forms of depreciation: linear depreciation and accelerated depreciation. Accelerated depreciation can be calculated in two ways, by adding up the year digits and by double reducing balance.

49. C. When analyzing a project continuity, sunk costs must not be considered, as they are performed costs.

50. D. Linear depreciation uses the same amount in each period.

Chapter 8

PROJECT QUALITY MANAGEMENT

1. Introduction
2. Project Quality Management processes
3. Quality management in project planning
4. Quality management in project executing
5. Quality management in project monitoring and controlling

Attachment I	Theorists of the quality and their principles
Attachment II	Tools of quality

- Additional information and reminders for the exam
- Supplementary exercises
- Questions
- Answer key

8.1 INTRODUCTION

This chapter will introduce the project management processes in the quality knowledge area, their relevant inputs, tools, techniques, and outputs.

8.2 PROJECT QUALITY MANAGEMENT PROCESSES

According to *PMBOK® Guide*, Project Quality Management includes processes and activities of the performing organization that determine quality policies, objectives, and responsibilities so that the project meets the needs for which it was undertaken.

Project Quality Management processes are

- **Plan Quality**

  The process of identifying the project and product quality requirements and/or standards in addition to the documentation of how the project will evidence compliance.

- **Perform Quality Assurance**

  The process of auditing quality requirements of the results of quality control measurement to ensure that quality standards and appropriate operational definitions are used.

- **Perform Quality Control**

  The process of monitoring and recording results of the quality activity execution to assess performance and recommend required changes

PMI® approach recognizes the importance of quality management project based on

- Customer satisfaction,
- Prevention over inspection,
- Management's responsibility, and
- Continua improvement.

In addition to compatibility with the ISO (International Organization for Standardization), the quality management in projects approach must be consistent with those recommended by Juran, Deming, and Crosby.

The following flowchart shows the relationship among the Project Quality Management processes and their locations across the project management process groups.

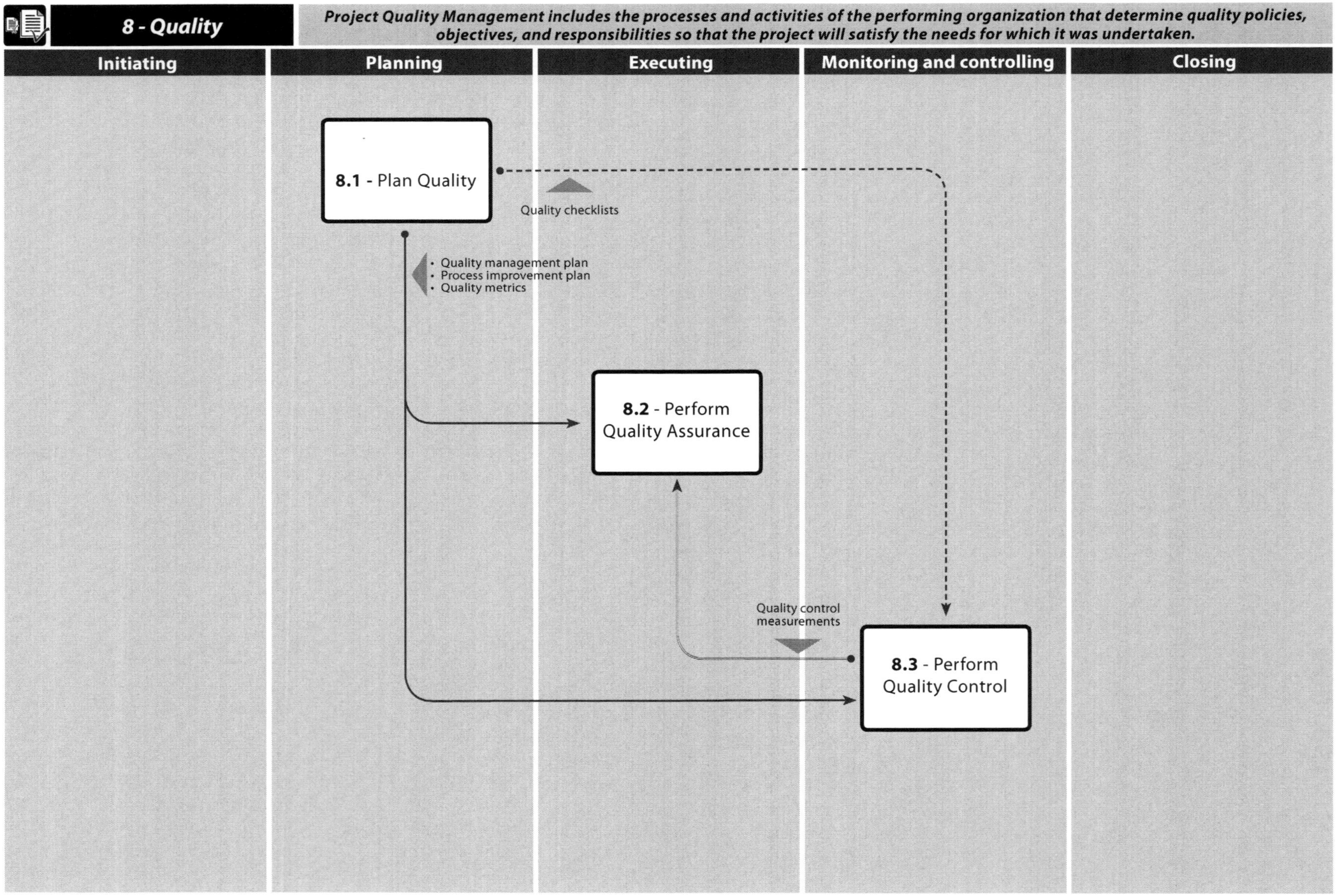
8 - Quality
Project Quality Management includes the processes and activities of the performing organization that determine quality policies, objectives, and responsibilities so that the project will satisfy the needs for which it was undertaken.
Initiating
Planning
Executing
Monitoring and controlling
Closing
8.1 - Plan Quality
Quality checklists
• Quality management plan
• Process improvement plan
• Quality metrics
8.2 - Perform Quality Assurance
Quality control measurements
8.3 - Perform Quality Control

8.3 QUALITY MANAGEMENT IN PROJECT PLANNING

According to PMI®, quality management in Project Planning is composed of a process, namely:

- *Plan Quality*

8.3.1 PLAN QUALITY (*PMBOK® GUIDE*, PROCESS 8.1)

The Plan Quality process involves identifying the project quality standards and determining how to deal with them. Quality Planning starts by defining quality goals and continues by defining actions, processes, and procedures required to meet the requirements of goals.

Taking into account the interaction between management processes and the significant quality impact on project management, any and all change in quality Planning must have its effects considered in other processes. Conversely, any and all change when Planning other processes must have its effects considered when Planning quality.

8.3.1.1 PLAN QUALITY: INPUTS, TOOLS AND TECHNIQUES, AND OUTPUTS

INPUTS

1 **Scope baseline**

- **Project scope statement**

  The project scope statement containing information on the project scope, such as assumptions and constraints, must be considered in this process.

- **Work Breakdown Structure (WBS)**

  The WBS, containing information on work packages and project deliverables, must be considered in this process.

- **WBS dictionary**

  The WBS dictionary, containing detailed information on the WBS components, must be considered in this process.

2 **Stakeholder register**

Registering stakeholders interested in quality or its requirements impacting quality.

3 **Cost performance baseline**

The cost performance baseline, which is the budget's final value, is appropriate and reconciled to the funding threshold and serves as a comparison for values of actual costs, must be considered in this process.

4 **Schedule baseline**

The schedule baseline, which contains activity deadlines, dates of project milestones, and other information, must be considered in this process.

5 **Risk register**

Risk register provides information on identified risks, their root causes, and project uncertain assumptions, and must be considered in this process.

6 **Enterprise environmental factors**

The enterprise environmental factors such as regulations, standards, and guidelines of government agencies, must be considered in this process.

7 **Organizational process assets**

Organizational process assets, such as quality policies and procedures, must be considered in this process.

TOOLS AND TECHNIQUES

1 **Cost-benefit analysis**

Plan Quality must take into account the cost-benefit of meeting quality requirements. It must consider that preventing problems is cheaper than fixing them. Meeting quality requirements provides less rework, which can result in cost savings, increased productivity, and increased satisfaction of stakeholders.

2 **Cost of quality**

The Cost of Quality (COQ) represents the sum of the compliance prevention cost added to the noncompliance cost. Such costs are related to prevention, assessment, and failure costs.

3 **Control charts**

Control charts are tools used to verify whether the process is statistically under control, that is, within the calculated limits. Generally, such graphics are used to monitor production processes in order to prevent defects, avoid wastes, and reduce costs.

4 **Benchmarking**

Benchmarking is the technique of checking practices used in previous projects to be implemented in the current project, including quality Planning. The objective is generating improvement ideas and obtaining benchmarks for performance measurement. This technique can be developed in previous projects of the company or with other companies which have performed similar projects.

5 **Design of experiments**

Design of Experiments (DOE) is a statistical technique used to simultaneously experiment changes to several variables in order to determine which combinations will cause the best result to the project.

For example, we can make a design of experiments to assess which combination of gasoline and alcohol mixture results in the lower mileage cost of a vehicle. In this experiment, with weight and speed parameters maintained constant, we could use several combinations of the alcohol and gasoline mixture and measure the distance traveled. By means of proportionate application of alcohol and gasoline costs to such combinations, we would obtain the lowest mileage cost combination.

6 **Statistical sampling**

Statistical sampling involves choosing a share of the population of interest for inspection, for example, selecting 10 engineering drawings from a total of one hundred drawings. The sampling frequency and size must be determined in the quality management plan.

7 **Flowcharting**

Flowcharting are graphical representations of sequencing activities of a process. The flowchart for using standardized symbols allows easily viewing process, identifying improvements, promoting information on the process, and easy communication among engaged people.

8 **Proprietary quality management methodologies**

Other methodologies applicable to quality management, such as 6 Sigma, can be used as tools of this process.

9 **Additional quality Planning tools**

Several Planning and quality control tools can be used in project management. The most common ones, in addition to above-mentioned control charts and flowcharting, are Pareto Chart, cause-and-effect diagrams, histograms, checklists, and scatter diagrams.

Other quality Planning tools are often used to better define quality requirements and plan effective quality management activities. They include, among others,

- Brainstorming (defined in section 5.4.1).
- Affinity diagrams, used to visually identify logical groupings based on natural relationships.
- Force field analysis, which are diagrams of forces for and against change.
- Nominal group techniques, to enable ideas to pass through brainstorming in small groups and then reviewed by a larger group.
- Matrix diagrams, which include two, three, or four information groups and show the relationships among factors, causes, and objectives. Data of a matrix are arranged in rows and columns with intersection cells that can be completed with information describing the relationships among items located in rows and columns.
- Prioritization matrices, which provide a way to classify a diverse set of problems and/or issues (usually generated during brainstorming) due to its importance.

OUTPUTS

1 **Quality management plan**

Quality management plan is the major output of this process. The plan must describe how the team will implement the quality policy in order to meet project requirements. Among other pieces of information, it must contain

- the quality team, its responsibilities, and assignments;
- the necessary resources for quality management;
- indication of processes and procedures to be used;

- indication of the major quality tools to be used;
- quality requirements (defined at the level of WBS deliverables); and
- information on quality assurance and control.

2 **Quality metrics**

Quality metrics, also referred to as operational definitions, are particular information of what it is and how a product or service must be measured in order to be accepted in accordance with the project requirements. While quality requirements are defined at the level of WBS deliverables, the metrics must be defined at levels below, namely, activities, in order to enable quality Monitoring and controlling of activities.

3 **Quality checklists**

Quality checklist is a tool used to verify whether quality criteria are being or will be complied with. The checklist must preferably be used as prevention, before the activity execution and, therefore, anticipating the occurrence of deviations or omissions. Often, using the checklist after the activity execution may not be so useful. For example, it is always desirable to verify the type of concrete to be used before applying it. After application and drying, this verification is only possible through destructive tests (taking specimens from the component itself), and, if unacceptable deviations as to the concrete type are found, the problem solution, whatever it may be, will have a dramatically higher cost.

Many companies have quality checklists for many activities, especially when they are frequently performed.

4 **Process improvement plan**

Process improvement plan is a plan aiming to detect and eliminate waste, stop non-earned value activities and identify the root cause of problems that occur when Executing activities. The plan must contain:

- **Process thresholds.** They describe the purpose of processes, their start and finish, inputs/outputs, data required, the owner, and stakeholders.
- **Process configuration.** A graphical representation of processes, with interfaces identified, used to make analysis easier.
- **Process metrics.** Along with control limits, it enables analyzing the process effectiveness.
- **Goals for enhanced performance.** They guide the process improvement activities.

5 **Project document updates**

The project documents that must be updated include stakeholder register and any other document related to this process.

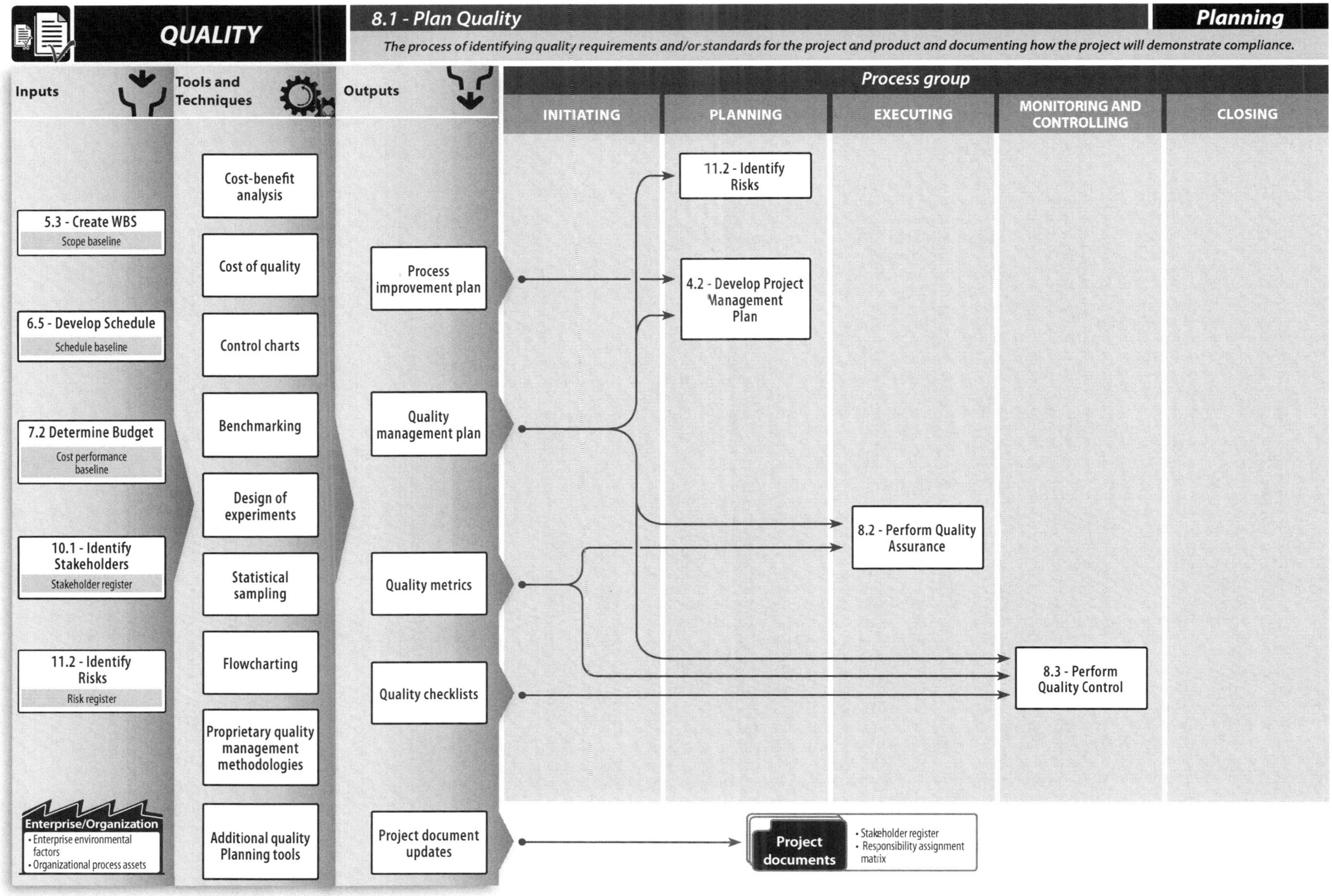

Chapter 8 - Project Quality Management

8.4 QUALITY MANAGEMENT IN PROJECT EXECUTING

According to PMI®, quality management in project executing is composed of a process called:

- ***Perform Quality Assurance***

8.4.1 PERFORM QUALITY ASSURANCE (*PMBOK® GUIDE*, PROCESS 8.2)

Quality Assurance (QA) is applying systematic and planned actions to ensure that the project will employ all processes necessary to meet requirements. Quality assurance is obtained by performing quality audits, whose function is verifying whether the project is being executed in accordance with quality policies and procedures. Such audits are generally performed by independent project teams and may be from other departments or even specialized companies hired for that purpose. However, the ultimate responsible for quality assurance is the project manager.

Quality assurance is also aimed at identifying process improvements, verifying nonearned value activities, identifying root causes of problems, and requesting preventive measures.

8.4.1.1 PERFORM QUALITY ASSURANCE: INPUTS, TOOLS, AND TECHNIQUES

INPUTS

1 **Project management plan**

The project management plan and, in particular, the quality management plan describing how quality assurance will be implemented in the project, must be considered in this process.

2 **Quality metrics**

Quality metrics describes how quality must be measured, and they must be considered in this process.

3 **Work performance information**

Information on work performance, such as technical performance measurements, current status of deliverables, schedule progress, and costs incurred, must be considered in this process.

4 **Quality control measurements**

Quality control measurements, performed in the quality control process, are used in this process as feedback and confirmation of the use of quality control processes expected.

TOOLS AND TECHNIQUES

1 **Plan Quality and Perform Quality Control tools and techniques**

Quality tools and techniques, such as the cause-and-effect diagrams, control charts, flowcharting, histograms, and others, are used in this process.

2 **Quality audits**

A quality audit is a structured independent review to determine whether project activities are in compliance with policies, processes, and procedures of the organization and the project. The objectives of a quality audit are

- Identifying all good/best practices being implemented,
- Identifying any gaps/deficiencies,
- Sharing good practices used or implemented in similar projects in the organization and/or the industry,
- Providing proactive support in a positive way to improve the implementation process in order to help the team increase productivity, and
- Highlighting contributions of each audit in the organization's repository of lessons learned.

3 **Process analysis**

Process analysis aims at detecting and eliminating waste, stopping nonearned value activities, and identifying the root cause of problems occurring when Executing activities.

OUTPUTS

1 **Organizational process assets updates**

The Perform Quality Assurance process can identify new processes or opportunities for improvements in the organization standards, quality procedures, and policies.

2 **Change requests**

The Perform Quality Assurance through audits, process analysis, and its tools and techniques may find opportunities for process improvements, which must be subject to change requests. Such changes must be submitted for review, and, if approved, they must be implemented.

3 **Project management plan updates**

The project management plan and in particular, plans for quality management, schedule management, and cost management must be updated according to the Perform Quality Assurance process.

4 **Project document updates**

Project documents must be updated, including quality audit reports, training plans, and process documentation.

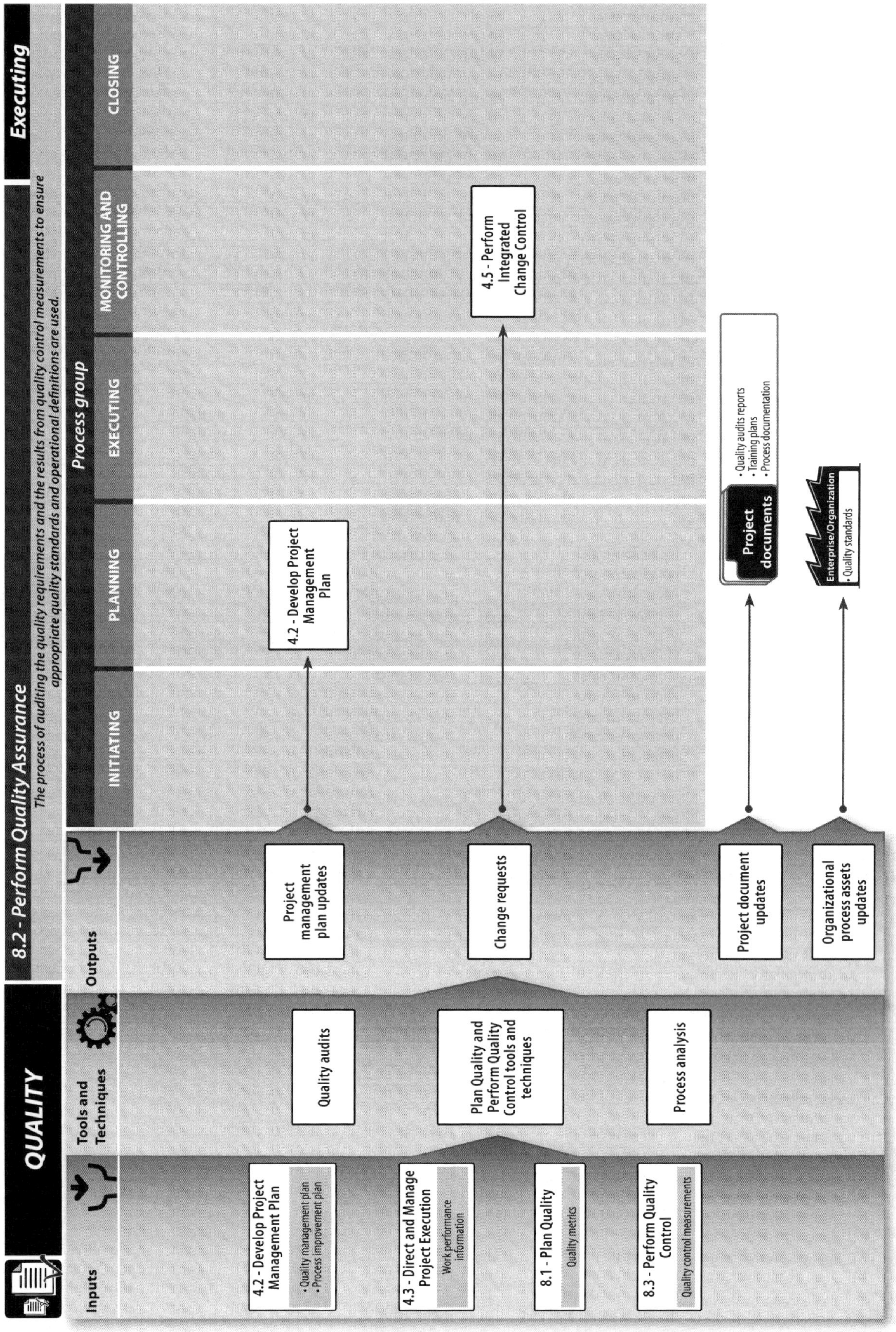
QUALITY
8.2 - Perform Quality Assurance
Executing
The process of auditing the quality requirements and the results from quality control measurements to ensure appropriate quality standards and operational definitions are used.
Inputs
Tools and Techniques
Outputs
Process group
INITIATING
PLANNING
EXECUTING
MONITORING AND CONTROLLING
CLOSING
4.2 - Develop Project Management Plan
• Quality management plan
• Process improvement plan
4.3 - Direct and Manage Project Execution
Work performance information
8.1 - Plan Quality
Quality metrics
8.3 - Perform Quality Control
Quality control measurements
Quality audits
Plan Quality and Perform Quality Control tools and techniques
Process analysis
Project management plan updates
Change requests
Project document updates
Organizational process assets updates
4.2 - Develop Project Management Plan
4.5 - Perform Integrated Change Control
Project documents
• Quality audits reports
• Training plans
• Process documentation
Enterprise/Organization
• Quality standards

8.5 QUALITY MANAGEMENT IN PROJECT MONITORING AND CONTROLLING

According to PMI®, quality management in project monitoring and controlling is composed of the following process:

- *Perform Quality Control*

8.5.1 PERFORM QUALITY CONTROL (*PMBOK® GUIDE*, PROCESS 8.3)

The process of monitoring and recording results of the quality activity execution to assess performance and recommend required changes. Quality control must be performed throughout the project. The procedures and tools of quality, defined in the quality management plan, must be considered in quality control.

8.5.1.1 CONTROL QUALITY: INPUTS, TOOLS AND TECHNIQUES, AND OUTPUTS

INPUTS

1 **Project management plan**

The project management plan and, in particular, the quality management plan, must be considered in this process.

2 **Quality metrics**

Quality metrics in the quality management plan must be considered in this process.

3 **Quality checklists**

Quality checklists are used to verify whether a set of required steps was performed, and they must be considered in this process.

4 **Work performance measurements**

Information on technical performance, schedule performance, and cost performance must be considered in this process.

5 **Approved change requests**

Approved change requests can influence the quality criteria and metrics and must be considered in this process.

6 **Deliverables**

Deliverables, which must be performed in compliance with the project requirements, must be considered in this process.

7 **Organizational process assets**

Organizational process assets, such as quality policies and procedures, must be considered in this process.

TOOLS AND TECHNIQUES

See the attachment to this chapter.

1 **Cause-and-effect diagrams**

2 **Control charts**

3 **Flowcharting**

4 **Histogram**

5 **Pareto chart**

6. **Run chart**

The run chart is a line chart showing data points plotted in the order they occur, showing trends in a process over time. Such trends may be related to technical performance (identified errors and defects) or to cost and time performance (not completed activities within the deadline or above the cost).

7 **Scatter diagram**

8 **Statistical sampling**

Statistical sampling is selecting and separating a data sample from a population of interest for inspection in order to verify whether they fit predefined quality requirements.

9 **Inspection**

Inspection is verifying the work product in order to determine whether it complies with the project requirements.

10 **Approved change requests review**

All approved change requests must be reviewed in order to verify whether if they have been implemented as approved.

OUTPUTS

1 **Quality control measurements**

Quality control measurements are the feedback to quality assurance and must be documented in this process.

2 **Validated changes**

Validated changes must be documented, and stakeholders must be notified.

3 **Validated deliverables**

Deliverables complying with defined quality requirements and those accepted must be documented in this process.

4 **Organizational process assets updates**

The Perform Quality Control process can identify new processes or opportunities for improvements in the organization standards, procedures, and quality policies.

5 **Change requests**

The Perform Quality Control process may find opportunities for improvements in processes, which must be subject to change requests. Such changes must be submitted for review and, if approved, they must be implemented.

6 **Project management plan updates**

The project management plan and, in particular, the quality management plan must be updated after changes are approved as a result of the Project management plan process.

7 **Project document updates**

All and any project document that have been influenced by the Perform Quality Control process must be updated, such as, quality standards.

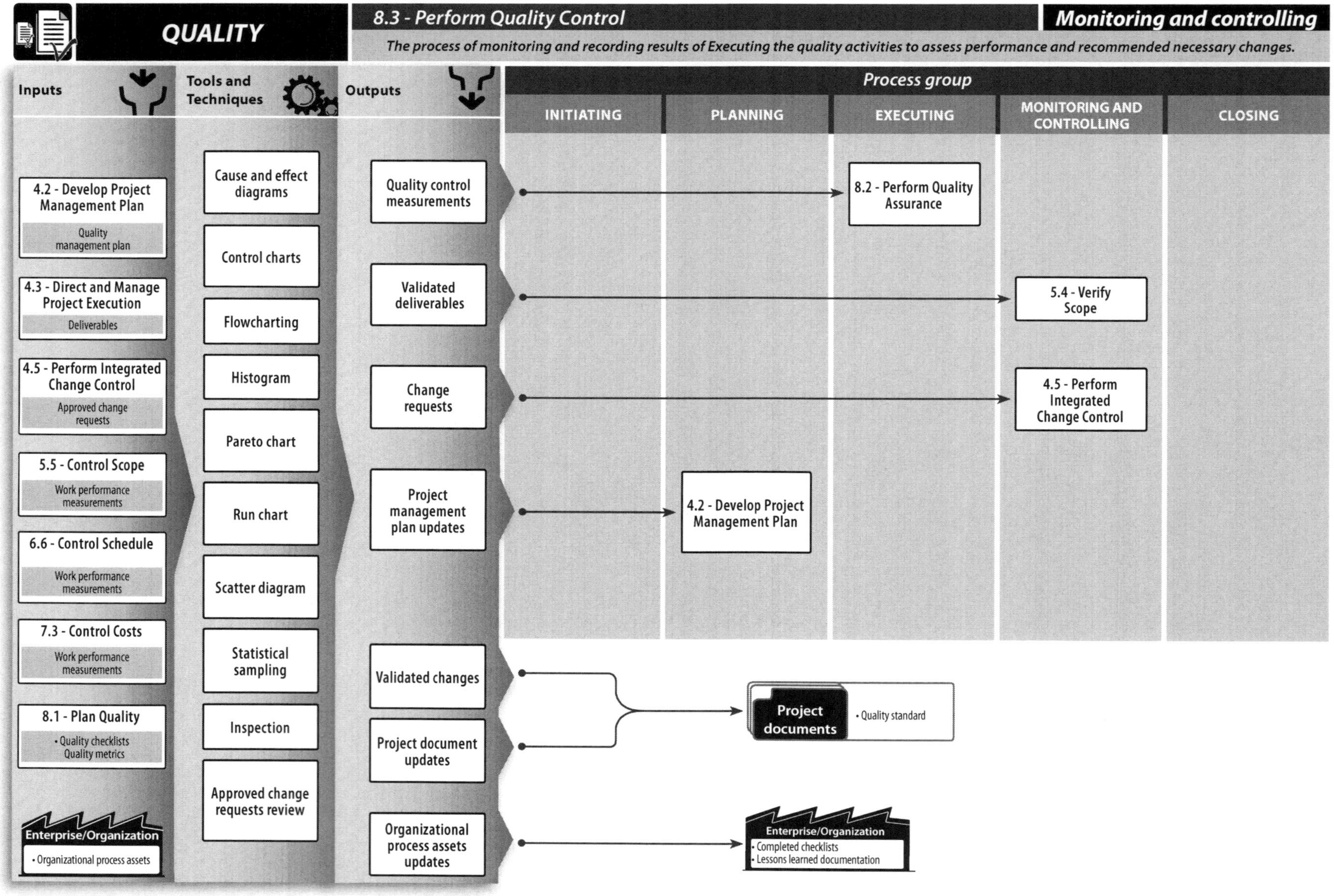

QUALITY
8.3 - Perform Quality Control
Monitoring and controlling
The process of monitoring and recording results of Executing the quality activities to assess performance and recommended necessary changes.
Inputs
Tools and Techniques
Outputs
Process group
INITIATING
PLANNING
EXECUTING
MONITORING AND CONTROLLING
CLOSING
4.2 - Develop Project Management Plan
Quality management plan
4.3 - Direct and Manage Project Execution
Deliverables
4.5 - Perform Integrated Change Control
Approved change requests
5.5 - Control Scope
Work performance measurements
6.6 - Control Schedule
Work performance measurements
7.3 - Control Costs
Work performance measurements
8.1 - Plan Quality
• Quality checklists
Quality metrics
Enterprise/Organization
• Organizational process assets
Cause and effect diagrams
Control charts
Flowcharting
Histogram
Pareto chart
Run chart
Scatter diagram
Statistical sampling
Inspection
Approved change requests review
Quality control measurements
Validated deliverables
Change requests
Project management plan updates
Validated changes
Project document updates
Organizational process assets updates
8.2 - Perform Quality Assurance
5.4 - Verify Scope
4.5 - Perform Integrated Change Control
4.2 - Develop Project Management Plan
Project documents
• Quality standard
Enterprise/Organization
• Completed checklists
• Lessons learned documentation

Attachment I

THEORISTS OF THE QUALITY AND THEIR PRINCIPLES

THEORISTS OF THE QUALITY AND THEIR PRINCIPLES

1 INTRODUCTION

The industrial revolution, which occurred from the mid-eighteenth century onward, implemented mass production of consumer goods with mechanization of production systems and the labor division system. With increased population and consumption of such goods, companies were seeking greater productivity without enough concern for the quality of products. However, with increased competition, companies are now forced to start controlling their raw materials and production lines.

In the early twentieth century, Frederick Taylor introduced the scientific management theories, proving it possible to apply scientific knowledge to the development of work processes in order to achieve the best service execution. In his studies, Taylor found that the continuous search for productivity was damaging product quality. Based on that, he created the inspector position, with the isolated action of production staff.

In the 20s, American mathematician Walter Shewhart introduced the Statistical Process Control (SPC) using sampling techniques and defining variance limits of product characteristics for acceptance.

In the early 50s, American statistician William Edwards Deming was invited to lecture in Japan for industrial workers and scientists interested in strengthening the productivity and quality of the Japanese industry seeking to recover their economy that had been shattered by World War II. He spread the concepts of SPC and PDCA (Plan-Do-Check-Action) created by Shewhart as well as other teachings, thus strengthening the Japanese production process.

In 1951, electrical engineer Joseph Juran, born in Romania and settled in the United States, launched his *Quality Control Handbook*, which became a quality management reference. In 1954, Juran was also invited to hold lectures in Japan in order to present his quality management concepts.

In the early 60s, American businessman and writer Philip B. Crosby defines quality as "compliance with requirements" and creates the "zero defect" and "doing it right the first time" concepts.

At that time, electrical engineer Armand V. Feigenbaum developed the Total Quality Control (TQC) concept and defined quality as a set of characteristics of a product or service that meets customers' expectations.

Also, at the time, Japanese Kaoru Ishikawa created the Quality Control Circle (QCC) concept. Ishikawa also developed the seven tools toward total quality.

In the 80s, because extreme competitiveness threatened by the Japanese industry, Americans begin to adopt the Japanese production and quality control model.

In 1987, the International Standardization Organization published ISO-9000, which became a standard for quality implementation, management, and assurance.

2 WILLIAM EDWARDS DEMING

In Deming's view, quality must be defined according to consumers' requirements and needs, and quality is a relative term changing its meaning as customers' needs evolve. In 1989, Deming defined 14 quality principles:

1 Create constancy of purpose, that is, permanent resources for continuous improvement of products and services so that the organization is competitive, stays in the market, and

creates jobs. The organization management must prioritize long-term concerns and invest in innovative ways to best meet the customers' need;

2 Adopt a new philosophy. Delays, errors and lack of a training policy can no longer be tolerated, requiring a transformation of the Western management approach.

3 Cease dependence on inspection as a means to achieve quality, since the consequence of this practice is accepting the defect. One must first invest in defect prevention and elimination by prioritizing the product quality and control by sampling.

4 End the practice of choosing suppliers through a single criterion - price. Price is just a cost that must be assessed along with quality or lack of quality of supply. The important thing is minimizing total costs. Therefore, there must be new rules on purchases, and long-term relationships with suppliers must be developed.

5 Constantly and forever improve the production system.

6 Institute modern training methods. New skills matching changes to materials, methods, design, equipment, and services are always required.

7 Institute leadership. Establish new ways of managing based on quality reports.

8 Drive out fear. Avoid an authoritarian management style so that everybody can work effectively. Encourage communication and give employees freedom to question, propose, and report problems.

9 Break down barriers between departments. People must work in teams and communication between services is essential. The existence of multidisciplinary quality circles contributes to enriching activities and solutions.

10 Eliminate slogans and numerical goals. Most quality problems have to do with processes and systems created by managers.

11 Eliminate management by objectives based on quantitative indicators. Such indicators highlight quantity over quality. Using statistical methods for continuous quality and productivity improvement.

12 Not to classify or order workers' performance.

13 Institute an education and self-improvement program.

14 Structure management in order to comply with 13 points above. Get the commitment of all employees toward change.

3 JOSEPH MOSES JURAN

Juran conceptualizes that quality is characterized by adapting the characteristics required by the customer (fitness for use) and the absence of flaws and deficiencies.

Juran believes quality management has three key points, the famous *Juran Trilogy*:

1 **Plan Quality**

Identify customers, determine their needs, and create product characteristics that meet such needs, create processes capable of meeting such needs and transfer leadership of such processes at the operational level.

2 **Quality improvement**

Recognize the need for improvement, transform opportunities for improvement in an activity shared by all workers, create a quality board to select improvement projects, promote quality training, assess project progression, award-winning teams, post results, review reward systems in order to increase the improvement level, and include improvement objectives in the company's business plans.

3 **Control quality**

Assess the current performance level, compare with objectives set, and take steps to reduce the difference between the expected, and the actual performance.

Juran bases his approach on customers' needs, not necessarily advocating the organization restructuring.

Juran's sequence:

- Justify the need for improvement
- Identity projects
- Organize to guide and direct projects
- Organize to diagnose and assess projects
- Diagnosis problem to identify root causes
- Corrective action for findings
- Break barriers in cultural resistance to change
- Control new levels

Juran also developed the principle that 80% of problems are due to 20% of their causes. Nevertheless, he stated that other causes must not be neglected or forgotten, under penalty of becoming major causes of problems.

4 PHILIP B. CROSBY

Crosby's approach is based on prevention. The idea that mistakes are inevitable is false. It is up to managers through their attitudes and practices, especially through recognition, developing commitment to prevention and defining "zero defects" as their main goal. If, for example, the execution time is prioritized over quality, then work will focus on that parameter.

For Crosby, quality is associated with the following concepts: zero defects, doing it right the first time, the four absolutes of quality, the prevention process, vaccine quality, and the 6 C's.

Zero defects concept does not mean that the product needs to be perfect. It means that all individuals in the organization are committed to meet the requirements the first time. This policy enables the senior management to reaffirm their commitment to quality.

The four absolutes of quality:

- Prevention must be the general line of conduct;
- Quality costs are a management tool to assess and allocate resources;

- Zero defects standard must be the work philosophy; and
- Compliance with specifications must the standardized language in relation to the intended quality level.

Crosby sees problems as noncompliance bacteria, hence the need for vaccines and antibodies to act so as to prevent the existence of problems. The quality vaccine consists of three management actions:

- Determination,
- Formation, and
- Implementation.

The responsibility for the continuous administration of the vaccine belongs to the senior management.

The six C's:

- Comprehension is the importance of realizing what quality means.
- Commitment of the senior management, which starts by defining the quality policy.
- Competence is the result of a critical training plan to implement the quality improvement movement in a methodical way.
- Communication is so that everyone in the organization acquire a corporate quality culture.
- Correction is based on prevention and performance.
- Continuation highlights the quality improvement process as a "way of being" of the organization.

For Crosby, quality means compliance with requirements. Quality must be defined in quantitative terms to help the organization to act based on tangible goals.

Quality must be measured regularly through the cost caused by botched items. In order to assist managers in assessing error costs, he developed the following formula:

Cost of Quality (COQ) = Price of Compliance (POC) + Price of Noncompliance (PONCE)

Where

POC - refers to the cost of doing it well the first time.

PONCE - provides information to management about the cost lost and an indication of progress as the organization improves.

Crosby defined quality as the mood of employees of an organization on how they should perform work. If there is no formal policy established by the management, each individual establishes its own.

Crosby set a sequence of steps toward a quality improvement program:

1. Senior management commitment to quality. The organization management must be convinced of the necessity of improving quality and express it clearly on a written document outlining the organization's quality policy. It must express what everyone should do in order to meet customers' needs.

2 Quality improvement teams. Management must establish a team to oversee quality improvement in all departments. The team's role is to assess what is needed in each department and to fulfill all that concerns the general policy of the organization's quality.

3 Quality measurement. Quality indicators must be introduced in order to identify needs for improvement.

4 Nonquality cost assessment. Quality improvement teams must estimate nonquality costs in order to identify priority areas where actions will be immediately profitable.

5 Awareness of quality needs. Employees must understand the importance of following specifications and noncompliance costs.

6 Corrective actions. Opportunities for corrective actions are triggered in steps 3 and 4.

7 Plan a "zero defects" program. An ad hoc committee must be constituted in the quality improvement team. This commission must start a "zero defects" program appropriate to the needs of the organization and its culture.

8 Training managers and inspectors. Since the program start until the different levels of responsibility, directors must be trained to implement what they are responsible for in the quality improvement global program.

9 Create the "zero defect day" so that the organization group of employees is made aware of the new performance rules.

10 Goal setting. In order to turn commitments into action, individuals and groups must be encouraged to set goals for improvement. For that, each responsible must define along with members of his or her team, the specific objectives to achieve measurable results. Such goals can be known by everyone, and their progress can be assessed at regular meeting.

11 Eliminate causes of errors. Employees must be encouraged to report difficulties in achieving the goals of streamlining and removing the causes of errors.

12 Recognition. Recognition must be publicly (but not financially) stated to those who attain goals on a regular basis.

13 Quality circles. Quality experts and people particularly motivated by the progress of quality improvement must meet regularly to exchange ideas and experiences.

14 Restart and always progress. The previous set of steps must be initiated regularly, renewing the commitment of former employees and introducing new ones in the process.

5 ARMAND VALLIN FEIGENBAUM

Feigenbaum defined, in the 50s, the Total Quality Control concept: "an effective system for integrating quality development, quality maintenance and quality improvement efforts of several groups in an organization, to allow more economical products and services that take consumer's total satisfaction into account."

For Feigenbaum, quality is a management philosophy and a commitment to excellence.

Quality:

- Is the only goal of the organization
- Is determined by customers

- Assumes group work (quality circles)
- Requires the senior management's commitment
- Requires *empowerment* (increased decision making capacity of workers and reduction of hierarchical levels)

Feigenbaum argues that quality must be designed and incorporated to products and cannot be obtained only from their inspection. In order to support this requirement, he holds that the company should introduce a Quality System.

He defines the Total Quality System as a combination of the work's operational structure across the organization documented in management procedures and techniques, effective and integrated toward the orientation of coordinated actions of manpower, machinery, and information of the organization, according to the best and most practical ways to ensure satisfaction as to quality and costs.

The Quality System must be structured and planned, not developed in a haphazard way. Those principles must include:

- Client orientation;
- Integration of activities across the organization;
- Clear assignments to staff, in order to achieve quality;
- Specific activities for suppliers' control;
- Total identification of quality equipment;
- Awareness throughout the organization;
- Real effectiveness of corrective actions;
- Continuous system control, including forecasts and feedback of information; and
- Periodic audit of system activities.

Feigenbaum suggests a number of basic component parts or subsystems that must be based on documented procedures, having the quality manual as a macro-reference:

- Quality assessment before production starts
- Plan Quality and process
- Planning, assessment, and quality control of purchased materials
- Product and process assessment and quality control
- Feedback of quality information
- Quality information equipment
- Training and orientation towards quality and staff development
- Quality technical assistance
- Management of the quality control function
- Special studies on quality

6 KAORU ISHIKAWA

Ishikawa is mainly associated with the Quality Circles concepts. Quality Circles are small teams usually composed of the same work area that voluntarily and regularly meet to identify, investigate, analyze, and solve problems they encounter at work.

In Quality Circles, the following characteristics are highlighted:

1 **Volunteering work**

Circles must be created on a voluntary basis, not by orders from senior management.

2 **Self development**

Circle members must have a willingness to learn.

3 **Mutual development**

Circle members must aspire to expand their horizons and cooperate with other circles.

4 **Possible full participation**

Circles need to establish their ultimate goal as full participation of all workers in the same workplace.

Basic ideas underlying Quality Circle activities are

- Contributing to the organization's improvement and development;
- Respecting humankind and creating an exciting workplace where proper working together is nice; and
- Exercising human capabilities to the fullest.

According to Ishikawa, practicing good quality control means developing, designing, producing, and marketing a cheaper, more useful and high-quality product that is satisfactory to the customer.

Ishikawa systematized the seven quality control tools:

- Pareto chart
- Cause-and-effect diagrams
- Histogram
- Checklists
- Scatter diagrams
- Flowcharting
- Control charts

Ishikawa noted that not all problems could be solved by these tools but at least 95% of the problems could be. And he found that any worker could use these tools, because of their simple and easy application. Some tools were already known, such as the Pareto chart. However, Ishikawa organized them so as to contribute to quality control. He created the cause-and-effect diagrams, also named Fishbone diagram, or Ishikawa diagram.

7 GENISHI TAGUSHI

In Tagushi's view, quality and cost of a product are determined largely by its design and its manufacturing process.

He defines quality in terms of losses generated by this product to society.

In general there are four quality concepts ascribed to Tagushi:

1 Quality must be incorporated in the product from day one, not through inspections. Improvements will occur in the design phase of a product or process and will continue throughout the production phase. Lack of quality cannot be improved by traditional inspection.

2 Best quality is reached by minimizing deviations in relation to goals. The product must be designed in a robust way and immune to uncontrollable environmental factors. Values must be specified for critical parameters and ensure that production meets these goals with the minimum deviation.

3 Quality must not be based on performance or product characteristics. This causes price and/or the market to fluctuate, but not quality. Product performance and characteristics may be related to quality, but they are not the basis of quality. Instead, performance is a measure of the product capabilities.

4 Quality costs must be measured in terms of deviations from the product performance. This includes rework costs, inspection, warranties, returns, and so forth.

Attachment II

TOOLS OF QUALITY

TOOLS OF QUALITY

1 INTRODUCTION

Tools of quality can be techniques, devices, graphical statements, execution schemes, and other procedures used to implement and verify quality of a product or service.

This attachment contains the following tools:

- Pareto chart
- Cause-and-effect diagrams
- Histograms
- Checklists
- Scatter diagrams
- Flowcharting
- Control charts
- Brainstorming
- 5W2H.

2 PARETO CHART

Pareto chart is a bar chart that organizes occurrence frequencies, from largest to smallest, prioritizing problems or causes for a problem.

Constructing the Pareto chart follows, in short, the following steps:

- Definition of problems to be analyzed

  Examples: noncompliance occurrences; production losses.

- Definition of problem data

  Examples: noncompliance due to dimensional deviation, noncompliance due to malfunction, loss of production due to low quality of raw materials, loss of production due to mechanical failure.

- Define the data collection method

  Examples: survey site, process, work shift.

- Perform data collection.

- Construction of a bar chart in decreasing order of occurrence. Indicate the sum of miscellaneous occurrences in the last chart on the right.

The following figure shows an example of a Pareto chart.

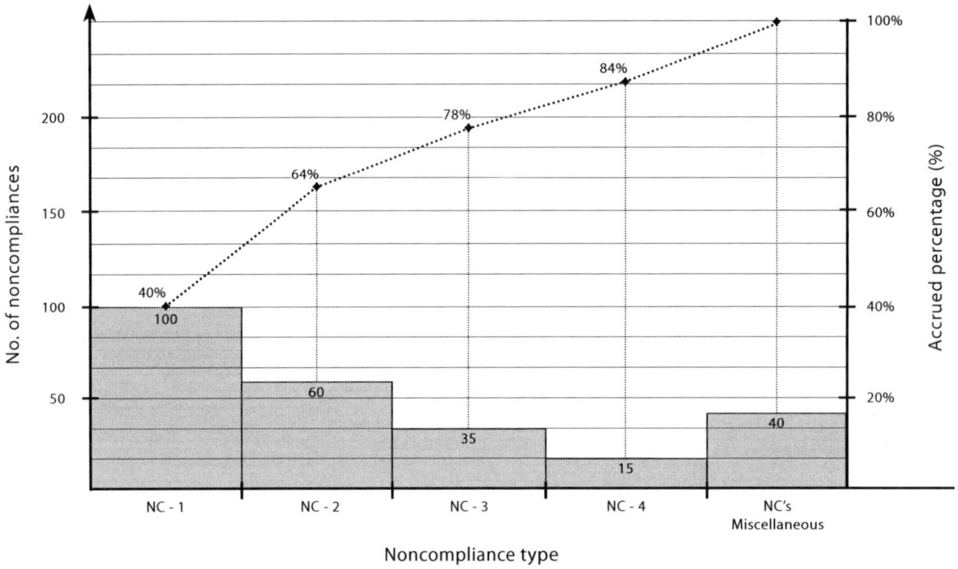

3 CAUSE-AND-EFFECT DIAGRAMS

The cause-and-effect diagrams (Fishbone diagram, or Ishikawa diagram) is a graphical tool that shows the relationship between a problem and possible causes that may contribute to it.

The diagram considers that problems can be classified into six types: method, raw material, manpower, machinery, measurement, and environment.

Constructing the cause-and-effect diagram follows, in short, the following steps:

- Clear definition of the problem to be analyzed
- Brainstorming to identify as many causes of the problem as possible – *What is happening?*
- Grouping causes into categories, preferably following the types above
- Placement of causes in the diagram
- Questioning (*Why does this happen?*) and identification of causes that appear repeatedly
- Obtaining consensus from the group or using voting to select the most likely and more important causes

The following figure shows an example of cause-and-effect diagrams.

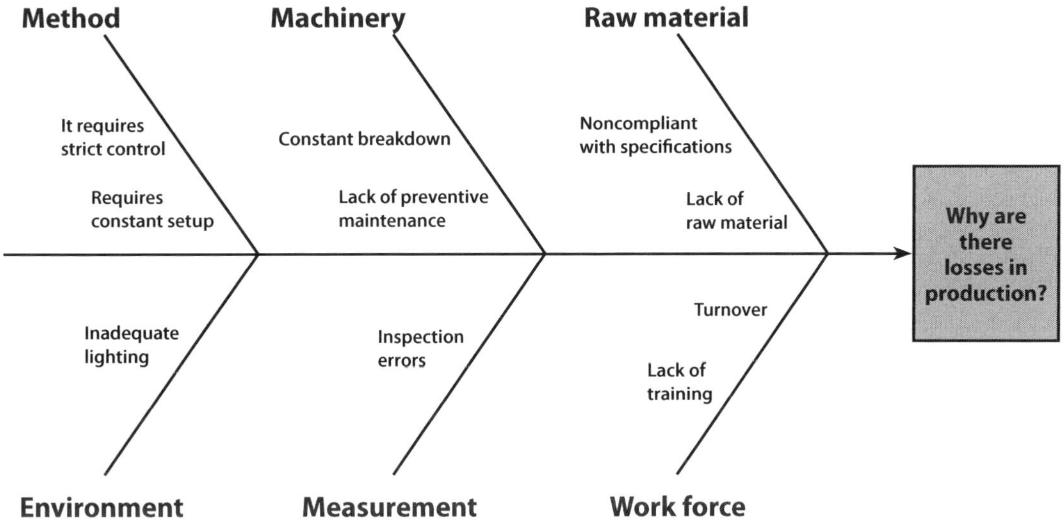

4 HISTOGRAM

Histograms are graphical representations describing the frequency distribution of a set of measurements, usually arranged in a vertical bar chart. In this chart, the base of rectangles corresponds to the class range and height corresponds to frequency. The construction of histogram has a preliminary character in any study and is an important indicator of a data distribution.

The following figure shows a histogram example.

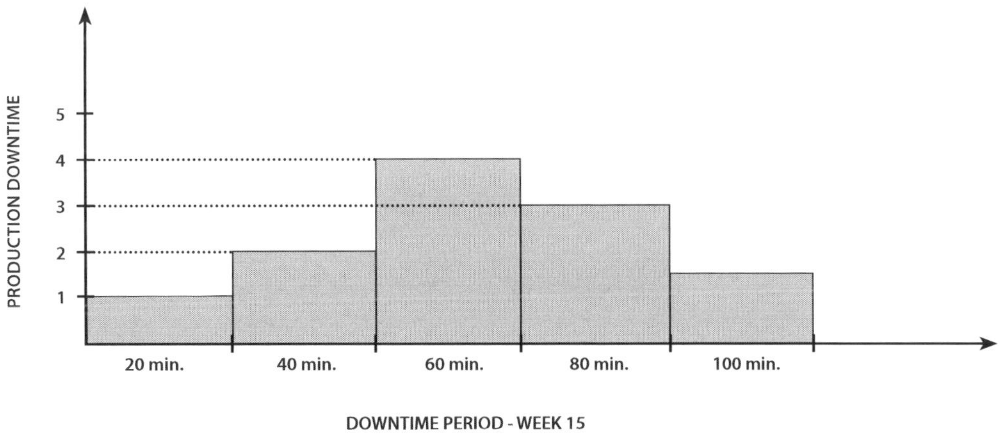

5 CHECKLISTS

Checklists are forms used to collect and analyze data. These lists can be used as follows:

- **Simple list**

  Simple checklists are used for verifying compliance with pre-established activities or to assess the level where they are.

The following figure shows an example of the simple checklist to verify activities in training.

CHECKLIST

	Training activities	Never	Most of the time	Always
1	Activities are being performed according to the training?			
2	Is everybody complying with established hours?			
3	Are instructions on the use of equipment being observed?			
4	Are operating instructions being followed?			
5	Are safety instructions being followed?			
6	Is productivity expected during the training being achieved?			
7	Do reports follow training definitions?			
8	Were occurred problems listed?			
9	Have problem root causes been defined?			
10	Were corrective actions taken to deal with occurred problems?			
11	Were preventive measures taken concerning the problems?			
12	Are results generally satisfactory?			

- **Frequency list**

  Frequency checklists are used to recognize how many times an event occurs over a period.

The figure below shows an example of the frequency checklist for losses on a production line.

NONCOMPLIANCE FREQUENCY CHECKLIST

Process: Manufacturing piece X		**Responsible:** David Leeman
Period: 9/1/2006 to 9/30/2006 - 2nd shift		**Production: 420 pieces**
NC - 1	///// ///// ///// ////	19
NC - 2	///// ///// ///// ///// //	22
NC - 3	///// ///// /////	15
NC - 4	///// ////	09
Several NCs	///// ////	08
	Total of NCs	73

6 SCATTER DIAGRAMS

The Scatter diagram is used to monitor what happens to one variable when another one is changed, in order to determine whether there is a relationship between them. Such variables can be related to quality, product characteristics, or any factor that may cause variance in another variable. The more aligned and continuous data are on the chart, the greater the possibility of their relationship.

The following figure shows a scatter diagram model that indicates the possibility of a relationship between variables A and B for the sample case.

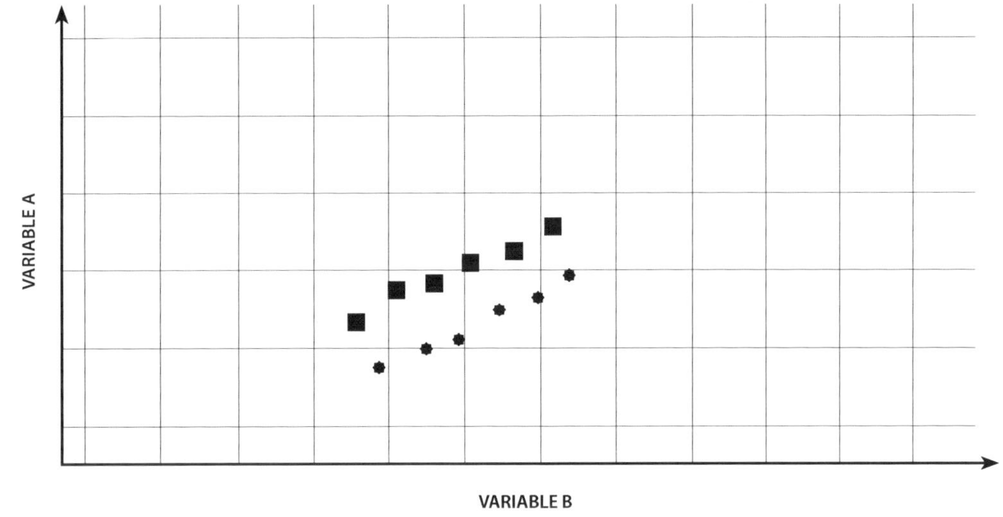

7 FLOWCHARTING

Flowcharting is a graphical representation of sequencing activities of a process. As the flowchart uses standardized symbols, it allows viewing, identifying improvements, promoting information on the process, and communicating easily among engaged people.

Flowchart symbols

Symbols used in flowcharting represent steps in the process or industries involved, sequence of activities, milestones, or verification questions (Yes/No). The most commonly used symbols are as follows:

Indicates a process start or finish

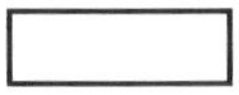
Indicates a process stage

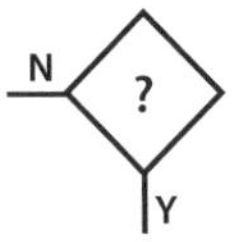

Indicates a process point when a decision must be reached.
The question is usually internal to the diamond, and two alternative outputs represent Yes or No answers

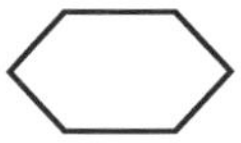
Indicates a preparation activity

Indicates the direction and sequence of activities in the process

Developing a flowchart follows, in short, the steps below:

- Gather a group of people involved in the process.
- Describe activities and build the flowchart, paying attention to decision points (Yes/No).
- Identify those responsible for performing each activity.
- Verify whether the flowchart corresponds to the way how the process is executed. If necessary, make corrections.

Important

To verify the current process of what could be done to improve the process, split the group into two subgroups of people. A subgroup produces the current process flowchart and another one produces the ideal process flowchart. Differences among flowcharting enable realizing potential improvement points in the process.

The following figure shows a critical flowchart example.

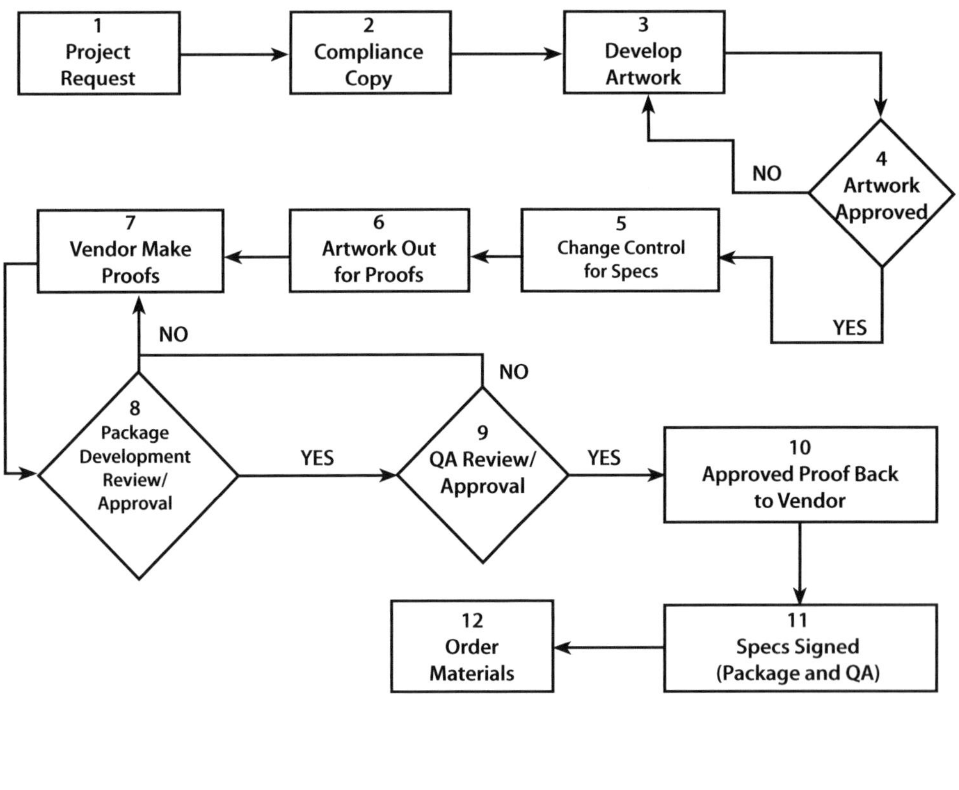

SOURCE: *PMBOK® Guide*, 3rd Edition

8 CONTROL CHARTS

Control charts are tools used to verify whether the process is statistically under control, that is, within the calculated limits. Generally, such graphics are used to monitor production processes in order to prevent defects, avoid waste, and reduce costs.

8.1 CONTROL CHARTS COMPONENTS

- *(Upper and lower) specification limits.* They represent customers' expectations or contractual requirements for product performance and quality.
- *(Upper and lower) control limits.* They represent limits established by the performing company related to the product average performance and quality based on statistical calculations.
- *Goal.* The chart midline representing the process midline based on statistical calculations.

The following figure shows the components of a control chart.

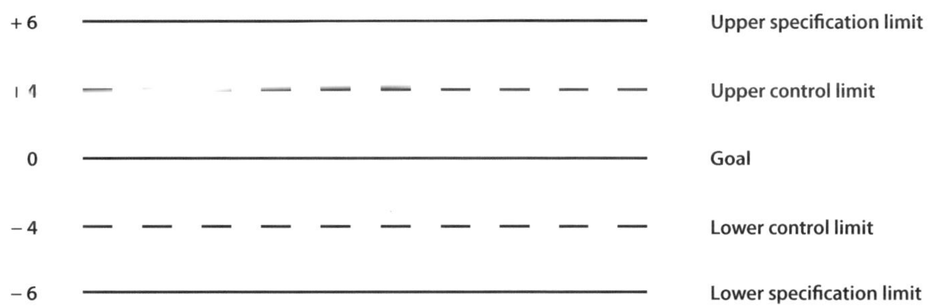

8.2 CONTROL CHARTS RESULTS

- *Process normal variance.* Results are within upper and lower control limits.
- *Process out of control.* The process is out of control when a point is outside the upper or lower control limit (assignable cause) or even when the rule of seven is taking place.
- *Rule of seven.* This rule sets that if seven points make up series above or below average, even within the control limits, they are not random and must be verified, since the process may be out of control.

The following figure illustrates a control chart with results.

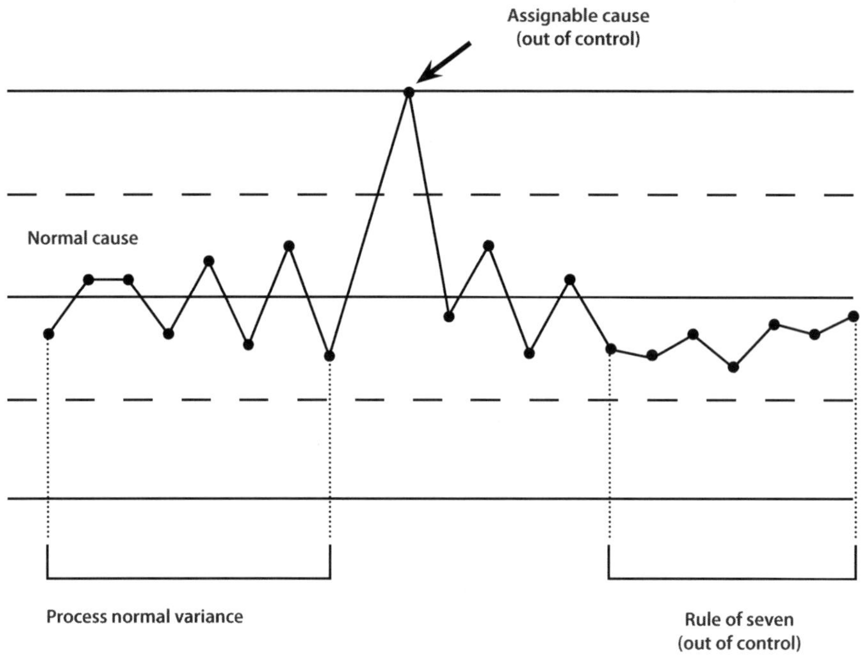

9 BRAINSTORMING

Brainstorming is a group work technique designed to release participants' imagination and creativity, by breaking down set paradigms toward ideas and solutions about a particular subject.

In addition to its easy use, brainstorming can generate a large number of ideas in a short period.

BRAINSTORMING TYPES

- **Structured**

  Everyone must come up with an idea each round or not suggest an idea until his or her next turn is up.

- **Nonstructured**

  Group members come up with ideas as they come in their minds. This tends to create a more relaxed atmosphere but at the risk of more extroverted participants leading the session.

BRAINSTORMING RULES

Basic rules are as follows:

- Emphasize quantity over quality of ideas.
- Avoid criticism, assessments, or judgments of the ideas of any participant.
- Present these ideas as they arise, bluntly, without any elaborations or further consideration. "Saying nonsense" must not be feared. Ideas considered crazy can provide links to other more creative ones.
- Encourage all ideas, no matter how outlandish they may seem.

- "Hitchhiking" others' ideas, creating from them.
- Write participants' words. Do not interpret them.

BRAINSTORMING SESSION

The brainstorming session must follow the following phases:

- **Phase 1 – Introduction**
  Session start, clarification of goals, and creation of a relaxed and pleasant atmosphere.
- **Phase 2 – Idea generation**
  Consecutive rounds of idea requests and records.
- **Phase 3 – List review**
  Verification of questions (without any judgment) and requests for clarification.
- **Phase 4 - Analysis and selection**
  Discussion, analysis, and preliminary selection of ideas.
- **Phase 5 - Sorting ideas**
  Analysis of preselected ideas, prioritization and selection of the three most important ideas.

10 5W2H

The 5W2H is a basic management tool aimed at establishing, on a table or spreadsheet, responsibilities, procedures, deadlines, goals, and costs about the execution of a particular action or activity.

Preparation develops based on answers to the following questions:

WHAT	What must be performed?
WHEN	When must it be performed?
WHO	Who is responsible for performing it?
WHERE	Where will it be performed?
WHY	Why must it be performed this way?
HOW	How will the action be performed?
HOW MUCH	How much will be spent?

The following figure shows an example of the 5W2H tool.

ACTION PLAN
OBJECTIVE:
WHAT?
WHEN?
WHO?
WHERE?
WHY?
HOW?
HOW MUCH?

Additional information and reminders for the exam

- Quality is defined as the degree according to which the project meets requirements.
- Exceeding customers' expectations with additional deliverables is usually related to additional or superfluous work — this is not allowed as it can generate additional deadlines and/or costs.
- Quality must be planned, not only inspected.
- Marginal analysis refers to the study in order to reach the point where the revenue obtained from improving quality equals the incremental cost to implement such quality. At this point, quality improvement must be stopped.
- Impact of poor quality: increased costs, rework, schedule delays, customers' and users' low satisfaction, increased risks.
- In an on-demand *Just in time* environment, inventory is almost zero, and supplies are delivered when needed for production. This requires more attention from companies and suppliers.
- Kaizen, or continuous improvement, is the continuous search for improvements in quality.
- **Theorists of quality**
  - Joseph Juran: developed the 80/20 principle and defined quality as *fitness for use*.
  - W. Edwards Deming: developed the PDCA (Plan–Do–Check–Act) cycle and 14 points for the total quality management;
  - Philip Crosby: advocated prevention over inspection and the zero defects concept. He used to state that quality is compliance to requirements.
- **The Cost of Quality (COQ) can be**:
  - Cost of compliance: training, studies, researches;
  - Cost of noncompliance: rework, lost production (scrap), loss of business, inventory costs, costs to cover guarantees.

  The cost of compliance must be less than the cost of noncompliance.

- **Control charts**

  The data on samples are collected and plotted on the chart to check whether they are within the limits.

  - Upper and lower control limits: the range of variance acceptable of a process. It generally considers ±3 Sigma or standard deviations. Points within this range are considered under control, except for the rule of seven. It represents the quality standard of the performing company. For safety reasons, this range must be less than the range of specification limits.
  - Average: the chart midline indicating the midpoint of the process acceptable variance range.
  - Specification limits: represent the customers' expectations or quality contractual requirements. During the exam, consider that specification limits are higher than the upper and lower control limits.
  - Process out of control: the absence of uniformity and predictability in the process. It can occur when given data are out of the upper or lower control limit or when the rule of seven is in place.
  - Rule of seven: a group of seven consecutive pieces of data to be located on one side of the average. This repetition states that the process may be out of control. The rule of seven is a general or heuristic rule.
  - Variance with assignable cause or special cause: the need to investigate a data point or rule of seven.

- Design of experiments: an experiment to determine, based on statistics, which variables can improve quality.

- Benchmarking: a review of other projects for ideas in order to improve the current project quality.

- Statistical sampling: a technique to measure a share of the population.

- Flowcharting: Show how a process or system is developed, from start to finish and how activities are related. They are used in the Perform Quality Control process in order to find potential quality problems.

- Quality metrics: they represent the quality acceptance criteria of a product, such as: maximum quantities of items failed during inspection, product weight variance and number of bugs found in a software application.

- Quality checklists: lists of items to be inspected or a list of stages to be observed. They are developed in the Plan Quality process and used in the Perform Quality Control process.

- Process improvement plan: quality improvement.

- Quality audits: procedure for verifying compliance with the company's policies, standards, and procedures. In addition, it verifies whether these documents are appropriate, efficient, and effective or need to be reviewed.

- Process analysis: identification of improvements that can be added to processes in order to improve quality.

- Statistical independence: the probability of an occurrence does not affect the occurrence of another event.

- Mutual exclusivity: two events are considered mutually exclusive when they cannot occur together in a single test.
- Normal distribution: a distribution chart of the most common probability density, usually in the form of a bell curve.

- **1, 2, 3, or 6 Sigma**

  They represent the quality level the company aims to achieve.

  - ±1 sigma (standard deviation) represents that 68.26% of occurrences will be within the control limits – less than 317,400 parts in a million may be outside the control limits.
  - ±2 sigma (two standard deviations) represents that 95.46% of occurrences will be within the control limits – less than 45,400 parts in a million may be outside the control limits.
  - ±3 sigma (three standard deviations) represents that 99.73% of occurrences will be within the control limits – less than 2,700 parts in a million may be outside the control limits.
  - ±6 sigma (six standard deviations) represents that 99.99985% of occurrences will be within the control limits – less than 1.5 parts in a million may be outside the control limits.

- **Seven basic tools of quality**

  Cause-and-effect diagrams, flowcharts, histograms, Pareto chart, sequential chart, scatter diagram, and control chart.

  1. Cause-and-effect diagrams (Ishikawa diagram, Fishbone diagram): it helps identify the root cause of the problem, organize ideas, stimulate thought, and generate discussion.
  2. Flowchart: described earlier in this section.
  3. Histogram: a chart displaying data in the form of bars or columns.
  4. Pareto chart: a chart similar to the histogram, which organizes the results of the most frequent to the least frequent, helping to identify root causes that generate most problems. It focuses attention on the most critical issues.
  5. Sequential chart: a chart with data plotting, which can analyze the history, the variance standard, and define trends.
  6. Scatter diagram: checks whether two variables are related.
  7. Control chart: described earlier in this section.

Supplementary exercises

1. In regards to the Project quality knowledge area, indicate to which management processes group(s) each element is related and explain why. Follow the example of quality audits.

1. Quality audits

☐ Initiating ☐ Planning ☒ Executing ☐ Monitoring/controlling ☐ Closing

Quality audits are tools/techniques of the Perform Quality Assurance process, developed in the project Executing.

2. Deliverables

☐ Initiating ☐ Planning ☐ Executing ☐ Monitoring/controlling ☐ Closing

3. Quality metrics

☐ Initiating ☐ Planning ☐ Executing ☐ Monitoring/controlling ☐ Closing

4. Process analysis

☐ Initiating ☐ Planning ☐ Executing ☐ Monitoring/controlling ☐ Closing

5. Pareto chart

☐ Initiating ☐ Planning ☐ Executing ☐ Monitoring/controlling ☐ Closing

6. Flowcharting

☐ Initiating ☐ Planning ☐ Executing ☐ Monitoring/controlling ☐ Closing

7. Quality control measurements

☐ Initiating ☐ Planning ☐ Executing ☐ Monitoring/controlling ☐ Closing

8. Quality checklists

☐ Initiating ☐ Planning ☐ Executing ☐ Monitoring/controlling ☐ Closing

9. Stakeholder register

☐ Initiating ☐ Planning ☐ Executing ☐ Monitoring/controlling ☐ Closing

10. Process improvement plan

☐ Initiating ☐ Planning ☐ Executing ☐ Monitoring/controlling ☐ Closing

11. Change requests

☐ Initiating ☐ Planning ☐ Executing ☐ Monitoring/controlling ☐ Closing

12. Approved change requests

☐ Initiating ☐ Planning ☐ Executing ☐ Monitoring/controlling ☐ Closing

13. Validated changes

☐ Initiating ☐ Planning ☐ Executing ☐ Monitoring/controlling ☐ Closing

14. Validated deliverables

☐ Initiating ☐ Planning ☐ Executing ☐ Monitoring/controlling ☐ Closing

15. Proprietary quality management methodology

☐ Initiating ☐ Planning ☐ Executing ☐ Monitoring/controlling ☐ Closing

2. Complete the sentences below, stating whether the option refers to an input, tool/technique, or output, and identify the corresponding project management process.

1. Quality audits are ______________________ of the ______________________ ______________________ process.
2. Validated deliverables are ______________________ of the ______________________ ______________________ process.
3. Quality metrics are ______________________ of the ______________________ ______________________ process.
4. Benchmarking is a ______________________of the ______________________ ______________________ process.
5. Validated changes are ______________________ of the ______________________ ______________________ process.
6. Change requests are ______________________ of the ______________________ ______________________ processes.
7. Process analysis is a ______________________ of the ______________________ ______________________ process.
8. Deliverables are ______________________ of the ______________________ process.
9. Quality metrics are ______________________ of the ______________________ ______________________ processes.
10. Pareto chart is a ______________________ of the ______________________ ______________________ processes.
11. Design of experiments is a ______________________ of the ______________________ ______________________ processes.
12. Quality checklists are ______________________ of the ______________________ ______________________ process.
13. Quality checklists are ______________________ of the ______________________ ______________________ process.
14. Approved change requests are ______________________ of the ______________________ ______________________ process.
15. Quality control measurements are ______________________ of the ______________________ ______________________ process.

Questions

1. All the processes listed provide inputs to the Plan Quality process, except
   a. Develop Project Management Plan
   b. Create WBS
   c. Identify Stakeholders
   d. Determine Budget

2. All the processes listed provide inputs to the Plan Quality process, except
   a. Develop Schedule
   b. Identify Risks
   c. Identify Stakeholders
   d. Estimate Costs

3. The Plan Quality process generates outputs that become inputs to the following processes:
   a. Perform Quality Control, Perform Quality Assurance, Identify Risks, Develop Project Management Plan, and Determine Budget
   b. Perform Quality Control, Perform Quality Assurance, Identify Risks, and Develop Project Management Plan
   c. Perform Quality Control, Perform Quality Assurance, Estimate Costs, and Develop Project Management Plan
   d. Perform Quality Control, Perform Quality Assurance, Identify Risks, and Determine Budget

4. All items listed are related to the cost of compliance, except
   a. Training
   b. Rework
   c. Document processes
   d. Time to execute the right way

5. The objective of a quality audit is all the options listed, except
   a. Identify all the good/best practices being implemented
   b. Record results of the quality activity execution in order to assess performance and recommend changes

c. Identify all deficiencies

d. Share good practices implemented in similar projects

6. The Perform Quality Control process receives inputs from all processes listed, except

a. Perform Integrated Change Control

b. Control Costs

c. Control Scope

d. Verify Scope

7. The Perform Quality Control process generates outputs that become inputs of all processes listed, except

a. Control Schedule

b. Perform Quality Assurance

c. Verify Scope

d. Perform Integrated Change Control

8. The difference between tolerances and control limits is

a. Tolerances refer to the result whether or not in compliance, and control limits refer to the classification of results in continuous scale measuring the compliance degree

b. Tolerances refer to the limits that can indicate whether a process is out of control, and control limits refer to the limits of a specified range of acceptable results

c. Tolerances refer to a specified range of acceptable results, and control limits refer to the limits that can indicate whether a process is out of control

d. Control limits refer to whether the result is in compliance or not, and tolerances refer to the classification of the results in continuous scale measuring the compliance degree

9. The reason given by a random pattern of points within the control limits of a control chart is named:

a. Abnormal cause

b. Special cause

c. Assignable cause

d. Common cause

10. The reason given by points beyond the control limits or by nonrandom patterns within control limits on a control chart is named

a. Special cause

b. Common cause

c. Random cause

d. Normal cause

11. The two major components of the COQ are

a. Internal failures and external failures

b. Cost prevention and assessment costs

c. Cost of compliance and cost of noncompliance

d. Tests and rework

12. The area consists of three standard deviations on both sides of the midline, or average, of a normal distribution of data plotted on a control chart reflecting the expected variance on data is named:

a. Control limits

b. Tolerance limits

c. Specification limits

d. Threshold lower limits

13. The area on both sides of the midline, or average, of data plotted on a control chart meeting customers' requirements for a product or service is named:

a. Control limits

b. Tolerance limits

c. Specification limits

d. Threshold lower limits

14. The theory stating that quality improvements must represent a continuous way of doing business, not an exclusive event of an activity or process is named:

a. Juran's theory

b. McGregor's theory

c. Maslow's theory

d. Total Quality Management

15. Quality checklists are outputs of the following process(es):

a. Perform Quality Assurance and Plan Quality

b. Perform Quality Control

c. Plan Quality

d. Perform Quality Assurance

16. Quality checklists are inputs of the following process(es):

a. Perform Quality Control and Perform Quality Assurance

b. Perform Quality Control

c. Plan Quality

d. Plan Quality and Perform Quality Control

17. The zero defects theory is ascribed to

a. Juran

b. Crosby

c. Deming

d. Ishikawa

18. All of the following options are inputs of the Plan Quality process, except

a. Scope baseline

b. Stakeholder register

c. Quality metrics

d. Organizational process assets

19. All of the following options are tools or techniques of the Plan Quality process, except

a. Cost of Quality

b. Benefit-cost analysis

c. Control charts

d. Quality metrics

20. All of the following options are tools or techniques of the Plan Quality process, except

a. Improvement plan in the process

b. Benefit-cost analysis

c. Control charts

d. Benchmarking

21. All of the following options are tools or techniques of the Plan Quality process, except

a. Cost of Quality

b. Benefit-cost analysis

c. Quality audits

d. Statistical sampling

22. All of the following options are inputs of the Plan Quality process, except

a. Quality management plan
b. Quality metrics
c. Process analysis
d. Process improvement plan

23. All of the following options are tools or techniques of the Plan Quality process, except

a. Quality metrics
b. Control charts
c. Enterprise environmental factors
d. Quality checklists

24. All of the following options are outputs of the Plan Quality process, except

a. Control charts
b. Quality metrics
c. Flowcharting
d. Statistical sampling

25. All the following options are inputs of the Perform Quality Assurance, except

a. Work performance information
b. Project management plan
c. Quality audits
d. Quality control measurements

26. All the following options are tools and techniques of the Perform Quality Assurance process, except

a. Quality control tools
b. Quality audits
c. Quality metrics
d. Process analysis

27. All the following options are outputs of the Perform Quality Assurance process, except

a. Work performance information
b. Change requests

c. Project document updates

d. Project management plan updates

28. All of the following options are inputs of the Perform Quality Control process, except

a. Project management plan

b. Quality metrics

c. Quality checklists

d. Statistical sampling

29. All of the following options are inputs of the Perform Quality Control process, except

a. Work performance measurement

b. Approved change requests

c. Quality control measurements

d. Project management plan

30. All of the following options are tools or techniques of the Perform Quality Control process, except

a. Cause-and-effect diagrams

b. Control charts

c. Flowcharting

d. Work performance measurements

31. All of the following options are tools or techniques of the Perform Quality Control process, except

a. Quality checklist

b. Review of approved change requests

c. Run chart

d. Pareto chart

32. All of the following options are tools or techniques of the Perform Quality Control process, except

a. Ishikawa diagram

b. Flowcharting

c. Statistical sampling

d. Quality control measurements

33. All of the following options are tools or techniques of the Perform Quality Control process, except

a. Validated deliverables

b. Fishbone diagram

c. Run charts

d. Inspection

34. All of the following options are outputs of the Perform Quality Control process, except

a. Quality control measurements

b. Validated changes

c. Validated deliverables

d. Deliverables

35. All of the following options are outputs of the Perform Quality Control process, except

a. Project document updates

b. Organizational process assets updates

c. Approved change requests

d. Project management plan updates

36. How can quality be defined?

a. The degree to which the project meets users' requirements

b. The degree to which the project meets requirements

c. The degree to which the project meets customers' requirements

d. The degree to which the project exceeds customers' expectations

37. The company where you work is revamping its production and has implemented an inventory system on demand. This means that:

a. The stock is reduced and requires more attention

b. The production level is based on demand

c. The stock is flexible and does not require as much attention

d. The stock is zero (Just in Time) and requires more attention

38. One of the most commonly used graphic in quality management, the Pareto chart, helps the project manager:

a. Determine whether a process is out of control

b. Identify the root cause of problems and focus on the most critical issues

c. Explore a desired future result

d. Stimulate thinking about a problem

39. The standard deviation refers to

a. Time deviation acceptable for the project

b. Deviation among estimates

c. Distance between the upper estimate and the lowest estimate

d. Distance between the measurement and the average

40. The control chart showed seven consecutive points above the average. Which action must be taken?

a. Verify the point distribution in the previous reading

b. Find an assignable cause

c. Develop a reading schedule

d. No action for the time being – this is the rule of seven

41. In a project Executing, a measurement was performed and found that the quality metrics of a work package was not complied with. The project manager gathered the entire team to discuss the problem and to find a solution that meets the project requirements. In which part of quality management is team engaged?

a. Perform Quality Control

b. Quality Planning

c. Project Monitoring and controlling

d. Perform Quality Assurance

42. The project manager found the solution to a problem occurred in the project, but the same problem occurred again after two months. What did the project manager probably failed to do?

a. Use the Pareto chart

b. Use the Ishikawa diagram

c. Project risk analysis

d. Use the control chart

43. One of the quality theorists, who developed the 80/20 principle, was

a. W. Edwards Deming

b. Kaoru Ishikawa

c. Joseph Juran

d. Philip Crosby

44. When an event occurrence probability does not affect the likelihood that another occurs, it refers to

a. Mutual exclusivity

b. Normal distribution

c. Statistical independence

d. Standard deviation

45. The production manager met with the organization's quality manager and they agreed to analyze 30 pieces per 1.000 ones produced, whenever the factory third shift is in operation. In other shifts, the analysis will continue to be made in 20 of the 1.000 parts produced. What kind of quality tools/techniques are they using?

a. Production incremental analysis

b. Checklist

c. Control charts

d. Statistical sampling

46. The project manager asked the project team to created record items to be inspected. This means that he intends to use which quality tool?

a. Design of experiments

b. Checklists

c. Statistical sampling

d. Flowcharting

47. The project team collected several data points to analyze the correlation between two variables and put them in graphic form to present to the project manager. What tool the team used for this presentation?

a. Pareto chart

b. Control chart

c. Gantt chart

d. Scatter diagram

48. The organization's quality team is collecting information and measuring comparisons with upper and lower variance limits defined for products of a particular production line. What quality tool are they using?

a. Statistical sampling

b. Cause-and-effect diagrams

c. Control chart

d. Checklist

Answer key

Supplementary exercises

2. 1 - Tool/technique - Perform Quality Assurance

2 - Outputs - Perform Quality Control

3 - Outputs - Plan Quality

4 - Tool/technique - Plan Quality

5 - Outputs - Perform Quality Control

6 - Outputs - Perform Quality Assurance and Perform Quality Control

7 - Tool/technique - Perform Quality Assurance

8 - Inputs - Perform Quality Control

9 - Inputs - Perform Quality Assurance and Perform Quality Control

10 - Tool - Perform Quality Assurance and Perform Quality Control

11 - Tool - Plan Quality and Perform Quality Assurance

12 - Outputs - Plan Quality

13 - Inputs - Perform Quality Control

14 - Inputs - Perform Quality Control

15 - Inputs - Perform Quality Assurance

Questions

1. A. According to *PMBOK® Guide*, the Develop Project Management Plan process does not provide outputs to the Plan Quality process. However, Scope baseline is considered an output of the Create WBS process, not a component of the Project management plan. Therefore, inputs of the Plan Quality process are the scope baseline of the Create WBS process; stakeholder register in the Identify Stakeholders process; cost performance baseline of the Determine Budget process; schedule baseline of the Develop Schedule process; risk register of the Identify Risks process. Organizational process assets and the enterprise environmental factors are also inputs of the process.

2. D. The Estimate Costs process does not provide inputs to the Plan Quality process. The inputs of the Plan Quality process are the scope baseline of the Create WBS process; stakeholder register in the Identify Stakeholders process; cost performance baseline of the Determine Budget process; schedule baseline of the Develop Schedule process; risk register of the Identify Risks process. Organizational process assets and the enterprise environmental factors are also inputs of the process.

3. B. The Plan Quality process provides the following outputs for processes: quality management plan for the Identify Risks, Develop Project Management Plan and Perform Quality Assurance processes;

process improvement plan for the Develop Project Management Plan process; quality metrics for the Perform Quality Control and Perform Quality Assurance processes; quality checklists for the Perform Quality Control process.

4. B. Rework is a cost of noncompliance. The cost of compliance – money spent during the project to avoid failures can be obtained from

- Cost prevention (manufacturing a high-quality product): training, document processes, equipment, time to correct execution.
- Assessment cost (assess quality): tests, loss of destructive test, inspections.

5. B. Option B refers to the process Perform Quality Control. Audits are performed in the Perform Quality Assurance process. All other options refer to quality audits.

6. D. The Perform Quality Control process receives inputs of the following processes: Develop Project Management Plan, Direct and Manage Project Execution, Perform Integrated Change Control, Control Scope, Schedule control, Cost control and Quality Planning.

7. A. The Perform Quality Control process generates the following outputs: quality control measurements for the Perform Quality Assurance process; project management plan updates for the Develop Project Management Plan process; change requests for the Perform Integrated Change Control process; validated deliverables for the Verify Scope process; validated changes and project document updates for the project documents; organizational process assets updates for the company/organization.

8. C. Tolerances refer to a specified range of acceptable results, and control limits refer to the limits that can indicate whether a process is out of control (*PMBOK® Guide*).

9. D. The reason given by a random pattern of points within the control limits of a control chart is called a common cause. It is also referred to as random cause.

10. A. The reason given by points beyond the control limits or by nonrandom patterns within the control limits on a control chart is named special cause. It is also referred to as assignable cause.

11. C. The two major components of COQ are

- Cost of compliance, including 1) cost prevention (manufacturing a high-quality product) through training, process documentation, equipment, time to correct execution; 2) assessment costs (assess quality), through testing, loss of destructive testing and inspections.
- Cost of noncompliance, including 1) cost of internal failures (failures found in the project), causing rework and disposal; 2) cost of external failures (found by the customer), causing responsibilities, warranty work and lost business.

12. A. The area consisting of three standard deviations on both sides of the midline, or average, of a normal distribution of data plotted on a control chart reflecting the expected data variance is called control limits.

13. C. The area on both sides of the midline, or average, of data plotted on a control chart meeting customers' requirements for a product or service is called specification limits.

14. D. The Total Quality Management theory, created by W. Edwards Deming.

15. C. Quality checklists are outputs of the Plan Quality process. They show a series of steps that a certain process must follow.

16. B. Checklists are inputs of the Perform Quality Control process.

17. B. The zero defects theory is ascribed to Crosby. Zero defects means performing a task right the first time in order to avoid rework, lost productivity, and increased costs.

18. C. In order to Plan Quality, you must consider the scope baseline (scope statement, WBS and WBS dictionary), verify quality requirements contained in the stakeholder register, refer to the company's quality policies and procedures (organization process assets), and other actions. However, quality metrics will only be obtained, as a formal document, at the end (output) of the Plan Quality process.

19. D. The quality metrics are defined in this process, therefore, they represent a product (output) of the process.

20. A. The process improvement plan is developed in this process; therefore, it is a product (output) of the process.

21. C. Quality audits are performed in the Perform Quality Assurance process. When you find "Quality audit" in the exam, think about Quality assurance!

22. C. A good tip for the exam: when you come across the term "analysis," it denotes the tool or technique. Process analysis is a tool of the Perform Quality Assurance process.

23. B. The question, asked more clearly, is "Which of the following options IS a tool or technique of the Plan Quality process?" Enterprise environmental factors are always inputs of processes. The quality metrics and checklists are products (outputs) of this process. During the exam, note the term "graphic" is always related to tools and techniques.

24. B. The question, asked more clearly, is "Which of the following options IS an output of the Plan Quality process?" Remember in the exam: when you come across the terms control charts, flowcharting, and sampling, they refer to tools and techniques. Quality metrics are defined in the Plan Quality process.

25. C. Keep in mind in the exam: Quality assurance is related to audits! And vice versa! Audits are tools, not an input, of the Perform Quality Assurance process. The other options are process inputs.

26. C. Note that the term "quality metrics" are always inputs and outputs of the Quality management processes. The other options are process tools and techniques.

27. A. Keep in mind in the exam: the term "updates" always refers to process outputs. Change requests (generated in this process) are also outputs of the process. The information on the work performance are process inputs.

28. D. Statistical sampling (choice of one part of the population of interest for inspection) is a tool of the Perform Quality Control process. The other options are process inputs.

29. C. Quality Control Measurements are the documented results (outputs) of the activities of quality control. The other options are process inputs.

30. D. Work performance measurement (technical, deadlines and costs performance) are inputs of the Perform Quality Control process – even if you do not agree with that! The other options are process tools.

31. A. Quality checklists are outputs of the Plan Quality process and inputs of the Perform Quality Control process. The other options are process tools and techniques.

32. D. Quality control measurements are the documented results (outputs) of the Quality control activities. The other options are process tools and techniques.

33. A. One of the goals of quality control is validating deliverables. The results (outputs) of the execution of quality control processes are validated deliverables. The other options are process tools.

34. D. Deliverables are outputs of the Direct and Manage Project Execution process and inputs of the Perform Quality Control process. The products (outputs) of the Perform Quality Control process are, among others, quality control measurements, validated changes, and validated deliverables.

35. C. Keep in mind in the exam: the term "updates" always refers to process outputs. You may not eliminate all the question options in the exam, but it will help you save time. The only option that is not an output is C, approved change requests, a process input.

36. B. Memorize this definition for the exam: Quality is defined as the degree according to which the project meets requirements. That is, all the requirements! Not only users' and customer's requirements (options A and C). In general, option D refers to additional or superfluous work.

37. D. In an on-demand environment (Just in Time), inventory is almost zero, the supplies are delivered when needed for production. This requires more attention from the company and suppliers.

38. B. The last two options relate to the Fishbone diagram (or Ishikawa diagram). Option A refers to control charts. Option B refers to the Pareto chart.

39. D. The standard deviation is an interval measurement around the average.

40. B. The rule of seven applies here: if there were seven consecutive points in one side of the average, an action would be required to correct the problem.

41. A. Measurements are part of the Perform Quality Control process. Note that the question refers to quality management, not to project management (option C).

42. B. The problem root cause was not probably identified – therefore, there was a problem recurrence. The Ishikawa diagram (Fishbone) helps recognize the problem root cause.

43. C. The 80–20 rule – 80% of problems are due to 20% of the causes – was developed by Joseph Juran.

44. C. Keep in mind for the exam: statistical independence means that the occurrence probability of one event in no way affects the occurrence probability of another event. For example, when a playing card is launched into the air and falls face up, it is statistically independent of the playing card falling back up the next time it is launched.

45. D. The population measurement technique is named statistical sampling.

46. B. A checklist contains items that must be checked during an inspection.

47. D. The scatter diagram is used to analyze the correlation between two variables. In the chart, independent and dependent variables are plotted. The closer the points are in relation to a diagonal line, the closer their relationship.

48. C. Control charts shows the upper and lower variance limits.

Chapter 9

PROJECT HUMAN RESOURCE MANAGEMENT

1. Introduction
2. Project Human Resource Management processes
3. Human resource management in project planning
4. Human resource management in project executing

Attachment I	Further reading on conflicts in projects
Attachment II	Supplementary study for the exam

- Additional information and reminders for the exam
- Supplementary exercises
- Questions
- Answer key

9.1 INTRODUCTION

This chapter will introduce the project management processes in the human resource area, their relevant inputs, tools, techniques, and outputs.

9.2 PROJECT HUMAN RESOURCE MANAGEMENT PROCESSES

According to *PMBOK® Guide*, the Project Human Resource Management includes the processes organizing and managing the project team. The project team consists of people with assigned roles and responsibilities to complete the project. This team is also called core team, executive team, or leadership team.

The project cost human resource processes are

- **Develop Human Resource Plan**
  Process identification and documentation of required roles, responsibilities, skills, and hierarchical relationships of the project as well as the creation of a staffing management plan.

- **Acquire Project Team**
  The process of confirming the availability of human resources and obtaining the team required to complete the project assignments.

- **Develop Project Team**
  The skill enhancement, team interaction, and team global environment process in order to improve the project performance.

- **Manage Project Team**
  The process of monitoring the performance of team members, providing *feedback*, dealing with issues, and managing changes in order to optimize the project performance.

The following flowchart displays the relationship among the Project Human Resource Management processes and their locations across the project management process groups.

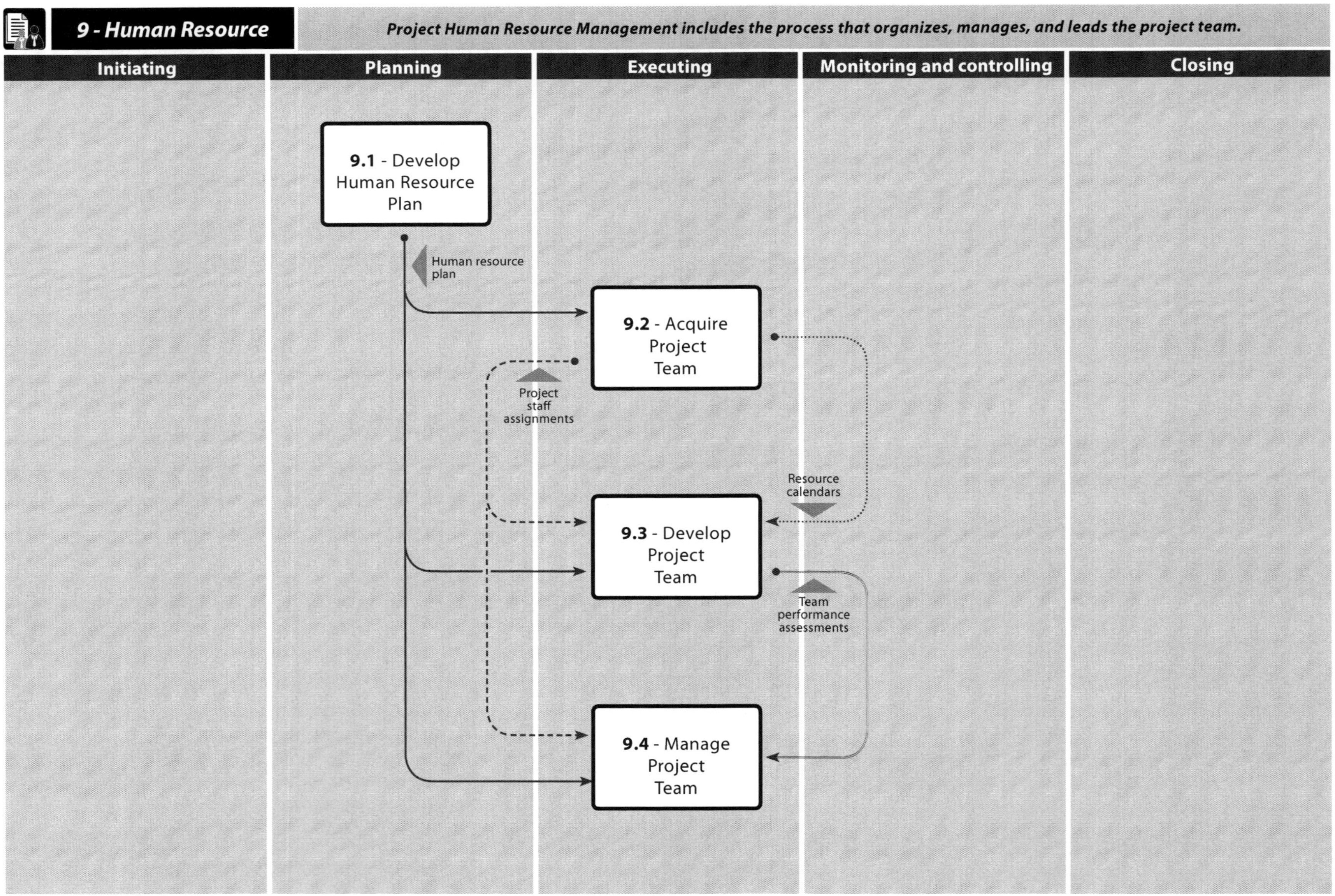
9 - Human Resource
Project Human Resource Management includes the process that organizes, manages, and leads the project team.
Initiating
Planning
Executing
Monitoring and controlling
Closing
9.1 - Develop Human Resource Plan
Human resource plan
9.2 - Acquire Project Team
Project staff assignments
Resource calendars
9.3 - Develop Project Team
Team performance assessments
9.4 - Manage Project Team

9.3 HUMAN RESOURCE MANAGEMENT IN PROJECT PLANNING

According to PMI®, the human resource management in project planning is composed of a process, namely:

- ***Develop Human Resource Plan***

9.3.1 DEVELOP HUMAN RESOURCE PLAN (*PMBOK® GUIDE*, PROCESS 9.1)

Develop Human Resource Plan basically involves

- Determining roles and responsibilities of each team member, usually defined in a responsibility assignment matrix;
- Representing the team members and their hierarchical relationships graphically, usually defined in an organization chart; and
- Executing the Project Human Resource Management.

9.3.1.1 DEVELOP HUMAN RESOURCE PLAN: INPUTS, TOOLS AND TECHNIQUES, AND OUTPUTS

INPUTS

1 **Activity resource requirements**

The necessary resources and their requirements must be considered in this process.

2 **Enterprise environmental factors**

Recognizing enterprise environmental factors is extremely important to the project human resource Planning. The organization type, the relationship between internal departments and the organization, between the organization and other companies participating in the project, between the organization and government bodies as well as logistics and politics-related issues, should be checked for their impact on this process.

A few important factors to be considered include:

- **Organizational factors**

  Consider which departments or sectors are involved in the project; check for external organizations participating in the project; check for the influence of these organizations in the project; check the existence of labor agreements.

- **Technical factors**

  Consider the technical disciplines and expertise required to execute the project; consider the need to use special software applications and equipment; check for challenges in the project transition or transfer phases to production.

- **Interpersonal factors**

  Consider experience, skills and hierarchical relationships of candidates to the project team; consider cultural and language differences; consider the level of trust and respect in relation to subordinates and superiors.

- **Logistics-related factors**

  Consider the location of people to join the project team; consider the workplace conditions; consider strengths and weaknesses of the workplace resource supply. In order to perform remote work, consider the existence of communication such as e-mail, videoconferencing system, management system of electronic documents, and others.

- **Political factors**

  Consider the powers and influence of stakeholders on the project.

In addition to these factors, constraints must be considered in the project human resource Planning, such as

- **Organizational structure**

  Consider what type of organizational structure in the company directly influences the project. For example, a strong matrix structure provides more power to a project manager than a weak matrix structure or a functional structure.

- **Collective agreement negotiations**

  Consider the collective agreement negotiations and their influences on the project.

- **Economic conditions**

  Consider fund availability for training, hiring, travel, and other project needs.

3 **Organizational process assets**

Human resource Planning should consider lessons learned from previous projects and the existence of templates and standards within the company in order to reduce the Planning preparation time and avoid potential omissions. Organization charts, job descriptions, checklists, and other documents from previous projects are examples of these assets.

TOOLS AND TECHNIQUES

1 **Organization charts and position descriptions**

Organizational charts and position descriptions can be performed in several formats as hierarchy charts, responsibility assignment matrix charts, or a text-oriented format.

- **Hierarchy charts**

  The project organization chart can be presented as a hierarchy chart. Similarly to breaking down work packages performed in the Work Breakdown Structure (WBS), this organization chart can be broken down from top to bottom, with departments, units or teams existing within the project organization. Another type of hierarchy chart is the Resource Breakdown Structure (RBS), which breaks down the project work into all types of resources. RBS allows for viewing the location of each type of resource within the project and may be associated with the organization's accounting system and is also useful for monitoring project costs.

HIERARCHY CHART

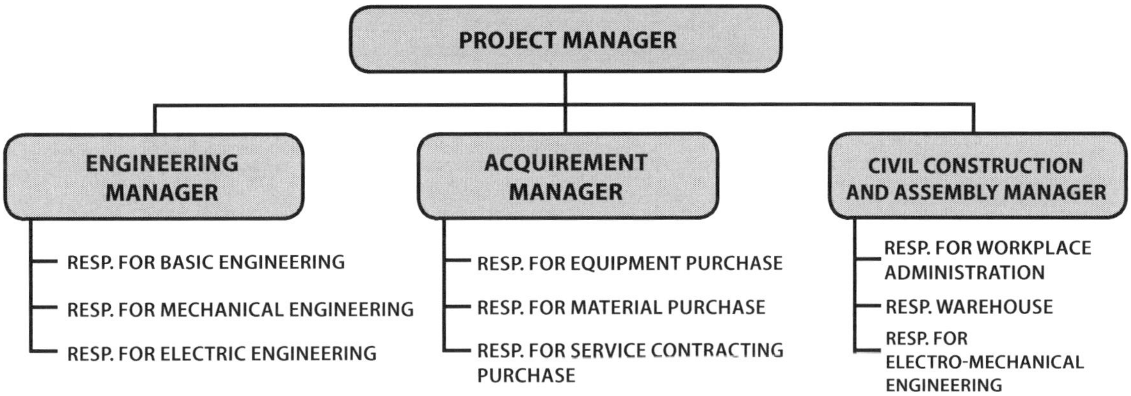

- **Matrix charts**

  Matrix charts are usually performed in a Responsibility Assignment Matrix (RAM) format, which shows links between the project team and the work to be developed. RAM can use the RACI (Responsible, Accountable, Consult, Inform) format, which identifies the Responsible, Accountable, Consult, and Inform functions. This matrix can use a particular resource or a group of resources. The following figure shows an example of a RACI responsibility assignment matrix.

RACI MATRIX

	PAUL	JOHN	MARY	ANNA
Activity A	R	A	C	C
Activity B	I	R	A	A
Activity C	C	I	R	A
Activity D	R	A	C	I

Legend:	R = Responsible	C = Consult
	A = Accountable	I = Inform

- **In text formats**

  Job descriptions and other documents with large amounts of data can be performed in text-oriented formats. The figure on the next page shows a job description form example.

LOGO	PROJECT	JOB DESCRIPTION	Rev.: Data: Sheet ___ of ___
JOB TITLE:			
RESPONSIBILITY:			
AUTHORITY:			
COMPETENCE:			
PROJECT:			**DATE:**
JOB TITLE:			**DATE:**

2 **Networking**

Networking is an informal way of interacting with others from or outside the organization, aimed to better understand political and interpersonal factors. This interaction can occur through informal conversations, meetings with colleagues, fairs, conferences, among others.

3 **Organizational theory**

The organizational theory is the study of how organizations work and how they affect and are affected by the environment where they operate.

The organizational theory helps understand the behavior patterns of individuals, teams, and organizational units. The application of motivation techniques, for example, increases the likelihood of success in managing human resources.

OUTPUTS

1 **Human resource plan**

1.1 **Roles and responsibilities**

Roles and responsibilities of team members and some stakeholders should be prepared by using, for example, the functions illustrated below:

- **Project team roles**

  The project team roles are usually related to project implementation and may include the following:

  - Provide support and guidance to complete the project
  - Elaborate project Planning, including resource and duration estimates, network diagrams, and schedules
  - Perform the project budget
  - Assist in project activity implementation
  - Ensure compliance with the project quality requirements
  - Ensure compliance with the work safety procedures
  - Ensure compliance with the environment use and protection requirements
  - Identify and assess risks and suggest solutions to these risks
  - Assess change requests and implement approved changes
  - Identify and assess suppliers
  - Perform contract management in order to achieve the project objectives
  - Account for project resource use
  - Prepare and distribute reports
  - Prepare the project file
  - Perform the project administrative closure

- Perform the contract closure; and
- Prepare the file and promote lessons learned.

- **Project manager roles**

  The project manager role is broad and can vary depending on the size and complexity of the project as well as the type of organizational structure adopted, however, we can briefly determine as his roles:

  - Lead and hold together the project team;
  - Clearly define the project objectives to the project team;
  - Cause everyone to use the project standards and procedures;
  - Manage the project team to ensure that all members fulfill their roles and responsibilities;
  - Manage schedule to ensure that the project meets the schedule and cost objectives;
  - Identify risks and take risk response measures;
  - Ensure the implementation of the assurance and quality control processes;
  - Identify, manage, and resolve conflicts that may exist in the project;
  - Provide efficient and effective communication to all project stakeholders;
  - Be proactive and have the authority with stakeholders interested in the project; and
  - Be responsible for the project success and failure.

1.2 Project organization charts

The project organization charts are outputs of the project human resource Planning.

1.3 Staffing management plan

The staffing management plan describes how the project human resources will be treated and managed. It should deal with the following considerations:

- **Recruitment and selection**

  Inform the source of resources, their levels of expertise, their costs, the workplace, the benefits provided for in the organization, and other considerations related to resource provision.

- **Timetables and histograms**

  Inform the existence of particular times for certain resources, if any. Submit a resource use histogram. These histograms can be presented separately by resource supply area (for example, a histogram of the engineering area staff and a histogram of the supply department staff). This makes it possible to forecast and control the resource supply by both the functional manager and the project manager. The following figure shows a resource histogram example.

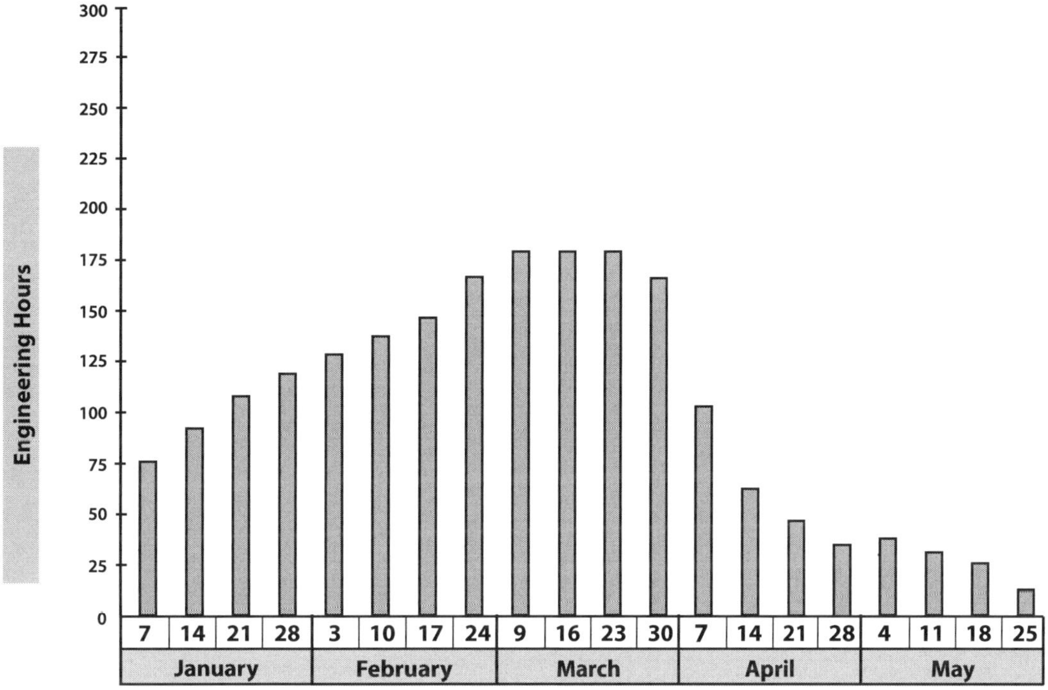

- **Need for training**

  Inform, if any, the need for training resources in order to adjust them to the project requirements.

- **Recognition and rewards**

  Indicate recognition and awards plans for the project allocated resources.

- **Release criteria**

  Indicate the project resource release forecast, separately by resource supply area. This allows for better resource management by functional managers, when their employees return.

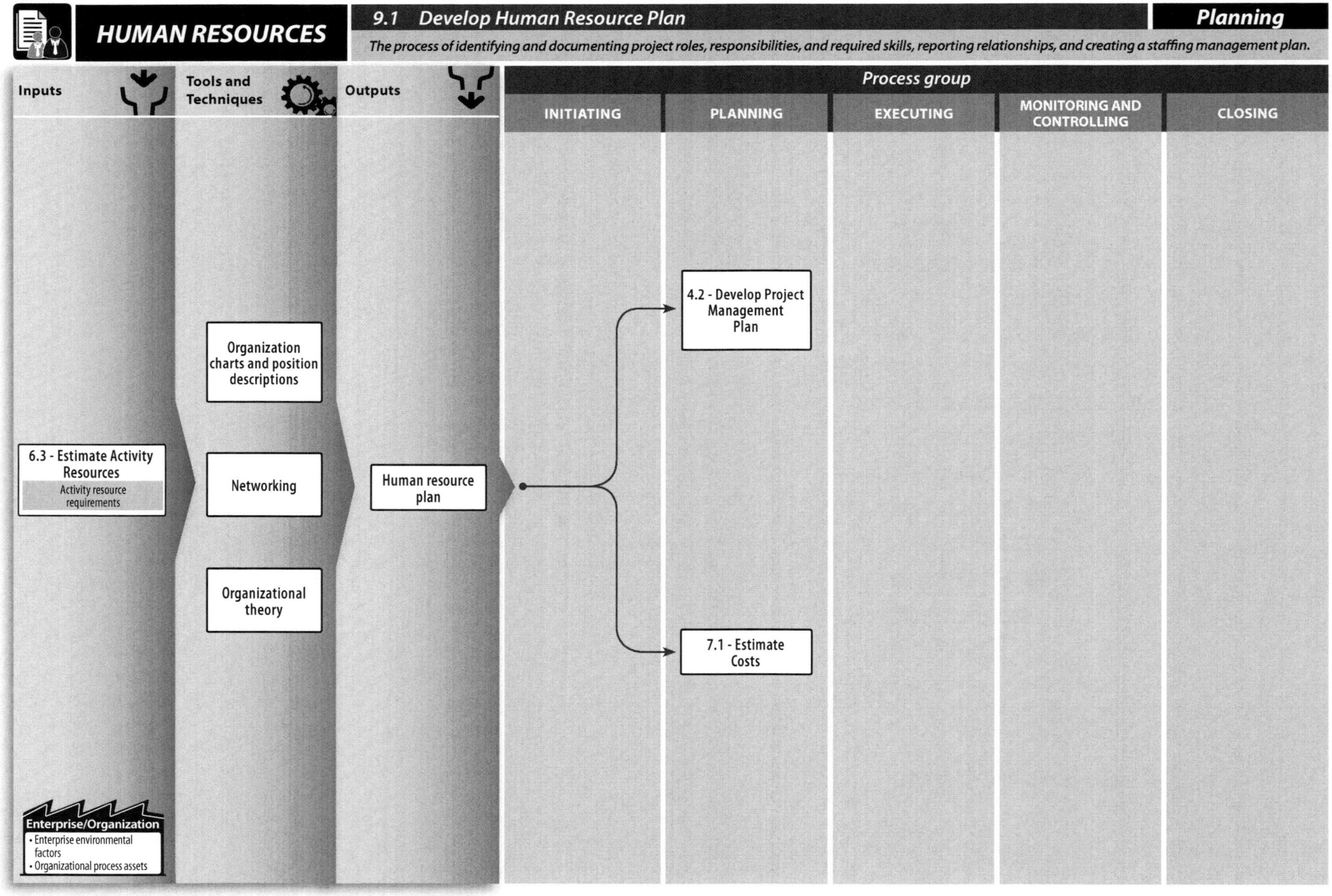
HUMAN RESOURCES
9.1 Develop Human Resource Plan
Planning
The process of identifying and documenting project roles, responsibilities, and required skills, reporting relationships, and creating a staffing management plan.
Inputs
Tools and Techniques
Outputs
Process group
INITIATING
PLANNING
EXECUTING
MONITORING AND CONTROLLING
CLOSING
6.3 - Estimate Activity Resources
Activity resource requirements
Enterprise/Organization
• Enterprise environmental factors
• Organizational process assets
Organization charts and position descriptions
Networking
Organizational theory
Human resource plan
4.2 - Develop Project Management Plan
7.1 - Estimate Costs

9.4 HUMAN RESOURCE MANAGEMENT IN PROJECT EXECUTING

According to PMI®, human resource management in project executing comprises the following processes, namely

- ***Acquire Project Team***
- ***Develop Project Team***
- ***Manage Project Team***

9.4.1 ACQUIRE PROJECT TEAM (*PMBOK® GUIDE*, PROCESS 9.2)

Acquire Project Team consists in obtaining and allocating the human resources required to implement project activities. These resources can be obtained from within the organization or specialized companies. The process involves recognizing which resources were preassigned to the project, negotiating the acquisition of appropriate and qualified resources from the individuals responsible for providing such resources, contracting resources at the appropriate time and working with virtual teams. Toward the process effectiveness, an assessment of the following factors should be performed, namely, resources, skills, experience, and cost and, ultimately, the interest of the individuals selected to participate in the project.

9.4.1.1 ACQUIRE THE PROJECT TEAM: INPUTS, TOOLS AND TECHNIQUES, AND OUTPUTS

INPUTS

1 **Project management plan**

The project management plan provides information on how human resources should be identified, assigned, managed, and controlled, including

- Roles and responsibilities related to positions, skills, and competencies required by the project;
- Organizational charts, indicating the number of individuals required for the project; and
- Team management plan defining the period of time required to each team member during the project as well as other information.

2 **Enterprise environmental factors**

Consideration of environmental factors should involve the organization itself and outside companies that will make professionals available for the project and this should be performed before allocating resources to the project. Such criteria will include:

- **Availability**

  Both functional managers and contractors should inform about available professionals and the likely availability of other professionals.

Chapter 9 - Project Human Resources Management

- **Capacity**

  Functional managers and contractors should inform about the skills of professionals recommended to compose the project team so that the project manager can assess it.

- **Experience**

  Functional managers and contractors should inform about the experience and achievements of professionals recommended to compose the project team so that each professional is assessed and adjusted to the project needs.

- **Interest**

  Functional managers and contractors should inform about the real interest of professionals in taking part in the project as well as the reasons for that interest. The project manager should check this information in detail with professionals and seek to identify the existence of potential conflicts with other recommended professionals or members of the project team.

- **Cost**

  The project manager should check cost allocation of professionals and compare it with the project cost estimates.

3 **Organizational process assets**

Organizational process assets may include procedures for hiring and training, the company's human resources policy, among others, and must be considered in this process.

TOOLS AND TECHNIQUES

1 **Preassignment**

Preassignment may be

- **Internal**

  Internal preassignment occurs when the organization professionals are assigned in advance to compose the project team, and this may be due to the project need, availability of the professional at the organization, or by appointment of managers and the senior management.

- **External**

  External assignment occurs when professionals from external companies are assigned to compose the project team.

2 **Negotiation**

The project manager must negotiate resources with functional managers and companies that will make professionals available for the project, in order to provide staff with appropriate skills and experience to the project and within the requested schedule.

During the organization's internal negotiations, it is important that the project manager:

- Demonstrates the real need of using the resources requested by means of organization charts, schedules, and job descriptions;

- Develop a good relationship with functional managers and departments that make the professionals available, based on the organization and project objectives and goals, preferably by their individual goals; and
- Try to recognize the abilities and skills of professionals and the reasons that led to them being appointed to make up the project team.

3 **Acquisition**

When the organization does not have the professionals necessary to the project, such service may be performed by contractors.

4 **Virtual teams**

Virtual teams are groups of people participating in the project without being necessarily present most of the time. The use of electronic communication, such as the Internet and videoconferencing, enables the existence of virtual teams. This team format enables using professionals who live in remote locations, working in home-based offices as well as professionals with mobility impairments. Composing virtual teams can make feasible projects that would otherwise be discarded because of the high cost of travel expenses.

OUTPUTS

1 **Project staff assignments**

After hiring the necessary professionals, the project will have its work team defined. Assignment consists of determining the roles and responsibilities of each team professional, according to the staffing management plan.

2 **Resource calendars**

The resource availability consists of verifying and documenting the period of time that each professional may be allocated to the project, including holidays and commitments to other projects.

3 **Project management plan updates**

The project management plan and especially the human resource plan should be updated with information from the project's assigned professionals. Organization charts, role descriptions, and other documents should be revised to depict the current team building.

HUMAN RESOURCE

9.2 Acquire Project Team

Executing

The process of confirming human resource availability and obtaining the team necessary to complete project assignments.

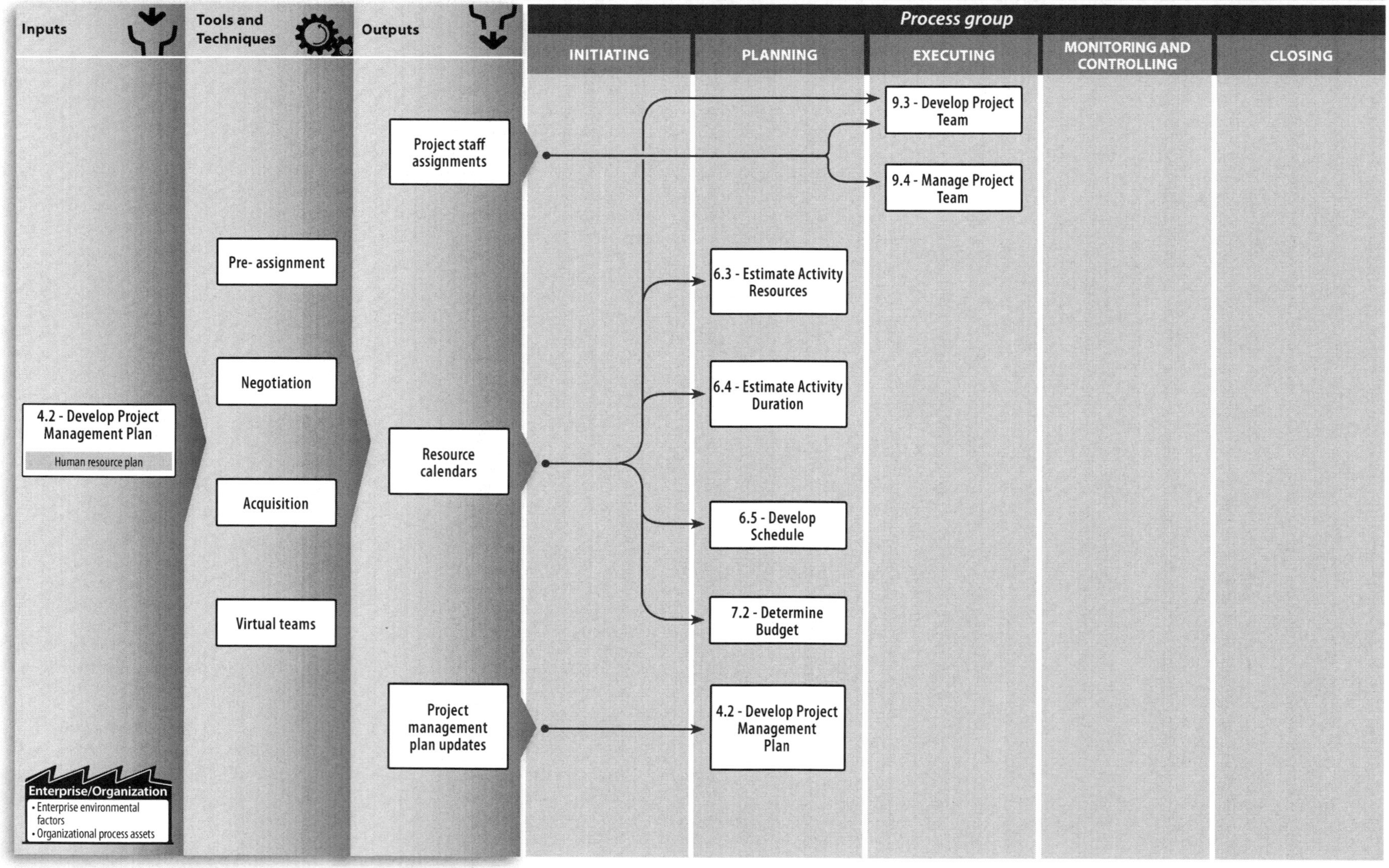

9.4.2 DEVELOP PROJECT TEAM (*PMBOK® GUIDE*, PROCESS 9.3)

Develop Project Team consists of improving professionals' skills and promoting their integration in order to increase productivity and deliver quality work. This process may include the following activities:

- Recognition of skills and weaknesses of professionals composing the team;
- Promoting the integration of professionals among themselves;
- Promoting the integration of professionals in the work environment and the organization; and
- Training required to team members so that they can perform the activities under their responsibility.

The team development efforts should be started as soon as possible after the team is formed and should be continuously developed throughout the project.

9.4.2.1 DEVELOP PROJECT TEAM: INPUTS, TOOLS AND TECHNIQUES, AND OUTPUTS

INPUTS

1 **Project staff assignments**

Staff assignments are the major inputs of this process.

2 **Project management plan**

Project management plan and especially the human resource plan provide guidelines for the team development process with recommended training, disciplinary actions, and awards.

3 **Resource calendars**

Information on resource availability is crucial to this process.

TOOLS AND TECHNIQUES

1 **Interpersonal skills**

Interpersonal skills such as leadership, ability to foster motivation, listening skills, ability to solve problems and resolve conflicts among team members and stakeholders should be used by the project manager throughout the project life cycle. Recognizing feelings and needs of team members is the initial factor to be considered by the project manager in this process.

2 **Training**

Training consists of developing activities to enhance team skills in order to implement activities according to the project need. Training should focus not only on enhancing the team skills but also on reducing the project cost toward improving efficiency. Training can be developed individually or in groups, within the organization team, or in specialized companies outside the organization. For example, training courses can be directed to schedules and network diagrams, project Planning and control, quality control, risk analysis, particular training related to the project product, and so forth.

The project manager may, according to the staffing management plan and the project needs, develop a training plan per team member, as explained in the following spreadsheet.

PROJECT:			
TRAINING PLANS			
ELABORATED BY:		**DATE:**	
Name/Course	**Scheduled date**	**New scheduled date**	**Programming date**
1. Mr. John Wash			
Course A			
Course D			
2. Mr. Brian Wilson			
Course C			
3. Mr. Steve Smith			
Course A			
Course B			
Course D			

After performing the training plan, the project manager should take it to the attention of the manager of each functional team member. Among other participations, the functional manager may suggest the joint execution of courses with professionals assigned to other projects, which can reduce the project training costs.

3 Team-building activities

The project team building will include people who know each other and probably people who have never seen one another before. Even the project manager cannot know all team members. The project manager's role is promoting team integration, direct it to the project objectives, and provide motivation and recognition to its members.

In general, team building goes through four stages:

- **Forming**

  Forming is the initial stage, where members are gathered together, introduced, and informed of the project objectives and their roles and responsibilities. In summary, this meeting will answer the following questions:

  - What is the project team mission?
  - Which are the team objectives and goals?
  - How is the team organized? What is the team organizational structure?
  - What are the roles and responsibilities of each team member?

- Which resources are available to the team?
- Which resources are necessary to the team? When are they necessary?
- Which are the organization policies and procedures to be complied with?
- Which are the risks forecast by the team members?

- **Storming**

  Storming is the stage where team members are excited and they will confront each other in order to attain power and status within the team.

- **Norming**

  Norming is the stage when members are calmer, and team members are more aware and more interested in the project problems.

- **Performing**

  Performing is the stage where the team is mature and capable of doing great things for the project.

- **Adjourning**

  Adjourning is the stage where the team completes the job and leaves the project.

4 **Ground rules**

Defining ground behavior rules promotes the education of team members as to conduct and behavior requirements. Rules can be internal to the project, such as start and finish working hours, adequate behavior in meetings and other events, or external to the project, such as safety and use of the organization facilities and resources.

5 **Co-location**

Co-location consists of the physical allocation of team members in the same building or physical space. Although virtual teams have their advantages, including reducing project costs, it is not always possible to use them in only one project. Co-location, however, enables the team to function more efficiently rather than if members were in different places. Co-location makes communication easier and reduces conflicts, precisely because participants are face to face. The co-location strategy may be used in a meeting room, also called "war room", to gather team members together and discuss project issues.

6 **Recognition and rewards**

Recognition and awards consist of formal methods of recognizing and rewarding team members as to their desirable behavior. The recognition and awards plan, which is part of the staffing management plan, must be impartial and relate to all team members so that they do not jeopardize team cohesion. Recognition and awards must be directly related to professionals' performance and achieving or exceeding the project objectives. Awards should be win-win, where all members can win, as opposed to win-lose, where only a few ones win. The award for completing the work breakdown structure at the expected date is a prize example where all members participated and deserve the award. The "team members of the month" award, where only a few win, is not recommended, as it harms team cohesion.

OUTPUTS

1 **Team performance assessments**

Team performance assessment consists of collecting indication data to assess the team, while it is formed, integrated, and receives the required training. Such indicators may include skill enhancement of a team member, enhanced team competences, and feelings and a low staff turnover rate of team members.

2 **Enterprise environmental factors updates**

The Develop Project Team process can identify new processes or opportunities in the organization human resource standards, procedures, and policies.

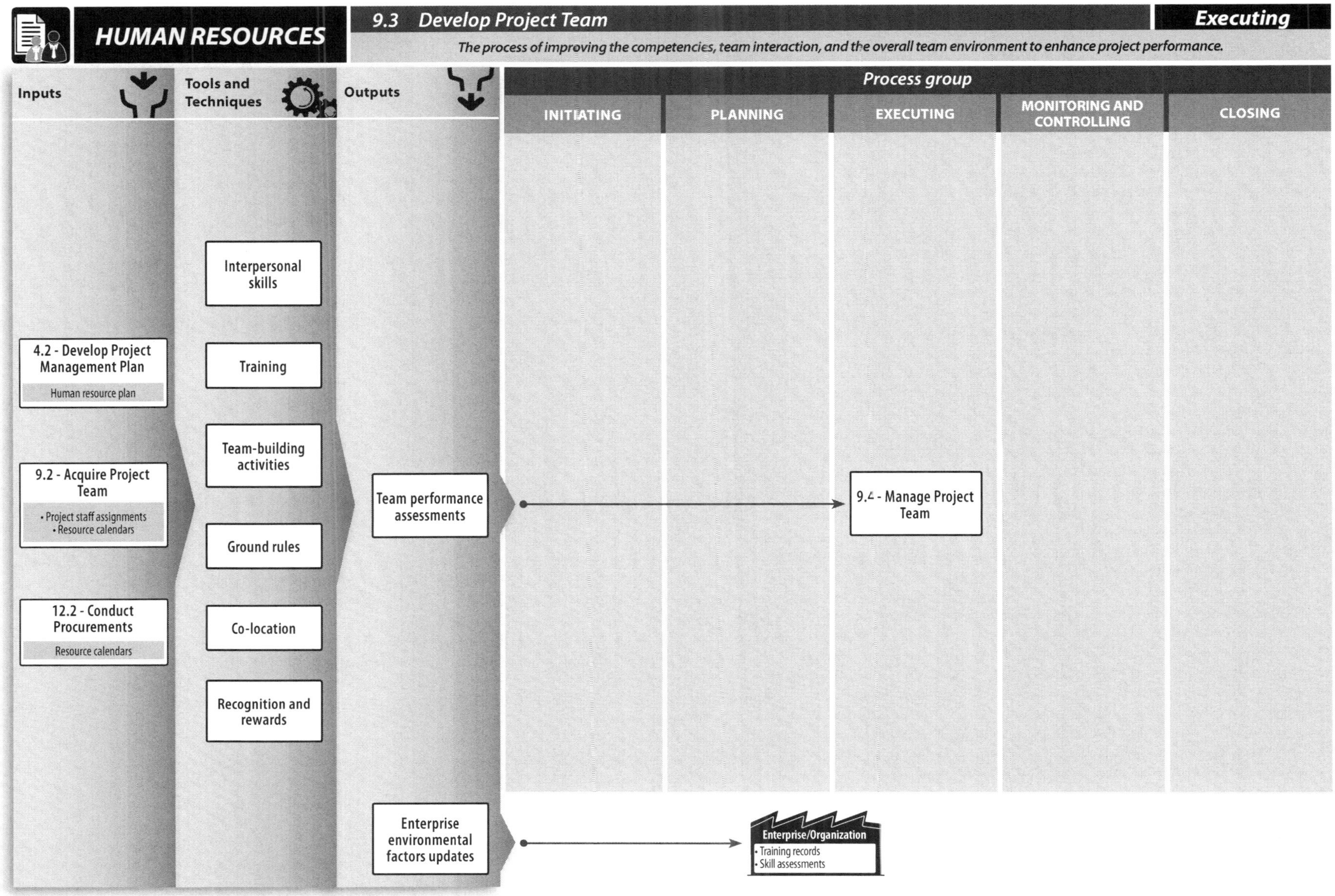
HUMAN RESOURCES
9.3 Develop Project Team
Executing
The process of improving the competencies, team interaction, and the overall team environment to enhance project performance.
Inputs
Tools and Techniques
Outputs
Process group
INITIATING
PLANNING
EXECUTING
MONITORING AND CONTROLLING
CLOSING
4.2 - Develop Project Management Plan
Human resource plan
9.2 - Acquire Project Team
• Project staff assignments
• Resource calendars
12.2 - Conduct Procurements
Resource calendars
Interpersonal skills
Training
Team-building activities
Ground rules
Co-location
Recognition and rewards
Team performance assessments
Enterprise environmental factors updates
9.4 - Manage Project Team
Enterprise/Organization
• Training records
• Skill assessments

9.4.3 MANAGE PROJECT TEAM (*PMBOK® GUIDE*, PROCESS 9.4)

The Manage Project Team process consists in monitoring the performance of team members in resolving problems and conflicts among them as well as coordinating changes to improve the project performance.

9.4.3.1 MANAGE PROJECT TEAM: INPUTS, TOOLS AND TECHNIQUES, AND OUTPUTS

INPUTS

1 **Project staff assignments**

Staff assignments for the project determine roles and responsibilities of each professional of the team and must be considered in this process.

2 **Project management plan**

The project management plan and especially the human resource plan provides guidelines for the Manage Project Team process, such as roles and responsibilities, project organization, and staffing management plan.

3 **Team performance assessments**

The team performance assessment must be considered in this process. This analysis can assist in resolving problems and conflicts and in improving communication and interaction among team members.

4 **Performance reports**

Performance reports may assist in assessing the project team performance, forecasting human resources necessary to the project as well as in recognitions and awards.

5 **Organizational process assets**

Organizational process assets, such as policies and procedures related to human resources, must be considered in this process.

TOOLS AND TECHNIQUES

1 **Observation and conversation**

Observing the behavior of the team members by the project manager can result in obtaining information related to their grievances, needs, and desires as well as helping manage the team. Defining a cordial relationship policy with team members can be obtained through informal discussions between the project manager and them.

2 **Project performance appraisals**

Project performance appraisals, in general terms, consist of assigning scores to team members based on their performances in the project. The successful completion of assessments depends on the project size, complexity, and scope, the organization policy as well as how resources were contracted or allocated to the project. One of the techniques used is the "360 feedback", which collects information from all team members and other people interacting in the project, such as functional managers, the organization human resources analysts, customers, and other stakeholders. This technique has the disadvantage of causing discomfort among team members when assigned scores are disclosed and comments are made by colleagues. However, this and other assessment techniques are always helpful in detecting training needs, clearing up responsibilities, and setting new goals for team members and the project.

3 **Conflict management**

Conflict management in a project is one of the major responsibilities of a project manager, because when properly performed, it will result in higher productivity and greater integration of people participating in the project. Conflicts are the result of different goals and objectives of stakeholders and resistance against establishing procedures for project management. In general, the following are the ways of dealing with conflicts:

- Confrontation, also called coping or troubleshooting
- Negotiation
- Withdrawal, also called escape or retreat
- Imposition, also called strength
- Agreement, also called temporary solutions

4 **Issue log**

Issue log should be developed to enable monitoring and controlling problems. Particular worksheets or minutes of meetings can be used, that contain a clear definition of the problem, who is facing the problem, the resolution deadline, and possible impacts if problems are not dealt with.

5 **Interpersonal skills**

The project manager must use technical, human, and conceptual skills to analyze project situations and interact appropriately with the project team members.

Some of the interpersonal skills most often used by project managers are briefly discussed below.

- **Leadership.** Successful projects require strong leadership skills. Leadership is important across all stages of the project life cycle. It is especially important to convey the vision and inspire the project team to achieve high performance.
- **Influence.** Because project managers often have little or no direct authority over team members in a matrix environment, their ability to appropriately influence stakeholders is essential to the project success. The major influence skills include:
    - Ability to be persuasive and clearly articulate viewpoints and stances,
    - High levels of active and effective listening skills,
    - Consider the several perspectives in any situation, and
    - Collect relevant and critical information to address important issues and reach agreements, maintaining mutual trust.

- **Effective decision-making process.** It involves the ability to negotiate and influence the organization and the project management team. A few guidelines for decision-making include:
    - Focus on goals to be achieved
    - Follow a process for the decision-making process
    - Study environmental factors
    - Develop team members' personal qualities
    - Encourage the team's creativity
    - Managing opportunity and risk

OUTPUTS

1 **Enterprise environmental factors updates**

The Manage Project Team process can identify new improvement processes or opportunities related to enterprise environmental factors, such as organizational performance assessments and personal skill updates.

2 **Organizational process assets updates**

The Manage Project Team process can identify new improvement processes or opportunities for the organization procedures and human resource policies. All documentation related to the project human resources, such as organization charts, job descriptions, individual information on team members and others must be documented as lessons learned from the project.

3 **Change requests**

The Manage Project Team process may detect opportunities or needs for changes in the staffing management plan, roles, and responsibilities and even the number of people allocated to the project, which should be subject to request changes. These changes must be submitted for review, and, if approved, they should be implemented.

4 **Project management plan updates**

The project management plan and, in particular, the human resource management plan must be updated after changes are approved as a result of this process.

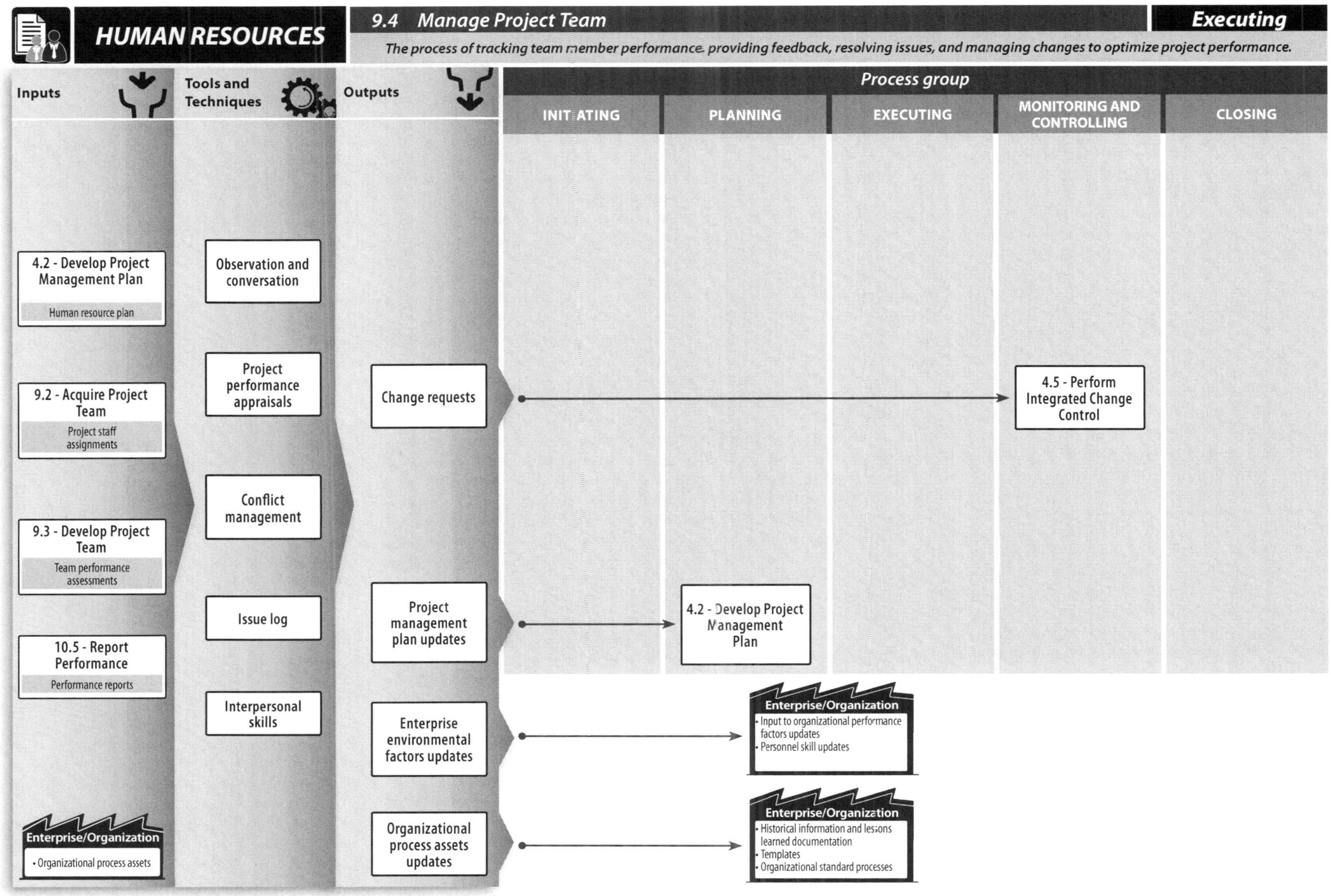
HUMAN RESOURCES
9.4 Manage Project Team
Executing
The process of tracking team member performance, providing feedback, resolving issues, and managing changes to optimize project performance.
Inputs
Tools and Techniques
Outputs
Process group
INITIATING
PLANNING
EXECUTING
MONITORING AND CONTROLLING
CLOSING
4.2 - Develop Project Management Plan
Human resource plan
9.2 - Acquire Project Team
Project staff assignments
9.3 - Develop Project Team
Team performance assessments
10.5 - Report Performance
Performance reports
Enterprise/Organization
• Organizational process assets
Observation and conversation
Project performance appraisals
Conflict management
Issue log
Interpersonal skills
Change requests
Project management plan updates
Enterprise environmental factors updates
Organizational process assets updates
4.5 - Perform Integrated Change Control
4.2 - Develop Project Management Plan
Enterprise/Organization
• Input to organizational performance factors updates
• Personnel skill updates
Enterprise/Organization
• Historical information and lessons learned documentation
• Templates
• Organizational standard processes

Attachment I

FURTHER READING ON CONFLICTS IN PROJECTS

CONFLICTS IN PROJECTS

1 INTRODUCTION

Conflicts in projects are the result of different goals and objectives of stakeholders as well as resistance against the establishment of project management procedures. The project temporary nature and dynamics, its complexity, and the number of interfaces contribute to the natural existence of conflicts. They occur across all projects and take a long time from the project manager, but they should not be considered only as harmful to the project. A conflict can be beneficial to the project when it results in discussions and solutions to project problems. What is important when managing conflicts is the project manager always seeking to make decisions aimed at successfully achieving the project goal.

2 SOURCES OF CONFLICT IN PROJECTS

Conflict sources may be related to

- **Schedules**

  Defining delivery dates, activity execution priorities, and other issues related to time are constantly conflicts sources among stakeholders.

- **Project priorities**

  Project priorities in relation to others within the organization are conflict sources among project managers and functional managers, among managers, and the senior management and even between a project manager and his customer.

- **Resources**

  Resource allocation, its use, and the time expected to remain in the project may generate conflicts between the project manager and functional managers as well as between the project manager and contractors to allocate resources to the project.

- **Expert opinion**

  Different technical opinions on certain technical issues may generate conflicts among team members, among them and suppliers, and among hired consultants.

- **The organization and the project procedures**

  Procedures established by the organization and those specific to the project may generate conflicts among several project stakeholders. The organization human resource management policies, such as position and wage plan, employee transfer policy, and others, are often causes of conflicts between the project manager, functional managers, and the project team.

- **Cost**

  The project cost limitations may generate conflicts among several project stakeholders. Such limitations may interfere with performance, quality, and other factors established for the project deliverables, which may not fully meet the requirements desired by stakeholders.

- **Personality**

  As with any interpersonal relationship, conflicts related to stakeholder personality may occur in a project.

3 CONFLICT ANALYSIS

Conflict analysis can, in summary, encompass the following steps:

- Recognition of facts triggering the conflict
- Verification of the conflict impact on the project and the project team
- Identification of alternative conflict solutions among team members and stakeholders
- Verification of the cost, benefits, and impacts on the project of alternative conflict solutions

4 CONFLICT RESOLUTION METHODS

Overall, five conflict resolution methods are considered:

- **Confronting (problem solving)**

  Confronting, also called problem solving, is the best conflict resolution method. This method consisting in ascertaining facts causing the conflict, analyze them, and reaching the decision about the only correct solution to the conflict. For example, an explanation from the project manager as to a particular procedure can resolve a conflict between two project team members.

- **Compromising**

  Compromising is a less efficient method than confronting, as it is based on the lose-lose system, where conflicting parties receive only a part of what they wanted. This method typically uses phrases like "let's do a part of what everybody is suggesting."

- **Withdrawal (avoidance)**

  Withdrawal, also known as escape, or avoidance, is not a good conflict resolution option, as it consists in postponing the problem. Withdrawal usually occurs when one of the conflicting parties refuses to discuss the issue.

- **Imposition**

  Imposition, also called force, not always represents a good conflict resolution option, as it is the unconditional acceptance by stakeholders of a solution imposed by the management. This method typically uses phrases like "let's do it this way!"

- **Accommodating**

  Accommodating, also called "temporary solution", is a method that seeks to reach an agreement among conflicting parties without emphasizing different opinions. This method usually results in loss of enthusiasm and reluctance to accept the solution. For example, when the project manager uses the phrase "let's calm down and do our job", he is actually using this conflict resolution method.

5 AVOIDING CONFLICTS

Despite the inevitable existence of conflicts in projects, the project manager can develop actions and adopt attitudes to minimize the occurrence of conflicts harmful to the project, such as

- Being a facilitator and clarifier for the project team;
- Clearly defining roles and responsibilities of each team member;
- Being responsive to team members;
- Respecting views and personality of team members;
- Developing, since the project start, a pleasant working environment where team members feel free to expose ideas and suggestions;
- Minimizing cultural differences among team members;
- Developing and implementing an efficient communication system among team members;
- Promoting informal relationship among team members through informal conversations, meetings outside the company, social gatherings, and other activities.

Attachment II

SUPPLEMENTARY STUDY FOR THE EXAM

MOTIVATION THEORIES

1 HIERARCHY'S NEEDS THEORY BY MASLOW

Abraham Maslow, an American psychologist, created a pyramid-shaped hierarchical division, in which lower-level needs must be met before higher-level ones. Such needs have been categorized by Maslow in groups, as mentioned below:

- **Physiological (basic) needs:** food, water, sex, sleep, shelter
- **Safety needs:** personal and family security, stable employment, health (health insurance or life insurance, for example)
- **Love and relationship needs:** having an affection and love relationship, belonging to a group or being part of a club
- **Esteem needs:** self-esteem, confidence, respect from others, and respect for others
- **Personal achievement:** becoming what one can be or "What humans can be, they must be. They must be true to their own nature". Morality, spontaneity, no prejudice, and others

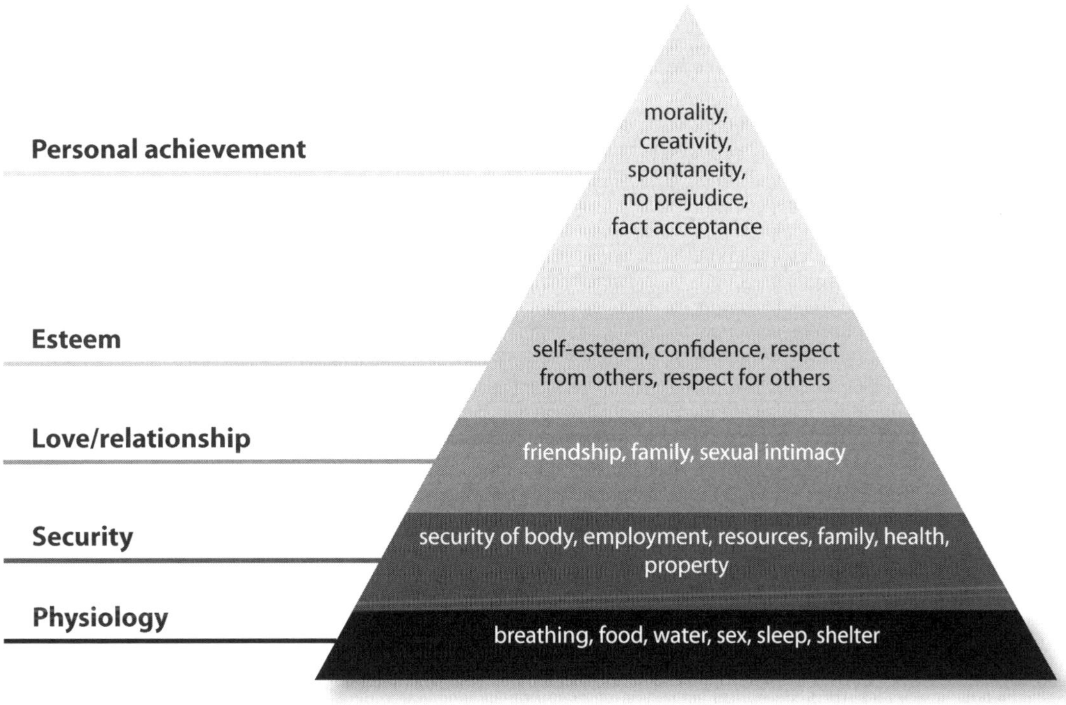

2 THEORY OF EXPECTATIONS

The theory of expectations, attributed to Victor Vroom, a Canadian psychologist and professor, based on the assumption that people choose from different behaviors, according to expectations.

- Effort versus performance. *"If I make an effort, will I have a good performance?"*
- Performance versus reward. *"If I reach this level of performance, will I be rewarded?"*
- Reward validity or attractiveness. *"How much do I really value this reward?"*

3 HERZBERG'S THEORY

Frederick Herzberg, an American sociologist, was the author of "Theory of Two Factors," also called "Hygiene Theory", which considers:

- Hygiene factors. These are factors that can cause dissatisfaction in a certain position and may arise from the work environment, supervision, co-workers, safety in the work environment, salary, and others.
- Motivating factors. These are the factors that cause work-related motivation, such as position content, challenging and stimulating activities necessary to perform the function, professional growth, and recognition.

4 THEORY OF NEEDS

David McClelland, an American psychologist, upholds that people's motivation comes from the necessity of three factors:

- Achievement. The need to feel capable in view of acceptable challenges, the need for achievement, and the need for recognition.
- Affiliation or socialization. The need to belong to a group, to cooperate with the group, and to be approved by the group.
- Power. The need to influence people, to become a leader.

HUMAN BEHAVIOR THEORIES

The following human behavior theories can be addressed in the exam:

1 THEORY X AND THEORY Y

Douglas McGregor, an American economist and university professor, was the creator of Theory X and Theory Y, which states that workers follow two behavioral patterns, and, based on that, they are analyzed by managers.

Theory X. It states that human beings dislike and avoid work whenever possible; human beings prefer to be directed rather than directing; the average human being is little ambitious; people are unable and unwilling to take responsibility.

Theory Y. People can learn to take responsibility; people can be motivated; people can work without being constantly monitored; the intellectual capability of the average human being can be increased.

2 THEORY Z

Dr. William Ouchi, an American author and professor, created Theory Z, which states that humans do not unlink their human condition from their employee condition, and that the humanization of the work environment increases the company productivity and employees' self-esteem.

THE POWER OF THE LEADERS

The types of power that can be used by leaders and project managers to convince others to cooperate and perform things in a certain way are

1. Legitimate or formal power. Power comes from the position of the manager and the decisions that he can reach.
2. Reward or prize power. Power comes from rewards to desirable behaviors, through incentives or bonuses.
3. Punishment or penalty power. Power comes from the threat of punishment for undesirable behavior or actions, or for failing to meet goals set.
4. Expert's power. Power comes from the technical knowledge on the subject or the manager's personal skills.
5. Reference power. Power comes from the charisma, the leadership, and the respect that a manager naturally exerts on team members, causing them to respect and admire him.

Additional information and reminders for the exam

- At the exam, consider that You are the project manager and directly responsible for the project team.
- Organizational breakdown structure: a chart showing the responsibilities by department.
- Resource breakdown structure: a chart showing the work divided by resource.
- Virtual teams: people from the project team who never or rarely meet one another.
- Halo effect: a tendency to consider a team member for his skills in a particular factor, such as competent in other factors.
- Team formation and development stages: training, conflict, agreement, performance, dispersion.
- Ground rules: these are the behavior norms and rules applicable to the project team, as defined by the project manager. Examples: conduct during project meetings, honest information, and conflict resolution.
- The co-location or war room helps communication, reduces the impact of conflicts, and identifies the project team with the organization and the customer.
- Powers of the project manager: legitimate (or formal) power; awarding (or rewarding) power; punishment (or penalty) power; expert's power; reference power. The manager's most effective powers are the awarding and the expert's ones. The manager's least effective power is the punishment power.
- Conflict resolution methods: confrontation (or troubleshooting); negotiation; withdrawal (or escape); agreement (temporary solution or accommodation); imposition (or force); collaboration.
- In general, 50% of conflicts are caused by resources, schedules, and priorities.
- The best conflict resolution method is confrontation — or troubleshooting.
- Arbitration: a neutral party, accepted by the parties, is consulted to resolve the dispute.
- **Motivation Theories**
  - Hierarchy's needs theory by Maslow: Physiological needs, safety needs, love and relationship needs, esteem needs, personal achievement.
  - Theory of Expectations (Victor Vroom): People choose from different behaviors according to expectations.

- Herzberg Theory (or the Hygiene Theory): Hygiene factors can cause dissatisfaction; motivation factors are the position contents, challenging activities, professional growth, and recognition.
- Theory of Needs (David McClelland): Motivation stems from the need for achievement, socialization, and power.

- **Human Behavior Theories**

  - Theory X and Theory Y (Douglas McGregor): Theory X states that human beings dislike and avoid work; they prefer to be directed rather than directing; the average human being is little ambitious. Theory Y states that people can learn, take responsibility, be self-motivated, and work without constant supervision.
  - Theory Z (William Ouchi): Human beings do not unlink their human condition from their employee condition and humanization of the work environment increases the company's productivity and employees' self-esteem.

Supplementary exercises

1. In regards to the Project Human Resources area of knowledge, indicate to which management processes group(s) each element is related and explain why. Follow the example of Training.

1. Training

☐ Initiating ☐ Planning ☒ Executing ☐ Monitoring/controlling ☐ Closing

Training is a tool of the Develop Project Team process — developed during the project Executing.

2. Preassignment

☐ Initiating ☐ Planning ☐ Executing ☐ Monitoring/controlling ☐ Closing

3. Organizational theory

☐ Initiating ☐ Planning ☐ Executing ☐ Monitoring/controlling ☐ Closing

4. Observation and conversations

☐ Initiating ☐ Planning ☐ Executing ☐ Monitoring/controlling ☐ Closing

5. Resource calendars

☐ Initiating ☐ Planning ☐ Executing ☐ Monitoring/controlling ☐ Closing

6. Negotiation

☐ Initiating ☐ Planning ☐ Executing ☐ Monitoring/controlling ☐ Closing

7. Conflict management

☐ Initiating ☐ Planning ☐ Executing ☐ Monitoring/controlling ☐ Closing

8. Networking

☐ Initiating ☐ Planning ☐ Executing ☐ Monitoring/controlling ☐ Closing

9. Virtual teams

☐ Initiating ☐ Planning ☐ Executing ☐ Monitoring/controlling ☐ Closing

10. Project staff assignments

☐ Initiating ☐ Planning ☐ Executing ☐ Monitoring/controlling ☐ Closing

11. Project performance appraisals

☐ Initiating ☐ Planning ☐ Executing ☐ Monitoring/controlling ☐ Closing

12. Organization charts and position descriptions

☐ Initiating ☐ Planning ☐ Executing ☐ Monitoring/controlling ☐ Closing

13. Resource calendars

☐ Initiating ☐ Planning ☐ Executing ☐ Monitoring/controlling ☐ Closing

14. Interpersonal skills

☐ Initiating ☐ Planning ☐ Executing ☐ Monitoring/controlling ☐ Closing

15. Record of questions

☐ Initiating ☐ Planning ☐ Executing ☐ Monitoring/controlling ☐ Closing

2. Complete the sentences below, stating whether the option refers to input, tool/technique, or output, and identify the corresponding project management process.

1. Preassignment is a ______________________ of the ______________________ ______________________ process.
2. Team performance assessment is a ______________________ of the ______________________ ______________________ process.
3. Organization charts and position descriptions are ______________________ of the ______________________ process.
4. Negotiation is a ______________________ of the ______________________ ______________________ process.
5. Issue log is a ______________________ of the ______________________ ______________________ process.
6. Observations and conversations are ______________________ of the ______________________.
7. Resources calendar is a ______________________ of the ______________________ ______________________ process.
8. Resources calendar is a ______________________ of the ______________________ ______________________ process.
9. Networking is a ______________________ of ______________________ ______________________ processes.
10. Conflict management is a ______________________ of the ______________________ ______________________ process.
11. Project staff assignments are ______________________ of the ______________________ ______________________ process.
12. Project staff assignments are ______________________ of ______________________ ______________________ processes.

Questions

1. A chart represented as a matrix showing the resource types and the corresponding responsibilities in the project is
   a. Resource breakdown structure
   b. RACI chart
   c. Description of roles and responsibilities
   d. Project resource structure

2. Formal means, tools, and techniques of the Develop Project Team process, for which the project manager recognizes and promotes the project team desirable behavior are called
   a. Promotions
   b. Halo effect
   c. Recognition and reward
   d. Special remuneration

3. The theory that upholds that people will want to give their best if they receive adequate motivation and expectations is called
   a. Theory of Achievement
   b. Theory of Expectations
   c. Theory X
   d. Theory Y

4. The motivational theory stating that most people do not like working and try to evade their obligations is called
   a. Theory of Achievement
   b. Theory of Expectations
   c. Theory X
   d. Theory Y

5. The theory that upholds that people have little or no ambition, that they need constant supervision, and that they will only fulfill their duties if they are threatened is called
   a. Theory of Achievement
   b. Theory of Expectations

c. Theory X

d. Theory Y

6. All the following are inputs of the Develop Human Resource Plan process, except

a. Organization charts and position descriptions

b. Resources required for activities

c. Organizational process assets

d. Enterprise environmental factors

7. All of the following are tools or techniques of the Develop Human Resource Plan process, except

a. Organization charts and position descriptions

b. Resources required for activities

c. Networking

d. Organizational theory

8. All of the following are tools or techniques of the Develop Human Resource Plan process, except

a. Historical records of other projects

b. The company's human resource plan

c. Organizational theory

d. Project human resource plan

9. All of the following are inputs of the Acquire Project Team process, except

a. Project management plan

b. Enterprise environmental factors

c. Organizational process assets

d. Hiring

10. All of the following are inputs of the Develop Project Team process, except

a. General management skills

b. Project staff assignment

c. Project management plan

d. Resource calendars

11. All of the following are inputs of the Manage Project Team process, except

a. Assigning staff to the project

b. Project management plan

c. Organizational process assets

d. Observations and conversations

12. All the following are tools and techniques of the Acquire Project Team process, except

a. Preassignment

b. Negotiation

c. Project staff assignments

d. Hiring

13. All the following are tools and techniques of the Develop Project Team process, except

a. Training

b. Team performance assessment

c. Team building activities

d. Recognition

14. All the following are tools and techniques of the Manage Project Team process, except

a. Observations

b. Team performance assessments

c. Project performance appraisals

d. Conversations

15. All the following are tools and techniques of the Manage Project Team process, except

a. Recognition and rewards

b. Problem register

c. Observations and conversations

d. General management skills

16. All the following are tools and techniques of the Manage Stakeholder Expectations process, except

a. General management skills

b. Interpersonal skills

c. Stakeholder management strategy

d. Communication methods

17. All of the following are outputs of the Acquire Project Team process, except

a. Project staff assignments

b. Resource calendars

c. Hiring

d. Project management plan updates

18. All the following are tools and techniques of the Develop Project Team process, except

a. Team-building activities

b. Resource calendars

c. Awards

d. Rewards

19. All of the following are outputs of the Manage Project Team process, except

a. Conflict management

b. Change requests

c. Enterprise factors update

d. Project management plan updates

20. All of the following are inputs of the Acquire Project Team process, except

a. Project management plan

b. Preassignment

c. Organizational process assets

d. Enterprise environmental factors

21. All of the following are inputs of the Acquire Project Team process, except

a. Project management plan

b. Enterprise environmental factors

c. Negotiation

d. Organizational process assets

22. All of the following are inputs of the Acquire Project Team process, except

a. Virtual teams

b. Enterprise environmental factors

c. Organizational process assets

d. Project management plan

23. All of the following are inputs of the Develop Project Team process, except

a. Resource calendar

b. Project staff assignment

c. Project management plan

d. Training

24. All of the following are inputs of the Develop Project Team process, except

a. Recognition and rewards

b. Project staff assignment

c. Project management plan

d. Resource calendars

25. All of the following are inputs of the Manage Project Team process, except

a. Project management plan

b. Project performance appraisals

c. Organizational process assets

d. Team performance assessments

26. Maslow's hierarchy of needs emphasizes

a. Self-achievement

b. Association need

c. Physiological satisfaction

d. Self-esteem

27. The project manager is resolving a conflict and would like to apply a technique to generate a solution as long-lasting as possible. Which technique should he apply?

a. Confronting

b. Temporary solutions

c. Force

d. Compromising

28. In the midst of a discussion among members of the project team, the project manager said, "I'll deal with that problem later." Which conflict resolution technique is he using?

a. Withdrawal

b. Force

c. Troubleshooting

d. Temporary solutions

29. The project resource histogram shows a factor not displayed by the responsibility assignment matrix. Which factor is that?

a. Those responsible for the activities

b. Activity

c. Interrelationship among activities

d. Time

30. Confronting, force, and withdrawal are conflict resolution techniques that can be used in a project as well as

a. Discussion

b. Control

c. Temporary solution

d. Ordination

31. The theory proposing that employees should be rewarded for their achievements is

a. McGregor's

b. Compensatory effort

c. Maslow's

d. The expectation theory

32. The "halo effect" refers to

a. Transferring project management people to other areas because they are good in their area of expertise

b. Transferring people to project management because they are good in their area of expertise

c. Transferring people among technical areas because they are good in their area of expertise

d. Internally promoting people as soon as a new project is started

33. A team member is not having the performance expected by the project manager. Who should he contact to solve the problem?

a. Senior management

b. Functional manager

c. Sponsor

d. Program manager

34. Using a war room during a project has several advantages, except

a. It helps communication

b. It improves the project identity

c. It increases the impact of conflicts due to personalities

d. It reduces the impact of conflicts, as people are together

35. The conflict resolution technique in which parties try to incorporate several viewpoints to reach a consensus is called

a. Confronting

b. Accommodation

c. Compromising

d. Collaboration

36. The new organization project manager believes that people need to be monitored at all times, are incapable, do not take responsibility, and avoid work whenever possible. He follows:

a. Herzberg's Theory

b. McGregor's Theory X

c. McGregor's Theory Y

d. David McClelland's Theory

37. The project manager recently hired by the organization, in a conversation with the project director, explained that he follows McGregor's Theory Y. What did he mean by that?

a. He believes that people avoid work whenever possible

b. He believes that people are incapable and do not take responsibilities

c. He believes that people are willing to work without supervision, that they can direct their own efforts, and that they wish to be succesful

d. He believes that hygiene factors can destroy motivation, but in general improving these factors does not increase motivation

38. The acquired needs theory (David McClelland's Theory) states that the people's primary motivation is one of the three requirements listed in the following option:

a. Physiological, safety, social

b. Achievement, socialization, power

c. Need for food, shelter and clothing

d. Their own satisfaction, friends, approval

Answer key

Supplementary exercises

2. 1 - Tool/technique - Acquire Project Team

2 - Output - Develop Project Team

3 - Tools - Develop Human Resource Plan

4 - Tool/technique - Acquire Project Team

5 - Tool/technique - Manage Project Team

6 - Tools/techniques - Manage Project Team

7 - Output - Acquire Project Team

8 - Input - Develop Project Team

9 - Tool - Develop Human Resource Plan

10 - Technique - Manage Project Team

11 - Outputs - Acquire Project Team

12 - Inputs - Develop Project Team and Manage Project Team

Questions

1. B. RACI chart shows resources and the corresponding project responsibilities. The acronym RACI means Responsible, Accountable, Consult, and Inform. It is a tool and a technique of the Develop Human Resource Plan process.

2. C. Recognition and rewards are tools and techniques of the Develop Project Team process, and they are used when a team member has a higher than expected performance or his behavior is desirable when performing his functions.

3. B. Theory of Expectations upholds that people will want to give their best if they receive adequate motivation and expectations.

4. C. Theory X states that most people do not like working and try to evade their obligations.

5. C. Theory X states that people have little or no ambition, that they need constant supervision and that they will only fulfill their duties if they are threatened.

6. A. In order to develop the human resource plan, you will need inputs to check the human resources necessary to the activities, the enterprise environmental factors (the enterprise human resourced culture, among others), and the organizational process assets (productivity indices, hiring procedures, among others). Organizational charts and job descriptions are products (outputs) of the process.

7. B. The resources required for the activities were defined in the Estimate Activity Resources process, and they are inputs of the Develop Human Resource Plan process.

8. A. The question, asked more clearly, is "Which of the following options IS a tool or technique of the Develop Human Resource Plan process?" The company's historical records and human resource plan are active processes; therefore, they are inputs of processes! The project human resource plan is the product (output) of this process. The organizational theory is used as a tool of the process.

9. D. Remember that, in Executing, Monitoring and controlling, and Closing, the project management plan is an input of all processes. Hiring is one of the tools of the of the Acquire Project Team process, not an input. The other options are inputs of this process.

10. A. Remember that in Executing, Monitoring and controlling, and Closing, the project management plan is an input of all processes. The general management skills are tools of the Develop Project Team process, not an input. The other options are inputs of this process.

11. D. Remember that, in Executing, Monitoring and controlling, and Closing, the project management plan is an input of all processes. Observations and conversations are tools of the process. The other options are inputs of this process.

12. C. In the Acquire Project Team process, you perform this process when assigning (mobilizing) the team. This represents the product (output) of the process. Preassignment, negotiation (with human resource assignment companies, for example), and hiring are tools and techniques of the process.

13. B. The project team development is performed through training, team-building activities, and recognition, among other tools and techniques. The result of team development (output) is the team performance assessment.

14. B. The project management team is developed through observations, conversations, project performance appraisals, among other tools. Team performance assessments are outputs of the Develop Project Team process and inputs of this process.

15. A. Recognition and rewards are tools of the Develop Project Team process. The other options are tools and techniques of this process.

16. C. Note that the terms "skills" and "methods" always relate to tools and techniques (options A, B, and D). The Stakeholder management strategy, developed in the Identify Stakeholders process, is an input of this process.

17. C. Hiring is a tool of the process, while other options are outputs of the process.

18. B. The project team is developed through building activities, awards, rewards, and other tools and techniques. Resource calendar is not a tool or technique; rather, it is a source of information in this process; therefore, it is an input.

19. A. Keep in mind that on the exam: the term "updates" always refers to process outputs. Change requests (generated in this process) are also outputs of the process. Conflict management is a technique of the process.

20. B. Remember that in Executing, Monitoring and controlling, and Closing, the project management plan is an input of all processes. Preassignment is one of the tools of the of the Acquire Project Team process, not an input. The other options are inputs of this process.

21. C. Remember that in Executing, Monitoring and controlling, and Closing, the project management plan is an input of all processes. Negotiation (with functional managers, suppliers, service providers) is one of the tools of the Acquire Project Team process, not an input. The other options are inputs of this process.

22. A. Remember that in Executing, Monitoring and controlling, and Closing, the project management plan is an input of all processes. The use of virtual teams (a group of people with a common goal who perform their roles and do not meet very often) is one of the tools of the Acquire Project Team process, not an input. The other options are inputs of this process.

23. D. Remember that, in Executing, Monitoring and controlling, and Closing, the project management plan is an input of all processes. Training is a tool of the Develop Project Team process, not an input. The other options are inputs of this process.

24. A. Remember that in Executing, Monitoring and controlling, and Closing, the project management plan is an input of all processes. Recognition and rewards are tools of the Develop Project Team process, not an input. The other options are inputs of this process.

25. B. Remember that in Executing, Monitoring and controlling, and Closing, the project management plan is an input of all processes. Another reminder to help you succeed in the exam: memorize that the team performance assessments are an input of the process, and project performance appraisals are a tool of the Manage Project Team process. Organizational process assets are inputs of this process.

26. A. Maslow's pyramid shows, from bottom to top: physiological - safety - social - esteem self achievement.

27. A. The problem solution, although it takes longer, is the more lasting solution to a conflict.

28. A. Delaying a conflict resolution is also called withdrawal (temporary withdrawal — postponement).

29. D. The responsibility assignment matrix does not show the use of resources over time, what is shown in the histogram — by resource or group of resources.

30. C. Confrontation, force, withdrawal, and temporary solutions are conflict resolution techniques.

31. D. The expectation theory is: "Employees who believe that their efforts will lead to effective performance and who expect to be rewarded for their accomplishments remain productive as rewards meet their expectations."

32. B. The "halo effect" refers to transferring people to project management because they are technically good in their areas of expertise. However, as these people may not be qualified for the position, this can have negative impacts on the project — and should be avoided.

33. B. The control of team members is the responsibility of the functional manager.

34. C. The war room (or co-location) is a central site for project coordination. Usually, this room has the WBS, the schedule, and the network diagram posted on walls. As people are gathered in one place, conflicts among the team members are smaller, due to their continuous and joint exposure.

35. D. Troubleshooting (confronting) represents "facing" the problem and solving it, as it is the best technique. Accommodation (temporary solutions) emphasizes agreement over different opinions, and is not a good technique. Compromising involves finding solutions that partially meet the parties, and is not the best technique (it occurs after confrontation). Collaborating is a technique in which parties try to incorporate several viewpoints to reach a consensus.

36. B. McGregor's Theory X is described in this question. McGregor's Theory Y is that people are willing to work without supervision, they think they can direct their own efforts, and they want to be successful.

37. C. Option C represents McGregor's Theory Y. Options A and B refer to McGregor's Theory X. Option D refers to Herzberg's Theory.

38. B. David McClelland's Theory considers motivation based on one of three requirements: achievement (they like recognition), socialization (they work better in groups), and power (they like to influence others). All other options refer to Maslow's hierarchy of needs.

Chapter 10

PROJECT COMMUNICATIONS MANAGEMENT

1. Introduction
2. Project Communications Management processes
3. Communications management in project initiating
4. Communications management in project planning
5. Communications management in project executing
6. Communications management in project monitoring and controlling

---

Attachment I	Identification and management of stakeholders
Attachment II	Further reading on communication in projects

- Additional information and reminders for the exam
- Supplementary exercises
- Questions
- Answer key

10.1 INTRODUCTION

This chapter will introduce the project management processes in the Communications knowledge area, their relevant inputs, tools, techniques, and outputs.

10.2 PROJECT COMMUNICATIONS MANAGEMENT PROCESSES

According to *PMBOK® Guide*, Project Communications Management includes the processes required to ensure that project information is generated, collected, distributed, stored, retrieved, and organized in a timely and appropriate manner.

Project Communications Management processes are

- **Identify Stakeholders**

  The process of identifying all people or organizations that may be affected by the project and documenting information relevant to their interests, engagement, and impact on the project success.

- **Plan Communications**

  The process of determining the project stakeholder information needs and defining a communication approach.

- **Distribute Information**

  The process of making necessary information available to project stakeholders, as planned.

- **Manage Stakeholder Expectations**

  The communication and interaction process with stakeholders in order to meet their needs and deal with issues as they occur.

- **Report Performance**

  The process of collecting and distributing performance information, including progress reports, progress measurements, and forecasts.

The following flowchart displays the relationship among the Project Communications Management processes and their locations across the project management process groups.

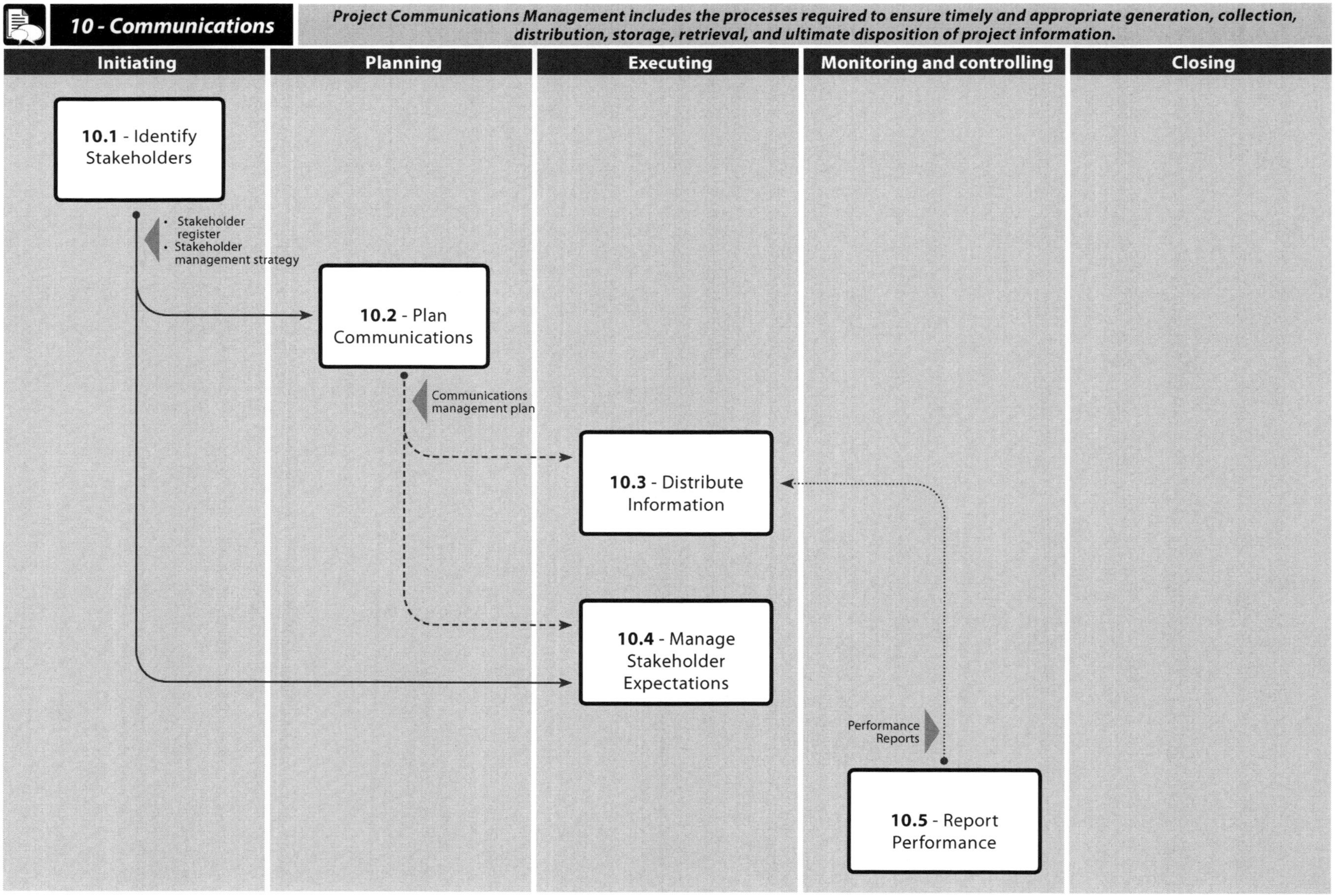
10 - Communications
Project Communications Management includes the processes required to ensure timely and appropriate generation, collection, distribution, storage, retrieval, and ultimate disposition of project information.
Initiating
Planning
Executing
Monitoring and controlling
Closing
10.1 - Identify Stakeholders
• Stakeholder register
• Stakeholder management strategy
10.2 - Plan Communications
Communications management plan
10.3 - Distribute Information
10.4 - Manage Stakeholder Expectations
Performance Reports
10.5 - Report Performance

10.3 COMMUNICATIONS MANAGEMENT IN PROJECT INITIATING

According to PMI®, the integration management in project initiating is composed of a process, namely,

- ***Identify Stakeholders***

10.3.1 IDENTIFY STAKEHOLDERS (*PMBOK® GUIDE*, PROCESS 10.1)

Identifying stakeholders is essential to successfully complete the project since, based on this identification, it is possible for the project manager to recognize and document the expectations of each stakeholder and be aware that these expectations should be, if not exceeded, at least complied with.

A stakeholder can be defined as someone with interests that may be impacted, positively or negatively, by the project. Generally, a project can have, for example, the following stakeholders:

- A sponsor
- A customer (which can also be the sponsor)
- The project manager
- The project scope
- The administrative staff
- Contractors
- Suppliers
- People in the project implementation environment

10.3.1.1 IDENTIFY STAKEHOLDERS: INPUTS, TOOLS AND TECHNIQUES, AND OUTPUTS

INPUTS

1 **Project charter**

The project charter can provide information on stakeholders, such as the sponsor, users, team members, functional, and operational managers.

2 **Procurement documents**

Procurement documents provide information on vendors, contractors, and other project stakeholders.

3 **Enterprise environmental factors**

Enterprise environmental factors can provide information on the company's departments, government agencies, and other project stakeholders.

4 **Organizational process assets**

The organizational process assets can provide examples and information on records of previous project stakeholders and must be considered in this process.

TOOLS AND TECHNIQUES

1 Stakeholder analysis

See Attachment I of this chapter.

2 Expert judgment

The expert judgment of consultants, managers, and other professionals in the organization and interest groups among other, can help identify stakeholders.

OUTPUTS

1 Stakeholder register

See Attachment I of this chapter.

2 Stakeholder management strategy

See Attachment I of this chapter.

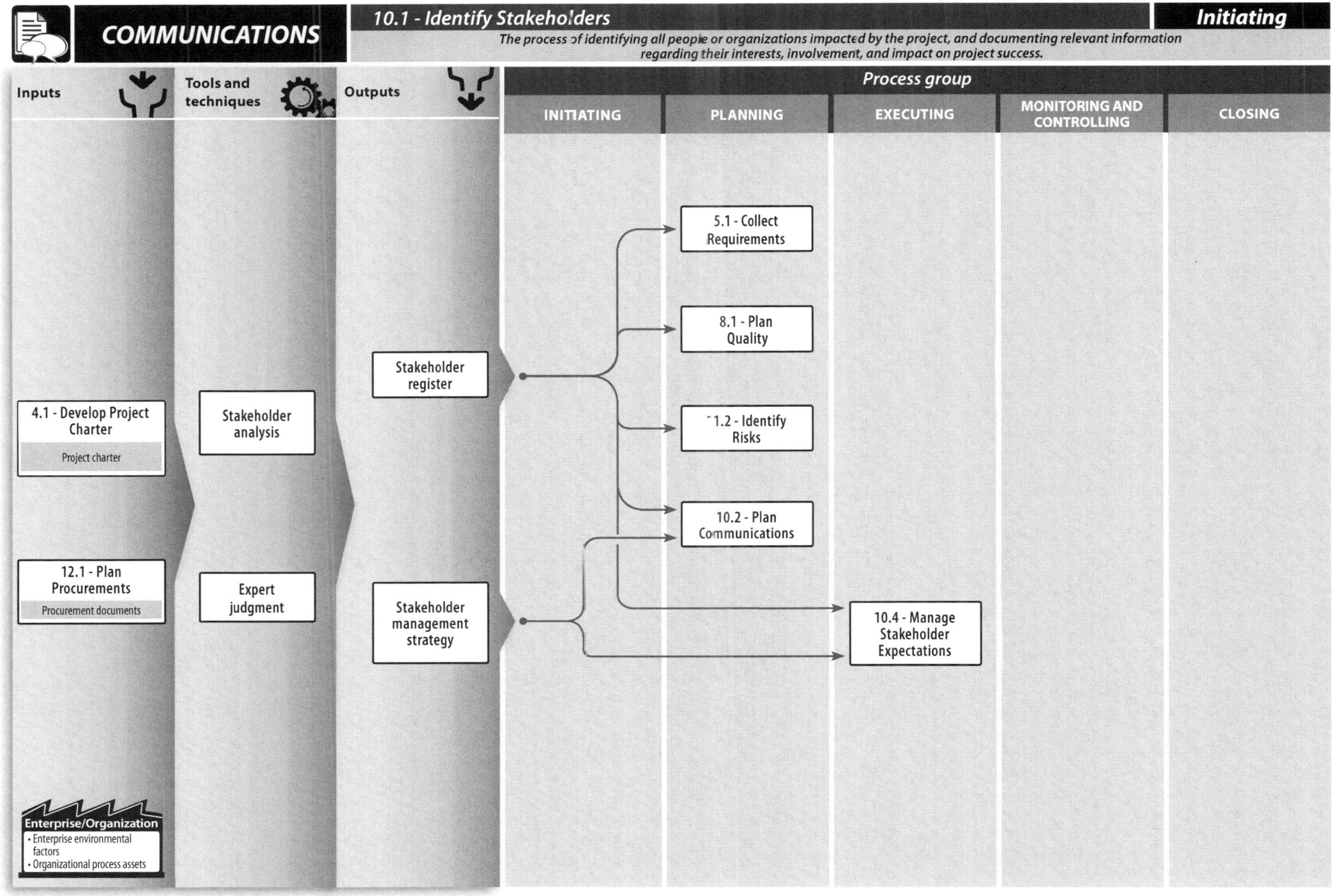
COMMUNICATIONS
10.1 - Identify Stakeholders
Initiating
The process of identifying all people or organizations impacted by the project, and documenting relevant information regarding their interests, involvement, and impact on project success.
Inputs
Tools and techniques
Outputs
Process group
INITIATING
PLANNING
EXECUTING
MONITORING AND CONTROLLING
CLOSING
4.1 - Develop Project Charter
Project charter
12.1 - Plan Procurements
Procurement documents
Enterprise/Organization
• Enterprise environmental factors
• Organizational process assets
Stakeholder analysis
Expert judgment
Stakeholder register
Stakeholder management strategy
5.1 - Collect Requirements
8.1 - Plan Quality
11.2 - Identify Risks
10.2 - Plan Communications
10.4 - Manage Stakeholder Expectations

10.4 COMMUNICATIONS MANAGEMENT IN PROJECT PLANNING

According to PMI®, the management integration in project planning is composed of a process, namely,

- ***Plan Communications***

10.4.1 PLAN COMMUNICATIONS (*PMBOK® GUIDE*, PROCESS 10.2)

A process to determine information and communication needs of project stakeholders as well as establish a communication approach.

10.4.1.1 PLAN COMMUNICATIONS: INPUTS, TOOLS AND TECHNIQUES, AND OUTPUTS

INPUTS

1 **Stakeholder register**

The record of the stakeholders must be considered in this process.

2 **Stakeholder management strategy**

The stakeholder management strategy must be considered in this process.

3 **Enterprise environmental factors**

The enterprise environmental factors, such as communication system for example, must be considered in this process.

4 **Organizational process assets**

The organizational process assets as policies and procedures related to human resources must be considered in this process.

TOOLS AND TECHNIQUES

1 **Communication requirements analysis**

Communication requirements analysis aims at determining stakeholder needs, defining the best communication manner, and deciding whether to implement such communication manner. The following figure is an example form used for that analysis.

STAKEHOLDERS	TYPE OF REQUIRED INFORMATION	COMMUNICATION METHOD	PERIODICITY
Sponsor			
Customer			
Senior management			
Functional managers			
Departments			
Project team			
Seller			
Government agencies			

2 **Communication technology**

Communication technology is related to methods and tools to be used to transmit and manage project information. Based on the analysis of the communication requirements and the project characteristics (complexity, duration, value, development dynamic, and others), the technology available in the organization should be analyzed in terms of meeting the project communication requirements. If this technology meet the requirements, should be listed hardware requirements and software application project and, if necessary, training of project team. If this technology does not meet or partially meet these requirements, a cost-benefit study on implementing additional or new technology should be performed. For example, a project may require videoconferencing for some team members located in different regions of the country.

3 **Communication models**

Communication models is a graphical representation of how communication occurs between the sender and receiver of a message.

4 **Communication methods**

For each type of project communication, the communication method to be used to transmit the message needs to be defined. Communication methods can be formal writing, formal speech, informal writing, and verbal speech.

Attachment I provides further reading on communication methods

OUTPUTS

1 Communications management plan

The communications management plan must indicate stakeholder communication requirements, the type of information to be provided, the information transmission method, and any and all information related to the project communication.

2 Project document updates

Project documents that need to be updated include but are not limited to

- Stakeholder register, and
- Stakeholder management strategy.

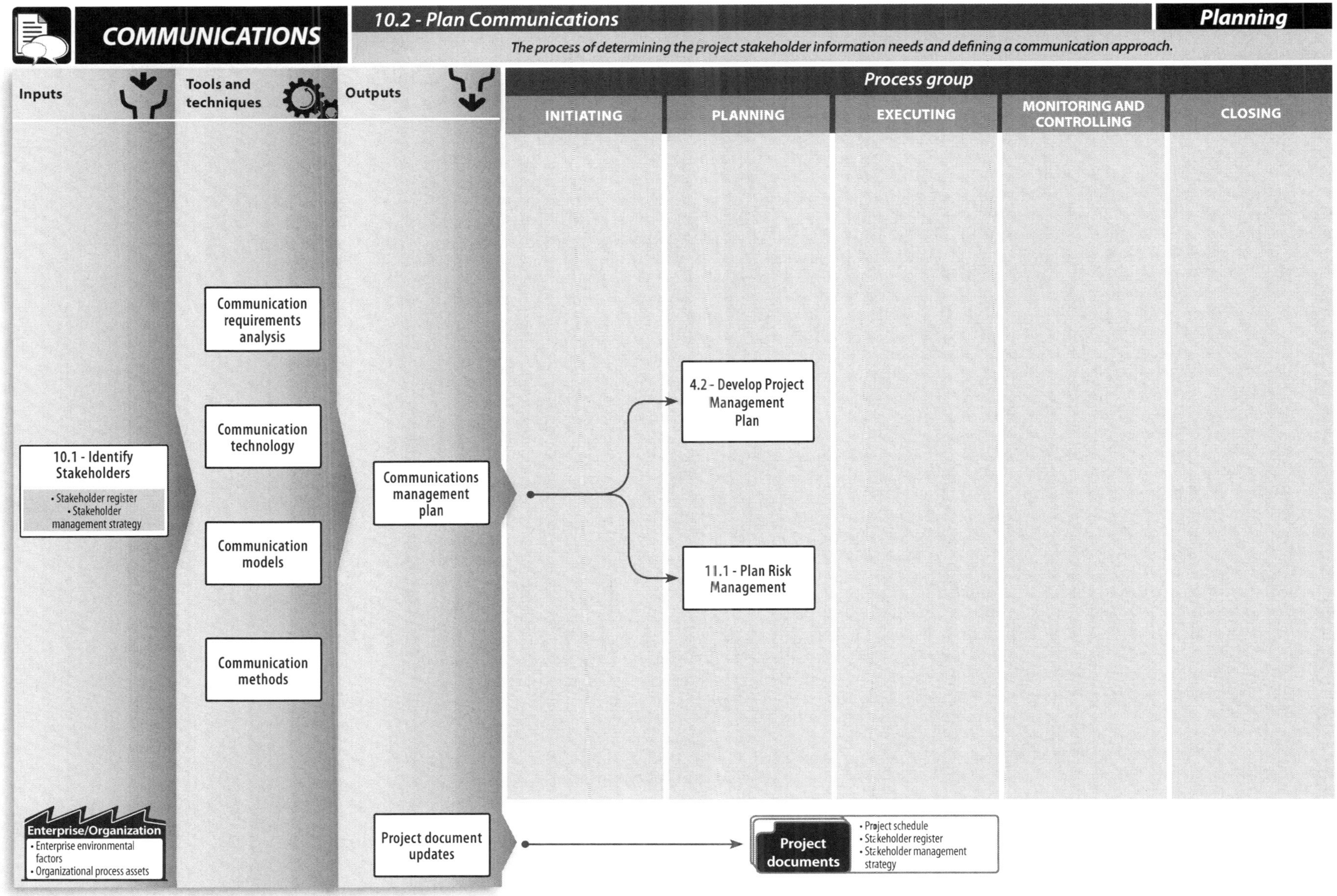
COMMUNICATIONS
10.2 - Plan Communications
Planning
The process of determining the project stakeholder information needs and defining a communication approach.
Inputs
Tools and techniques
Outputs
Process group
INITIATING
PLANNING
EXECUTING
MONITORING AND CONTROLLING
CLOSING
10.1 - Identify Stakeholders
• Stakeholder register
• Stakeholder management strategy
Enterprise/Organization
• Enterprise environmental factors
• Organizational process assets
Communication requirements analysis
Communication technology
Communication models
Communication methods
Communications management plan
Project document updates
4.2 - Develop Project Management Plan
11.1 - Plan Risk Management
Project documents
• Project schedule
• Stakeholder register
• Stakeholder management strategy

10.5 COMMUNICATIONS MANAGEMENT IN PROJECT EXECUTING

According to PMI®, the management integration in project executing is composed of two process:

- ***Distribute Information***
- ***Manage Stakeholder Expectations***

10.5.1 DISTRIBUTE INFORMATION (*PMBOK® GUIDE*, PROCESS 10.3)

The process of making necessary information available to project stakeholders, as planned. Distribution can be performed in several ways, such as status reports, monitoring meetings, and others.

10.5.1.1 DISTRIBUTE INFORMATION : INPUTS, TOOLS AND TECHNIQUES, AND OUTPUTS

INPUTS

1 **Project management plan**

The project management plan and especially the communications management plan should be distributed to inform the project information.

2 **Performance reports**

Performance reports are used to distribute the project status and performance information.

3 **Organizational process assets**

Organizational process assets may influence the Distribute Information process by means of information distribution policies and procedures, communication templates, historical information, and lessons learned from previous projects.

TOOLS AND TECHNIQUES

1 **Communication methods**

Communication templates can be meetings, presentations, video and audio conferencing, and others.

2 **Information distribution tools**

Project information can be distributed using several tools, including

- Project meetings, presentations, printed copies of documents, and databases shared access;
- Fax, e-mail, telephone, video conferencing tools, and publications on the Internet; and
- Software project management, portals, and management tools for collaborative work.

OUTPUTS

1 **Organizational process assets updates**

The outputs of the process of distributing information related to the organizational process assets may include:

- **Documentation of lessons learned**

  This documentation must include problem root causes, corrective action selected, results obtained and how this can be useful to the current and future projects.

- **Project records and reports**

  This documentation should include correspondence, memoranda, minutes of meetings, project progress reports and other documents, which must be properly filed for future reference by the project team and others in the organization.

- **Project presentations**

  Presentations made in the project must be properly filed for future reference by the project team and others in the organization.

- **Notifications and feedback from stakeholders**

  The information transmitted and received by stakeholders must be filed for future reference by the project team. They can also provide important data for future projects of the organization.

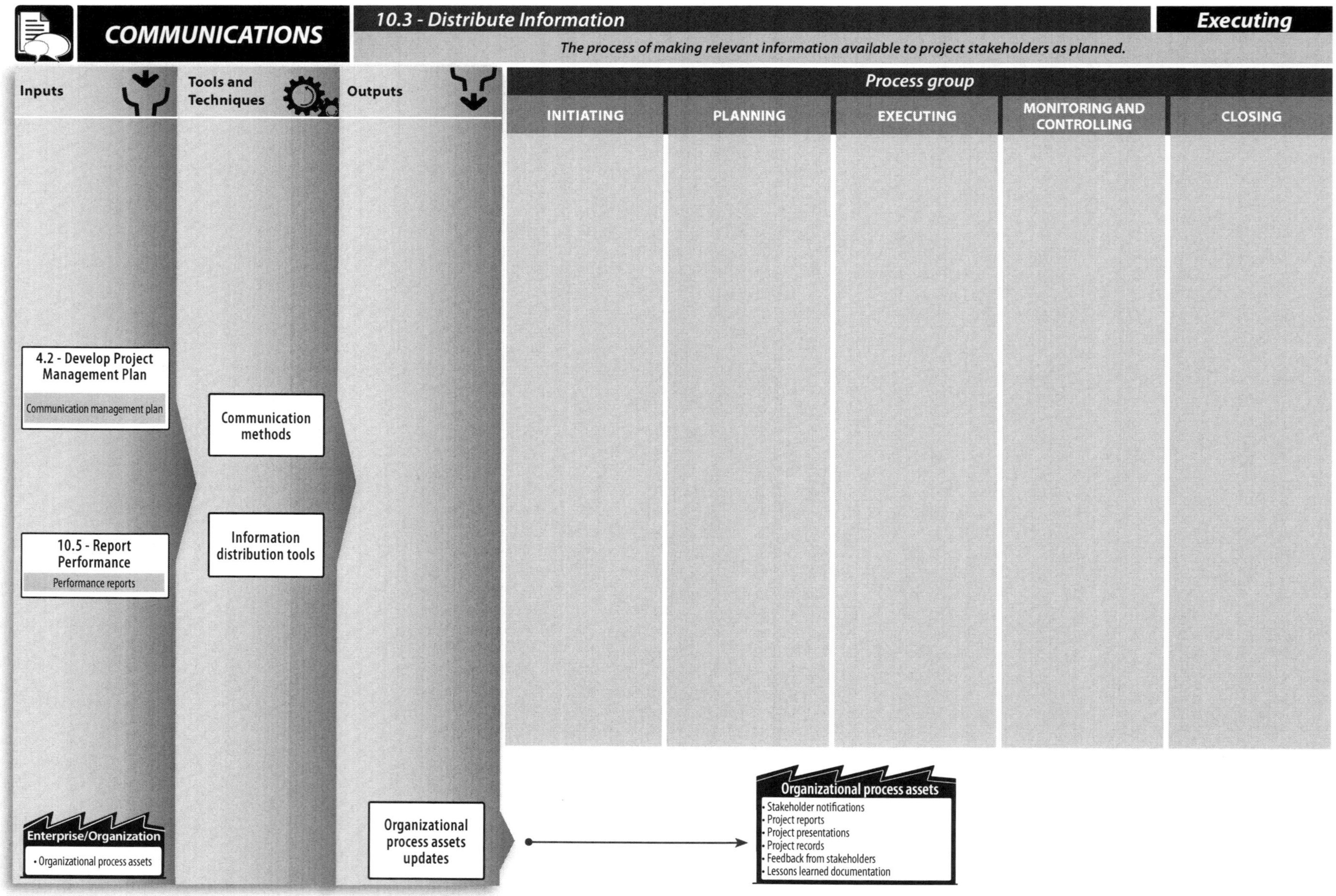
COMMUNICATIONS
10.3 - Distribute Information
Executing
The process of making relevant information available to project stakeholders as planned.
Inputs
Tools and Techniques
Outputs
Process group
INITIATING
PLANNING
EXECUTING
MONITORING AND CONTROLLING
CLOSING
4.2 - Develop Project Management Plan
Communication management plan
10.5 - Report Performance
Performance reports
Enterprise/Organization
• Organizational process assets
Communication methods
Information distribution tools
Organizational process assets updates
Organizational process assets
• Stakeholder notifications
• Project reports
• Project presentations
• Project records
• Feedback from stakeholders
• Lessons learned documentation

10.5.2 MANAGE STAKEHOLDER EXPECTATIONS (*PMBOK® GUIDE*, PROCESS 10.4)

The Manage Stakeholder Expectations process consists in managing communications in order to meet stakeholder needs and apply troubleshooting on them. This management should follow the definitions in the communications management plan, the policies established by the organization, and the particular needs of each stakeholder.

10.5.2.1 MANAGE STAKEHOLDER EXPECTATIONS: INPUTS, TOOLS AND TECHNIQUES, AND OUTPUTS

INPUTS

1 **Stakeholder register**

The record of the parties is a list of project stakeholders and must be considered in this process.

2 **Stakeholder management strategy**

The stakeholder management strategy must be considered in this process.

3 **Project management plan**

The project management plan and especially the communications management plan describes stakeholder needs and expectations and must be considered in this process.

4 **Issue log**

Issue log is used to document and monitor the resolution of issues in order to make communication easier among project team members and ensure common understanding of issues.

5 **Change log**

Change log, used to document changes occurring during the project, must be considered in this process.

6 **Organizational process assets**

The organizational process assets, such as procedures for problem management, change control procedures, historical information from previous projects, and others, must be considered in this process.

TOOLS AND TECHNIQUES

1 **Communication methods**

The communications management plan establishes the means of communication and troubleshooting to be used, such as meetings, video conferences, Internet media, and others.

2 **Interpersonal skills**

The project manager must apply appropriate interpersonal skills to Manage Stakeholder Expectations.

3 **Management skills**

The project manager must apply management skills, such as appropriate negotiation, presentation, writing, and others, to Manage Stakeholder Expectations.

OUTPUTS

1 **Organizational process assets updates**

The Manage Project Team process can identify new opportunities to improve processes or procedures and human resources policies of the organization.

2 **Change requests**

Troubleshooting can generate recommendations for changes in communication policy or plan of the Project Communications Management. Such recommendations must be analyzed and, if approved, must be recorded in this process.

3 **Project management plan updates**

The project management plan and, in particular, the scope management plan must be updated after changes are approved as a result of the Control Scope process.

4 **Project document updates**

Any and all project documents that have been influenced by this process must be updated, such as:

- Stakeholder management strategy,
- Stakeholder register, and
- Issue log.

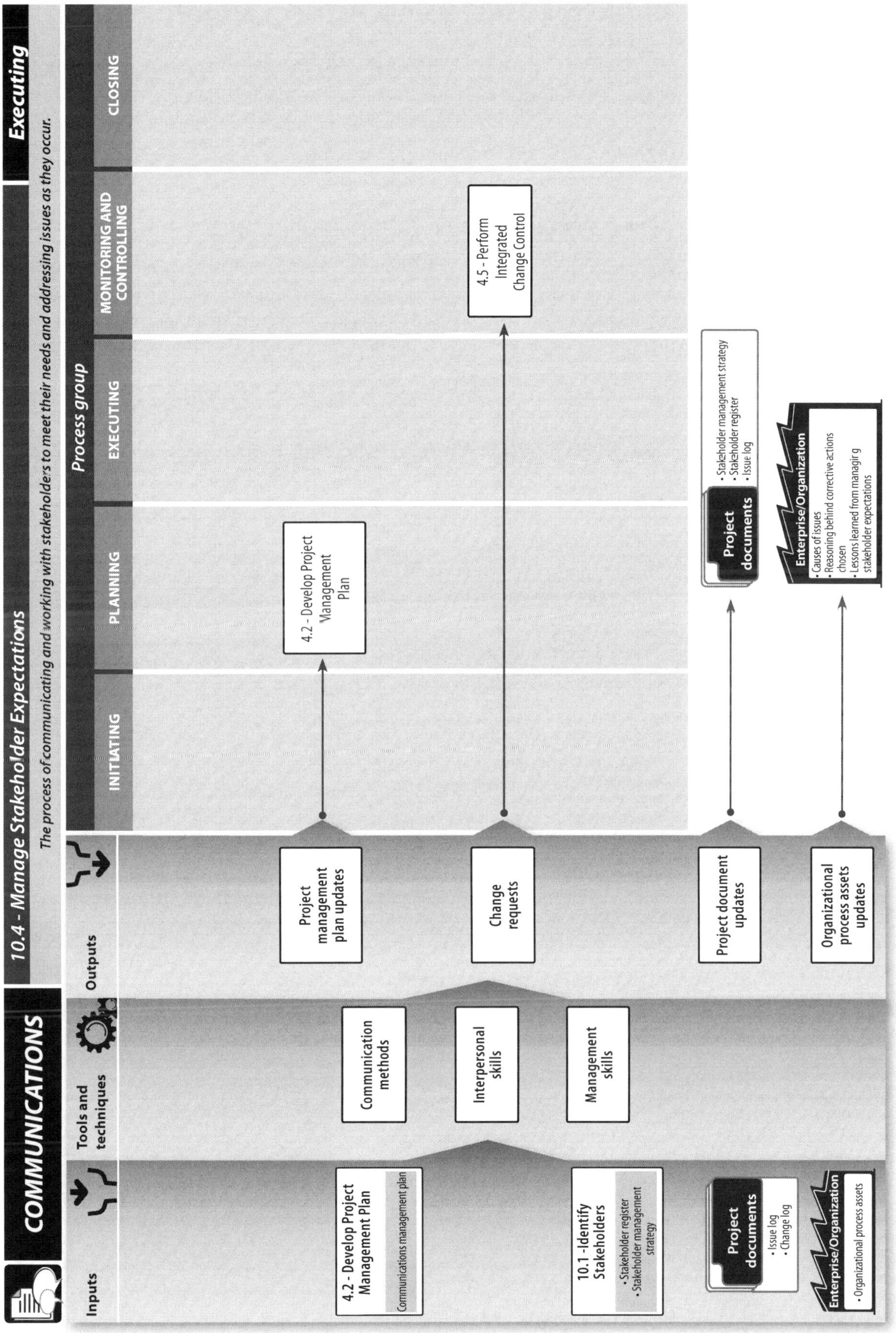
COMMUNICATIONS
10.4 - Manage Stakeholder Expectations
Executing
The process of communicating and working with stakeholders to meet their needs and addressing issues as they occur.
Inputs
Tools and techniques
Outputs
Process group
INITIATING
PLANNING
EXECUTING
MONITORING AND CONTROLLING
CLOSING
4.2 - Develop Project Management Plan
Communications management plan
10.1 -Identify Stakeholders
• Stakeholder register
• Stakeholder management strategy
Project documents
• Issue log
• Change log
Enterprise/Organization
• Organizational process assets
Communication methods
Interpersonal skills
Management skills
Project management plan updates
Change requests
Project document updates
Organizational process assets updates
4.2 - Develop Project Management Plan
4.5 - Perform Integrated Change Control
Project documents
• Stakeholder management strategy
• Stakeholder register
• Issue log
Enterprise/Organiztion
• Causes of issues
• Reasoning behind corrective actions chosen
• Lessons learned from managir g stakeholder expectations

10.6 COMMUNICATIONS MANAGEMENT IN PROJECT MONITORING AND CONTROLLING

According to PMI®, communications management in project monitoring and controlling is composed of the following process:

- ***Report Performance***

10.6.1 REPORT PERFORMANCE (*PMBOK® GUIDE*, PROCESS 10.5)

Report Performance consists in the collection and distribution of timely and appropriate information on project performance to stakeholders. This information can be related to deadlines, costs, quality, procurements, risks, and other project factors. It should reflect the conditions prevailing at the time when the report is performed, enabling, therefore, information to be validated.

10.6.1.1 REPORT PERFORMANCE: INPUTS, TOOLS AND TECHNIQUES, AND OUTPUTS

INPUTS

1 **Project management plan**

Information on scope, time, and cost management plan contained in the project and its subsidiary plans and baselines of the project, must be considered in this process.

2 **Work performance information**

Information on work performance are important elements for the preparation of performance reports and must be considered in this process.

3 **Work performance measurements**

Measurements of performance of work as technical performance, schedule performance, and cost performance must be considered in this process.

4 **Budget forecasts**

The budget forecasts, obtained from the Earned Value Management (EVM), must be considered in this process.

5 **Organizational process assets**

Organizational process assets, such as report issuance procedures, report templates, and others, must be considered in this process.

TOOLS AND TECHNIQUES

1 **Variance analysis**

Variance analysis is performed to verify the causes of differences between the baseline and the current performance. In general, it is developed through the following steps:

- Check the quality of information collected in order to ensure that it is complete, consistent with historical data and reliable when compared with information from other projects;

- To determine the variation, comparing current information with the baseline project and noting any differences, whether favorable or unfavorable to the project outcome. EVM uses particular formulas for determining the variation.
- Determine the impact of changes on the cost, project schedule, and any other area of the project.

2 **Forecasting methods**

Forecasting is the process of predicting the project future based on actual performance until today. Forecast methods can be classified into different categories:

- **Time series methods.** Time series methods is based on historical data to estimate future results. Example methods in this category may include earned value, moving average, extrapolation, linear forecast, trend estimation, and growth curve.
- **Causal/econometric methods.** A few forecast methods use the assumption that it is possible to identify the underlying factors that may influence the variable being forecast. For example, umbrella sales might be associated with climatic conditions. If causes are understood, it is possible to forecast the influencing variables and use them in forecasting. Example methods in this category include linear or nonlinear regression analysis.
- **Subjective methods.** Subjective forecast methods incorporate insights, opinions, and probably estimates. Examples of methods in this category are compound forecasts, polls, Delphi technique, scenario creation, and forecast by analogy.
- **Other methods.** Other methods may include simulation, probabilistic forecast, and forecasts by group.

3 **Communication methods**

Communication methods may include reports, letters, memos, and e-mails, among others.

4 **Reporting systems**

Information distribution systems may be tools or software applications used for report presentation and may include spreadsheets, graphical presentation software application, and others.

OUTPUTS

1 **Performance reports**

Performance reports are the major output of this process. They must contain the information and test results related to cost and time compared with the baseline of performance measurement. For example, these reports may contain schedules, milestone schedules, resource use histograms, and earned value management, among others.

2 **Organizational process assets updates**

The performance analysis can identify new processes or opportunities for improvement in standards, policies, and procedures related to the organization's project performance report.

3 **Change requests**

The performance analysis can generate implementation needs in the process, with the goal of recovery time and reduce costs. Such changes must be submitted for review, and, if approved, they should be implemented.

COMMUNICATIONS

10.5 - Report Performance

Monitoring and controlling

The process of collecting and distributing performance information, including status reports, progress measurements, and forecasts.

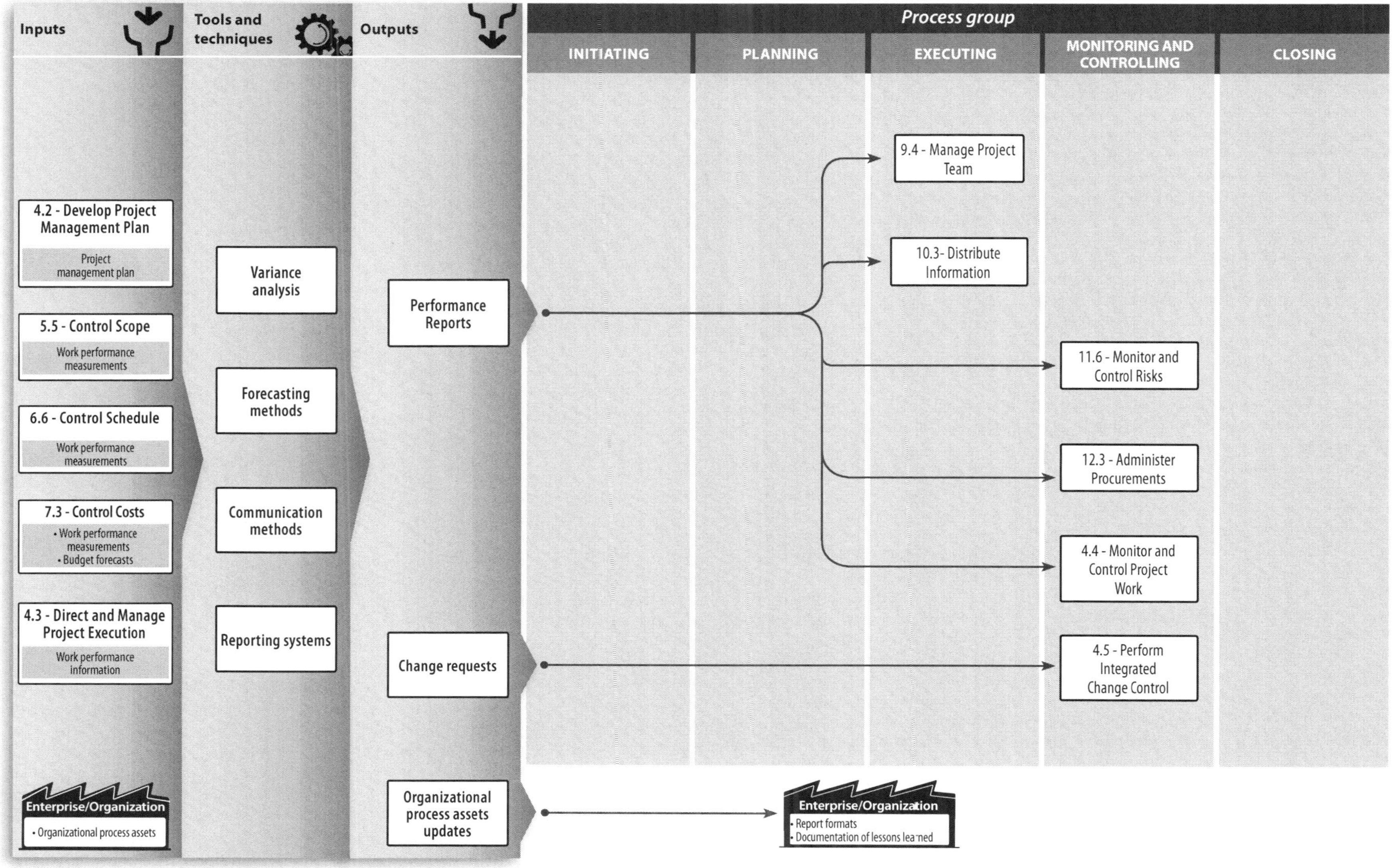

Attachment I

IDENTIFICATION AND MANAGEMENT OF STAKEHOLDERS

IDENTIFICATION AND MANAGEMENT OF STAKEHOLDERS

1 INTRODUCTION

A stakeholder is any individual or organization that can influence, either positively or negatively, the project performance.

Stakeholders may be internal to the organization, as the project manager, functional managers, and senior management or external to the organization as the customer, suppliers and government agencies.

The identification of project stakeholders, the recognition of the roles they play in the organization and the project, their requirements and expectations, and the implementation of a management plan of their influences is essential to the project. The project manager must, *as soon* as possible, develop these activities, covering the largest number of stakeholders at the stage of initiating project. Some stakeholders, such as companies to be contracted to supply equipment, will be identified only later. When the effective engagement of these parties, the same activities described above should be developed for them.

2 STAKEHOLDER IDENTIFICATION

The identification of stakeholders will cover two different stages: the primary identification of stakeholders and the recognition of their requirements and expectations.

2.1 PRIMARY IDENTIFICATION OF PRIMARY STAKEHOLDERS

Primary identification is the high-level recognition of major stakeholders and the roles they play. This activity should be made by the project manager with senior management, sponsor, or customer and is an interview where they will be raised the following information:

- Who are the project stakeholders?
- What is their interest in the project?
- What is their influence on the project as a whole?
- How can they influence the project resources?
- How can they influence the project requirements?
- How can they influence the project process?
- How can they influence the project performance and success?
- How must their participation in the project be?

2.2 RECOGNITION OF STAKEHOLDER REQUIREMENTS AND EXPECTATIONS

This activity consists in a direct interview with each stakeholder in order to obtain their requirements and expectations related to the project, including the recognition of particular activities to be developed, information on project deliverables, project constraints, required communication methods, risk forecast, and mitigation as well as other information.

3 STAKEHOLDER ANALYSIS

The stakeholder analysis is the process of qualitative and quantitative analysis of stakeholder requirements and expectations in order to identify the potential impact of each stakeholder in the project and how that impact should be managed. This analysis will enable including stakeholders in impact classification grids that may be, among others, the following:

- **Power and interest grid.** It classifies stakeholders according to the authority (power) and interest level in the project.
- **Power and influence grid.** It classifies stakeholders according to their authority (power) and interest level in the project.
- **Grid influence and impact.** It classifies stakeholders according to their influence and impact level on the project.
- Other grids that can classify stakeholders based on power, urgency to meet requirements and expectations, and legitimate influences, among others.

The figure below is an example of a power and interest grid to a group of six stakeholders (A, B, C, D, E, F).

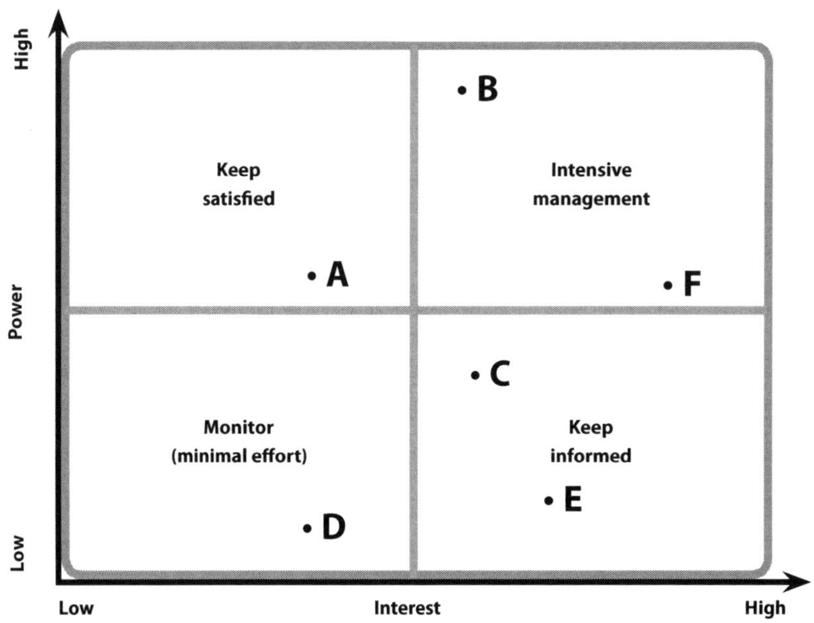

Attachment II

FURTHER READING ON COMMUNICATION IN PROJECTS

COMMUNICATION IN PROJECTS

1 INTRODUCTION

The origin of the word communication is Latin *comunicare* whose meaning is share, associate, exchange ideas, converse. Communication can be defined as the process of exchanging thoughts and opinions between a transmitter and a receiver by using sound, written, gesture and behavioral symbols.

In projects, communication affects all stakeholders and is a determining factor of success or failure. Communication processes are started in the first thinking about the project execution and they only cease after all other management processes are completed. Communication in project environment uses almost all the symbols through presentations, letters, reports and even informal conversations between those involved in the project. The recognition of the stakeholder communication requirements and the establishment of proper symbols are the major factors to be considered in implementing and managing the project communication processes.

2 COMMUNICATION TEMPLATE

A communication template comprises three components: sender, message, and receiver. The sender is the message originator, who uses a means to transmit it to the receiver. The message is what the sender wishes to inform, namely, the idea coded in a language understood by the receiver. The receiver is the message, who must decode it and give feedback on understanding it. The figure below shows a communication template diagram.

COMMUNICATION TEMPLATE

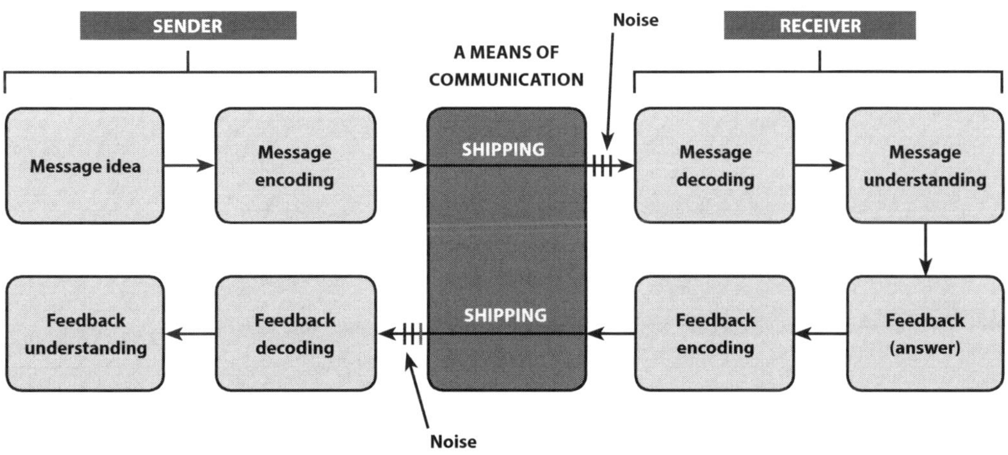

For effective communication, it is important that the sender encodes the message to make the message purpose clear. For effective listening, it is important that the receiver decodes the message, confirms that he has understood its objective, or requests clarification from the sender.

3 COMMUNICATION CHANNELS

Communication channels are the communication possibilities among the parties involved in the project. If a project existed only between two people, there would be only one communication channel between them. If more than one person were added to the project, there would be three communication channels among them.

The calculation of the amount of communication channels can be performed by the formula:

$$C = [n (n - 1)] \div 2$$

Where

C = number of communication channels

n = number of participants

In the figure below, nodes represent participants and lines represent the communication channels among them.

COMMUNICATION CHANNELS - A GROUP OF SIX PEOPLE

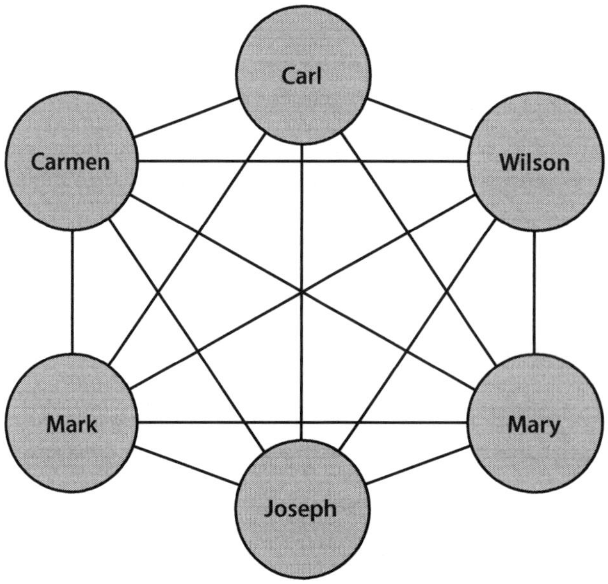

By applying the formula in the figure above, we have:

C = [6 (6 – 1)] ÷ 2 = 15 communication channels.

4 COMMUNICATION TYPES

The table below shows communication types and when they should be used.

COMMUNICATION METHODS	WHEN THEY ARE USED
Formal writing	Complex problems, project management plans, project charter, communication over long distances
Formal speech	Presentations and lectures
Informal writing	Memos, e-mails, and reminders
Informal speech	Meetings and conversations

5 COMMUNICATION METHODS

There are several methods used to share information among the project stakeholders. These methods can be generally classified in

- **Interactive communication.** Between two or more parties performing a multidirectional information exchange. It is the most efficient way to ensure a common understanding by all participants on particular topics. It includes meetings, phone calls, videoconferences, and so forth.
- **Active communication *(push)*.** Sent to particular recipients of the information they need to know. It ensures that information is distributed but does not check whether they are delivered or understood by the audience. Active communication includes letters, memos, reports, *emails*, faxes, voice mail, press releases, and so forth.
- **Passive communication *(pull)*.** It is used for very large volumes of information or for a very large audience and requires recipients to access the communication content at their discretion. These methods include *intranet* websites, *e-learning*, knowledge repositories, and so forth.

The project manager decides, based on the requirements of communications, which communication methods are used in the project, how, and when.

6 PROJECT MEETINGS

Project meetings are designed as information exchanges among participants in order to Distribute Information, project progress analysis, variance analysis, corrective and preventive measures, risk identification, and risk response Planning, and others. Meeting types include:

- **Kick-off meeting**

  It is the project's first meeting. During this meeting, the project team members will be introduced. It presents the project and product objectives and requirements as well as the procedures to be used in project management.

- **Technical monitoring meeting**

  It is the meeting where it will be discussed whether product requirements are being met by the project and which modifications and revisions are required for this service.

- **Progress assessment meeting**

  It is the meeting where the project progress will be discussed, deadline compliance, deviation correction, and preventive measures for new deviations. It is important that in all of these meetings, participants are encouraged to forecast possible risks to the project and enabled to prepare proper responses to them.

- **Meeting with suppliers**

  Such a meeting may be used for suppliers' proposal assessment, supply kick-off, technical monitoring, and supply progress assessment.

- **Coordination meeting**

  It is the meeting where representatives of the project team and other stakeholders as well as contractors are represented. Here are the topics discussed coordination of the workplace, which can be related to occupational safety, environmental protection, internal movement of materials, procedures for input and exit of staff from the workplace, set hours for work and others.

7 THE PROJECT MANAGER CHALLENGE

The project manager's biggest challenge is communication. Statistically, the project manager spends up to 90% of his time in communication. The search for effective communication between stakeholders in all stages of the project must be one of the major functions of project manager. Effective communication helps to solve problems and conflicts, and, especially, it is a prevailing factor while maintaining the project team cohesion. Therefore, the project manager is responsible for

- Recognizing stakeholder communications requirements,
- Developing Planning communications in a clear and comprehensive manner,
- Obtaining approval from stakeholders in order to Plan Communications,
- Managing the information distribution correctly and in a timely manner, and
- Managing stakeholder interests in order to meet the requirements and solution of problems and conflicts between them.

Additional information and reminders for the exam

- **Types of communication**
  - Formal writing: project important records, complex problems, communicate over long distances.
  - Formal speech: presentations and lectures.
  - Informal writing: memos, e-mails.
  - Informal speech: meetings and conversations.

- The communication template comprises three components: the sender (the message originator), the message (what the sender wants to inform), and the receiver (the message recipient).

- The number of communication channels is given by:

  C = [n(n−1)] / 2, where **n** is the number of participants.

- Communication methods: interactive communication, active communication (push), and passive communication (pull).

Supplementary exercises

1. In regards to the Project Communications area of knowledge, indicate to which management processes group(s) each element is related and explain why. Follow the Communication methods example.

1. Communication methods

☐ Initiating ☒ Planning ☒ Executing ☒ Monitoring/controlling ☐ Closing

Communication methods are tools of the Plan Communications (Planning), Distribute Information, Manage Stakeholder Expectations (Executing), and Report Performance (Monitoring and controlling) processes.

2. Communication templates

☐ Initiating ☐ Planning ☐ Executing ☐ Monitoring/controlling ☐ Closing

3. Stakeholder register

☐ Initiating ☐ Planning ☐ Executing ☐ Monitoring/controlling ☐ Closing

4. Variance analysis

☐ Initiating ☐ Planning ☐ Executing ☐ Monitoring/controlling ☐ Closing

5. Interpersonal skills

☐ Initiating ☐ Planning ☐ Executing ☐ Monitoring/controlling ☐ Closing

6. Change requests

☐ Initiating ☐ Planning ☐ Executing ☐ Monitoring/controlling ☐ Closing

7. Stakeholder management strategy

☐ Initiating ☐ Planning ☐ Executing ☐ Monitoring/controlling ☐ Closing

8. Communication requirements analysis

☐ Initiating ☐ Planning ☐ Executing ☐ Monitoring/controlling ☐ Closing

9. Forecast methods

☐ Initiating ☐ Planning ☐ Executing ☐ Monitoring/controlling ☐ Closing

10. Management skills

☐ Initiating ☐ Planning ☐ Executing ☐ Monitoring/controlling ☐ Closing

11. Procurement documents

☐ Initiating ☐ Planning ☐ Executing ☐ Monitoring/controlling ☐ Closing

12. Work performance measurements

☐ Initiating ☐ Planning ☐ Executing ☐ Monitoring/controlling ☐ Closing

13. Budget forecasts

☐ Initiating ☐ Planning ☐ Executing ☐ Monitoring/controlling ☐ Closing

14. Performance reports

☐ Initiating ☐ Planning ☐ Executing ☐ Monitoring/controlling ☐ Closing

15. Information distribution tools

☐ Initiating ☐ Planning ☐ Executing ☐ Monitoring/controlling ☐ Closing

2. Complete the sentences below, stating whether the option refers to input, tool/technique, or output, and identify the corresponding project management process.

1. Stakeholder register is a ______________________ of the ______________________ process.
2. Stakeholder register is a ______________________ of ______________________ processes.
3. Communication requirements analysis is a ______________________ of the ______________________ process.
4. Work performance measurements are ______________________ of the ______________________ process.
5. Communication templates are ______________________ of the ______________________ process.
6. Forecasts methods are ______________________ of the ______________________ process.
7. Procurement documents are ______________________ of the ______________________ process.
8. Performance reports are ______________________ of the ______________________ process.
9. Performance reports are ______________________ of the ______________________ process.
10. Change requests are ______________________ of ______________________ processes.
11. Variance analysis is a ______________________ of the ______________________ process.
12. Issue log is a ______________________ of the ______________________ process.

Questions

1. In general, how much of their time do project managers spend in communications?
    a. 80%
    b. 90%
    c. 70%
    d. 50%

2. The determination of information and communication methods that stakeholders will need in the project is developed in the following process:
    a. Report Performance
    b. Plan Communications
    c. Distribute Information
    d. Identify Communication Requirements

3. Every communication has the following components:
    a. Sender, message, receiver, and feedback
    b. Sender, message, and receiver
    c. Sender, message, receiver, and noise
    d. Sender, message, receiver, and environment.

4. The document defining the types of stakeholder information needs, how information should be distributed and how often, as well as which communication method must be used is:
    a. Communications management plan
    b. Stakeholder management plan
    c. Project requirements registration
    d. Stakeholder requirements registration

5. All of the following are inputs of the Sequence Activities process, except
    a. Stakeholder register
    b. Stakeholder management strategy

c. Analysis of communication requirements

d. Enterprise environmental factors

6. All of the following are tools or techniques of the Define Activities process, except

a. Analysis of communication requirements

b. Communication technology

c. Communication strategies

d. Communication methods

7. All of the following are not outputs of the Define Scope process, except

a. Project scope statement

b. Project charter

c. Project requirements

d. Stakeholder register

8. All of the following are not inputs of the Sequence Activities process, except

a. Analysis of communication requirements

b. Stakeholder register

c. Communication template

d. Communication methods

9. All of the following are not tools or techniques of the Sequence Activities process, except

a. Communication methods

b. Stakeholder management strategy

c. Expert judgment

d. Communications management plan

10. All of the following are not outputs of the Define Activities process, except

a. Communication methods

b. Communications management plan

c. Analysis of communication requirements

d. Communication technology

11. All of the following are inputs of Distribute Information process, except

a. Project management plan

b. Performance Reports

c. Communication methods

d. Organizational process assets

12. All of the following are inputs of the Manage Stakeholder Expectations process, except

a. Organizational process assets updates

b. Performance reports

c. Change requests

d. Project document updates

13. All of the following are inputs of the Manage Stakeholder Expectations process, except

a. Stakeholder register

b. Change log

c. Change requests

d. Organizational process assets

14. All of the following are inputs of Distribute Information process, except

a. Project management plan

b. Performance Reports

c. Organizational process assets

d. Information distribution tools

15. All of the following are inputs of the Manage Stakeholder Expectations process, except

a. Stakeholder management strategy

b. Interpersonal skills

c. Issue register

d. Stakeholder register

16. All of the following are inputs of the Manage Stakeholder Expectations process, except

a. General management skills

b. Issue log

c. Change log

d. Stakeholder register

17. All of the following are inputs of the Manage Stakeholder Expectations process, except

a. Stakeholder management strategy

b. Organizational process assets

c. Communication methods

d. Stakeholder register

18. All of the following are inputs of the Develop Schedule process, except

a. Project management plan

b. Work Performance Information

c. Work performance measurements

d. Performance Reports

19. All of the following are tools or techniques of the Control Schedule process, except

a. Variance analysis

b. Forecast methods

c. Work performance information

d. Communication methods

20. All of the following are outputs of the Develop Schedule process, except

a. Performance reports

b. Information distribution system

c. Change requests

d. Organizational process assets updates

21. If there are four people in a project and a fifth one is added, how many additional communication channels will there be?

a. 6

b. 10

c. 20

d. 4

22. The solution to complex problems can be helped by the extensive use of what kind of communication?

a. Nonverbal

b. Verbal

c. Written

d. Formal

23. The organization acquisitions department is preparing a contract to acquire equipment for a project. A few questions are being cleared up with the engineering staff and the legal department. What kind of communication must be employed in this case?

a. Informal verbal communication

b. Formal written communication

c. Formal speech communication

d. Informal writing communication

24. One team member is not getting the performance that you, as project manager, expected of him. What type of communication will you use to deal with the problem?

a. Formal written communication

b. Formal speech communication

c. Informal verbal communication

d. Informal writing communication

25. A new project manager is trying to improve communication within the project team. For this, he uses the argument that communications tend to improve when the sender ________________ the receiver.

a. has communication skills with

b. is straightforward with

c. sets clear objectives and transmits them to

d. seeks to understand the viewpoint of

26. The project is in the group of Planning processes, particularly focused on the end of the schedule, and a member of the team recommended that after this time, were not identified new stakeholders so there are no major changes in the schedule. The project manager gave his opinion about that suggestion by saying that:

a. The suggestion is valid, since the project is over and new stakeholders may interfere with the project's critical path.

b. The suggestion is valid, since the project already has multiple critical paths, and new stakeholders may interfere with the project deadlines.

c. The suggestion is not valid because the stakeholder identification can occur in any project management process group.

d. The suggestion is valid, since the stakeholder identification has been made in the beginning and during Planning.

27. During a project progress meeting, the manager is dissatisfied with its progress: everyone speaks at the same time, others do not take part, and even others discuss other issues. What should the project manager have actually done?

a. He should have called only the right people and interested in the project.

b. He should have created meeting control rules and a meeting agenda, and shared it in advance.

c. He should control those who are allowed to speak and be polite with everybody.

d. He should have told everyone that he would like to have order in the meeting.

28. A project manager was recently assigned to a project lasting 2 years and that is in half of that period. He has many suppliers and involves about 20 members on the project team. The manager wants to know quickly the current status of the project. Which report should he consult?

a. The project change report

b. The forecast report

c. The progress report

d. The report of works planned for the next period

29. In project management, formal writing is used in the following except

a. Memos

b. Attempts to deal with complex problems

a. Project documents

d. E-mail messages

30. In project management, speech communication is used in

a. Presentations

b. Meetings

c. Memos

d. Conversations

31. In project management, informal written communication refers to

a. Complex problems

b. E-mail messages

c. Presentations

d. Meetings

32. All of the following options are components of the communication basic template, except

a. Encoding and decoding

b. Message, feedback, means

c. Noise

d. Technology

Answer key

Supplementary exercises

2. 1 - Output - Identify Stakeholders

2 - Input - Plan Communications and Manage Stakeholder Expectations

3 - Tool/technique - Plan Communications

4 - Inputs - Report Performance

5 - Tools - Plan Communications

6 - Tools/techniques - Report Performance

7 - Inputs - Identify Stakeholders

8 - Inputs - Distribute Information

9 - Outputs - Report Performance

10 - Outputs - Manage Stakeholder Expectations and Report Performance

11 - Tool/technique - Report Performance

12 - Input - Manage Stakeholder Expectations

Questions

1. B. Project managers spend about 90% of their time in communications, including project meetings, e-mails, presentations, etc.

2. B. The determination of the communication needs among stakeholders as well as the definition of technology, communication methods, and templates is performed in the Plan Communications process.

3. B. All communication has three components: sender, message, and receiver.

4. A. The communications management plan defines the types of stakeholder information needs, how information should be distributed and how often, and which communication method should be used.

5. C. In order to prepare the communication planning, you need (inputs) analyze communication requirements contained in Stakeholder register, check the communication strategy defined in the Stakeholder management strategy document, and analyze the Enterprise environmental factors (such as the company communication). The analysis of communication requirements is one of the actions (tool/technique) to be performed in order to complete the communications Planning.

6. C. The words communication strategies are not used as input, tool/technique, or output of processes, rather as stakeholder management strategy, which is an input of the Plan Communications process.

7. B. Note that the question is "Which of the following options IS an input of the Identify Stakeholders process?" In this type of question, the first thing to do is to identify which group of project management processes you are in and, so far, what has been developed in the project. In this case, you are at the Project Initiating; therefore, the scope statement has not been developed yet and no requirements were collected. Stakeholder register is the output of the corresponding process.

8. B. Note that the question is "Which of the following options IS an input of the Plan Communications process?" The only input of this process is option B. Note during the exam: the terms "analysis", "template," and "method" always refer to tools and techniques.

9. A. The question, asked more clearly, is "Which of the following options IS a tool or technique of the Plan Communications process?" The Stakeholder management strategy is an input of the process. Expert judgment is not a tool of this process. The communications management plan is the product (output) of this process. Communication methods (meetings, e-mails, memos, letters, etc.) are tools of the process.

10. B. The question, asked more clearly, is "Which of the following options IS an output of the Plan Communications process?" The process name leads us to believe that we should have a communications plan. The other options are process tools and techniques.

11. C. Remember that in Executing, Monitoring and controlling, and Closing, the project management plan is an input of all processes. Communication methods are tools of the process. The other options are inputs of this process.

12. A. Keep in mind during the exam: the term "updates" always refers to outputs of the process. Change requests (generated in this process) are also outputs of the process. Performance reports are outputs of the Report Performance process.

13. C. Change requests (generated in this process) are an output of the process. The other options are process inputs.

14. D. Remember that, in Executing, Monitoring and controlling, and Closing, the project management plan is an input of all processes. Options B and C are inputs of this process. Information distribution tools, as the name implies, are tools that process.

15. B. Note, during the exam, that term "register" always refers to an input or output of processes – questions C and D are inputs of this process as well as option A. Interpersonal relationship skills are tools of the process.

16. A. Note, during the exam, that the term "register" always refers to an input or output of processes – options B, C, and D are inputs of the process. General management skills are tools of the process.

17. C. Communication methods are tools of the process. The other options are inputs of this process.

18. D. The very name of the process leads to think about "report". The major product (output) Report of the process performance are performance reports.

19. C. Remember in the exam: the terms "analysis" and "method" refers to tools and techniques of processes. Option C is an input of the process performance report.

20. B. The information distribution system is one of the tools used in the Report Performance process, enabling information collection, storage, and distribution to stakeholders about the schedule progress, about costs and the project performance. The other options are process outputs.

21. D. The number of communication channels is given by [N(N–1)]/2, where N is the number of people. With four people, there are six channels, and with five people, there are 10 channels. Therefore, there are four additional channels.

22. C. When there is a complex problem and you would like to explain or document it in detail, it is better doing it in written form – so that all stakeholders receive the same information.

23. B. When information is usually needed from other organization departments, such as professionals in the technical or legal areas, you should resort to formal written communication.

24. C. The project manager first action should be talking to the team member (option C). If this fails, formal written communication should be applied.

25. D. Communications tend to improve when the sender tries to understand the receiver's viewpoint – this allows us to recognize the receiver's needs.

26. C. Obviously, the sooner they are identified stakeholders and their requirements known, it is best for the project – in terms of scope, cost, schedule, quality and other project factors. However, **things in projects do not happen quite so!** The identification of stakeholders can happen in any project management process group, even during closure! Here's an example: You are Closing your project and your company has been hired to perform a new project, similar to yours. The new project manager has become a stakeholder of your new project: he will want to know about the lessons you learned in each phase of the project or the project as a whole.

27. B. It is understood that only the right people interested in the project were called, which crosses out option A. Option C is not a rule for effective meetings. Option D does not guarantee discussion about the meeting subjects only. Creating a set of control rules is important to properly deal with meetings. Creating an agenda and sharing it to people helps them focus on the meeting subjects.

28. C. In order to quickly view the project's current status, the summary report is the progress report – containing information such as the planned physical progress = x%; actual physical progress = y%.

29. D. Information interfering with the project must be formalized, such as memos, correspondence on complex issues, documents, etc. E-mails, and handwritten notes are considered informal writing.

30. A. Meetings and conversations (options B and D) are examples of informal verbal communication. Memos are examples of formal written communication. Presentations and lectures are examples of formal speech communication.

31. B. Complex problems must be addressed through formal written communication. Presentations are examples of formal speech communication. Meetings are examples of informal verbal communication. E-mails and handwritten notes are considered examples of informal written communication.

32. D. The basic communication template consists of items in options A, B, and C (*PMBOK® Guide*). Technology is a factor that may affect the project communications.

Chapter 11

PROJECT RISK MANAGEMENT

1. Introduction
2. General considerations on Project Risk Management
3. Risk management in project planning
4. Risk management in project monitoring and controlling

Attachment I   Risks in projects

- Additional information and reminders for the exam
- Supplementary exercises
- Questions
- Answer key

11.1 INTRODUCTION

This chapter will introduce project management processes in the Risk knowledge area, their relevant inputs, tools, techniques, and outputs.

11.2 GENERAL CONSIDERATIONS ON PROJECT RISK MANAGEMENT

Project Risk Management includes the execution of the activities of identification, analysis, response Planning, Monitoring and controlling of risks in order to decrease the probability and impact of negative risks (threats) and increased probability as well as impact of positive risks (opportunities). Risk management involves prioritizing risks according to their occurrence and impact probability, given that it would not be possible to allocate resources in order to counteract the action of all risks envisioned for the project. Risk management should be initiated *as early* as possible and should be a continuous and iterative process throughout the project life cycle.

According to PMI®, the Project Risk Management must include the following processes:

- **Plan Risk Management**

  The process to define how the Project Risk Management activities should be performed.

- **Identify Risks**

  Determine risks that may affect the project and document their characteristics.

- **Perform Qualitative Risk Analysis**

  Prioritizing risks for subsequent further analysis or action by assessing and combining the occurrence probability and impact.

- **Perform Quantitative Risk Analysis**

  Numerical analysis of the effect of identified risks on the project overall goals.

- **Plan Risk Responses**

  Developing options and actions in order to increase opportunities and reduce threats to the project objectives.

- **Monitor and Control Risks**

  Monitoring identified risks, monitoring residual risks, identifying new risks, Executing risk response plans, and evaluating the effectiveness throughout the project life cycle.

Attachment I provides further reading on risks in projects

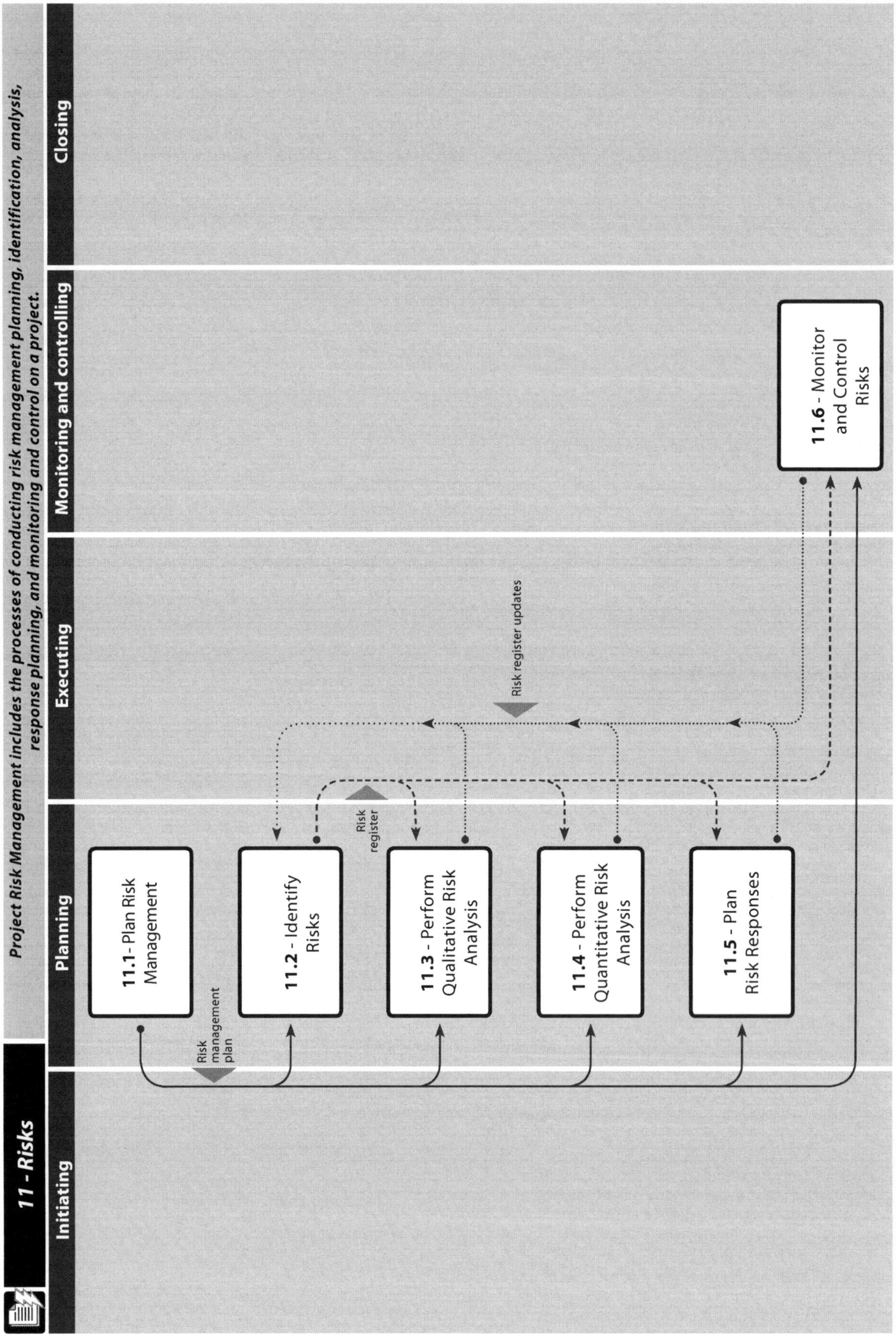
11 - Risks
Project Risk Management includes the processes of conducting risk management planning, identification, analysis, response planning, and monitoring and control on a project.
Initiating
Planning
Executing
Monitoring and controlling
Closing
11.1 - Plan Risk Management
11.2 - Identify Risks
11.3 - Perform Qualitative Risk Analysis
11.4 - Perform Quantitative Risk Analysis
11.5 - Plan Risk Responses
11.6 - Monitor and Control Risks
Risk management plan
Risk register
Risk register updates

11.3 RISK MANAGEMENT IN PROJECT PLANNING

According to PMI®, risk management in project planning comprises the following processes, namely,

- *Plan Risk Management*
- *Identify Risks*
- *Perform Qualitative Risk Analysis*
- *Perform Quantitative Risk Analysis*
- *Plan Risk Responses*

11.3.1 PLAN RISK MANAGEMENT (*PMBOK® GUIDE,* PROCESS 11.1)

Plan Risk Management is the process of deciding how to approach and execute risk management activities of the project. The output of this process is the risk management plan, which shows how implementation, Monitoring and controlling of all other risk management processes will occur, without detailing the definition of responses to particular risks.

11.3.1.1 PLAN RISK MANAGEMENT: INPUTS, TOOLS AND TECHNIQUES, AND OUTPUTS

INPUTS

1 **Project scope statement**

The project scope statement may include risks defined by the customer or sponsor and other risks identified in this stage, which may influence the development of the risk management Planning.

2 **Cost management plan**

The cost management plan presents the relative risks to the budget, contingencies and reserves management, must be considered in this process.

3 **Schedule management plan**

The management plan provides information on the schedule activity durations, and other restrictions, must be considered in this process.

4 **Communications management plan**

The communications management plan defines the interactions that must occur in the project and must be considered in this process.

5 **Enterprise environmental factors**

The enterprise environmental factors must be analyzed as to influence on the risk management Planning. The culture of the company in relation to risk, existence of policies and guidelines related to risks must be considered as well as levels of risk tolerance of the company and stakeholders in the project. These tolerance levels refer to how strongly the project manager and stakeholders are willing to expose themselves to a risk based on the benefits it can bring about or how much a risk will be avoided in view of the impact it may cause on the project.

6 Organizational process assets

The organizational process assets that can influence the risk management plan, including, but not limited to, the following:

- Risk categories defined by the organization
- Definitions and common terms used by the organization
- Risk reporting formats used by the organization
- Standard templates
- Roles and responsibilities defined
- Levels of authority for decisions
- Lessons learned from previous projects
- Stakeholder register of previous projects

TOOLS AND TECHNIQUES

1 Planning meetings and analysis

Planning meetings and analysis are the basic tool to implement risk Planning. Those attending these meetings are stakeholders, including the project manager, the team, functional managers, representatives of other departments with some influence on the project, and others who may contribute to this process. At these meetings, the basic plans and tools to be used in risk management should be defined as well as risk responsibilities.

OUTPUTS

1 Risk management plan

Risk management plan is the only output of this process. It documents structuring and implementation of the Project Risk Management. According to PMI®, risk management plan should provide the following elements:

- **Methodology**

  It defines the procedures and tools to be used in the management of project risks as well as data sources for references of selected risks.

- **Roles and responsibilities**

  It defines the team responsible for managing identified risks and their responses.

- **Budgeting**

  It defines resources to be used and performs a cost estimate of risk management activities. This estimate should be included in the project cost baseline.

- **Times**

  It defines when and how often the risk management process will be executed and which risk-related activities will be part of the project schedule.

- **Risk category**

  The execution of a risk listing and risk analytical framework enables to categorize risks, helping us to identify and understand them.

- **Probability and impact matrix**

  It is the establishment of criteria to classify probability (chance of occurrence) and impact (consequence faced by the project) of a certain risk. Numerical values can be used (degree 1, degree 2..., degree 10, for example) or textual definitions (low degree, medium degree, high degree, for example) for each risk. The use of a probability and impact matrix helps visualizing risks that must be prioritized and they need to respond faster and in more detail.

- **Review of stakeholders' tolerances**

  According to the project progress, stakeholders can increase or decrease risk-related tolerances. If this change occurs, risk management plan should be updated.

- **Report formats**

  It indicates document formats to be used in the Project Risk Management.

- **Follow-up**

  It describes how risks and the corresponding replies will be documented in benefit of the project or future projects. It also indicates whether risk processes will be audited and how they will be performed.

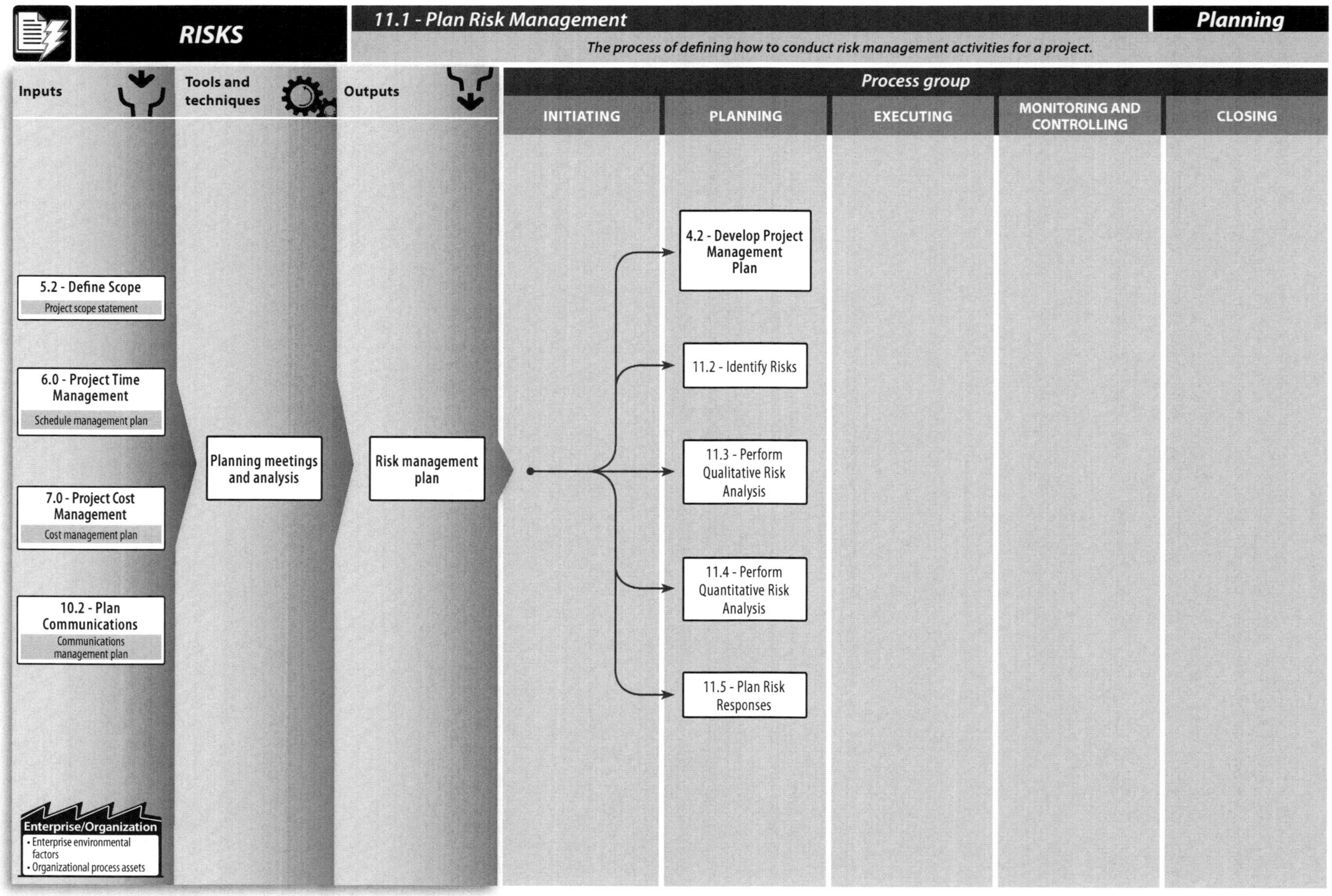
RISKS
11.1 - Plan Risk Management
Planning
The process of defining how to conduct risk management activities for a project.
Inputs
Tools and techniques
Outputs
Process group
INITIATING
PLANNING
EXECUTING
MONITORING AND CONTROLLING
CLOSING
5.2 - Define Scope
Project scope statement
6.0 - Project Time Management
Schedule management plan
7.0 - Project Cost Management
Cost management plan
10.2 - Plan Communications
Communications management plan
Enterprise/Organization
• Enterprise environmental factors
• Organizational process assets
Planning meetings and analysis
Risk management plan
4.2 - Develop Project Management Plan
11.2 - Identify Risks
11.3 - Perform Qualitative Risk Analysis
11.4 - Perform Quantitative Risk Analysis
11.5 - Plan Risk Responses

11.3.2 IDENTIFY RISKS (*PMBOK® GUIDE*, PROCESS 11.2)

Identify Risks is the process determining risks that may impact the project and documenting its characteristics. This process involves the project team and stakeholders and may have the participation of others in the organization itself who were part of the risk management in previous projects and even experts outside the organization. The Identify Risks process should be developed as soon as possible and it should be the reason behind assessment and revision throughout the project life cycle, with the inclusion of new risks as the project progresses.

11.3.2.1 IDENTIFY RISKS: INPUTS, TOOLS AND TECHNIQUES, AND OUTPUTS

INPUTS

1 **Risk management plan**

The risk management plan, which guides the implementation of all risk management processes, must be considered when identifying risks.

2 **Activity cost estimates**

Cost estimates of activities should be analyzed to Identify Risks related to possible variations in costs arising from estimates.

3 **Activity duration estimates**

Activity duration estimates must be analyzed to Identify Risks related to possible schedule variations arising from the estimate.

4 **Scope baseline**

The scope baseline (project scope statement, WBS, and the WBS dictionary) should be analyzed to Identify Risks related to the establishment of the project scope.

5 **Stakeholder register**

Stakeholder register should be analyzed to Identify Risks related to stakeholder expectations and requirements.

6 **Cost management plan**

The cost management plan must be analyzed to Identify Risks related to project costs.

7 **Schedule management plan**

The schedule management plan must be analyzed to Identify Risks related to deadlines, resources, assumptions and the restrictions placed on the schedule.

8 **Quality management plan**

The quality management plan must be analyzed to Identify Risks related to metrics established, control, and quality assurance.

9 **Project documents**

Project documents that must be analyzed to Identify Risks include, but are not limited to, the following:

- Work performance reports,
- Earned Value Reports,
- Network diagrams,
- Project baseline, and
- Any other document that enables the identification of risks.

10 Enterprise environmental factors

The enterprise environmental factors must be considered when identifying risks. The company culture in relation to risk, and risk-related policies and guidelines must be considered as well as the company and the project stakeholders' risk tolerance levels. Factors outside the organization must also be considered, such as those related to politics, the environment and the economy.

11 Organizational process assets

Historical risk registers of previous projects and lessons learned in the past can help identify project risks.

TOOLS AND TECHNIQUES

1 Documentation reviews

It consists in checking all the project documentation, such as the project management plan and its subplans, specifications, cost estimates, resources, the network diagram, and schedule.

2 Information gathering techniques

Information gathering techniques may include *brainstorming*, Delphi technique, interviews, root cause identification, and SWOT analysis.

3 Checklist analysis

Checklists used in this process refer to risk lists developed on information from previous projects and the team experience.

4 Assumptions analysis

Assumptions analysis is identifying risks that may occur if assumptions are not true or do not occur.

5 Diagramming techniques

Diagramming techniques involve cause-and-effect diagrams, flowcharts, and influence diagrams.

Attachment I provides further reading on diagramming techniques

6 **SWOT analysis**

SWOT analysis is a scenario analysis technique, which can be used to Identify Risks. The term SWOT is an acronym for *Strengths*, *Weaknesses*, *Opportunities*, and *Threats*.

7 **Expert judgment**

Expert judgment to define the project scope can be obtained from several sources, including

- Other units of the organization;
- Consultants;
- Stakeholders, including users, sponsors, and others;
- Technical and professional associations;
- Industrial groups;
- Suppliers and manufacturers; and
- Project Management Office (PMO).

OUTPUTS

1 **Risk register**

Risk register is the description of risks identified, their root causes, and the project's uncertain assumptions. These risks can be recorded in a spreadsheet or database in order to allow Monitoring and controlling.

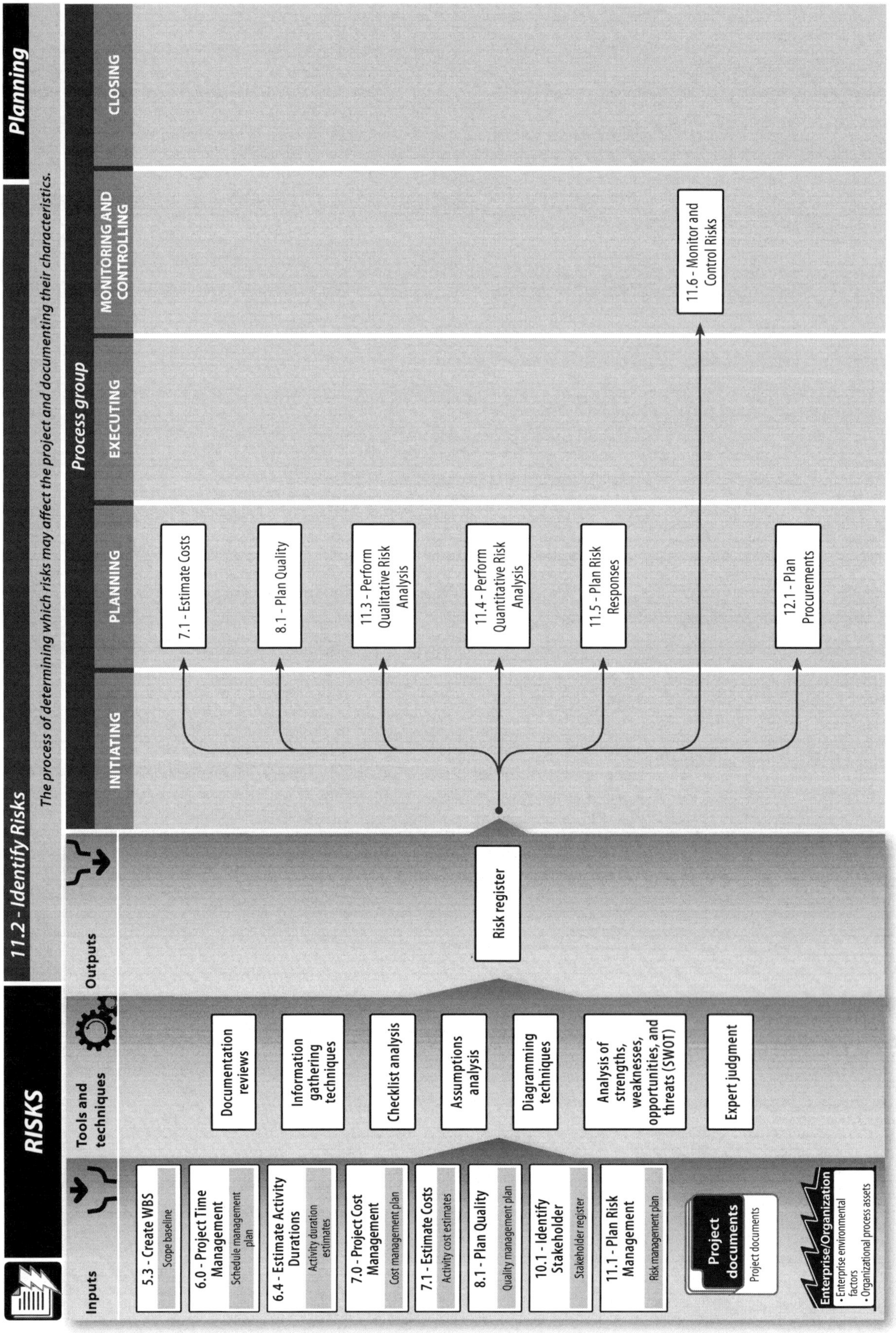

RISKS
11.2 - Identify Risks
Planning
The process of determining which risks may affect the project and documenting their characteristics.
Inputs
Tools and techniques
Outputs
Process group
INITIATING
PLANNING
EXECUTING
MONITORING AND CONTROLLING
CLOSING
5.3 - Create WBS
Scope baseline
6.0 - Project Time Management
Schedule management plan
6.4 - Estimate Activity Durations
Activity duration estimates
7.0 - Project Cost Management
Cost management plan
7.1 - Estimate Costs
Activity cost estimates
8.1 - Plan Quality
Quality management plan
10.1 - Identify Stakeholder
Stakeholder register
11.1 - Plan Risk Management
Risk management plan
Project documents
Project documents
Enterprise/Organization
• Enterprise environmental factors
• Organizational process assets
Documentation reviews
Information gathering techniques
Checklist analysis
Assumptions analysis
Diagramming techniques
Analysis of strengths, weaknesses, opportunities, and threats (SWOT)
Expert judgment
Risk register
7.1 - Estimate Costs
8.1 - Plan Quality
11.3 - Perform Qualitative Risk Analysis
11.4 - Perform Quantitative Risk Analysis
11.5 - Plan Risk Responses
12.1 - Plan Procurements
11.6 - Monitor and Control Risks

11.3.3 PERFORM QUALITATIVE RISK ANALYSIS (*PMBOK® GUIDE*, PROCESS 11.3)

Perform Qualitative Risk Analysis is assessing the occurrence probability of a risk and the impact corresponding to the project objectives. This process also considers other factors such as deadline and risk tolerance of the project cost, schedule, scope, and quality constraints. The important emphasis in this process is choosing tools and techniques to prioritize risks.

11.3.3.1 PERFORM QUALITATIVE RISK ANALYSIS: INPUTS, TOOLS AND TECHNIQUES, AND OUTPUTS

INPUTS

1 **Risk register**

Risk register is an essential element for risk qualitative analysis.

2 **Risk management plan**

The risk management plan provides information on risk roles and responsibilities, risk categories, probability, and impact definition and other information that must be considered in qualitative risk analysis.

3 **Project scope statement**

The project scope statement provides information that enables the project uncertainty level to be assessed. If the project is similar to others already executed by the organization, the uncertainty degree is probably small and risks are better well known. In contrast, if the project has a high uncertainty level or complexity greater than previous ones, risks will require more careful analysis in this process.

4 **Organizational process assets**

Risk information from previous projects and lessons learned must be considered in qualitative risk analysis.

TOOLS AND TECHNIQUES

1 **Risk probability and impact assessment**

This technique consists in assessing the probability of a given risk occurring and its impact on project objectives. According to this assessment, a risk may be assigned a more urgent response and action priority than others.

2 **Probability and impact matrix**

This technique consists in classifying risk according to the level of probability and impact values defined. Each risk is assigned a score that will help risk responses. This technique can be used for both negative risks (threats) and positive risks (opportunities).

3 **Risk data quality assessment**

This technique consists in checking the quality and usefulness level of risk data. Risk assessment in previous projects, their root causes, conditions contributing to that occurrence, and other factors can be compared with the project's current conditions and help this evaluation.

4 **Risk categorization**

Project risks can be categorized by risk source (according to the Risk Breakdown Structure), and they are (based on the WBS), by phase, by project specialty, or another useful category.

5 **Risk urgency assessment**

This technique consists in recognizing risks with earlier occurrence probability dates, to which a more urgent response is defined. The response definition must consider the time required for the response development and application.

6 **Expert judgment**

The use of expert opinion to Perform Qualitative Risk Analysis of the project can originate in several sources, as indicated in the Identify Risks processes presented earlier.

OUTPUTS

1 **Risk register updates**

The risk register prepared in the Identify Risks process must be updated according to the results of qualitative risk analysis and contain the following information:

- Classification (or priority) of project risks
- Risks grouped by categories
- List of risks requiring a short-term response
- List of risks for further analysis and response
- Low-priority risk observation list
- Trends of results of qualitative risk analysis

With this information, Risk register will enable better visualization and better understanding of the project risks. Risks requiring additional analysis and responses to complement their understanding and enable appropriate responses to them deserve special attention. Low-priority risks must be systematically assessed as to possible probability and impact changes on the project objectives.

11.3 - Perform Qualitative Risk Analysis

Planning

The process of prioritizing risks for further analysis or action by assessing and combining their probability of occurrence and impact.

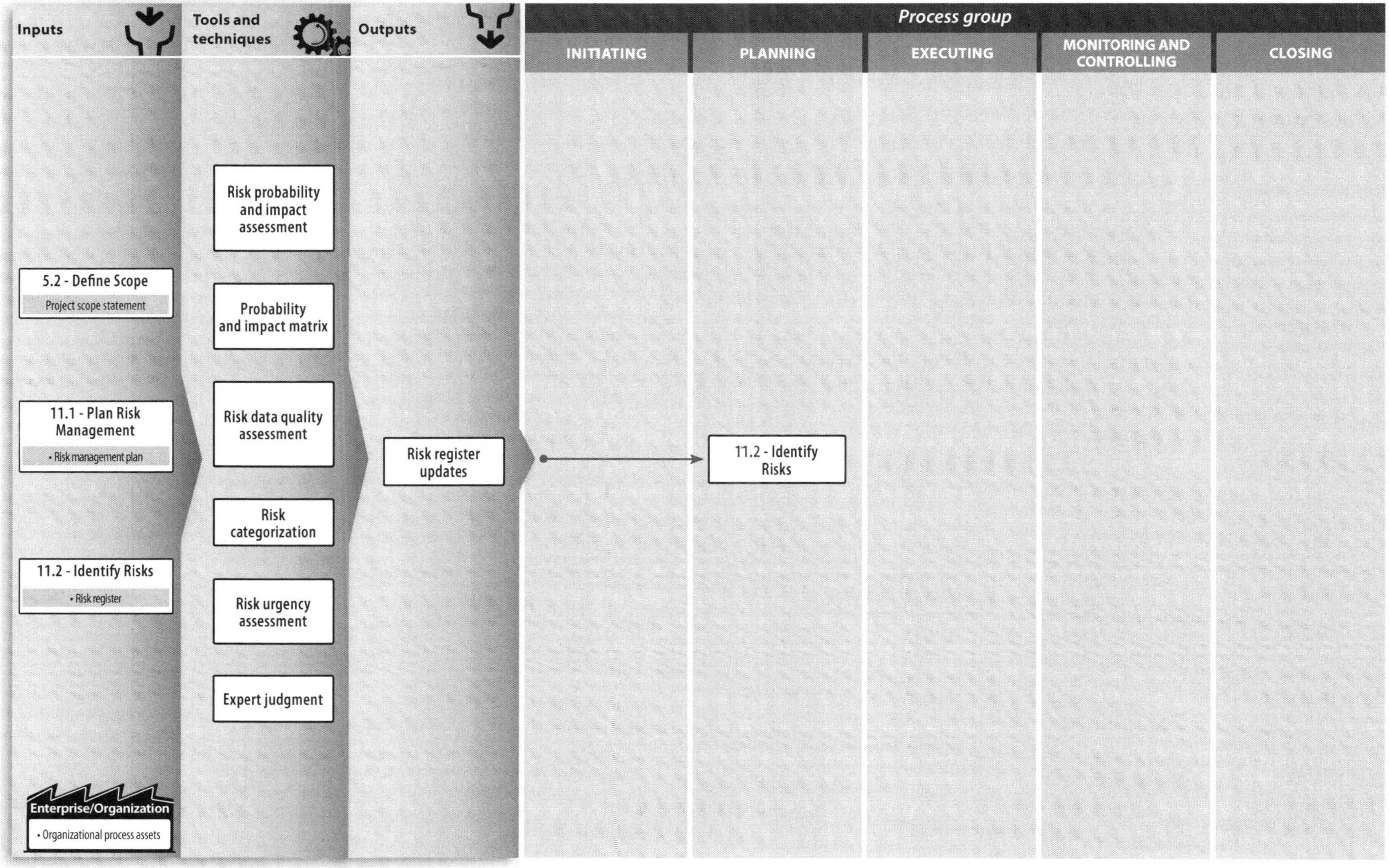

11.3.4 PERFORM QUANTITATIVE RISK ANALYSIS (*PMBOK® GUIDE*, PROCESS 11.4)

Perform Quantitative Risk Analysis means assessing the impacts and the numerical classification of risks identified in the Perform Qualitative Risk Analysis. It can use techniques such as the expected value analysis, probability distribution, the Monte Carlo analysis, and the decision tree analysis. The analysis enables identifying risks that should have further attention or a faster response, probabilities of reaching the project objectives, and determining the project cost and time reserves.

11.3.4.1 PERFORM QUANTITATIVE RISK ANALYSIS: INPUTS, TOOLS AND TECHNIQUES, AND OUTPUTS

INPUTS

1 **Risk register**

Risk register, updated in the Perform Quantitative Risk Analysis process, is the essential input to the quantitative risk analysis.

2 **Risk management plan**

Information from the risk management plan must be considered in this process.

3 **Cost management plan**

Information from the cost management plan must be considered in this process.

4 **Schedule management plan**

Information from the schedule management plan must be considered in this process.

5 **Organizational process assets**

Risk information from previous projects and lessons learned must be considered in this process.

TOOLS AND TECHNIQUES

The tools and techniques of quantitative risk analysis are only listed in this section. The complete description can be found in Attachment I.

1 **Data gathering and representation techniques**

Data gathering and representation techniques include:

- Interviews
- Probability distributions

2 **Quantitative risk analysis and modeling techniques**

Techniques commonly used in quantitative analysis include:

- Sensitivity analysis,
- Expected monetary value analysis,
- Decision tree analysis, and
- Modeling and simulation.

3 **Expert judgment**

The use of expert opinion to Perform Quantitative Risk Analysis of the project can originate in several sources, as indicated in the Identify Risks processes presented earlier.

OUTPUTS

1 **Risk register updates**

Risk register must be updated according to the results of the quantitative risk analysis with the following information:

- **Project probability analysis.** It is the forecast of results of the project deadline and costs, providing data to establish contingency reserves for such objectives.
- **Execution probability of cost and time objectives.** It is the forecast of reaching particular cost and time objectives.
- **Prioritized list of quantified risks.** It is a list of risks that pose the largest threats or the largest opportunities to the project objectives.
- **Trends of results of qualitative risk analysis.** The trend analysis of quantitative analysis results may help define risk responses.

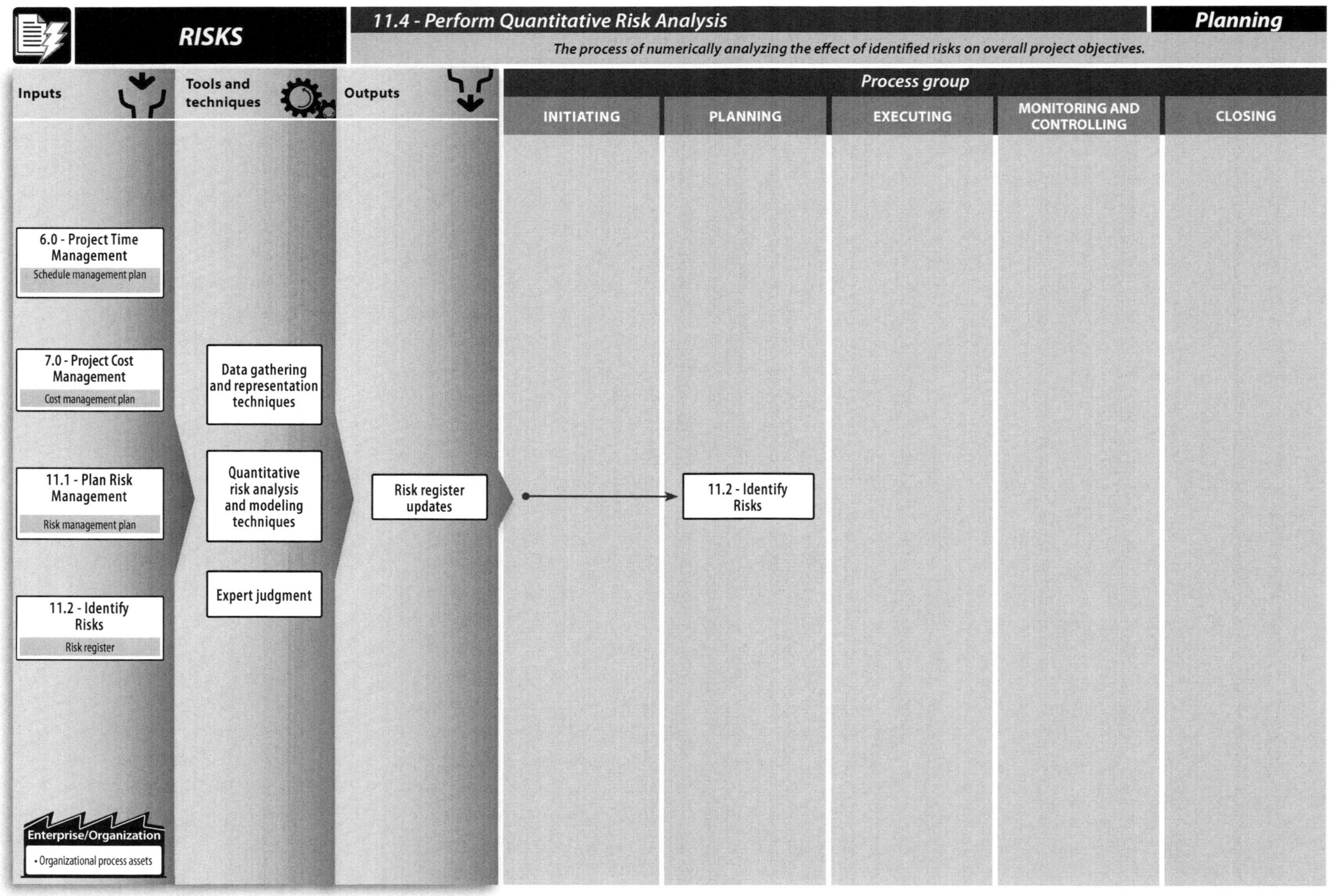
RISKS
11.4 - Perform Quantitative Risk Analysis
Planning
The process of numerically analyzing the effect of identified risks on overall project objectives.
Inputs
Tools and techniques
Outputs
Process group
INITIATING
PLANNING
EXECUTING
MONITORING AND CONTROLLING
CLOSING
6.0 - Project Time Management
Schedule management plan
7.0 - Project Cost Management
Cost management plan
11.1 - Plan Risk Management
Risk management plan
11.2 - Identify Risks
Risk register
Enterprise/Organization
• Organizational process assets
Data gathering and representation techniques
Quantitative risk analysis and modeling techniques
Expert judgment
Risk register updates
11.2 - Identify Risks

11.3.5 PLAN RISK RESPONSES (*PMBOK® GUIDE*, PROCESS 11.5)

The risk response plan is defining actions to reduce threats and increase opportunities found in risk analysis processes. This plan also defines individuals or departments with responsibilities for risk responses, called "risk owners". Planning preparation must consider combining occurrence probability with the impact on the project. A high occurrence probability risk with high impact on the objectives must be a priority in terms of time and response Planning detailing.

11.3.5.1 PLAN RISK RESPONSES: INPUTS, TOOLS AND TECHNIQUES, AND OUTPUTS

INPUTS

1 **Risk register**

Risk register, updated in the risk analysis processes, is the fundamental gateway for Planning risk responses.

2 **Risk management plan**

The risk management plan, developed in the Plan Risk Management process, must be considered when Planning risk responses.

TOOLS AND TECHNIQUES

Tools and techniques of Planning risk responses are only listed in this section. A detailed description can be found in Attachment I.

Attachment I contains further reading on tools and techniques of Plan Risk Responses

1 **Strategies for negative risks or threats**

Strategies for negative risks or threats include

- Avoid
- Transfer
- Mitigate

2 **Strategies for positive risks or opportunities**

Strategies for positive risks or opportunities include

- Exploit
- Share
- Enhance

3 **Contingent responses strategies**

It is an alternative strategy defined in case a particular event takes place.

4 **Expert judgment**

The use of expert opinion to Perform Quantitative Risk Analysis of the project can originate in several sources, as indicated in the Identify Risks process presented above.

OUTPUTS

1 **Risk register updates**

Risk register must be updated and contain information from Risk response Planning, including

- Risk owners and their responsibilities.
- Risk responses strategies agreed.
- Specific actions to implement risk responses.
- Cost and time estimates to implement the risk responses plan.
- Cost and time contingency reserves.
- Residual risks. These are the minimum risks expected to continue after implementing the response plan.
- Secondary risks. These are the risks caused by implementing a risk response.

2 **Risk-related contract decisions**

Contracting supplies and services can provide for transferring a threat or sharing an opportunity with the contractor. Contracting insurance or a company specialized in a particular service are examples of such types of agreements.

3 **Project management plan updates**

The project management plan must be updated, taking into account the influences of the risk responses Planning. Direct influences on the project time and cost can be the reason to update the corresponding time and cost management plan.

4 **Project documents updates**

Any and all project document that have been influenced by the Plan Risk Responses process must be updated, such as

- Assumption register and
- Technical documentation.

11.5 Plan Risk Responses

The process of developing options and actions to enhance opportunities and to reduce threats to project objectives.

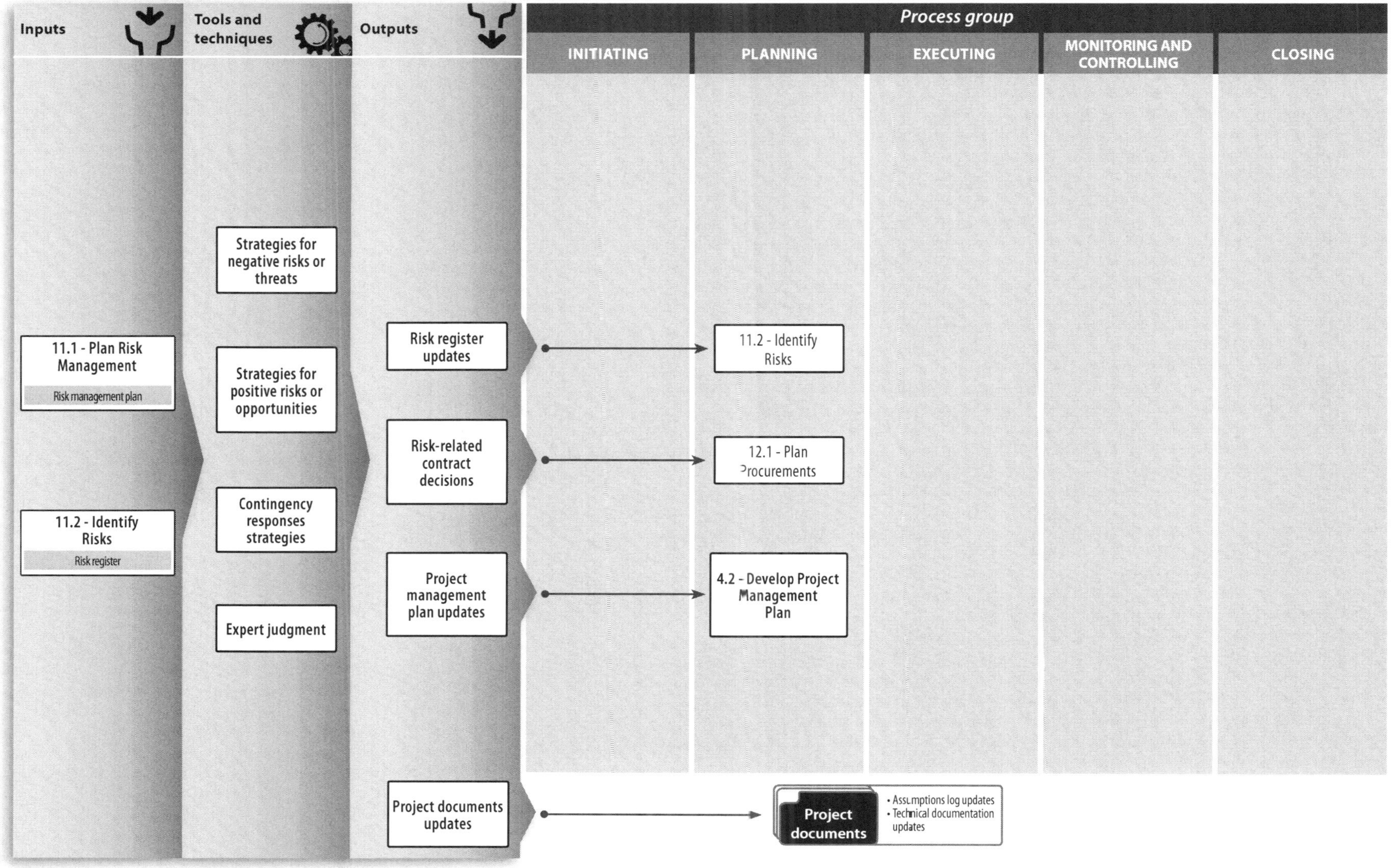

11.4 RISK MANAGEMENT IN PROJECT MONITORING AND CONTROLLING

According to PMI®, risk management in project risk management is comprised by the following process:

- *Monitor and Control Risks*

11.4.1 MONITOR AND CONTROL RISKS (*PMBOK® GUIDE*, PROCESS 11.6)

Monitor and Control Risks means tracking and monitoring risks identified and identifying as well as Planning responses to new project risks. Tracking and monitoring identified risks involving analysis and assessment of risk response plans, reassessing existing risks, identification of possible risk triggers, monitoring residual risks, and updating cost and scheduling contingency reserves. Risk Monitoring and controlling occurs throughout the project life cycle and must be a factor of constant attention by the project manager.

11.4.1.1 MONITOR AND CONTROL RISKS: INPUTS, TOOLS AND TECHNIQUES, AND OUTPUTS

INPUTS

1 **Risk register**

Risk register contains information on identified risks, owners of such risks, expected actions for risk responses and other information important for such process.

2 **Project management plan**

The project management plan and, in particular, the risk management plan, must be considered in this process.

3 **Work performance information**

Work performance information can help assess the risks identified and identify new project risks.

4 **Performance reports**

Performance reports can help assess risks and identify new project risks.

TOOLS AND TECHNIQUES

1. **Risk reassessment**

Risk reassessment must be periodically performed by the members of the project team, preferably during the project meetings. The purpose is to identify the current legitimacy of each risk previously identified regarding the occurrence possibility and, if it would occur, which impacts it would cause to the project.

2 **Risk audits**

Risk audits are generally performed by professionals not belonging to the project team and, at times, they are hired outside the company. The purpose of such audits is checking the effectiveness of the risk management plan implementation by the project team and how new risks are identified and addressed. Risk auditors can also identify new risks and suggest preventive actions to the project manager. Risk audit reports must be simultaneously forwarded to the project manager and the organization senior management.

3 **Variance and trend analysis**

The project actual performance variance in relation to the expected performance in the project baseline must be analyzed from standpoint of possibility of new risks caused by this variance and the need to implement preventive measures.

4 **Technical performance measurement**

Technical performance measurement compares technical performances with the technical performance expected in the project baseline. Deviations, for example, from functionality or performance, may indicate risks related to schedule delays, increased costs, and other factors.

5 **Reserve analysis**

The management reserve analysis must be performed during the project execution phase in order to confirm whether the remaining amounts of such reserves are sufficient to complete the project.

6 **Status meetings**

Including "risk" subjects in all tracking meetings is considered as good management practice, aimed at always remembering and addressing the corresponding subject.

OUTPUTS

Variance in the project actual performance in relation to performance expected in the scope baseline must be analyzed in order to verify the need for corrective or preventive actions.

1 **Risk register updates**

Risk register must be updated in order to depict the reality of risks and include the results of risk reassessment and risk audits.

2 **Organizational process assets updates**

The Monitor and control project risks can identify new ways of identifying risks, new risk responses, and other related information that must be documented, such as project lessons learned.

3 **Change requests**

The Monitor and control project risks process can identify new opportunities or confirm needs for changes in the project in order to decrease or stop certain risks from occurring, which must be subject to change requests. These changes must be submitted for review and, if approved, they should be implemented.

4 **Project management plan updates**

The project management plan and, in particular, the risk management plan, must be updated after changes are approved as a result of the Monitor and Control Risks process.

5 **Project document updates**

Any and all project document that have been influenced by the Monitor and Control Risks process must be updated, not limited to the following:

- Assumption register
- Technical documentation

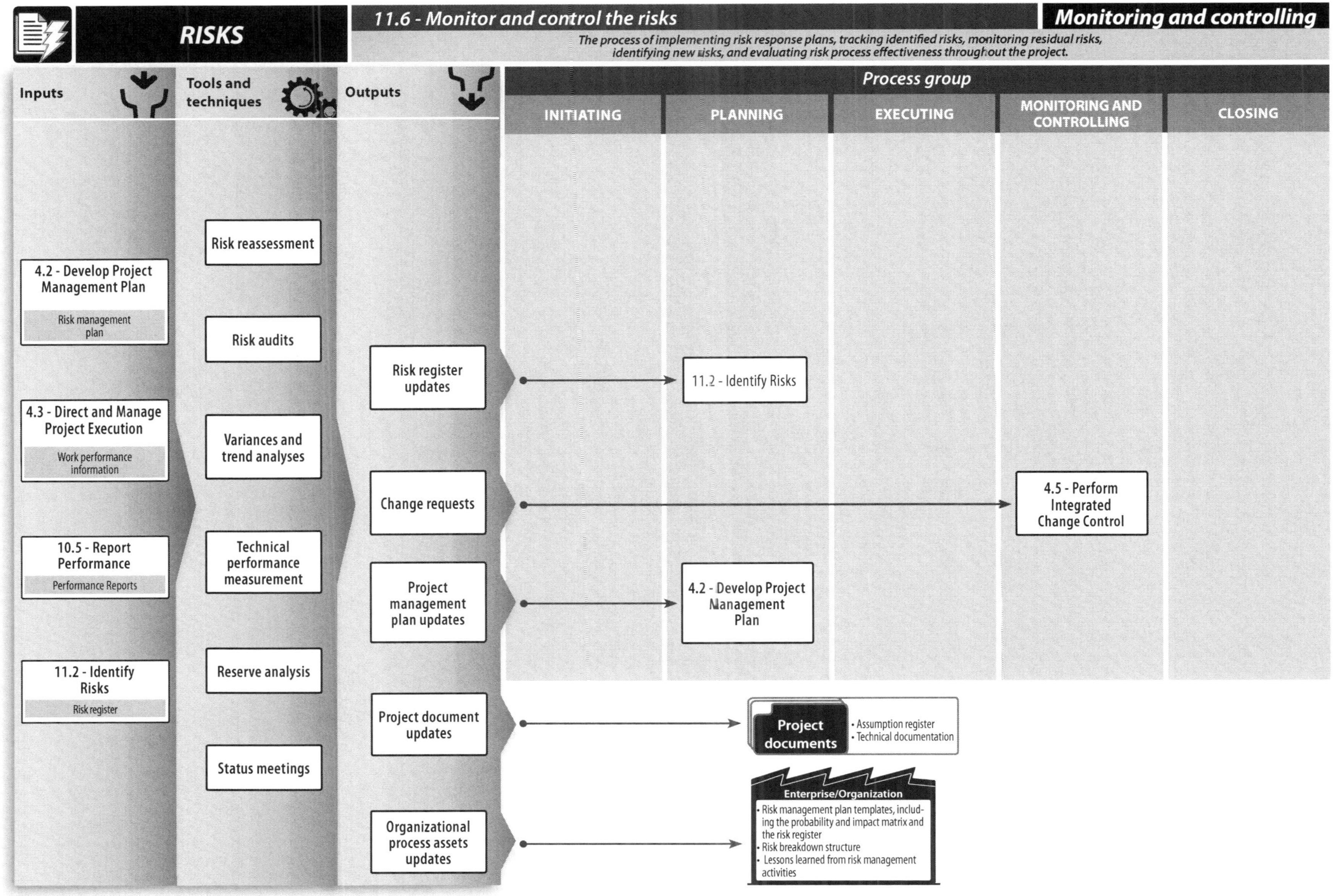
RISKS
11.6 - Monitor and control the risks
Monitoring and controlling
The process of implementing risk response plans, tracking identified risks, monitoring residual risks, identifying new risks, and evaluating risk process effectiveness throughout the project.
Inputs
Tools and techniques
Outputs
Process group
INITIATING
PLANNING
EXECUTING
MONITORING AND CONTROLLING
CLOSING
4.2 - Develop Project Management Plan
Risk management plan
4.3 - Direct and Manage Project Execution
Work performance information
10.5 - Report Performance
Performance Reports
11.2 - Identify Risks
Risk register
Risk reassessment
Risk audits
Variances and trend analyses
Technical performance measurement
Reserve analysis
Status meetings
Risk register updates
Change requests
Project management plan updates
Project document updates
Organizational process assets updates
11.2 - Identify Risks
4.5 - Perform Integrated Change Control
4.2 - Develop Project Management Plan
Project documents
• Assumption register
• Technical documentation
Enterprise/Organization
• Risk management plan templates, including the probability and impact matrix and the risk register
• Risk breakdown structure
• Lessons learned from risk management activities

Attachment I

RISKS IN PROJECTS

RISKS IN PROJECTS

1 INTRODUCTION

Risk is an uncertain event or condition that, if occurring, will have positive or negative effects on the project. Risks originate in the very uncertainty inherent to the project. They appear throughout the project life cycle, with larger occurrence in the early stages and smaller occurrence in the final stages. Generally speaking, a risk is assessed by the occurrence probability and the impact it causes. A risk occurrence can affect any project objective, such as time, cost, quality, or scope. A risk can originate by one or more causes and may generate one or more impacts on one or more project objective(s). However, not all risks are bad. They can represent threats, while others may represent improvement opportunities related to the objectives. Recognizing risk causes and taking appropriate action to minimize threats and increase opportunities is essential to the project successful completion.

2 RISK IDENTIFICATION

Risk identification determines risks that may impact the project and documents their characteristics. In addition to using information from inside the project, this process must use historical records and lessons learned from other projects as well as the expert opinion of sources outside the organization. It is an interactive process, involving the project team and other stakeholders throughout the project life cycle.

2.1 RISK CATEGORIES

Risk categories are a way of identifying and classifying risks, which makes it easier to analyze and understand them. This classification varies from organization to organization and even from project to project. A classification could consider, for example, the following risk factors:

- Technological
- Schedules
- The customer
- The stakeholders
- Scope changes
- Project management problems
- The sponsor
- Purchasing and contracting
- Resource availability
- Political and legal issues
- Environment-related issues
- The company and stakeholders' culture

One of the most common classifications considers the following risks:

- **Technical risks**

  Are risks related to technology or a technology change, quality, or performance defined for the project components? For example, a change in the specification of certain project equipment may result in delayed delivery by the manufacturer.

- **Project Risk Management**

  Risks are related to the implementation of management activities, such as schedule execution, preparation of resource, and cost estimates. Errors or inadequate considerations when Executing such activities may pose risks to the project.

- **Risks inside the organization**

  These are risks associated with the company organization itself. Risk-related culture, risk tolerance level, the real interest of the senior management in the project, and resource release toward the project are a few examples of this kind of risk.

- **Risks outside the organization**

  These are risks related to outside factors, over which the organization has no control. Defining a new governmental law, labor union agreements, and the environment policy in place at the project site are a few of these kinds of risk. Risks related to catastrophes such as earthquakes, and floods, are not usually considered in the project management.

- **Residual risks**

  A risk that continues after risk responses have been implemented.

2.2 RISK INFORMATION INTERNAL SOURCES

Risk information internal sources are all the documentation generated in the project, such as the project scope statement, the project management plan, and management auxiliary plans. In general, such consideration must include the following:

- **The project objectives**

  The project objectives may determine additional risks and the need for specific Planning for such risks.

- **The project assumptions**

  Assumptions (beliefs and opinions about the project) can help identify additional risks as well as increase or decrease the impact of risks already identified.

- **Restrictions**

  Imposed restrictions can pose time, cost, and quality risks as well as increase or decrease the impact of risks already identified.

- **The Work Breakdown Structure (WBS)**

  WBS must be considered, since risk must be identified at the project and work packages levels.

- **The network diagram**

  The network diagram must be considered to find multiple convergences of predecessors, which increases the successor activity risk. The project objectives shown in the diagram can define risks related to the project deadline execution.

- **The resource estimates**

  Checking the actual resource availability and productivity considered in estimates can generate time-related risks.

- **The duration estimates**

  Verification of the methods used in duration estimates may generate time-related risks.

- **The cost estimates**

  Checking cost estimates may generate cost-related risks.

In a more specific way in relation to management plans, risk consideration must include the following:

- **Scope management plan**

  The scope recognition and the identification of specific or special activities may promote the definition of new risks. An activity usually not performed by the company as well as an activity that depends on supply of an exclusive supplier may pose a risk on the project.

- **Time management plan**

  Assumptions and restrictions related to deadlines can promote the definition of new risks. The need to verify a certain area on a certain date by the customer may pose a risk on the project.

- **Cost management plan**

  Assumptions and restrictions related to costs can promote the development of new risks. Changing the cost of an activity as a result of market changes or changing the human resource cost as a result of labor union agreements may pose a risk on the project.

- **Quality management plan**

  Quality requirements and metrics can promote the development of new risks. The performance requirement of equipment to be acquired can compromise the deadline and the cost as well as pose a risk on the project.

- **Human resource management plan**

  Resource availability and the need for special skills for certain resources in order to develop activities may pose time and cost risks to the project.

- **Communications management plan**

  Forecasting communication difficulties may promote the identification of new risks. Communication with a supplier located abroad may pose a risk to the project.

- **Procurement management plan**

  Procurement and hiring can promote the development of new risks related to time, cost and project quality. In addition, procurements and hiring can contribute to risk mitigation or transference to suppliers and contractors.

2.3 RISK IDENTIFICATION TOOLS

In addition to analyzing the project documentation and assumptions, as previously addressed, data collection techniques and diagram techniques are generally used.

2.3.1 Data gathering techniques

Data gathering can be performed by brainstorming, the Delphi technique, interviews, root cause identification, and SWOT analysis:

- **Brainstorming**

  Brainstorming is the most widely used technique in data risk collection. It is a group work technique designed to release participants' imagination and creativity, by breaking down set paradigms toward ideas and solutions about a particular subject. In addition to being easy and usable, brainstorming can generate a large number of ideas in a short period.

- **Delphi technique**

  The Delphi technique is a way of reaching the consensus of experts on a particular subject of the project, including risks. It is a technique that consists of creating a questionnaire to be sent to experts, who can be in different locations, in order to obtain ideas on the subject concerned. Answers are summarized and redistributed to experts for further comment. One of the advantages of this technique is participants' anonymity, which rules out the possibility of judging ideas and helps them be more genuine.

- **Interviews**

  Interviews with people who participated in other projects, with stakeholders, customers, suppliers, users, and risk experts represent a form of risk identification.

- **Root cause identification**

  An investigation of the essential causes of the project risks enables a clearer risk definition and the classification of these causes. This classification allows for the Planning risk response by type of question, which might allow the reduction or elimination of the impact of several risks to the treatment or disposal of only one question.

- **SWOT analysis**

  The SWOT analysis is a tool used in the scenario analysis as a basis for strategic management and Planning of an organization. Being quite simple, it can be used in any kind of scenario analysis, including risk identification. The term SWOT is an acronym for the words strengths, weaknesses, opportunities, and threats.

  This scenario analysis is split into internal environment (strengths and weaknesses) and external environment (opportunities and threats), as shown in the figure below.

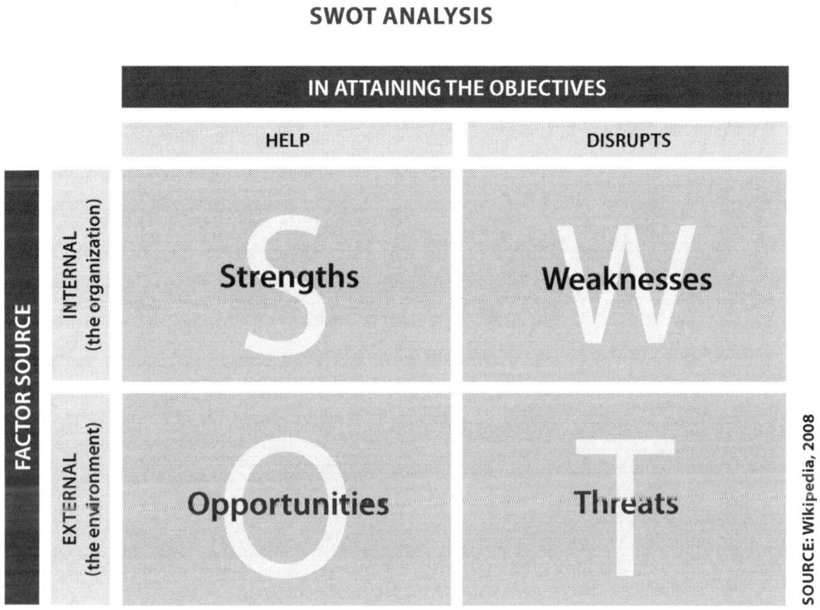

  Strengths and weaknesses are determined by the company's current position and relate almost exclusively to internal factors. On the other hand, opportunities and threats are anticipations of the future and are related to external factors.

  In the risk scenario, opportunities and strengths represent positive forces, and the organization must overemphasize their possible occurrence and impact. Threats and weaknesses represent negative risks, and the organization must Monitor and control them in order to avoid or minimize their effects.

2.3.2 Diagramming techniques

Diagramming techniques for risk study may include the cause-and-effect diagram, flowcharts, and influence diagrams:

- **Cause-and-effect diagram**

  The cause and effect diagram (Fishbone diagram or Ishikawa diagram) is a graphical tool showing the relationship between a problem and possible contributing causes.

- **Flowcharts**

  Flowchart is a graphical representation of sequencing process activities, which can be used as a tool for risk identification.

- **Influence diagrams**

  Influence diagrams show causal influences and the relationship between variables and their outcomes. The figure below shows, as a simplified example, an influence diagram of variables that impact the performance of an activity.

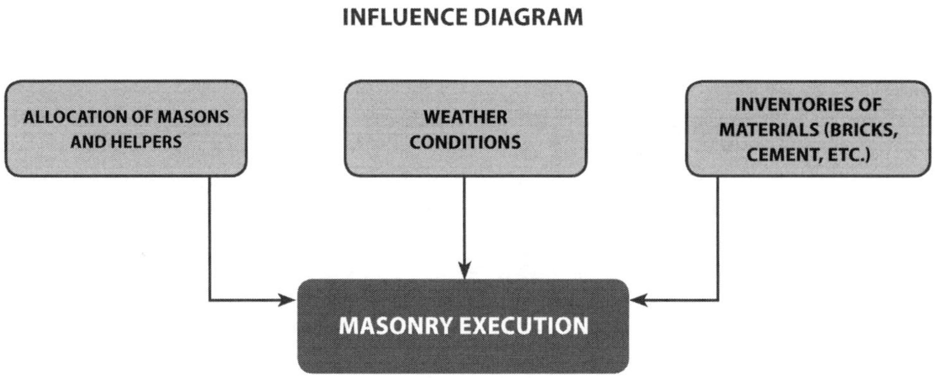

2.4 QUALITATIVE RISK ANALYSIS

Qualitative risk analysis is assessing the occurrence probability of a risk and the impact corresponding to the project objectives. This process also considers other factors, such as deadline and risk tolerance of the project cost, schedule, scope, and quality constraints.

2.4.1 Tools and techniques of qualitative risk analysis

The techniques used in this analysis are the risk probability and impact assessment and the probability and impact matrix execution:

- **Probability and risk impact assessment**

  This technique consists of assessing the probability of a given risk occurring and its impact on project objectives. This assessment is performed individually for each identified risk and is usually implemented through meetings among team members and interviews with experts. According to this assessment, a risk may be assigned a more urgent response and action priority than others. Other risks, with low probability and impact are not classified, but they will be included in a watch list for future monitoring.

- **Probability and impact matrix**

  This technique consists of classifying risk according to the level of probability and impact values defined. Each risk is assigned a score that will help risk responses. This technique can be used for both negative risks (threats) and positive risks (opportunities).

  Practically, the technique consists in choosing a risk assessment that can be related to time, cost, or scope, for example. Then, this risk probability is assessed, usually by guessing or, preferably, by means of expert judgment. This probability is usually expressed by a number between 0.0 (0% probability of occurring) and 1.0 (100% probability of occurring). Impact can also be expressed as a numerical scale from 0.0 to 1.0, with risk impact low, medium, and high classification degrees. The figure below shows a probability and impact matrix with the representation of threats and opportunities.

PROBABILITY	THREATS					OPPORTUNITIES				
0.90	0.90	1.80	2.70	3.60	4.50	4.50	3.60	2.70	1.80	0.90
0.70	0.70	1.40	2.10	2.80	3.50	3.50	2.80	2.10	1.40	0.70
0.50	0.50	1.0	1.50	2.00	2.50	2.50	2.00	1.50	1.0	0.50
0.30	0.30	0.60	0.90	1.20	1.50	1.50	1.20	0.90	0.60	0.30
0.10	0.10	0.20	0.30	0.40	0.50	0.50	0.40	0.30	0.20	0.10
IMPACT	1.0	2.0	3.0	4.0	5.0	5.0	4.0	3.0	2.0	1.0

Impact (ratio) on an objective (e.g., cost, time, scope or quality)

2.5 QUANTITATIVE RISK ANALYSIS

The quantitative risk analysis is assessing the impacts and the numerical classification of the risks identified in the Perform Quantitative Risk Analysis. The techniques used in this analysis enables identifying risks that should have further attention or a faster response, probabilities of reaching the project objectives and determining the project cost and time reserves.

2.5.1 Tools and techniques of quantitative risk analysis

The tools and techniques used in quantitative risk analysis can be divided into two types: data representation and collection techniques and modeling techniques.

2.5.1.1 Data gathering and representation techniques

Data gathering and representation techniques include interviews, probability distribution, and expert judgment:

- **Interviews**

  This technique is the same as that presented in the quantitative risk analysis. Interviews with people who participated in other projects, with stakeholders, customers, suppliers, users, and risk experts may be helpful during the risk quantitative analysis.

- **Probability analysis**

  The continuous probability distributions are graphical representations showing the uncertainty in values, which may be related to activity durations and costs, for example. Continuous distributions include the normal, normal logarithmic, triangular, beta, and uniform distributions. Triangular distributions use the three-point estimates (pessimistic, most likely and, optimistic) obtained in interviews and by means of expert judgment. Normal and normal logarithmic distributions use the three-point estimates obtained by calculating the average deviation and the standard deviation of estimates. The figure below shows two examples of probability distributions, where horizontal axes (x) represent time values and vertical axes (y) represent the relative probability.

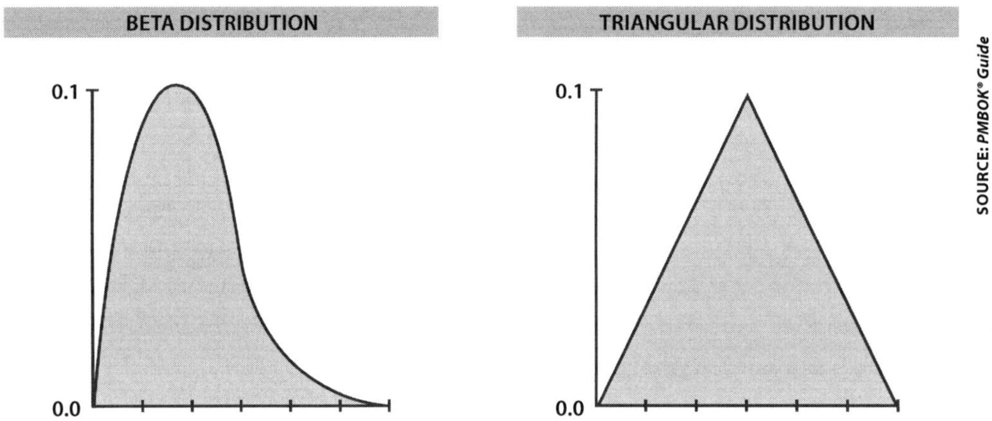

- **Expert judgment**

  This technique is the same as discussed in other project management processes. Experts, inside or outside the organization, can contribute to the quantitative risk analysis.

2.5.1.2 Quantitative risk analysis and modeling techniques

The quantitative analysis techniques and modeling techniques include sensitivity analyses, expected monetary value, decision tree and modeling, and simulation.

- **Sensitivity analysis**

  Sensitivity analysis consists in determining which risks cause a larger potential impact on the project, based on the evaluation of uncertainties of their elements. A usual representation of this analysis is the Tornado Diagram. This chart shows possible values for risks, arranged in horizontal bars, always downward obeying the decreasing order of values. It is named like that as it resembles a tornado, a hurricane, or an inverted cone. The following figure shows an example of this diagram for costs of a project.

TORNADO DIAGRAM

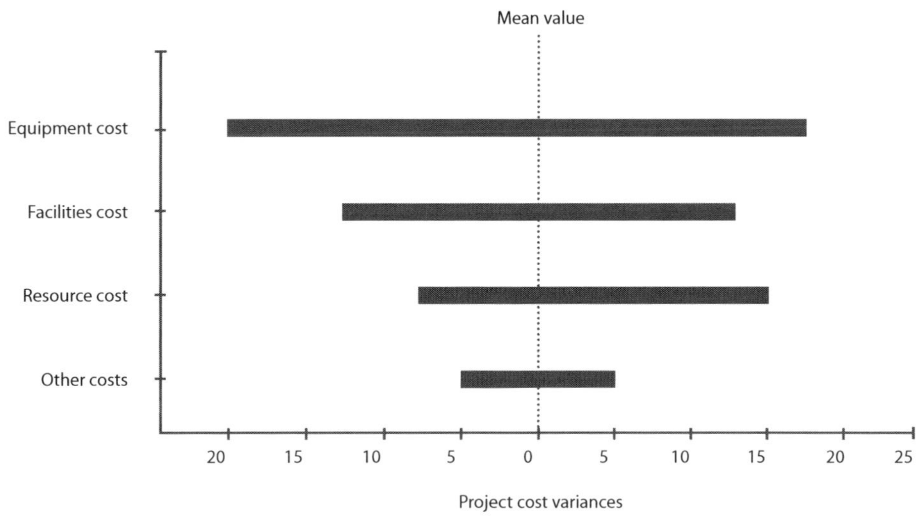

- **Expected monetary value analysis**

  The Expected Monetary Value (EMV) analysis is a statistical technique to calculate the decision average impact. In simple terms, EMV is calculated by multiplying the value of each possible result by its occurrence probability. Positive impact values represent opportunities, and negative values represent threats. The following table is an example of negative impact (threat) and a positive impact (opportunity). Note that the sum of EMVs is a negative value, representing the need for an increased contingency reserve fund to the project.

RISK	PROBABILITY	IMPACT	EMV
RISK A	25%	– $10,000	– $2,500
RISK B	40%	$4,000	$1,600
		TOTAL Expected Monetary Value	– $900

- **Decision tree analysis**

  The decision tree analysis is a technique showing the sequence of possible decisions and expected outcomes according to the selected alternative. It incorporates the cost of each choice, probabilities of each scenario, and the return of each alternative logical path. The following figure is a decision tree example, where the expected value is the decision impact in monetary values, calculated by multiplying the occurrence probability of risk versus impact. Note that the best decision, in this example, is option A, the result of which is a higher value.

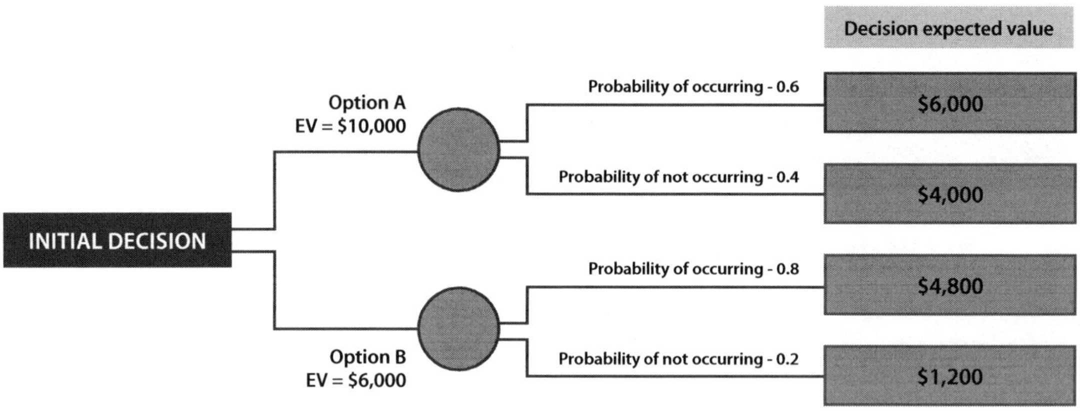

- **Modeling and simulation**

  These techniques use several inputs, such as costs or schedule duration, in order to define the probability distribution for the selected variable. For example, the determination of the total project cost would be obtained through simulations as input variables with the elements of the project costs through several simulations. One of the most widely used techniques is the Monte Carlo Method, usually developed on computers with particular software application due to the complexity and number of simulations that the method performs.

2.7 RISK RESPONSE STRATEGIES

Risk response strategies include strategies for negative risks or threats, positive risks, or opportunities, as well as acceptance and strategies for contingent responses.

2.7.1 Strategies for negative risks or threats

Strategies for negative risks or threats include the following:

- **Avoid**

  It consists in eliminating the threat posed by a risk. It can be executed by changing the project management plan and auxiliary plans, adopting known methodologies instead of unknown ones, extending schedule, contracting additional members to the project team, experienced in the technology in question, removing the work package, removing a team member and other measures.

- **Transfer**

  It is transferring a risk to a third party, with the response ownership. This strategy does not eliminate risk, but only transfers the responsibility to others. The most common examples are insurance policies, contracted with specialized companies, and equipment warranties, contracted with manufacturers.

- **Mitigate**

  It consists in the action taken to minimize the probability of the risk occurring or reducing the impact to an acceptable limit. The use of less complex processes, prototyping, implementation of a larger amount of tests, and the use of more reliable and stable suppliers are examples of this technique.

2.7.2 Strategies for positive risks or opportunities

Strategies for positive risks or opportunities include:

- **Exploit**

  It consists in removing the uncertainty of a risk, making the opportunity happen. An example is the opportunity to appoint more qualified resources with better sales and profit figures in order to reduce project time.

- **Share**

  It consists in assigning the ownership to third parties so they can better seize the opportunity and benefit the project. For example, they can be partnerships and contracting companies with a particular purpose in mind.

- **Enhance**

  It consists in increasing probabilities or impacts by identifying and maximizing the major drivers of these risks. Perform a training specific to a particular team, seeking proper performance of its functions is an example of this strategy.

2.7.3 Acceptance

Another threats and opportunities strategy is acceptance. Acceptance may be passive or active. It is passive when no action is taken, leaving the team to deal with the problem if it occurs. It is active when a time, money, or resource reserve is determined in order to deal with the problem if it occurs.

2.7.4 Contingent response strategies

It is an alternative strategy defined in case a particular event takes place. The project team executes a plan that will only be executed on certain predefined conditions.

2.7.5 Workarounds

Workarounds are responses to unplanned risks, developed in the event of unforeseen risk events.

Additional information and reminders for the exam

- Risks can be either positive (opportunities) or negative (threats).
- Data gathering techniques (for risk identification): brainstorming, Delphi technique, interviews, root cause analysis.
- SWOT Analysis: analysis to Identify Risks considering strengths, weaknesses, opportunities, and threats.
- Expected Monetary Value (EMV) = P × I (probability × impact).
- **Monte Carlo analysis**
    - It is used to assess impacts of costs and schedule, providing the probability of the project to be completed on a particular date and its cost.
    - It indicates the probability of any activity being present in the critical path.
    - It provides the project general risk assessment.
    - It works with a large number of simulations and provides a probability distribution.
- **Risk response negative (threats) strategies**
    - Avoid
    - Mitigate
    - Transfer
- **Positive risk responses (opportunities) strategies**
    - Exploit
    - Enhance
    - Share
- **Negative and positive risk response strategies**
    - Accept
- Noncritical risks should be recorded on a checklist and must be periodically reviewed. Some of them have their importance increased and become critical.
- Trigger risks are events triggering the response contingency.
- Risks related to the environment and government laws are classified as external.

- Risks related to meeting deadlines, scope changes, and inadequate Planning are classified as internal risks.
- Workarounds: responses to unplanned risk, developed in the event of unforeseen risk events.
- During the project budget, contingencies reserves are values related to known risks.
- During the project budget, management reserves are amounts related to unknown risks.
- Risks must be addressed in all meetings of the project team.

Supplementary exercises

1. In regards to the Project Risks area of knowledge, indicate to which management process group(s) each element is related and explain why. Follow the Risk Register example.

1. Risk Register

   ☐ Initiating ☒ Planning ☐ Executing ☒ Monitoring/controlling ☐ Closing

   Risk register is the output of the Identify Risks process (Planning) and an input of the Perform Qualitative Risk Analysis and Perform Quantitative Risk Analysis (Planning) processes, and an input of the Monitor and Control Risks (Monitoring and controlling).

2. Planning meetings and analysis

   ☐ Initiating ☐ Planning ☐ Executing ☐ Monitoring/controlling ☐ Closing

3. Risk audits

   ☐ Initiating ☐ Planning ☐ Executing ☐ Monitoring/controlling ☐ Closing

4. Data gathering and representation techniques

   ☐ Initiating ☐ Planning ☐ Executing ☐ Monitoring/controlling ☐ Closing

5. SWOT analysis

   ☐ Initiating ☐ Planning ☐ Executing ☐ Monitoring/controlling ☐ Closing

6. Risk reassessment

☐ Initiating ☐ Planning ☐ Executing ☐ Monitoring/controlling ☐ Closing

7. Diagramming techniques

☐ Initiating ☐ Planning ☐ Executing ☐ Monitoring/controlling ☐ Closing

8. Status meetings

☐ Initiating ☐ Planning ☐ Executing ☐ Monitoring/controlling ☐ Closing

9. Checklist analysis

☐ Initiating ☐ Planning ☐ Executing ☐ Monitoring/controlling ☐ Closing

10. Performance reports

☐ Initiating ☐ Planning ☐ Executing ☐ Monitoring/controlling ☐ Closing

11. Variance and trend analysis

☐ Initiating ☐ Planning ☐ Executing ☐ Monitoring/controlling ☐ Closing

12. Probability and impact matrix

☐ Initiating ☐ Planning ☐ Executing ☐ Monitoring/controlling ☐ Closing

13. Reserve analysis

☐ Initiating ☐ Planning ☐ Executing ☐ Monitoring/controlling ☐ Closing

14. Risk categorization

☐ Initiating ☐ Planning ☐ Executing ☐ Monitoring/controlling ☐ Closing

15. Technical performance measurement

☐ Initiating ☐ Planning ☐ Executing ☐ Monitoring/controlling ☐ Closing

2. Complete the sentences below, stating whether the option refers to input, tool/technique, or output, and identify the corresponding project management process.

1. Probability and impact matrix is a ______________________________ of the ______________________________ process.
2. Risk register is a ______________________________ of the ______________________________ process.
3. Information gathering techniques are ______________________________ of the ______________________________ process.
4. Modeling techniques are ______________________________ of the ______________________________ process.
5. Risk urgency assessment is a ______________________________ of the ______________________________ process.
6. SWOT analysis is a ______________________________ of the ______________________________ process.
7. Risk probability and impact assessment is a ______________________________ of the ______________________________ process.
8. Status meetings are ______________________________ of the ______________________________ process.
9. Risk-related contract decisions are ______________________________ of the ______________________________ process.
10. Risk audit is a ______________________________ of the ______________________________ process.
11. Risk categorization is a ______________________________ of the ______________________________ process.
12. Contingency response strategies are ______________________________ of the ______________________________ process.
13. Variance and trend analysis are ______________________________ of the ______________________________ process.
14. Assumption analysis is a ______________________________ of the ______________________________ process.
15. Change requests are ______________________________ of the ______________________________ process.

Questions

1. You are working in the Project Risk Management processes and have been finding it hard to define the relationship between the causes and effects of the problems. At this point, you must remember that you should use the
   a. Scatter diagram
   b. Simulation diagram
   c. Ishikawa diagram
   d. Decision tree diagram

2. Activities related to assigning an overall risk classification to the project and creating a list of risks by order of priority are developed in the process
   a. Plan Risk Responses
   b. Perform Quantitative Risk Analysis
   c. Plan Risk Management
   d. Perform Qualitative Risk Analysis

3. You are at the risk identification process. All of the following are techniques of Data gathering, except
   a. Checklist analysis
   b. Delphi technique
   c. Root cause analysis
   d. Brainstorming

4. All of the following are techniques of Data collection, except
   a. Interviews
   b. SWOT analysis
   c. Delphi technique
   d. Flowcharts

5. In the risk identification process, diagram techniques include the following options, except
   a. Cause-and-effect diagram
   b. Influence diagram

c. SWOT analysis

d. Flowchart

6. Your project team found that a risk event, should it occur, could save $125,000 in project costs. Based on that, which is the best answer to the question?

a. The risk is positive (an opportunity) and must be mitigated

b. The risk is negative (a threat) and must be explored

c. The risk is positive (opportunity) and must be explored

d. The risk is positive (opportunity) and must be accepted

7. Your project team found that a risk event, should it occur, could save $350,000 in project costs. Senior management decided to hire a company to help the project team make this risk happen. Based on that, which is the best answer to the question?

a. The risk is positive (an opportunity) and must be mitigated

b. The risk is negative (a threat) and must be explored

c. The risk is positive (opportunity) and must be improved

d. The risk is positive (opportunity) and must be shared

8. The supplier of project equipment called you to inform that a potential storm at the sea may prevent it arrives on time. Anyway, the supplier will continue keeping you abreast of developments. This fact about the storm possibility is a

a. Contingency plan

b. Recurring risk

c. Residual risk

d. A risk trigger

9. Some stakeholders are concerned about the project cost risk analysis, given the project high cost. With this in mind, senior management decided to approve the purchase of an application software specific to the Monte Carlo analysis. All options below are true, except

a. The Monte Carlo analysis is developed on computers with specific software applications

b. The Monte Carlo analysis is a modeling and simulation technique

c. The Monte Carlo analysis is a modeling technique and calculates the costs once

d. The Monte Carlo analysis is a great method to be used when determining risk costs

10. The supplier of a large power generator of the project informed the manager that transportation and delivery would possibly be delayed by the rain possibility this time of year. This generator is required for emergency lighting of an area to be inaugurated with the presence of state authorities. Considering this, the project manager decided to rent a generator from a rental company, so that no surprise occurs on the opening day. This is a response to risk of type

a. Mitigate

b. Eliminate

c. Transfer

d. Accept

11. Your project team is performing sensitivity analysis on the project quantitative risk analysis. Which is the diagram often used to graphically demonstrate the risks of this analysis?

a. Cause-and-effect diagram

b. Control diagram

c. Influence diagram

d. Tornado diagram

12. The project team is identifying project risks and intends to use all of the following tools and techniques, except

a. Decision tree diagram

b. Cause-and-effect diagram

c. Process flowcharts

d. Influence diagram

13. The project manager is talking to the manager responsible for the functional resources on the possibility of the network administrator quitting, which could cause a risk of delaying the project schedule. Although there is an explicit manifestation of the administrator, there are rumors that this will happen in about two weeks. Even so, the project manager and the functional manager chose to deal with this risk only after the network administrator's intent is completed. So, which of the following statements is true?

a. It is a risk response strategy called active acceptance

b. It is a risk response strategy called passive acceptance

c. It is a strategy to respond to contingencies

d. It is a negative risk response strategy

14. All of the following are inputs of the Plan Risk Management, except

a. Risk register

b. Project scope statement

c. Schedule management plan

d. Cost management plan

15. All of the following are inputs of the Perform Qualitative Risk Analysis process, except

a. Risk management plan

b. Project scope statement

c. Risk register updates

d. Organizational process assets

16. All of the following are inputs of the Perform Quantitative Risk Analysis process, except

a. Risk management plan

b. Risk data collection

c. Organizational process assets

d. Cost management plan

17. All of the following are NOT tools or techniques of the Plan Risk Management process, except

a. Risk management plan

b. Planning meetings and analysis

c. Risk register

d. Risk assessment

18. All of the following are tools or techniques of the Identify Risks process, except

a. Expert judgment

b. SWOT analysis

c. Diagramming techniques

d. Risk categorization

19. All of the following are tools or techniques of the Perform Qualitative Risk Analysis process, except

a. Probability and risk impact assessment

b. Risk categorization

c. SWOT analysis

d. Responsibility assignment and impact matrix

20. All of the following are tools or techniques of the Perform Qualitative Risk Analysis process, except

a. Risk urgency assessment

b. Risk strategies

c. Risk data quality assessment

d. Risk categorization

21. All of the following are tools or techniques of the Perform Quantitative Risk Analysis process, except

a. Data gathering and representation techniques

b. Quantitative risk analysis and modeling techniques

c. Expert judgment

d. Risk quantity assessment

22. All of the following are tools or techniques of the Plan Risk Responses process, except

a. Strategies for negative risks or threats

b. SWOT analysis

c. Expert judgment

d. Strategies for positive risks or opportunities

23. All of the following are outputs of the Plan Risk Responses process, except

a. Risk register updates

b. Risk-related contractual decisions

c. Project document updates

d. Strategies for negative risks or threats

24. All of the following are not inputs of the Plan Risk Management process, except

a. Planning meetings and analysis

b. SWOT analysis

c. Communications management plan

d. Diagramming techniques

25. All of the following are not inputs of the Identify Risks process, except

a. Expert judgment

b. Risk register

c. Assumptions analysis

d. Risk management plan

26. All of the following are not inputs of the Perform Qualitative Risk Analysis process, except

a. Risk register

b. Risk categorization

c. Risk probability and impact assessment

d. Risk urgency assessment

27. All of the following are not inputs of the Perform Quantitative Risk Analysis process, except

a. Data gathering and representation techniques

b. Expert judgment

c. Schedule management plan

d. Modeling techniques

28. All of the following are not inputs of the Plan Risk Responses process, except

a. Strategies for positive risks

b. Risk register

c. Strategies for negative risks

d. Contingency response strategies

29. All of the following are not tools or techniques of the Plan Risk Management process, except

a. SWOT analysis

b. Information gathering techniques

c. Expert judgment

d. Planning meetings and analysis

30. All of the following are not tools or techniques of the Identify Risks process, except

a. Expert judgment

b. Risk register

c. Risk register from previous projects

d. Risk response plan from previous projects

31. All of the following are not tools or techniques of the Perform Qualitative Risk Analysis process, except

a. Risk register

b. SWOT analysis

c. Information gathering techniques

d. Risk urgency assessment

32. All of the following are not tools or techniques of the Perform Quantitative Risk Analysis process, except

a. SWOT analysis

b. Risk register updates

c. Expert judgment

d. Performance variance analysis

33. All of the following are not tools or techniques of the Plan Risk Responses process, except

a. Risk register updated

b. Strategies for opportunities

c. Negative risk quantitative analysis

d. Risk management plan

34. All of the following are not outputs of the Plan Risk Management process, except

a. Risk register

b. SWOT analysis

c. Risk management plan

d. Documentation revisions

35. All of the following are not outputs of the Identify Risks process, except

a. Risk register

b. Updated risk register

c. Risk categorization

d. Risk impact assessment

36. All of the following are not outputs of the Perform Qualitative Risk Analysis process, except

a. Risk reassessment

b. Risk register updates

c. Risk urgency assessment

d. Change requests due to risks

37. All of the following are not outputs of the Perform Quantitative Risk Analysis process, except

a. Quantitative risk analysis

b. Data gathering and representation techniques

c. Risk register updates

d. Expert judgment

38. All of the following are not outputs of the Plan Risk Responses process, except

a. Risk-related contract decisions

b. Strategies for threats

c. Strategies for opportunities

d. Risk reassessment

39. All of the following are tools and techniques of the Monitor and Control Risks process, except

a. Risk reassessment

b. Updated risk register

c. Variance and trend analysis

d. Risk audits

40. All of the following are tools and techniques of the Monitor and Control Risks process, except

a. Status meetings

b. Reserve analysis

c. Work performance information

d. Technical Performance Measurement

41. All of the following are tools and techniques of the Monitor and Control Risks process, except

a. Change requests

b. Risk reassessment

c. Technical performance measurement

d. Reserve analysis

42. Performing the analysis of a project, you find that it has 70% probability of obtaining a profit of $200,000 and 30% probability of obtaining a loss of $200,000. What is the expected monetary value of the project that you get?

a. $140,000

b. $80,000

c. $60,000

d. $40,000

43. A risk event can cause a result of $20,000 and has 80% probability of occurring. What does $16,000 represent?

a. Value of contingency risk

b. Risk amount

c. Expected present value

d. Expected monetary value

44. In a project estimated to take five months, has been identified a risk with 25% probability of occurring in a month. What is the probability of this risk in the third month of the project?

a. 5%

b. 8.33%

c. 25%

d. 4%

45. In the management of project risks, hiring insurance policy is the best example

a. Acceptance

b. Mitigate

c. Transfer

d. Avoid

46. Which of the following is one of the main features of the Delphi technique?

a. Expert opinion

b. Verification of historical records

c. Polls

d. Decomposition of work packages

47. The person responsible for electromechanical equipment of the project says: "There may be a need to add work packages to the WBS in order to install new equipment in the 10 area. If this occurs, we may have an additional cost of approximately $23,500 in the project and a schedule delay of 15 days!" This is an example of risk related to

a. Scope

b. Cost

c. Schedule

d. Resources

48. All options are techniques of risk identification, except

a. Brainstorming

b. Delphi technique

c. Root cause analysis

d. Analysis of the risk register

49. The technique of interviewing experts gathered in a meeting room to Identify Project Risks is called

a. Delphi technique

b. Root cause analysis

c. Interview

d. SWOT analysis

50. The qualitative risk analysis tools may include the following except

a. Probability and impact matrix

b. Monte Carlo analysis

c. Assessing the quality of risk data

d. Risk urgency assessment

51. A company is considering whether it is worth doing a prototype project. The project team decided to use the decision tree as a decision tool, with the following data:

- Prototype cost = $80,000 – in case the prototype is made, the probability of failure is 30% and the impact of this failure is $60,000.
- In the case of not making the prototype, the probability of failure is 70% and the impact of this failure will be $200,000. What must be the company's attitude?

a. Make the prototype, because this option has a higher expected monetary value

b. Make the prototype, because this option has a lower expected monetary value

c. Do not make the prototype, because this option has a higher expected monetary value

d. Do not make the prototype, because this option has a lower expected monetary value

52. You have an appointment in three days in another town and is deciding whether to go there using your car or by plane. You decided to use the decision tree as a tool of analysis, with the following information:

- Car travel: travel costs $1,100, 10% probability of delay
- Air travel: travel costs $800, 30% probability of delay
- Delay impact: $600

a. Traveling by car, because this option has a higher expected monetary value

b. Traveling by plane, because this option has a lower expected monetary value

c. Traveling by plane, because this option has a higher expected monetary value

d. Traveling by car, because this option has a lower expected monetary value

53. All options are strategies for response to threats to the project, except

a. Mitigate

b. Enhance

c. Eliminate

d. Transfer

54. Removing the package of work that is a major cause of project risk is the risk response strategy called

a. Transfer

b. Mitigate

c. Enhance

d. Eliminate

55. Creating a partnership is a response strategy called positive risk:

a. Share

b. Enhance

c. Explore

d. Transfer

56. When performing the project budget, it was detected that there is a 30% probability that the equipment will cost $40,000 less than anticipated. What you should do regarding the project contingency reserves?

a. Add $12,000

b. Subtract $12,000

c. Subtract $40,000

d. Subtract $28,000

57. There is a 20% probability that the production is less complex than expected, generating savings of $40,000 in the project. What should be done concerning the project contingency reserves?

a. Reduce $32,000

b. Add $8,000

c. Reduce $8,000

d. Add $32,000

58. The "What is the risk status?" and "Is there any new risk?" questions are approaches to be asked in

a. Deadline control meetings

b. Cost control meetings

c. All meetings of the project team

d. Risk meetings

59. The closure of a risk no longer applicable will result in

a. Reducing the cost of control accounts

b. The possibility of using the reserve value in another activity

c. Returning the reserve value corresponding to the risk to the company

d. Rewarding the project team for monitor and control risks

60. All of the following options are related to errors in the Project Risk Management, except

a. The risk description is generic and not specific, making perfect identification harder

b. Noncritical risks are recorded in a checklist

c. Contracts are signed before completing their risk studies

d. Risk identification results in a brief list

Answer key

Supplementary exercises

2. 1 - Tool/technique - Perform qualitative analysis

2 - Output - Identify Risks

3 - Techniques - Identify Risks

4 - Techniques - Perform Qualitative Risk Analysis

5 - Technique - Perform Qualitative Risk Analysis

6 - Tool/technique - Identify Risks

7 - Tool/technique - Perform Qualitative Risk Analysis

8 - Tools - Monitor and Control Risks

9 - Outputs - Plan Risk Responses

10 - Tools/techniques - Monitor and Control Risks

11 - Tool/technique - Perform Qualitative Risk Analysis

12 - Tools/techniques - Plan Risk Responses

13 - Tools/techniques - Monitor and Control Risks

14 - Tool/technique - Identify Risks

15 - Outputs - Monitor and Control Risks

Questions

1. C. The Ishikawa diagram, also called Fishbone diagram, and cause-and-effect diagram.

2. D. The Perform Qualitative Risk Analysis creates a list in order of priority and assigns a risk classification to the project.

3. A. Data gathering techniques include brainstorming, Delphi technique, interviews, root cause identification, and SWOT analysis.

4. D. Data gathering techniques include brainstorming, Delphi technique, interviews, root cause identification, and SWOT analysis. Flowcharts are diagramming techniques.

5. C. When identifying risks, diagram techniques used are cause-and-effect diagram, flowchart and influence diagram. SWOT analysis is a data collection technique.

6. C. Risk is positive (opportunity), since it reduces the project costs. Exploring is eliminating the uncertainty of this risk, making it happen.

7. D. Risk is positive (opportunity), since it reduces the project costs. Sharing includes the involvement of third parties to help eliminate the uncertainty of this risk, making it happen.

8. D. Triggers are warning signs of an imminent event.

9. C. The Monte Carlo analysis is a modeling and simulation technique, which simulates project costs many times.

10. A. Mitigation seeks to reduce the impact of a risk implementation. The plan to rent another equipment reduces the risk consequences.

11. D. The diagram is the graph generally used in sensitivity analysis. This chart shows possible values for risks, arranged in horizontal bars, always downward obeying the decreasing order of values. It is so named because it resembles a tornado, a hurricane, or an inverted cone.

12. A. The decision tree diagram is used in quantitative risk analysis. When identifying risks, the following tools and techniques are used:

    - Data gathering techniques (brainstorming, Delphi technique, interviews, and root cause identification as well as SWOT analysis)
    - Diagramming techniques (cause-and-effect diagram, flowchart, influence diagram)

13. B. Passive acceptance is a risk response strategy so named because parties have not agreed on any action related to that risk. Only take action if the risk occurs. This response can be used both for negative risks and positive risks.

14. A. The scope, schedule, and costs are factors related to risks and must be considered in the Plan Risk Management process. Afterward, the Identify Risks process will be started, the output of which is Risk register.

15. C. A good tip for the exam: whenever you come across the term updates, it is related to OUTPUTS! Updates to risk registers are outputs of the qualitative analysis, quantitative analysis, risk response plan and monitor, and control risks processes.

16. B. Risk data collection is technique of the Perform quantitative analysis process and may be performed through interviews, expert judgment, and the decision tree analysis.

17. B. The question is, "Which is the tool of the Plan Risk Management process?" The most predictable answer is related to planning, i.e., Planning meetings and analysis.

18. D. Risk categorization is developed during the Perform Qualitative Risk Analysis process.

19. C. Tip for the exam: when using the terms SWOT analysis, the reference is Identify Risks!

20. B. Remember that strategy refers to a plan, a planning. The definition of risk strategies are developed in the Plan Risk Responses process.

21. D. The terms Risk amount assessment are not used as names of inputs, tools, and techniques or outputs of project management processes.

22. B. The SWOT analysis is a technique used in the Identify Risks process.

23. D. Negative risks strategies are tools of the Plan Risk Responses process.

24. C. Maybe, for this question, the last option you should choose would be C, don't you agree? First, note that the question is "Which of the following IS an input of the Plan Risk Management process?" In this case, the best thing to do is eliminating alternatives. Well, keep in mind during the exam: the terms "analysis" and "technique" (options A, B, and D) always refer to tools and techniques. Why is the Communications Management Plan an input of this process? See *PMBOK® Guide* item 11.1.1.4: The Project Communications Management Plan defines interactions to occur in the project and determines who will be available to share information on several risks and responses in different times and places.

25. D. Note that the question is "Which of the following is an input of the process to Identify Risks!" The risk management plan, defined in process prior to this one (Risk management plan) is the only input of the Identify Risks process. Expert opinion and Assumption analysis are tools and techniques. Risk register is the output of this process.

26. A. Note that the question is "Which of the following options IS an input of the Perform Qualitative Risk Analysis process?" Risk register is the only input of this process. Risk categorization is a tool. Remember during the exam: when you see the term assessment (as well as analysis), it always refers to tools and techniques.

27. A. Note that the question is "Which of the following options IS an input of the Perform Quantitative Risk Analysis process?" Let's eliminate alternatives one by one: techniques (options A and D) are, as the name implies, techniques, not inputs. Expert judgment (option B), regardless of any related process, is always a tool. Option C was left – the schedule management plan, which is an input of the process.

28. B. Note that the question is "Which of the following IS an input of the Plan Risk Responses process. Remember during the exam: the term "strategy" always refers to tools and techniques. The only input of the process is Risk register.

29. B. The question, asked more clearly, is "Which of the following options IS a tool or technique of the Plan Risk Management process?" The first three options are tools and techniques of the Identify Risks process. The only technique of the Plan Risk Management process is Planning meetings and analysis.

30. A. The question, asked more clearly, is "Which of the following options IS a tool or technique of the Identify Risks process?" Risk register is the product (output) of this process. Options C and D refer to organizational process assets, which are inputs of project management processes.

31. D. The question, asked more clearly, is "Which of the following options IS a tool or technique of the Perform Qualitative Risk Analysis process?" Risk register is an output of the Identify Risks process

and an input of this process. Options B and C are techniques of the Identify Risks process. The risk urgency assessment is a tool of the corresponding process.

32. D. The question, asked more clearly, is "Which of the following options IS a tool or technique of the Perform Quantitative Risk Analysis process?" The SWOT analysis is a risk identification technique. Documents updates, in project management, are always related to outputs. The terms "Performance variance analysis" are not used in tools and techniques of this process. Expert judgment is one of the tools to be used in the process.

33. B. The question, asked more clearly, is "Which of the following options IS a tool or technique of the Plan Risk Responses process?" Risk register (option A) and the risk management plan (option D) are inputs of this process. The quantitative risk analysis (option C) is a technique of the Perform Quantitative Risk Analysis process. Strategies for opportunities or positive risks are tools of this process.

34. C. The question, asked more clearly, is "Which of the following options IS an output of the Plan Risk Management process?" The process name itself leads us to believe that we should have a risk management plan. Risk register is an output of the Identify Risks process. Options B and D are techniques of the Identify Risks process.

35. A. The question, asked more clearly, is "Which of the following options IS an output of the Identify Risks process?" The only output of the Identify Risks process is Risk register. Risk register updates will only occur from the next process (Perform Qualitative Risk Analysis). Options C and D are tools and techniques of this next process.

36. B. The question, asked more clearly, is "Which of the following options IS an output of the Perform Qualitative Risk Analysis process?" Note that You are at the project Planning. Options A and D can only occur during risk Monitoring and controlling. Risk urgency assessment is a tool of the process.

37. C. The question, asked more clearly, is "Which of the following options IS an output of the Perform Qualitative Risk Analysis process?" Please note: after Risk register is prepared in the Identify Risks process, this document will be updated in all of the next risk processes. The other options are process tools and techniques.

38. A. The question, asked more clearly, is "Which of the following options IS an output of the Plan Risk Responses process?" One of the negative risks strategies is transferring risk to a supplier by means of a contractual agreement with a risk clause. Options B and C are tools and techniques of the process. Risk reassessment (option D) occurs on the Monitor and Control Risks process.

39. B. The updated risk register is just the major product (output) of the Monitor and Control Risks process. This document will record new risks identified, reassessed current risks, and closed risks.

40. C. Remember during the exam: the term information always refers to the inputs of project management processes. The other options are tools and techniques of processes.

41. A. The Monitor and Control Risks process can identify the need for changes in scope, costs, deadlines, procurements, and other project components. The request for change (output) will be forwarded to the Perform Integrated Change Control process.

42. B. The expected monetary value is calculated by the following formula: EMV = probability × impact. By calculating the positive value (profit) and the negative value (loss) and adding them together, we will have the EMV.

$0.7 \times 200{,}000 = 140{,}000$

$0.3 \times 200{,}000 = 60{,}000$

$EMV = 140{,}000 - 60{,}000 = \$80{,}000$

43. D. The expected monetary value is calculated by the following formula: EMV = probability × impact. EMV = $20,000 × 0.8 = $16,000

44. C. If risk is 25% likely to occur in one month, the occurrence probability in the third month is 25%.

45. C. Transfer means to pass the risk forward to another party. Acceptance would not include the policy contracting. Mitigate refers to reducing the occurrence probability or the impact. Eliminate refers to a change in the project, so that this risk no longer exists.

46. A. The Delphi technique consists in obtaining expert judgment on the project technical subjects, such as scope, cost, and others, including risks.

47. A. Although additional cost and schedule delay are mentioned, the risk cause is related to the scope – work packages to be added to the WBS.

48. D. Risk register already identifies risks. Risk identification techniques include: brainstorming, Delphi technique, root cause analysis, interviews, SWOT analysis, checklist analysis, assumption analysis, cause-and-effect diagrams, flowcharts, and others.

49. C. When it comes to interview with experts, two techniques can be used: the Delphi technique (experts participate anonymously in the process) and interview (experts meet face to face in order to Identify Risks).

50. B. The Monte Carlo analysis is one of the risk quantitative analysis tools. The qualitative risk analysis tools are probability and impact matrix, risk data quality assessment, risk urgency assessment, and risk categorization.

51. B. After inserting the data in the decision tree, we (have):

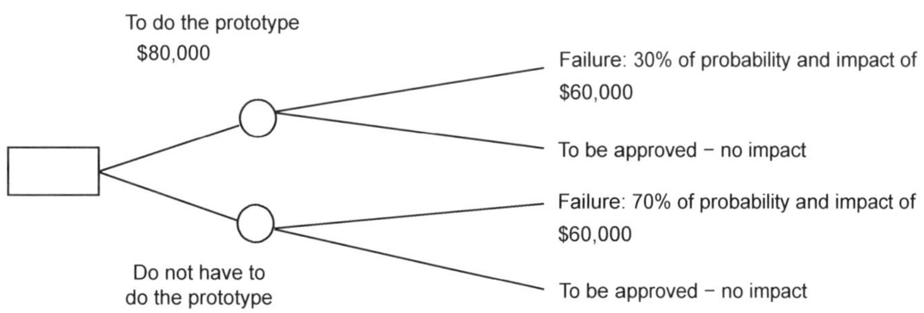

Expected monetary value:

- Make this prototype: $80,000 + (0.3 × $60,000) = $98,000
- Do not make this prototype: 0.70 × $200,000 = $140,000

Conclusion is that the company must make the prototype, since the expected monetary value (which, in this case, is loss) is lower.

52. B. After inserting the data in the decision tree, we have

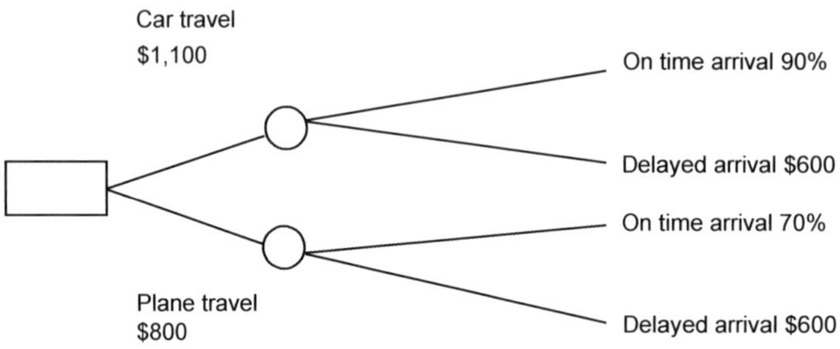

Expected monetary value:

- Car travel: $1,100 + (0.1 × $600) = $1,160
- Air travel: $800 + (0.30 × $600) = $980

The conclusion is that you should travel by plane, because the expected monetary value (in this case referring to expenses) is lower.

53. B. Enhance is a project opportunity response strategy (as opposed to mitigate). Mitigate, improve, transfer (divert, allocate) are threat (negative risk) response strategies of the project.

54. D. When removing the risk root cause, you are eliminating risk.

55. A. Create a partnership, a joint venture or a joint team with a third party, which is better qualified to complete the opportunity, are examples of the share opportunity technique.

56. B. If there is a lower cost probability, you should reduce any amount of the contingency reserves. This amount is = 0.30 × $40,000 = $12,000.

57. C. If there is a lower cost probability, you should reduce any amount of the contingency reserves. This amount is = 0.20 × $40,000 = $8,000.

58. C. Memorize this for the exam: risks must be addressed in all meetings held by the project team. Although there are specific risks meetings, in other meetings they must also be addressed.

59. C. Option A is not true, since control accounts do not include contingency reserves. Option B is not a good project management practice. Option D is not applicable, because the risk closure may not be due to the project team, and it would only be acceptable upon approval of the sponsor and/or customer. Risk closure should result in returning the company the reserve value corresponding to the risk. During the exam, think about "direct" project management, according to the procedures, without deviations like "as we already saved on this item, we can spend it on that one" or "as we are ahead of schedule here, we can rest assured about completing the next activities." Have you seen any budgeting procedure stating that "if any expected risk does not occur, the contingency reserve value of this risk may be used in another activity or there will be grounds for rewarding the project team"?

60. B. Noncritical risks must be recorded on a checklist to enable continuous monitoring throughout the project to check whether they tend to become critical. The other options are common mistakes when managing project risks.

Chapter 12

PROJECT PROCUREMENT MANAGEMENT

1. Introduction
2. General considerations on Project Procurement Management
3. Procurement management in project planning
4. Procurement management in project executing
5. Procurement management in project monitoring and controlling
6. Procurement management in project closing

Attachment I   Procurements in projects

- Additional information and reminders for the exam
- Supplementary exercises
- Questions
- Answer key

12.1 INTRODUCTION

This chapter will introduce project management processes in the Procurements knowledge area and their relevant inputs, tools, techniques, and outputs.

12.2 GENERAL CONSIDERATIONS ON PROJECT PROCUREMENT MANAGEMENT

Project Procurement Management includes the processes required to implement the purchase of goods and service contracting from external suppliers and contractors. Such processes include Planning procurements, offer request and analysis, selection of suppliers and procurement and management of resulting contracts. These processes appear at least once in the project and interact with each other and with processes of other areas. The perspective to be considered in the development of processes is that of a buyer.

According to PMI®, the Project Procurement Management must include the following processes:

- **Plan Procurements**

  The process of documenting the project procurement decisions and identifying potential suppliers.

- **Conduct Procurements**

  Obtaining information, quotations, prices, bids or proposals, as appropriate, offer analysis, choice among potential suppliers and negotiation of a written contract with each supplier.

- **Administer Procurements**

  Contract management and the relationship between the buyer and the supplier, analysis and documentation of current or past performance of a supplier in order to establish the necessary corrective actions and provide the basis for future relations with the supplier, management of contract-related changes, and, when appropriate, management of the contractual relationship with a buyer outside the project.

- **Close Procurements**

  Close and settle each contract, including resolution of any outstanding items and closing each contract applicable to a project or a project phase.

Attachment I provides further reading on procurements in projects

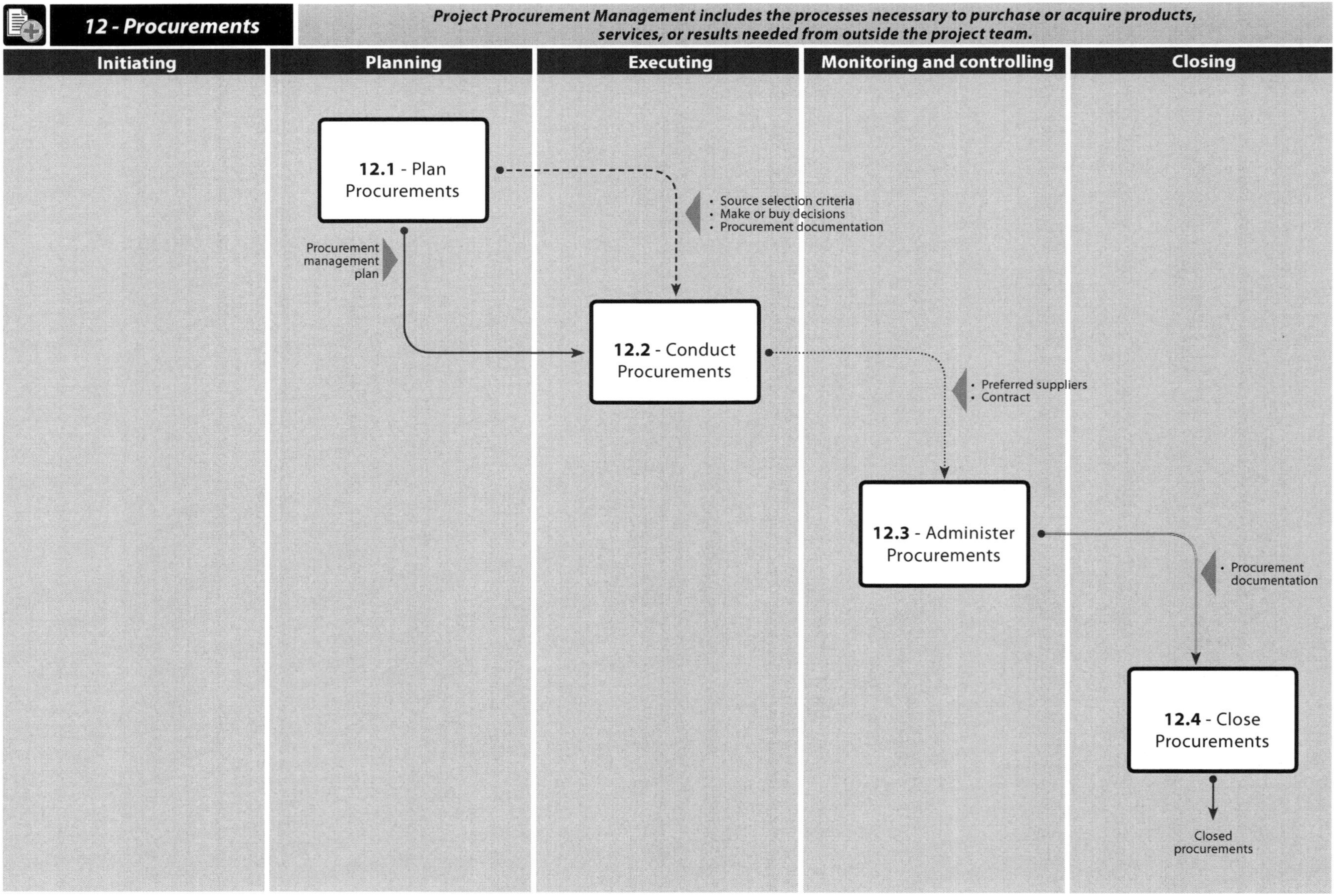
12 - Procurements
Project Procurement Management includes the processes necessary to purchase or acquire products, services, or results needed from outside the project team.
Initiating
Planning
Executing
Monitoring and controlling
Closing
12.1 - Plan Procurements
Procurement management plan
• Source selection criteria
• Make or buy decisions
• Procurement documentation
12.2 - Conduct Procurements
• Preferred suppliers
• Contract
12.3 - Administer Procurements
• Procurement documentation
12.4 - Close Procurements
Closed procurements

12.3 PROCUREMENT MANAGEMENT IN PROJECT PLANNING

According to PMI®, procurement management in project planning is comprised by the following process:

- ***Plan Procurements***

12.3.1 PLAN PROCUREMENTS (*PMBOK® GUIDE*, PROCESS 12.1)

The Plan Procurements process includes the activities of defining what will be purchased or acquired outside the organization, the definition of what will be performed in house, the analysis of related risks and the analysis of contract types to be used.

12.3.1.1 PLAN PROCUREMENTS: INPUTS, TOOLS AND TECHNIQUES, AND OUTPUTS

INPUTS

1 **Scope baseline**

The scope baseline (project scope statement, WBS, and WBS dictionary) provides information related to the needs, requirements, acceptance criteria, and other technical information that must be the basis for this process.

2 **Requirements documentation**

The requirements documentation may include

- Important information on the project requirements that must be taken into account when Planning procurements.
- Other requirements and contractual and legal implications related to safety, health, environment, insurance, intellectual and proprietary rights, licenses and permits, among others.

3 **Teaming agreements**

The existence of partnerships agreements or a *joint venture* between suppliers or between the customer and one or more suppliers must be taken into account in this process.

4 **Risk register**

Risk register provides information on identified risks, their root causes and the project uncertain assumptions, and must be taken into account in this process.

5 **Risk-related contract decisions**

Contractual decisions related to risks can include risk transference clauses for contractors and must be taken into account in this process.

6 **Activity resource requirements**

The required resources for activities provide the needs for personnel, equipment and materials to perform activities and must be taken into account in this process.

7 **Project schedule**

The project schedule provides information on the deadline of activities, contractual milestones and others, and must be taken into account in this process.

8 **Activity cost estimates**

The activity cost estimate provides the cost values expected for each activity and must be taken into account in this process.

9 **Cost performance baseline**

The project cost performance baseline provides the project planned budget and must be taken into account in this process.

10 **Enterprise environmental factors**

The enterprise environmental factors must be analyzed as to influence on the Plan Procurements process. The current availability of products and services in the market and other market conditions can influence this process.

11 **Organizational process assets**

Policies, guidelines and procedures related to procurements must be taken into account in the Plan Procurements process. A supplier's assessment system, its criteria, and assessment frequency as well as the existence of accredited suppliers can provide important information for this process. Procurement historical records of previous projects and lessons learned in the past may also help this process.

TOOLS AND TECHNIQUES

1 **Make-or-buy analysis**

The make-or-buy analysis is a technique used to determine whether a product or service will be performed within the organization or contracted or purchased from third parties. When the decision reached is purchasing, it involves further study of the buy or rent analysis, based on the company's cost and strategy considerations.

See Attachment I for more information on the make-or-buy analysis

2 **Expert judgment**

Expert opinion may play a major role in the Purchasing and procurement Planning process. It can involve specialized technicians of the products and services to be purchased, specialized in the purchasing area, lawyers to review special contracts, and other professionals.

3 **Contract types**

According to PMI®, contracts are usually included in three categories:

- Fixed price contracts or lump sum
- Cost-reimbursable contracts, subdivided into

  a. Cost-Plus-Fee (CPF) or Cost-Plus-Percentage of Cost (CPPC)

  b. Cost-Plus-Fixed-Fee (CPFF)

  c. Cost-Plus-Incentive-Fee (CPIF)

- Time and Material (T&M) contract.

OUTPUTS

1 **Procurement management plan**

The procurement management plan describes how procurements will be managed, since the development of specific documentation to contract closure. This plan may include

- Types of contracts to be used;
- Constraints and assumptions influencing the procurements;
- Standardized procurement documents, such as general supply conditions and others;
- Roles and responsibilities of the management team in relation to procurements;
- Definitions related to deadlines to execute procurement or contracting processes;
- Setting dates for major deliverables in line with the project schedule;
- Criteria for contract management and suppliers' assessment; and
- Further information on procurements and contracting.

2 **Procurement statements of work**

The contract Statement of Work (SOW) defines, for each contract, what is being acquired or contracted, based on the WBS, the WBS dictionary, and the project scope statement. The statement of work must contain detailed information about the product or service to be provided and can include drawings, rules and specifications, progress measurement, and assessment criteria, among other relevant documents. Each procurement or contracting item must be related to a SOW. However, a SOW can include multiple procurement or contracting items.

3 **Make-or-buy decisions**

Make-or-buy decisions must be documented as outputs of the Plan Procurements process, aiming not only at guiding the development of contracts and purchase orders but also the historical record for future projects.

4 **Procurement documents**

Procurement documents include a call for proposal, a request for quotation, contract templates, drawings, and specifications as well as other documents enabling the perfect understanding of the procurement or contracting subject matter by potential suppliers. Details of this documentation will be according to the product or service level of complexity as well as the purchase or procurement amount. The issuance of this documentation must meet the organization's standards and can be performed by means of direct invitations to suppliers or by means of open disclosure to stakeholders through newspapers, magazines, and the Internet.

5 **Source selection criteria**

The criteria for source selection must be established at this stage and must be taken into account in the Conduct Procurements process. Such criteria may be related to the subject matter of the procurement or contracting or even to the supplier. Regarding the subject matter of the procurement or contracting, these criteria may include price, product performance, delivery deadline, equipment life (if any), and others. Regarding the supplier, these criteria may be the supplier's technical capability, production capacity, interest in supply, and references of other supplies.

6 **Change requests**

The Plan Procurements process may result in change request in the project management plan and its subsidiary plans. Such requested changes must be processed and forwarded to the change integrated control.

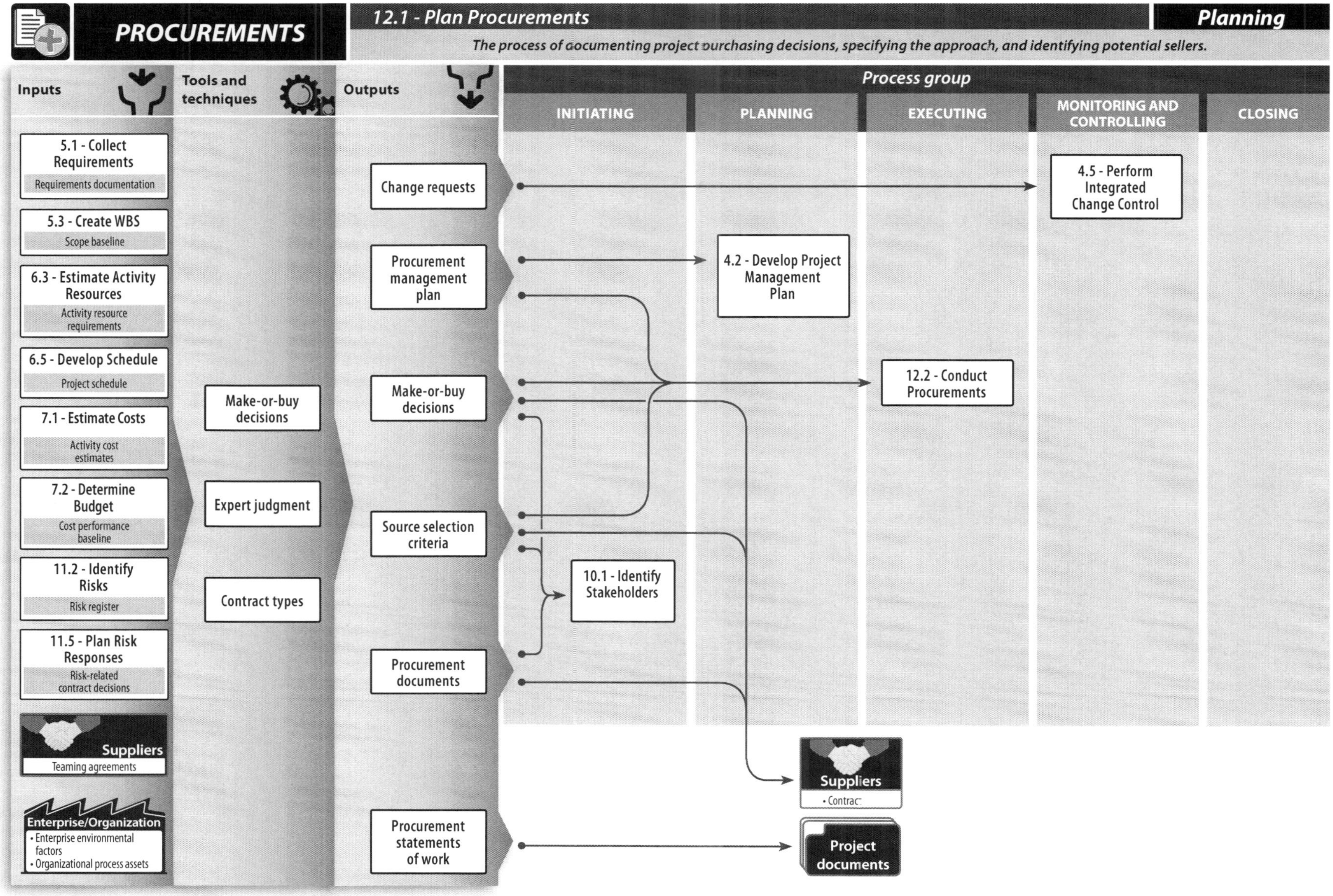
PROCUREMENTS
12.1 - Plan Procurements
Planning
The process of documenting project purchasing decisions, specifying the approach, and identifying potential sellers.
Inputs
Tools and techniques
Outputs
Process group
INITIATING
PLANNING
EXECUTING
MONITORING AND CONTROLLING
CLOSING
5.1 - Collect Requirements
Requirements documentation
5.3 - Create WBS
Scope baseline
6.3 - Estimate Activity Resources
Activity resource requirements
6.5 - Develop Schedule
Project schedule
7.1 - Estimate Costs
Activity cost estimates
7.2 - Determine Budget
Cost performance baseline
11.2 - Identify Risks
Risk register
11.5 - Plan Risk Responses
Risk-related contract decisions
Suppliers
Teaming agreements
Enterprise/Organization
• Enterprise environmental factors
• Organizational process assets
Make-or-buy decisions
Expert judgment
Contract types
Change requests
Procurement management plan
Make-or-buy decisions
Source selection criteria
Procurement documents
Procurement statements of work
4.5 - Perform Integrated Change Control
4.2 - Develop Project Management Plan
12.2 - Conduct Procurements
10.1 - Identify Stakeholders
Suppliers
• Contrac
Project documents

12.4 PROCUREMENT MANAGEMENT IN PROJECT EXECUTING

According to PMI®, procurement management in project executing is composed of the following process:

- *Conduct Procurements*

12.4.1 CONDUCT PROCUREMENTS (*PMBOK® GUIDE*, PROCESS 12.2)

The Conduct Procurements process is obtaining responses from suppliers, selecting a supplier, and awarding a contract. In this process, the project team will receive quotations and proposals and will apply the selection criteria previously set to one or more suppliers qualified to perform the work.

Obtaining responses from suppliers is obtaining proposals and quotations for project services and products to be contracted or purchased. The process considers the definitions of what must be purchased or contracted, which occurred in previous procurement processes, and it begins by sending bidding documents to potential suppliers as a request for proposal and a request for quotation. The process's main objective is ensuring that all potential suppliers have complete understanding of the objectives of contracting or procurement. Another objective is developing the qualified seller list, which can be used for the project and other projects of the organization.

12.4.1.1 CONDUCT PROCUREMENTS: INPUTS, TOOLS AND TECHNIQUES, AND OUTPUTS

INPUTS

1 **Project management plan**

The project management plan and its subsidiary plans must be taken into account in this process, including risk register and potential risk-related contractual agreements.

2 **Procurement documents**

Procurement documents, such as the Request for Quotation and the Request for Proposal, must be taken into account when developing this process.

3 **Source selection criteria**

The organization assessment criteria or those included in the procurement management plan must be taken into account in this process. These criteria are used to classify and sort proposals. For example, when preparing a price quotation for commercial items, where the product characteristics are perfectly known, the price criterion may be the deciding factor when contracting. Therefore, the company submitting the lowest price would be placed first, the one with the second lowest price second, and so on. The criteria are also used for early decommissioning of suppliers not meeting the assessment basic requirements.

A screening system uses specific predetermined criteria for the suppliers' initial selection. For example, it can be determined that the first selection criterion be the allocation of a professional with proven experience in developing the contract subject matter. Suppliers not submitting this professional in the proposal must be automatically disqualified, regardless of other criteria.

4 **Qualified seller list**

In general, companies have a historical database of supplies and suppliers qualified in previous projects, which allows quick reference for the current project procurements. This database can be simple, such as a list of suppliers, or sophisticated, containing assessments related to the performance of the supplied product, suppliers' performance, project cooperation, on-time deliverables, and other information. Even with the existence of this database, the project team can develop its qualified seller list, based on the project's specific needs and update of the existing database.

The qualified seller list contains suppliers who will be required to submit a proposal or quotation. It is always desirable that this list contains a fair amount of qualified suppliers. However, in a given project, the following conditions may also occur: single source and preferred source.

- **Exclusive source**

  Exclusive source occurs when there is only one supplier for the bid subject matter. In this case, the supplier's monopoly enables it to create its own supply rules, including minimum delivery deadlines, little chance of reducing bid amounts, performance and quality requirements set unilaterally by the supplier, among others. Negotiation possibilities tend to be lower, while risks tend to be higher for the buyer.

- **Preferred source**

  Preferred source occurs when there are several possible suppliers, but the corporate decision is choosing a supplier in advance, for reasons that must be documented. One reason may be the long relationship between the organization and the supplier. In this case, results of previous projects must be checked, such as concerns about cost, deadline, quality, and performance of the product and the supplier. The actual qualification of the supplier for the supply in question must also be checked. The degree of research and the assessment of the factors above determine the supply risk degree.

5 **Seller proposals**

Proposals are documents prepared by potential suppliers outlining their plans for compliance with the contract, including proposals for cost, deadlines, compliance with performance and quality criteria as well as all other requirements included in procurement documentation. The Request suppliers' response process is completed when proposals are received and potential requests for oral presentations from suppliers.

6 **Project documents**

Any and all project document containing information that influences procurements must be taken into account in this process, such as drawings, specifications, procedures, policies, and others.

7 **Make-or-buy decisions**

Make-or-buy decisions must be taken into account in this process.

8 **Teaming agreements**

The existence of partnerships agreements or a *joint venture* between suppliers or between the customer and one or more suppliers must be taken into account in this process.

9 **Organizational process assets**

Organizational process assets may contain information about suppliers, prices and quotations from previous projects as well as information on suppliers qualified or selected by the organization.

TOOLS AND TECHNIQUES

1 **Bidder conferences**

Bidder conferences, also called prebid meetings, are a common practice for major project purchases. These are meetings with potential suppliers of the project, aiming to strengthening the requirements to be included in the request for proposal and enabling questioning suppliers. Generally, these meetings are attended by the project manager, those responsible for procurements, and a representative of the technical area of the bid subject matter. All potential suppliers must be equally treated by the project team in order to produce the best results possible. Important questions and their responses must be sent to all potential suppliers. One of the major advantages of such meetings is enabling the incorporation of improvements in the request for proposal prior to its issuance.

2 **Proposal evaluation techniques**

Proposal assessment techniques include tools and techniques dealt with above as well as a combination of them. In all techniques, some expert opinion and some form of assessment criteria must be used. Anyway, the offer price or cost must be analyzed in terms of type of expected contract.

- **Fixed-price contract**

  In the request for proposal, it is important to indicate prices for each item of the contract in order to compare suppliers' offers. Specific and special contractual items, such as price of replacement items, the amount determined for warranty, and special tests, may represent a high-value proposal for suppliers.

- **Agreement for cost-reimbursable or time and material**

  This contract type demands in-detail analysis of the costs submitted by suppliers. The analysis must involve direct costs (materials, labor, and others), indirect costs (travel, accommodation, management personnel, and others), and *overhead* (apportionment of the supplier's office expenses, high costs of salaries of the supplier's senior management, and profit, among others).

3 **Independent estimates**

Independent estimates, also named achievable cost estimates, are used to compare the prices offered. Generally, these estimates are developed for major purchases or contracting of the project, a professional with experience in estimating costs in similar works. These estimates can be performed by examining the request for proposal and preparing bottom-up estimating and must be preferably performed without the responsible professional being aware of the suppliers' estimating. Independent estimate is used to create a comfort zone in procurement analysis and management.

If differences are significant, this may indicate that the contract statement of work was not appropriate, that the supplier skipped considerations and activities or that there was a market change.

4 **Expert judgment**

Expert opinion may be used as the basis for selecting suppliers. It can be inside the organization, such as advice legal, finance, accounting, engineering and maintenance, or outside the organization by using consultants and specialized companies.

5 **Advertising**

Publishing advertisements in specialized newspapers and publications helps expand the list of existing suppliers and can assist in the Conduct Procurements process.

6 **Internet search**

The Internet can be used as a tool for finding suppliers, materials, and equipment.

7 **Procurement negotiations**

Procurement negotiations include a discussion between the buyer and potential suppliers in order to obtain a consensus on the several criteria of the contract, such as cost, deadline, quality and performance criteria, and acceptance of known risks. Negotiation must also include addressing other factors such as property rights, product warranty, contract management, and other payment methods. In order to negotiate major contracts for the project, it is desirable that both the organization and the supplier have a multifunctional negotiation team, with representatives of technical and commercial areas and even the participation of the legal area. Negotiations will be conducted under the *win-win* view in order to enable both parties to benefit from the contract. Negotiations under the *win-lose* view, seeking maximum concessions by the other party is detrimental to the project, and, if performed, they would tend to be cause for contract revisions and changes. Negotiations are completed when an agreement with a supplier is reached and the final contract is drawn up and signed by both parties.

OUTPUTS

1 **Selected sellers**

Selected sellers are those selected to participate in the project, resulting from previous assessments and negotiations.

2 **Procurement contract award**

The contract is a legal instrument entered into between the buyer and supplier which governs the purchase of goods or services. Generally, the contract must contain the following:

- Scope of services
- Location facilities or found difficulties where the services will be performed
- Mobilization deadlines, performance of services and demobilization
- Documents contained in the contract (drawings, specifications, quantity spreadsheets, etc.)
- Contractor's obligations and responsibilities – related to labor, material, and equipment supply and performance of services
- Contractor's obligations and responsibilities
- Contracting and payment method
- The bank letter of guarantee requirement
- Price adjustment
- Measurement criteria of services performed
- Acceptance criteria of services performed or of products
- Considerations of extra-contractual services
- Fine-related provisions
- Assurance criteria of services performed or of products
- Criteria for contract termination
- Any other information relevant to procurement

3 **Resource calendars**

The contract and additional documents define dates for mobilization and demobilization of major resources to be allocated in the contract execution.

4 **Change requests**

If changes occur during this process, they will be forwarded for review and approval and, if approved, they must be implemented.

5 **Project management plan updates**

The project management plan and especially the procurement management plan must be updated according to procurements executed. In addition, the contract management plan must be executed and used for procurements or significant purchases. This plan consists in defining how provision will be assessed and audited according to the aspects defined during contracting and the statement of work. This plan will be developed during this phase, and its activities will be developed as part of Monitoring and controlling processes.

6 Project document updates

Any and all project document that have been influenced by the Conduct Procurements process must be updated; this is not limited to the following:

- Requirements documentation
- Requirements traceability matrix
- Risk register

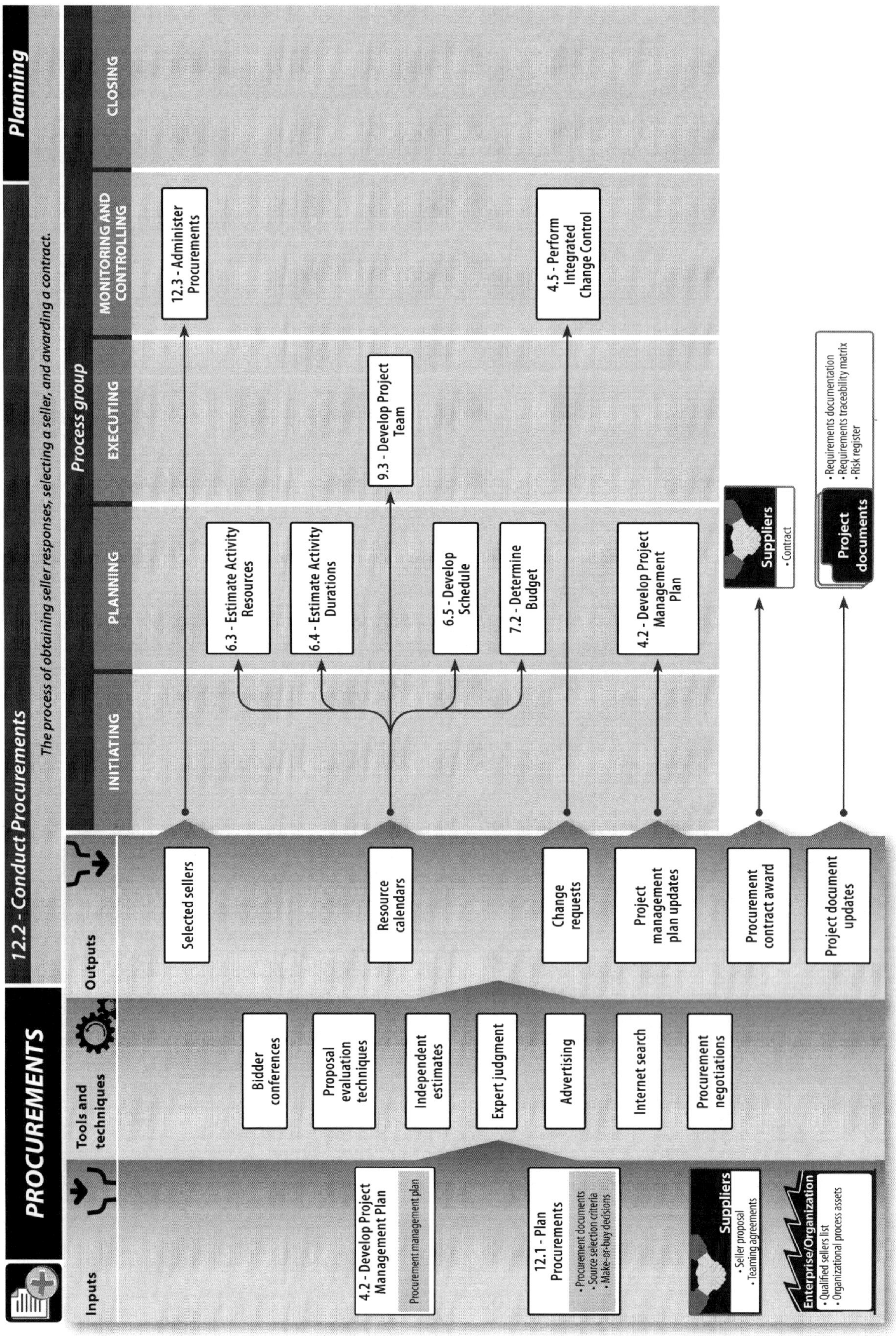
PROCUREMENTS
12.2 - Conduct Procurements
Planning
The process of obtaining seller responses, selecting a seller, and awarding a contract.
Inputs
Tools and techniques
Outputs
Process group
INITIATING
PLANNING
EXECUTING
MONITORING AND CONTROLLING
CLOSING
4.2 - Develop Project Management Plan
Procurement management plan
12.1 - Plan Procurements
• Procurement documents
• Source selection criteria
• Make-or-buy decisions
Suppliers
• Seller proposal
• Teaming agreements
Enterprise/Organization
• Qualified sellers list
• Organizational process assets
Bidder conferences
Proposal evaluation techniques
Independent estimates
Expert judgment
Advertising
Internet search
Procurement negotiations
Selected sellers
Resource calendars
Change requests
Project management plan updates
Procurement contract award
Project document updates
6.3 - Estimate Activity Resources
6.4 - Estimate Activity Durations
6.5 - Develop Schedule
7.2 - Determine Budget
4.2 - Develop Project Management Plan
9.3 - Develop Project Team
12.3 - Administer Procurements
4.5 - Perform Integrated Change Control
Suppliers
• Contract
Project documents
• Requirements documentation
• Requirements traceability matrix
• Risk register

12.5 PROCUREMENT MANAGEMENT IN PROJECT MONITORING AND CONTROLLING

According to PMI®, procurement management in project monitoring and controlling is composed by the following process:

- ***Administer Procurements***

12.5.1 ADMINISTER PROCUREMENTS (*PMBOK® GUIDE,* PROCESS 12.3)

The Administer Procurements process includes monitoring suppliers' performance related to meeting contractual requirements and verifying that contractual requirements are complied with. The Administer Procurements process must focus not only on managing the contract of each particular supplier but also on managing the relationships between all project suppliers. Procurement management is usually performed by a professional from the procurement department assigned to the project or inside the procurement department. Whichever way you choose, it is the project manager's responsibility for managing project contracts.

According to PMI®, several processes are applied to procurement management, including

- ***Direct and Manage Project Execution*** to authorize the work of the contractor in a timely manner
- ***Report Performance*** to monitor costs, schedule, and the contractor technical performance
- ***Perform Quality Control*** to inspect and verify the contractor product suitability
- ***Perform Integrated Change Control*** to ensure that changes are properly approved and that all people who need to know them are aware of such changes
- ***Monitor and Control Risks*** to ensure that risks are mitigated

In addition to these processes, procurement management has a contract financial management component, in order to ensure that contractually determined payment conditions are in compliance with and that payments to the supplier are consistent with the work progress compliance, as defined in the contract.

12.5.1.1 ADMINISTER PROCUREMENTS: INPUTS, TOOLS AND TECHNIQUES, AND OUTPUTS

INPUTS

1 **Procurement documents**

Procurement documents provide the information necessary to procurement management, such as specifications, measurement criteria, and acceptance of services or products, and must be taken into account in this process.

2 **Project management plan**

The project management plan and especially the procurement management plan must be taken into account in this process.

3 **Contract**

The contract provides the information necessary for procurement management, such as scope, deadlines, warranties and others, and must be taken into account in this process.

4 **Performance reports**

Suppliers' performance reporting inform on the suppliers' actual performance as compared to the performance expected at baseline and determined in the contract. Analyzing results of suppliers' performance can bring about change requests or recommendations for corrective and preventive actions.

5 **Approved change requests**

Analysis of approved change requests can influence contract management and result in new change requests or recommendations for corrective and preventive actions.

6 **Work performance information**

Work performance information are provided by performance reporting and it must be taken into account in this process.

TOOLS AND TECHNIQUES

1 **Contract change control system**

The contract change control system is intended to establish a formal process in which the contract can be changed. It describes how requests must be made to change the contract, how requests must be analyzed, and who has the authority to approve these changes. It must also include procedures for monitoring changes and dispute resolution.

2 **Procurement performance reviews**

Procurement performance reviews conducted by the buyer is aimed at comparing suppliers' performance as compared to contractual requirements. This analysis must be performed periodically in order to prevent that deviations are discovered only when it became stranded. Contractual requirements to be compared include, but are not limited to

- Scope compliance,
- Meeting deadlines,
- Compliance with quality requirements,
- Compliance with expected costs, and
- Treatment of supplier liability risks.

Failure to meet contractual requirements by the supplier can result in fines, as provided by the contract, and even termination.

3 **Inspections and audits**

Inspections and audits are requested by the buyer to check for deficiencies in the product or the service subject matter of the supplier's contract. These activities can be developed by the purchaser, the project team members, or by a specialized company contracted for that purpose.

4 **Performance reporting**

Performance reporting provides information on suppliers' performance, which can be compared to contractual requirements and can identify the need for corrective or preventive actions.

5 **Payment systems**

The payment system is intended to establish a formal process by which payments will be made to the supplier. This system may be the organization's own system or a system developed exclusively for the project. Whatever its form, the contract manager is responsible for releasing payments to the supplier.

6 **Claims administration**

Claims administration is intended to establish a formal process for handling claims and complaints from the supplier that have not been accepted by the buyer. These claims are usually caused by changes implemented in contractual requirements, for which the supplier requires the right to receive an additional value to the contract and the buyer deems to be the suppliers' responsibility. These claims can be dealt with through the following ways:

- Meetings between the supplier and the buyer in order to reach a consensus and agreement
- Arbitration, consisting of a meeting between the supplier, the buyer and a third party, named mediator, in order to reach a consensus and an agreement
- Legal action, usually brought by the supplier for trial in a court of law.

7 **Records management system**

The records management system is intended to establish a formal process by which all contract documentation is properly filed. The system purpose, in addition to being a source of lessons learned, is safeguarding the information for complaints and lawsuits from suppliers.

OUTPUTS

1 **Procurement documentation**

Procurement documentation may be, among others, the actual contract and its attachments, the contract schedule, the services measurement bulletin, contractual amendments, and the provisional and final acceptance terms.

2 **Organizational process assets updates**

The Administer Procurements process of the contract can identify new processes or opportunities for improvements in the organization's contract management procedures and policies. All documentation related to contract management, such as the contract and its attachments, services measurement bulletins and contractual amendments, must be documented as lessons learned from the project.

3 **Change requests**

Procurement management can generate implementation change needs in the processes towards deadline recovery or cost reduction. These changes must be submitted for review, and, if approved, they must be implemented.

4 **Project management plan updates**

The project management plan and, in particular, the procurement management plan must be updated after changes are approved as a result of the procurement management.

PROCUREMENTS

12.3 - Administer Procurements

Monitoring and controlling

The process of managing procurement relationships, monitoring contract performance, and making changes and corrections as needed.

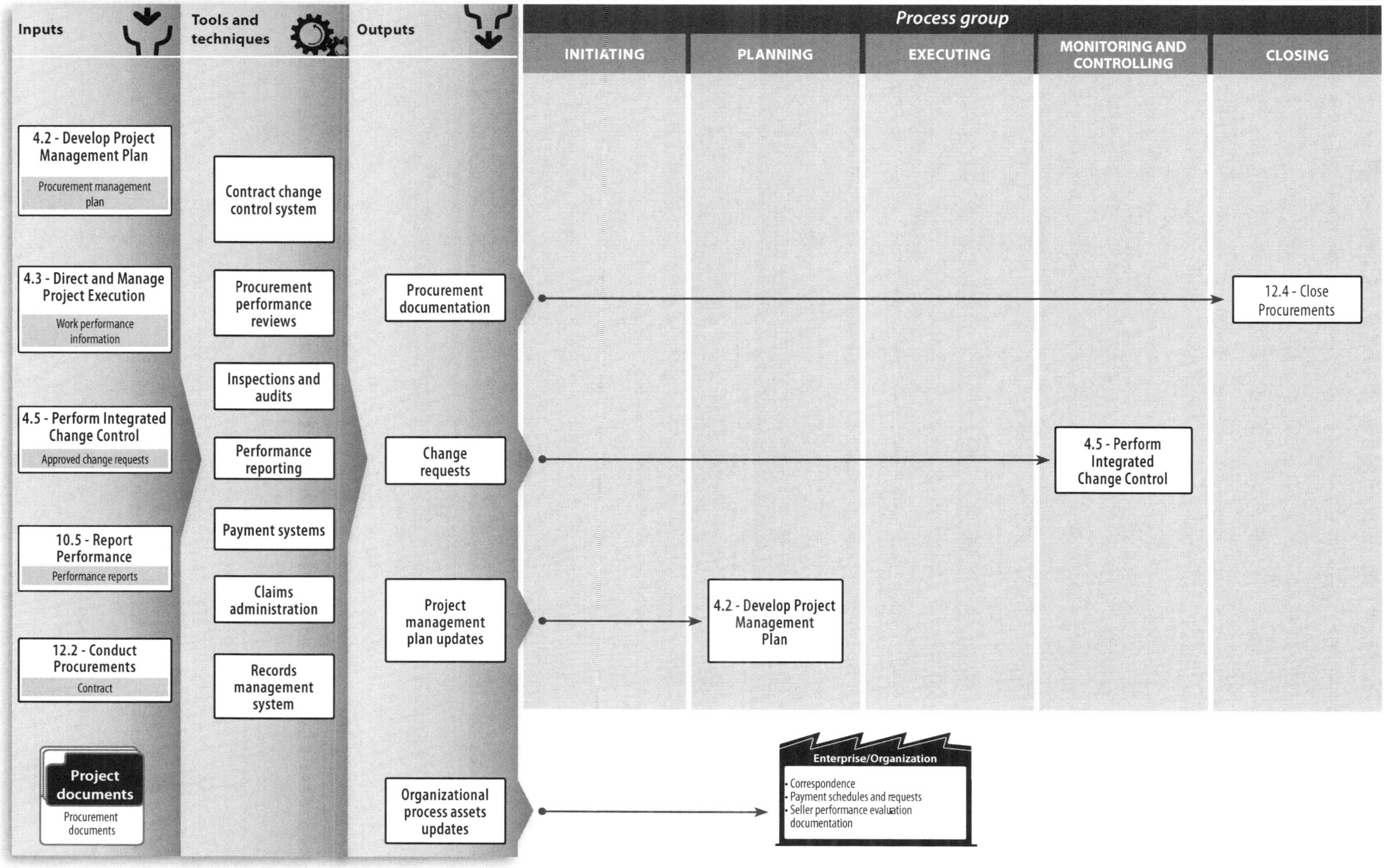

12.6 PROCUREMENT MANAGEMENT IN PROJECT CLOSING

According to PMI®, the procurement management in project closing is composed of by a process, namely,

- ***Close Procurements***

12.6.1 CLOSE PROCUREMENTS (*PMBOK® GUIDE*, PROCESS 12.4)

The Close procurement process consists of checking the product and arranging the settlement of contractual terms. Product verification can occur at any stage of the project and may comprise one or multiple deliverables. Settlement of contractual terms is checking that all contractual requirements have been met and approved changes, accepted by the supplier, were implemented. This process also involves updating records related to the contract management, for future reference in case of suppliers' claims and also to serve as lessons learned for other projects. Contract termination is also considered in this process and may result from a mutual agreement between the parties or noncompliance of obligations by either party. In this case, contract termination must follow termination instructions set forth in the contract.

12.6.1.1 CLOSE PROCUREMENTS: INPUTS, TOOLS AND TECHNIQUES, AND OUTPUTS

INPUTS

1 **Project management plan**

The project management plan and, in particular, the procurement management plan, must be taken into account in this process.

2 **Procurement documentation**

All procurement documentation must be collected, indexed and filed. Information on schedule, scope, quality, contract cost performance, payment record, results of inspections and others must be cataloged. This information can be used as lessons learned and as a basis for assessing suppliers for future contracts.

TOOLS AND TECHNIQUES

1 **Procurement audits**

Procurement audits consist in assessing the results obtained in the contract, in order to record information on the procurement process and the supplier and to serve as a reference for future procurements.

2 **Negotiated settlements**

It is desirable that all disagreements, complaints, claims, and disputes between the parties are discussed, negotiated, and agreed at the end of procurement. This prevents the parties from taking alternative measures such as mediation, external arbitration, and even lawsuits.

3 **Records management system**

The records management system helps to fill the project documentation and must be used in this process.

OUTPUTS

1 Closed procurements

The major output of the Close Procurements process is formalization, performed by the buyer to the supplier, at the end of the contract and obtaining formal acceptance from such supplier.

2 Organizational process assets updates

The Close Procurements process can identify new processes or opportunities for improvements in the procurement closure procedures and policies. All documentation related to the contract termination must be considered and filed as lessons learned from the project.

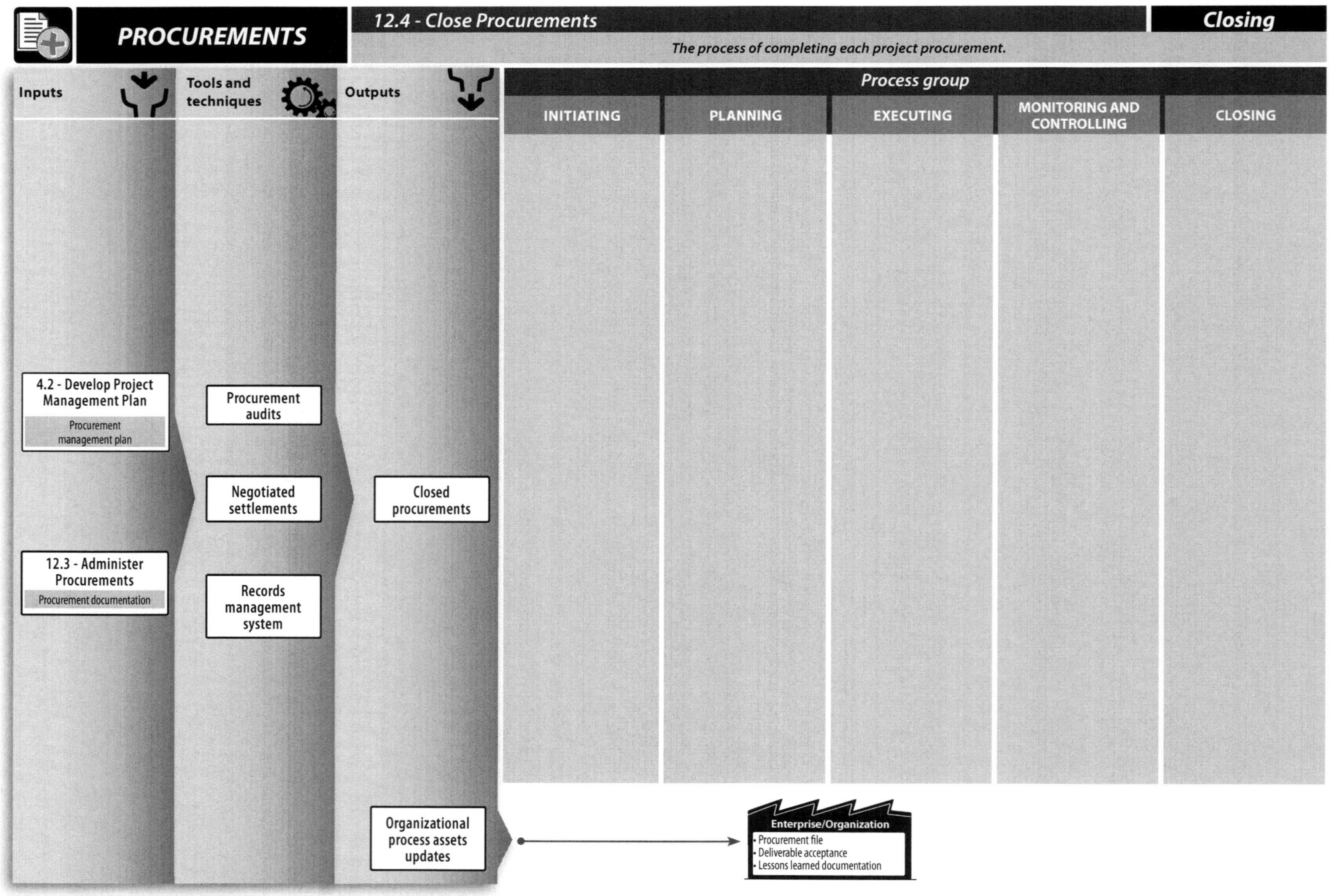
PROCUREMENTS
12.4 - Close Procurements
Closing
The process of completing each project procurement.
Inputs
Tools and techniques
Outputs
Process group
INITIATING
PLANNING
EXECUTING
MONITORING AND CONTROLLING
CLOSING
4.2 - Develop Project Management Plan
Procurement management plan
12.3 - Administer Procurements
Procurement documentation
Procurement audits
Negotiated settlements
Records management system
Closed procurements
Organizational process assets updates
Enterprise/Organization
• Procurement file
• Deliverable acceptance
• Lessons learned documentation

Attachment I

PROCUREMENTS IN PROJECTS

PROCUREMENTS IN PROJECTS

1 INTRODUCTION

In projects, in addition to specific activities of the project team, we often find the need for purchasing materials, equipment, and other supplies as well as contracting services. This need arises from the very complexity of projects and the variety of activities comprising them. In general, an organization does not have, by itself, full knowledge and the technical capacity to produce all necessary materials and equipment or the qualified and/or available personnel to implement all project activities. Therefore, procurements and contracting play a fundamental role in successfully completing a project.

2 MAKE-OR-BUY ANALYSIS

The *make-or-buy* analysis aims at defining which project elements will be executed by the project team and which elements will be contracted or purchased outside the organization. These elements, in general, refer to the work packages defined in the Work Breakdown Structure (WBS). Factors influencing this analysis may include the service complexity, technical knowledge, suppliers' expertise, the organization production capacity, risk, deadline, costs and quality, among others. In general, this analysis covers the following definitions:

- **Make mandatory**

  This definition is often used for activities involving the company's own technology or when a high control level to perform the activity is desired. Another reason for this definition is the labor availability within the organization, provided that it meets the level of expertise required to perform the activity.

- **Compulsory purchase**

  This definition is usually made for activities that the company is unable to perform or when qualified people are not available to perform them at the required time.

- **Make-or-buy**

  Definitions are related to activities that can be performed both inside the organization and outside by contractors. Selecting one or another definition will depend on factors interfering in these activities, such as time, cost, deadline, and quality. The organization may also choose to perform part of the activity and contract the remaining part with third parties.

This must generate a list of activities to be performed internally, with activities to be contracted. In order to be valid, this analysis must use reliable and cost data regarding the project date. When the decision reached is purchasing, it involves further study of the buy or rent analysis, based on the company's cost and strategy considerations.

Example of exam question

Question: It is necessary to use a piece of equipment in your project. This equipment has a daily lease cost of $240. The equipment purchase involves $2,000 plus a daily cost of $40. How long will it take for the purchase cost to equal the lease?

Answer: Making "d" and the number of days, we have:

$\$240d = \$2000 + \$40d$

$\$240d - \$40d = \$2000$

$\$200d = \$2000$

$d = 2000/200$

$d = 10$ days

3 PROCUREMENT CATEGORIES

In a project, procurements can have a wide range of features. Some procurements may be complex and others simpler or routine. Some purchases may have a high-risk degree, while others do not. Some purchases require that the buyer and the supplier enter into a contract, while others can be made by sending e-mail or even online via the Internet. Purchase categorization helps managing them according to their characteristics, risk, and complexity. In general, procurements can be included in the following categories:

- **High-complexity procurements (high risk)**

  These are procurements of something not existing yet, with a high monetary value and which generally have a high risk for the project. Such procurements may require the need for specifications, drawings, and other documents defining the project objective related to this procurement. As examples, we can have contracting a company to build a bridge or a commercial building and contracting a company to develop a software application exclusively for the organization.

- **Low-complexity procurements (low risk)**

  These are procurements of commercially available products, with a high monetary value and usually do not have a high risk for the project. As examples, we may have buying a car and buying a group of new computers.

- **Routine procurement**

  These are purchases of routinely used materials and contracting simple services not critical to successfully completing the project. As examples, we may have buying a small quantity of screws and contracting catering for the project.

- **Strategic procurements**

  These are purchases of goods or services considered as strategic by the organization, usually defined by the senior management. As an example, we have purchasing a plot of land for the company's future industrial unit.

4 CONTRACT TYPE SELECTION

Selecting the contract type is essential to both the buyer and the supplier. The contract type and its conditions define the degree of risk assumed by both of them. In this selection, in addition of the contract scope, other factors must be taken into account, such as the project life cycle, known risks and the ability of the project team to define exactly what it wishes to contract in a clear and definite way.

According to PMI®, contracts are usually included in three categories:

- Fixed price contracts or lump sum
- Cost-reimbursable contracts, subdivided into
    a. Cost-Plus Fee (CPF) or Cost-Plus-Percentage of Cost (CPPC)
    b. Cost-Plus-Fixed-Fee (CPFF)
    c. Cost-Plus-Incentive-Fee (CPIF)
- Time and Material (T&M) contract

4.1 FIXED-PRICE CONTRACTS OR LUMP SUM

Fixed-price contracts or lump sum define a fixed total price for a well-defined product. However, sometimes such contracts may include incentives for the supplier based on its achievement of the goals and objectives established in the contract. Longtime contracts may also include adjustment clauses to prevent losses due to changes to economic conditions.

The key element of this type of contract is the requirement the contractor to provide the subject matter of the contract, regardless of the circumstances. If the contract execution demanded more resources or cost more to the supplier, he or she alone is responsible for the losses. Therefore, when selecting this type of contract, the buyer must have a complete and clearly defined SOW of the contract.

Fixed-price contracts require, in general, less management effort by the buyer. However, if periodic payments to the supplier are expected, the buyer must contractually establish how the work progress will be assessed or measured as well as restrain payments to reach the expected result in each period.

Main risks related to fixed-price contracts may be related to inaccuracy when defining the subject matter of the contract. If the SOW of the contract is not complete or raises doubts, the supplier will probably increase the value to cover this risk. Another possible risk is breach of contract if the supplier finds or glimpses financial losses in it. Changes in scope are almost always harmful when using this contract type, since these changes are usually considered by the supplier as opportunities to increase its earnings.

The current trend of private companies is increasing the use of this contract type to the detriment of other types of contracts.

4.2 COST-REIMBURSABLE CONTRACTS

Cost-reimbursable contracts define the payment (refund) to the supplier of the actual cost plus a fee that usually represents the supplier's profit. These contracts are generally used when it is not possible to detail the contract service by the buyer. The buyer knows the final project need, but who will describe the SOW will be the contract supplier. For that purpose, there are virtually no risks, what can make the contract price cheaper than if it were a fixed-price contract. A typical example is contracts of research and development projects.

Cost-reimbursable contracts require, in general, higher management effort by the buyer. Given that costs are reimbursed, there is no interest from the supplier in seeking alternatives that are more economical. This often requires frequent analysis of the supplier's invoicing. However, if periodic payments to the supplier are expected, the buyer must contractually establish it how the work progress will be assessed or measured as well as restrain payments to reach the expected result in each period. In order to establish that, it is necessary to request from the supplier, at the time of bidding, a preliminary SOW containing the percentage weights of each work phase.

The most common types of cost-reimbursable contracts are:

a. Cost-Plus Fee (CPF) or Cost-Plus-Percentage of Cost (CPPC)

This type of contracts define the payment (refund) to the supplier for the actual cost-plus fee calculated as a percentage of the actual cost. This type of contract is detrimental to the project because there is no incentive to the supplier in lowering costs, since the fee increases when costs are higher. This type of contract is forbidden in the United States and many government agencies.

b. Cost-Plus-Fixed-Fee (CPFF)

Such contracts define the payment (refund) to the supplier for the actual costs plus a fixed percentage over the estimated costs. This percentage does not vary with actual costs, unless changes are made in the work to be performed. These are generally used when it is difficult obtaining cost estimates or when they have a high uncertainty degree. In such contracts, the supplier has no incentive to Control Costs, since cost variances do not affect the fee.

c. Cost-Plus-Incentive-Fee (CPIF)

Such contracts define the payment (refund) to the supplier for the actual costs plus a predetermined fee rate usually subject to achieving the contract of goals and objectives. This fee can also have a maximum and minimum value related to the contract actual costs. This means that the supplier has an incentive to reduce costs. CPIF contracts, in general, may have five components, namely, target cost, target fee, minimum fee, and the rate adjustment formula for variance of the supplier's performance. This formula, usually shown as the quotient of two numbers (90/10, 80/20, for instance) represents the sharing proportion of a value agreed between the contractor and the supplier if the latter reaches one or more project objectives. These goals, which can be related to reducing the target cost or advance deadlines, set the contractor and the supplier in line with each other in order to achieve the same goal. An example of this compensation contract can be seen below.

COMPONENT	AMOUNT
Target cost	$100,000
Target fee rate	10%
Minimum rate (related to the target cost)	7%
Maximum rate (related to the target cost)	14%
Sharing formula	80/20
Total contract cost	$110,000

This contract, therefore, has the following considerations:

- If the supplier reaches the target cost, its fee will be $10,000, related to 10% of the target cost, and the contract will cost $110,000.
- If the supplier is able to reduce the cost target, the difference between that and the actual cost will be shared between the contractor (80%) and the supplier (20%), limited to a maximum value, corresponding to 14% of target cost.
- If the supplier exceeds the target cost, the difference between this cost and the actual one will be deducted from the supplier's target fee, at the proportion of 20%, limited to a maximum of 3% of the target cost.

The following examples demonstrate these considerations:

a. **Actual cost amount = $90,000**

Amount to be paid to the supplier:

$10,000 + 20% of (100,000 – 90,000) = $12,000

Contract total cost = **$102,000**

b. **Actual cost amount = $78,000**

Amount to be paid to the supplier:

$10,000 + 20% of (100,000 – 78,000) – over 14% = $10,000 + $4,400 – 400 = $14,000 (14% limit)

Contract total cost = **$92,000**

c. **Actual cost amount = $110,000**

Amount to be paid to the supplier:

$10,000 – 20% of (110,000 – 100,000) = $8,000

Contract total cost = **$118,000**

d. **Actual cost amount = $120,000**

Amount to be paid to the supplier:

$10,000 – 20% of (120,000 – 100,000) + 3% surplus of $10,000 – $4,000 + $1,000 = $7,000 (7% limit)

Contract total cost = **$127,000**

These types of contracts may also have, in addition to costs, other incentive clauses, for example, compliance with delivery dates, and product performance. To be effective, these incentives must be related to something that can be measured or observed, and rates must be subject to addition or discount of the amounts expected for the supplier.

4.3 TIME AND MATERIAL (T&M) CONTRACT

Time and material contracts define the payment to the supplier based on a fixed price per hour (fixed-price contract) and material costs (cost-reimbursable contract). Generally, these contracts are used in short-term, small monetary value contracts, and is a good option, for example, to increase labor in a work team, but it required the contractor's supervision. They are appropriate when it is not possible to estimate the contract amount of work, its cost, or duration. However, in view of the possibility of exceeding cost values, a limit for the contract is usually set, which can only be revoked by the project manager.

4.4 CONTRACT TYPE VARIANCES

There are contracts that are variances of the contracts presented above. Among them, the following ones can be mentioned:

- **Fixed-price with incentive**

  This contract defines a fixed payment to the supplier, plus an incentive amount if the supplier meets the contract goals and objectives. These objectives and targets may be related to cost, time, and quality. It is used when the buyer has the SOW of the contract, but it is not necessarily detailed to use the fixed-price contract. Such incentive fee may be performed in the same way as the CPIF contracts.

- **Fixed-price with a reward fee**

  This contract defines a fixed payment to the supplier, plus an amount related to a fixed rate if the supplier meets the contract goals and objectives. These objectives and targets may be related to cost, time, and quality. The difference in relation to the previous item is that the rate is fixed and not dependent on cost variance.

- **Fixed price with adjustment clause**

  This contract defines a fixed payment to the supplier, plus an adjustment amount to cover economic contingencies. Such contracts are generally used in long-term services, and adjustment values are defined based on variances in economic indices.

- **Fixed price with indefinite quantity**

  This contract defines the payment of an amount to the supplier, resulting from multiplying the fixed unit amount by the item's actual amount of service performed. It is generally used when the work to be performed is known, but not the exact quantities. The supplier's services are required to be supervised by the contractor, especially in activities with measurements made possible only during the activity execution, for example, piling of a building.

- **Cost and cost participation**

  This contract defines the payment of an amount (refund) to the supplier for costs incurred, without any additional profit or incentive fee or a rate significantly lower than that applied commercially by other companies. This contract type is generally used when the supplier will obtain future gains from the contract product.

- **Men-hours**

  This contract differs from the time and material contract since all materials are provided by the contractor and only the supplier's labor is contracted.

5 PROCUREMENT MANAGEMENT PLAN

The procurement management plan may be, according to the complexity of the purchasing needs and the amount of contracts, simple and summarized in a materials quotation page or complex and with a large volume of descriptive pages of all the items to be purchased, with specifications, drawings, and other project documents. Anyway, the management plan must go through three distinct phases. Initially, the project must define what must be purchased or contracted and how procurement will be made. Later on, the project will select and contract the product or service supplier. Finally, it will trigger the supplier's management for execution of the contract or service hired and complete planned deliverables.

5.1 DECIDING WHAT TO BUY

The decision of what must be purchased by the project and preparing the procurement management is crucial to successfully complete the project.

This activity must be based on the project scope statement, the WBS, the WBS dictionary, cost estimates, and must involve the make or buy analysis. After defining what will be performed internally and issuing the list of products or services to be purchased, they must be divided into categories according to complexity, risks, costs, and other factors. This categorization enables viewing the need of people who must work in the preparation of procurement documents, and other necessary resources, such as rooms, furniture, computers, and more. One of the most important activities in this phase is preparing specifications for products or services to be acquired. After such definitions are completed, those in charge of purchasing may seek to identify potential suppliers for the project and define the most appropriate contract type for each procurement.

5.2 DEFINING WHEN PURCHASING

The next step in developing the procurement management plan is defining *when* purchases must be made to meet the project schedule. This definition must take into account all procurement activities, ranging from the preparation of specifications and documentation, issuance of requests for quotation, receipt of proposals, analysis of proposals, negotiations, issuance of the contract or purchase order, manufacture or execution time of the purchased object, to the delivery date according to the project schedule. One technique that can be applied is using a timeline where the delivery required date will be launched and, retroactively, the estimated durations for other activities are released, until the preparation of specifications and documentation. The following figure illustrates this technique used to purchase equipment for the project.

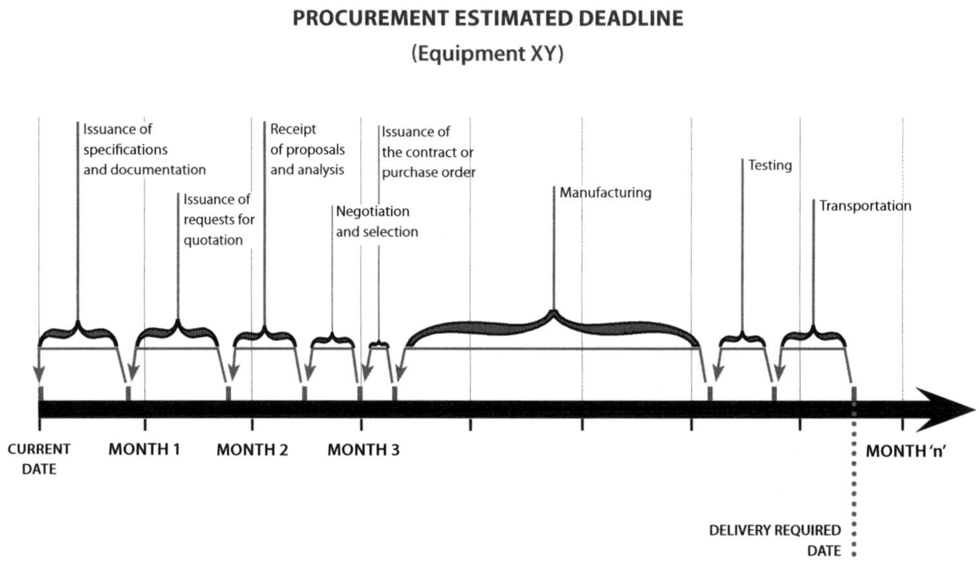

The estimated duration of each activity must be based on historical supply records of items similar to the one being considered in the project or the expert opinion. This technique enables viewing how much time is left until each procurement process starts or if we are already behind schedule in some procurements. In this case, duration estimates of each activity must be reviewed and negotiated with those responsible for each activity in order to meet the date required in the project schedule. In that case, it is also observed that it is always better to have a preview of activities internal to the organization when preparing the specifications and issuance of purchase orders, thus obtaining more time for potential manufacturing problems, rather than simply negotiating a reduced manufacturing deadline with the supplier. Since this is one of the last activities to be performed and should a delay occur, there will hardly be any chance to recover the deadline.

5.3 DEFINING HOW IT WILL BE ACQUIRED

The process of defining how project purchases will be made must consider whether the procurement will be centralized or decentralized, the procedures and specific procurement documents to be used, and the proposal assessment criteria.

5.3.1 CENTRALIZED AND DECENTRALIZED PROCUREMENTS

Centralized procurements are conducted by a department that performs all purchases of all projects in the organization. In this type of organization, a purchasing manager may be responsible for the purchases of several projects. Decentralized purchases are those made within the project environment, with the appointment of a professional or a team of professionals to carry out purchasing activities exclusively for the project. In some cases, a mixed strategy can be established, where important equipment and specific services are contracted by professionals within the project team, and materials considered as "shelf" are purchased by the company's purchase department team, along with materials from other projects. This strategy enables the project team to focus on items important to the project and enables the organization to have better prices when purchasing larger quantities of shelf items.

From the organization viewpoint, the benefits of centralized procurements may be obtaining better prices due to the volume of purchases, easy implementation of specific policies and procedures for purchases, and the expertise of professionals acquired based on several historical projects.

From the project viewpoint, the benefits of decentralized purchase may be full dedication of purchase professionals to the project and easy resolution of technical problems related to the project procurements. Still, in this type of procurement, the project manager's involvement in procurement processes is more frequent, which greatly contributes to the success of procurement management.

5.3.2 REQUEST FOR PROPOSALS

A request for proposal is prepared for each type of procurement and sent to the selected suppliers. Preparation of documents must comply with procurement policies and procedures, and the organization must consider the specific characteristics of each product or service to be acquired. Generally, a request for quotation or an offer refers to procurements that must take into account only the price factor of the product offered and usually largely applies to procurements of commercial items. Also, in general, a request for proposal is used when other factors must be taken into account such as the supplier's experience, delivery time, and proposed quality requirements. However, regardless of any factor, the documentation of the request for proposals must contain all the material necessary for clear understanding of the subject matter of the procurement by the supplier.

A *request for quotation* for commercial items can be simple and functional. However, in this type of procurement, it is important that the commercial item description is clear and complete, preferably standardized as technical standards or usual market standards. The use of nonstandard or incomplete descriptions is a causative factor of nonconformities and differences in the receipt of such materials, which can delay the project implementation.

A *request for proposal* usually comprises several components, including

- An order presentation letter, briefly explaining the purpose of the request, the subject matter of the purchase, the proposal deadline and delivery site, the person responsible for issuing the request, and to whom the proposal must be addressed.

- The statement of work of the subject matter of the procurement.
- Drawings and specifications, when required.
- Specific requirements to be met, such as deadlines, quality, performance, and others.
- The template contract to be signed with the selected supplier.
- A request for submitting the description of executive methods proposed by the supplier.
- A request for submitting Planning and service coordination rules by the supplier.
- Certifications and other requirements to be confirmed by the supplier.
- Other requirements that must be provided by the supplier to meet the project objectives.

Another point to be considered in requests for proposal is avoiding the incorporation of redundant activities or unnecessary requirements, for example, the request for highly qualified labor if the subject matter of the contract does not require it.

5.3.4 ASSESSMENT CRITERIA FOR PROPOSALS

When starting the project procurement, one of the first actions to be accomplished by the project manager is determining the formation of a committee, which will function to establish the assessment criteria to be considered in case of a procurement process as well as the percentage weight of each criterion considered. After receiving seller proposal, the committee receives their assessment function. The assessment committee composition must consider the characteristics and requirements of the subject matter of each contract and may include representatives of the technical, commercial, and quality areas as well as, crucially, the project manager.

Defining criteria for evaluating seller proposal must be performed in advance or in conjunction with the procurement documentation preparation. Preferably, these criteria must be forwarded to potential suppliers for information and confirmation that the assessment does not consider only the cost factor. However, the assessment committee composition must not be reported to suppliers.

Defining criteria for assessing proposals must consider the project procurement categories. Therefore, while a request for quotation may consider criteria such as the materials cost and delivery deadline, a high-value equipment, for example, may consider criteria such as cost, delivery deadline, quality, product performance, warranty, supplier's experience and reliability, supplier's production capacity, financial status, execution team composition, and others.

A scoring system example based on the weights of assessment criteria for proposals is shown in the following example.

ASSESSMENT CRITERIA AND WEIGHT SET	SUPPLIER 1		SUPPLIER 2	
	SCORE (MIN. 1/MAX. 5)	SCORE	SCORE (MIN. 1/MAX. 5)	SCORE
Proposal price 20%	3	0.6	4	0.8
Understanding customers' needs 25%	2	0.5	5	1.25
Life cycle cost 15%	3	0.45	2	0.3
Technical capacity 20%	5	1.0	4	0.8
Manageability capability 15%	4	0.6	4	0.6
Financial resources 5%	4	0.2	5	0.25
Final score Maximum score = 5		3.35		4

Additional information and reminders for the exam

- During the exam, consider yourself as a buyer, unless it is clearly defined that you are the supplier.
- During the exam, consider the term *seller* as *supplier*.
- The primary objective of negotiations with potential suppliers must be to develop a serious and lasting relationship, so that it becomes a benefit to the project.
- In a centralized contracting environment, there is a procurement department, and buyers execute contracts for several projects.
- In a decentralized contracting environment, the buyer is assigned exclusively for project purchases, reporting directly to the project manager.
- **"Make-or-buy" analysis**

  1. ***Making* is better when**
     - The work involves sensitive information,
     - If you would like to have a high level of control, and
     - Labor is available or idle.
  2. ***Buying* is better when**
     - There is not a full command of the execution technology,
     - People qualified for the execution are not available, and
     - If you would like to reduce the risks of this work, transfer some of them to the supplier.
- Price: the amount the supplier charges the buyer.
- Target price: the value that the buyer deems adequate and reasonable for a particular procurement.
- Ceiling limit: the maximum amount the buyer is willing to pay for a certain procurement.
- Point of total assumption: a valid consideration for fixed-price contracts with an incentive fee, where the supplier assumes the loss if it exceeds the budget above a certain amount (total assumption point).

$$\text{PTA} = \frac{(\text{ceiling limit} - \text{target price})}{\text{buyer's share ratio}} + \text{target cost}$$

- **Fixed-price contracts**
  - The procurement statement of work must be complete in order to avoid additional requests by the supplier.
  - It is easier to be managed by the buyer. The audit level is low.
  - The buyer knows the total price before starting work.
  - Risks are assumed by the supplier, which can make the contract more expensive than in other contract forms.
- **Time and Material contracts**
  - Used for short contracts and small projects.
  - The contract creation is fast.
  - Requires daily supervision by the purchaser, in order to check hours and resources used.
- **Cost-Reimbursable Contracts**
  - The procurement statement of work may be simpler, and scope can be simplified.
  - The total price is unknown.
  - Requires more work than the buyer. Requires auditing all supplier invoices.
  - Risks are assumed by the buyer.
- Privity: the contractual relationship. For example, the customer contracted company A, which subcontracted company B. If the customer contacts company B directly, a contractual relationship can be established between the customer and company B. If this damages company A, it can apply for refund.
- **Noncompetition procurement forms**
  - Single source: a known company already working for the buyer that always performs the same services.
  - Exclusive source: only one supplier for the procurement. Companies with patents are examples of exclusive sources.
- Procurements are closed when the contract is completed or when the contract is terminated prior to completion.
- Fait accompli: the supplier claim that the issue has already been decided or is not relevant and therefore must not be discussed further.

Supplementary exercises

1. In regards to the Project Procurements area of knowledge, indicate to which management processes group(s) each element is related and explain why. Follow the example of make-or-buy decisions.

1. Make-or-buy decisions

   ☐ Initiating ☐ Planning ☐ Executing ☐ Monitoring/controlling ☐ Closing

   Make-or-buy decisions are outputs of the Plan Procurements process (Planning) and inputs of the Plan Procurements process (Executing).

2. Procurement documentation

   ☐ Initiating ☐ Planning ☐ Executing ☐ Monitoring/controlling ☐ Closing

3. Negotiated settlements

   ☐ Initiating ☐ Planning ☐ Executing ☐ Monitoring/controlling ☐ Closing

4. Performance reporting

   ☐ Initiating ☐ Planning ☐ Executing ☐ Monitoring/controlling ☐ Closing

5. Proposal evaluation techniques

   ☐ Initiating ☐ Planning ☐ Executing ☐ Monitoring/controlling ☐ Closing

6. Procurement documentation

☐ Initiating ☐ Planning ☐ Executing ☐ Monitoring/controlling ☐ Closing

7. Procurement audits

☐ Initiating ☐ Planning ☐ Executing ☐ Monitoring/controlling ☐ Closing

8. Claims administration

☐ Initiating ☐ Planning ☐ Executing ☐ Monitoring/controlling ☐ Closing

9. Internet search

☐ Initiating ☐ Planning ☐ Executing ☐ Monitoring/controlling ☐ Closing

10. Contract

☐ Initiating ☐ Planning ☐ Executing ☐ Monitoring/controlling ☐ Closing

11. Teaming agreements

☐ Initiating ☐ Planning ☐ Executing ☐ Monitoring/controlling ☐ Closing

12. Seller proposal

☐ Initiating ☐ Planning ☐ Executing ☐ Monitoring/controlling ☐ Closing

13. Payment systems

☐ Initiating ☐ Planning ☐ Executing ☐ Monitoring/controlling ☐ Closing

14. Closed procurements

☐ Initiating ☐ Planning ☐ Executing ☐ Monitoring/controlling ☐ Closing

15. Qualified seller list

☐ Initiating ☐ Planning ☐ Executing ☐ Monitoring/controlling ☐ Closing

2. Complete the sentences below, stating whether the option refers to input, tool/technique, or output, and identify the corresponding project management process.

1. Risk-related contract decisions are ________________ of the ________________ process.
2. Inspections and audits are ________________ of the ________________ process.
3. Procurement negotiations are ________________ of the ________________ process.
4. Closed procurements are ________________ of the ________________ process.
5. Statement of work of procurements is a ________________ of the ________________ process.
6. Bidder conferences are ________________ of the ________________ process.
7. Negotiated settlements are ________________ of the ________________ process.
8. Procurement performance reviews is a ________________ of the ________________ process.
9. Make-or-buy decisions are ________________ of the ________________ process.
10. Teaming agreements are ________________ of the ________________ process.
11. Procurement audits are ________________ of the ________________ process.
12. Contract is a ________________ of the ________________ process.
13. Procurement documentation are ________________ of the ________________ process.
14. Payment systems are ________________ of the ________________ process.
15. Proposal evaluation techniques are ________________ of the ________________ process.

Questions

1. All listed processes generate outputs that become inputs of the Plan Procurements process, except
   a. Identify Risks
   b. Collect Requirements
   c. Develop Project Management Plan
   d. Create WBS

2. All listed processes generate outputs that become inputs of the Plan Procurements process, except
   a. Estimate Activity Resources
   b. Develop Schedule
   c. Estimate Costs
   d. Identify Stakeholders

3. The Plan Procurements process provides outputs to the Conduct Procurements process and to all procurement processes listed in the options, except
   a. Perform Integrated Change Control
   b. Administer Procurements
   c. Develop Project Management Plan
   d. Identify Stakeholders

4. All of these options are inputs of Conduct Procurements process, except
   a. Qualified seller list
   b. Seller proposals
   c. Risk register
   d. Procurement management plan

5. All of these options are inputs of Conduct Procurements process, except
   a. Activity resource estimates
   b. Make or buy decisions
   c. Source selection criteria
   d. Procurement documents

6. The Conduct Procurements process provides outputs that become inputs of all processes listed, except

a. Estimate Activity Resources

b. Estimate Activity Durations

c. Develop Schedule

d. Direct and Manage Project Execution

7. The Conduct Procurements process provides outputs that become inputs of all processes listed, except

a. Administer Procurements

b. Develop Project Team

c. Control Schedule

d. Perform Integrated Change Control

8. All listed processes generate outputs that become inputs of the Administer Procurements process, except

a. Develop Project Management Plan

b. Direct and Manage Project Execution

c. Conduct Procurements

d. Control Costs

9. The Administer Procurements process generates outputs that become inputs of the following processes

a. Develop Project Management Plan, Conduct Procurements and Close Procurements

b. Perform Integrated Change Control and Close Procurements

c. Develop Project Management Plan and Close Procurements

d. Develop Project Management Plan, Perform Integrated Change Control and Close Procurements

10. The Close Procurements process provides outputs to the process(es) below

a. Plan Procurements and Develop Project Management Plan

b. None of the above

c. Administer Procurements and Conduct Procurements

d. Develop Project Management Plan

11. The type of cost-reimbursable contract where the buyer reimburses the supplier for allowable costs plus a fixed profit amount is called

a. Cost plus fixed fee

b. Cost plus incentive fee

c. Reimbursable costs

d. Fixed price plus incentive fee

12. The contract type where the buyer pays the supplier a certain amount (set by contract) and for which the contractor may receive an additional amount to meet the performance criteria set is called

a. Cost plus fixed fee

b. Cost plus incentive fee

c. Reimbursable costs

d. Fixed price plus incentive fee

13. The contract type where the buyer pays the supplier a certain amount (as defined by the contract), regardless of the supplier's costs, is called

a. Time and material

b. Guaranteed fixed price

c. Fixed-price plus incentive fee

d. Cost plus fixed fee

14. The project procurement team is organizing bidder conferences in order to listen to and answer questions from them. Which statement is true regarding bidder conferences?

a. They are tools of the Administer Procurement process

b. They are outputs of the Conduct Procurements process

c. They are tools and techniques of the Conduct Procurements process

d. They are inputs of the Conduct Procurements process

15. For some items of the project, the procurement team decided to use an independent estimate made by an external professional to serve as verification of prices offered by suppliers. At which project management process is the team?

a. Manage Procurements

b. Administer Procurements

c. Plan Procurements

d. Conduct Procurements

16. Which of the following tools is used in the Conduct Procurements process to check prices offered by suppliers?

a. Independent estimates

b. Proposal assessment techniques

c. Weighting system

d. Classification system

17. During negotiations with a prospective supplier, he used the fait accompli technique. To what does this technique refers?

a. A party claims that the issue has already been decided and cannot be changed

b. A party claims that the issue has not been decided yet

c. A party claims that the issue will be decided later and nothing can be done at the moment

d. A party claims that the issue is not dependent on a decision, since it is a contractual item

18. What must be the preferred method to be used in resolving project claims and demands?

a. Negotiation

b. Arbitration

c. Collaboration

d. Imposition

19. The application of assessment criteria to proposals received from prospective suppliers is performed in the following process:

a. Administer Procurements

b. Conduct Procurements

c. Plan Procurements

d. Control procurements

20. Procurement audits are performed in the following process(es):

a. Plan Procurements and Conduct Procurements

b. Conduct Procurements and Administer Procurements

c. Administer Procurements and Close Procurements

d. Conduct Procurements and Close Procurements

21. All of the following options are inputs of the Administer Procurements process, except

a. Procurement documentation

b. Contract

c. Selected suppliers

d. Project management plan

22. All of the following options are inputs of the Administer Procurements process, except

a. Work performance information

b. Payment systems

c. Performance reporting

d. Approved change requests

23. All of the following options are tools and techniques of the Administer Procurements process, except

a. Contract change control system

b. Procurement performance reviews

c. Inspections and audits

d. Procurement documentation

24. All of the following options are tools and techniques of the Administer Procurements process, except

a. Payment systems

b. Claims management

c. Change requests

d. Procurement performance reviews

25. All of the following options are outputs of the Administer Procurements process, except

a. Organizational process assets updates

b. Approved change requests

c. Project management plan updates

d. Change requests

26. The contract was drawn up without a complete statement of work. The supplier has completed the work and would like to formally deliver the work. The buyer is not satisfied with the result and would like to review the statement of work. In that case, the contract will be considered:

a. Incomplete

b. Complete

c. Null

d. Void

27. The company to which the project belongs and a supplier entered into an equipment supply contract, therefore establishing a legal obligation to each other, unless:

a. The supplier cannot fulfill the contract

b. The company cannot fulfill the contract

c. Impossibility is declared by either party

d. Applicable laws are violated

28. The project manager and the procurement team started equipment purchase negotiations for the project. The major objective of these negotiations must be:

a. Obtaining the best price possible

b. Getting the most for the best possible price

c. Obtaining the best price and the best payment terms

d. Protecting the relationship between the company and the supplier

29. In a fixed-price contract type, profit is:

a. A fixed amount

b. Unknown

c. An amount set on each invoice

d. Defined in the contracting phase

30. In relation to a cost-reimbursable contract, what should the buyer remember to continually do, specifically for this contract type, until this procurement is closed?

a. Check whether the supplier is up to date with services

b. Check whether the supplier is performing deliverables

c. Check whether the supplier is not inserting unnecessary resources

d. Check whether the supplier is meeting its contractual obligations

31. In one of the project is large procurements, the project manager would like to adopt a fixed-price contract type. For the buyer, this type of contract:

a. Poses a shared risk

b. Poses no risks

c. Poses a higher-cost risk

d. Poses a lower-cost risk

32. The project procurement sector meets with one of the potential suppliers to discuss the proposal amounts. Suddenly, the supplier states that the meeting must end within an hour, since he needs to catch a plane. Which of the following negotiation strategies is he using?

a. Advance

b. Deadline

c. Cost

d. Lag

33. In a make-or-buy analysis, you must choose to buy if

a. There is idle labor

b. It reduces the risk of project constraints

c. You wish to retain control

d. The work involves proprietary information

34. The project team is deciding on purchasing or leasing a certain equipment for the project. The equipment purchase involves $2,000 in cash and a daily cost of $40. The lease cost is $240 per day. How long will it take for the purchase cost to equal the lease?

a. 15 days

b. 12 days

c. 10 days

d. 8 days

35. For a cost-reimbursable contract, what should a detailed procurement statement include?

a. It needs to be detailed so that the supplier knows exactly what needs to be performed

b. It needs to be detailed so that the supplier knows how to determine the price

c. There is no need for a statement of work for this contract type

d. It does not need to be detailed, since the supplier provides the knowledge to perform the work

36. What audit level should the buyer apply on a fixed-price contract?

a. High – analyzing all costs and receipts in detail

b. Low – the most important is ensuring that the work has been completed

c. Average – analyzing all high costs

d. None – no need to audit this contract type

37. In your project, you need to contract a specialized company to conduct research and development. What type of contract should you use in this contracting?

a. Fixed-price

b. Cost-reimbursable

c. Unit prices

d. Purchase order

38. In relation to a given work package of the project, the project team knows exactly what must be done. If it decides to contract a supplier for this package, what type of contract is the most recommended?

a. Cost-reimbursable

b. Unit prices

c. Fixed cost

d. Reimbursable costs plus incentive fee

39. The project manager has decided to directly contract a company to provide a particular service, without performing the competition process. The reason is that the company has performed several services, which were all satisfactory. What type of procurement is the manager doing?

a. Historical source

b. Single source

c. Exclusive source

d. Mutual source

40. The project manager decided to contract a company as an "exclusive source". How will he report this to the sponsor?

a. The company has performed previous services and has preference

b. The company has experience and always presents reasonable costs

c. The company holds the work patent necessary to the project

d. The company is a partner of the organization

41. When a supplier says, "I was only authorized to approve a maximum reduction of up to 2 months on the schedule," which negotiation tactic is he using?

a. Limited authority

b. Deadline

c. Lag

d. Withdrawal

42. In procurements, the Total Assumption Point (TAP) means

a. The sharing ratio between the supplier and the buyer

b. An amount above which the supplier assumes an entire loss of cost overruns

c. Price ceiling

d. Fixed price

43. In procurements, price ceiling means

a. The total assumption point

b. The target cost plus the target fee

c. The highest price that the buyer will pay for a certain procurement

d. The higher cost that the buyer will pay for a certain procurement

44. In procurements, the target price means

a. The highest price that the buyer will pay for a certain procurement

b. Thc total assumption point

c. The lowest price that the buyer will pay for a certain procurement

d. The expected price for a certain procurement

45. In your project, you identified the need for a programmer to join the project team who must be contracted from a company. What happens is that you cannot specify exactly for how long the program will develop its functions. What type of contract are you supposed to use?

a. Cost plus incentive fee

b. Time and material

c. Fixed cost

d. Cost-reimbursable

46. You are buying stationery materials for your project. What type of contract should you use for that purpose?

a. Cost-reimbursable contract plus incentive

b. Purchase order

c. Cost-reimbursable contract

d. Time and material contract

Answer key

Supplementary exercises

2. 1 - Inputs - Plan Procurements

2 - Tools/techniques - Administer Procurements

3 - Tools/techniques - Conduct Procurements

4 - Outputs - Close Procurements

5 - Outputs - Plan Procurements

6 - Tools - Conduct Procurements

7 - Tools/techniques - Close Procurements

8 - Tools/techniques - Administer Procurements

9 - Outputs - Plan Procurements

10 - Tools - Monitor and Control Risks

11 - Tools/techniques - Conduct Procurements

12 - Input - Administer Procurements

13 - Outputs - Plan Procurements

14 - Tools - Administer Procurements

15 - Techniques - Conduct Procurements

Questions

1. C. The Develop Project Management Plan process does not provide an input to the Plan Procurements process. The Identify Risks process provides the risk register input. The Collect Requirements process provides requirements documentation input. The Create WBS process provides the scope baseline.

2. D. The Identify Stakeholders process does not provide an input to the Plan Procurements process. The Estimate Activity Resources process provides the activity resource requirements input. The Develop Schedule process provides the project schedule input. The Estimate Costs process provides the activity cost estimates input.

3. B. The Plan Procurements process does not provide a direct input to the Administer Procurements process. The outputs of the Plan Procurements process are: selection criteria for sources and make or buy decisions to the Conduct Procurements process; change requests to the Perform Integrated Change Control process; procurement management plan to the Develop Project Management Plan and Conduct Procurements processes; procurement documents to the Identify Stakeholders process; and procurement statements of work to the project documents.

4. C. Risk register is not an input of the Conduct Procurements process. The other options are inputs of this process.

5. A. Estimates of activity resources are not inputs of the Conduct Procurements. The other options are inputs of this process.

6. D. The Conduct Procurements process provides the following outputs: selected suppliers to the Administer Procurements process; resource calendar to the Estimate Activity Resources, Estimate Activity Durations, Develop Schedule, Determine Budget, and Develop Project Team processes; change requests to the Perform Integrated Change Control process; updates of the project document; updates of the project management plan of the Develop Project Management Plan process; and procurement contract award to suppliers.

7. C. The Conduct Procurements process provides the following outputs: selected suppliers to the Administer Procurements process; resource calendar to the Estimate Activity Resources, Estimate activity durations, Develop Schedule, Determine Budget, and Develop Project Team processes; change requests to the Perform Integrated Change Control process; updates of the project documents; updates of the project management plan of the Develop Project Management Plan process; procurement contract award to suppliers.

8. D. Inputs of the Administer Procurements process are procurement management plan, the Develop Project Management Plan process; work performance information of the Direct and Manage Project Execution process; approved change request of the Perform Integrated Change Control process; performance reporting of the Report Performance process; contract of the Performance reporting process; procurement documents of the project documents.

9. D. The Administer Procurements process generates the following outputs: updates of the project full management to the Develop Project Management Plan process; change requests to the Perform Integrated Change Control process; procurement documents to the Close Procurements process; updates to organizational process assets to the company/organization.

10. B. The Close procurement process provides the following outputs: closed procurements and updates to the organizational process assets.

11. A. The type of cost-reimbursable contract where the buyer refunds the supplier for allowable costs plus a profit fixed amount is named cost plus fixed fee contract.

12. D. The contract type where the buyer pays the supplier a certain amount (set by contract) and for which the contractor may earn an additional amount to meet the performance criteria set is called a fixed-price incentive fee contract.

13. B. The contract type where the buyer pays the supplier a certain amount (as defined by the contract), regardless of the supplier's costs, is called a guaranteed fixed-price contract.

14. C. Bidder conferences are tools and techniques of Conduct Procurements process.

15. D. Independent estimates are tools and techniques of the Conduct Procurements process.

16. A. Independent estimates prepared by the organization itself or by a third-party professional are used to check prices proposed by suppliers.

17. A. Fait accompli refers to claim by one of the parties that the issue has already been decided or is not relevant and that it must not be discussed further.

18. A. Negotiation is the most effective method in resolving claims and demands of a contract.

19. B. The assessment of proposals from prospective suppliers is performed in the Conduct Procurements process.

20. C. Procurement audits are tools and techniques of Administer Procurements and Close Procurements processes.

21. C. Suppliers were selected (output) and contracted in the Conduct Procurements process. Documents of this contracting in addition to the project management plan are references (inputs) of the Administer Procurements process.

22. B. Remember during the exam: the term system always refers to tools of project management processes.

23. D. Documents can be information sources (inputs) or results (outputs) of the project management processes.

24. C. In the Administer Procurements process, the need for change in procurements can be identified, such as contractual amendments, new procurements, changes in contractual terms, and others. This request for change (process output) will be forwarded to the Perform Integrated Change Control process.

25. B. The Administer Procurements process can identify a need and make a change request. This request approval can only be made in the Perform Integrated Change Control process.

26. B. If the supplier performed the work expected in the statement of work, the contract is considered complete. It does not mean that the contract must be terminated. The contract may have a contractual amendment. But the original contract work is considered complete.

27. D. The impossibility of performing a contract does not exempt either party from their legal obligation! The contract cannot violate applicable laws.

28. D. During negotiations, the project manager must seek to develop a serious and lasting relationship with the supplier so that it becomes a benefit to the project.

29. B. Remember during the exam that you must be on the buyer's side, not the supplier's one. For the buyer, the profit amount is unknown (to the supplier, it is known).

30. C. In a cost-reimbursable contract type, the buyer must remember to continually check whether the supplier is not inserting unnecessary characteristics. The other options are common actions performed by the buyer to all types of contracts.

31. D. Remember during the exam that you must be on buyer's side, not the supplier's one. In a fixed-price contract type, cost risk is lower, from the buyer viewpoint. For the supplier, the cost risk is higher.

32. B. The strategy of determining a time limit for negotiation is a deadline strategy.

33. B. When you purchase or contract, you are transferring part of the risk to the supplier. There is no reason to buy there is idle labor, when you would like to retain control over the work or when the work involves the company's confidential information.

34. C. By regarding "d" as the number of days, we have:

$240d = $2000 + $40d
$240d – $40d = $2,000
$200d = $2,000 – therefore d = 10 days.

35. D. The scope statement must describe the performance criteria of what is being purchased, but it does not need to be detailed. Options A and B refer to fixed-price contracts. For a unit price contract, there is no need for a detailed statement of work; working sets being displayed is sufficient.

36. B. In this contract type, audit focuses more on checking whether the work was performed, no need to analyze costs and receipts in detail. In cost-reimbursable contracts (option A), there is the need to audit all costs in detail.

37. B. Remember during the exam: if the company does not master a certain work to be performed, it must contract a specialized company, with the best option being to contract a cost-reimbursable type.

38. C. If the work scope to be contracted is well known, the best option is contracting the fixed-price contract type. Remember that for the exam.

39. B. Single source refers to a preferred supplier – for several reasons, such as previous experience, previously proven quality and others. Exclusive source refers to the existence of a single supplier. A company holding a patent is an exclusive source example. Terms used in options A and D have been made up.

40. C. Exclusive source contracting refers to the existence of a single supplier. A company holding a patent is a "single source" example. Option A refers to a single source.

41. A. The supplier is using the limited authority tactic by declaring stating something that may or may not be true. The deadline tactic would be using a sentence similar to "our flight leaves at 5:00 p.m. and we must complete this negotiation soon". The lag tactic would be using a sentence similar to "let's review this issue at our the next meeting". Withdrawal can be emotional or physical and can usually indicate reduced interest of the supplier.

42. B. The total assumption point is the value above which the supplier assumes the entire loss of cost overruns. It only applies to Fixed-Price Incentive Fee (FPIF) contracts.

43. C. Price ceiling means the price (cost plus fee) higher than the buyer will pay for a particular procurement. Note that option D refers only to suppliers' costs.

44. D. Target price means the price expected for a given procurement. It is used to compare the result of a procurement to the expected. Target price represents the sum of the target cost and the target fee.

45. B. Since you do not know the exact time during which the programmer will work, it is desirable that you use the Time and Material (unit price) contract type.

46. B. The purchase order is the simplest fixed-price contract type (not mentioned in the other options). It is usually used for simple purchases.

Chapter 13

ETHICS AND PROFESSIONAL RESPONSIBILITY

1. Introduction
2. Vision and purpose of the Code of Ethics and Professional Conduct
3. Areas addressed by the Code of Ethics and Professional Conduct
4. Responsibility
5. Respect
6. Fairness
7. Honesty

- Additional information and reminders for the exam
- Questions
- Answer key

13.1 INTRODUCTION

This chapter presents the areas and topics related to ethics and professional conduct of project management, based on the PMI® Code of Ethics and Professional Conduct.[1]

13.2 VISION AND PURPOSE OF THE CODE OF ETHICS AND PROFESSIONAL CONDUCT

As practitioners of project management, we are committed to doing what is right and honorable. We set high standards for ourselves and aspire to meet them in all aspects of our lives – at work, at home, and in service to our profession.

The Code of Ethics and Professional Conduct describes the expectations we have of ourselves and our fellow practitioners in the global project management community. The Code articulates the ideals to which we aspire as well as behaviors that are mandatory in our roles as both professionals and volunteers.

The purpose of this Code is to instill confidence in the project management profession and to help an individual to become better practitioner. We do this by establishing a clear understanding of appropriate behavior related to the profession. We believe that the credibility and reputation of the project management profession are shaped by the collective conduct of individual practitioners.

13.3 AREAS ADDRESSED BY THE CODE OF ETHICS AND PROFESSIONAL CONDUCT

There are four areas addressed by the PMI® Code of Ethics and Professional Conduct:

- Responsibility
- Respect
- Justice
- Honesty

13.4. RESPONSIBILITY

- **Description of Responsibility**

  Responsibility is our duty to take ownership for the decisions we make or fail to make, the actions we take or fail to take, and the consequences that result.

- **Responsibility: desired standards**

  As practitioners in the global project management community, we must

  1 Make decisions and take actions based on the best interests of society, public safety, and the environment.

  2 Accept only those assignments that are consistent with our background, experience, skills, and qualifications.

1 The PMI® website (www.pmi.org) contains the official version, in English, of the PMI® Code of Ethics and Professional Conduct.

For competition contracts, only compete in activities for which our organization is qualified to perform and we must also appoint only individuals qualified to perform such activities.

3 Fulfill the commitments that we undertake – we do what we say we will do.

4 When we make errors or omissions, we take ownership and make corrections promptly. When we discover errors or omissions caused by others, we notify the interested party immediately.

We accept accountability for any issues resulting from our errors or omissions and any resulting consequences;

5 Protect proprietary information or confidential information that has been entrusted to us.

- **Responsibility: mandatory standards**

As practitioners in the global project management community, we require the following of ourselves and our fellow practitioners:

Regulations and legal requirements:

1 Keep all members informed and uphold the policies, rules, regulations, and laws that govern our work and professional and volunteer activities.

2 Report any unethical or illegal conduct to appropriate management and, if necessary, to those affected by the conduct.

NOTE: These provisions have several implications. Specifically, we do not engage in any illegal behavior, including, but not limited to theft, fraud, corruption, embezzlement, or bribery. Further, we do not to be or abuse the property of others, including intellectual property, we do not engage in slander or libel. As doers and representatives of our occupation, we do not endorse or encourage others to practice any illegal behavior. We report any illegal and/or unethical conduct.

Ethics complaints:

3 We bring violations of the Code to the attention of the appropriate body for resolution.

4 We only file ethics complaints when they are substantiated by facts.

Refrain from accusing others from misconduct or unethical behavior when not all the facts are available.

Additionally, require that disciplinary action is taken against individuals who knowingly produce false allegations against others.

5 Demand disciplinary sanctions against any individual who retaliates against a person who is reporting suspected breach of ethics.

13.5 RESPECT

- **Description of respect**

Respect is our duty to show a high regard for ourselves, others, and the resources entrusted to us.

Resources entrusted to us may include people, money, reputation, the safety of others, and natural and environmental resources.

- **Respect: desired standards**

  As practitioners in the global project management community, we must

  1 Inform ourselves about norms and customs of others and avoid engaging in behaviors they might consider disrespectful.

  2 Listen to others' points of view, seeking to understand them.

  3 We approach directly those persons with whom we have a conflict or disagreement.

  4 Conduct ourselves in a professional manner, even when there is no reciprocity.

  NOTE: An implication of these provisions is that we avoid engaging in gossip and avoid making negative remarks to undermine another person's reputation.

- **Respect: mandatory standards**

  As practitioners in the global project management community, we require the following of ourselves and our fellow practitioners:

  1 Negotiations in good faith.

  2 Not to exercise the power of our expertise or position to influence the decisions or actions of others in order to benefit at their expense.

  3 Not to act in an abusive manner toward others.

  4 Respect the property rights of others.

13.6 FAIRNESS

- **Description of fairness**

  Fairness is our duty to make decisions and act impartially and objectively. Our conduct must be free from competing self-interests, prejudice, and favoritism.

- **Fairness: desired standards**

  As practitioners in the global project management community, we must:

  1 Demonstrate transparency in decision-making process.

  2 Constantly reexamine our impartiality and objectivity, taking corrective action as appropriate.

  Act positively seeking to identify potential conflicts and help each other, identifying potential conflicts of mutual interest and insist on their resolution.

  3 Provide equal access to information to those who are authorized to have that information.

- **Fairness: mandatory standards**

  As practitioners in the global project management community, we require the following of ourselves and our fellow practitioners:

  Conflicts of interest situations:

  1 Disclose any real or potential conflict of interest to the appropriate stakeholders.

2 We realize that we have a real or potential conflict of interest, we refrain from engaging in the decision-making process or otherwise attempt to influence outcomes, unless or until. We have an approved mitigation plan for the problem and obtain the consent of stakeholders to proceed.

Favoritism and discrimination:

3 We do not hire, fire, reward, punish, award, or deny contracts based on personal considerations, including but not limited to, favoritism, nepotism, or bribery.

4 We do not discriminate against others based on, but not limited to, gender, race, age, religion, disability, nationality, or sexual orientation.

5 We apply the rules of the organization – employer, the Project Management Institute, or other group – without any favoritism or prejudice.

13.7 HONESTY

- **Description of honesty**

  Honesty is our duty to understand the truth and act in a truthful manner both in our communication and in our conduct.

- **Honesty: desired standards**

  As practitioners in the global project management community, we must

1 Earnestly seek to understand the truth.

2 Be truthful in our communications and in our conduct.

3 Provide accurate information in a timely manner.

When results are negative, avoid hiding information or shifting blame to others. When results are positive, avoid being credited for the accomplishments of others. Such determinations reinforce the commitment to be honest and responsible.

4 Make commitment and promise, implied, or explicit, in good faith.

5 Strive to create an environment in which others feel safe to tell the truth.

- **Honesty: mandatory standards**

  As practitioners in the global project management community, we require the following of ourselves and our fellow practitioners:

1 We do not engage in or agree with any behavior that is designed to deceive others, including but not limited to, making false statements, stating half-truths, providing information out of context or withholding information that, if known, would render our statements as misleading or incomplete;

2 We do not engage in dishonest behavior with the intention of personal gain at the expense of another.

NOTE: Desired standards exhort us to be truthful. Half-truths and misinformation with the intent to mislead stakeholders are as unprofessional as making an intentional misrepresentation. We develop credibility by providing complete and accurate information.

Additional information and reminders for the exam

The project manager must

- Make decisions based on the interests of the organization and the team, not for his own benefit,
- Only accept positions and functions for which he is qualified,
- Follow the organization and the project confidentiality requirements,
- Comply with laws, including those related to copyright,
- Communicate to management any unethical behavior he may have witnessed,
- Report any violation of the PMI® Code of Ethics and Professional Conduct that may have witnessed,
- Respect cultural differences of the project team and stakeholders,
- Respect people,
- Not to engage in negotiations that are not performed in good faith,
- Not to gossip and create an environment where it is unacceptable,
- Be direct in dealing with conflict,
- Not to accept any kind of bribes,
- Not to perform any act of discrimination against people,
- Be loyal to the organization where he works,
- Telling the truth in all communications,
- Create an environment where people always tell the truth, and
- Not to use his position for personal gain.

Questions

1. You have been assigned as the project manager in another country and realized that there are more holidays in that country than in your home country. In addition, team members have an extra week of vacation per year. How should you deal with that?

a. Set a new work schedule, according to your country of origin

b. Set that the staff productivity must compensate holidays and additional vacation

c. Use the holiday and vacation calendar as a restriction in your schedule

d. Try to relocate part of the project to a different country

2. You are starting a project to build an office in another country, when you were told that obtaining an additional license from the city hall is necessary. This license may take 4-5 weeks to be issued. However, one of the city hall officials informed that, if an urgency fee of $300 is paid, the license would be issued within five days. This emergency fee is declared in the procedure for obtaining a license. What should you do?

a Wait 4 to 5 weeks until the license is usually issued

b. Pay the emergency fee

c. Offer a smaller amount to the city hall official

d. Ask a team member to best talk with the official

3. You are a project manager and the senior management has requested that you participate in the assessment committee of products to be supplied to a given project. When you start taking part in the committee, you realize that one of the products being assessed is manufactured by the company where your wife works. What is your first action in this case?

a. Not to say anything about it to the committee

b. Proceed with your usual work, without any impartiality

c. Notify your wife about the situation

d. Notify the product assessment committee about the situation

4. You have been appointed as the manager of a project that will require members from two foreign countries with big cultural differences. In order to ensure that such cultural differences do not affect the project development, which should your first action be?

a. Undertake specific training on cultural diversity for all team members

b. Develop the team based on cultural differences

c. Set standards and procedures for this new project

d. Prepare a team grouping (war room) to reduce conflicts

5. Based on professional responsibility, all options refer to actions of the project manager, except

a. Making decisions based on the interests of the company, the team, and the society

b. Only take assignments for which you are qualified

c. Making decisions in your own interest

d. If assigned to a project beyond your qualifications, ensure that the sponsor is aware of these gaps before accepting the position

6. Based on professional responsibility, all options refer to actions of the project manager, except

a. Recognize your own mistakes

b. Respect the project confidentiality requirements

c. Comply with laws

d. Not to report violations of the PMI® Code of Ethics and Professional Conduct

7. All options below relate to attitudes about the project manager, except

a. Respecting cultural differences

b. Being indirect when dealing with conflicts

c. Maintaining a cooperation attitude between project team members

d. Respect other people

8. All options below relate to attitudes about the project manager, except

a. Not to use your position to influence people for your own benefit

b. Engage in negotiations in good faith

c. Not to say anything that might damage the reputation of others

d. Not to recognize your own mistakes

9. All options below relate to justice attitudes inherent to the position of a project manager, except

a. Acting impartially, without any favoritism

b. Using your position for personal or commercial gain

c. Not to discriminate against others

d. Acting without nepotism, bribery, or prejudice

10. All options below relate to justice attitudes inherent to the position of a project manager, except

a. Not to use your position for personal gain

b. Being loyal to the company where you work and to organizations to which you are affiliated

c. Act with prejudice against team members

d. Identify conflicts of interest and disclose them

11. All options below relate to honesty attitudes inherent to the position of a project manager, except

a. Working to create an environment of people who tell the truth

b. Not to share false information

c. Try to understand the truth

d. Not to ensure that the information you are using are true

12. The company project office has issued a preliminary monthly report on the progress of projects that you are tasked to analyze. You realize that a project manager is not being truthful when he says that a delivery was performed because you know that the delivery will take place within ten days. What should your attitude about it be?

a. Report the truth in your analysis, rendering the project manager responsible for the incorrect information

b. Let the information as it is, since the project manager is supposed to know what he is doing

c. Let the information as it is, since this delivery does not influence the project development

d. Make a phone call to the project manager and call his attention so that he does not make these mistakes again

13. You provided a project cost estimate to the sponsor, who was dissatisfied and asked for a 10% reduction. What should you do about it?

a. Notify the project team

b. Reduce the project cost estimates by 10%

c. Find new estimates or a scope change to enable the 10% reduction

d. Notify the sponsor that it is not possible

14. You have been assigned to make a presentation to the customer on the project progress within three days. Although the project was going well, yesterday you heard of a problem in the manufacture of imported equipment, which will cause a delay of three weeks on the project. You and your team have already studied all the possibilities of reducing the delay, but you were not able to reach a conclusion about the matter. This supply lag risk has not been included in the risk management processes by the team. What should you do during the presentation to your client?

a. You tell the customer that this risk was not foreseen in the project since the supplier was considered reliable

b. You should present the actual situation of the problem that occurred and the delay of the project, informing the risk was not predicted by you

c. You tell the customer that you will take strong measures regarding the supplier

d. You tell the customer that this usually happens in projects

15. Your company has been invited to participate in a project in a foreign country. You are preparing the proposal, when you are is informed that, to be considered in the project participation, your company must pay a high value to a government minister from the foreign country. What should be the attitude of the company?

a. Not pay the amount and take part of the bidding

b. Consider the amount as a participation rate to lower the competition expenses

c. Pay the amount and take part in the bidding

d. Not pay the amount, since it is a bribe

16. You have been assigned as the project manager of the electromechanical assembly of a plant located a foreign city. Since you need to transport large equipment through city traffic, you have been notified by the local traffic engineer that a fee must be paid related to the monitoring of this transportation by the team. What should you do about it?

a. Eliminate equipment transport transportation

b. Consider the fee as bribery and not pay it

c. Give a directly lower amount to the traffic official

d. Pay the fee

17. You are a project manager in an organization as well as a professor. The university asks for confidential information of projects in which you have already taken part to be used in internal research. This concession might give you more power and work within the university. In addition, this information will not be published, and the university ensures confidentiality regarding its clients. What is your attitude toward this?

a. Provide part of the information

b. Provide only information related to work packages

c. Ask your customers for permission to disclose the information

d. Provide the information, since this will help you in college

18. You are the manager of an ongoing project, and the administration demands that a company that has completed several jobs for the organization is hired. In this case, you should be more concerned primarily with

a. Obeying the administration

b. The contracted work cost

c. Checking whether the company is able to provide the service

d. Checking the contractual terms and conditions

19. You have received concrete technological control reports of a part of your construction and found that, in some points, the resistance found is less than desired. You know that this resistance found in some minor points do not affect the project as a whole. What are you supposed to do?

a. Just not to mention these low-resistance points

b. Lower quality metrics in such points, so that the results are compliant

c. Report the problem and seek a solution to them

d. Followup the remaining concrete in a better way

20. The code of ethics established by PMI® to ensure personal and professional conduct by PMP® is named:

a. Project Management Professional Code of Personal and Professional Conduct

b. PMI® Code of Management Conduct and Ethics

c. PMI® Code of Ethics and Professional Conduct

d. PMI® Code of Policy and Professional Conduct

Answer key

1. C. The PMI® professional responsibility states that respect for other cultures must be highly regarded. In this case, you should accept the holiday and vacation calendar in your schedule.

2. B. You must pay the urgency fee – it is not a bribe to the employee! It is a fee established by the agency and stated in the procedure to get the a license.

3. D. The first action to be taken by you is saying that your wife works at the company of the product being assessed. Therefore, you are acting ethically.

4. A. The first question concerns the action to be taken. Taking a specific training on cultural diversity will allow members to know and respect their cultural differences. Grouping is not possible, since there are members from other nations. The team development (option B) can be applied, but this requires time. Option C can also take time to be implemented.

5. C. This is an easy question. The most important thing is knowing the other options, which are your responsibility as a project manager. The project manager should not make decisions based on his own interests.

6. D. This is a very easy question. As a PMI® member, you have a duty to report violations of the PMI® Code of Ethics and Professional Conduct. The most important thing is knowing the other options, which are your responsibility as a project manager.

7. B. The best way to deal with conflicts is being straightforward! The important aspect in this question is knowing the other attitude options regarding the project manager, which are your responsibility.

8. D. Very easy question, is not it? A project manager (or anyone) must recognize his own mistakes. The important aspect in this question is knowing the other attitude options regarding the project manager, which are your responsibility.

9. B. The project manager should not use his position for personal or commercial gain. The important aspect in this question is knowing the other justice attitude options inherent to the position of a project manager.

10. C. The project manager must not act with prejudice against anyone. The important aspect in this question is knowing the other justice attitude options inherent to the position of a project manager.

11. D. A project manager must continually ensure that the information you are using is true, so that false information is not distributed to project stakeholders. The other options are honesty attitudes inherent to the position of a project manager.

12. A. The project manager must bear the truth in mind! Neither you nor the project manager is being true.

13. C. Alternatives to reduce the cost of a project may involve scope changes and demand for new estimates.

14. B. The project manager must present the problem and take responsibility for any error committed by himself of his project team.

15. D. The company must refuse to make that payment, since it is a bribe.

16. D. This fee is not a bribe. It is a fee so that the traffic engineering can monitor and supervise the equipment transportation.

17. C. Any and all project information can be disclosed only under express authorization of the customer and other stakeholders.

18. C. The first thing to check is whether it does not violate ethics or any standard of the company, or even a law. Afterward, the more consistent action would be checking whether the company is able to provide the service.

19. C. The problem cannot be hidden. The project manager must show the problems and seeking solutions to them. Note that options A and B are unethical. Option D does not solve the problem which has already occurred.

20. C. The PMI® Code of Ethics and Professional Conduct is named PMI® Code of Ethics and Professional Conduct.

Appendix 1

PREPARATION FOR THE EXAM DAY

1. During the study phase
2. The day before the exam
3. On the exam day
4. At the exam time
5. The result
6. Review
7. Certification maintenance

1 DURING THE STUDY PHASE

1. Only schedule the exam when you are aware that you are prepared and getting an average of 85% of correct answers in the mock tests.
2. Schedule the exam to be taken in the afternoon. Therefore, even if you do not have a good night's sleep, something common because of the anxiety caused by the exam, you will have the morning to relax and concentrate for the exam.
3. Visit the exam site in advance. Check traffic conditions, parking lot, and cafés.
4. TAKE AS MANY MOCK TESTS AS YOU CAN. This is quite important for you to learn and become familiar with the exam.
5. Some formulas must be memorized! But first try to understand them so that memorization becomes easier.

2 ON THE DAY BEFORE THE EXAM

1. Do not overstudy on this day! Take the opportunity to take a general look at reminders of each chapter in the book.
2. Prepare the sheet of formulas to memorize and write down during the exam.
3. Separate your personal documents (2 documents with photo, containing your name exactly as entered in your application) and the PMI® letter of authorization. Make sure you have cash or a bank card for parking expenses and meals.
4. If you sometimes have headaches, bring the medicine you are used to take during these situations. In addition, bring a bottle of water with you.
5. Plan to arrive at the exam site (at least) one hour ahead of the exam time. Consider the traffic you may face.
6. Do not study on the night before the exam! Do some relaxing activity and enjoy a little more sleep.

3 ON THE EXAM DAY

1. Get up a little earlier than usual. Take a warm shower and have a light breakfast! Wear light and comfortable clothes. Wear comfortable shoes or sneakers.
2. Read reminder pages of the chapters and check formulas that must be memorized.
3. Be aware that you studied enough and that you are ready for the exam. And... relax!
4. Bring together all the material (the letter from the PMI®, 2 documents, cash or bank card, medicine, water, formula note sheets, this book, a sweater, etc.) and head for the exam site.
5. At the site, introduce yourself and know the room where you take the exam and the time when you will be able to enter.
6. Have a snack or a light meal.
7. If you have time, take a look at the reminders of chapters and the formulas.

4 AT THE EXAM TIME

1. Introduce yourself in the exam room, with the letter received from the PMI® and the two documents. You will receive the locker key to store your belongings – all of your belongings! You are not allowed to bring any material into the examination room, except for the key to your locker.
2. The examination room contains several camcorders. Do not even consider bringing reminders into the exam room.
3. You will receive a pencil and two sheets of blank paper. The calculator will be available on the computer. Note sheets will be returned at the end of the exam.
4. When entering the exam room, you will have 15 minutes to familiarize yourself with the computer and the test. Make the sheet of memorized formulas, using the blank sheets of paper. Take deep breaths to make relaxation easier.
5. Start the exam! Do not worry if you have any queries in the first questions of the exam! That is normal and happens to everyone! Go ahead and answer the questions with queries later on.
6. Answer the questions from the PMI® point of view!
7. Notice terms appearing in questions, such as: except for, not, always, never, more likely, less likely, first, last, next, best, major, and others.
8. In questions with lots of information, focus on what is relevant. In general, the last paragraph of the question is very important.
9. You can leave the room to go to the bathroom, drink water, and rest a little. But do that consciously, after being in control of the exam time.
10. Use all of the time assigned to the exam. Carefully read the questions marked for review!

5 THE RESULT

1. The result is known immediately after the examination is completed, with a printed report being provided, stating whether the applicant has passed or not.
2. Applicants also receive a percentage of correctly answered questions in each process group. The answer template will not be provided. It is possible not reaching the average mark in one of the process groups and still pass the exam.
3. In case of pass, the PMI® will send the certificate to the applicant's mailing address.

6 NEW EXAM

1. In case of failure, the applicant must download the new examination form from the PMI® website (www.pmi.org), complete it, and send it to the PMI®. Alternatively, the applicant can e-mail it to customercare@pmi.org and request the form, which can be completed directly via the Web.
2. The applicant has three chances to pass the exam within the eligibility period. If not approved at the third attempt, the applicant must wait a year to resume the process.
3. The new examination fee is US$275 for members and US$375* for nonmembers and can be paid with an international credit card.

* Fees in effect when this book was edited.

7 CERTIFICATION MAINTENANCE

1. The PMP® certification is valid for 3 years. Within that period, the PMP® must meet the requirements of PMI® Professional Development Program in order to maintain the PMP® certificate.
2. During the validity period, the PMP® must submit information to the PMI® demonstrating at least 60 PDUs (Professional Development Units). This can be performed directly on the PMI® website. Keep your e-mail updated with the PMI® so that end of your cycle can be properly informed.
3. PDUs are regarded as participation in courses, academic activities, community and association activities, lectures, PMI® leader, a member of committees, professional activities, or self-study hours.
4. The certification renewal fee is US$60 for PMI® members and US$150 for nonmembers.

Appendix 2

GLOSSARY

B.1 INCLUSIONS AND EXCLUSIONS

These glossary terms are:

- Unique or nearly unique to project management (e.g., project scope statement, work package, work breakdown structure, critical path method).
- Not unique to project management, but used differently or with a narrower meaning in project management than in general everyday usage (e.g., early start date, schedule activity).

This glossary generally does not include

- Application area-specific terms (e.g., project prospectus as a legal document – unique to real estate development).
- Terms used in project management which do not differ in any material way from everyday use (e.g., calendar day, delay).
- Compound terms whose meaning is clear from the combined meanings of the component parts.
- Variants when the meaning of the variant is clear from the base term (e.g., exception report is included, exception reporting is not).

As a result of the above inclusions and exclusions, this glossary includes:

- A preponderance of terms related to Project Scope Management, Project Time Management, and Project Risk Management, since many of the terms used in these Knowledge Areas are unique or nearly unique to project management.
- Many terms from Project Quality Management, since these terms are used more narrowly than in their everyday usage.
- Relatively few terms related to Project Human Resource Management and Project Communications Management, since most of the terms used in these Knowledge Areas do not differ significantly from everyday usage.
- Relatively few terms related to Project Cost Management, Project Integration Management, and Project Procurement Management, since many of the terms used in these Knowledge Areas have narrow meanings that are unique to a particular application area.

B.2 COMMON ACRONYMS

AC	Actual Cost
ACWP	Actual Cost of Work Performed
BAC	Budget at Completion
BCWP	Budgeted Cost of Work Performed
BCWS	Budgeted Cost of Work Scheduled
CCB	Change Control Board
COQ	Cost of Quality
CPAF	Cost Plus Award Fee
CPF	Cost Plus Fee

CPFF	Cost Plus Fixed Fee
CPI	Cost Performance Index
CPIF	Cost Plus Incentive Fee
CPM	Critical Path Methodology
CPPC	Cost-Plus-Percentage of Cost
CV	Cost Variance
EAC	Estimate at Completion
EF	Early Finish Date
EMV	Expected Monetary Value
ES	Early Start Date
ETC	Estimate to Complete
EV	Earned Value
EVM	Earned Value Management
FF	Finish-to-Finish
FFP	Firm Fixed Price
FMEA	Failure Mode and Effect Analysis
FP-EPA	Fixed Price with Economic Price Adjustment
FPIF	Fixed Price Incentive Fee
FS	Finish-to-Start
IFB	Invitation for Bid
LF	Late Finish Date
LOE	Level of Effort
LS	Late Start Date
OBS	Organizational Breakdown Structure
PDM	Precedence Diagramming Method
PMBOK®	Project Management Body of Knowledge
PMIS	Project Management Information System
PMP®	Project Management Professional
PV	Planned Value
QA	Quality Assurance
QC	Quality Control
RACI	Responsible, Accountable, Consult, and Inform
RAM	Responsibility Assignment Matrix
RBS	Risk Breakdown Structure
RFI	Request for Information
RFP	Request for Proposal

RFQ	Request for Quotation
SF	Start-to-Finish
SOW	Statement of Work
SPI	Schedule Performance Index
SS	Start-to-Start
SV	Schedule Variance
SWOT	Strengths, Weaknesses, Opportunities, and Threats
T&M	Time and Material
TQM	Total Quality Management
WBS	Work Breakdown Structure

B.3 DEFINITIONS

Many of the words defined here have broader and, in some cases different, dictionary definitions.

The definitions use the following conventions:

- In some cases, a single glossary term consists of multiple words (e.g., risk response Planning).
- When synonyms are included, no definition is given and the reader is directed to the preferred term (i.e., see preferred term).
- Related terms that are not synonyms are cross-referenced at the end of the definition (i.e., see also related term).

A

Acceptance Criteria
Those criteria, including performance requirements and essential conditions, which must be met before project deliverables are accepted.

Acquire Project Team [Process]
The process of confirming human resource availability and obtaining the team necessary to complete project assignments.

Activity
A component of work performed during the course of a project.

Activity Attributes [Output/Input]
Multiple attributes associated with each schedule activity that can be included within the activity list. Activity attributes include activity codes, predecessor activities, successor activities, logical relationships, leads and lags, resource requirements, imposed dates, constraints, and assumptions.

Activity Code
One or more numerical or text values that identify characteristics of the work or in some way categorize the schedule activity that allows filtering and ordering of activities within reports.

Activity Duration
The time in calendar units between the start and finish of a schedule activity. See also *duration*.

Activity Identifier
A short unique numeric or text identification assigned to each schedule activity to differentiate that project activity from other activities. Typically, unique within any one project schedule network diagram.

Activity List [Output/Input]
A documented tabulation of schedule activities that shows the activity description, activity identifier, and a sufficiently detailed scope of work description so project team members understand what work is to be performed.

Actual Cost (AC)
Total costs actually incurred and recorded in accomplishing work performed during a given time period for a schedule activity or work breakdown structure component. Actual cost can sometimes be direct labor hours alone, direct costs alone, or all costs, including indirect costs. Also referred to as the Actual Cost of Work Performed (ACWP). See also *earned value management* and *earned value technique*.

Actual Cost of Work Performed (ACWP)
See Actual Cost (AC).

Actual Duration
The time in calendar units between the actual start date of the schedule activity and either the data date of the project schedule if the schedule activity is in progress or the actual finish date if the schedule activity is complete.

Administer Procurements [Process]
The process of managing procurement relationships, monitoring contract performance, and making changes and corrections as needed.

Analogous Estimating [Technique]
An estimating technique that uses the values of parameters, such as scope, cost, budget, and duration or measures of scale such as size, weight, and complexity from a previous, similar activity as the basis for estimating the same parameter or measure for a future activity.

Application Area
A category of projects that have common components significant in such projects but are not needed or present in all projects. Application areas are usually defined in terms of either the product (i.e., by similar technologies or production methods) or the type of customer (i.e., internal versus external, government versus commercial) or industry sector (i.e. utilities, automotive, aerospace, information technologies, etc.). Application areas can overlap.

Approved Change Request [Output/Input]
A change request that has been processed through the integrated change control process and approved.

Assumptions
Assumptions are factors that, for Planning purposes, are considered to be true, real, or certain without proof or demonstration.

Assumptions Analysis [Technique]
A technique that explores the accuracy of assumptions and identifies risks to the project from inaccuracy, inconsistency, or incompleteness of assumptions.

Authority
The right to apply project resources, expend funds, make decisions, or give approvals.

B

Backward Pass
The calculation of late finish dates and late start dates for the uncompleted portions of all schedule activities. Determined by working backward through the schedule network logic the project's end date. See also *schedule network analysis*.

Baseline
An approved plan for a project, plus or minus approved changes. It is compared to actual performance to determine whether performance is within acceptable variance thresholds. Generally, refers to the current baseline, but may refer to the original or some other baseline. Usually used with a modifier (e.g., cost performance baseline, schedule baseline, performance measurement baseline, technical baseline).

Bottom-up Estimating [Technique]
A method of estimating a component of work. The work is decomposed into more detail. An estimate is prepared of what is needed to meet the requirements of each of the lower, more detailed pieces of work, and these estimates are then aggregated into a total quantity for the component of work. The accuracy of bottom-up estimating is driven by the size and complexity of the work identified at the lower levels.

Brainstorming [Technique]
A general data gathering and creativity technique that can be used to identify risks, ideas, or solutions to issues by using a group of team members or subject-matter experts.

Budget
The approved estimate for the project or any work breakdown structure component or any schedule activity. See also *Estimate*.

Budget at Completion (BAC)
The sum of all the budgets established for the work to be performed on a project or a work breakdown structure component or a schedule activity. The total planned value for the project.

Budgeted Cost of Work Performed (BCWP)
See *Earned Value (EV)*.

Budgeted Cost of Work Scheduled (BCWS)
See *Planned Value (PV)*.

Buffer
See *reserve*.

Buyer
The acquirer of products, services, or results for an organization.

C

Calendar Unit
The smallest unit of time used in scheduling a project. Calendar units are generally in hours, days, or weeks, but can also be in quarter years, months, shifts, or even in minutes.

Change Control
Identifying, documenting, approving or rejecting, and controlling changes to the project baselines.

Change Control Board (CCB)
A formally constituted group of stakeholders responsible for reviewing, evaluating, approving, delaying, or rejecting changes to a project, with all decisions and recommendations being recorded.

Change Control System [Tool]
A collection of formal documented procedures that define how project deliverables and documentation will be controlled, changed, and approved. In most application areas, the change control system is a subset of the configuration management system.

Change Request
Requests to expand or reduce the project scope, modify policies, processes, plans, or procedures, modify costs or budgets, or revise schedules.

Charter
See *project charter.*

Claim
A request, demand, or assertion of rights by a seller against a buyer, or vice versa, for consideration, compensation, or payment under the terms of a legally binding contract, such as for a disputed change.

Close Procurements [Process]
The process of completing each project procurement.

Close Project or Phase [Process]
The process of finalizing all activities across all of the Project Management Process Groups to formally complete the project or phase.

Closing Processes [Process Group]
Those processes performed to finalize all activities across all Project Management Process Groups to formally close the project or phase.

Code of Accounts [Tool]
Any numbering system used to uniquely identify each component of the work breakdown structure.

Collect Requirements [Process]
Collect Requirements is the process of defining and documenting stakeholders' needs to meet the project objectives.

Co-location [Technique]
An organizational placement strategy where the project team members are physically located close to one another in order to improve communication, working relationships, and productivity.

Common Cause
A source of variation that is inherent in the system and predictable. On a control chart, it appears as part of the random process variation (i.e., variation from a process that would be considered normal or not unusual) and is indicated by a random pattern of points within the control limits. Also referred to as random cause. Contrast with *special cause.*

Communication Management Plan [Output/Input]
The document that describes: the communications needs and expectations for the project; how and in what format information will be communicated; when and where each communication will be made; and who is responsible for providing each type of communication. The communication management plan is contained in, or is a subsidiary plan of, the project management plan.

Conduct Procurements [Process]
The process of obtaining seller responses, selecting a seller, and awarding a contract.

Configuration Management System [Tool]
A subsystem of the overall project management system. It is a collection of formal documented procedures used to apply technical and administrative direction and surveillance to identify and document the functional and physical characteristics of a product, result, service, or component; control any changes to such characteristics; record and report each change and its implementation status; and support the audit of the products, results, or components to verify conformance to requirements. It includes the documentation, tracking systems, and defined approval levels necessary for authorizing and controlling changes.

Constraint [Input]
The state, quality, or sense of being restricted to a given course of action or inaction. An applicable restriction or limitation, either internal or external to a project, which will affect the performance of the project or a process. For example, a schedule constraint is any limitation or restraint placed on the project schedule that affects when a schedule activity can be scheduled and is usually in the form of fixed imposed dates.

Contingency
See *reserve*.

Contingency Allowance
See *reserve*.

Contingency Reserve [Output/Input]
The amount of funds, budget, or time needed above the estimate to reduce the risk of overruns of project objectives to a level acceptable to the organization.

Contract [Output/Input]
A contract is a mutually binding agreement that obligates the seller to provide the specified product or service or result and obligates the buyer to pay for it.

Control
Comparing actual performance with planned performance, analyzing variances, assessing trends to effect process improvements, evaluating possible alternatives, and recommending appropriate corrective action as needed.

Control Account [Tool]
A management control point where scope, budget (resource plans), Actual cost, and schedule are integrated and compared to earned value for performance measurement. See also *work package*.

Control Chart [Tool]
A graphic display of process data over time and against established control limits, and that has a centerline that assists in detecting a trend of plotted values toward either control limit.

Control Costs [Process]

The process of monitoring the status of the project to update the project budget and managing changes to the cost baseline.

Control Limits

The area composed of three standard deviations on either side of the centerline, or mean, of a normal distribution of data plotted on a control chart that reflects the expected variation in the data. See also specification limits.

Control Schedule [Process]

The process of monitoring the status of the project to update project progress and managing changes to the schedule baseline.

Control Scope [Process]

The process of monitoring the status of the project to product scope and managing changes to the scope baseline.

Controlling

See *control.*

Corrective Action

Documented direction for Executing the project work to bring expected future performance of the project work in line with the project management plan.

Cost Management Plan [Output/Input]

The document that sets out the format and establishes the activities and criteria for Planning, structuring, and controlling the project costs. The cost management plan is contained in, or is a subsidiary plan of, the project management plan.

Cost of Quality (COQ) [Technique]

A method of determining the costs incurred to ensure quality. Prevention and appraisal costs (cost of conformance) include costs for quality Planning, quality control (QC), and quality assurance to ensure compliance to requirements (i.e., training, QC systems, etc.). Failure costs (cost of nonconformance) include costs to rework products, components, or processes that are noncompliant, costs of warranty work and waste, and loss of reputation.

Cost Performance Baseline

A specific version of the time-phased budget used to compare actual expenditures to planned expenditures to determine whether preventive or corrective action is needed to meet the project objectives.

Cost Performance Index (CPI)

A measure of cost efficiency on a project. It is the ratio of earned value (EV) to Actual Costs (AC). CPI = EV divided by AC.

Cost-Plus-Fixed-Fee (CPFF) Contract

A type of cost-reimbursable contract where the buyer reimburses the seller for the seller's allowable costs (allowable costs are defined by the contract) plus a fixed amount of profit (fee).

Cost-Plus-Incentive-Fee (CPIF) Contract

A type of cost-reimbursable contract where the buyer reimburses the seller for the seller's allowable costs (allowable costs are defined by the contract), and the seller earns its profit if it meets defined performance criteria.

Cost-Reimbursable Contract

A type of contract involving payment to the seller for the seller's Actual costs, plus a fee typically representing seller's profit. Cost-reimbursable contracts often include incentive clauses, where, if the seller meets or exceeds selected project objectives, such as schedule targets or total cost, then the seller receives from the buyer an incentive or bonus payment.

Cost Variance (CV)

A measure of cost performance on a project. It is the difference between Earned Value (EV) and Actual Cost (AC). CV = EV minus AC.

Crashing [Technique]

A specific type of project schedule compression technique performed by taking action to decrease the total project schedule duration after analyzing a number of alternatives to determine how to get the maximum schedule duration compression for the least additional cost. Typical approaches for crashing a schedule include reducing schedule activity durations and increasing the assignment of resources on schedule activities. See also fast tracking and schedule compression.

Create WBS (Work Breakdown Structure) [Process]

The process of subdividing project deliverables and project work into smaller, more manageable components.

Criteria

Standards, rules, or tests on which a judgment or decision can be based, or by which a product, service, result, or process can be evaluated.

Critical Activity

Any schedule activity on a critical path in a project schedule. Most commonly determined by using the critical path method. Although some activities are "critical", in the dictionary sense, without being on the critical path, this meaning is seldom used in the project context.

Critical Chain Method [Technique]

A schedule network analysis technique that modifies the project schedule to account for limited resources.

Critical Path

Generally, but not always, the sequence of schedule activities that determines the duration of the project. It is the longest path through the project. See also *critical path methodology*.

Critical Path Methodology (CPM) [Technique]

A schedule network analysis technique used to determine the amount of scheduling flexibility (the amount of float) on various logical network paths in the project schedule network, and to determine the minimum total project duration. Early start and finish dates are calculated by means of a forward pass, using a specified start date. Late start and finish dates are calculated by means of a backward pass, starting from a specified completion date, which sometimes is the project early finish date determined during the forward pass calculation. See also *critical path*.

D

Data Date

The data up to or through which the project's reporting system has provided actual status and accomplishments. Also called as-of date and time-now date.

Decision Tree Analysis [Technique]

The decision tree is a diagram that describes a decision under consideration and the implications of choosing one or another of the available alternatives. It is used when some future scenarios or outcomes of actions are uncertain. It incorporates probabilities and the costs or rewards of each logical path of events and future decisions, and uses expected monetary value analysis to help the organization identify the relative values of alternate actions. See also *expected monetary value analysis*.

Decomposition [Technique]

A Planning technique that subdivides the project scope and project deliverables into smaller, more manageable components, until the project work associated with accomplishing the project scope and providing the deliverables is defined in sufficient detail to support Executing, Monitoring, and Controlling the work.

Defect

An imperfection or deficiency in a project component where that component does not meet its requirements or specifications and needs to be either repaired or replaced.

Defect Repair

The formally documented identification of a defect in a project component with a recommendation to either repair the defect or completely replace the component.

Define Activities [Process]

The process of identifying the specific actions to be performed to produce the project deliverables.

Define Scope [Process]

The process of developing a detailed description of the project and product.

Deliverable [Output/Input]

Any unique and verifiable product, result, or capability to perform a service that must be produced to complete a process, phase, or project. Often used more narrowly in reference to an external deliverable, which is a deliverable that is subject to approval by the project sponsor or customer. See also *product* and *result*.

Delphi Technique [Technique]

An information gathering technique used as a way to reach a consensus of experts on a subject. Experts on the subject participate in this technique anonymously. A facilitator uses a questionnaire to solicit ideas about the important project points related to the subject. The responses are summarized and are then recirculated to the experts for further comment. Consensus may be reached in a few rounds of this process. The Delphi technique helps reduce bias in the data and keeps any one person from having undue influence on the outcome.

Dependency

See *logical relationship*.

Determine Budget [Process]
The process of aggregating the estimated costs of individual activities or work packages to establish an authorized cost baseline.

Develop Human Resource Plan [Process]
The process of identifying and documenting project roles, responsibilities, and required skills, reporting relationships, and creating a staffing management plan.

Develop Project Charter [Process]
The process of developing a document that formally authorizes a project or a phase and documenting initial requirements that satisfy the stakeholder's needs and expectations.

Develop Project Management Plan [Process]
The process of documenting the actions necessary to define, prepare, integrate, and coordinate all subsidiary plans.

Develop Project Team [Process]
The process of improving the competencies, team interaction, and the overall team environment to enhance project performance.

Develop Schedule [Process]
The process of analyzing sequences, durations, resource requirements, and schedule constraints to create the project schedule.

Direct and Manage Project Execution [Process]
The process of performing the work defined in the project management plan to achieve the project's objectives.

Distribute Information [Process]
The process of making relevant information available to project stakeholders as planned.

Duration (DU or DUR)
The total number of work periods (not including holidays or other nonworking periods) required to complete a schedule activity or work breakdown structure component. Usually expressed as workdays or workweeks. Sometimes incorrectly equated with elapsed time. Contrast with *effort.*

E

Early Finish Date (EF)
In the critical path method, the earliest possible point in time on which the uncompleted portions of a schedule activity (or the project) can finish, based on the schedule network logic, the data date, and any schedule constraints. Early finish dates can change as the project progresses and as changes are made to the project management plan.

Early Start Date (ES)
In the critical path method, the earliest possible point in time on which the uncompleted portions of a schedule activity (or the project) can start, based on the schedule network logic, the data date, and any schedule constraints. Early start dates can change as the project progresses and as changes are made to the project management plan.

Earned Value (EV)
The value of work performed expressed in terms of the approved budget assigned to that work for a schedule activity or work breakdown structure component. Also referred to as the budgeted cost of work performed (BCWP).

Earned Value Management (EVM)
A management methodology for integrating scope, schedule, and resources, and for objectively measuring project performance and progress. Performance is measured by determining the budgeted cost of work performed (i.e., earned value) and comparing it to the Actual Cost of Work Performed (i.e., Actual Cost).

Earned Value Technique (EVT) [Technique]
A specific technique for measuring the performance of work and used to establish the performance measurement baseline (PMB).

Effort
The number of labor units required to complete a schedule activity or work breakdown structure component. Usually expressed as staff hours, staff days, or staff weeks. Contrast with *duration*.

Enterprise Environmental Factors [Output/Input]
Any or all external environmental factors and internal organizational environmental factors that surround or influence the project's success. These factors are from any or all of the enterprises involved in the project, and include organizational culture and structure, infrastructure, existing resources, commercial databases, market conditions, and project management software.

Estimate [Output/Input]
A quantitative assessment of the likely amount or outcome. Usually applied to project costs, resources, effort, and durations and is usually preceded by a modifier (i.e., preliminary, conceptual, feasibility, order-of-magnitude, definitive). It should always include some indication of accuracy (e.g., ± x percent). See also *budget* and *cost*.

Estimate Activity Durations [Process]
The process of approximating the number of work periods needed to complete individual activities with estimated resources.

Estimate Activity Resources [Process]
The process of estimating the type and quantities of material, people, equipment, or supplies required to perform each activity.

Estimate at Completion (EAC) [Output/Input]
The expected total cost of a schedule activity, a work breakdown structure component, or the project when the defined scope of work will be completed. The EAC may be calculated based on performance to date or estimated by the project team based on other factors, in which case it is often referred to as the latest revised estimate. See also *earned value technique* and *estimate to complete*.

Estimate Costs [Process]
The process of developing an approximation of the monetary resources needed to complete project activities.

Estimate to Complete (ETC) [Output/Input]
The expected cost needed to complete all the remaining work for a schedule activity, work breakdown structure component, or the project. See also *earned value technique* and *estimate at completion*.

Execute
Directing, managing, performing, and accomplishing the project work, providing the deliverables, and providing work performance information.

Executing Processes [Process Group]
Those processes performed to complete the work defined in the project management plan to satisfy the project objectives.

Expected Monetary Value (EMV) Analysis
A statistical technique that calculates the average outcome when the future includes scenarios that may or may not happen. A common use of this technique is within decision tree analysis.

Expert Judgment [Technique]
Judgment provided based expertise in an application area, knowledge area, discipline, industry, and so forth as appropriate for the activity being performed. Such expertise may be provided by any group or person with specialized education, knowledge, skill, experience, or training.

F

Failure Mode and Effect Analysis (FMEA) [Technique]
An analytical procedure in which each potential failure mode in every component of a product is analyzed to determine its effect on the reliability of that component and, by itself or in combination with other possible failure modes, on the reliability of the product or system and on the required function of the component; or the exam of a product (at the system and/or lower levels) for all ways that a failure may occur. For each potential failure, an estimate is made of its effect on the total system and of its impact. In addition, a review is undertaken of the action planned to minimize the probability of failure and to minimize its effects.

Fast Tracking [Technique]
A specific project schedule compression technique that changes network logic to overlap phases that would normally be done in sequence, such as the design phase and construction phase, or to perform schedule activities in parallel. See also *crashing* and *schedule compression*.

Finish Date
A point in time associated with a schedule activity's completion. Usually qualified by one of the following: actual, planned, estimated, scheduled, early, late, baseline, target, or current.

Finish-to-Finish (FF)
The logical relationship where completion of work of the successor activity cannot finish until the completion of work of the predecessor activity. See also *logical relationship*.

Finish-to-Start (FS)
The logical relationship where initiation of work of the successor activity depends the completion of work of the predecessor activity. See also *logical relationship*.

Firm-Fixed-Price (FFP) Contract
A type of fixed price contract where the buyer pays the seller a set amount (as defined by the contract), regardless of the seller's costs.

Fixed-Price-Incentive-Fee (FPIF) Contract
A type of contract where the buyer pays the seller a set amount (as defined by the contract), and the seller can earn an additional amount if the seller meets defined performance criteria.

Float
Also called *slack*. See *total float* and *free float*.

Flowcharting [Technique]
The depiction in a diagram format of the inputs, process actions, and outputs of one or more processes within a system.

Forecast
An estimate or prediction of conditions and events in the project's future based on information and knowledge available at the time of the forecast. The information is based on the project's past performance and expected future performance and includes information that could impact the project in the future, such as estimate at completion and estimate to complete.

Forward Pass
The calculation of the early start and early finish dates for the uncompleted portions of all network activities. See also *schedule network analysis* and *backward pass*.

Free Float
The amount of time that a schedule activity can be delayed without delaying the early start date of any immediately following schedule activities. See also *total float*.

Functional Manager
Someone with management authority over an organizational unit within a functional organization. The manager of any group that actually makes a product or performs a service. Sometimes called a line manager.

Functional Organization
A hierarchical organization where each employee has one clear superior, and staff are grouped by areas of specialization and managed by a person with expertise in that area.

G

Gantt Chart [Tool]
A graphic display of schedule-related information. In the typical bar chart, schedule activities or work breakdown structure components are listed down the left side of the chart, dates are shown across the top, and activity durations are shown as date-placed horizontal bars.

Grade
A category or rank used to distinguish items that have the same functional use (e.g., "hammer") but do not share the same requirements for quality (e.g., different hammers may need to withstand different amounts of force).

H

Hammock Activity
See *summary activity*.

Historical Information
Documents and data on prior projects, including project files, records, correspondence, closed contracts, and closed projects.

Human Resource Plan
A document describing how roles and responsibilities, reporting relationships, and staffing management will be addressed and structured for the project. It is contained in or is a subsidiary plan of the project management plan.

I

Identify Risks [Process]
The process of determining which risks may affect the project and documenting their characteristics.

Identify Stakeholders [Process]
The process of identifying all people or organizations impacted by the project and documenting relevant information regarding their interests, involvement, and impact on project success.

Imposed Date
A fixed date imposed on a schedule activity or schedule milestone, usually in the form of a "start no earlier than" and "finish no later than" date.

Influence Diagram [Tool]
A graphical representation of situations showing causal influences, time ordering of events, and other relationships among variables and outcomes.

Initiating Processes [Process Group]
Those processes performed to define a new project or a new phase of an existing project by obtaining authorization to start the project or phase.

Input [Process Input]
Any item, whether internal or external to the project that is required by a process before that process proceeds. May be an output from a predecessor process.

Inspection [Technique]
Examining or measuring to verify whether an activity, component, product, result, or service conforms to specified requirements.

Invitation for Bid (IFB)
Generally, this term is equivalent to request for proposal. However, in some application areas, it may have a narrower or more specific meaning.

Issue
A point or matter in question or in dispute or a point or matter that is not settled and is under discussion or over which there are opposing views or disagreements.

L

Lag [Technique]
A modification of a logical relationship that directs a delay in the successor activity. For example, in a finish-to-start dependency with a 10-day lag, the successor activity cannot start until 10 days after the predecessor activity has finished. See also *lead*.

Late Finish Date (LF)
In the critical path method, the latest possible point in time that a schedule activity may be completed based upon the schedule network logic, the project completion date, and any constraints assigned to the schedule activities without violating a schedule constraint or delaying the project completion date. The late finish dates are determined during the backward pass calculation of the project schedule network.

Late Start Date (LS)
In the critical path method, the latest possible point in time that a schedule activity may begin based the schedule network logic, the project completion date, and any constraints assigned to the schedule activities

without violating a schedule constraint or delaying the project completion date. The late start dates are determined during the backward pass calculation of the project schedule network.

Lead [Technique]
A modification of a logical relationship that allows an acceleration of the successor activity.
For example, in a finish-to-start dependency with a 10-day lead, the successor activity can start 10 days before the predecessor activity has finished. A negative lead is equivalent to a positive lag. See also lag.

Lessons Learned [Output/Input]
The learning gained from the process of performing the project. Lessons learned may be identified at any point. Also considered a project record, to be included in the lessons learned knowledge base.

Lessons Learned Knowledge Base
A store of historical information and lessons about both the outcomes of previous project selection decisions and previous project performance.

Leveling
See *resource leveling*.

Life Cycle
See *project life cycle*.

Log
A document used to record and describe or denote selected items identified during execution of a process or activity. Usually used with a modifier, such as issue, quality control, action, or defect.

Logical Relationship
A dependency between two project schedule activities, or between a project schedule activity and a schedule milestone. The four possible types of logical relationships are Finish-to-Start, Finish-to-Finish, Start-to-Start, and Start-to-Finish. See also *precedence relationship*.

M

Manage Project Team [Process]
The process of tracking team member performance, providing feedback, resolving issues, and managing changes to optimize project performance.

Manage Stakeholder Expectations [Process]
The process of communicating and working with stakeholders to meet their needs and addressing issues as they occur.

Master Schedule [Tool]
A summary-level project schedule that identifies the major deliverables and work breakdown structure components and key schedule milestones. See also *milestone schedule*.

Material
The aggregate of things used by an organization in any undertaking, such as equipment, apparatus, tools, machinery, gear, material, and supplies.

Matrix Organization
Any organizational structure in which the project manager shares responsibility with the functional managers for assigning priorities and for directing the work of persons assigned to the project.

Methodology
A system of practices, techniques, procedures, and rules used by those who work in a discipline.

Milestone
A significant point or event in the project.

Milestone Schedule [Tool]
A summary-level schedule that identifies the major schedule milestones. See also *master schedule*.

Monitor
Collect project performance data with respect to a plan, produce performance measures, and report and disseminate performance information.

Monitor and Control Project Work [Process]
The process of tracking, reviewing, and regulating the progress to meet the performance objectives defined in the project management plan.

Monitor and Control Risks [Process]
The process of implementing risk response plans, tracking identified risks, monitoring residual risks, identifying new risks, and evaluating risk process throughout the project.

Monitoring and Controlling Processes [Process Group]
Those processes required to track, review, and regulate the progress and performance of the project, identify any areas in which changes to the plan are required, and initiate the corresponding changes.

Monte Carlo Analysis
A technique that computes or iterates the project cost or project schedule many times using input values selected at random from probability distributions of possible costs or durations, to calculate a distribution of possible total project cost or completion dates.

Monte Carlo Simulation
A process which generates hundreds or thousands of probable performance outcomes based on probability distributions for cost and schedule on individual tasks. The outcomes are then used to generate a probability distribution for the project as a whole.

N

Near-Critical Activity
A schedule activity that has low total float. The concept of near-critical is equally applicable to a schedule activity or schedule network path. The limit below which total float is considered near critical is subject to expert judgment and varies from project to project.

Network
See *project schedule network diagram*.

Network Analysis
See *schedule network analysis*.

Network Logic
The collection of schedule activity dependencies that makes up a project schedule network diagram.

Network Path
Any continuous series of schedule activities connected with logical relationships in a project schedule network diagram.

Node
One of the defining points of a schedule network; a junction point joined to some or all of the other dependency lines.

O

Objective
Something toward which work is to be directed, a strategic position to be attained, or a purpose to be achieved, a result to be obtained, a product to be produced, or a service to be performed.

Opportunity
A condition or situation favorable to the project, a positive set of circumstances, a positive set of events, a risk that will have a positive impact on project objectives, or a possibility for positive changes. Contrast with *threat.*

Organizational Breakdown Structure (OBS) [Tool]
A hierarchically organized depiction of the project organization arranged so as to relate the work packages to the performing organizational units.

Organizational Process Assets [Output/Input]
Any or all process related assets, from any or all of the organizations involved in the project, that are or can be used to influence the project's success. These process assets include formal and informal plans, policies, procedures, and guidelines. The process assets also include the organizations' knowledge bases such as lessons learned and historical information.

Output [Process Output]
A product, result, or service generated by a process. May be an input to a successor process.

P

Parametric Estimating [Technique]
An estimating technique that uses a statistical relationship between historical data and other variables (e.g., square footage in construction, lines of code in software development) to calculate an estimate for activity parameters, such as scope, cost, budget, and duration. An example for the cost parameter is multiplying the planned quantity of work to be performed by the historical cost per unit to obtain the estimated cost.

Pareto Chart [Tool]
A histogram, ordered by frequency of occurrence, that shows how many results were generated by each identified cause.

Path Convergence
The merging or joining of parallel schedule network paths into the same node in a project schedule network diagram. Path convergence is characterized by a schedule activity with more than one predecessor activity.

Path Divergence
Extending or generating parallel schedule network paths from the same node in a project schedule network diagram. Path divergence is characterized by a schedule activity with more than one successor activity.

Percent Complete
An estimate, expressed as a percent, of the amount of work that has been completed on an activity or a work breakdown structure component.

Perform Integrated Change Control [Process]
The process of reviewing all change requests, approving changes, and managing changes to the deliverables, organizational process assets, project documents, and project management plan.

Performance Measurement Baseline
An approved integrated scope-schedule-cost plan for the project work against which project execution is compared to measure and manage performance. Technical and quality parameters may also be included.

Performance Reports [Output/Input]
Documents and presentations that provide organized and summarized work performance information, earned value management parameters and calculations, and analyses of project work progress and status.

Performing Organization
The enterprise whose personnel are most directly involved in doing the work of the project.

Perform Qualitative Risk Analysis [Process]
The process of prioritizing risks for further analysis or action by assessing and combining their probability of occurrence and impact.

Perform Quality Assurance [Process]
The process of auditing the quality requirements and the results from quality control measurements to ensure appropriate quality standards and operational definitions are used.

Perform Quality Control [Process]
The process of monitoring and recording results of Executing the quality activities to assess performance and recommend necessary changes.

Perform Quantitative Risk Analysis [Process]
The process of numerically analyzing the effect of identified risks on overall project objectives.

Phase
See *project phase.*

Plan Communications [Process]
The process of determining project stakeholder information needs and defining a communication approach.

Plan Procurements [Process]
The process of documenting project purchasing decisions, specifying the approach, and identifying potential sellers.

Plan Quality [Process]
The process of identifying quality requirements and/or standards for the project and product, and documenting how the project will demonstrate compliance.

Plan Risk Management [Process]
The process of defining how to conduct risk management activities for a project.

Plan Risk Responses [Process]
The process of developing options and actions to enhance opportunities and to reduce threats to project objectives.

Planned Value (PV)
The authorized budget assigned to the scheduled work to be accomplished for a schedule activity or work breakdown structure component. Also referred to as the budgeted cost of work scheduled (BCWS).

Planning Package
A work breakdown structure component below the control account with known work content but without detailed schedule activities. See also *control account*.

Planning Processes [Process Group]
Those processes performed to establish the total scope of the effort, define and refine the objectives, and develop the course of action required to attain those objectives.

Portfolio
A collection of projects or programs and other work that are grouped together to facilitate effective management of that work to meet strategic business objectives. The projects or programs of the portfolio may not necessarily be interdependent or directly related.

Portfolio Management [Technique]
The centralized management of one or more portfolios, which includes identifying, prioritizing, authorizing, managing, and controlling projects, programs, and other related work, to achieve specific strategic business objectives.

Practice
A specific type of professional or management activity that contributes to the execution of a process and that may employ one or more techniques and tools.

Precedence Diagramming Method (PDM) [Technique]
A schedule network diagramming technique in which schedule activities are represented by boxes (or nodes). Schedule activities are graphically linked by one or more logical relationships to show the sequence in which the activities are to be performed.

Precedence Relationship
The term used in the precedence diagramming method for a logical relationship. In current usage, however, precedence relationship, logical relationship, and dependency are widely used interchangeably, regardless of the diagramming method used. See also *logical relationship*.

Predecessor Activity
The schedule activity that determines when the logical successor activity can begin or end.

Preventive Action
A documented direction to perform an activity that can reduce the probability of negative consequences associated with project risks.

Probability and Impact Matrix [Tool]
A common way to determine whether a risk is considered low, moderate, or high by combining the two dimensions of a risk: its probability of occurrence and its impact on objectives if it occurs.

Procurement Documents [Output/Input]
The documents used in bid and proposal activities, which include the buyer's Invitation for Bid, Invitation for Negotiations, Request for Information, Request for Quotation, Request for Proposal, and seller's responses.

Procurement Management Plan [Output/Input]
The document that describes how procurement processes from developing procurement documentation through contract closure will be managed.

Product
An artifact that is produced, is quantifiable, and can be either an end item in itself or a component item. Additional words for products are material and goods. Contrast with result. See also *deliverable*.

Product Life Cycle
A collection of generally sequential, nonoverlapping product phases whose name and number are determined by the manufacturing and control needs of the organization. The last product life cycle phase for a product is generally the product's retirement. Generally, a project life cycle is contained within one or more product life cycles.

Product Scope
The features and functions that characterize a product, service, or result.

Product Scope Description
The documented narrative description of the product scope

Program
A group of related projects managed in a coordinated way to obtain benefits and control not available from managing them individually. Programs may include elements of related work outside of the scope of the discrete projects in the program.

Program Evaluation and Review Technique (PERT)
A technique for estimating that applies a weighted average of optimistic, pessimistic, and most likely estimates when there is uncertainty with the individual activity estimates.

Program Management
The centralized coordinated management of a program to achieve the program's strategic objectives and benefits.

Progressive Elaboration [Technique]
Continuously improving and detailing a plan as more detailed and specific information and more accurate estimates become available as the project progresses, and thereby producing more accurate and complete plans that result from the successive iterations of the Planning process.

Project
A temporary endeavor undertaken to create a unique product, service, or result.

Project Calendar
A calendar of working days or shifts that establishes those dates on which schedule activities are worked and nonworking days that determine those dates on which schedule activities are idle. Typically defines holidays, weekends, and shift hours. See also *resource calendar*.

Project Charter [Output/Input]
A document issued by the project initiator or sponsor that formally authorizes the existence of a project and provides the project manager with the authority to apply organizational resources to project activities.

Project Communications Management [Knowledge Area]
Project Communications Management includes the processes required to ensure timely and appropriate generation, collection, distribution, storage, retrieval, and ultimate disposition of project information.

Project Cost Management [Knowledge Area]
Project Cost Management includes the processes involved in estimating, budgeting, and controlling costs so that the project can be completed within the approved budget.

Project Human Resource Management [Knowledge Area]
Project Human Resource Management includes the processes that organize and manage the project team.

Project Initiation
Launching a process that can result in the authorization of a new project.

Project Integration Management [Knowledge Area]
Project Integration Management includes the processes and activities needed to identify, define, combine, unify, and coordinate the various processes and project management activities within the Project Management Process Groups.

Project Life Cycle
A collection of generally sequential project phases whose name and number are determined by the control needs of the organization or organizations involved in the project. A life cycle can be documented with a methodology.

Project Management
The application of knowledge, skills, tools, and techniques to project activities to meet the project requirements.

Project Management Body of Knowledge
An inclusive term that describes the sum of knowledge within the profession of project management. As with other professions, such as law, medicine, and accounting, the body of knowledge rests with the practitioners and academics that apply and advance it. The complete project management body of knowledge includes proven traditional practices that are widely applied and innovative practices that are emerging in the profession. The body of knowledge includes both published and unpublished materials. This body of knowledge is constantly evolving. PMI®'s *PMBOK® Guide* identifies that subset of the project management body of knowledge that is generally recognized as good practice.

Project Management Information System (PMIS) [Tool]
An information system consisting of the tools and techniques used to gather, integrate, and disseminate the outputs of project management processes. It is used to support all aspects of the project from initiating through Closing and can include both manual and automated systems.

Project Management Knowledge Area
An identified area of project management defined by its knowledge requirements and described in terms of its component processes, practices, inputs, outputs, tools, and techniques.

Project Management Office (PMO)
An organizational body or entity assigned various responsibilities related to the centralized and coordinated management of those projects under its domain. The responsibilities of a PMO can range from providing project management support functions to actually being responsible for the direct management of a project.

Project Management Plan [Output/Input]
A formal, approved document that defines how the project is executed, monitored, and controlled. It may be a summary or detailed and may be composed of one or more subsidiary management plans and other Planning documents.

Project Management Process Group
A logical grouping of project management inputs, tools and techniques, and outputs. The Project Management Process Groups include initiating processes, Planning processes, Executing processes, Monitoring and controlling processes, and Closing processes. Project Management Process Groups are not project phases.

Project Management System [Tool]
The aggregation of the processes, tools, techniques, methodologies, resources, and procedures to manage a project.

Project Management Team
The members of the project team who are directly involved in project management activities. On some smaller projects, the project management team may include virtually all of the project team members.

Project Manager (PM)
The person assigned by the performing organization to achieve the project objectives.

Project Organization Chart [Output/Input]
A document that graphically depicts the project team members and their interrelationships for a specific project.

Project Phase
A collection of logically related project activities, usually culminating in the completion of a major deliverable. Project phases are mainly completed sequentially but can overlap in some project situations. A project phase is a component of a project life cycle. A project phase is not a Project Management Process Group.

Project Procurement Management [Knowledge Area]
Project Procurement Management includes the processes to purchase or acquire the products, services, or results needed from outside the project team to perform the work.

Project Quality Management [Knowledge Area]
Project Quality Management includes the processes and activities of the performing organization that determine quality policies, objectives, and responsibilities so that the project will satisfy the needs for which it was undertaken.

Project Risk Management [Knowledge Area]
Project Risk Management includes the processes concerned with conducting risk management Planning, identification, analysis, responses, and monitoring and control on a project.

Project Schedule [Output/Input]
The planned dates for performing schedule activities and the planned dates for meeting schedule milestones.

Project Schedule Network Diagram [Output/Input]
Any schematic display of the logical relationships among the project schedule activities. Always drawn from left to right to reflect project work chronology.

Project Scope
The work that must be performed to deliver a product, service, or result with the specified features and functions.

Project Scope Management [Knowledge Area]
Project Scope Management includes the processes required to ensure that the project includes all the work required, and only the work required, to complete the project successfully.

Project Scope Statement [Output/Input]
The narrative description of the project scope, including major deliverables, project assumptions, project constraints, and a description of work, that provides a documented basis for making future project decisions and for confirming or developing a common understanding of project scope among the stakeholders.

Project Team Directory
A documented list of project team members, their project roles, and communication information.

Project Time Management [Knowledge Area]
Project Time Management includes the processes required to manage the timely completion of a project.

Projectized Organization
Any organizational structure in which the project manager has full authority to assign priorities, apply resources, and direct the work of persons assigned to the project.

Q

Quality
The degree to which a set of inherent characteristics fulfills requirements.

Quality Management Plan [Output/Input]
The quality management plan describes how the project management team will implement the performing organization's quality policy. The quality management plan is a component or a subsidiary plan of the project management plan.

R

Regulation
Requirements imposed by a governmental body. These requirements can establish product, process, or service characteristics, including applicable administrative provisions that have government-mandated compliance.

Report Performance [Process]
The process of collecting and distributing performance information, including status reports, progress measurements, and forecasts.

Request for Information (RFI)
A type of procurement document whereby the buyer requests a potential seller to provide various pieces of information related to a product or service or seller capability.

Request for Proposal (RFP)
A type of procurement document used to request proposals from prospective sellers of products or services. In some application areas, it may have a narrower or more specific meaning.

Request for Quotation (RFQ)
A type of procurement document used to request price quotations from prospective sellers of common or standard products or services. Sometimes used in place of request for proposal and in some application areas, it may have a narrower or more specific meaning.

Requested Change [Output/Input]
A formally documented change request that is submitted for approval to the integrated change control process.

Requirement
A condition or capability that must be met or possessed by a system, product, service, result, or component to satisfy a contract, standard, specification, or other formally imposed document. Requirements include the quantified and documented needs, wants, and expectations of the sponsor, customer, and other stakeholders.

Requirements Traceability Matrix
A table that links requirements to their origin and traces them throughout the project life cycle.

Reserve
A provision in the project management plan to mitigate cost and/or schedule risk. Often used with a modifier (e.g., management reserve, contingency reserve) to provide further detail on what types of risk are meant to be mitigated.

Reserve Analysis [Technique]
An analytical technique to determine the essential features and relationships of components in the project management plan to establish a reserve for the schedule duration, budget, estimated cost, or funds for a project.

Residual Risk
A risk that remains after risk responses have been implemented.

Resource
Skilled human resources (specific disciplines either individually or in crews or teams), equipment, services, supplies, commodities, material, budgets, or funds.

Resource Breakdown Structure
A hierarchical structure of resources by resource category and resource type used in resource leveling schedules and to develop resource-limited schedules, and which may be used to identify and analyze project human resource assignments.

Resource Calendar
A calendar of working days and nonworking days that determines those dates on which each specific resource is idle or can be active. Typically defines resource-specific holidays and resource availability periods. See also *project calendar*.

Resource Histogram

A bar chart showing the amount of time that a resource is scheduled to work over a series of time periods. Resource availability may be depicted as a line for comparison purposes. Contrasting bars may show actual amounts of resources used as the project progresses.

Resource Leveling [Technique]

Any form of schedule network analysis in which scheduling decisions (start and finish dates) are driven by resource constraints (e.g., limited resource availability or difficult-to-manage changes in resource availability levels).

Responsibility Assignment Matrix (RAM) [Tool]

A structure that relates the project organizational breakdown structure to the work breakdown structure to help ensure that each component of the project's scope of work is assigned to a person or team.

Result

An output from performing project management processes and activities. Results include outcomes (e.g., integrated systems, revised process, restructured organization, tests, trained personnel, etc.) and documents (e.g., policies, plans, studies, procedures, specifications, reports). Contrast with product. See also *deliverable*.

Rework

Action taken to bring a defective or nonconforming component into compliance with requirements or specifications.

Risk

An uncertain event or condition that, if it occurs, has a positive or negative effect on a project's objectives.

Risk Acceptance [Technique]

A risk response Planning technique that indicates that the project team has decided not to change the project management plan to deal with a risk or is unable to identify any other suitable response strategy.

Risk Avoidance [Technique]

A risk response Planning technique for a threat that creates changes to the project management plan that is meant to either eliminate the risk or to protect the project objectives from its impact.

Risk Breakdown Structure (RBS) [Tool]

A hierarchically organized depiction of the identified project risks arranged by risk category and subcategory that identifies the various areas and causes of potential risks. The risk breakdown structure is often tailored to specific project types.

Risk Category

A group of potential causes of risk. Risk causes may be grouped into categories, such as technical, external, organizational, environmental, or project management. A category may include subcategories such as technical maturity, weather, or aggressive estimating.

Risk Management Plan [Output/Input]

The document describing how Project Risk Management will be structured and performed on the project. It is contained in or is a subsidiary plan of the project management plan. Information in the risk management plan varies by application area and project size. The risk management plan is different from the risk register that contains the list of project risks, the results of risk analysis, and the risk responses.

Risk Mitigation [Technique]
A risk response Planning technique associated with threats that seeks to reduce the probability of occurrence or impact of a risk to below an acceptable threshold.

Risk Register [Output/Input]
The document containing the results of the qualitative risk analysis, quantitative risk analysis, and risk response Planning. The risk register details all identified risks, including description, category, cause, probability of occurring, impact(s) on objectives, proposed responses, owners, and current status.

Risk Tolerance
The degree, amount, or volume of risk that an organization or individual will withstand.

Risk Transference [Technique]
A risk response Planning technique that shifts the impact of a threat to a third party, together with ownership of the response.

Role
A defined function to be performed by a project team member, such as testing, filing, inspecting, and coding.

Rolling Wave Planning [Technique]
A form of progressive elaboration Planning where the work to be accomplished in the near term is planned in detail at a low level of the work breakdown structure, while the work far in the future is planned at a relatively high level of the work breakdown structure, but the detailed Planning of the work to be performed within another one or two periods in the near future is done as work is being completed during the current period.

Root Cause Analysis [Technique]
An analytical technique used to determine the basic underlying reason that causes a variance or a defect or a risk. A root cause may underlie more than one variance or defect or risk.

S

Schedule
See *project schedule* and see also *schedule model.*

Schedule Baseline
A specific version of the schedule model used to compare actual results to the plan to determine whether preventive or corrective action is needed to meet the project objectives.

Schedule Compression [Technique]
Shortening the project schedule duration without reducing the project scope. See also *crashing* and *fast tracking.*

Schedule Management Plan [Output/Input]
The document that establishes criteria and the activities for developing and controlling the project schedule. It is contained in, or is a subsidiary plan of, the project management plan.

Schedule Model [Tool]
A model used in conjunction with manual methods or project management software to perform schedule network analysis to generate the project schedule for use in managing the execution of a project. See also *project schedule.*

Schedule Network Analysis [Technique]
The technique of identifying early and late start dates, as well as early and late finish dates, for the uncompleted portions of project schedule activities. See also *critical path method, critical chain method,* and *resource leveling.*

Schedule Performance Index (SPI)
A measure of schedule efficiency on a project. It is the ratio of earned value (EV) to planned value (PV). The SPI = EV divided by PV.

Schedule Variance (SV)
A measure of schedule performance on a project. It is the difference between the earned value (EV) and the planned value (PV). SV = EV minus PV.

Scheduled Finish Date (SF)
The point in time that work was scheduled to finish on a schedule activity. The scheduled finish date is normally within the range of dates delimited by the early finish date and the late finish date. It may reflect resource leveling of scarce resources. Sometimes called planned finish date.

Scheduled Start Date (SS)
The point in time that work was scheduled to start on a schedule activity. The scheduled start date is normally within the range of dates delimited by the early start date and the late start date. It may reflect resource leveling of scarce resources. Sometimes called planned start date.

Scope
The sum of the products, services, and results to be provided as a project. See also *project scope* and *product scope.*

Scope Baseline
An approved specific version of the detailed scope statement, work breakdown structure (WBS), and its associated WBS dictionary.

Scope Change
Any change to the project scope. A scope change almost always requires an adjustment to the project cost or schedule.

Scope Creep
Adding features and functionality (project scope) without addressing the effects on time, costs, and resources, or without customer approval.

Scope Management Plan [Output/Input]
The document that describes how the project scope will be defined, developed, and verified and how the work breakdown structure will be created and defined, and that provides guidance on how the project scope will be managed and controlled by the project management team. It is contained in or is a subsidiary plan of the project management plan.

S-Curve
Graphic display of cumulative costs, labor hours, percentage of work, or other quantities, plotted against time. Used to depict planned value, earned value, and actual cost of project work. The name derives from the S-like shape of the curve (flatter at the start and finish, steeper in the middle) produced on a project

that starts slowly, accelerates, and then tails off. Also a term used to express the cumulative likelihood distribution that is a result of a simulation, a tool of quantitative risk analysis.

Secondary Risk
A risk that arises as a direct result of implementing a risk response.

Seller
A provider or supplier of products, services, or results to an organization.

Sensitivity Analysis
A quantitative risk analysis and modeling technique used to help determine which risks have the most potential impact on the project. It examines the extent to which the uncertainty of each project element affects the objective being examined when all other uncertain elements are held at their baseline values. The typical display of results is in the form of a tornado diagram.

Sequence Activities [Process]
The process of identifying and documenting relationships among the project activities.

Simulation
A simulation uses a project model that translates the uncertainties specified at a detailed level into their potential impact on objectives that are expressed at the level of the total project. Project simulations use computer models and estimates of risk, usually expressed as a probability distribution of possible costs or durations at a detailed work level, and are typically performed using Monte Carlo analysis.

Slack
Also called float. See *total float* and *free float.*

Special Cause
A source of variation that is not inherent in the system, is not predictable, and is intermittent. It can be assigned to a defect in the system. On a control chart, points beyond the control limits, or nonrandom patterns within the control limits, indicate it. Also referred to as assignable cause. Contrast with *common cause.*

Specification
A document that specifies, in a complete, precise, verifiable manner, the requirements, design, behavior, or other characteristics of a system, component, product, result, or service and, often, the procedures for determining whether these provisions have been satisfied. Examples are requirement specification, design specification, product specification, and test specification.

Specification Limits
The area, on either side of the centerline, or mean, of data plotted on a control chart that meets the customer's requirements for a product or service. This area may be greater than or less than the area defined by the control limits. See also *control limits.*

Sponsor
The person or group that provides the financial resources, in cash or in-kind, for the project.

Staffing Management Plan
The document that describes when and how human resource requirements will be met. It is contained in, or is a subsidiary plan of, the human resource plan.

Stakeholder

Person or organization (e.g., customer, sponsor, performing organization, or the public) that is actively involved in the project, or whose interests may be positively or negatively affected by execution or completion of the project. A stakeholder may also exert influence over the project and its deliverables.

Standard

A document that provides, for common and repeated use, rules, guidelines, or characteristics for activities or their results, aimed at the achievement of the optimum degree of order in a given context.

Start Date

A point in time associated with a schedule activity's start, usually qualified by one of the following: actual, planned, estimated, scheduled, early, late, target, baseline, or current.

Start-to-Finish (SF)

The logical relationship where completion of the successor schedule activity is dependent on the initiation of the predecessor schedule activity. See also *logical relationship.*

Start-to-Start (SS)

The logical relationship where initiation of the work of the successor schedule activity depends on the initiation of the work of the predecessor schedule activity. See also *logical relationship.*

Statement of Work (SOW)

A narrative description of products, services, or results to be supplied.

Strengths, Weaknesses, Opportunities, and Threats (SWOT) Analysis

This information gathering technique examines the project from the perspective of each project's strengths, weaknesses, opportunities, and threats to increase the breadth of the risks considered by risk management.

Subnetwork

A subdivision (fragment) of a project schedule network diagram, usually representing a subproject or a work package. Often used to illustrate or study some potential or proposed schedule condition, such as changes in preferential schedule logic or project scope.

Subphase

A subdivision of a phase.

Subproject

A smaller portion of the overall project created when a project is subdivided into more manageable components or pieces.

Successor Activity

The schedule activity that follows a predecessor activity, as determined by their logical relationship.

Summary Activity

A group of related schedule activities aggregated at some summary level, and displayed/ reported as a single activity at that summary level. See also *subproject* and *subnetwork.*

T

Team Members

See *project team members.*

Technical Performance Measurement [Technique]
A performance measurement technique that compares technical accomplishments during project execution to the project management plan's schedule of planned technical achievements. It may use key technical parameters of the product produced by the project as a quality metric. The achieved metric values are part of the work performance information.

Technique
A defined systematic procedure employed by a human resource to perform an activity to produce a product or result or deliver a service, and that may employ one or more tools.

Template
A partially complete document in a predefined format that provides a defined structure for collecting, organizing, and presenting information and data.

Threat
A condition or situation unfavorable to the project, a negative set of circumstances, a negative set of events, a risk that will have a negative impact on a project objective if it occurs, or a possibility for negative changes. Contrast with *opportunity*.

Three-Point Estimate [Technique]
An analytical technique that uses three cost or duration estimates to represent the optimistic, most likely, and pessimistic scenarios. This technique is applied to improve the accuracy of the estimates of cost or duration when the underlying activity or cost component is uncertain.

Threshold
A cost, time, quality, technical, or resource value used as a parameter, and which may be included in product specifications. Crossing the threshold should trigger some action, such as generating an exception report.

Time and Material (T&M) Contract
A type of contract that is a hybrid contractual arrangement containing aspects of both cost-reimbursable and fixed-price contracts. Time and material contracts resemble cost-reimbursable type arrangements in that they have no definitive end, because the full value of the arrangement is not defined at the time of the award. Thus, time and material contracts can grow in contract value as if they were cost-reimbursable-type arrangements. Conversely, time and material arrangements can also resemble fixed-price arrangements. For example, the unit rates are preset by the buyer and seller when both parties agree on the rates for the category of senior engineers.

Time-Scaled Schedule Network Diagram [Tool]
Any project schedule network diagram drawn in such a way that the positioning and length of the schedule activity represents its duration. Essentially, it is a bar chart that includes schedule network logic.

To-Complete-Performance-Index (TCPI)
The calculated projection of cost performance that must be achieved on the remaining work to meet a specified management goal, such as the budget at completion (BAC) or the estimate at completion (EAC). It is the ratio of "remaining work" to the "funds remaining."

Tool
Something tangible, such as a template or software program, used in performing an activity to produce a product or result.

Total Float

The total amount of time that a schedule activity may be delayed from its early start date without delaying the project finish date, or violating a schedule constraint. Calculated using the critical path method technique and determining the difference between the early finish dates and late finish dates. See also *free float.*

Trend Analysis [Technique]

An analytical technique that uses mathematical models to forecast future outcomes based on historical results. It is a method of determining the variance from a baseline of a budget, cost, schedule, or scope parameter by using prior progress reporting periods' data and projecting how much that parameter's variance from baseline might be at some future point in the project if no changes are made in Executing the project.

Triggers

Indications that a risk has occurred or is about to occur. Triggers may be discovered in the risk identification process and watched in the risk monitoring and control process. Triggers are sometimes called risk symptoms or warning signs.

V

Validation

The assurance that a product, service, or system meets the needs of the customer and other identified stakeholders. It often involves acceptance and suitability with external customers. Contrast with *verification.*

Value Engineering

An approach used to optimize project life cycle costs, save time, increase profits, improve quality, expand market share, solve problems, and/or use resources more effectively.

Variance

A quantifiable deviation, departure, or divergence away from a known baseline or expected value.

Variance Analysis [Technique]

A method for resolving the total variance in the set of scope, cost, and schedule variables into specific component variances that are associated with defined factors affecting the scope, cost, and schedule variables.

Verification

The evaluation of whether a product, service, or system complies with a regulation, requirement, specification, or imposed condition. It is often an internal process. Contrast with validation.

Verify Scope [Process]

The process of formalizing acceptance of the completed project deliverables.

Virtual Team

A group of persons with a shared objective who fulfill their roles with little or no time spent meeting face to face. Various forms of technology are often used to facilitate communication among team members. Virtual teams can comprise of persons separated by great distances.

Voice of the Customer

A Planning technique used to provide products, services, and results that truly reflect customer requirements by translating those customer requirements into the appropriate technical requirements for each phase of project product development.

W

Work Authorization

A permission and direction, typically written, to begin work on a specific schedule activity or work package or control account. It is a method for sanctioning project work to ensure that the work is done by the identified organization, at the right time, and in the proper sequence.

Work Authorization System [Tool]

A subsystem of the overall project management system. It is a collection of formal documented procedures that defines how project work will be authorized (committed) to ensure that the work is done by the identified organization, at the right time, and in the proper sequence. It includes the steps, documents, tracking system, and defined approval levels needed to issue work authorizations.

Work Breakdown Structure (WBS) [Output/Input]

A deliverable-oriented hierarchical decomposition of the work to be executed by the project team to accomplish the project objectives and create the required deliverables. It organizes and defines the total scope of the project.

Work Breakdown Structure Component

An entry in the work breakdown structure that can be at any level.

Work Breakdown Structure Dictionary [Output/Input]

A document that describes each component in the work breakdown structure (WBS). For each WBS component, the WBS dictionary includes a brief definition of the scope or statement of work, defined deliverable(s), a list of associated activities, and a list of milestones. Other information may include responsible organization, start and end dates, resources required, an estimate of cost, charge number, contract information, quality requirements, and technical references to facilitate performance of the work.

Work Package

A deliverable or project work component at the lowest level of each branch of the work breakdown structure. See also *control account*.

Work Performance Information [Output/Input]

Information and data, on the status of the project schedule activities being performed to accomplish the project work, collected as part of the direct and manage project execution processes. Information includes: status of deliverables; implementation status for change requests, corrective actions, preventive actions, and defect repairs; forecasted estimates to complete; reported percent of work physically completed; achieved value of technical performance measures; start and finish dates of schedule activities.

Workaround [Technique]

A response to a negative risk that has occurred. Distinguished from contingency plan in that a workaround is not planned in advance of the occurrence of the risk event.

PMP® PREPARATORY BOOK

Study Tracking Sheet

Name:

EVALUATION	THEME	DATE	START/END	NUMBER OF QUESTIONS	RIGHT QUESTIONS	% OF RIGHT QUESTIONS	NOTES
Starting evaluation	General		S - E -	50			
			S - E -				
			S - E -				
			S - E -				
			S - E -				
			S - E -				
			S - E -				
			S - E -				
			S - E -				
			S - E -				
			S - E -				
			S - E -				
			S - E -				

General notes:

D.

E.

F.

G.

H.

I.

Q.

R.

S.

T.

V.

W.

Z.